social problems
in a diverse society

Canadian Edition

Diana Kendall
Baylor University

Vicki L. Nygaard
University of Victoria

Edward G. Thompson
McMaster University

PEARSON
and

Toronto

National Library of Canada Cataloguing in Publication

Kendall, Diana Elizabeth
     Social problems in a diverse society / Diana Kendall, Vicki L. Nygaard,
Edward G. Thompson. — Canadian ed.

Includes bibliographical references and index.
ISBN 0-205-36518-3

    1. Social problems.   I. Nygaard, Vicki Leanne, 1964– II.   Thompson, Edward G., 1945– III. Title.

HN17.5.K45 2004   361.1   C2003-903651-0

Statistics Canada information is used with the permission of the Minister of Industry, as Minister responsible for Statistics Canada. Information on the availability of the wide range of data from Statistics Canada can be obtained from Statistics Canada's Regional Offices, its World Wide Web site at http://www.statcan.ca, and its toll-free access number 1-800-263-1136.

ISBN 0-205-36518-3

Vice President, Editorial Director: Michael J. Young
Executive Acquisitions Editor: Jessica Mosher
Senior Developmental Editor: Martina van de Velde
Senior Marketing Manager: Judith Allen
Signing Representatives: Patty Riediger/Marc Sourrisseau
Production Editor: Cheryl Jackson/Richard di Santo
Copy Editor: Margaret McClintock
Proofreader: Tara Tovell
Production Manager: Wendy Moran
Page Layout: Debbie Kumpf
Permissions Manager: Susan Wallace-Cox
Photo Researcher: Lisa Brant
Art Direction: Julia Hall
Cover and Interior Design: Amy Harnden
Cover Image: Steve Puetzer/Photonica

1 2 3 4 5   08 07 06 05 04
Printed and bound in Canada.

DEDICATION

This book is dedicated to my dearest loves, Gary, Freja, Phoenix, Natasha and Maya, to my wonderful family and friends, and to the countless, but not nameless or faceless, Sociology 100, 202 and 430 students who rekindle my hope for a better world, year after year.

Vicki L. Nygaard

This book is dedicated to my dear partner, Helen.

Edward G. Thompson

CONTENTS

CHAPTER THIRTEEN

PROBLEMS IN POLITICS AND THE
GLOBAL ECONOMY   294

CHAPTER FOURTEEN

PROBLEMS IN THE MEDIA   318

[A social problems course] can provide a mind-opening . . . overview of a field of study, providing a method of perceiving and understanding the social realities we construct, playing a central role in leading students through the cognitive developmental processes that turn unchallenged dualism and other oversimplifications about everyday life into the complex formulations that better represent the social world in which we live.

Sociologists Michael Brooks and Kendal Broad describe the social problems course in the Instructor's Resource Manual on Social Problems *(Brooks and Broad, 1997:1)*

This statement sums up the main reasons why we wrote *Social Problems in a Diverse Society*. Learning about social problems can be a highly rewarding experience. Although we live in difficult and challenging times, the social problems course provides an excellent avenue for developing patterns of critical thinking and for learning how to use sociological concepts and perspectives to analyze specific social concerns ranging from drug addiction, violence, and war to inequalities of racialization and ethnicity, class, age, sexual orientation, and gender.

Our first and foremost goal in writing this book is to make the study of social problems interesting and relevant for students. To stimulate interest in reading the chapters and participation in class discussions, we have used lived experiences (personal narratives of real people) and statements from a wide variety of analysts to show how social problems impinge on people at the individual, group, and societal levels. Moreover, we have applied sociological imagination and relevant sociological concepts and perspectives to all the topics in a systematic manner.

The Canadian edition of *Social Problems in a Diverse Society* focuses on the significance of racialization and ethnicity, age, sexual orientation, class, and gender in understanding social problems in Canada and around the globe. Throughout the text, people—especially those from marginalized groups—are shown not merely as "victims" of social problems, but as individuals who resist discrimination and inequality and seek to bring about change in families, schools, workplaces, and the larger society. To facilitate the inclusion of previously excluded perspectives, Chapters 2 through 6 examine wealth and poverty, racialized/ethnic inequality, gender inequality, and inequalities based on age and sexual orientation. Thereafter, concepts and perspectives related to racialization and ethnicity, class, sexual orientation, age, and gender are intertwined in the discussion of specific social problems such as education, health care, and the media.

This Canadian edition is balanced in its approach to examining social problems. However, it includes a more comprehensive view of feminist and postmodern perspectives on a vast array of subjects—such as the effect of new technologies and how the media depict social issues—than other social problems textbooks. As sociologists who integrate social theory into our lectures, we were disheartened by the minimal use of sociological theory in most social problems texts. Those that discuss theory typically do so in early chapters but then fail to use these theories as a systematic framework for examining specific social issues in subsequent chapters. Similarly, many texts give the impression that social problems can be solved if people reach a consensus on what should be done, but *Social Problems in a Diverse Society*, Canadian Edition, emphasizes that how people view a social problem is related to how they believe the problem should be reduced or solved. Consider poverty, for example: people who focus on individual causes of poverty typically believe that individual solutions (such as teaching people the work ethic and reforming welfare) are necessary to reduce the problem, whereas those who focus on structural causes of poverty (such as chronic unemployment and inadequate educational opportunities) typically believe that solutions must come from the larger society. Moreover, what some people see as a problem, others see as a solution for a problem (e.g., the sex industry as a source of income, or abortion to terminate a problematic pregnancy). The final chapter (Chapter 18) allows students to fully explore the question, "Can social problems be solved?"

Finally, we wrote *Social Problems in a Diverse Society*, Canadian Edition, in hopes of providing students and instructors with a text that covers all the major social concerns of our day but does not leave them believing that the text—and perhaps the course—was a "depressing litany of social problems that nobody can do anything about anyway," as many students have stated about different texts. We have written this book in hopes of resolving those students' concerns, because we believe the sociological perspective has much to add to our national and global dialogues on a host of issues, such as environmental degradation; international terrorism; discrimination based on racialization and ethnicity, class, gender, age, sexual orientation, or other attributes; and problems in education. Welcome to an innovative examination of social problems—one of the most stimulating and engrossing fields of study in sociology!

ORGANIZATION OF THIS TEXT

Social Problems in a Diverse Society, Canadian Edition, has been organized with the specific plan of introducing disparities in wealth and poverty, racialization and ethnicity, gender, age, and sexual orientation early on, so that the concepts and perspectives developed in these chapters may be applied throughout the text. All chapters offer theoretical analyses from structural functionalism, conflict or Marxist perspectives, symbolic interactionism, and feminist theories. In addition, other theories are introduced where relevant.

- Chapter 1 explains the sociological perspective and highlights the issue of worldwide violence to draw students into an examination of debates about gun control or the influence of media violence.

- Chapter 2 looks at wealth and poverty in Canada and around the world. Students will gain new insights into disparities between the wealthy and the poor and about problems such as workfare, homelessness, food insecurity, and poverty. The chapter concludes with a thematic question, "Can class-based inequality be reduced?" This question will be asked throughout the text as new topics are discussed.

- Chapter 3 integrates the previous discussion of class-based inequalities with an examination of racialized and ethnic inequality. The chapter looks at issues of democratic racism and white privilege in Canada, and at the ways that racism manifests itself throughout Canadian institutions and practices.

- Chapter 4 highlights factors such as mainstream gender socialization and social barriers that contribute to the unequal treatment of women in the workplace, in the family, at school, and at other social institutions. Transgender issues and global gender issues are also introduced for discussion.

- Ageism and inequality based on age are discussed in Chapter 5, and inequality based on sexual orientation is examined in Chapter 6, placing these important topics in a context similar to the studies of prejudice and discrimination rooted in racism and sexism in contemporary societies. In addition, Queer theory is highlighted as a way of analyzing sexual orientation issues.

- Chapter 7 links previous discussions of racialization and ethnicity, class, and gender to an analysis of prostitution, pornography, and the sex trade. The chapter provides up-to-date information on the globalization of prostitution and gives students insights on "johns" and on how sex workers view themselves, why they engage in this line of work, and why some people view sex workers as a social problem.

- In Chapter 8, social problems caused by the use of alcohol and other drugs are discussed in depth, and students are provided with information about the drug commonly called the "date rape" drug and the abuse of prescription drugs, over-the-counter drugs, and caffeine.

- Chapter 9 discusses crime and criminal justice and takes an incisive look at sociological explanations of crime.

- Beginning with Chapter 10, a look at health care and its problems, we examine some of the major social institutions in our society and note aspects of each that constitute a social problem for large numbers of people.

- Chapter 11 explores the changing family, emphasizing diversity in intimate relationships and families, and child-related family issues.

- Chapter 12 presents contemporary problems in education, tracing the problems to such issues as what schools are supposed to accomplish, how they are financed, and why higher education may become less widely accessible with increasing tuition fees.

- Chapter 13 focuses on problems in politics and the global economy and provides a variety of perspectives on the economy and political power, trade agreements, and the power of the anti-globalization movement.

- Chapter 14, a discussion of problems in the media, looks at how the recent concentration in the media industries affects the news and entertainment that people receive.

- Chapter 15 provides a survey of problems associated with population and the environmental crisis, focusing particularly on the causes and consequences of high rates of global migration and particular types of pollution.

- Chapter 16, a look at urban problems, details the powerful impact of urbanization on both high-income and low-income nations of the world.

- Chapter 17 discusses global social problems related to war and terrorism. After examining such topics as militarism, war and terrorism, the environmental impacts of war, and racial profiling, the text concludes by talking about the emerging peace movement in response to war in the 21st century.

- Chapter 18 asks, "Can social problems be solved?" and includes a review of the four main sociological theories used to explain social problems, plus an analysis of attempts at problem solving at the microlevel, mid-range, and macrolevel of society.

DISTINCTIVE FEATURES

A number of special features have been designed to incorporate racialization and ethnicity, class, and gender into our analysis of social problems and to provide students with new insights on the social problems that they hear about on the evening news. The following sections discuss the text's distinctive features.

Lived Experiences throughout Each Chapter

These authentic, first-person accounts are used as vignettes—"real words from real people"—to create interest and show how the problems being discussed affect people as they go about their daily lives. Lived experiences provide opportunities for students to examine social life beyond their own experiences ("to live vicariously," as one student noted) and for instructors to systematically incorporate into lectures and class discussions examples of relevant, contemporary issues that have recently been on the evening news and in newspaper headlines.

- Fyre Jean Graveline, a college professor, describes her experience teaching in a "Native-controlled" college in Canada where nevertheless dominant White values are implicit and must be adhered to (Chapter 3, Racism and Ethnic Inequality).

- Gordon Brent Ingram discusses how his views of public spaces are informed by his sexual orientation (Chapter 6, Inequality Based on Sexual Orientation).
- Anonymous Canadian youth from across the country speak about how they became involved in the sex trade (Chapter 7, The Sex Industry in Canada and Beyond).
- Helen Stauffer, former Vice President of PRIDE (People to Reduce Impaired Driving Everywhere), and mother of a son who was killed by an impaired driver describes how that driver "took the sunshine from [her] life" (Chapter 8, Alcohol and Other Drugs).
- Ainsworth Morgan, an inner-city teacher and former Toronto Argonauts football player, outlines his ideas and projects to help his students succeed and help others (Chapter 12, Problems in Education).
- His Holiness the Dalai Lama speaks about pathways to peace, while President George W. Bush outlines his declaration of war against terrorism (Chapter 17, Global Social Problems: Our Common Humanity—Addressing War and Terrorism).

Interesting and Highly Relevant Boxed Features

Four different boxes—Social Problems and Information Technology, Social Problems in the Media, Social Problems and Social Policy, and Social Problems in Global Perspective—highlight current hot topics involving various long-term social problems. Examples of each type of box are:

- *Social Problems and Information Technology:* "Cracking Down on Internet Child Pornography" (Chapter 7, "The Sex Industry in Canada and Beyond");
- *Social Problems in the Media:* "Media Ageism: Reporting on and Preferring Age Groups " (Chapter 5, "Inequality Based on Age");
- *Social Problems and Social Policy:* "The Battle over Marijuana: Medicalization; Availability; Decriminalization; Legalization?" (Chapter 8, Alcohol and Other Drugs); and

- *Social Problems in Global Perspective:* "The Lysistrata Project" (Chapter 18, Can Social Problems Be Solved?).

Built-in Study Features

These pedagogical aids promote students' mastery of sociological concepts and perspectives:

- **Chapter Outlines:** A concise outline at the beginning of each chapter gives students an overview of major topics.
- **What Can You Do?** This section gives students suggestions about how they can tackle social problems on their own, as individuals, or collectively in a group.
- **Key Terms:** Major concepts and key terms are defined and highlighted in bold print within the text. Definitions are also available in the glossary at the back of the text.
- **Summary in question-and-answer format:** Each chapter concludes with a concise summary in a convenient question-and-answer format, to help students master the key concepts and main ideas in each chapter.
- **Questions for Critical Thinking:** End-of-chapter questions provide opportunities for students to develop important critical-thinking skills about the issues raised in each chapter.
- **Weblinks:** Several websites are listed to encourage students to pursue their interests, from a variety of perspectives, and gain more up-to-date material on social issues they are interested in following up.

Supplements

- **For the Instructor:** A variety of supplements is offered, including an Instructor's Manual, Test Bank, Test Generator and PowerPoint Slides (on the Companion Website). Please contact your local sales representative for more information on these items.
- **For the Student:** A wealth of online resources can be found on the Companion Website with Online Practice Tests (**www.pearsoned.ca/kendall**).

ACKNOWLEDGMENTS

We wish to thank personally the many people who have made this Canadian edition a reality. First, we offer our profound thanks to the following reviewers who provided valuable comments and suggestions on how to make this text outstanding. Whenever possible, we have incorporated their suggestions into the text. The reviewers are:

> Winston Barnwell, Dalhousie University
> Donald Clairmont, Dalhousie University
> Kimberley Ducey, McGill University
> Joy Emmanuel, Acadia University and Saint Mary's University
> Rick Grant, Loyalist College
> Richard Haigh, Grant MacEwan College
> Kate Krug, Acadia University
> Carmen Perillo, Centennial College and York University
> Peter Urmetzer, Okanagan University College
> Madine VanderPlaat, Saint Mary's University

The Canadian edition of *Social Problems in a Diverse Society* has also involved the co-operative efforts of many people who have made this book possible. We wish to thank Jessica Mosher, Executive Acquisitions Editor; Martina van de Velde, Senior Developmental Editor; Cheryl Jackson and Richard di Santo, Production Editors; and Margaret McClintock, Copy Editor.

I could not have written this book without the assistance of my husband, Terrence Kendall, who has done so much outstanding advising, editing—and sometimes consoling—on this and other texts I have written that I have declared him to be not only a lawyer but also an "Honorary Sociologist."

—Diana Kendall

My heartfelt thanks go my amazing partner, Gary Zubick, my beautiful daughters, Freja Aramaia, Phoenix Taran, and Natasha Claire, and my dearest friend, Maya Gislason, who endured much while continuing to offer love and support (and chocolate!) throughout the research and writing of this book. My appreciation also goes to my many friends, family members, and students in my classes who, over the years, have raised critical questions, gently educated me, and each other, and inspired hope . . . This one's for you!

—Vicki L. Nygaard

I could not have written this book without the assistance of my partner, Helen Barron, who has not only provided continuing support, but also edited each of my chapters. I would also like to thank a former student, Daisy Mae Hamelinck, for her comments on the Family and Education chapters.

—Edward G. Thompson

To each of you reading this preface, we wish you the best in teaching or studying social problems and hope that you will share with us any comments or suggestions you have about *Social Problems in a Diverse Society*, Canadian Edition. The text was written with you in mind, and your suggestions (with appropriate attribution) will be included whenever possible in future editions. Let's hope that our enthusiasm for "taking a new look at social problems" will spread to others so that together we may seek to reduce or solve some of the pressing social problems we encounter during our lifetime.

Diana Kendall
Vicki L. Nygaard
Edward G. Thompson

TAKING A NEW LOOK AT SOCIAL PROBLEMS

1

Gosset did something wrong, we all knew that. Gosset murdered my son. He used the law. He hid behind it. There's no way we could have gotten justice . . . . I'm not a racist person but I believe that both juries did not give us justice and I'm going to say freely that I do not think white people can give justice to black people . . . I think in their hearts they just can't.

Orberth Griffin, speaking out after the acquittal of the police officer who fatally shot Griffin's son (Pedicelli, 1998:94)

In no way am I racist. Where I used to live in Lasalle, there were many black people and I often vacation in countries that are predominantly black.

Constable Allan Gosset in response to accusations of racism in the shooting death of Anthony Griffin (Pedicelli, 1998:78)

To steal that [the touch of her son] away from you, it's like death to you.

Julia Farquharson speaks of her son's shooting to people trying to deal with the killing of over 100 Black youths by other Black youths in Toronto since 1996 (CBC, 2003)

Whether it takes place in an inner-city schoolyard or on a city street or in Iraq, Afghanistan, or Kosovo, violence leaves shock and anguish behind. ***Violence* is the use of physical force to cause pain, injury, or death or damage to property.** Around the world, violence is a major social problem. On an almost daily basis, the Internet and television news channels quickly spread word of the latest bombing, the latest massacre, the latest sexual assault, the latest murder. In Canada, a place not known for the violence reported daily in the United States, murders of youth by other youth have made headlines. Besides recent murders of youth in Toronto, a young South Asian woman, Reena Virk, was harassed and later killed by a group of peers in Victoria, B.C. The other youth were white, adding a racialized dimension to the tragedy. Additionally, following the Columbine High School murders in Littleton, Colorado, April 20, 1999, a 14-year-old Taber, Alberta, boy brought a gun to school and shot 17-year-old Jason Lang to death and injured another boy.

In the wake of each new episode of violence, a renewed call for gun control goes out from advocates of restricted access to guns and other weaponry. Advocates of gun control point to Department of Justice information showing that the province with the highest percentage of homes with guns is Alberta, followed by New Brunswick and Saskatchewan; the provinces with the highest rate of youth, aged 15 to 25, killed by firearms are, in order, New Brunswick, Saskatchewan, and Alberta (CBC, 1999). A corresponding cry arises from gun enthusiasts across the country and such organizations as the National Firearms Association, who oppose further tightening of gun laws. In fact, in a recent news release, the National Firearms Association (2002) called the federal government's newest gun control program "a dog and pony show."

Many of us are ambivalent about violence. We condemn drive-by shootings and cold-blooded murders, yet enjoy watching action movies with lots of "blood and guts" or contact sports such as wrestling, hockey, football, and boxing. However we explain this contradictory behaviour, violence is seen by many as a major social problem, in this country and around the world.

WHAT IS A SOCIAL PROBLEM?

Although not all sociologists agree about what constitutes a social problem, most would agree with this general definition: A *social problem* **is a social condition (such as poverty) or a pattern of behaviour (such as violence against women) that people believe warrants public concern and collective action to bring about change.** Social conditions or certain patterns of behaviour are defined as social problems when they systematically disadvantage or harm a significant number of people (or number of "significant" people?) or when they are seen as harmful by many of the people who wield power, wealth, and influence in a group or society. To put it another way, social problems are social in their causes, consequences, and possible sources of resolution.

The study of social problems is one area of inquiry within *sociology—***the academic and scholarly discipline that engages in systematic study of human society and social interactions.** A sociological examination of social problems focuses primarily on issues that affect an entire *society*—**a large number of individuals who share the same geographical territory and are subject to the same political authority and dominant cultural expectations**—and the groups and organizations that make up that society. Because social problems are social in their causes, public perception of what constitutes a social problem can change. Consider, for example, how public perception of what constitutes a social problem has changed over the last 50 years. In the 1950s, people worried about the problem of nuclear war. More recently, people have been worried about unemployment (early 1980s and early 1990s), government debt (mid-1990s), and, in the last few years, cutbacks to health care, education, and social services (*Maclean's*, 1999, 2002).

Sociologists apply theoretical perspectives and use a variety of research methods to examine social problems. Some social problems—such as violence and crime—are commonly viewed as conditions that affect all members of a population. Other social problems—such as racialized discrimination and sexual harassment—may be viewed (correctly or incorrectly) as conditions that affect some members of a population more than others. However, all social problems may be harmful to all members in a society whether they realize it or not. Sociological research, for example, has documented the extent to which white racism wastes the energies and resources of people who engage in racist actions as well as those of the targets of the actions (see Feagin and Sikes, 1994; Feagin and Vera, 1995).

Social problems often involve significant discrepancies between the ideals of a society and their actual achievement. For example, in Canada, the rights of individuals are guaranteed by the *Charter of Rights and Freedoms*, which also provides the legal basis for remedying injustices. Significant discrepancies exist, however,

SOCIAL PROBLEMS IN GLOBAL PERSPECTIVE

BOX 1.1 Violence around the World

In its first *World Report on Violence and Health,* released in October 2002, the World Health Organization (WHO) stated that violence kills 1.6 million people annually. About one-half of these deaths are due to suicide; one-third are due to homicide; and 20 percent are due to armed conflict. One person commits suicide every 40 or so seconds; one person is the victim of a homicide every minute; and one person is killed in armed conflict every two minutes. During the 20th century, about 191 million people were killed in armed conflict. Many more people are injured, physically and psychologically. Young people aged 15 to 44 are especially affected. Violence is a major cause of death for this group: 14 percent of young males and 7 percent of young females die violently.

Some patterns of victimization are experienced worldwide. For example, in Canada, nearly half of murdered women are killed by an intimate or former intimate partner (see Chapter 9); about 20 percent of women and 5 to 10 percent of men experience sexual abuse (see Chapter 11); and about 4 percent of the elderly experience abuse (see Chapter 5). Other patterns show wide differences in rates of victimization. For example, the rate of violent death is twice as high in low- and middle-income countries than in high-income countries; in some countries, up to 70 percent of women are killed by intimate or former intimate partners, and one-third of adolescent girls report forced sexual initiation. Patterns also vary by region. In Europe and Asia, suicides exceed homicides; in Latin America, homicides exceed suicides.

Following its mandate, the WHO promotes a public health approach to understanding the problem of violence. Thus, its *World Report on Violence and Health* could be considered as part of the process of the medicalization of crime and deviance (see Chapter 9). To solve the problem of violence, the report recommends dealing with the social, cultural, economic, and psychological root causes of violence and taking advantage of opportunities to prevent violence. Developing community projects such as parent training and gun-safety training, strengthening responses of victims to violence, collecting better data on violence, and seeking practical international agreements to combat the drug and arms trades are among the recommendations put forward.

This book offers you an opportunity to explore these and other problems in greater depth—and to learn some of the things you can do about them.

Source: World Health Organization (WHO), 2002. World Report on Violence and Health. *Retrieved February 15, 2003, from* http://www5.who.int/violence_injury_prevention/main.cfm?P=0000000117

between the democratic ideal and its achievement. One such discrepancy is *discrimination*—**actions or practices of dominant group members (or their representatives) that have a harmful impact on members of subordinate groups.** Sociologists define the *dominant group* as **the group whose members are disproportionately at the top of the hierarchy, "with maximal access to the society's power resources, particularly political authority and control of the means of economic production"** (Marger, 1999:273). *Subordinate groups* are all **those whose members, in relation to the dominant group (or groups), do not occupy such positions of power.** The term usually used for a subordinate group is *minority group* (see Chapter 3).

Discrimination may be directed along a number of lines—class, racialization, gender, and age. It also may be directed against subordinate group members whose sexual orientation, religion, nationality, disability, or other attributes or characteristics are devalued by those who discriminate against them. Sometimes, discrimination is acted out in the form of violence. This type of violent act is referred to as a *hate crime*—**an act of violence motivated by prejudice against people on the basis of racialized identity, ethnicity, religion, gender, or sexual orientation. This can include the dissemination of materials intended to incite hatred.** Although hate crimes have been added to the *Criminal Code* only quite recently, the crimes themselves date back hundreds of years (see Chapters 3, 6, and 9 for further discussion of hate crimes).

What does this photo show us about the discrepancies that exist between the democratic ideals and the social realities of our society? Does discrimination against subordinate group members take place in other societies as well?

Subjective Awareness and Objective Reality

A subjective awareness that a social problem exists usually emerges before the objective reality of the problem is acknowledged. Subjective awareness tends to be expressed as a feeling of uneasiness or skepticism about something, but the feeling may not correspond to concrete evidence about that problem. On the other hand, concrete measures, like those used in recognized national data, for example, may not be the best measures to indicate social problems for particular groups of people or for the future. For example, for several years the Canadian Council on Social Development (CCSD) has been comparing the data and perception indexes of the Personal Security Index (Schetagne, Jackson, and Harman, 2001). The data index contains

national data about economic (e.g., disposable income, unemployment rates, and debt level), health (e.g., potential years of life lost of the population, and work and traffic injuries), and crime (e.g., property and violent crime rates) problems. The perception index contains Canadians' perceptions about their economic security (e.g., adequacy of household income and chance of losing their job), health security (e.g., stress levels and self-ratings of health), and crime security (e.g., the safety of the neighbourhood and household exposure to crime). Different weightings were given to these measures and both indexes were set at 100 in 1998. Since 1998, the data index has risen over 15 percent, indicating we are more secure by the national measures. However, the perception index, after rising initially, has returned almost to 100. Is it the case that people have a mistaken notion of how secure they are? Or do they have a feeling of impending problems that the data index cannot yet measure? Perhaps people are over-reacting to problems in the economy, health care system, and crime because of media bias or over-reporting of certain kinds of situations. This textbook will study both people's subjective awareness of social problems, more objective measures of these problems, and, finally, the question of objectivity itself.

Why Study Social Problems?

Studying social problems helps us to understand the social forces that shape our lives on both personal and societal levels. In our daily lives, we rely on common sense—"what everybody knows"—to guide our conduct and make sense of human behaviour. But many commonsense notions about why people behave the way they do, who makes the rules, and why some people break rules and others follow them are *myths*—beliefs that persist even when the actual truth is different. Myths about social problems frequently garner widespread acceptance and, sometimes, extensive media coverage.

A sociological examination of social problems enables us to move beyond commonsense notions, to gain new insights into ourselves, and to develop an awareness of the connection between our own world and the worlds of other people. According to sociologist Peter Berger (1963:23), a sociological examination allows us to realize that "things are not what they seem." Indeed, most social problems are multifaceted. When we recognize this, we can approach pressing local, national, and global concerns in new ways and make more effective decisions about those concerns. In taking a global perspective on social problems, we soon realize that the lives of all people are closely intertwined, and that any one nation's problems are part of a larger global problem.

THE SOCIOLOGICAL IMAGINATION AND SOCIAL PROBLEMS

Just like other people, sociologists usually have strong opinions about what is "good" and "bad" in society and what might be done to improve conditions. However, sociologists know their opinions are subjective. Thus,

they use systematic research techniques and report their findings to other social scientists for consideration. In other words, sociologists strive to view social problems *objectively*. Of course, complete objectivity may not be an attainable—or desirable—goal in studying human behaviour. Max Weber (1864–1920), an early German sociologist, acknowledged that complete objectivity might be impossible and pointed out that *verstehen* ("understanding," or "insight") was critical to any analysis of social problems. According to Weber, *verstehen* enables individuals to see the world as others see it and to empathize with them. *Verstehen*, in turn, enables us to develop what is called the sociological imagination.

According to sociologist C. Wright Mills (1959b), the **sociological imagination is the ability to see the relationship between an individual's experiences and the larger society in which they are contextualized.** The sociological imagination enables us to connect the private troubles of individuals to the public issues of a society. Public issues (or social problems) are matters beyond a person's control that originate at the regional or national level and can be resolved only by collective action. In *The Sociological Imagination*, Mills used unemployment as an example of how people may erroneously separate personal troubles from public issues in their thinking. The unemployed individual may view his or her unemployment as a personal trouble concerning only the individual, other family members, and friends. However, widespread unemployment resulting from economic changes, corporate decisions (downsizing or relocating a plant abroad), or technological innovations (computers and advanced telecommunications systems displacing workers) is a public issue. The sociological imagination helps us to shift our focus to the larger social context and see how personal troubles may be related to public issues.

Sociologists make connections between personal and public issues in society through microlevel and macrolevel analysis. **Microlevel analysis focuses on small-group relations and social interaction among individuals.** Using microlevel analysis, a sociologist might investigate how fear of unemployment affects workers and their immediate families. In contrast, **macrolevel analysis focuses on social processes occurring at the societal level, especially in large-scale organizations and major social institutions such as politics, government, and the economy.** Using macrolevel analysis, a sociologist might examine how globalization, and the attendant labour market restructuring, has impacted Canadian workers and their families.

As Mills suggested, a systematic study of a social problem such as unemployment gives us a clearer picture of the relationship between macrolevel structures such as the Canadian economy and microlevel social interactions among people in their homes, workplaces, and communities. It does not get the individual his or her job back, but provides a better understanding of how the situation happened. With a clearer understanding of how we find ourselves in the situations we do, more effective levels of prevention and intervention may be possible.

SOCIOLOGICAL PERSPECTIVES ON SOCIAL PROBLEMS

To determine how social life is organized, sociologists develop theories and conduct research. A **theory is a set of logically related statements that attempt to describe, explain, or predict social events.** Theories are useful for explaining relationships between social concepts or phenomena, such as "ethnicity and unemployment" or "gender and poverty." They also help us to interpret social reality in a distinct way by giving us a framework for organizing our observations. Sociologists refer to this theoretical framework as a **perspective—an overall approach or viewpoint toward some subject.** Four major theoretical perspectives have emerged in sociology: the functionalist perspective, which views society as a basically stable and orderly entity; the conflict perspective, which views society as an arena of competition and conflict; the interactionist perspective, which focuses on the everyday, routine interactions among individuals; and, the feminist perspective, which focuses on the gendered (and racialized and classed) inequalities between groups and on strategies for positive social change. The functionalist and conflict perspectives are based on macrolevel analysis because they focus on social processes occurring at the societal level. The interactionist perspective is based on microlevel analysis because it focuses on small-group relations and social interaction. The feminist perspective involves both macro- and microlevel analysis by looking at the ways, for example, that the dominant gender ideology (macro) impacts the specific interactions (micro) between woman X and man Y within a capitalist and patriarchal, white-dominant culture.

The Functionalist Perspective

The functionalist perspective grew out of the works of early social thinkers such as Auguste Comte (1798–1857), the founder of sociology. Comte compared society to a living organism. Just as muscles, tissues, and organs of the human body perform specific functions that maintain the body as a whole, the various parts of society contribute to its maintenance and preservation. According to the **functionalist perspective, society is a stable, orderly system composed of a number of interrelated parts, each of which performs a function that contributes to the overall stability of society** (Parsons, 1951). These interrelated parts are social institutions (such as families, the economy, education, and the government) that a society develops to organize its main concerns and activities so that social needs are met. Each institution performs a unique function, contributing to the overall stability of society and the well-being of individuals (R.K. Merton, 1968). For example, the functions of the economy are producing and distributing goods (such as food, clothing, and shelter) and services (such as tourism services and dry-cleaning), whereas the government is responsible for coordinating activities of other institutions directed to such ends as health care, education, maintaining law and order, dealing with unmet social needs, and handling international relations and peace.

Manifest and Latent Functions

Though the functions of the economy and the government seem fairly clear-cut, functionalists suggest that not all the functions of social institutions are intended and overtly recognized. In fact, according to the functionalist perspective, social institutions perform two different types of societal functions: manifest and latent. *Manifest functions* are intended and recognized consequences of an activity or social process. A manifest function of education, for example, is to provide students with knowledge, skills, and cultural values. In contrast, *latent functions* are the unintended consequences of an activity or social process that are hidden and remain unacknowledged by participants

(R.K. Merton, 1968). The latent functions of education include the babysitter function of keeping young people off the street while their parents work and out of the full-time job market and the matchmaking function whereby schools provide opportunities for students to meet and socialize with potential marriage partners. These functions are latent because schools were not created for babysitting or matchmaking, and most organizational participants do not acknowledge that these activities take place.

Dysfunctions and Social Disorganization

From the functionalist perspective, social problems arise when social institutions do not fulfill their functions or when dysfunctions occur. *Dysfunctions* are the undesirable consequences of an activity or social process that inhibit a society's ability to adapt or adjust (R.K. Merton, 1968). For example, a function of education is to prepare students for jobs, but if schools fail to do so, then students have problems finding jobs, employers or governments have to spend millions of dollars on employee training programs, and consumers have to pay higher prices for goods and services to offset worker training costs. In other words, dysfunctions in education threaten other social institutions, especially families and the economy.

Dysfunctions can occur in society as a whole or in a part of society (a social institution). According to functionalists, dysfunctions in social institutions create social disorganization in the entire society. *Social disorganization* **refers to the conditions in society that undermine the ability of traditional social institutions to govern human behaviour.** Early in the 20th century, sociologists Robert E. Park (1864–1944) and Ernest W. Burgess (1886–1966) developed a social disorganization theory to explain why some urban areas had higher rates of *social deviance,* which they defined as a pattern of rule violation, than other areas had. Social disorganization causes a breakdown in the traditional values and norms that serve as social control mechanisms, which, under normal circumstances, keep people from engaging in nonconforming behaviour. *Values* **are collective ideas about what is right or wrong, good or bad, and desirable or undesirable in a specific society** (R.M. Williams, 1970). Although values provide ideas about behaviour, they do not state explicitly how we should behave. Norms, on the other hand, have specific behavioural expectations. *Norms* **are estab-**

lished rules of behaviour or standards of conduct. French sociologist Emile Durkheim (1858–1917) suggested that social problems arise when people no longer agree on societal values and norms. According to Durkheim, periods of rapid social change produce *anomie*—a loss of shared values and sense of purpose in society. During these periods, social bonds grow weaker, social control is diminished, and people are more likely to engage in nonconforming patterns of behaviour, such as crime.

Early sociologists, examining the relationship between social problems and rapid industrialization and urbanization in Britain, Western Europe, and the United States in the late 19th and early 20th centuries, noted that rapid social change intensifies social disorganization. *Industrialization* **is the process by which societies are transformed from a dependence on agriculture and handmade products to an emphasis on manufacturing and related industries.** At the beginning of the Industrial Revolution, thousands of people migrated from rural communities to large urban centres to find employment in factories and offices. New social problems emerged as a result of industrialization and *urbanization,* **the process by which an increasing proportion of a population lives in cities rather than in rural areas.** During this period of rapid technological and social change, a sharp increase occurred in urban social problems such as poverty, crime, child labour, inadequate housing, unsanitary conditions, overcrowding, and environmental pollution.

Applying the Functionalist Perspective to Problems of Violence

Some functionalists believe that violence arises from a condition of anomie, in which many individuals have a feeling of helplessness, normlessness, or alienation. Others believe that violence increases when social institutions such as the family, schools, and religious organizations weaken, and the main mechanisms of social control in people's everyday lives are external (i.e., law enforcement agencies and the criminal justice system).

Other functionalist explanations of violence focus on how changes in social institutions put some people at greater risk of being victims of violent crime than others. According to the *lifestyle–routine activity approach,* **the patterns and timing of people's daily** movements and activities as they go about obtaining such necessities of life as food, shelter, companionship, and entertainment are the keys to understanding violent personal crimes and other types of crime in our society** (L.E. Cohen and Felson, 1979). Among the changes over the past 50 years that have put people at increased risk for violent crime victimization in Canada may be more people living by themselves, shopping hours extended into the night, and more people eating outside the home (Parker, 1995). Social structure may also put constraints on behaviour, thus making certain people more vulnerable to violent attack (e.g., people who are required to work at night). The lifestyle– routine activity approach suggests that people who willingly put themselves in situations that expose them to the potential for violent crime should modify their behaviour or that society should provide greater protection for people whose lifestyle routine leaves them vulnerable to attackers. The lifestyle–routine activity approach is good as far as it goes, but it does not address the issue of violence in the home and other supposedly safe havens in society. Further, there is no explanation for the actual violence, just that people are at risk, which tells us nothing that would assist in eliminating violence.

How would a functionalist approach the problem of violence? Most functionalists emphasize shared moral values and social bonds. They believe that when rapid social change or other "disruptions" occur, moral values may erode and problems such as school violence or hate crimes are likely to occur more frequently. Functionalists believe that to reduce violence, families, schools, religious organizations, and other social institutions should be strengthened so that they can regenerate shared values and morality. Most functionalists also believe that those who engage in violent criminal behaviour should be prosecuted to the full extent of the law.

The Conflict Perspective

The *conflict perspective* **is based on the assumption that groups in society are engaged in a continuous power struggle for control of scarce resources.** Unlike functionalist theorists, who emphasize the degree to which society is held together by a consensus on values, conflict theorists emphasize the degree to which society is characterized by conflict and discrimination. According to some conflict theorists, certain groups of

The brutal murder of 14-year-old Reena Virk, a high-school student of South Asian descent, in Victoria, B.C., in 1997 by eight other youths produced an outcry in her community. Some people were concerned that hate crimes against individuals because of ethnic origin, class, or gender might go unpunished, or that the punishment of Virk's attackers would be too lenient because they were young, white, and middle-class.

people are privileged while others are disadvantaged through the inequitable use of political, economic, or social power. Not all conflict theorists hold the same views about what constitutes the most important form of conflict. We will examine two principal perspectives: the value conflict perspective and the critical-conflict perspective.

The Value Conflict Perspective

According to value conflict theorists, social problems are conditions that are incompatible with group values. From this perspective, value clashes are ordinary occurrences in families, communities, and the larger society, in which individuals commonly hold many divergent values. Although individuals may share certain core values, they do not share all values or a common culture. *Culture* refers to the knowledge, language, values, customs, and material objects that are passed from person to person and from one generation to the next in a human group or society.

Discrepancies between ideal and real culture are a source of social problems in all societies. *Ideal culture* refers to the values and beliefs that people claim they hold; *real culture* refers to the values and beliefs that they actually follow. In Canada, members of such diverse groups as B'nai Brith, the Heritage Front, the Aryan Nations, and the Urban Alliance on Race Relations all claim to adhere to ideal cultural values of equality, freedom, and liberty; however, these ideal cultural values come into direct conflict with real cultural values when issues of racialized/ethnic relations arise.

The value conflict perspective has been criticized by critical-conflict theorists, who argue that it overlooks the deeper social problems of inequality and oppression based on class, "race," and gender.

Critical-Conflict Perspective

Unlike the value conflict approach, critical-conflict theorists suggest that social problems arise out of the major contradictions inherent in the way societies are organized. Some critical-conflict perspectives focus on class inequalities in the capitalist economic system; others focus on inequalities based on "race"/ethnicity or gender.

Most class perspectives on inequality have been strongly influenced by Karl Marx (1818–1883), a German economist and activist, who recognized that the emergence of capitalism had produced dramatic and irreversible changes in social life. **Capitalism is an economic system characterized by private ownership of the means of production, from which personal profits can be derived through market competition and without government intervention.** According to Marx, members of the *capitalist class* (the *bourgeoisie*), who own and control the means of production (e.g., the land, tools, factories, and money for investment), are at the top of a system of social stratification that affords them different lifestyles and life chances from those of the members of the *working class* (the *proletariat*), who must sell their labour power (their potential ability to work) to capitalists. In selling their labour power, members of the working class forfeit control over their work, and the capitalists derive profits from the workers' labour.

Marx believed that capitalism led workers to experience increased levels of impoverishment and *alienation*—a feeling of powerlessness and estrangement from other people and from oneself (Marx and Engels, 1847/1971:96). He predicted that the working class would eventually overthrow the capitalist economic system. Although Marx's prediction has not come about, Erik Olin Wright (1997) and other social scientists have modified and adapted his perspective to apply to contemporary capitalist nations. In today's capitalist nations, according to Wright (1997), ownership of the means of production is only one way in which people gain the ability to exploit others. Two other ways in which individuals gain control are through *control* of property and *control* over other people's labour. In this view, upper-level managers and others in positions of authority gain control over societal resources and other individuals' time, knowledge, and skills in such a manner that members of the upper classes are able to maintain their dominance.

Some critical-conflict perspectives focus on racialized and gender subordination instead of class-based inequalities. Critical-conflict theorists who emphasize discrimination and inequality based on "race" or ethnicity note that many social problems are rooted in the continuing exploitation and subordination of people of colour and Indigenous people by white people, or more accurately, by institutions and systems set up by and for white people. For example, Frideres (1999:142–44) has shown how Indigenous people in Canada are greatly disadvantaged relative to any other ethnic groups; they have considerably lower family incomes and substantially higher rates of unemployment than non-Indigenous people.

Throughout this text, where we discuss conflict theory, we will use critical-conflict theory (rather than the value conflict approach) to highlight the power relations that result in social problems.

Applying the Conflict Perspective to Problems of Violence

Conflict theorists who focus on class-based inequalities believe that the potential for violence is inherent in capitalist societies. In fact, say these theorists, the wealthy engage in one form of violence, and the poor engage in another. They note that the wealthy often use third parties to protect themselves and their families from bodily harm as well as to secure their property and investments in this country and elsewhere in the world. For example, the wealthy who live in Canada or other high-income nations and own factories (or own stock in factories) in middle- and low-income nations, use the governments and police of those nations—third parties—to control workers who threaten to strike. The wealthy also influence Canadian government policy, by supporting or not supporting peacekeeping or military intervention in nations where they may have investments or desire to have investments.

In contrast, these theorists say, when the poor engage in violence, the violence is typically committed by the individual and may be a reaction to the unjust social and economic conditions he or she experiences daily on the bottom rung of a capitalist society. The economic exploitation of the poor, these theorists note, dramatically affects all aspects of the individual's life, including how the person reacts to daily injustices, stress, and other threatening situations. In violent street crimes, the vast majority of offenders—as well as victims—are poor, unemployed, or working in low-level, low-paying jobs. In fact, most violent street crime is an intraclass phenomenon: Poor and working-class people typically victimize others who are like themselves. In part, this is due to the fact that violence committed by middle- and upper-class individuals is not investigated and/or prosecuted, on par. Moreover, middle- and upper-class individuals are likely to obtain the services of people from lower classes when they wish to commit violence. For example, in a televised interview, Brett Hayes, a past member of a neo-Nazi skinhead organization in Canada, stated that certain individuals are targeted for violence by the organization's elite (many allegedly in prominent positions in society) but the actual violence is commissioned and carried out by the "foot soldiers," or "dogs," of the movement, the mainly working-class and youthful "skins" (CTV, 1995).

The conflict perspective argues that the criminal justice system is biased in favour of the middle and upper classes. Because it is, its definition of violence depends on where a person's ethnicity, class, and gender locate him or her in the system of stratification. In this way, violent crimes are but one part of a larger system of inequality and oppression. Sexism and racism are reinforced by the overarching class structure that benefits the powerful at the expense of the powerless. The conflict perspective that focuses on racialized/ethnic inequalities points out that racism is an important factor in explaining such violent acts as hate crimes. Recently, a number of white supremacists spouting racist and anti-Semitic dogma have been convicted of violent crimes. This kind of brutality, for example the murder of a Sikh man in Surrey, British Columbia, by a group of white supremacists, is fuelled by racist ideologies that suggest that problems with the economy and growing unemployment for young people are due to increased immigration. Leaders of white supremacist groups foster these discourses as a way of fuelling hate and inciting violence (see Chapter 3).

No matter what approach conflict theorists take, they all agree on one thing: Violence is unlikely to diminish significantly unless inequalities based on class and ethnicity are reduced at the macrolevel in society.

The Interactionist Perspective

Unlike the conflict perspective, which focuses on macrolevel inequalities in society, the interactionist perspective focuses on microlevel analyses of how people act toward one another and how they make sense of their daily lives. The **interactionist perspective views society as the sum of the interactions of individuals and groups.** Most interactionists study social problems by analyzing how certain behaviour comes to be defined as a social problem and how individuals and groups come to engage in activities that a significant number of people and/or a number of significant people view as a major social concern.

German sociologist Georg Simmel (1858–1918), a founder of the interactionist approach, investigated the impact of industrialization and urbanization on people's values and behaviour within small social units. Simmel (1902/1950) noted that rapid changes in technology and dramatic urban growth produced new social problems by breaking up the "geometry of social life," which he described as the web of patterned social interactions among the people who constitute a society. According to Simmel, alienation is brought about by a decline in personal and emotional contacts. How people *interpret* the subjective messages that they receive from others and the situations that they encounter in their daily life greatly influences their behaviour and perceptions of what constitutes a social problem.

Labelling Theory and the Social Construction of Reality

While Simmel focused on how people interpret their own situations, other interactionists have examined how people impose their shared meanings on others. According to sociologist Howard Becker (1963), *moral entrepreneurs* are people who use their own views of right and wrong to establish rules and *label* others as deviant (nonconforming). *Labelling theory*, as this perspective is called, suggests that behaviour that deviates from established norms is deviant *because* it has been labelled as such by others. According to this theory, deviants (nonconformists) are people who have been successfully labelled as such by others. Labelling theory raises questions about why certain individuals and certain types of behaviour are labelled as deviant but others are not. The answer is suggestive of an analysis of power, which this theory has no real view of.

According to some interaction theorists, many social problems can be linked to the *social construction of reality*—the process by which people's perception of reality is shaped largely by the subjective meaning that they give to an experience (P. Berger and Luckmann, 1967). From this perspective, little shared reality exists beyond that which people socially create. It is, however, this social construction of reality that influences people's beliefs and actions. Other interactionists suggest that how we define a situation affects our reactions to it. According to sociologist W.I. Thomas (1863–1947), when people define situations as real, the situations become real in their consequences. Elaborating on the Thomas Theorum, as it has come to be called, sociologist Robert Merton (1968) has suggested that when people perceive a situation in a certain way and act according to their perceptions, the end result may be a *self-fulfilling prophecy*—**a false definition of a situation that evokes a new behaviour that makes the original false conception become true.** For example, a teenager who is labelled a "juvenile delinquent" may accept the label and adopt the full-blown image of a juvenile delinquent as portrayed in television programs and films: wearing "gang" colours, dropping out of school, and participating in violence or other behaviour that is labelled

as deviant. If the teenager is subsequently arrested, the initial label becomes a self-fulfilling prophecy.

Applying Interactionist Perspectives to Problems of Violence

Interactionist explanations of violence begin by noting that human behaviour is learned through social interaction. Violence, interactionists state, is a learned response, not an inherent characteristic, in the individual. Some of the most interesting support for this point of view comes from studies done by social psychologist Albert Bandura (1973), who studied aggression in children. Showing children a film of a person beating, kicking, and hacking an inflatable doll produced a violent response in the children, who, when they were placed in a room with a similar doll, duplicated the behaviour shown in the film and engaged in additional aggressive behaviour. Others have noted that people tend to repeat their behaviour if they feel rewarded for it. Thus, when people learn that they can get their way by inflicting violence or the threat of violence on others, their aggressive behaviour is reinforced. It is important to point out that the "reward" may only be perceived as a reward in the eyes of that person.

Interactionists also look at the types of social interactions that commonly lead to violence. According to the *situational approach*, **violence results from a specific interaction process, termed a "situational transaction."** Criminologist David Luckenbill (1977) has identified six stages in the situational transaction between victim and offender. In the first stage, the future victim does something behavioural or verbal that is considered an affront by the other (e.g., a glare or an insult). In the second, the offended individual verifies that the action was directed at him or her personally. In the third, the offended individual decides how to respond to the affront and may issue a verbal or behavioural challenge (e.g., a verbal threat or a raised fist). If the problem escalates at this point, injury or death may occur in this stage; if not, the participants enter into the fourth stage. In this stage, the future victim further escalates the transaction, often prodded on by onlookers siding with one party or the other. In the fifth stage, actual violence occurs when neither party is able to back down without losing face. At this point, one or both parties produce weapons (if they have not already appeared), which may range from guns and knives to bottles, pool cues, or other bludgeoning devices, and the offender kills the victim. The sixth and final stage involves the offender's actions after the crime; some flee the scene, others are detained by onlookers, and still others call the police themselves.

The situational approach is based, first, on the assumption that many victims are active participants in the violence perpetrated against them and, second, on the idea that confrontation does not inevitably lead to violence or death. As Robert Nash Parker (1995) has noted, in the first four stages of the transaction, either the victim or the offender can decide to pursue another course of action and most often does.

According to interactionists, reducing violence requires changing those societal values that encourage excessive competition and violence. These changes must occur at the microlevel, which means agents of socialization must transmit different attitudes and values toward violence. The next generation must learn that it is an individual's right—regardless of gender, racialized status, class, religion, or other attributes or characteristics—to live free from violence and the devastating impact it has on individuals, groups, and the social fabric of society.

Feminist Perspectives

Feminist theorists begin their analysis by pointing out that mainstream sociological thought and theory is both *androcentric* and *Eurocentric* (Alvi, DeKeseredy, and Ellis, 2000:19). This means most sociological theory is based on the experiences, ideas, and issues of concern for males of European and Western extraction. European and male perspectives are valid, of course, *and* they are partial. All perspectives are partial but, in the past, these perspectives were treated as though they were representative of the experiences, ideas, and issues of all people. Today, we know this is impossible; hence, feminist theories, anti-racist theories, post-colonial theories, Indigenous theories, and so on have been created and employed to account for more of social life, in addition to maintaining the mainstream theories previously discussed.

There are no "feminist issues" per se. Every issue is a feminist issue. Basically, when feminist theorists engage in analysis, they "gender" the issues under study. This means that theorists look at the differential impacts of social phenomena for men and women, and more

recently for transgendered or non-gendered people as well. This does not mean that feminists study only gender, although, in the past, that may have been more true than today. Feminist theories typically examine dynamics of power in relationships between individuals, roles, structures, and so on. This focus on power differentials is shared with conflict and Marxist theories, but feminist theories add a focus on gendered power and patriarchy. A final defining feature of feminist theories is the idea of beginning one's analysis from a particular "standpoint." This is to say that social life is examined from the situated vantage points of the individuals and/or groups involved.

As there is no one feminist perspective, there is no one feminist perspective on social problems. Many authors put forth summaries of numerous variations of feminist theory (liberal, Marxist, radical, socialist, anti-racist, lesbian, cultural, and so on); however, it may be more useful to distinguish between the types of theories instead of the specific variants. Lengermann and Niebrugge-Brantley (1992:319) provide a classification system that categorizes various feminist theories either as (a) theories of difference, (b) theories of inequality, or (c) theories of oppression. Theories are distinguished from one another by the approach taken to answering the question, Why are women's situations as they are? Theories of difference are premised on the idea that men and women experience different realities, based on their differential locations within most situations. Theories of inequality assert that women's situations are not only different from men's but are also less privileged or are disadvantaged relative to men's. Theories of oppression suggest that not only are women's situations different from and unequal to men's but that women are actively subordinated and kept disadvantaged, both by patriarchal structures and individuals reinforcing sexist socialization and ideologies.

Feminist theories and the people who advance them have been appropriately criticized for perpetuating the same kinds of injustice based on "difference" that mainstream sociological theories perpetuated because of their androcentrism and Eurocentricity. Most feminist theory in the past (and today) comes from a white, middle-class, heterosexual, educated women's bias. The issues assumed to be central by these theories, then, are the issues of interest and concern to these groups of people. Criticism arose, for example, because where white and educated feminists saw men and patriarchy denying them reproductive freedom (e.g., access to birth control and abortion), Indigenous women and women of colour saw racism and acts of discrimination (e.g., in employment or housing) affecting both the men and the women of racialized groups as *the* issue of importance. Poor feminists saw academic elitism and poverty as *the* issue of importance for men and women. Lesbians and women with disabilities saw their perspectives silenced or marginalized. So, the locations or situations of the particular theorists determine what issues are defined as the quintessential feminist issues to be taken up.

Modern-day feminist theories, if they are reflexive, turn the lenses back upon themselves. If one is supporting a particular theory, is it sexist? Is it racist? Is it homophobic? Is it classist? Is it ableist? Many contemporary feminists spend a good deal of time deconstructing the theories they favour; the underlying assumptions, the exclusions, the inclusiveness, the impacts of the analysis, the dissemination of the analysis, and so on. While this exercise may seem academic—and it is, in some senses—it is also important to know where the theory is weak, where it cannot be used to see an issue clearly, what the bias is, whose voice is missing, and so on. Several feminist theorists today call for simultaneous analyses of interlocking oppressions (see Chapter 3). These feminist theorists view the social world as a matrix of domination, where sexism, racism, heterosexism, classism, and other marginalized statuses meet in myriad ways over issues. Theoretical analysis focuses on the various ways that these interlocking oppressions play out in different contexts. Other important concepts focused on by contemporary feminist theorists are "public and private spheres, ideology [and] relations of ruling" (Swingewood, 2000:240). A focus on these concepts allows us to analyze macro and micro issues and the interplay between the two, an important feature if we are to have the ability to understand social life from a broader perspective. This leads to a final defining feature of feminist theory—a propensity to propel its adherents toward engaged social action.

Applying Feminist Perspectives to Problems of Violence

Feminist perspectives of violence highlight issues of dominance and power. Inequalities between groups result in violence. People who enjoy power and privilege likely commit as many acts of violence as those who are disenfranchised. The main difference between groups is that those without power are disproportionately targeted as the perpetrators or viewed as bringing it on themselves. So, for example, in an analysis of Reena Virk's November 14, 1997, murder in Victoria, B.C., the media chose to focus on personal characteristics of the murdered young woman—her apparent "flaws"—while ignoring structures of domination and sexist and racist ideologies that create the context for this type of violence and that support and perpetuate gendered and racialized violence. In an incisive antiracist feminist analysis, Yasmin Jiwani (1997:2–3) concludes that

> [the murderers'] power and dominance, legitimized by and rooted in the sexism and racism of the dominant white culture and its attendant sense of superiority, was used to force [Virk] into submission—a submission that amounted to her death and erasure from society . . . . The implicit message [in the media] was that had she been white and had she been thin, she would have fit in, and there would have been no reason for her to be killed . . . . What happened to Reena could have happened to any number of us who are visibly different and doubly or triply marked in this society by virtue of race (sic), gender, sexual orientation and disability.

Feminists also add social class oppression as a location of domination. For example, in Chapter 4, the fact that the Montreal Massacre gained such notoriety is contrasted with the relatively little stir created by the murders of many women from the downtown East Side of Vancouver.

Finally, one feminist perspective suggests that violence against women is a means of reinforcing patriarchy. According to the feminist perspective, in a patriarchal system, the sexual marketplace is characterized by unequal bargaining power, making transactions between men and women potentially coercive in nature. Gender stratification is reinforced by powerful physical, psychological, and social mechanisms of control, including force or the threat of force. Fear of violence forces women to adapt their ways of being in the world—living, acting, and dressing—to ensure they are not in a position to be victimized by men, and thus, they are deprived of many basic freedoms (see C.B. Gardner, 1995).

SOCIAL RESEARCH METHODS FOR STUDYING SOCIAL PROBLEMS

Sociologists use a variety of research methods to study social problems such as violence. *Research methods* are strategies or techniques for systematically collecting data. Some methods produce quantitative data that can be measured numerically and lend themselves to statistical analysis. For example, the *Uniform Crime Report (UCR)*, published annually by the Canadian Centre for Justice Statistics (CCJS), provides crime statistics that sociologists and others can use to learn more about the nature and extent of violent crime in Canada. Other research methods produce qualitative data that are reported in the form of interpretive descriptions (words) rather than numbers. For example, qualitative data on violence in Canada can provide new insights on how the victims or their families and friends and communities cope in the aftermath of violent attacks, such as the school shooting in Taber, Alberta, or the fatal torture and drowning of Reena Virk. It may also be important, in these situations, to hear the words of those youth who committed the murders, not only to attempt an understanding, but to discover how to avoid such situations ever happening again.

Sociologists use three major types of research methods: field research, survey research, and secondary analysis of existing data. Although our discussion focuses on each separately, many researchers use a combination of methods, an approach known as *triangulating*, to enhance their understanding of social issues.

Field Research

Field research is the study of social life in its natural setting: observing and interviewing people where they live, work, and play. When sociologists want first-hand information about a social problem, they often use *participant observation*—field research in which researchers collect systematic observations while participating in the activities of the group they are studying. Field research on social problems can take place in many settings, ranging from schools and neighbourhoods to universities, prisons, and large corporations.

Field research is valuable because some kinds of behaviour and social problems can be studied best by

being there; a more complete understanding can be developed through observations, face-to-face discussions, and participation in events than through other research methods. For example, field research on gang violence led sociologist Martin Sánchez Jankowski (1991) to conclude that violence attributed to gangs is often committed by members who are acting as *individuals* rather than as agents of the organization. According to Jankowski, most gang members do not like violence and fear that they may be injured or killed in violent encounters. As a result, gang members engage in collective violence only to accomplish specific objectives, such as asserting authority or punishing violations by their own members who are incompetent or who break the gang's code. Violence against other gangs occurs primarily when gang members feel threatened or need to maintain or expand their operations in a certain area. According to Jankowski, gang members use collective violence to achieve the goals of gang membership (proving their masculinity and toughness, providing excitement, and maintaining their reputation) mainly when they have been provoked by others or feel fearful.

Sociologists using field research must have good interpersonal skills. They must be able to gain and keep the trust of the people they want to observe or interview. They also must be skilled interviewers who can keep systematic notes on their observations and conversations. Above all, they must treat research subjects fairly and ethically. Every research university, research organization, and sociological association has an established Code of Ethics and an ethics review panel or board, if its members are engaged in research with humans. Typically, a panel will review an application to do social research and, if there are ethical issues, will determine whether the benefit of the research outweighs the costs of potentially violating ethics. Most social research does not carry serious potential ethical infractions with it.

Survey Research

Survey research is probably the research method most frequently used by social scientists. **Survey research is a poll in which researchers ask the research participants a series of questions about a specific topic and record their responses.** Survey research is based on the use of a sample of people who are thought to represent the attributes of the larger population from which they are selected. Survey data are collected by using self-administered questionnaires or by interviewers who ask questions of people in person or by mail, telephone, or the Internet.

Statistics Canada conducts the General Social Survey (GSS) every five years. This survey contains a victimization component to fill in some of the gaps in the *UCR* data. The GSS interviews 10 000 randomly selected households to learn more about the victims of crimes, whether the crime has been formally reported or not. These surveys indicate that the number of crimes committed is substantially higher than the number reported in the *UCR*.

Survey research allows sociologists to study a large population without having to interview everyone in that population. It also yields numerical data that may be compared between groups and over periods of time. However, this type of research does have certain limitations. The use of standardized questions limits the types of information researchers can obtain from participants. Also, because data can be reported numerically, survey research may be misused to overestimate or underestimate the extent of a specific problem such as violence.

Secondary Analysis of Existing Data

Whereas the GSS contains primary data—data that researchers collected specifically for that study—sociologists often rely on **secondary analysis of existing data**—**a research method in which investigators analyze data that originally were collected by others, often for some other purpose.** This method is also known as *unobtrusive research* because data can be gathered without the researcher having to interview or observe research participants. Secondary data include public records such as birth and death records, official reports of organizations or governmental agencies such as Statistics Canada, and information from large databases such as the GSS and the Census.

Secondary analysis often involves *content analysis*, a systematic examination of cultural artifacts or written documents to extract thematic data and draw conclusions about some aspect of social life. For example, for the *National Television Violence Study* (1998) in the U.S., researchers at several universities conducted content analyses of violence in television programming. During a nine-month period each year, from October 1994 to June 1997, researchers selected a variety of programs, including drama, comedy, movies, music videos, reality programs, and children's shows, on 23 television channels, thus creating a composite of the content in a week of television viewing. The viewing hours were from 6:00 A.M. until 11:00 P.M., for a total of 17 hours a day across the seven days of the week. Some of the findings from this study are discussed in Box 1.2.

Some strengths of secondary analysis are its unobtrusive nature and the fact that it can be used even when people refuse to be interviewed or the researcher does not have the opportunity to observe research participants firsthand. However, secondary analysis also has inherent problems. Because the data originally were gathered for some other purpose, they may not fit the exact needs of the researcher, and they may be incomplete or inaccurate.

SOCIAL PROBLEMS AND INFORMATION TECHNOLOGY

BOX 1.2   Studying Violence in Television Programming and Increasing Public Awareness to Achieve a Healthier Environment

The overwhelming weight of evidence points to harmful effects of media violence, though nay-sayers will always persist particularly when funded by media giants like the Motion Picture Association of America. What is needed is a firm commitment to promote media literacy and to stop supporting, with tax credits, the production of media that depict violence.

Rose Dyson, Chair of Canadians Concerned About Violence in Entertainment, in a statement made to one of the authors.

Although many of us learn about the latest acts of violent behaviour from the media, we are less inclined to think about the amount of violence shown on television. In the interest of discovering how much violence is depicted in television programming overall, researchers at the University of California, Santa Barbara; the University of Texas at Austin; the University of Wisconsin, Madison; and the University of North Carolina, Chapel Hill, decided to conduct the *National Television Violence Study* (NTVS). Between 1994 and 1997, more than 300 researchers videotaped approximately 10 000 hours of television programming, and 1600 participants took part in five separate experiments (Federman, 1998). The purpose of the study was to investigate how television portrays violence. The researchers explained their approach in this way (in NTVS, 1998:20):

> We examined three different aspects of the program when assessing how violence is portrayed on television. First, we identified each *violent incident,* or interaction between a perpetrator and a victim. Second, we analyzed each *violent scene,* or instance of ongoing, uninterrupted violence. A violent scene, such as a bar fight, often contains several violent incidents between different types of characters. Finally, we analyzed the entire *violent program . . . .* By analyzing violence at all of these levels—the incidence, the scene, and the overall program—we provide rich information about the meaning of violence in television programming.

Although their findings are too numerous to discuss in total, here are a few:

■ Much of television violence is glamorized, sanitized, and trivialized. Characters seldom show remorse for their actions, and there is no criticism or penalty for the violence at the time that it occurs. Those who are victimized do not show physical harm or pain even though the serious physical aggression they have experienced would be lethal or incapacitating if such actions were to occur in real life (NTVS, 1998:26).

■ Across the three years of the study, violence was found in 60 percent of the television programs taped and few of these programs carried anti-violence themes (NTVS, 1998:29).

■ In the three-year period of the study, broadcast networks and basic cable stations increased the proportion of programs containing violence during prime time (the three-hour period each night that draws the most viewers) (NTVS, 1998:29).

■ "High risk" depictions (those that may encourage aggressive attitudes and behaviours) often involve: (1) "a perpetrator who is an attractive role model"; (2) "violence that seems justified"; (3) "violence that goes unpunished"; (4) "minimal consequences to the victims"; and, (5) "violence that seems realistic to the viewer" (NTVS, 1998:29). According to the study, for young viewers (particularly those under age seven), these factors often come together in cartoons (NTVS, 1998:30).

■ The typical preschool child who watches cartoons regularly will come into contact with more than 500 high-risk portrayals of violence each year. For preschoolers who watch television for two to three hours a day, there will be, on average, about one high-risk portrayal of violence per hour in cartoons. As a result, a child who watches two hours of cartoons each day will see more than 500 high-risk portrayals that encourage aggression each year (NTVS, 1998:31).

Is violence on television anything to be concerned about? These researchers believe that it is. Does violence on television encourage or discourage the learning of aggression? While researchers acknowledge that such factors as "peer influences, family role models, social and economic status, educational level, and the availability of weapons can significantly alter the likelihood of a particular reaction to viewing violence on television" (Federman, 1998), they feel their study supports other research findings that indicate viewing televised violence contributes to "learning aggressive attitudes and behaviours." Researchers note that the same graphic depiction of violence that elicits aggression in some people brings about fear of victimization by violence in others (Federman, 1998). Finally, they suggest that television violence serves as a form of "desensitization to violence" (NTVS, 1998:7).

Ironically, depictions of violence have also increased on news programs in recent years, as journalists have spent hours covering the string of shootings that have taken place across the nation. In the final analysis, perhaps the mantra "If it bleeds, it leads" applies to both news coverage and popular, prime-time television shows that attract a young—and often impressionable—audience (R. Turner, 1999).

A Canadian study by Wendy Josephson (1995), of young people of different ages and ethnic backgrounds and who had various kinds of social problems, found that children with limited resources were the most defenseless against the negative effects of televised violence; the effects lead the "'at-risk' children to be even more aggressive than they would otherwise be."

Will television producers, directors, and advertisers become more aware of this problem and do something about it? The answer to this question may be similar to one given by the NTVS researchers, who concluded that the portrayal of violence on television had changed relatively little over the three-year period of their study. If this is true, we can probably expect to see few, if any, changes in the nature and extent of the violence depicted on television in the near future. But, scholars will continue to examine the depiction and document what they believe to be the possible effects of these depictions, particularly on young people.

In Canada, several projects have been initiated to help people study the effects of media violence, increase public awareness of the effects, and promote a healthier environment.

First, the Media Awareness Network (**www.media-awareness. ca/eng/issues/violence/default.htm**) provides a general introduction to media violence in Canada, links to concerned groups, legislation, codes, and ratings, resources, and quick facts.

Second, the Violence and the Media Theme Page (**www.cln.org/themes/media_violence.html**) provides several links for children and violence and the history of the federal government's activities on the topic.

Third, Canadians Concerned About Violence in Entertainment (C-CAVE) (**www.communityradio.org/ C-CAVE.htm**) is an organization committed to increasing public awareness about the effects of cultural violence and bringing about a healthier environment. Since 1986, C-CAVE has been chaired by Rose Dyson (quoted above), author of *Mind Abuse:*

Media Violence in an Information Age (2000), about the nature of the problem and some of the work being done to deal with it.

INTERNET ACTIVITY

Read more about the National Television Violence Study. Then, develop an informal coding system and conduct your own content analysis of the television programs that you like to watch. An executive summary of the NTVS report can be found at **www.ccsp.ucsb.edu/execsum.pdf**. For additional information, contact the Centre for Communication and Social Policy at University of California, Santa Barbara: **http://research. ucsb.edu/cori/ccsp.html**.

Then, with the help of the information on the Canadian Web sites, create a media awareness program to increase public awareness of the effects of media violence.

In Sum

Sociologists view social problems from a variety of perspectives. Each perspective involves different assumptions. Functionalists, who emphasize social cohesion and order in society, commonly view social problems as the result of institutional and societal dysfunctions, social disorganization, or cultural lag, among other things. Conflict theorists, who focus on value conflict or on structural inequalities based on class, ethnicity, or other socially constructed attributes, suggest that social problems arise either from disputes over divergent values or from exploitative relations in society, such as those between capitalists and workers or between different ethnic groups. In contrast, interactionists focus on individuals' interactions and on the social construction of reality. For interactionists, social problems occur when social interaction is disrupted and people are dehumanized, when people are labelled deviant, or when the individual's definition of a situation causes him or her to act in a way that produces a detrimental outcome. Feminist theorists focus on gendering their analyses of inequalities that are maintained and perpetuated by structures and ideologies of domination. The ways that individuals play out oppressive relationships together can be traced to the unequal ways that structures and relations are organized in a capitalist, patriarchal society. This is the root of social problems, according to feminist theorists. We will use

these theoretical perspectives, along with selected others, throughout the book.

No matter what perspectives sociologists employ, they use research to support their ideas. All research methods have certain strengths and weaknesses, but taken together, they provide us with valuable insights that go beyond commonsense knowledge about social problems and stereotypes of people. Using multiple methods and approaches, sociologists can broaden their knowledge of social problems such as violence in Canada and other nations.

In this chapter, we have looked at violence from four sociological perspectives. Like many other social problems, people do not always agree on the causes of violence. They also do not always agree on what should be done about violence. However, this does not mean that we should simply give up and do nothing. The perspective taken by the authors of this text is that Canadians do have a number of pressing social problems to address and that it is our responsibility to work toward a better world, however we conceive that world and however we decide to do that work. In this book, we explore a range of social issues—and ways by which we may eliminate or reduce the harmful effects of those issues we collectively define as "problems." If an issue sparks something in you and you want to get involved, you will find some ideas for social action in the "What Can You Do?" section of each chapter. Of course, there are many more ideas and ways of being involved in the issue(s) of your choice than what we have indicated. Feel free to explore and do your part to make the world a better place. We would love to hear about it! As summarized by UNICEF in 1995, in *The Progress of Nations* (Ecumenical Coalition for Economic Justice, 1996):

> The day will come when the progress of nations will not be judged by their military or economic strength, nor by the splendour of their capital cities and public buildings, but by the well-being of their peoples: by their levels of health and education; by their opportunities to earn a fair reward for their labours; by their ability to participate in the decisions that affect their lives; by the respect that is shown for their political and civil liberties; by the provision that is made for those who are vulnerable and disadvantaged; and by the protection that is afforded to the growing minds and bodies of their children.

Please join us now in exploring many of the crucial issues of the 21st century.

SUMMARY

HOW DO SOCIOLOGISTS DEFINE A SOCIAL PROBLEM?

According to sociologists, a social problem is a social condition (such as poverty) or a pattern of behaviour (such as substance abuse) that people believe warrants public concern and collective action to bring about change.

HOW DO SOCIOLOGISTS VIEW VIOLENCE?

Sociologists view violence as a social problem that involves both a subjective awareness and objective reality. We have a subjective awareness that violence can occur in such public settings as schools, day-care centres, businesses, and churches. Our subjective awareness becomes an objective reality when we can measure and experience the effects of violent criminal behaviour.

HOW DO SOCIOLOGISTS EXAMINE SOCIAL LIFE?

Sociologists use both microlevel and macrolevel analyses to examine social life. Microlevel analysis focuses on small-group relations and social interaction among individuals; macrolevel analysis focuses on social processes occurring at the societal level, especially in large-scale organizations and major social institutions.

HOW DOES THE FUNCTIONALIST PERSPECTIVE VIEW SOCIETY AND SOCIAL PROBLEMS?

In the functionalist perspective, society is a stable, orderly system composed of interrelated parts, each of which performs a function that contributes to the overall stability of society. According to functionalists, social problems such as violence arise when social institutions do not fulfill the functions that they are supposed to perform or when dysfunctions occur.

HOW DOES THE CONFLICT PERSPECTIVE VIEW SOCIETY AND SOCIAL PROBLEMS?

The conflict perspective asserts that groups in society are engaged in a continuous power struggle for control of scarce resources. This perspective views violence as a response to inequalities based on "race," class, gender, and other power differentials in society.

HOW DOES THE VALUE CONFLICT PERSPECTIVE DIFFER FROM THE CRITICAL-CONFLICT PERSPECTIVE?

According to value conflict theorists, social problems are conditions that are incompatible with group values.

From this perspective, value clashes are ordinary occurrences in families, communities, and the larger society, in which people commonly hold many divergent values. In contrast, critical-conflict theorists suggest that social problems arise out of major contradictions inherent in the way societies are organized.

WHY ARE THERE SO MANY DIFFERENT APPROACHES IN THE CONFLICT PERSPECTIVE?

Different conflict theorists focus on different aspects of power relations and inequality in society. Perspectives based on the works of Karl Marx emphasize class-based inequalities arising from the capitalist economic system.

HOW DOES THE INTERACTIONIST PERSPECTIVE VIEW SOCIETY AND SOCIAL PROBLEMS?

Unlike the functionalist and conflict perspectives that focus on society at the macrolevel, the interactionist perspective views society as the sum of the interactions of individuals and groups. For interactionists, social problems occur when social interaction is disrupted and people are dehumanized, when people are labelled deviant, or when the individual's definition of a situation causes him or her to act in a way that produces a detrimental outcome.

WHAT IS THE FEMINIST PERSPECTIVE?

Feminist perspectives focus on patriarchy—a system of male dominance in which males are privileged and women are oppressed. Other perspectives emphasize that "race," class, and gender are interlocking systems of privilege and oppression that result in social problems. However, these perspectives are based on the assumption that inequality and exploitation, rather than social harmony and stability, characterize contemporary societies.

HOW DO SOCIOLOGICAL RESEARCH METHODS DIFFER?

In field research, sociologists observe and interview people where they live, work, and play. In survey research, sociologists use written questionnaires or structured interviews to ask respondents a series of questions about a specific topic. In secondary analysis of existing data, sociologists analyze data that originally were collected by others for some other purpose.

KEY TERMS

capitalism,   p. 9
conflict perspective,   p. 8
discrimination,   p. 4
dominant group,   p. 4
field research,   p. 14
functionalist perspective,   p. 6
hate crime,   p. 4
industrialization,   p. 7
interactionist perspective,   p. 10
lifestyle–routine activity approach,   pp. 7–8
macrolevel analysis,   pp. 5–6
microlevel analysis,   p. 5
norms,   p. 7
perspective,   p. 6

secondary analysis of existing data,   p. 15
self-fulfilling prophecy,   p. 11
situational approach,   p. 11
social disorganization,   p. 7
social problem,   p. 2
society,   p. 3
sociological imagination,   p. 5
sociology,   p. 2
subordinate group,   p. 4
survey research,   p. 14
theory,   p. 6
urbanization,   p. 7
values,   p. 7
violence,   p. 2

QUESTIONS FOR CRITICAL THINKING

1.   What are some of the impacts on a nation when high levels of violence exist within its borders?

2.   Value conflict theorists suggest that social problems are conditions that are incompatible with group values. How would value conflict theorists view debates over gun control laws?

3.   Some critical-conflict theorists believe that social problems arise from the major contradictions inherent in capitalist economies. What role does violence play in a capitalist economy?

4.   Using feminist and interactionist perspectives, what kind of arguments can you make to explain why males are more frequently involved in acts of physical violence than females? What do your own observations tell you about the relationship between social norms and violent behaviour?

2
WEALTH AND POVERTY

CANADIAN AND GLOBAL ECONOMIC INEQUALITIES

Poverty is not just the outstretched hand or the figure slumped in a doorway. It's not just the single mother down on her luck in line at the food bank, or the street kid looking for a safe place to spend the night. It isn't always genteel or hopeful, the person who might turn his life around with a little well-timed, benevolent help. It's a face that, no matter how charitable we might feel, we would probably rather not see.

Pat Capponi(1999:xi)

In the 21st century, our economic and social goals will be pursued hand-in-hand. Let the world see in Canada a society marked by innovation and inclusion, by excellence and justice.

Prime Minister Jean Chrétien, Reply to the Speech from the Throne, January 2001

Miraculously, my sister-in-law sent me some money in the mail. The boys came home from school to find me cooking a big supper. They were so happy! One of them said, "Mom, we were just talking about how hungry we were and how great it would be if we came home to find you making mashed potatoes and gravy and meat!" I felt so sad and so worthless.

Phyllis (Ontario Association of Interval and Transition Houses, 1998:36)

We keep hearing threats of more things being taken away, like "snow suit allowance" or we'll have to pay $2 prescription fees. That $2 buys two cans of juice, or two loaves of bread, or bus fare.

A participant in the YWCA of Metropolitan Toronto's Teen Mother Program (Ricciutelli et al., 1998:57)

The Child Tax Benefit is supposed to go to the child—for clothing etc.—but it has to go for food. That's not fair.

A participant in the YWCA of Metropolitan Toronto's Teen Mother Program (Ricciutelli et al., 1998:57)

Last week I went two days without food (I had some for the kids) until I got my cheque. They want me to get a job but I can't afford to send out resumes or take the bus to deliver them, as well as there is the cost of photocopying.

A participant in the YWCA of Metropolitan Toronto's Teen Mother Program (Ricciutelli et al., 1998:57)

The cuts have augmented my struggles against the constant pressure of economic survival, part-time attendance at the University of Toronto, a part-time job, and full-time work as a single parent. I really can see no sense in cutting funding for subsidized childcare, funding for the Ontario Student Assistance Program, and funding for the Family Benefits Act. For women like myself, such increased economic and emotional stress makes it more difficult, if not near impossible, to imagine a successful future for myself and my child.

Diane Aiken (Flynn, 1998:147)

Out of a Women of Action Day meeting, held in Ontario in 1996, a resource book was put together to document some of the impacts of the social services cuts on the daily lives of women and children in that province. Several groups and organizations participated in doing research and writing the pieces from which several of the above quotations were taken. The cuts in federal funding and provincial funding in several provinces today make the realities described in the Ontario resource book a reality for people right across Canada. Decreases in real wages, as well as unemployment and underemployment, mean that cuts to services not only impact those people who are on income assistance but also mean increased poverty for those who work full- and part-time. This chapter will look at these issues as well as how poverty is measured, who lives in poverty in Canada today, differences in wealth and income among Canadians, and how we deal with poverty and income inequalities as a nation.

For decades, Canada has been described as the "land of opportunity"—or a place where the "American Dream" can be realized. Simply stated, the *American Dream* is the belief that the members of each generation can have a higher standard of living than that of their parents (Danziger and Gottschalk, 1995). Implicit in the American Dream is the belief that all people—regardless of ethnicity, colour, national origin, gender, ability, age, sexual orientation, or religion—should have an equal opportunity for success. This is the same as saying that Canadians view themselves as living in a **meritocracy, a nation where the best person can rise to the top in any situation, despite his or her antecedents.** Sociologists John Macionis and Linda Gerber (2002:257) define a meritocracy as a "system of social stratification based on personal merit." But do all the people in this nation and other parts of the world really have an equal opportunity for success? How equally divided are national and global resources? What kinds of inequalities exist in the Canadian and worldwide class system today?

A *class system* **is a system of social inequality based on the ownership and control of resources and on the type of work people do** (Rothman, 1993). A primary characteristic of any class system is social mobility. *Social mobility* refers to the upward or downward movement in the class structure that occurs during a person's lifetime and from one generation to another.

WEALTH AND POVERTY IN GLOBAL PERSPECTIVE

On a global basis, there is a vast disparity in economic resources both across nations and within nations. In any one nation, there are both very wealthy and very poor individuals and families. When sociologists conduct research on these disparities, they frequently analyze secondary data that originally were collected by the World Bank and the United Nations. These data focus on quality-of-life indicators such as wealth, income, life expectancy, health, sanitation, the treatment of women, and education, for high-income, middle-income, and low-income nations. *High-income* **nations are countries with highly industrialized economies; technologically advanced industrial, administrative, and service occupations; and relatively high levels of national and per capita (per person) income.** Examples include Australia, New Zealand, Japan, the European nations, Canada, and the United States. *Middle-income nations* **are countries undergoing transformation from agrarian to industrial economies.** Columbia, Guatemala, Panama, Poland, and Romania are examples of middle-income nations. These nations still have many people who work the land, and national and per capita incomes remain relatively low. *Low-income nations* **are primarily countries with agrarian economies, little industrialization, and low levels of national and personal income.** For example, the countries in sub-Saharan Africa have experienced little or no benefit from recent changes in global economic markets (United Nations Development Programme, 1999). Examples of low-income nations include Rwanda, Mozambique, Ethiopia, Nigeria, Cambodia, Vietnam, Afghanistan, Bangladesh, Honduras, and Nicaragua.

Comparisons of high-income and low-income nations reveal a growing gap between the rich and the poor, both within and among nations. Indeed, throughout the world today, the wealthiest and poorest people are living in increasingly separate worlds (Crossette, 1996b). By the late 1990s, the fifth of the world's population living in the highest-income countries had 86 percent of the world's gross domestic product. The gross domestic product (GDP) is all of the goods and services produced *within* a country's economy during a given year (revenue from sources outside the country is not included in the GDP). The world's GDP, then, is the total of the GDP for each nation. By contrast, the bottom fifth of the world's population had only 1 percent of the world's GDP. Similarly, the highest-income countries contained 82 percent of world export markets, whereas the lowest-income countries had only 1 percent of those markets (United Nations Development Programme, 1999). Perhaps the easiest way to bring these statistics to life is to think in terms of the common telephone line: 74 percent of all the telephone lines in the world are in the highest-income countries; the bottom one-fifth of the world's nations have only 1.5 percent of all the telephone lines.

Disparity in the GDPs of high-income and low-income nations reflects disparity in the life chances of the populations of these nations. *Life chances* **are the extent to which individuals have access to important societal resources such as food, clothing, shelter, education, and health care.** Poverty, food shortages, hunger, and rapidly growing populations are pressing problems in many middle- and low-income nations. Today, more than 1.3 billion people live in *absolute poverty,* **a condition that exists when people do not have the means to secure the most basic necessities of life (food, clothing, and shelter).** Absolute poverty is life threatening. People living in absolute poverty may suffer from chronic malnutrition or die from hunger-related diseases. Current estimates suggest that more than 600 million people suffer from chronic malnutrition and more than 40 million people die each year from hunger-related diseases. To put this figure in perspective, the number of people worldwide dying from hunger-related diseases each year is the equivalent of more than 300 jumbo jet crashes *per day* with no survivors and half the passengers being children (Kidron and Segal, 1995). In recent years, the numbers of people living in absolute poverty in high-income nations like Canada has also been increasing, drawing the criticism of many worldwide, including the United Nations.

Magnifying the problems of the disparity in life chances and the prevalence of absolute poverty, experts project that the populations of middle- and low-income nations will increase by almost 60 percent by the year 2025, while the populations of high-income nations increase by about 11 percent. Because half of the world's population of about 6 billion people already lives in low-income nations, this rapid increase in population can only compound existing problems and increase inequality on a global basis.

How do social scientists explain the disparity between wealth and poverty in high-income and low-income nations? According to the "new international division of labour" perspective, the answer lies in the global organization of manufacturing production (Bluestone and Harrison, 1982). Today, workers in a number of low-income nations primarily produce goods such as clothing, electrical machinery, and consumer electronics for export to Canada and other developed nations (see Box 2.1). Using this global assembly line, transnational corporations find they have an abundant supply of low-cost (primarily female) labour, no corporate taxes, few or no environmental regulations, and no labour unions or strikes to interfere with their profits (Petras, 1983). Owners and shareholders of transnational corporations, along with subcontractors and managers in middle- and low-income nations, thus benefit while workers remain in poverty despite long hours in sweatshop conditions.

SOCIAL PROBLEMS IN GLOBAL PERSPECTIVE

BOX 2.1   "Cheap Labour" and Global Wealth and Poverty

Jakarta, Indonesia. "I think maybe I could work for a month and still not be able to buy one pair [of Reebok sneakers]"—Tini Heyun Alwi, an assembly-line worker at the Dong Joe shoe factory where Reeboks are made. Although Tini Heyun Alwi works 10-hour shifts six days a week (in a poorly ventilated factory in stifling heat), she earns only 2600 Indonesian rupiah ($1.28) a day. With overtime, her monthly wages are about $39, less than half of the $110 retail price of a pair of the Reeboks (Goodman, 1996:F1, F6).

San Salvador, El Salvador. When a U.S. journalist asked a woman who works in an assembly plant (located behind cinderblock walls and barbed wire and patrolled by armed guards) whether her three-year-old daughter had enough to eat, the woman replied, "Oh no. We are very poor." Asked whether her daughter drinks milk, the woman answered, "No. We can't afford it. We give her coffee." According to the woman, her daughter's diet is an egg for breakfast and boiled or fried beans for dinner. Meals with meat or vegetables are extremely rare. "My daughter is very thin and also weak, sometimes she falls down," the woman said (Herbert, 1995:A11).

United States of America. Professional basketball player Michael Jordan earns $20 million a year endorsing Nike sneakers, a sum that is greater than the total annual payroll for the thousands of Indonesian workers who assemble the shoes. When he was asked about recent allegations that Nike exploits its Indonesian workers, Jordan replied, "I'm not really aware of that. My job with Nike is to endorse the product. Their job is to be up on that" (Gibbs, 1996:29). According to a spokesperson, Nike owns no plants in Indonesia; it hires Korean- and Taiwanese-owned factories to make its products, which earned profits of more than $397 million in 1995 alone (*Time*, 1996:79).

What do these examples tell us about global wealth and poverty? Over the past three decades, many companies have closed their plants and factories in Canada and the United States and set up business in nations where wages are low, environmental and worker safety standards are weak, and local government officials offer assurances that strikes and independent unions will not be tolerated. Today, Canadian and U.S.-based multinational corporations employ more than 8 million workers in other nations. Many executives believe that the use of cheap labour is a survival strategy that they must use to be competitive in the global marketplace. Although some labour activists and social analysts call for a shutdown of global sweatshops, one analyst has pointed out that a crucial irony exists in the demand to end the exploitation of workers in middle- and low-income nations: Demanding that corporations either shut down plants or pay higher wages could mean that people who currently live in near poverty will have no wages at all in the future (Gibbs, 1996). What do you think will happen when corporations run out of nations where labour is cheap? What part does technology play in the global factory of the 21st century?

ANALYZING CANADIAN CLASS INEQUALITY

Despite the notion that anyone can get ahead if only she or he tries hard enough, one of this country's most persistent social problems is that Canada is a highly stratified society. *Social stratification* **is the hierarchical arrangement of large social groups on the basis of their control over basic resources** (Feagin and Feagin, 1997). Today, the gap between the rich and the poor in this nation is wider than it has been for decades.

This widening gap, which is linked with global systems of stratification, has a dramatic impact on everyone's life chances and opportunities. Affluent people typically have better life chances than the less affluent because the affluent have greater access to quality education, safe neighborhoods, high-quality nutrition and health care, police and private security protection, and an extensive array of other goods and services. In contrast, people who have low and poverty-level incomes tend to have limited access to these resources.

How are social classes determined in Canada? Most contemporary research on class has been influenced by either Karl Marx's means of production model or Max Weber's multidimensional model. In Marx's model, class position is determined by people's relationship to the means of production. Chapter 1 described Marx's division of capitalist societies into two classes: the bourgeoisie, or capitalist class, which owns the means of production; and, the proletariat, or working class, which sells its labour power to the capitalists to survive. According to Marx, inequality and poverty are inevitable by-products of the exploitation of workers by capitalists (Vanneman and Cannon, 1987:39).

Like Karl Marx, the German sociologist Max Weber (1864–1920) believed that economic factors were important in determining class location and studying social inequality, but he also believed that other factors were important. Weber developed a multidimensional class model that focused on the interplay of wealth, power, and prestige as determinants of people's class position. *Wealth* **is the value of all economic assets, including income and savings, personal property, and income-producing property, minus one's liabilities or debts.** While some people have great wealth and are able to live off their investments, others must work for wages. *Power* **is the ability of people to achieve their goals despite opposition from others.** People who hold positions of power can achieve their goals because they can control other people; on the other hand, people who hold positions that lack power must carry out the wishes of others. *Prestige* **is the respect, esteem, or regard accorded to an individual or group by others.** Individuals who have high levels of prestige tend to receive deferential and respectful treatment from those with lower levels of prestige.

Recent theorists have modified Marx's and Weber's theories of economic inequality. According to the sociologist Erik O. Wright (1997), neither Weber's

Although most people are aware of the wide disparity in lifestyles and life chances between the rich and the poor, far fewer of us stop to analyze the differences between middle-class and poverty-level living arrangements in Canada. Should social policies be implemented to equalize opportunities for the young people shown in these photos? Why or why not?

multidimensional model of wealth, power, and prestige nor Marx's two-class system fully define classes in modern capitalist societies or explain economic inequality. Wright sets forth four criteria for placement in the class structure: (1) ownership of the means of production; (2) purchase of the labour of others (employing others); (3) control of the labour of others (supervising others on the job); and (4) sale of one's own labour (being employed by someone else). Based on these criteria, Wright (1979, 1985) has identified four classes: the capitalist class, the managerial class, the small-business class, and the working class.

Wealth and Income Inequality

According to Forbes.com, a U.S. business e-publication, Kenneth J. Thomson is the richest Canadian, with a total net worth in 2002 of $14.9 billion (USD), or approximately $22.4 billion (CDN). No other Canadian comes close to owning that kind of wealth, although Canada has a respectable number of billionaires (see Table 2.1), like the Westons, the Bronfmans and the Irvings, and even British Columbia's own "rags to riches" storymaker, Jimmy Pattison. The vast majority of Canadians will never amass even a fraction of the wealth these people live with. In fact, although wealth for Canadian families increased by 10 percent overall between 1984 and 1999, it did not increase for all family types (Statistics Canada, 2002w). Wealth, or "net worth" for young families (aged 25 to 34) with children, for example, dropped a dramatic 30 percent in this 15-year period (from a net worth of $44 000 in 1984 to $30 800 in 1999). Additionally, the proportion of families with a zero net worth rose from 10 percent in 1984 to 16 percent in 1999. Conversely, families where the main income earner has a university degree rose 18 percent in this time period, for a net worth in 1999 of $118 000. Families in which the main income earner is 65 or older had an increase of 56 percent to a net worth of $126 000. Among immigrants to Canada, those who have been in Canada fewer than 10 years saw wealth fall 25 percent, while those who have been in Canada for 20 years or more saw wealth rise (Statistics Canada, 2002w). The face of poverty is increasingly diverse with regard to family type, as more Canadians experience layoffs, lack of real wage gains, and reduced work hours. We will look at this in more depth later in the chapter.

TABLE 2.1   Canada's Billionaires, 2002[1]

Rank	Name	Worth ($bil)
13	Thomson, Kenneth and family	14.9
82	Weston, Galen and family	4.2
84	Irving, James, Arthur & son	4.1
157	Bronfman, Charles	2.5
157	Sherman, Bernard (Barry)	2.5
191	Skoll, Jeffrey S.	2.2
208	Pattison, Jim	2.0
234	Melnyk, Eugene	1.8
258	McCain, Wallace	1.7
277	Desmarais, Paul and family	1.6
293	McCain, Harrison	1.5
351	Coutu, Jean	1.3
378	Rogers, Edward S.	1.2
413	Chagnon, Andre	1.1
413	Lee-Chin, Michael	1.1

[1]Rank = "rank in world"

Source: Forbes.com (September 2002). Reprinted by permission of Forbes Magazine © 2003 Forbes Inc.

How is the unequal distribution of wealth associated with social problems? According to sociologists Melvin L. Oliver and Thomas M. Shapiro (1995:2), wealth is a particularly important indicator of individual and family access to life chances:

> Wealth signifies the command over financial resources that a family has accumulated over its lifetime along with those resources that have been inherited across generations. Such resources, when combined with income, can create the opportunity to secure the "good life" in whatever form is needed—education, business, training, justice, health, comfort, and so on. Wealth is a special form of money not used to purchase milk and shoes and other life necessities. More often it is used to create opportunities, secure a desired stature and standard of living, or pass class status along to one's children.

Like wealth, income is extremely unevenly divided in Canada. ***Income* is the economic gain derived from wages, salaries, and income transfers (governmental aid such as income assistance [welfare], or ownership of property)** (Beeghley, 1989). In 2000, in Canada, the median income, adjusted for inflation, for families of two persons or more was $51 000, finally after a decade starting to creep closer to the 1990 median income of $51 900 (Statistics Canada, 2002g). Median income is where exactly one-half of families make below $51 000 and one-half make above $51 000. When looking at market wages in comparison, average market wages, again adjusted for inflation, were $61 634 in 2000, the equivalent of an annual increase of 2.5 percent per year since 1993. This average market wage is, however, exactly that—an average. When examining which families are benefiting most from market increases, a clearer picture emerges. The distribution of market income for each quintile of the Canadian population has remained amazingly stable since 1951 (see Figures 2.1 and 2.2). The share of income in the highest quintile rose from 42.8 percent in 1951 to 44.5 percent in 1996. The share for the lowest quintile went from 4.4 percent in 1951 to 4.6 percent in 1996. It is noteworthy that in 1998, the share for the highest quintile was up

to 45.2 and down to 3.1 for the lowest (Statistics Canada, 2000). The gap between the richest and the poorest in the nation continues to widen.

Divisions in the Canadian Class Structure

Canada has a number of class divisions that are characterized by widely diverse lifestyles and life chances. The upper, or capitalist, class, the wealthiest and most powerful class, is made up primarily of those whose wealth is inherited. In Canada, this accounts for fewer than 1 percent of Canadians. The children of these elite Canadians attend private schools and exclusive universities, studying liberal arts, not vocations (Macionis

FIGURE 2.1   Percentage Distribution of Total Income of Families and Unattached Individuals by Quintiles, Canada, 1951–1996

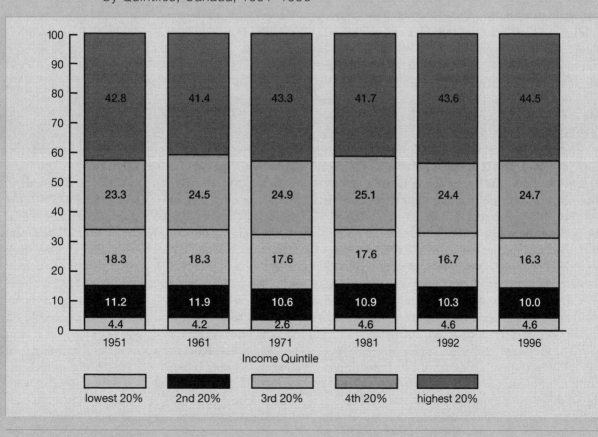

Source: Adapted from Income Distribution by Size in Canada, *Statistics Canada (Catalogue no. 13-207);* Income Distributions by Size in Canada 1996, *Centre for International Statistics at the Canadian Council on Social Development, Statistics Canada (Catalogue no. 13-207-XPB). Reproduced by permission of the Minister of Industry.*

and Gerber, 2002:77). Elite women often involve themselves in charity work, which, as Macionis and Gerber point out, "also builds networks that put these families at the center of the nation's power elite." The "lower upper" class, the remaining two to 4 percent of the capitalist class, derive their income from investments in income-producing property, such as media conglomerates, high-rise hotels, apartment buildings, and office parks; others earn their wealth as entrepreneurs, presidents of major corporations, sports or entertainment celebrities, or top-level professionals.

The middle class in Canada, approximately 40 to 50 percent of the population, is more ethnically diverse than the WASPish upper class. The upper-middle class is composed typically of university-educated professionals (for example, physicians and attorneys), business analysts, owners of small businesses, stockbrokers, and corporate managers. These individuals generally do not own the means of production but have substantial control over production and other workers and can amass considerable wealth (Wright, 1979, 1985). The "middle-middle" class includes white-collar office workers, middle-management personnel, and people in support positions (for example, medical technologists, nurses, and legal and medical secretaries), semiprofessionals, and non-retail salesworkers. Typically people in this class are high-school graduates and homeowners who are able to accumulate a small amount of wealth.

The working class, approximately one-third of the Canadian population, is composed of people who work as semiskilled machine operators in industrial settings and in non-manual, semiskilled positions (for example, day-care workers, checkout clerks, cashiers, and counter help in fast-food restaurants). People in this class have little or no accumulated wealth and, if they are homeowners, typically own homes in low-cost neighbourhoods. They are unlikely to go to university or have incomes above the national average (unless unionized) and their jobs are often highly supervised and give little personal satisfaction (Macionis and Gerber, 2002)

The lower class in Canada, approximately 20 percent of the population, is comprised of the working poor and the chronically poor. The working poor are those who work full-time in unskilled positions, such as seasonal or migrant agricultural workers or the lowest-paid service sector workers, but still remain at the edge of poverty. When the minimum wage was introduced in Canada in 1974, an individual with full-time, full-year

employment, earning minimum wage, could expect to be 10 percent above the poverty line. Today, an individual needs to earn at least $10 per hour, full-time, full-year to even get up to the poverty line. It is easy, therefore, to see why so many Canadians fall into this class, despite the overall wealth of the nation. In an interview with sociologist Mark Robert Rank (1994:43), Jack Collins, a married father with six children, described the transitory nature of work for the working poor:

> You name it, I've done it. I started out cooking. I've been a janitor. I've been an auto mechanic. I drove a school bus for five years. I drove a semi [truck] coast to coast. I've worked in a foundry. I've worked in a shoe factory. I've worked in other factories, warehouses. I'll do just about anything. . . . The main problem was findin' [a job] with starting pay that's enough to really get by on.

Jack Collins and his family may be only one paycheque away from the chronically poor, the very bottom of the Canadian class system.

The National Council of Welfare (2001b) demonstrated, by way of examples, how working people can remain poor in Canada. The poverty line for a two-person family in a large city in 1998 was $22 452. Working 40 hours per week at minimum wage in Ontario ($6.85/hour), a person could earn $14 248. These wages can keep people just above the poverty line if there are two adults working 52 weeks per year. However, if the other person in the two-person family is a child, even with the federal child tax benefit of $1625 for one child, plus a GST refund of $503, the family only receives $16 376 per year to live on—a figure not even close to the poverty line. In 1999 in Winnipeg, a single parent would have to work 80 hours per week to get to the poverty line, while a two-parent family with two children would have to work 118 hours per week to reach the poverty line. There are only 168 hours in a week, so this scenario assumes each parent could get the equivalent of a 59-hour-per-week job (not easy in the current economy) and also assumes that childcare or after-school care is not needed. Vancouver had the highest minimum wage and still a single parent had to work 61 hours per week while a couple with two children had to work 89 hours per week to get to the poverty line. Minimum wages in this country no longer keep people out of poverty, despite the fact that that was what they were designed to do.

Although the poor constitute almost 20 percent of the Canadian population, they receive only about 4 percent of the overall Canadian income. Individuals who are chronically poor include people of working age who are unemployed or outside the labour force and children who live in poor families caught in long-term deprivation. Overrepresented among low-income and poverty-level individuals are those who are unable to work because of age or disability and lone-parent mothers who are heads of households, along with their children. The term *underclass* is sometimes used to refer to people who are chronically poor, but this term not only negatively labels poor people, it also puts them outside the mainstream of society.

POVERTY IN CANADA

The fact that Canada is such a wealthy nation, but one in which such a high proportion of the population lives in low income and poverty situations, has made Canada the target of international criticism, particularly by the United Nations. In Canada, the picture of poverty is multifaceted. Estimates of the homeless population range in the hundreds of thousands (Duffy and Mandell, 2001), while people trying to survive on social assistance number in the hundreds of thousands as well. Along with affordable housing, one of the most critical issues facing people on a limited or poverty level income is food security. As a woman interviewed by the Peterborough Social Planning Council (1998:126) reported, "I've been visiting my doctor regularly. He feels I'm not eating properly. My kids are fed three times per day, whereas I eat three times per week. I've lost 60 lbs. in the last year."

In *Hunger Count 2002—Eating Their Words: Government Failure on Food Security*, the Canadian Association of Food Banks (2002:4) outlined some of the impacts of poverty and deprivation:

Food insecurity . . . elicits feelings of alienation, impoverishment and social exclusion. While parents deprive themselves in order to protect their children from the impacts of poverty and food insecurity, some simply do not have the resources to ensure an adequate diet for their children. Inadequately nourished children are more likely to experience compromised health, iron deficiency, frequent stomach aches and

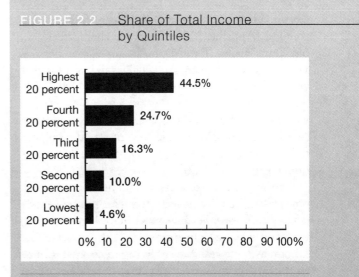

FIGURE 2.2   Share of Total Income by Quintiles

Highest 20 percent — 44.5%
Fourth 20 percent — 24.7%
Third 20 percent — 16.3%
Second 20 percent — 10.0%
Lowest 20 percent — 4.6%

0% 10 20 30 40 50 60 70 80 90 100%

Source: "Percentage Distribution of Total Income of Families and Unattached Individuals by Quintile, Canada, 1980–1996," Canadian Council on Social Development, 1996, www.ccsd.ca/factsheets/quint96.html. Reprinted by permission of the Canadian Council on Social Development.

head aches, colds, ear infections, anemia, and asthma. Children with poor diets also have slower recovery periods from illness and reduced immune systems. Food insecurity is associated with major depression in adults, hyperactivity in children, and dysthymia, suicidal ideation and attempted suicide in adolescents.

Recently, in many provinces, governments have been introducing severe cuts, disqualifying many previous recipients, and changing criteria so fewer people qualify for benefits. The result has been, in some provinces, a reduction in the numbers of people receiving income assistance benefits but not a reduction in need. What happens to people who no longer qualify for social assistance? Evidence suggests that more people are joining the ranks of the homeless, erecting cardboard huts, sleeping in cars, or staying in urban shelters. In fact, one-third of all homeless people are entire families. Children are the fastest growing group of homeless people in Canada (Macionis and Gerber, 2002:289) and recent studies of shelter use indicate that one-fifth of shelter users are children under the age of 18 (Duffy and Mandell, 2001:95). In Toronto, the issue of inclusion has surfaced in a challenging way: There are approximately 100 homeless transgendered people (see Chapter 4) who have trouble finding even temporary shelter. In February 2001, the Salvation Army banned "trans" people from its facility because it was contracted "to provide space for only '100 percent females' and couples" (Appelbe, 2001). Everyone should feel safe, but "trans" males (F to M), for example, may not feel safe in shelters for men. An equally valid point is that women in women's shelters may not feel safe in close quarters with females who they perceive are men (M to F). Advocates for "trans" people say "the only acceptable solution is education and legal action that results in full acceptance of all trans-gender people in any situation" (Appelbe, 2001:2).

Sociologists make a distinction between absolute poverty and relative poverty. ***Relative poverty* exists when people may be able to afford basic necessities, such as food, clothing, and shelter, but cannot maintain an average standard of living in comparison to that of other members of their society or group** (Ropers, 1991). Many Canadians do not suffer from absolute poverty, but do experience relative poverty on the basis of what is available to other people in Canada.

Canada has a very high rate of poverty compared with other advanced industrial nations, although the United States has the highest (Rothchild, 1995). The *poverty rate* **is the proportion of the population whose income falls below the government's official poverty line—the level of income below which a family of a given size is considered to be poor.** In Canada, the government has never actually established a formal "poverty line" as such, but rather has created a Low Income Cut-Off (LICO) line, which allows us to see how many people in Canada spend significantly more than the average on the necessities of life (see Table 2.2). LICOs also allow us to see how far below the cut-off some people live. As stated by the National Council of Welfare (2001b) in a recent report: "All measures of poverty are relative. The issue is not so much about measurement as it is about values. How poor and excluded are we willing to allow some people to be in our wealthy society?"

The number of families who live below the unofficial poverty (LICO) line in Canada increased throughout the 1980s and 1990s, although since 1996, the numbers have dropped marginally each year, signifying better overall economic conditions in more recent years (Statistics Canada, 2002h). The National Council of Welfare (2001b) cautions, though, that the drop in numbers living in poverty is not equivalent to the economic increases experienced by the nation overall, suggesting, for poor people, stagnation at best.

Poverty Lines: LICOs and LIMs

The Canadian government, through Statistics Canada, has established two measures that are commonly used to measure poverty in Canada, although neither measure is an actual measure of poverty per se. The first is the Low Income Cut-Off line, discussed earlier. It uses information on family spending patterns and family and community size from a specified base year. The base year is updated periodically. Currently, Statistics Canada is using 1992 data for its base-spending year. Every year, the LICO is updated to reflect changes in inflation, as per the Consumer Price Index. When the LICO was first established in 1959, the average Canadian family spent 50 percent of its pre-tax income on food, shelter and clothing, according to the FAMEX (Family Expenditures Survey). Twenty points were added to this number with the rationale that a family spending 70 percent of its pre-tax income on these necessities would be "in strained circumstances" (Statistics Canada, 2002*l*:11). Using the 70 percent, LICOs for five community sizes and seven family sizes are then calculated. Another measure often used to calculate the well-being of the population is the Low Income Measure, or LIM. The LIM takes a fixed percentage of per capita family income and adjusts it for family size *and* the age of family members. The rationale is that a family of two adults and one child is cheaper to feed than a family of three adults. LIMs are calculated on a before-tax and an after-tax basis. Neither LICOs nor LIMs are measures of poverty, although they are typically used as such, as they do indicate relative circumstances for citizens. Furthermore, we lack other measures, a curious fact given that such a high proportion of Canadians live below the LICOs set by the federal government.

Who Are the Poor?

If poverty were equally distributed among all social groups in Canada, all people regardless of their age, ethnicity, gender, household composition, ability, or other attributes would have an equal chance of being among the poor in any given year. However, poverty is not distributed equally: People in some categories are at greater risk for poverty than are people in other categories.

Age, Gender, Household Composition, and Poverty

The vast majority of poor people in Canada are women and children, particularly lone parent women and their children. Sociologist Diana Pearce (1978) refers to the association between gender and poverty as the *feminization of poverty*—**the trend whereby women are disproportionately represented among individuals living in poverty.** On the basis of research on the feminization of poverty, some sociologists suggest that high rates of female poverty are related to women's unique vulnerability to event-driven poverty—poverty resulting from the loss of a job, disability, desertion by a spouse, separation, divorce, or widowhood (Bane, 1986; Kurz, 1995; Weitzman, 1985) (see Chapter 4 for a full discussion of the feminization of poverty). In Canada in 2000, there were 531 000 lone parent families headed by women. Four out of five of those women had earnings and over one-third (34 percent) of them lived in low-income situations. Of the lone parent women who had no earnings, 88 percent had low income (Statistics Canada, 2002h). Statistics Canada estimates that families below the low-income line would have needed, on average, an additional $6707 per year, after tax, to rise above that line.

In 2000, 868 000 children lived in poverty in Canada, an appalling number given the federal government's commitment to the United Nations during the mid-1990s to eradicate "child poverty" by the year 2000. The term *child poverty* is an Orwellian exercise in language use—clearly, children are poor *because* their parents are poor. By having governments speak of "child poverty," we are able to simultaneously hold children blameless (appropriately) for their situations while targeting their parents as "shiftless," "lazy," "welfare cheats" (see Box 2.2). As Freiler and Cerny (1998:17) point out, "child and family poverty is being redefined as a personal problem arising out of immoral or irresponsible behaviour, rather than out of external social and economic factors." Similarly, by speaking of "lone-parent" women, we do not focus on the behaviours of the men they may have been involved with and their potential contributions to the rise in the lone-parent female population or the relative poverty of lone-parent females in comparison with lone-parent males.

Ethnicity, Racialization, and Poverty

As of the May 15, 2001, Census, Canada experienced its greatest number of foreign-born citizens (18.4 percent of the total population) since 1931 (22.2 percent). Along with people reporting "aboriginal identity" (approximately 3.3 percent of the population) and those reporting "visible minority" status (13.4 percent of the population), foreign-born people have a heightened risk of poverty over Canadian-born individuals. There are many confounding reasons for the overrepresentation of people from marginalized groups at or below the Low Income Cut-Off line: discrimination due to racism, education level, age, unemployment, labour market attachment, language, and culture, to name a few (see Chapter 3). Consistently, Indigenous people in

TABLE 2.2   Low Income Cut-Off Lines, 2001[1]

	Population				
	30 000	30 000 to 99 999	100 000 to 499 999	500 000+	Rural Areas
Family size[2]					
1 person	$14 940	$16 055	$16 167	$18 849	$13 026
2 persons	18 674	20 070	20 209	22 561	16 283
3 persons	23 224	24 958	25 134	29 303	20 151
4 persons	28 113	30 214	30 424	35 471	24 513
5 persons	31 425	33 773	34 010	39 651	27 402
6 persons	34 737	37 333	37 595	43 830	30 292
7+ persons	38 049	40 893	41 181	48 010	33 181

[1] National Council of Welfare Estimates of Statistics Canada's Before-Tax Low Income Cut-Offs (1992 base) for 2001 based on 2.6 percent inflation in 2001.
[2] Does not distinguish between adults and children as family members

Source: "Fact Sheet: Poverty Lines 2001," National Council of Welfare, 2002 (March), **www.ncwcnbes.net/htmdocument/principales/povertyline.htm.**
Reproduced with permission of the Minister of Public Works and Government Services Canada, 2003.

Canada have the highest unemployment rates of all Canadians and the lowest employment incomes. In 1995, 60 percent of Indigenous children under age six lived in poor families, compared to a poverty rate for all children under age six of 25 percent (National Council of Welfare, 2001b). A Centre for Social Justice study, using Statistics Canada income data from 1996 and 1998, showed that white Canadians had a poverty rate of 17.6 percent, compared to 35.6 for racialized minorities (Fleras and Elliott, 2003:120). The dramatic differences in poverty rates between white Canadians and members of racialized minorities have been referred to as "economic apartheid" (Galabuzi, in Fleras and Elliott, 2003:120).

The contrast in poverty rates within racialized categories becomes especially evident if household composition is considered. According to sociologist Demie Kurz (1995), the feminization of poverty is intensified by the racialization of poverty—the process by which the effects of low income are made even worse by racialized discrimination, which is experienced by all people of colour and Indigenous people but is particularly acute for women who are single heads of household. This phenomenon (discussed in Chapter 3) is known as *intersectionality*: **when people experience oppression in more than one aspect of their lives (e.g., sexism plus racism plus homophobia), the resulting oppression is greater than the sum of these oppressions.**

Education Level, Ability, and Poverty

Statistics from 1998 show that even higher education does not protect Canadians from poverty. Nearly one-half of the major income earners in two-parent families and over one-half of impoverished female lone parents attained more than a high-school education (National Council of Welfare, 2001b). In fact, an emergent problem seems to be the difficulty many students today are having in paying back enormous student loans. One Canadian Web site, in fact, is dedicated to recording people's student loan experiences (see "Canadian Student Loans Discussion Site" in Web Links at end of chapter). The site is divided into two sections, "bad experiences" and "good experiences"—which it labels "the loneliest site on the Internet"! Structural shifts in the labour market are responsible for many people's inability to get a job that pays more than minimum wage, even when they hold a baccalaureate degree. People

with a master's degree do fare better, but the question is, for how long? Many, particularly those who have amassed a small fortune in student loan debt, wonder if they would have been better off financially without the postsecondary education.

The impact intersectionality has on the population's risk of poverty is clear. In addition to risks of poverty associated with education, according to the 2001 Participation and Activity Limitation Survey (PALS), 12.4 percent of the Canadian population lives with a disability. Indigenous people have significantly higher rates of disability than the population generally (as reported in the 2000–01 Canadian Community Health Survey); the most common disabilities experienced by Canadians are mobility, agility, and pain conditions (HRDC, 2002). For people with disabilities in Canada, many lack the education to participate fully in the workforce. In 2001, just over one-half had completed high school (46 percent for Indigenous) and only 7 percent (2 percent for Indigenous) had a university degree. This is contrasted with the population at large, in which over 70 percent graduate from high school and 17 percent hold university degrees. As noted by Human Resources Development Canada, stable employment is a critical factor in financial security. The employment rate in 1996 for men with a disability was 41 percent and for women was 32 percent. Again, compared to the Canadian population as a whole, this is abysmal. In Canada, among people without a disability, 83 percent of men and 70 percent of women were employed in 1996. Looking at the Indigenous population, 56 percent of the general population was employed while only 28 percent of Indigenous people with a disability were employed. Lastly, looking at 1998 income, working-age people with a disability earned 76 percent of what nondisabled Canadians earned, after taxes, while Indigenous people with disabilities earned only half. People with a disability are doubly disadvantaged here as well, as they often have extra expenses that accompany the disability itself, besides having dramatically lower after-tax incomes.

Consequences of Poverty

Poverty statistics are more than just a snapshot of who is poor and how the poor live: These statistics are predictors. As such, they tend to predict a grim future for individuals who live below the poverty line and for the entire nation (Gleick, 1996). As one social analyst

(Ropers, 1991:25) has noted, "Poverty narrows and closes life chances. . . . Being poor not only means economic insecurity, it also wreaks havoc on one's mental and physical health."

Health and Nutrition

According to the Canadian Association of Food Banks (2002:5), "[w]ithin a domestic context, hunger and food insecurity are best understood as consequences of extreme poverty."

Good nutrition, which is essential to good health, depends on the food purchased, and when people are poor, they are more likely to go without food or to purchase cheap but filling foods such as beans, rice, and potatoes that may not meet all daily nutritional requirements. Poor children particularly are at risk for inadequate nutrition and hunger (Community Childhood Hunger Identification Project, 1995). According to a study of Toronto and area food bank use, child hunger increased to 32 percent in 2002 from 18 percent in 1995 (CAFB, 2002:14). Increasing numbers of people annually are relying on food banks to meet their needs. Evaluating the contents of food bank hampers, nutritionists found that the donated groceries did not allow a person to meet basic daily nutritional requirements (CAFB, 2002:15). When these hampers are used in emergency situations, as they were originally intended, that does not present as many problems. However, when people are reliant on food bank hampers over the long term, the consequences are detrimental and severe. Prolonged malnutrition can contribute to or result in such medical problems as rickets, scurvy, parasitic worms, and developmental disabilities. Between one-third and one-half of all children living in poverty consume significantly less than the federally recommended guidelines for caloric and nutritional intake (Children's Defense Fund, 1999). Problems associated with food and shelter are intricately linked. When parents have to decide between paying the rent and putting food on the table, many choose to pay the rent in hopes of keeping a roof over their children's head. Sometimes, however, they cannot afford to do either.

Housing

The lack of affordable housing in many regions in Canada is becoming an increasing problem. Over the last decade, low-cost housing units in many areas have been replaced by expensive condominiums or single-family residences for affluent residents in a process known as "gentrification." This shift to condominiums and single-family residences has made finding housing even more difficult for individuals and families living in poverty. When low-income housing is available, it may be located in high-density, often overcrowded areas. The housing often has inadequate heating and plumbing facilities, infestations of insects or rodents, and dangerous structural problems due to faulty construction or lack of adequate maintenance. Studies conducted by food banks in Canada show that most food-bank users spend more than 30 percent of their income on housing (CAFB, 2002:14). The Canadian Mortgage and Housing Corporation (CMHC) describes people in this situation as "in core housing need and at risk of becoming homeless" (CAFB, 2002:14).

Recently, the federal government signed agreements with seven provincial and territorial governments to match $680 million over five years for social housing. This is a welcome shift away from funding cuts but unfortunately still does not meet need. The Federation of Canadian Municipalities and the National Housing and Homelessness Network have estimated that an annual budget of $2 billion over 10 years is what is needed (CAFB, 2002:15). With the provision of additional social housing in Canada, a central question remains regarding affordability. As the Canadian Association of Food Banks points out in *HungerCount 2002*, "There is no suggestion that federal government will intervene to ensure affordability of this new housing" (CAFB, 2002:15).

In recent years, increasing rates of homelessness reflect one of the most devastating effects of poverty. As described earlier, the composition of the homeless population has shifted to include many more families, young children, youth, and elderly (see studies by Liebow, 1993; Lundy, 1995; Rossi, 1989). Regardless of age or marital status, homeless people are among the poorest of the poor.

Education

A crucial relationship exists between educational opportunities and life chances. Children from low-income families tend to have inadequate educational opportunities; this keeps them at the bottom of the

The sight of homeless individuals and families has become all too familiar in Canada, primarily in larger cities, but also in rural areas. What social factors do you think have caused an increase in homeless families in recent years?

class system (Bowles and Gintis, 1976). They get fewer years of schooling and are less likely to graduate from high school or a post-secondary institution than are children from more affluent families. The schools that poor children attend are more likely to be in areas with lower property values and more limited funding bases for education than are the schools attended by more affluent students, who often live in property-rich suburbs. Schools located in high-poverty rural areas or central cities often are dilapidated, have underpaid and overworked teachers, and must rely on outdated equipment and teaching materials.

Lack of educational opportunity can result in lower levels of educational attainment among people from lower-income and poverty-level families and tends to perpetuate poverty by making it significantly more difficult for these individuals to acquire well-paying jobs or a more secure economic future.

How Canada Deals with Poverty

In Canada, as part of an overall retrenchment of government programs and services, structural poverty is dealt with as though it is an individual problem. Rather than examine ways of eliminating poverty or dealing with poverty at a societal level, we offer temporary assistance, not through our governments, but through charity—both individual charity, such as serving a meal at a soup kitchen on Christmas day and making a donation of money or goods, or through the existence of charitable organizations, such as soup kitchens like the Open Door and food banks like The Mustard Seed in Victoria, B.C., which typically rely on volunteer labour and community donations and, sometimes, some base year-to-year funding from government. In 1980 in Canada, there were no food banks. In 2002, 620 food banks, along with 2192 affiliated agencies, provided "emergency" food rations and meals to Canadian citizens. Food bank use in Canada has increased an incredible 97.8 percent since 1989, although Canada made a commitment in 1996, as a signatory to the Rome Declaration on World Food Security, to attain food security and end hunger (CAFB, 2002). Forty-one percent of food bank users are children, despite the federal government's 1989 pledge to end "child poverty." The numbers of shelters has grown in recent years as well and, still, there are not enough available beds for all who need them. Sociologists Ann Duffy and Nancy Mandell (2001:1995) state that Toronto frontline workers estimate that two to four homeless people die each week in the city and, as mentioned earlier, that the number of homeless in Canada in the late 1990s was approximately 200 000, one-third of whom are whole families (Macionis and Gerber, 2002:289).

We temporarily fund shelters and food banks in Canada, as though the problems associated with poverty in our nation are fleeting aberrations. Yet, poverty is not significantly decreasing, despite overall economic growth. The gap between rich and poor in Canada continues to grow. State welfare programs, such as Employment Insurance (EI) and Social Assistance, continue to be retrenched, resulting in heightened risks of poverty for income-insecure individuals. As Macionis and Gerber (2002:289) state:

> Structural changes in the Canadian economy coupled with declining government support for lower-income people have all contributed to homelessness.

By way of example, revisions to the employee- and employer-funded Employment Insurance program have resulted in drastically narrowed eligibility criteria and shorter benefit periods, even though the program has always run at a surplus. Most recent data demonstrate that a mere 38.5 percent of the applicants meet new criteria compared to more than 74 percent one decade ago (Canadian Labour Congress, 2002). Additionally, waiting periods for benefit receipt have been lengthened and individuals who must be in receipt of social assistance while waiting for a decision about their EI claim must agree to pay that money back when they receive EI benefits. In the past, when unemployed workers were able to achieve EI benefits of up to 75 percent of their previous earnings, this would not be as problematic in the short term. Today, however, workers typically are only able to receive *up to* 55 percent of their previous earnings. If you were laid off tomorrow, what would you do to survive for a month or more while eligibility was being determined? How well could you make ends meet on half of your current monthly income? What about your parents, if they are still in the labour market?

SOCIAL WELFARE IN CANADA

Canada, like many other advanced capitalist nations, is a *welfare state*—**a nation in which the government intervenes in the welfare of its citizens through various social policies, programs, standards, and regulations** (see Olsen, 2002, and Teeple, 2000, for a thorough discussion). Most Canadians are so accustomed to the benefits of the Canadian welfare state that we take them for granted. All of our social programs, such as universal health care, education, pension plans, worker's compensation, minimum wage, employment standards, environmental regulations, health and safety standards, social or income assistance, child tax benefits and so on, are subsumed under the mantle of the welfare state. From their inception, government programs have been viewed as "good" if recipients are thought to be deserving of assistance and "bad" if recipients are considered undeserving (see Box 2.2).

The modern welfare state, or Keynesian welfare state, came into existence in Canada following World War II. The economist John Maynard Keynes proposed that nation states intervene between their citizens and capitalism in order to create

> a political compromise with the working classes. This compromise included the goals of moderating the business cycle (to prevent a repeat of the unrest of the 1930s), helping rebuild the war-destroyed economies of Europe (to ensure the re-establishment of capitalism), and containing or diminishing the growing interest in socialism stemming from the experience of the 1930s and the devastation of war. (quoted in Teeple, 2000:440)

One of the unintended, but useful, consequences of the welfare state has been to ameliorate the worst contradictions created by capitalism's normal "ebb and flow" cycle; therefore, as Teeple (2000:442) points out, the welfare state soothes "the worst effects of economic inequality and . . . placate[s] resistance to all political and social implications of such inequality." A harsher view of this is proposed by sociologists Shahid Alvi, Walter DeKeseredy, and Desmond Ellis (2000:60), who observe that capitalists and conservatives view the poor as

> "social junk" because they are not formally attached to the capitalist economy, . . . [and] are seen by the ruling class as requiring discipline. Thus, the "invisible hand" of the capitalist market is replaced by the "visible fist" of the government. For example, the government intervenes to ensure that the process of capital accumulation is not hindered by these potential troublemakers.

In the early 1970s, capitalism shifted from a national to an international economic system—in short, capitalism became global. Capitalist enterprises were no longer reliant on the purchasing power of any particular nation-state when a whole world was now the market. Additionally, workers in any particular nation no longer had to be placated when capitalist enterprises could easily move production from nation to nation. Under various trade agreements, capitalists sought to level ("harmonize") social and economic policies between nations so as to facilitate easier, and more profitable, trade (see Chapter 13). A newly internationalized capitalism put increased pressure on governments to enact new neo-liberal policies that would have the effect of reducing government interventions, sometimes called "barriers to trade" by neo-liberals. These "interventions," in the form of social programs and public protections, are being retrenched or cut back more each year, using a variety of justifications, from "deficit-mania" hysteria to superficially convincing arguments that Canadian health care is "just too expensive" when the facts underlying these sophisticated advertising campaigns demonstrate much different realities. Can a welfare state provide a solution to poverty? The answer to this question may depend on how poverty itself is explained.

SOCIAL PROBLEMS AND SOCIAL POLICY

BOX 2.2   Workfare in Canada: Betraying a National Trust

In 1966 the federal government brought into effect the Canada Assistance Plan (CAP). The purpose of the plan was to outline the ways the federal government would cost-share income assistance with the provinces and to establish national social assistance standards. The criterion upon which people could access CAP was need, based on the idea that all Canadian citizens had certain basic human rights. These rights, enshrined in CAP, were: (a) the right to income assistance when in need; (b) the right to an amount of income assistance that meets basic requirements; (c) the right to appeal decisions if the person disagrees; (d) the right not to have to work or train in order to collect income assistance; and (e) the right to collect income assistance, regardless of the province of origin (Swanson, 2001:108). Historically derived from a charity model, income assistance based upon need became a right for all citizens in Canada.

Following a Keynesian economic model, the government had great incentive to stabilize the domestic market. Unemployment had to be kept low. Business cycles needed to be stabilized. All of which protected corporations and citizens from the worst of the cyclical nature of capitalism (Shragge,

1997). CAP was just one of many social programs that were part of the welfare state, along with universal health care and education, pension plans and unemployment insurance.

In July 1995, the Liberal government passed Bill C-76, which signalled the end of the Canada Assistance Plan, and on April 1, 1996, they replaced it with the Canada Health and Social Transfer Act (CHST). Replacing CAP with CHST was part of a broader strategy of retrenchment by the government, decreasing its responsibilities in general for the welfare of citizens through the reduction of various social services (Morel, 2002). Sociologist Gregg M. Olsen (2002), in a comparative analysis between Canada, the United States, and Sweden, states that while all three are advanced capitalist nations, Canada has always existed somewhere between the other two with regard to policies and programs and their effects. With globalization stepping up, Canada has been becoming increasingly more similar to the United States in terms of social policies, cost-cutting measures, and cutbacks in social services and programs (Olsen, 2002:3). Welfare state retrenchment in Canada has had farther reaching, and more "acute, punitive, and brutal" changes, because we are becoming more like the United States than like

Sweden (Olsen, 2002:3). Political scientist Sylvie Morel (2002:19) has noted that one of the distinctive features of Canadian welfare policy reform is the classification of social assistance recipients according to a criterion of fitness for work. One of the major effects of replacing CAP with the CHST was that it ended our participation in the United Nations Covenant of Social, Economic, and Cultural Rights, which we signed in 1976. Among other things, the covenant declared that all citizens have the right to "freely chosen" employment and to "an adequate standard of living . . . including adequate food, clothing and housing and . . . the continuous improvement of living conditions" (UN, 1992, in Swanson, 1997:158). Every five years, each nation that has signed the covenant must report to the UN how it is complying. In the past, Canada used the CAP Act to demonstrate its commitment to the covenant. Another and related effect of the CHST was to make workfare legal in Canada.

The term *workfare* is generally used to describe a particular direction taken by governments as they reform social assistance, with a particular focus on the shift from income assistance based on need to some type of mandatory employment activity in exchange for benefits (Morel, 2002; Shragge, 1997). Workfare programs are based on the assumption that there are two groups of poor: the deserving and the undeserving. The deserving poor are those who, for reasons completely beyond their control (for example, extreme old age or extreme disability) are unable to work. The undeserving poor, rated as the vast majority of people on income assistance, are those who suffer from the "damaging consequences of dependence on the welfare system" (Shragge, 1997:17). According to proponents of workfare schemes, the undeserving poor need the "tough love of workfare" to give them a hand up and not merely a hand out (Shragge, 1997:19). Ideally, this tough love would improve the moral conduct of the undeserving poor, who, it is supposed, must be taught "appropriate sexual conduct" and a "life of thrift and humility," rather than squandering their meager incomes on alcohol, tobacco, bingo, and other luxuries (Hardina, 1997; Shragge, 1997; Swanson, 2001).

The official rationale for retrenchment and for workfare is to save money and reduce welfare dependency. It is believed by many that "the poor" are unmotivated, or do not value work, or have no work ethic, or have, through a "culture of poverty," "cultural values and attitudes which preclude a commitment to work" (Hardina, 1997:132). In fact, social scientist Donna Hardina, following a comprehensive analysis of U.S. workfare programs, noted that conservatives throughout the 1990s have blamed "single mothers [on income assistance] for both the federal deficit and moral decay." Swanson (1997) calls this "Newspeak," based on the language made up by government officials in George Orwell's famous novel *1984.* In Orwell's novel, new terms are created in order to shape and direct citizen's understandings of social life in particular ways. Activist Jean Swanson (1997:151)

argues that "social policy 'experts,' corporate lobby groups, and right-wing politicians" have devised a new language of blame that serves to obscure the truth about welfare and workfare programs and to create a climate where cuts can be justified. Newspeak about workfare is based on two myths, one, that people on welfare need to be forced to take employment because they are lazy and, two, that enough employment, paying living wages, exists. A coalition of social justice groups concerned with poverty, End Legislated Poverty, catalogued at least 15 Newspeak terms currently in use and their meanings (Swanson, 1997). The following reflects a small sampling of some of these terms. Have you heard these expressions before?

Breaking the Cycle of Poverty: This phrase implies that children are taught to be poor by poor adults who pass their preference for poverty onto their children. ELP notes that "no one is exhorted to 'break the cycle of wealth' where rich people pass their wealth on to children who pass it on to their children, perpetuating inequality of income distribution" (Swanson, 1997:152–153).

Bring Social Programs into the 21st Century: This phrase typically means to "cut and slash social programs so that people will have to work at low-wage jobs [if they can find them] so they can compete with people in Mexico making $5 a day" (Swanson, 1997:153).

Self Esteem: This phrase is most often used in conjunction with the idea that people need employment to build and maintain their self-esteem. "It implies that a single parent must build her self-esteem at a low-wage, exploitative paid job, rather than by staying home to raise her children to be good citizens" (Swanson, 1997:154).

Training for the Jobs of the Future: Swanson (1997) states this one best, saying that this "phrase is used to imply that if only we got ourselves trained in computer programming or air traffic controlling, we could get off welfare or UI and be set for the future. In fact, we don't need 1.5 million (the number of unemployed in Canada) people in new high-tech jobs. Training does not create jobs. Available jobs are mostly low wage. Tens of thousands of people get trained and then can't find work. They are pushed out into the labour force to compete with those who do have jobs and pull wages down . . ." (Swanson, 1997:154–155).

Newspeak therefore attempts to suggest that workfare programs are good for people on welfare, as a way of curbing their dependence on the system, on "taxpayers." Nowhere does Newspeak suggest that people's, usually short-term and temporary, sojourns on income assistance are caused by the lack of decent-paying jobs, by downsizing and restructuring and other structural shifts in the paid labour market.

This reflects an individualizing of poverty, where the cause of poverty is viewed as resting with the individual instead of being found in social and structural factors. Critics of workfare point to these structural factors as the reason workfare schemes and the retrenchment of other social programs and services will not work to eradicate poverty.

In fact, long-term research in the U.S. and in Canada has shown that workfare programs are not successful in moving people off of income assistance in the long term (Hardina, 1997; Shragge, 1997; Swanson, 1997). As Hardina (1997:131) states:

> There is no sound empirical research that confirms that mandatory work and job training programs are effective in helping people leave the welfare system. On the contrary, most evaluations of welfare state reform projects have not produced statistically significant differences in job acquisition, earnings or decreases in welfare benefits.

Swanson (1997:150), citing 40 years of research in British Columbia, makes the further point that "welfare benefits are so low, the welfare system so controlling and demeaning, that the vast majority of people engineer their own escapes from it as soon as they can." Her comments are based on research showing that only 10 percent of assistance recipients stay on it for more than two years. Hardina (1997:137) further points out that conservative politicians assert that income assistance is the "cause" of deficits, but in Canada, *all* social program spending (including health and education spending) accounts for a mere 2 percent of the budget, and in the United States, AFDC (Aid to Families with Dependent Children) spending accounts for less than 1 percent. Income assistance programs in Canada cost taxpayers as much money as tax breaks to RRSP holders do and yet, the latter class of citizens is not held to blame for Canadian deficit problems (Swanson, 1997, 2001). If it is true, that most people only use income assistance as a safety net in times of real need, as was intended, and if forced work programs have not been shown to be effective for their stated purpose (to save money and reduce welfare rolls), and if these social programs do not cost us much money, why do governments persist in moving ahead with workfare programs and the like?

Several writers have developed incisive critiques of workfare, putting forth alternative reasons for governmental promotion of workfare programs while cutting benefits and eligibility for income assistance and EI. Tying people's income assistance benefits to training and/or to low-waged, temporary employment threatens existing jobs and wages and depresses labour standards throughout society (ACTEW, 1998; Hardina, 1997; Morel, 2002; Shragge, 1997; Swanson, 1997, 2001). Basically, these programs create a pool of cheap, subsidized, and "flexible" (disposable) labour that governments, the private sector, and community organizations can access. In effect, workfare creates the perfect reserve army of labour, a pool of workers who can be moved into and out of the labour market as needed,

without regard to the creation of permanent jobs, living wages, or benefits. This pool of labour is not only flexible (available to serve the cyclical expansion and contraction of a capitalist market), but is also used to undermine so-called good jobs (those with decent wages, labour practices, stability, and benefits) and help bust unions. Social scientist Eric Shragge (1997:30–31) summarizes, "Workfare becomes a means of mobilizing a surplus population to undermine the conditions of public sector and community employment."

What are the social policy implications following from these analyses? Long-term forecasts for employment predict that, with globalization, generally, unemployment in Canada will get worse. Shragge (1997) suggests that in shaping future social policy we need to look at the polarizations that are taking place in the labour market and in society in general between those with wealth and employment and those without. Many people find themselves forced to work longer hours and take more jobs while others are being "downsized" right out of the labour market. In order to create a more equitable distribution of income and employment, then, some policies may need to address restrictions on overtime and shorter average work weeks (Shragge, 1997). Further, the National Council of Welfare recently conducted a study that found that if minimum wage was raised to $10 or $11 dollars per hour, people would have no disincentive to work, as they could live on that wage (Swanson, 1997).

Canadian social welfare policy has been based, in the past, on two distinct traditions. The first of these is the British Poor Laws of the 1600s, which established notions of deserving and undeserving poor (Graham et al., 2000:64). Social scientist Francis J. Turner (1995:6), in an overview of social welfare in this country, described the nature of this historical dichotomy:

> The *deserving* were those persons and groups who, through no fault of their own, but by birth, accident, or disaster, were not able to care for themselves, either temporarily or permanently. Since they were deemed not to be responsible for their state of need, it was considered fitting that society, through one of its subsystems, provide assistance to them. What has never been clear in this matter is who decided, and on what grounds, what criteria could be applied in determining who was deserving or undeserving.
>
> The *undeserving* were those people who, in the opinion of persons of influence, were in need through their own fault or failings. Such persons were considered to be lazy, irresponsible, improvident—and indeed, evil— members of society and thus were not considered to have a claim on assistance. To help such persons was considered as an unfair drain on the resources of society and as a way of contributing to further indolence. Any help that was made available was provided only

grudgingly, was made as unattractive as possible, and was kept to an absolute minimum.

The second tradition informing Canadian social welfare policies has been the racist Social Darwinism of the 19th century, which helped to establish ideas about hierarchies and majority–minority relations (Graham et al., 2000:64). Poverty in

Canada kills more people than cancer, despite the fact that we have a cure for poverty, through changes to social policies (see Table 2.3), should we choose to exercise it (Swanson, 2001:185). So far, however, we have chosen not to. What do you think will happen in the future if we refuse to intervene in the problem of poverty in Canada?

PERSPECTIVES ON POVERTY AND CLASS INEQUALITY

Social class inequality and poverty can be understood from various perspectives and are explained in individualistic, cultural, or structural terms. The framework that is applied influences people's beliefs about how poverty might be reduced. We will look at each perspective separately.

The Symbolic Interactionist Perspective

Symbolic interactionists examine poverty from the perspective of meanings, definitions, and labels. How is poverty defined? How are people who are poor viewed by non-poor society members? How do people who are poor define themselves and their situations? What stigma is attached to poverty and how do people live with, or manage, that stigma? What are the consequences of being labelled as "poor" or "low income"?

Canada is a meritocracy, and much of contemporary rhetoric suggests, then, that if people wish to succeed, they can. Definitions of *success* are rarely explicitly discussed but, rather, a common understanding of the term is assumed and taken for granted. If they fail to succeed, the fault lies with the individual who is "irresponsible," "lazy," "immoral," "lacking in motivation," and so on. This is the "land of opportunity," and people who do not succeed have none but themselves to blame for their lacks and flaws (Feagin, 1975). Workfare programs for social assistance recipients are based on individualistic explanations for poverty. To many sociologists, however, individual explanations of poverty

amount to *blaming the victim*—**a practice used by people who view a social problem as emanating from within the individual who exhibits the problem** (Ryan, 1976). Conversely, symbolic interactionists also examine what it means to be wealthy. How are those with wealth viewed by others? While impoverished people tend to be negatively stigmatized, wealthy individuals tend to be seen as hard working and deserving of their wealth. Where do we get information about the relative merits of whole groups of people? As author and journalist Jeremy Seabrook (2002:129) points out, "while it is easy to find a table of the 20 richest people in the world, it would be impossible to do the same with the 20 poorest."

Symbolic interactionists are also interested in what it means to people to be poor and the impact of stigma on people's self-concepts. Some researchers have focused on how cultural background affects people's values and behaviour. Among the earliest of these explanations is the "culture of poverty" thesis by anthropologist Oscar Lewis (1966). According to Lewis, poor people have different values and beliefs than people from the middle and upper classes and so develop a separate and self-perpetuating system of attitudes and behaviours that keeps them trapped in poverty. Among these attitudes and behaviours are the inability to defer gratification or plan for the future; feelings of apathy, hostility, and suspicion toward others, deficient speech and communication patterns, female-headed households, and a decided lack of participation in major societal institutions. People trapped in the "culture of poverty" socialize their children into this cycle of poverty, and hence the culture perpetuates. The "culture of poverty" thesis has provided political leaders, social analysts, and many ordinary Canadian citizens with a reasonable-sounding rationale for blaming the situations endured by poor people on the poor themselves. The

TABLE 2.3   Differences in Canadian and Western European Family Policies

	Canada	Western Europe
Value assigned to children and the role of parents	• children considered "life style choices" or "private commodities" to be pursued with private means • family presumed to be essentially private and self-sufficient • government role/community support only when children are "at risk" or families "in need" • parenting role is undervalued because children are undervalued	• children considered collective responsibility or "public goods" who contribute to the well-being of the whole society • important contribution parents make to the larger society is recognized • state commitment to contribute to the cost of raising children
Ideas about who should benefit from social programs	• "public charity" model results in growing unwillingness to contribute to "undeserving" welfare poor • pits modest-income families against poor families; threatens social cohesion • privatization of child rearing and targeting basic benefits primarily to the poor • median-income families excluded from significant benefits	• willingness of people to contribute public revenues for the common good of *all* families • not only those with the lowest incomes benefit from social programs • policies provide significant benefits to all or most families, reflecting sense of collective responsibility. • universality and higher family allowances
Ways of supporting families/women	• reducing/preventing poverty are explicit goals of public policy, yet unsuccessful at preventing poverty • women not supported adequately as mothers or workers • mothers of young children expected to be in the labour market yet very little support is provided (income support, child care, parental leave programs) • gender-neutral individual responsibility model	• reduction/prevention of poverty among families with children are by-products of family support policies and programs • two different approaches: family-oriented or employment-oriented • both approaches extremely successful at preventing poverty, even among lone parents • social responsibility model to support family ethic and/or care ethic for women
Different outcomes	• social assistance primary form of income support for many families with children • high poverty rates for children, particularly in female lone-parent families • large income gaps and inequalities	• social assistance truly residual • low poverty rates even for female lone-parent families • smaller income disparities generally

Source: **Benefiting Canada's Children: Perspectives on Gender and Social Responsibility,** *by Christa Freiler and Judy Cerny, 1998 (March), Ottawa, ON: Research Directorate, Status of Women Canada. Reproduced with the permission of the Minister of Public Works and Government Services.*

"culture of poverty" thesis, while popular, is not without criticism. Critics point out that people who are poor, just like people who are not poor, develop attitudes and behaviours as responses and ways of coping with stigma and other limitations and barriers placed on their participation. The "culture of poverty" thesis has also been critiqued for suggesting that poor people both enjoy their impoverished situations and do not know any better. Both notions are paternalistic and erroneous.

More recent cultural explanations of poverty have focused on the lack of *cultural capital*—**social assets, such as the values, beliefs, attitudes, and competencies in language and culture, that are learned at home and required for success and social advancement**

(Bourdieu and Passeron, 1990). From this perspective, low-income people do not have adequate cultural capital to function in a competitive global economy. According to some sociologists, cultural explanations again deflect attention from the true sources of poverty (unemployment, racism, sexism, and so on) and shift blame from the affluent and powerful to the poor and powerless (Sidel, 1996:xvii–xviii).

The Structural Functionalist Perspective

Unlike individual and cultural explanations of poverty, which operate at the microlevel, structural explanations of poverty focus on the macrolevel, the level of social organization that is beyond an individual's ability to change. One structural explanation of poverty (Wilson, 1996) points to changes in the economy that have dramatically altered employment opportunities for people, particularly those who have the least wealth, power, and prestige. According to the functionalists who espouse this explanation, social inequality serves an important function in society because it motivates people to work hard to acquire scarce resources. In 1945, Kingsley Davis and Wilbert Moore published a paper explaining that social stratification exists in every society in some form and must, therefore, be functional. Davis and Moore asserted that some occupations require more training and investment than others, or are difficult or unpleasant to do, so should be compensated more, through prestige and pay. This explains, they felt, why doctors and judges have high prestige and pay, while restaurant servers and truck drivers do not. This thesis has been criticized for several reasons, among them the idea that inequities in pay and prestige are functional for society. Why are women paid less than men? Who is this functional for? Is the work of a childcare provider really worth millions of dollars less, per year, than the "work" of an NHL star? Why are occupations that are dirty or dangerous not rewarded with high salaries? Functionalists also assert that it is functional to maintain a pool of more desperate workers in order to fill the occupations that no one wants to do. This is deemed "functional" but is likely problematic for those who are forced to work in unfavourable conditions for low wages. This is a main criticism of functionalist perspectives generally—we must always ask the question, functional for whom?

Lastly, sociologists Linda Mooney, David Knox, Caroline Schacht, and Adie Nelson (2001:312) point out that functionalists may see poverty as functional for those who work in the "poverty industry" (for example, financial assistance workers) and for those who need a market for second-rate or "inferior goods such as older dilapidated homes and automobiles."

The Conflict Perspective

Another structural explanation for poverty is based on a conflict perspective that suggests poverty is a side effect of the capitalist system. Using this explanation, analysts note that workers are increasingly impoverished by the wage squeeze and high rates of unemployment and underemployment. The *wage squeeze* is the steady downward pressure on the real take-home pay of workers that has occurred over the past two decades. During these same decades, shareholders in major corporations have had substantial increases in dividends and chief executive officers have received extremely lucrative salaries and compensation packages (Gordon, 1996). For example, in 1992, the *Edmonton Journal* reported that the salary of the average worker in North America had decreased by 10 percent. At the same time, executive pay increased 75 percent, raising the pay gap between these workers' salaries to three times what it was 15 years earlier. Corporate downsizing and new technologies that take the place of workers have further enhanced capitalists' profits and contributed to the impoverishment of middle- and low-income workers by creating a reserve army of unemployed people whom the capitalists use for labour and as a means to keep other workers' wages low. Corporations' intense quest for profit results in low wages for workers, a wide disparity in the life chances of affluent people and poor people, and the unemployment and impoverishment of many people. Sociologist Harley D. Dickinson (2000) notes that unemployment is a normal consequence of capitalism and, in fact, is necessary for capitalism. Conflict between the capitalists (Marx's bourgeoisie) and the workers (Marx's proletariat) has, in part, been ameliorated in past decades by welfare state programs like EI or social assistance (Dickinson, 2000). What effect will continued retrenchment have on class conflict in Canada? Although some analysts suggest that high rates of poverty will always exist in advanced capitalist societies, others believe that inequality and poverty could be reduced, if not eliminated, if the political will existed.

Feminist Perspectives

Many feminist perspectives on poverty or class inequality focus in on the gendered character of stratification and poverty. Most of the people living in poverty are women and their children. This has been called the "feminization of poverty." Feminist theorists look at the differential valuing of occupations and roles within Canadian society, noting who has power and prestige, which occupations are deemed more or less valuable, and so on. In work that later became the foundation of a socialist–feminist analysis of the intersection of gender and class, or patriarchy and capitalism, Engels theorized that the fact of private property was at the heart of patriarchy. With capitalism came private property. With private property came the desire to pass it and the wealth it generated on to the children of the bourgeoisie. This then made knowing who one's genetic offspring were very important to the bourgeoisie, which then made the establishment of a system for ensuring paternity very important. In order to ensure a man's children were indeed his own, monogamy and the subjugation of women became necessary. Engels (1884/1972:120) referred to this, in a famous phrase, as "the world-historical defeat of women." One of the criticisms of a socialist–feminist perspective is that it is deterministic; it lacks an explanation of why capitalism must unfold this way (Muszynski, 2000). More recently, instead of seeing women and men as oppositional classes, scholars have analyzed the variety of ways that gender, racialization, and class intersect within a capitalist economic system, recognizing the complexities in an analysis of who is poor and who is wealthy, who is an oppressor and who is oppressed. In addition to the fact that poverty is gendered, Kazemipur and Halli (2000:112) point out in their recent book on poverty in Canada that

> poverty is too diverse and complicated a phenomenon to be adequately explained by a uni-dimensional theory. It varies, for example, from one city to another; from one ethnic group to another; from one segment of population (e.g., immigrants) to another; and even within each segment, it varies from one generation to another.

If we are going to understand poverty, if indeed this is a necessary precursor to ending it, our explanations will need to become more comprehensive. Is it possible to reduce or eliminate class inequality and poverty without a theoretical understanding?

CAN CLASS-BASED INEQUALITY BE REDUCED?

Chapter 1 made the point that how people view a social problem is related to how they believe the problem should be reduced or solved. Poverty and social inequality are no exceptions. Analysts who focus on individualistic explanations of poverty typically suggest individual solutions: "Low-income and poverty-level people should change their attitudes, beliefs, and work habits." For example, economist George Gilder (1981) has stated that "the only dependable route from poverty is always work. . . . The poor must not only work, they must work harder than the classes above them."

Similarly, people who use cultural explanations seek cultural solutions; they suggest that poverty can be reduced by the enhancement of people's cultural capital. They urge the development of more job training and school enrichment programs to enhance people's cultural capital and counteract negative familial and neighbourhood influences. Seeking cultural solutions, the federal government developed job training and young entrepreneur programs to provide children and adolescents from low-income families with the cultural capital (white middle-class values, for example) that they need to succeed in the (white, middle class) world (see Quadagno and Fobes, 1995).

Although some analysts seeking structural solutions suggest that poverty can be eliminated only if capitalism is abolished and a new means of distributing valued goods and services is established, others state that poverty can be reduced by the creation of "a truly open society—a society where the life chances of those at the bottom are not radically different from those at the top and where wealth is distributed more equitably" (MacLeod, 1995:260). These analysts feel that federal, territorial, and provincial governments should play a vital role in reducing poverty and lessening people's need for social assistance. Recent proposals based on this structural solution include the following strategies:

- establishing a coordinated employment policy that emphasizes the creation of jobs with livable wages and benefits;
- building individual assets through government policies that provide incentives and resources for low-income families to acquire and build economic assets;
- providing tax benefits to assist low-income workers;
- giving economic assistance to help families deal with divorce, unwanted pregnancies, and child-care; and
- investing in lower-income areas of communities and empowering residents to organize and address problems such as affordable housing and better schools (Rank, 1994).

Although these proposals, if enacted, would not "solve" the problem of poverty, they might temper and reduce the price poor people pay for living in the "land of opportunity" (Rank, 1994).

WHAT CAN YOU DO?

- Lobby politicians to support real job-creation strategies, higher minimum wages, universal child-care, and affordable housing.
- Volunteer at a local food bank or shelter or soup kitchen.
- Donate money, food, or time to an organization such as a food bank or an anti-poverty organization.
- Write a letter to the local newspaper or your university or college paper, outlining some little known facts about poverty or welfare or "wealthfare" or workfare or hunger in your region. Send a copy of your letter to the Canadian Association of Food Banks at info@cafb-acba.ca.
- Participate in alternate economies like food-share programs and car-share programs.
- Bookmark on a computer you use some of the Web sites for organizations that keep up-to-date statistics on hunger and homelessness in Canada (see below).
- Engage a homeless person in conversation and find out about his or her life.

- Make a phone call to your local city hall and ask what programs the municipality has in place for homeless people. Use your voice!
- Become a member of the Canadian Association of Food Banks or a local anti-poverty organization.
- Attend demonstrations and protests on poverty issues in order to gain information about what the issues are locally. For example, recently in Victoria, B.C., a group of temporary shelters made of cardboard, erected in an out-of-the-way place, was torn down by police at the directive of the municipality. Taking away people's belongings and a semi-dry place to sleep did not stop the problem of homelessness in that city. Use your privilege, as a literate person with more media access than most homeless people, to get these issues heard.
- Organize a food drive for a local food bank. For example, at Christmas time in some urban centres, municipal garbage collection workers, organized through the Canadian Union of Public Employees (CUPE), ask citizens to leave wrapped, nonperishable food donations outside on garbage collection days and they will ensure they get to the local food bank.
- Visit a local grocery store, deli, or bakery and ask if they donate leftover food to the local food banks or soup kitchens. Call places that do and thank the managers of those stores. This encourages people to continue to operate with their civic responsibilities in mind.
- Send a donation to the Canadian Association of Food Banks (an organization that represents 90 percent of national food banks). For every dollar you donate, the CAFB can move $75 worth of food.
- Intervene when you hear someone poor-bashing or negatively stereotyping poor people. Educate friends, family members, and classmates or professors who are not as knowledgeable about the issues. Keep up to date about the facts so you are comfortable educating others.

SUMMARY

WHY IS SOCIAL STRATIFICATION A SOCIAL PROBLEM?

Social stratification refers to the hierarchical arrangement of large social groups based on their control over basic resources. In highly stratified societies, low-income and poor people have limited access to food, clothing, shelter, education, health care, and other necessities of life.

WHAT ARE THE MAJOR PROBLEMS OF THE LOW-INCOME NATIONS?

Studies of global inequality distinguish between high-income nations—countries with highly industrialized economies and relatively high levels of national and per capita (per person) income, middle-income nations—countries that are undergoing transformation from agrarian to industrial economies, and low-income nations—countries that are primarily agrarian with little industrialization and low levels of national and personal income. Poverty, food shortages, hunger, and rapidly growing populations are pressing problems in many low-income nations.

HOW DOES THE "NEW INTERNATIONAL DIVISION OF LABOUR" PERSPECTIVE EXPLAIN GLOBAL INEQUALITY?

According to this perspective, transnational corporations have established global assembly lines of production in which workers in middle- and low-income nations, earning extremely low wages, produce goods for export to high-income nations such as Canada, the United States, and Japan.

HOW IS THE CANADIAN CLASS STRUCTURE DIVIDED?

The Canadian population is divided into a number of classes. The upper, or capitalist, class, the wealthiest and most powerful class, is made up of investors, heirs, and executives. The upper-middle class is composed of professionals, business analysts, owners of small businesses, stockbrokers, and business analysts. The middle class includes white-collar office workers, middle-management personnel, people in technical support positions, semiprofessionals, and non-retail salesworkers. Members of the working class hold occupations such as semiskilled machine operator or counter help in a fast-food restaurant. The poor include the working poor and the chronically poor. The working poor are those who are attached to the labour market but whose wages are not sufficient to provide them with the necessities. The chronically poor include individuals of working age who are outside the labour force and children who live in poor families.

WHO ARE THE POOR IN CANADA?

While poverty cuts across every gender, age, sexual orientation, ethnicity, and ability, the major categories of poor people in Canada are women, children under age 18, people with disabilities, and visible minorities, especially Indigenous people.

WHAT ARE INDIVIDUAL AND CULTURAL EXPLANATIONS OF POVERTY?

Individual explanations of poverty focus on the attitudinal and motivational problems of individuals or the amount of human capital a person possesses. Cultural explanations of poverty focus on how cultural background affects people's values and behaviour. These explanations focus on the microlevel, and many sociologists view them as attempts to blame the victim for the problem.

WHAT ARE STRUCTURAL EXPLANATIONS OF POVERTY?

Structural explanations of poverty focus on the macrolevel, the level of social organization that is beyond an individual's ability to change. These explanations consider how changes in the economy have altered employment opportunities or how inequality and exploitation are inherent in the structure of class relations in a capitalist economy.

WHAT SOLUTIONS HAVE BEEN SUGGESTED FOR POVERTY?

Most individual and cultural solutions focus on the importance of work. Individual perspectives suggest that people should work harder. Cultural perspectives suggest enhancing people's cultural capital to make them better prepared for employment. Structural perspectives are based on the assumption that society can reduce poverty by creating real jobs and training programs and investing in people through provision of childcare, health care, and affordable housing. Intersectionality approaches highlight the need for multipronged strategies.

KEY TERMS

absolute poverty,   p. 23
blaming the victim,   p. 39
class system,   p. 23
cultural capital,   p. 40
feminization of poverty,   p. 31
high-income nations,   p. 23
income,   p. 26
intersectionality,   p. 32
life chances,   p. 23
low-income nations,   p. 23

meritocracy,   p. 22
middle-income nations,   p. 23
poverty rate,   p. 30
power,   p. 25
prestige,   p. 25
relative poverty,   p. 30
social stratification,   p. 25
wealth,   p. 25
welfare state,   p. 35

QUESTIONS FOR CRITICAL THINKING

1.   You have decided to study wealth and poverty in your community. Which of the research method(s) described in Chapter 1 would provide the best data for analysis? What secondary sources might provide useful data? What kinds of information would be easiest to acquire? What kinds of information would be most difficult to acquire and why?

2.   What would happen if all the wealth in Canada were redistributed so that all adults had the same amount? Some analysts suggest that within five years most of the wealth would be back in the possession of the people who hold it today. What arguments can you give to support this idea? What arguments can you give to refute this idea?

3.   How do the lives of assembly-line workers in middle- and low-income nations compare with the lives of people who live in poverty in central cities and rural areas of Canada? Should Canadian foreign policy include provisions for reducing the problems of people in middle- and low-income nations? Should it be Canadian government policy to help disadvantaged people in our own country? Why or why not?

4.   Pretend that cost is no object and develop a plan for solving the problem of poverty in Canada. What are your priorities and goals? How long will your plan take to implement? Who will be the primary beneficiaries of your plan? Will the plan have any effect on you?

5.   Forcese (1997:215) stated that "Employers can, if obliged, produce jobs as well as products. Educational institutions, if obliged, can generate mobility. Political parties, if obliged, can legislate benefits." Assess the implications of "obliging" employers, educational institutions, and political parties to do these things.

WEBLINKS

Caledon Institute for Social Policy

www.caledoninst.org

The Caledon Institute for Social Policy is a think tank that produces research, analysis, and practical proposals and seeks to inform public opinion on social policy and reform social programs. It contributes articles, some of which are available on the site in PDF format, to major newspapers and media institutions.

Canadian Association of Food Banks (CAFB)

www.icomm.ca/cafb

The CAFB represents member food banks in every province in Canada. It coordinates the distribution of goods to food banks throughout the country and works to find solutions to Canada's growing hunger problem. The site enables you to get involved in its activities.

Canadian Centre for Policy Alternatives (CCPA)

www.policyalternatives.org

The Canadian Centre for Policy Alternatives is a national organization that undertakes and promotes research on issues of social and economic justice. The centre produces various publications that offer accurate facts and ideas on how to best understand and choose the policies that affect our lives.

Canadian Council on Social Development (CCSD)

www.ccsd.ca

The Canadian Council on Social Development is a nonprofit social policy and research unit whose work, focusing on issues such as poverty, disability, cultural diversity, housing and employment, seeks to improve social and economic security. The site offers links to many other social organizations.

Centre for Social Justice

www.socialjustice.org

The Centre for Social Justice is an advocacy organization that seeks to make policy changes that promote economic and social justice. The site offers information, lists of publications and articles, and opportunities to join and make donations.

Canadian Student Loans Discussion Site

www.members.shaw.ca/frasie/

This site, committed to exposing the harsh realities of dealing with banking institutions while repaying student loans, gives Canadians an opportunity to give their side of the story and to ask questions.

National Anti Poverty Organization (NAPO)

www.napo-onap.ca

NAPO works to foster awareness of and respect for low-income people across Canada. Its aim is to eradicate poverty by researching, mobilizing, and lobbying.

National Council of Welfare

www.ncwcnbes.net

The National Council of Welfare is a citizens' advisory body that advises the Minister of Human Resources Development on the needs and problems of low-income Canadians. The site offers welfare incomes reports, publications, and public statements in HTML and PDF formats.

Poverty Network

www.povnet.org

The PovNet site provides general, up-to-date information about welfare and housing laws in Canada. It is designed for advocates and people on welfare or involved in anti-poverty work. It also offers numerous links to other anti-poverty organizations and resources in Canada and worldwide.

Statistics Canada

www.statcan.ca/Daily/English

Statcan.ca is the official source for Canadian social and economic statistics and products. It provides detailed information on nearly every aspect of Canada's products and services. Some of the content is also available in PDF format.

3

RACISM AND ETHNIC INEQUALITY

We looked around at the other women at the table. Nobody said hello. They looked and I looked back. . . . We sat and we waited. The other women talked amongst themselves in what resembled a huddle. They glanced furtively in our direction. We sat and waited—I watched. Whispers. Whispers coming from the huddle. Whispers that called out, too loud, clanging around in my ears, "Smells like Indians!" Instinctively I breathed in deeply. Did they mean us? I could see them staring at us. My mother's head was down. Tears? I looked back at them. I knew it was us. We moved to another table. We do not speak about what was said about us. We do not recognize them. We cannot give them more power. My anger grows. My mother's spirit staggers. . . . How can they make a judgment about Native people without knowing or caring to know about us?—judgments made in ignorance. I decided that someday I would tell them about things they did not want to hear, about things they were afraid to ask. I decided to talk back. There was nothing to lose. People hated us anyway.

Valerie Bedassigae Pheasant recollecting "growing up different" in Canada (2001:39–40)

I grew a second head—an English one. Depending on the time or issue, I would inhabit one or the other of my two heads. But for many of my interlocutors, this meant at times exhibiting behaviours that appeared to be, or were effectively, "out of place"—that of a Quebecoise in Toronto, and a somewhat Torontonian in Quebec. . . . Since moving to Hullottawa, where living a bilingual existence has meant spending about 70 percent of my time speaking English, I have found myself (still), and not without paradox, a Quebecoise francophone. This situation makes me wonder if I can escape Papineau's fate, and at this point in history the question remains pertinent not only for me as an individual but also on the collective and political levels.

Angele Denis, speaking of her experience coming to English Canada from Quebec. She theorizes about the potential similarities between her experience, Canada's experience, and Papineau's experience. In a novel by Jacques Godbout, the character Papineau is a person with two heads, one French and one English. When deciding to merge, as half-French and half-English, the English persona takes over the French, resulting in an Anglo personality (2001:135, 137).

"We're all the same. Just because you're Black doesn't matter." I realized there was a lot more work to do than just explaining my feelings. I was shocked to realize that many of my classmates—professional people living in Canada, one of the most multicultural countries in the world—simply didn't get it. For them, the Canadian Mosaic was not much of a reality. . . . I asked my classmates, "How can I, an African, be the same as you, an Irish immigrant?". . . "Our experiences are not the same, our lives are not the same, and by God I am thankful that we are not the same." My reaction surprised them.

Gifty Serbeh-Dunn speaking about when she realized that many Canadians had no desire to discuss culture and "race" (Dunn and Dunn, 2001:270)

I expect that being an interracial couple in Toronto would be a very different experience. Our smaller community seems at times to exoticize my Indianness and at other times to ostracize us as a couple. I remember when we decided to tell my parents about our relationship and felt as though the burden of the world had been lifted from our shoulders. Walking down the street for the first time, hand-in-hand, without fear that we would be seen was like walking on cloud nine. Do you remember? What popped my balloon was that guy on the park bench who yelled out to us, "You fucking White bastard, what are you doing with that Paki woman?" It jarred me into a reality that our differences were not just cultural but also racial, and that we would not only have to deal with the problem of my family's acceptance of you as my husband, but also that of society's acceptance of us. This is the difference that has been the most difficult with which to cope. The cultural stuff like food, language and clothing can be negotiated. But racism is something not so easily negotiated.

Bina Mehta in a dialogue with her husband, Kevin Spooner (2000:155)

I am always unprepared for the backlash of White authority. How the words and actions of myself and my students were twisted and used against me. Twisted and used against the students. Twisted and used against our traditions. . . . "You are to teach in the expected mode, exactly what the calendar says." Why is White monocultural reality now the expected norm on our ancestral lands, I want to know.

Fyre Jean Graveline, describing an experience teaching in a "Native-controlled college [that] was not" (2000:284)

It is not enough to imagine a better and more just future; without a commitment to action, we will continue to suffer. . . . We cannot expect a better future in the absence of a commitment to take action, to attack and destroy the heart of colonialism. There is no hope—or sense—in attacking the state with physical force, or in seeking peace by unpeaceful means. The goals that flow from our traditions demand an approach based on undermining the intellectual and moral foundations of colonialism and exposing internal contradictions of states and societies that promise justice and practice oppression. Non-Indigenous people need to be brought to the realization that their notion of power and its extension over Indigenous peoples is wrong by any moral standard. This approach holds the greatest promise for the freedom of Indigenous people.

Taiaiake Alfred, Director of the Indigenous Governance Program at the University of Victoria (1999:144)

As the preceding quotations illustrate, racism in Canada continues unabated in both subtle and overt forms. While many in Canada know that racism is unacceptable, their privileged positions blind them to ways they participate in and perpetuate it. Non-White Canadians, regardless of class position, gender, sexual orientation, ability, age, size, educational level, or occupation, all experience prejudice and discrimination every day in what many people claim is a multicultural society. We know from experience that right now several people reading this are wondering if we are non-White people writing this, because our socialization in Canada teaches us that issues of racialized prejudice and discrimination are not White issues; that they are issues for Indigenous people or visible minorities only. We are White people, and therefore are every bit as implicated in the racism we speak about as are most of the readers. This chapter will not only discuss the many manifestations of racist discrimination in Canada, it will also raise issues of privilege and dominance and examine possibilities for change.

As described in Chapter 1, *discrimination* is the actions or practices of dominant group members that have a harmful impact on members of subordinate groups (Feagin and Feagin, 1999). Like many other social problems, racialized and ethnic discrimination signals a discrepancy between the ideals and realities of Canadian society today. While equality and freedom for all—regardless of country of origin, skin colour, creed, or language—are stated ideals of this country, many subordinate group members experience oppression based on racializing factors, regardless of their other statuses.

RACISM AND ETHNIC INEQUALITY AS A SOCIAL PROBLEM

As we enter the 21st century, racism is among the most divisive social problems facing Canada. At the same time, sociologists such as William J. Wilson (1996) suggest that we all—regardless of racialized or ethnic background—share certain common interests and concerns that cross "race" and class boundaries. Some of the problems are unemployment and job insecurity, declining real wages, escalating medical and housing costs, a scarcity of good-quality childcare programs, worries about the quality of public education, and violence in many neighbourhoods. From this perspective, racialized and ethnic inequality is a problem for everyone, not only for people of colour. Additionally, all people can be allies in working toward the elimination of racism. While the anti-racism torch has been lit and carried by non-White people for many years in Canada, it is time for White people to exercise some of their considerable privilege to join this campaign. Who better to speak out against racism than those who benefit most from it? Who better than those who are viewed as credible sources (as opposed to those viewed as "whining special interest groups") to take up this discussion publicly and to press for the necessary changes? Changes for the better have already been made and there is no doubt, despite backlash, that they will continue. The process of change could however, move more quickly when alliances are formed.

What Are Ethnicity, "Race," and Racialization?

In Canada, the terms *ethnicity* and *"race"* are often used interchangeably, while *racialization* is a term many people have never heard of. It is useful therefore, to define these concepts at the outset. In Canada, we talk mainly of "ethnicity," and Statistics Canada Censuses have, historically, collected data based primarily on eth-nic group. An *ethnic group* **is a category of people who are distinguished, by others or by themselves, on the basis of cultural or nationality characteristics** (Feagin and Feagin, 1999). **These can include language, country of origin, and adherence to a culture.** Briefly stated, members of an ethnic group share five main charac-teristics: (1) unique cultural traits; (2) a sense of community; (3) a feeling that one's own group is dis-tinct; (4) membership from birth; and, (5) a tendency, at least initially, to occupy a distinct geographic area (such as a Chinatown, Little Italy, or Greektown). "White ethnics," such as Norwegian Canadians, Ukrainian Canadians, and Jewish Canadians, are also examples of ethnic groups. Ethnicity can be, and often is, used as a basis to judge an individual or group as inferior or superior. Ethnicity is a contested issue. Some, like sociologist J. Milton Yinger (1994), support a more narrow definition of ethnicity based on three criteria: members of a group must view themselves as distinct; others must view the group as distinct; and group mem-bers must participate in collective "activities that have the intent or the effect of affirming their distinctive-ness" (Fleras and Elliott, 1999:104). Sociologists Augie Fleras and Jean Leonard Elliott (1999) point out that these criteria would leave out the most dominant group—White Canadians—a conclusion they find problematic. It is problematic to assert that most mem-bers of the dominant group have no ethnicity. It presents White existence as a neutral standard and masks the ethnicized nature of our institutions, practices, and beliefs (see Box 3.2 on page 59). Moreover, it suggests that ethnicity is really a euphemism for "minority group," which again puts White experience at the cen-tre, a standard against which "others" (non-White ethnics) are measured. Fleras and Elliott (1999:104) caution, "To ignore white ethnicity is to redouble its hegemony by naturalizing whiteness."

Where ethnic groups are defined on the basis of cultural or nationality characteristics, sociologists note that racialized groups are usually defined on the basis of real or alleged physical characteristics. Many sociologists view "race" as a *social construct*—**a classi-fication of people based on social and political values—rather than a biological given** (see Omi and Winant, 1994). How does a sociological definition of "race" differ from a biological one? A *biological defini-tion of a "race"* is "a population that differs from other populations in the incidence of some genes." In the past, some anthropologists classified diverse categories of peoples into "races" on the basis of skin colour (pig-mentation) and features and build (morphology). Contemporary anthropologists classify "races" in terms of genetically determined immunological and bio-chemical differences. There exist clusters of phenotypes (observable characteristics) and genotypes (more inter-nal attributes that are not as easily discernable) that can occur more frequently if a subpopulation has been isolated for quite a long time. However, humans have not existed long enough, in isolated groups, for speci-ation to occur. Anthropologists and other scientists have therefore concluded that, because of multiple gen-erations of interbreeding, no "pure races" exist. In humans, genetic differences by population do not exist—we share a generalized gene pool. The only "race" that exists with regard to humans is the "human race," or human species. Socioculturally, however, the con-cept of "race" has been salient. European, Chinese, and Arab people were active in attempting to classify humans into racialized groups as early as the 15th cen-tury, although Europeans became the first to use "science" to legitimate and popularize "race" as a clas-sification system (Fleras and Elliott, 1999).

In contrast to an attempted biological definition of "race," sociologists define a *racialized group* **as a cat-egory of people who have been singled out, by others or themselves, as inferior or superior, on the basis of subjectively selected physical characteristics such as skin colour, hair texture, and eye shape.** Blacks, Whites, Asians, and "Aboriginals" are all examples of categories of people that have been racialized. Racialization is therefore a process that occurs to or with a group in that it becomes "racialized," or comes to be seen as having certain distinct traits that are sup-posed to mean something. In addition to persistent efforts to classify people along "racial" lines despite the continued lack of biological substantiation, it is in the definition and ranking of traits where racism can be seen, because definitions applied to certain features or characteristics are completely arbitrary: They vary across cultures and change over time. This is not the same as saying "race" doesn't matter. "Race" does matter, not because of innate differences between people, but because racialized individuals and groups have been treated as though certain characteristics matter in certain ways (see Box 3.2 on page 59).

Historical and Political Roots of "Race"

Fleras and Elliott (1999:47) define "race" as the classification of people into categories on the basis of preconceived attributes. . ... each group is defined as different by virtue of predetermined properties that are seen as fixed and permanent because of real or alleged characteristics.

Several classification schemes were developed from the 1700s onward, beginning with Swedish naturalist Carl von Linne's (Linnaeus') four-category scheme from 1735. Others since have come up with anywhere from 30 to 150 categories (Fleras and Elliott, 1999). The most well-known of these typologies is the one still employed today: Mongoloid (for Yellow people), Caucasoid (for White people), and Negroid (for Black people). It is curious that this three-category typology has remained so stubbornly in our lexicon when there are such serious flaws with its use, not the least of which is, under which category do we classify the Red people and the Brown people? There are several other arguments against the use of "racial" typologies that deserve mention. Discrete boundaries between so-called "races" are indefinable and, hence, arbitrary. "Racial" purity is a myth. The selection of traits defined as meaningful in some way is arbitrary. Why skin colour, for example, and not eye colour (Fleras and Elliott, 1999:48)? It is important to understand that there is more variation on any criterion within a supposed "race" than between "races"; for example, there are more variations in skin tone within any racialized grouping than between two racialized groupings.

The politics of "race" are hotly debated and highly divisive because people who are attached to "racial" classifications often attempt to "rank diversity along an ascending/descending order," with implicit and explicit messages about concomitant superiority or inferiority (Fleras and Elliott, 1999:49). Others acknowledge that racialization is what is significant and not the socially constructed notion of "race." In any case, no one disputes the significance of the concept in justifying or legitimating ways of treating people. The concept of "race" has, historically, been used to justify inequitable treatment—sometimes economic and social disadvantage, sometimes death—in all cases, not contributing anything satisfactory to our understanding of human behaviour. As summarized by Fleras and Elliott (1999:36), "Race matters because people perceive others to be different and rely on these perceptions to justify unequal treatment and condone indifference."

The Meaning of Majority and Minority Groups

When sociologists use the terms *majority group* and *minority group*, they are referring to power differentials among groups, not to the numerical sense in which the words *majority* and *minority* are generally used. A **majority (or *dominant*) group is one that is advantaged and has superior resources and rights in a society** (Feagin and Feagin, 1999). Majority groups often are determined on the basis of racialized factors or ethnicity, but they can also be determined on the basis of gender, sexual orientation (homosexuality, heterosexuality, or bisexuality), age, or physical ability. A **minority (or *subordinate*) group is one whose members, because of physical or cultural characteristics, are disadvantaged and subjected to negative discriminatory treatment by the majority group and regard themselves as objects of collective discrimination** (Wirth, 1945). In Canada, people of colour, all women, people with disabilities, and gay men, lesbians, and trans people tend to be considered minority group members, regardless of their proportion in the overall Canadian population.

White Privilege and Internalized Dominance

In Canada, the racialized and ethnic majority group is associated with *White privilege,* privilege that accrues to the people who have "white" skin, trace their ancestry to Northern and Western Europe, and think of themselves as European Canadians or WASPs (White Anglo-Saxon Protestants). Women's studies scholar Peggy McIntosh describes White privilege as "an invisible package of unearned assets that I can count on cashing in each day, but about which I was 'meant' to remain oblivious. White privilege is like an invisible weightless knapsack of special provisions, assurances, maps, guides, codebooks, passports, visas, clothes, compass, emergency gear, and blank cheques" (McIntosh, 1995:76–77)

In a paper called "Deconstructing Whiteness," Gabriel Bedard (2000:45) makes the point that "In

Canada, Whiteness holds political, economic and moral power." In addition, Whiteness is a condition that White people every day can count on to ease their lives *because* they are White. In general, having "white" skin in Canada confers two overarching benefits: the normalization of privilege and the choice of whether or not to struggle against oppression (Wildman and Davis, 2002). The normalization of privilege means that characteristics and attributes associated with Whiteness or White people's cultures are viewed as the standard, as the "normal" way of doing things. Normalization of privilege manifests when all members of a society are judged against the characteristics or attributes of those who are privileged, and typically this is seen as a neutral process—the standard is typically invisible to those who do the judging. Objectivity is the dominant group's subjectivity. In this system, when people—usually those who are most like the privileged norm—succeed, it is seen as the result of individual effort or merit, not due to privilege (Wildman and Davis, 2002:93). Janet Sawyer (1989) called this "*internalized dominance*": **all the ways that White people learn they are normal, feel included, and do not think of themselves as "other" or "different."** White people carry this privilege around with them at all times, everywhere they go, and they are generally unaware of it. Sawyer (1989:23) concludes a discussion of internalized dominance by saying:

> In any way we are in a dominant group, we have been taught to internalize our own dominance. That is not our fault. It does not mean we are bad people. It does mean that our learned values, assumptions and behaviours are actively hurting other people. It does mean that it is our responsibility to change.

The second benefit conferred on people with "white" skin is having the choice about whether to work against oppression. If White people choose, they do not have to engage in working against racist oppression. This privilege is commonly exercised as silence when witnessing racist behaviour or hearing racist comments. As legal scholars Stephanie Wildman and Adrienne D. Davis (2002:94) conclude, "Privilege is not visible to its holder; it is merely there, a part of the world, a way of life, simply the way things are. Others have a *lack,* an absence, a deficiency." Most White Canadians are unaware of the benefits that they derive from White privilege (see Frankenberg, 1993; Hacker,

1995; McIntosh, 1995; Wellman, 1993). Nevertheless, the advantage/disadvantage and power/exploitation relationships of majority and minority groups in this country are deeply rooted in patterns of prejudice and discrimination.

RACISM, PREJUDICE, AND DISCRIMINATION

Racism **is a set of attitudes, beliefs, and practices used to justify the superior treatment of one racialized or ethnic group and the inferior treatment of another racialized or ethnic group.** In sociology, racism is sometimes referred to as White racism. *White racism* refers to socially organized attitudes, ideas, and practices that deny visible minorities the dignity, opportunities, freedoms, and rewards that are typically available to White Canadians (Feagin and Vera, 1995:7). From this perspective, people of colour pay a direct, heavy, and immediately painful price for racism, while White discriminators pay an indirect and seldom-recognized price.

Prejudice **is a negative attitude about people based on such characteristics as racialization, gender, age, religion, or sexual orientation** (Allport, 1958). If we think of prejudice as a set of negative attitudes toward members of another group simply because they belong to that group, we quickly realize that all people have prejudices, whether or not they acknowledge them. Prejudice is rooted in *ethnocentrism*—**the assumption that one's own group and way of life are superior to all others.** For example, most school children are taught that their own school and country are the best. Singing the national anthem is a form of *positive ethnocentrism.* However, *negative ethnocentrism* can result if individuals come to believe, because of constant emphasis on the superiority of their own group or nation, that other groups or nations are inferior and should be treated accordingly (Feagin and Feagin, 1999). Negative ethnocentrism is manifested in stereotypes that adversely affect many people.

Stereotypes **are overgeneralizations about the appearance, behaviour, or other characteristics of all members of a group.** For example, non-White-looking Canadians, regardless of how many generations their families have been in Canada and who may even be of mixed ethnic origins, are assumed to be from somewhere other than Canada, in ways White-looking

Canadians are not. Greg Taylor (in Taylor, 2000:61), a man with a White mother and Black father, recollects a fairly typical experience he had growing up in Eastern Ontario:

> I was playing at a soccer game at a local high school in Grade 10 or 11 and developed what I thought was a friendly competitive rivalry between myself and the guy on their team I was always paired up against. This happens a lot and generally isn't much of a big deal. Anyway, this other guy decides to increase the competition by elbowing me. I (because I hate conflict) started walking away. To my back he says to me: "Why don't you go back to your own fucking country, you fucking nigger?". . . I always thought it was interesting that he told me to go back to my own country. Where would that be exactly, if not Canada? This is my country and I belong here as much as he does.

Discrimination may be carried out by individuals acting on their own or by individuals operating within the context of large-scale organizations or institutions, such as schools, corporations, and government agencies. *Individual discrimination* **consists of one-on-one acts by members of the dominant group that harm members of the subordinate group or their property** (Carmichael and Hamilton, 1967). Individual discrimination results from the prejudices and discriminatory actions of bigoted people who target one or more subordinate group members. The taxi driver who refuses to pick up passengers who are members of Indigenous groups in Canada is practicing individual discrimination. The neo-Nazi member of an organized racist group who paints a swastika on a synagogue is practicing individual discrimination.

In contrast, *institutional discrimination* **consists of the day-to-day practices of organizations and institutions that have a harmful impact on members of subordinate groups.** For example, many mortgage companies are more likely to make loans to White people than to people of colour or to members of Indigenous groups (see Squires, 1994). Institutional discrimination is carried out by the individuals who implement policies and procedures that result in negative and differential treatment of subordinate group members. Jewish immigrants in the late 1800s experienced institutional discrimination in accommodations and employment. Signs in hotel windows often read

"No Jews Allowed," and many "help wanted" advertisements stated "Christians Only" (Levine, 1992:55). Such practices are referred to as *anti-Semitism—***prejudice and discriminatory behaviour directed at Jews**. Anti-Semitism is not the same as racism, although both have to do with prejudice and discrimination against a group of people presumed to have certain characteristics.

Anti-Semitism is one of the longest standing forms of discrimination recorded in history (Fleras and Elliott, 1999). A little-known fact about Canada is that in 1939, authorities refused to admit to Canada, as refugees, 900 German Jews who were fleeing the Holocaust. They were forced to return to Nazi Germany where many were imprisoned in concentration camps. In Toronto, Jews (and dogs) were disallowed public beach access at Lake Ontario. Public signage warning Jews (and Catholics) not to apply for police work was posted by the Metropolitan Toronto Police Force, and many other types of employment and education in Canada were closed to Jews (see Abella, 1989; Abella and Troper, 1991). Today, discrimination against Jews is often carried out through the destruction and defacing of property and the distribution of hate propaganda, increasingly over the Internet. Based on the pernicious history of intolerance and overt discrimination against Jews in Canada, there is a longstanding debate about whether or not anti-Semitism should be taken up under the anti-racism banner. In defence of keeping the issues separate, but co-operating as allies with common interests, activist Joshua Goldberg (1998), a White Jew, wrote in correspondence to a friend, "Solidarity is not built on pretending we all experience the same struggles. As a white Jew, I get all the race-based privileges afforded Gentile white people." While this is no doubt true, Jewish people today still experience being on the receiving end of negative stereotyping, prejudice, and discrimination. In fact, with the upsurge of organized racist activity around the world, Jews are active targets of virulent hatred. In addition to this, they are often disbelieved when they try to raise issues of anti-Semitism. Short (1991:37), for example, states that even "anti-racists appear to have eschewed any interest in anti-Semitism." Reasons for the neglect of anti-Semitism in anti-racist work may be remnants of anti-Semitism amongst those who are active anti-racists or a belief in the stereotype of Jews as powerful people in society who are therefore not subject to economic

Anti-Semitism is one of the longest-standing recorded forms of discrimination in history. Today, in Canada and throughout the world, discrimination against Jews is often carried out in the destruction and defacing of property, as this photo illustrates, and in the distribution of hate propaganda.

and educational disadvantage in the same ways that people of colour (Jewish or not) or Indigenous people are. Racism and anti-Semitism come from different histories of oppression: colonization and slavery on the one hand and expulsion and persecution on the other.

In all anti-oppression work, it is important to acknowledge people's distinct histories and distinct struggles and not become complicit in furthering people's oppression through competition. Isobel Yrigoyei, a student of professor bell hooks, wrote:

> We are not equally oppressed. There is no joy in this. We must speak from within us, our own experiences, our own oppressions—taking someone else's oppression is nothing to feel proud of. We should

never speak for that which we have not felt. (in hooks, 1984:57)

This last point speaks also to the issue of analogizing, as a way of unintentionally furthering the oppression of people as we try to understand their situations. Legal scholars Tina Grillo and Stephanie Wildman (1996:86) talk about the contradictory use of analogies as both "the key to greater comprehension and the danger of false understanding." Trying to understand another's experience by comparing it with an experience one has had is common. This can ease the process of comprehension and pave the way for greater understanding. It can, however, perpetuate existing relations of domination and, thus, cause more pain by centring on and shifting the focus back to the analogizer's issues or by taking over or denying the existence of pain through the analogizer's belief that she or he understands the pain the other is experiencing. As Grillo and Wildman (1996:98) conclude:

> The use of analogy exacerbates this natural desire to have our own struggles receive recognition. For if we can convince ourselves that another's experience is "just like" ours, we are then exempt from having fully to comprehend that experience.

A final type of institutional discrimination that deserves mention occurs in what American anti-racism trainer and diversity consultant Byron Kunisawa (1996) refers to as an "institutional design of omission." Kunisawa points out that the design of the whole range of systems, from education through health care through not-for-profit organizations through government through judicial systems, reflects the needs, values, practices, and priorities of those who created them. Members of every group in society were not consulted. Their needs and priorities were not considered. It may have nothing to do with intentional exclusion but rather may reflect the (racist) protocols and values consistent with the era in which the systems were developed. Kunisawa's contribution to understanding and overcoming racism is that he points out that we have never actually dealt with the exclusionary nature of the system design. Rather, we attempt to remedy situations by "adding on" another piece. For example, in his model, Institutional Designs of Omission (see Figure 3.1), Kunisawa shows, in phase one, how a system or an organization gets designed by people who represent 70

FIGURE 3.1   Institutional Designs of Omission

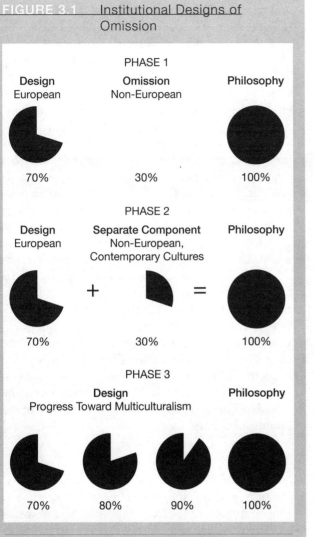

FIGURE 3.1   Institutional Designs of Omission

Source: Byron Kunisawa, **www.byronkunisawa.com**. *Reproduced by permission of the author.*

Historically, Canada and the United States have maintained a philosophy of equality and opportunity. However, our systems and institutions have never reflected the design to match this philosophy. The three phases illustrated here reflect the past and present system designs and future design for systemic change. If we are going to become truly, multicultural nations in the 21st century, we will need to work toward the model reflected in phase three.

percent of the population but who *think* they represent 100 percent. In phase two, those left out of the original design want inclusion. The way of balancing people's demands for inclusion is to create separate systems, add-ons, with the belief that these add-ons will suffi-

ciently meet the needs of those previously excluded. The add-ons do not, however, because people are still not included in systems. People are still set apart and, given how pervasive racism is, not treated equally. What we need to do, according to Kunisawa, is work toward changing the fundamental design criteria of the organizations and systems we take part in by including historically marginalized people in their redesign. This process will take time but will yield an inclusive, and truly multicultural, society; however, we still have a long way to go when one considers how little progress we have made historically.

Historical Roots of Racism

As Europeans participated in campaigns to expand their empires, they increasingly came into contact with "exotic others." Their responses to these others ranged from benign curiosity to outright hostility. As a way of making sense of the diversity they encountered, they employed the pseudoscientific "race" theories that were gaining a foothold in society. It was the time known as the Enlightenment, and people searched for rational and scientific ways to classify and explain their worlds. These theories explained, using the legitimacy of the scientific enterprise (but arbitrary criteria), that some people were superior to others. That these systems of classification also aided Europeans in colonization, by justifying the exploitation and domination of people all over the world, is not accidental.

> Europeans not only racialized the "other" as unassimilable or as a threat; they also racialized themselves by defining Europeans as a group held together by the inevitable superiority of white to non-white. (Fleras and Elliott, 1999:53)

The most common doctrine of "racial" supremacy used in colonization efforts was Social Darwinism, widely accepted in the first part of the 19th century (Fleras and Elliott, 1999). Using Darwin's propositions of "survival of the fittest" and the "struggle for survival" and the notion of unilinear evolution, overseas expansion was legitimated using the rationale that those who were better adapted would thrive; those less adapted would become extinct. As with all who have the power to define, the Europeans defined themselves at the top of the evolutionary hierarchy with all others ranked according to how closely they emulated

European civilization and Christianity. Therefore, colonialism was viewed as a "natural" and inevitable process, just as capitalism and imperialism were. Colonialists saw themselves as assisting those whom they were exploiting in their evolutionary progression from savagery through barbarism to civilization. Civilization meant European and Christian civilization, of course. This doctrine added legitimacy to many practices, such as slavery and forced labour, the appropriation of land and resources, and the destruction of whole cultures and ways of life.

The Many Forms of Racism in Canadian Society

Racism is not a uniform process. It has many permutations and varieties, demonstrating its complexity and multidimensionality. Several authors have created a typology of the diversity of forms of racism in Canada as a way of pointing to the necessity for a range of diverse solutions to the problem (Fleras, 2001; Fleras and Elliott, 1999; Henry et al., 2000). Fleras and Elliott (1999) outline three broad categories of racism, each with specific subcategories: interpersonal, which includes red-neck racism and polite racism; institutional, which includes systematic racism and systemic racism; and societal, which includes everyday racism and cultural racism.

Interpersonal Racism

Interpersonal racism occurs between individuals and gets directed at an individual because of who or what that individual stands for. The typical depiction of a racist is the red-neck racist whose racism is explicit and who, generally, is not intimidated by the label "racist." This is the "Bubba" stereotype of our collective view. "Bubba" participates in highly personalized attacks on others, such as name calling or "racial" slurs, based on the notion that his or her culture is superior. Examples of red-neck racism can be the type of racism exhibited by members of White supremacist groups in Canada, such as the Heritage Front or the Aryan Nations (see Box 3.1 for more discussion).

The use of the "Bubba" stereotype in our cultural view can be dangerous for two reasons. First, it is a stereotype and, as such, can be misleading and inaccurate and can be applied to people erroneously. Second,

and more subtly, is the fact that if we define racism as only the type of behaviour exhibited by "Bubba," we miss the majority of racism that goes on in Canada; the stereotype provides a cover for other harmful attitudes and practices. Human rights legislation and the *Charter of Rights and Freedoms* have done a great deal to erode red-neck racism in public discourse. In its place, due to increasing risks of legal and social consequences, polite racism has evolved. *Polite racism* refers to the ways that people may couch criticisms of racialized others in bland tones or use language that appears non-prejudicial on the surface. Polite racists are often good at phrasing a sentence so as to deliver the racist message to anyone looking for it but make it obscure enough to enable him or her to deny that there was any racist intent. Unsurprisingly perhaps, polite racists tend to be those with higher education. Polite racism can be difficult to prove and therefore difficult to combat. An example is when a member of a dominant group makes a comment to another member of a dominant group about a subordinate group that he or she would not make, knowingly, to a member of the subordinate group in question. The comment is often carefully benign on the surface, to allow room for the denial of racism, but the receptor of the comment *knows* what the thrust of the comment is.

Institutional Racism

Institutional racism refers to various organizational practices, policies, and procedures that discriminate, either purposely or inadvertently. If there is the intent to deny privilege or to exclude, it is referred to as systematic. If not, it is referred to as systemic. *Systemic racism* is embedded in the design of the organization, is formalized, and is legally sanctioned by the state. Discriminatory practices reflect the values of the dominant culture and act to deliberately prevent certain groups from participating in the culture. Examples are the exclusion of Black Canadians from movie theatres and restaurants until the 1950s, the restricting of the enrollment of Jewish Canadians in Canadian universities in the 1940s, and the disallowing of Japanese Canadians from voting in British Columbia until 1949 (Fleras and Elliott, 1999).

Systemic racism is also embedded in the organization, procedures, and norms of an organization. It tends to be impersonal and unconscious in that discrimination is unintended but has the effect of discriminating

BOX 3.1   Organized Racism—(Not) Only in Canada, You Say?

Organized racist groups have been increasing in membership around the world since the fall of apartheid in South Africa and the fall of Communism in Europe and the former U.S.S.R. Racist groups worldwide have fairly easily traceable links to a number of racists networks and groups in Canada. While it may be surprising to many Canadians, the history of organized hate groups in Canada is, unfortunately, a long one. The Ku Klux Klan (KKK), which began as a U.S. group, became a thriving organization in Canada in the 1920s and 1930s and has recently resurfaced here. Along with the KKK, however, we have seen the growth and proliferation of more of these groups, both in Canada and abroad. British Columbia and Ontario see the highest rates of organized racist activity, hardly surprising as these two provinces have, along with Quebec, the highest rates of immigration into Canada.

Organized racism is often referred to as neofascism, neoNazism, White supremacism, or organized hate. It differs from other forms of Canadian racism in both its virulence and its intent. Organized racists differ from regular racists in that their hatred of non-White people, and of Jews in particular, coupled with their active membership in a hate group gives them a predisposition to *act* on their racism, by committing violence, by publishing messages of hate, by recruiting others to their cause, and by participating in a host of other activities.

The intent of the many hate groups ranges; however, they do have one basic activity in common—to rid the province/state/nation/world of *undesirables*; to fight against what they view as the "racial takeover" of "their" geographic space. As anthropologists Frances Henry and Carol Tator, lawyer Winston Mattis, and race relations and diversity specialist Tim Rees (2000:99) state, "All these groups share an ideology that supports the view that the Aryan, or White, 'race' is superior to all others, morally, intellectually, and culturally, and that it is Whites' manifest destiny to dominate society." Also, as the term implies, organized racism is an organized activity. Typically, the group has a designated leadership and a well-established hierarchy of followers. Most Canadians are completely unaware of this kind of organized activity. Those who are aware of the existence of such groups tend to dismiss their adherents as "nutters" or people on the fringe. Contrary to what many people believe, or want to believe, about these groups, they do exist, they have resources, and they are dangerous. While many of us do not wish to believe it, when a 65-year-old Sikh janitor is beaten to death at a Surrey, B.C., temple, or an elderly Calgary journalist is beaten savagely in a surprise attack at his home, or Jewish synagogues are defaced across Canada, or burning crosses are placed on the lawns of people believed to be non-White or Jewish, it is difficult to discount these White supremacists as harmless.

Fleras and J.L. Elliott reported in 1999 that in Canada there may only be "1500 hard-core supremacists" who are members of a proliferation of groups including known racist groups such as the KKK, the Western Guard, the Aryan Nations, White Aryan Resistance, the Heritage Front, the Nationalist Party, Posse Comitatus, and the Church of the Creator, and alleged groups such as the Canadian Free Speech League, the Council on Public Affairs, and the Coalition for Humanistic British Canada. Information about organized hate groups in Canada is now easy to access, through the Internet and telephone call-in lines such as Canadian Liberty Net, although organized hate groups still carry out physical recruitment drives, as well.

The question is, What do these people want? Different groups have different aims. Some of the more radical right-wing groups desire the downfall of the Canadian state (viewed as traitorous because it has allowed non-White and Jewish immigration) and political control over a bounded territory (a sovereign "Aryan Nation") completely free of non-White and Jewish people and of "race traitors" (those who associate with non-Whites or Jews). For many, violence is an acceptable means for achieving these ends, and in preparation for the coming "race war," paramilitary training is carried out in several areas of Canada (for example, Northern British Columbia, Alberta, and Ottawa) and at some "Whites only" compounds in the United States (Hayden Lake, Idaho, and other areas in the southern United States, for example).

Organized hate groups adhere to an extreme right-wing, and very often Christian, ideology. Sociologist Stanley Barrett (1991:90–91) reports that the main tenets of the White supremacist's ideology are "anticommunism, antiliberalism, racism and anti-Semitism" and a belief that the "survival of the whites is precarious." Barrett (1991:90) also points out that, in contrast to their views of Jewish people, who are supposedly responsible for all of society's ills, "White supremacists see themselves as the saviours of the white race (sic) and Western Christian civilization." In this way, many right-wing racists interpret their racism as a positive force rather than a negative one, "a 'natural' preference of people for their own race and repugnance for other races" (Barrett, 1991:95). Many believe that it will take an extreme incident, like the near-extinction of Whites, before White people will wake up and realize they need to join supremacist groups and "take back" their nation. While some are content to wait for the majority of Whites to "wake up," many others take matters into their own hands by actively recruiting members.

Recruitment into hate groups takes many forms. It may be a simple pamphlet left in a mall washroom or on a city bus seat. It may be a racist comic book given out to elementary school children. It can be a book table at a public lecture. It can be a personal visit to a person's home. It can be through political platforms in legitimate democratic elections (Wolfgang Droege, Heritage Front leader, ran in a municipal election in Scarborough, Ontario in 1993 and won an alarming 14 percent of the vote). It can be through music. For example, the alternative rock band RaHoWa (which stands for Racial Holy War), is managed by George Burdi, who is also the band's lyricist and vocalist. Burdi is the self-proclaimed leader of the violent Church of the Creator and a Heritage Front member. Burdi's Ontario band and bands like Odin's Law from Surrey, B.C., distribute their hate-filled lyrics worldwide. While membership in organized hate groups tends to increase during economic recessions, membership is by no means restricted to the working class. On the contrary, while much of the membership may be from economically disenfranchised classes, the leadership and financial support are often from middle- and upper-middle classes (CTV, 1995).

Dhiru Patel (1980, cited in Barrett, 1991:85–86) distinguishes three explanations for racism. The first views racism from the perspective of the deviant individual. Acts like racist graffiti or the beating of a member of a minority group are seen as being caused by poorly socialized individuals. The second perspective, a social forces perspective, sees a rise in racism as accompanying aberrant social factors such as an increase in immigration, unemployment, or inflation. From this view, racism is, again, not integral to society but atypical, and will abate when the event abates. The third view, the institutional racism perspective, suggests that acts of racism can occur because there is widespread institutional and social structural support for racism. Based on this view, Barrett (1991:87) concludes "it is improbable that such organizations could exist unless there was some degree of compatibility with the institutional fabric of the larger society." This last view may best explain how it is that organized hate groups are able to access tolerance from many liberal thinkers who otherwise claim to be non-racist. The racists play on people's deep emotions about personal freedoms and democracy. Making a heartfelt case for an issue like freedom of speech, organized racists say that even if most Canadians do not like exactly what they are saying, as Canadians they should have the right not to be censored. Fleras and Elliott (1999:80) point out that, because of a deeply rooted history of racism and the ability of organized racists to hide behind this liberal façade, "these extremists have the potential to destabilize a society where prejudice is pervasive."

anyway. It occurs because seemingly neutral rules get applied evenly to all, even when this may be inappropriate. The impact is the favouring of certain groups whose members most closely resemble the rule makers while disadvantaging those who are different. An example is the height and weight requirements for police recruits in Canada, which inadvertently disallow most Asians, Indigenous people, and women from participation. A well-publicized example was the headgear policy for the RCMP that stated that members had to wear RCMP-issue headgear. This policy, which was fought and defeated, effectively disenfranchised Sikhs who, for religious reasons, must wear a turban.

Societal Racism

Societal racism refers to the generalized, and typically unconscious, patterns of interaction between people that perpetuate a racialized social order. It is part of the general functioning of the society and is said to precede other forms of racism (Henry et al., 2000). *Everyday racism* refers to general, and seemingly benign, ideas of the relative superiority and inferiority of certain groups. These ideas are widely accepted as normal by dominant group members. The main way that ideas are perpetuated is through language that is held to be neutral. Language, of course, is far from neutral, as through it we socially construct our reality. Words convey images and associations, both positive and negative, that we draw upon to order our worlds. As Fleras and Elliott (1999:84) point out, "[Language] provides a cultural frame of reference for defining what is desirable and important."

Some examples of everyday racism are found in the use of colour symbolism (e.g., associating white with good, black with evil) or the use of emotionally loaded terms like "Indian massacres" (Fleras and Elliott, 1999:85). Everyday racism can be further distinguished into active and passive racism (Henry et al., 2000:55). *Active racism*, according to social psychologist Philomena Essed (1990), includes any act (including the use of language) that is motivated by the intention of excluding or making a person or group feel inferior *because* of his/her/their minority group status. *Passive racism* includes being complicit in another's racism, for example laughing at a racist joke or "not hearing" racist comments (Essed, 1990). *Cultural racism* refers to cultural values that reinforce the interest of the dominant group while undermining the interests of subordinate groups. Cultural racism manifests in the notion that minority groups are acceptable in Canada, as long as they know and understand their place in society and act in ways the dominant majority wants them to. Cultural values support equality, but measures toward ensuring that it happens are resisted. An example can be cultural support for the notion of equal opportunity in employment in all sectors but hostility toward employment equity programs or the Canadian Employment Equity Act. This type of racism is discussed in depth in Box 3.2, below.

Racism manifests in a diversity of ways. This being so, it is imperative that strategies and measures to combat it be equally diverse and multidimensional.

What does the act of employing ethnic "seasonal" labourers for extremely low wages by Canadian businesses, especially in the agricultural sector, suggest about the existence of racist beliefs among Canadians?

SOCIAL PROBLEMS AND SOCIAL POLICY

BOX 3.2   Undermining Democratic Racism in Canada

Most non-White Canadians know that prejudice and discrimination based upon racializing factors is still very much alive and well in Canada. While there are many White Canadians who are aware of this as well, there are more who are perplexed when they hear allegations of racism in Canada. Pointing to our official multiculturalism policies, our recent hate crimes legislation, our Federal Employment Equity policy, and our *Charter of Rights and Freedoms,* people question how racism can coexist with policies and laws that enshrine people's rights to be culturally and linguistically different from the mainstream. The fact of these liberal democratic policies and laws may be precisely what makes racism in Canada so elusive. Frances Henry and Carol Tator (1999:107) have published a number of articles and books addressing this paradox. In fact, they assert "social inequality continues to operate and is reproduced and legitimated through the state." Racism in Canada, although often cloaked, is thus made possible by way of a process called "democratic racism."

Democratic racism refers to the tension between two contradictory sets of values, and the process enabling them to simultaneously exist (Henry and Tator, 1999, 2000; Henry et al., 2000). This gets played out in Canada through, on the one hand, ideologies consistent with liberal democracies, with ideals like "justice," "fairness," "equality," "tolerance," "acceptance," and individual rights," and, on the other hand, pervasive and widespread racist practices, beliefs, and attitudes. This racism is inherent in, and promoted by, not only individuals but also institutions and the Canadian state itself through its policies and practices. As Henry and Tator (1999:89–90) state:

> State responses have largely failed to achieve the goal of eliminating or even controlling racial bias and discrimination because racism and notions of racial superiority are deeply embedded in the collective belief system and in the norms and practices of Canadian society.

We typically think of racism as the attitudes and actions of individuals. More dangerous, perhaps, because it is more easily hidden, is the racism, rooted in our collective belief system, that holds up one culture's beliefs, values, norms, and practices as superior and others as inferior. Individuals' attitudes and practices are connected, however, to institutions and the whole system: "Racist attitudes are derivative in nature and grow out of and are sustained by the structures of social relations of which they are a mere reflection" (Henry and Tator, 2000:286).

We have developed a set of arguments in Canada that justify and rationalize racism. Philosopher Michel Foucault used the term *discourse* to describe these sets of arguments as a form of communication that is used as a "vehicle for social processes" (1980, in Henry and Tator, 2000:291). In deconstructing an overall discourse of domination, Henry and Tator (2000:292–298) outline 12 myths or discourses that support and perpetuate democratic racism. Each one is briefly featured below.

The Discourse of Denial: The main assumption underpinning this discourse is that racism simply does not exist here. The systemic nature and embeddedness of racism is ignored. Examples of this discourse include, "Canada is not a racist nation"; "I am not a racist"; "The justice system is not racist."

The Discourse of Political Correctness: The main feature of this neo-conservative discourse is that it discredits any moves toward social justice—for example, the inclusion of marginalized people or groups or critiques of exclusionary practices—as "overzealous" and "illegitimate" or "whining." The term *political correctness* (as in, "I don't even know what the 'politically correct' term for Indians is these days") is used derisively to "stifle dissent."

The Discourse of Colour Blindness: The overriding feature of this discourse is a lack of acknowledgment of the privileges that accompany skin colour in Canada. For example, many White people will insist they "don't even notice skin colour." Minimizing or ignoring the impact of skin colour allows people to ignore the very real power differences and the fact that "race matters" in terms of the experiences that people have had.

The Discourse of Equal Opportunity: The point of this discourse is to convey the message that, if we treat everyone equally, fairness will follow. The unexplored, ahistorical, and incorrect assumption is that everyone is coming from an equivalent place and has an equal opportunity to succeed or fail. This discourse ignores the power and privilege assigned to people based on gender, language, skin colour, sexual orientation, and so on.

The Discourse of "Blame the Victim": This discourse builds upon the assumption of equal opportunity. Any person or group who is not successful must therefore, clearly, be flawed in some way, due either to genetic inferiority or upbringing (for example, as promoted by the culture of poverty thesis discussed in Chapter 2).

The Discourse of White Victimization: The main tenet of this discourse is that White immigrants also have experienced prejudice and discrimination and that all immigrants should expect to start at the bottom and work their way up. One problematic piece of this argument is that it confounds "race," ethnicity, and immigrant experiences, lumping them all together, as though they are the same. Another problematic piece is the refusal to acknowledge that, for non-White immigrants, prejudice and discrimination do not go away in the second or third generation but are still in effect in ongoing oppressive practices.

The Discourse of Reverse Racism: The main point of this discourse is the assertion that White people are now on the receiving end of oppression and exclusion. Policies and programs that are designed to redress inequities in Canadian society are viewed as anti-democratic and symptomatic of a "creeping totalitarianism" that discriminates against Whites.

The Discourse of Binary Polarization: This discourse rests on the fragmenting of Canadian society into "us" and "them." An example of an implicit message is: "We are 'Canadian Canadians'—law-abiding, hard-working members of society. They are the "others" who, it must be assumed, have opposite characteristics" (Henry et al., 2000:384).

The Discourse of "Moral Panic": The major point underlying this discourse is that the dominant group, in the wake of economic and political uncertainty, is no longer in control. Instead of targeting processes that accompany the globalization of capital, for example, the threat to "the Canadian way of life" is seen to come from immigrants and other, usually racialized, "others." Henry and Tator (2000) refer to this sort of propaganda as a "moral panic."

The Discourse of Multiculturalism—Tolerance, Accommodation, Harmony, and Diversity: The main point of this discourse is that while the ways of "others" must be tolerated (but not necessarily accepted or enjoyed) in a multicultural society, the dominant ways are superior and people *should* adapt. Cultural practices that are viewed as too distant from those of the mainstream are viewed as disruptive to overall Canadian harmony. "Tolerance has its limits."

The Discourse of Liberal Values—Individualism, Truth, Tradition, Universalism, and Freedom of Expression: The main feature of this discourse is the notion that there is "a" truth, one overarching, authentic view. An example of this discourse is: "There is a universal form of expression that includes and transcends all cultural and racial boundaries." (Henry et al., 2000:385).

The Discourse on National Identity: The major feature of this discourse is the exclusion of all but English Canadians and French Canadians from the national identity. Despite the fact that groups other than the British or French settled in the region long before Confederation, the national identity is based on the two *Charter* groups. Everyone else is treated as "other." As Henry and Tator (2000:297) point out, "erasures, omissions and silences mark the discourse of Canada's national identity."

After identifying these 12 discourses that underlie democratic racism in Canada, Henry and Tator (2000:298) conclude:

> Many Canadians see themselves as egalitarian and have little difficulty in rejecting the more overt expressions of racism. They may make symbolic gestures of inclusivity. However, beyond these tokenistic efforts, the struggles of people of colour [and Indigenous people] are met with arbitrary use of political, economic, and cultural institutional power in the interest of "maintaining democracy."

Democratic racism plays out at all levels in Canadian society and carries with it many consequences for all citizens. One consequence of democratic racism is a general lack of support for anti-racist or equity initiatives. As an example, employment equity strategies, or affirmative action strategies by employers, get painted in mainstream society as "unfair" and "undemocratic." The argument is based on the idea that these hires are not based on "merit" but rather are based on some ascribed characteristic such as skin colour, ancestry, or gender. What is conveniently overlooked in this argument is that we have always had precisely this kind of affirmative action, *for members of dominant groups*. When people from the dominant groups are no longer automatically preferred or privileged, we hear the cries of "unfair," "*reverse* racism," "discrimination," and so on. While, strictly speaking, affirmative action is discriminating and selectively preferring, as an interim strategy, it is necessary if we are to build a truly fair and just society, based on something other than ascription. This is not to suggest that people hired through employment equity strategies are, in any way, unqualified. It is unfortunate, but often, a member of a minority group must be many times more qualified than a member of the dominant group in order to be hired. A message of "lack of qualifications" is often the implicit message in these complaints, however, and needs to be exposed for its underlying racism. We must make an effort, even if temporarily, to redress past exclusion and discrimination. When we have true equity, we will no longer need specific policies and legislation.

Many Canadians seem to resist equity and anti-racist initiatives because it is easier to believe the rhetoric of democratic racism. It is easier to believe that things are running smoothly for us all and blame the victim when we hear stories that contradict our beliefs. It is easier to do this than critically question our own deeply held beliefs and value systems because, ultimately, upon examination, if our real practices do not support our stated values, we are placed in an untenable position. If we know about this contradiction and we choose to do nothing, it makes us hypocrites, and if we choose to do something, where and how do we begin? Additionally, we may be in the uncomfortable predicament of having to give up some of our invisible, and often uncontested, privilege. As philosopher Elizabeth Kamarck Minnich (1995:424) noted more than a decade ago, "Most seem to want to give up the harm without giving up the privilege."

Given the pervasive and sometimes subtle nature of democratic racism, it is difficult to know how to approach meaningful change. Henry et al. (2000) offer five strategies as starting points that offer hope that we can work toward the elimination of racism in Canada. Each strategy will be reviewed briefly.

The Development of Reflective Skills and Practices

Most White people do not experience the marginalization, exclusion, and discrimination that non-White people in Canada do and, hence, it is very difficult for many White people to see or understand the kind of impact these everyday experiences have on a person. Much of the privilege that Whites in Canada have is invisible to them. As an example, Grillo and Wildman (1996) have pointed out that part of the privilege of Whiteness is the ability not to think about "race." One of the necessary skills that is absent from professional socialization and curricula is reflective practice. Incorporating critical thinking and reflection into university training for professionals (social workers, judges, lawyers, teachers, and so on) could have a widespread and beneficial effect of giving people the tools to deconstruct privilege, critically examine racism and its impacts, and allow people with privilege to gain a more complete understanding of what others in Canadian society face (Henry et al., 2000:390–392).

Responses to Allegations of Racism

Responses to allegations of racism are usually emotional for all parties concerned. First, the individuals involved (the person saying the complaint and the person hearing the complaint) both need to acknowledge that the issue is emotional, without getting defensive or distraught. Second, White people need to recognize that their realities, as dominant group members, can be quite different from those of non-White Canadians. Third, both parties need to make a "commitment to negotiate, implement, and institutionalize change." This process can also take place at the community and/or institutional levels (Henry et al., 2000:392–393).

The Empowerment of Communities

Communities should be empowered to push for peaceful social change, based on different groups' differing needs and interests. This may bring racialized communities into conflict with dominant structures and institutions. This should be regarded as a positive sign (within reason) as it may be indicative of more efforts to reduce inequality underway. Community pressure has always been a major impetus for change. Direct and sustained community actions should include "organizational resources (financial and human); legitimacy (support from media and other communities); expertise (legal, media, and organizational); and leadership (training and development) (Henry et al., 2000:393–395).

The Monitoring of Anti-Racism Initiatives

In Canada, a number of policies and acts of legislation have been put into place to address disadvantage occurring due to prejudice and discrimination. However, the main activities that have taken place have been around determining if racism is happening, how much is occurring, how it occurs and how it may be prevented.

While this is very important, it is equally important to emphasize the analysis of outcomes. "In other words, initiatives must show definable results that reduce racial injustices in a measurable way" (Henry et al., 2000:396). Anti-racist initiatives too often are based on vague (and immeasurable) concepts like "encouraging," "improving," and "promoting." Instead of attempting to measure the process of "promoting diversity" what is needed are ways to measure the *impact* of a particular program or policy in reducing disadvantage. Moreover, information about initiatives, processes, and impacts needs to be shared across the nation much more broadly than is currently occurring. If people have information about the problem and the impact of anti-racist measures, more can be achieved (Henry et al., 2000:395–397).

The Emphasis on the Role of Major Institutions

Institutions need to articulate specific statements regarding racism, coming from upper management first. Currently, they operate as though racism does not exist and is in no way connected with them, if it does exist. Coherent statements and measures need to be implemented in institutions so that people understand the ways in which racism negatively impacts all citizens (not just people "of colour" or "visible" minorities). Monitoring systems need to be set up in institutions so that people can assess the progress toward a racism-free institution. The development of a coherent anti-racism strategy in an institution requires "a total system effort that must be comprehensive, systematic, and long term with clearly enunciated goals, not so much concerned with maintaining order and harmony as with responding to grievances and correcting inequities." At a very basic level, ensuring that people from all groups are represented at the decision-making level of any organization is an important first step (Henry et al., 2000:399–400).

Despite measures that have been taken in Canada to reduce inequalities based on ethnicity and racialization, they persist at alarming levels. The concept of democratic racism, with its confounding discourses, allows us to understand how it is possible to hold two sets of conflicting values simultaneously. The impact of these values contradictions is not merely intellectual but, rather, has serious and derogatory impacts on the real material conditions of people's lives—their abilities to participate equally and be treated equally as citizens in a rich and prosperous land. We must all take action to eliminate racism. Besides being morally and ethically wrong, it is a shocking waste of human potential.

PERSPECTIVES ON RACIALIZED AND ETHNIC INEQUALITY

Over the course of the past 100 years, sociologists have developed different perspectives to explain why racialized and ethnic inequality occurs and why it persists. Some perspectives focus on sociological factors such as migration, assimilation, conflict, and exploitation.

The Symbolic Interactionist Perspective

Somewhat related to social-psychological explanations of prejudice and discrimination are theories based on the interactionist perspective. One interactionist approach emphasizes how racialized socialization contributes to feelings of solidarity with one's own racialized or ethnic group and hostility toward all others. *Racialized socialization* is a process of social interaction that contains specific messages and practices concerning the nature of one's racialized or ethnic status as it relates to: (1) personal and group identity; (2) inter-group and inter-individual relationships; and, (3) one's position in the social stratification system. Although racialized socialization may occur through direct statements about "race" made by parents, peers, teachers, and others, it may also include indirect modelling behaviours, which occur when children imitate the words and actions of parents and other caregivers (Thornton et al., 1990). Racialized socialization affects how people view themselves, other people, and the world. Here, for example, racialization and ethnic relations scholar and historian Manning Marable (1995:1) describes how racialized socialization makes "race" a prism through which Canadians who are Black or members of other visible minorities view their daily lives:

> Black and white. As long as I can remember, the fundamentally defining feature of my life, and the lives of my family, was the stark reality of race. . . . It was the social gravity which set into motion our expectations and emotions, our language and dreams. . . . Race seemed granite-like, fixed and permanent, as the centre of the social universe. The reality of racial discrimination constantly fed the pessimism and doubts that we as Black people felt about the apparent natural order of the world, the inherent unfairness of it all, as well as limiting our hopes for a better life somewhere in the distant future.

Though all groups practice racialized socialization, White racialized socialization emphasizes White "racial" bonding. According to multicultural education scholar Christine E. Sleeter (1996), White "racial" bonding occurs when White people act in ways that reaffirm the common stance on ethnic or cultural issues and draw "us-them" boundaries, thus perpetuating racism and discrimination. Such people choose to live near other Whites, to socialize with other Whites, and to vote for other Whites, thus maintaining racialized solidarity. Although many Whites do not support racist beliefs, actions, or policies, they fear breaking bonds with other Whites and may simply remain silent in the face of prejudice and discrimination (Sleeter, 1996).

The Structural Functionalist Perspective

To functionalists, social order and stability are extremely important for the smooth functioning of society. Consequently, "racial" and ethnic discord, urban unrest, and riots are dysfunctional and must be eliminated or contained. One functionalist perspective focuses on *assimilation*—**the process by which members of subordinate racialized and ethnic groups become absorbed into the dominant culture.** Functionalists view assimilation as a stabilizing force that minimizes differences that otherwise might result in hostility and violence (Gordon, 1964). In its most complete form,

assimilation becomes *amalgamation,* **a process in which the cultural attributes of diverse racialized or ethnic groups are blended together to form a new society incorporating the unique contributions of each group**. Amalgamation occurs when members of dominant and subordinate racialized or ethnic groups intermarry and procreate to produce "mixed-ethnicity" children.

Early assimilation in Canada focused primarily on the Anglo-conformity model, rather than amalgamation. The *Anglo-conformity model* **refers to a pattern of assimilation in which members of subordinate racialized/ethnic groups are expected to conform to the culture of the dominant (White) Anglo-Saxon population.** Assimilation does not always lead to full social acceptance. For example, many successful members of minority groups have been excluded from membership in elite private clubs and parties in the homes of coworkers.

Another functionalist perspective emphasizes *ethnic pluralism*—**the coexistence of diverse racialized/ethnic groups with separate identities and cultures within a society.** In a pluralistic society, political and economic systems link diverse groups, but members of some racialized/ethnic groups maintain enough separation from the dominant group to guarantee that their group and ethnic cultural traditions continue (Gordon, 1964). Ethnic pluralism is the formal model of ethnic relations in Canadian society, however, Anglo-conformity is such a strong force that pluralism may be more of a myth than a reality for ethnic groups. In Canada, pluralism can take the form of *segregation* because subordinate racialized/ethnic groups have less power and privilege than do members of the dominant group (Marger, 1994). *Segregation* **is the spatial and social separation of categories of people by racialization, ethnicity, class, gender, religion, or other social characteristics.** Recent sociological studies have found that when high levels of segregation based on racialization are followed by inter-ethnic contact, competition may ensue, tending to increase ethnic unrest and the potential for intense conflict between groups (Olzak et al., 1996).

The Conflict Perspective

Conflict theorists explain racialized and ethnic inequality in terms of economic stratification and access to power. As discussed in Chapter 1, there are a number of conflict perspectives. However, in this chapter we focus on the critical-conflict approach, which explains racialized and ethnic inequality in terms of economic stratification and unequal access to power. We will briefly examine class perspectives, split-labour market theory, internal colonialism, and the theory of "racial" formation.

Class perspectives on racialized and ethnic inequality highlight the role of the capitalist class in racialized exploitation. For example, according to sociologist Oliver C. Cox (1948), the primary cause of slavery was the capitalist desire for profit, not racialized prejudice. People were enslaved because, using force, they could be made to do heavy labour and other duties for, basically, the costs of feeding and housing them. A contemporary class perspective suggests that members of the capitalist class benefit from a split-labour market that promotes racialized divisions among workers and suppresses wages. According to the *split-labour market theory,* the economy is divided into two employment sectors: a primary sector composed of higher-paid workers in more secure jobs and a secondary sector composed of lower-paid workers in jobs that often involve hazardous working conditions and little job security (Bonacich, 1972, 1976). Dominant group members are usually employed in primary sector positions; subordinate group members are concentrated in the secondary sector. Workers in the two job sectors tend to have divergent interests and goals because of their different relations to the labour market; therefore worker solidarity is difficult (Bonacich, 1972, 1976). Members of the capitalist class benefit from these divisions because workers are less likely to band together and demand pay increases or other beneficial changes in the workplace. White workers in the primary sector who buy into racist arguments attempt to exclude subordinate group members from higher-paying jobs by barring them from labour unions, lobbying against employment equity, and opposing immigration.

A second critical-conflict perspective examines *internal colonialism*—**a process that occurs when members of a racialized/ethnic group are conquered or colonized and forcibly placed under the economic and political control of the dominant group.** According to sociologist Robert Blauner (1972), people in groups that have been subjected to internal colonialism remain in subordinate positions in society much longer than do people in groups that voluntarily migrated to this country. For example, Indigenous peoples were forced into subordination when they were colonized by Europeans. Hundreds of culturally and linguistically diverse Indigenous groups lost property, political rights, components of their culture, and often their lives; some Indigenous groups were virtually extinguished, victims of *genocide*—**the deliberate, systematic killing of an entire people or nation.** Meanwhile, the capitalist class acquired cheap labour and land, frequently through government-sanctioned racialized exploitation (Blauner, 1972). The legacy of internal colonialism remains visible today in the number of Indigenous people who live in poverty, particularly those who live on federal reserves, often lacking essential services such as water, electricity, and sewage disposal.

The last critical-conflict perspective we will look at is the *theory of racial formation,* **which states that the government substantially defines racialized and ethnic relations.** From this perspective, racialized bias and discrimination tend to be rooted in government actions ranging from passage of "race"-related legislation to imprisonment of members of groups that are believed to be a threat to society. According to sociologists Michael Omi and Howard Winant (1994), governments are responsible for shaping the politics of racialized inequality through actions and policies that have resulted in the unequal treatment of Indigenous people and visible minorities. Immigration legislation, for example, reveals specific racialized biases. Fleras and Elliott (1992:39–40), for example, note that "initial policies could be described as essentially racist in orientation, assimilationist in content, and segregationist in intent." As examples, Western Europeans were preferred as immigrants, and when this was extended to Eastern Europeans, Jewish and Mediterranean people required special permits. Further, Asians of Chinese and Indian origin were reluctantly admitted during times of capitalist expansion, when the state required large pools of cheap labour, and then, only males were permitted to come to work. Family members were not allowed. Overtly racially selective immigration policies, closely following Canada's nation-building requirements, were in force until the first major revision in 1962. As sociologist Victor Satzewich (1989) has pointed out:

> Racism is an ideology imposed from above by those who own the means of production on those who do not: racism acts to mystify social reality, justifies the

Reprinted by permission.

Feminist and Anti-Racist Perspectives

One feminist perspective is based on a critical-conflict perspective and links racialized inequality and gender oppression. ***Gendered racism* may be defined as the interactive effect of racism and sexism in exploiting Indigenous and visible minority women.** According to Essed (1991), not all workers are exploited equally by capitalists. For many years, the majority of jobs in the primary sector of the labour market were held by White men, while most people of colour and many White

women were employed in secondary sector jobs. Below the secondary sector, in the underground sector of the economy, many Indigenous women and women of colour worked as domestic servants and nannies, in sweat shops or the sex trade, to survive. Work in this underground sector is unregulated, and people who earn their income in it are vulnerable to exploitation by many people, including unscrupulous employers, greedy pimps, and corrupt police officers (Amott and Matthaei, 1991).

In Canada, anti-racist feminist theorizing, deconstructing the interconnectedness of racism and sexism, has been engaged in since the 19th century (Dua, 1999). Anti-racist feminist theorizing differs from mainstream feminist theorizing: it challenges the notion of a common experience that all women share

(Text continues, partial at left top:) exploitation of certain groups of people's labour power, and contributes to the maintenance of the status quo.

under capitalism; it focuses on the specific ways that class, gender, *and* ethnicity play out as interconnections. Anti-racist feminist scholar and critical theorist Hamani Bannerji (1995:77) points out that "the erasure of the factors 'race,' racism, and continual immigration prevents an adequate understanding of the Canadian economy." Building on this, women's studies scholar Enakshi Dua (1999:21) concludes that "the discourse of race is as 'foundational' to the creation and maintenance of the Canadian political economy as are capitalist relations and patriarchy." Dua (1999:16) outlines three priorities within much of Canadian anti-racist feminist thought: (1) to interrogate feminist theory and practice to assess its complicity in perpetuating racism; (2) to raise questions about ways in which to theorize the connections between gender and racialization; and, (3) to continue to document the ways that racialized differences are created and maintained amongst women.

Many proponents of anti-racist feminism also investigate the impacts of racism on women of colour, examining the ways that gender, racialization, and class intersect, for example, when well-to-do White women employ racialized and poor women from non-industrialized nations to do domestic labour for them on temporary work visas. Other impacts that have been examined are the wages of women of colour and Indigenous women compared to White women's wages and the ways that equity measures for women disproportionately privilege White women relative to non-White women. Some anti-racist feminist theorists have suggested a *standpoint analysis*, that is, beginning theorizing and analysis from the situated standpoint of the person and her experiences—employing a kind of "outsider-within" perspective (Dua, 1999:19). However, women's experiences with racialization vary along class lines, according to sexual orientation and personal history. Therefore, it is important to account for the whole of a person's identity or locations.

Taking anti-racist feminism a step further, sociologist and editor Daiva Stasiulis (1999) makes a convincing case for feminist intersectional theorizing. Feminist intersectional theorizing is a trend away from what Stasiulis (1999:350–351) calls the "race-gender-class trinity" or the "iron triangle of race-gender-class" and a move toward an understanding of the myriad ways that oppressions are linked and the impacts on individuals and groups of those intersections. In addition to a focus on the triad of issues mentioned, nationality, language, religion, sexuality, citizenship, ability, and so on are interrogated, with the emphasis on seeing the ways these social divisions play out. With the increase in economic globalization, interest in this mode of analysis was heightened and developed. In developing an analysis of intersectionality, the challenge, however, is to steer clear of the trap of essentializing all women as this way and all people of colour that way and so on as well as to avoid using terms euphemistically, as in gender means "women" and "racialized" means "brown," and so on.

CAN RACIALIZED AND ETHNIC INEQUALITIES BE REDUCED?

According to symbolic interactionists, prejudice and discrimination are learned, and what is learned can be unlearned. As sociologist Gale E. Thomas (1995:339) notes, "In the areas of race, ethnic, and human relations, we must learn compassion and also to accept and truly embrace, rather than merely tolerate, differences . . . through honest and open dialogue and through the formation of genuine friendships and personal experiential . . . exchanges and interactions with different individuals and groups across cultures." In other words, only individuals and groups at the grass-roots level, not government and political leaders or academic elites, can bring about greater "racial" equality. Many authors point to anti-racist education as an important means of promoting change and building alliances (Bishop, 2002; Fleras, 2001; Fleras and Elliott, 1999; Henry et al., 2000; Kivel, 1996; Robertson, 1999).

How do functionalists suggest reducing racialized/ethnic inequality? Because they believe a stable society requires smoothly functioning social institutions and people who have common cultural values and attitudes, functionalists suggest restructuring social institutions to reduce discrimination and diffuse racialized/ethnic conflict. According to sociologist Arnold Rose (1951), discrimination robs society of the talents and leadership abilities of many individuals, especially people of colour. Rose suggests that societies invest time and money fostering racialized/ethnic inclusion and eliminating institutionalized discrimination in education, housing, employment, and the criminal justice system. Employing a global perspective, functionalists argue that Canadian racialized discrimination should be reduced because it negatively affects diplomatic and economic relations with other nations made up of diverse racialized/ethnic groups (Feagin and Vera, 1995).

From a conflict perspective, racialized and ethnic inequality can be reduced only through struggle and political action. Conflict theorists believe that inequality is based on the exploitation of subordinate groups by the dominant group, and that political intervention is necessary to bring about economic and social change. They agree that people should mobilize to put pressure on public officials. According to social activist Paul Kivel (1996), racialized inequality will not be reduced until there is, in this country, significant national public support and leadership for addressing social problems directly and forcefully.

Feminists and anti-racist feminists advocate critical analysis that begins from the myriad standpoints and situated experiences of people. In addition to building on insights developed from various standpoints, they advocate rendering the connections between locations or standpoints visible so that silences can be heard, hypocrisies can be exposed, and myths can be evaporated. When White people become more clearly aware of their complicity in perpetuating racism and systems of domination, the foundation for solid alliances can be built. We must work toward those ends tirelessly if we intend to create a better place for all.

Whether or not the people of Canada will work for greater equality for all racialized-ethnic groups, one thing is certain: The Canadian population is rapidly becoming increasingly diverse. Statistics Canada released its latest analysis of 2001 Census data on ethnic diversity in January, 2003, and stated that 18.4 percent of the population in Canada today is foreign-born. This is the highest rate of foreign-born Canadians since 1931, when 22.2 percent of the population was foreign born. Foreign-born citizens are increasingly diverse, both culturally and linguistically, adding credence to the notion of a "Canadian mosaic," a concept that in recent decades has been little more than a catchphrase. For example, in 2001, 4 million people, or 13.4 percent of the population, claimed "visible minority" status. The population of Indigenous people in Canada has also been increasing, accounting for a total of 4.4 percent of the population (1.3 million people). In addition to responding to the challenges and richness accompanying increased diversity, we also need to deal with long-standing tensions between Indigenous peoples and White people based on a legacy of colonization. A vision of the future in Canada must be inclusive and be based on a collective endeavour to bring about the thorough eradication of racism at all levels of society—the individual, the institutional, and the societal. The time to begin is immediately.

WHAT CAN YOU DO?

- Join (or start) a local anti-racism group and develop or take part in a "social action" mandate.
- Learn how to address racist comments and jokes when you hear them.
- Join and/or monitor anti-racist discussion groups online.
- Make an effort to get to know people from cultural groups different from your own. Take stock of your friendship circle right now. Do you regularly hang out with people who are different from you?
- Report suspected or known hate crimes or White supremacist activity to CAERS online (see Web Links).
- Attend cultural activities that are open to the public in order to get to know people different from you and find out about cultures different from your own.
- Do not assume that eating sushi or falafel or listening to "world music" gives you broad enough cross-cultural experience!
- To begin to learn how to unlearn racism, enroll in an anti-racism or diversity course or workshop.
- Get educated about contemporary Indigenous issues such as sovereignty, land claims, and self-determination.
- Attend public forums on issues concerning immigration, refugees, and Indigenous people.
- Look at the cultural makeup of the boards and staff and volunteers at organizations you belong to. Where there is diversity, what positions do people fill in your organization? Are there any non-White people in positions of authority or working on the front lines (e.g., visible to the public as soon as they walk in?).

- Carefully read the policies of organizations you are part of. Are they inclusive? Are they welcoming of diversity? If you are unsure, contact a local anti-racism organization and have them come in to do a policy workshop, or consult with them, using your policies as examples.

- Address stereotypical comments that may be made by your family and friends. Do not let any such remarks go by. Ask them for more information about a stereotype they hold, or why they believe the stereotype to be true; or, if they really believe the stereotype to be true, ask them what evidence they have that it is.

- March in solidarity with people of all backgrounds when the opportunity to publicly declare your stance against racism arises.

- Write letters or editorials for your local or post-secondary newspaper, debunking stereotypes. Interview people of diverse groups.

- If you are White, do not make your unlearning of racism the work of people of colour or Indigenous people. Make this your own project. Read. Talk to other White people who are grappling with these issues. Be reflective about the biases and stereotypes you hold and analyze them critically. Do not wallow in guilt. This serves no one.

- Think about your locations and determine which of your statuses confer privilege and which ones confer disadvantage. Think carefully about what you are willing to give up or to do to ensure equality for all people in Canada. This is a hard one!

SUMMARY

HOW DO RACIALIZED AND ETHNIC GROUPS DIFFER?

According to sociologists, racialized groups are defined on the basis of arbitrarily selected characteristics, and ethnic groups are defined on the basis of cultural or nationality characteristics. "Race" does not exist biologically but does exist as a socio-cultural phenomenon.

WHAT ARE MAJORITY AND MINORITY GROUPS?

When sociologists use the terms *majority group* and *minority group,* they are referring to power differentials. A majority (or dominant) group is one that is advantaged and has superior resources and rights in a society. A minority (or subordinate) group is one whose members, because of physical or cultural characteristics, are disadvantaged and subjected to unequal treatment by the dominant group and regard themselves as objects of collective discrimination.

HOW ARE PREJUDICE AND DISCRIMINATION RELATED?

Prejudice is a negative attitude that may or may not lead to discrimination, which is an action or practice of dominant group members that has a harmful impact on subordinate group members.

HOW DO INDIVIDUAL DISCRIMINATION AND INSTITUTIONAL DISCRIMINATION DIFFER?

Although individual discrimination and institutional discrimination are carried out by individuals, individual discrimination consists of one-on-one acts by members of the dominant group; institutional discrimination refers to actions and practices that are built into the day-to-day operations of large-scale organizations and social institutions.

HOW DO THE INTERACTIONIST AND FUNCTIONALIST PERSPECTIVES VIEW RACIALIZED AND ETHNIC RELATIONS?

Interactionists focus on microlevel issues, such as how people develop a racialized/ethnic identity and how individuals from diverse racialized/ethnic groups interact with each other. Functionalists focus on macrolevel issues, such as how entire groups of people assimilate, or do not assimilate, into the mainstream of the society.

WHAT ARE THE MAJOR CONFLICT EXPLANATIONS FOR RACIALIZED/ETHNIC INEQUALITY?

Conflict perspectives include class perspectives, split-labour market theory, internal colonialism, and racial formation theory.

HOW DO FEMINIST AND ANTI-RACIST FEMINIST THEORIES EXPLAIN RACIALIZED/ETHNIC INEQUALITY?

Feminists and anti-racist feminists advocate using critical analysis, beginning from the lived experiences of people. Additionally, they advocate an analysis that examines the intersections of locations, like gender and ethnicity, for example.

WHAT TYPES OF DISCRIMINATION HAVE BEEN EXPERIENCED BY MINORITY GROUP MEMBERS IN CANADA?

Minority group members have experienced every type of discrimination in Canada, from exclusion and expulsion to cultural genocide, slavery, and internment, from discrimination in hiring and retention and in housing to physical violence on a personal level. The legacy of racism for Indigenous people is particularly acute.

WHAT COMMONALITIES CAN BE SEEN IN THE EXPERIENCES OF ALL SUBORDINATE RACIALIZED-ETHNIC GROUPS?

Members of most subordinate racialized-ethnic groups have these commonalities in their experiences in Canada: (1) Each has been the object of negative stereotypes and discrimination; (2) each has resisted oppression and continued to strive for a better life for their members and their children; and, (3) each has been the object of some government policy that has shaped its place (or lack thereof) in Canadian ethnic relations over the past four centuries.

KEY TERMS

amalgamation,   p. 63
Anglo-conformity model,   p. 63
anti-Semitism,   p. 53
assimilation,   p. 63
ethnic group,   p. 50
ethnic pluralism,   p. 63
ethnocentrism,   p. 52
gendered racism,   p. 65
genocide,   p. 64
individual discrimination,   p. 53
institutional discrimination,   p. 53

internal colonialism,   p. 64
internalized dominance,   p. 52
majority (dominant) group,   p. 51
minority (subordinate) group,   p. 51
prejudice,   p. 52
racialized group,   p. 50
racism, p. 52
segregation,   p. 63
social construct,   p. 50
stereotypes,   p. 52
theory of racial formation,   p. 64

QUESTIONS FOR CRITICAL THINKING

1. Do you consider yourself part of the majority or dominant racialized/ethnic group or part of a minority or subordinate racialized/ethnic group in Canada? Consider what specific ways your life might be different if you were in another group.

2. Sociologists suggest that we acquire beliefs about our self and others through socialization. What specific messages have you received about your racialized/ethnic identity? What specific messages have you received about dealing with people from other racialized-ethnic groups? What hidden messages have you received about your cultural group and others?

3. Have all White Canadians, regardless of class, gender, or other characteristics, benefited from racialized prejudice and discrimination in Canada? Why or why not? In what ways have White people benefited from racism against non-Whites? In what ways have they been harmed by racism against non-Whites?

4. Compare recent depictions of Indigenous people, Black Canadians, Asian Canadians, and other racialized ethnic groups in Canada in films, television shows, and advertisements. To what extent have we moved beyond the traditional stereotypes of those groups? To what extent have the stereotypes remained strong?

WEBLINKS

Assembly of First Nations (AFN)
www.afn.ca
The AFN represents over 630 First Nation's communities in Canada. The national lobby organization is designed to present the views of the various First Nations through their leaders in areas such as: Aboriginal and Treaty Rights, Economic Development, Education, and Health and Housing, among others.

Canadian Antiracism Education and Research Society
www.antiracist.com
Antiracist.com is a site committed to improving the respect of human rights and equality worldwide; it provides general information, news reports, and case studies to help people organize peacefully against hate groups.

Canadian Ethnic Studies Journal
www.ss.ucalgary.ca/ces
A tri-annual interactive journal dedicated to the study of ethnicity, immigration, inter-group relations and the history and cultural life of ethnic groups in Canada. It also offers book and film reviews, opinions, immigrants' memoirs, and other resources.

Canadian Race Relations Foundation
www.crr.ca
The CRRF seeks to strengthen the struggle for racial harmony, for the eradication of racism. The site presents the foundation's activities, research projects and other publications.

Canadian Research Centres in the Field of Ethnic Relations
www.ceetum.umontreal.ca/english/links/htm
The Centre for Research and Interdisciplinary Training in the Ethnic Studies Field's links page leading to other Canadian and international research centres.

Canadian Women's Internet Directory
http://directory.womenspace.ca/anti-racism
A directory of Internet links focusing on anti-racism and minority groups, some of them dedicated to women user groups.

Crosspoint Antiracism
www.magenta.nl/crosspoint/cnd/html
Magenta is a foundation that combats racism and discrimination. Its Crosspoint is the Internet's largest directory of links in the field of human rights and anti-racism.

National Antiracism Council of Canada

www.narc.freeservers.com

The National Antiracism Council of Canada brings together community-based organizations and individuals to ensure that the country actively contributes to the United Nations World Conference Against Racism and that work to fight racism is implemented locally.

The Nizkor Project

www.nizkor.org

The Nizkor project is devoted to shedding light on the phenomenon and history of hate (especially the Nazi Holocaust) and seeks to offer nonviolent methods for combatting such hate.

UN World Conference Against Racism: NGO Virtual Forum

www.unwcar.freeservers.com

This site offers a discussion forum and an online community fighting to eliminate racism. Also available are a search engine and a variety of links.

4

GENDER INEQUALITY

Would you note that if I commit suicide today 89-12-06 it is not for economic reasons (for I have waited until I have exhausted all my financial means, even refusing jobs) but for political reasons. Because I have decided to send the feminists, who have always ruined my life, to their Maker. For seven years life has brought me no joy and being totally blasé, I have decided to put an end to those viragos . . . Even if the Mad Killer epithet will be attributed to me by the media, I consider myself a rational erudite that only the arrival of the Grim Reaper has forced to take extreme acts. . . . The feminists have always enraged me. They want to keep the advantages of women . . . while seizing for themselves those of men.. . .

Partial text of the suicide letter left by the shooter who killed 14 women on December 6th, 1989 at Montreal's École Polytechnique. The letter was followed by a list of names of 19 women and the following appended note . . . "The lack of time (because I started too late) has allowed these radical feminists to survive." (Printed in Malette and Chalouh, 1991:180–181)

The killing of 14 women in Montreal, Quebec, on December 6th, 1989, shocked the nation. Most news reports in the days and weeks following cited the act as that of a madman—an isolated, bizarre event carried out by a deranged individual. While there can be no doubt that the act was extreme, feminists and other analysts continue to question this individualistic analysis, pointing instead to the pervasiveness of sexism in a patriarchal society, a pervasiveness they say creates a climate for actions such as this, and other forms of violence against women, to play out. **Sexism is the subordination of one sex, female, based on the assumed superiority of the other sex, male,** while *patriarchy* **refers to a hierarchical system of social organization in which cultural, political, and economic structures are controlled by men.** According to some social analysts, problems of sexism have been overblown: Sexism was a problem in the past when women were underrepresented in organizations and the paid labour force generally; now, however, women have made significant inroads in education and employment. In 2000, for example, 56 percent of women aged 15 and over were employed for pay, up from 42 percent in 1976. Many more women today have gained postsecondary degrees and are employed in an increasing variety of professional fields; women are also increasingly represented among the self-employed. With increases such as these,

some people believe that women should just be happy and stop complaining about the "past." Many feel that, while the events of December 6, 1989, were tragic, conditions that may (assuming a social vs. an individualized analysis) have caused such an event to occur are over now—they are historical conditions that we have overcome in recent years. These people believe that women and men in Canada today are equal.

However, despite women's advances in the labour market and education and so on, gender inequality persists. Nowhere is this more clearly illustrated than in the persistence of violence against women. As Charlotte Bunch, past president of MATCH, a Canadian NGO, stated in a public speech in the early 1990s, "Violence against women is the most pervasive human rights abuse in the world today. If any other group in society were as systematically battered and killed in order to be controlled, it would be a civil emergency . . . the war on women must end."

The 1993 National Violence Against Women Survey conducted by Statistics Canada represents the only comprehensive report on women's experience of violence. The survey, which asked a sample of 12 300 women to report their lifetime experiences of assault, sexual assault, and sexual harassment, found that most assaults go unreported to police. Only 14 percent of all assaults had been reported; wife assaults were reported at a rate of 26 percent. Fifty-one percent of Canadian women had, since the age of 16, experienced at least one incidence of physical or sexual assault. Forty-five percent of these women were assaulted by men known to them, and an additional 23 percent were assaulted by a stranger. Thirty-nine percent of women experienced sexual assault; 34 percent of women experienced nonsexual assault. Some of the sexual assaults and most of the nonsexual assaults were perpetrated by the women's spouses (Johnson, 1996:49).

Just as women are not viewed as equal to men, not all women are viewed as equal to one another. For example, the murders of the 14 women in Montreal sparked annual December 6th memorials to raise awareness of the violence against women that continues today. The White Ribbon campaign, begun and carried out by men to raise awareness of violence against women, continues to gain support each year. And a National Monument in Vancouver's Thornton Park commemorates women's deaths at the hands of male violence. Women's groups from Vancouver's downtown East Side question why the disappearances of at least 63 Vancouver women since 1983 has not created the same kind of public concern. No one criticizes the increased attention to issues of violence against women, but many point out the difference in public interest and attention the two groups of women have received. Analysts highlight the class, ethnic, and lifestyle differences between the groups; for instance, the Montreal Massacre, as it quickly came to be called, involved 14 young, White, middle-class women, most of whom were enrolled as students in Engineering at the "Poly." The disappearances in Vancouver have mainly involved women believed to be drug users and/or sex-trade workers, many of whom are also Indigenous. These women are commonly viewed as "disposable" people, societal "throwaways." In a critique of the way the 63 disappearances have been handled by RCMP to date, John Lowman of Simon Fraser University's Department of Criminology stated in a February 2002 newspaper interview, "If [63] women in any other category, whether housewives or women of a certain age or anyone else, went missing, believe me; the police reaction would have been entirely different" (Editorial, *Globe and Mail*, Feb 9, 2002, p. A4).

Violence against women in its many forms is one result of sexism and gender inequality. Other manifestations of sexism that are discussed on the following pages include inequalities in the paid labour force and in domestic labour. The ways that gender socialization perpetuates these inequalities is highlighted, as are various theories for analyzing gender inequality.

GENDER INEQUALITY AS A SOCIAL PROBLEM

Similar to the ways that racialized ethnic group members experience discrimination based on supposed innate characteristics, women experience discrimination based on their sex. Since 51 percent of the people in Canada are female, women constitute a numerical majority. However, they are sometimes referred to as the country's largest minority group because, as a group, they do not possess as much wealth, power, or prestige as men. As a telling example involving income alone, for all full-time workers in Canada in 1991, women earned 69.4 percent of what men earned. In 1995, this increased to 73.0 percent and by 2000, it had decreased again, although marginally, to 72.0 percent (Statistics

Canada, 2002a). The differences between women's and men's earnings are more striking when we examine all earners' wages, as women are more often only employed part-time. Sometimes this is by choice, though often it is not by choice but is the result of persistent gender stereotypes that women's incomes are "pin money" or otherwise merely "supplemental" to men's. In 1991, for all Canadian earners, full- and part-time, women earned 61.3 percent of men's earnings. In 1995, a banner year, they earned 64.8 percent, and in 2000, women earned 64.0 percent of what men earned (Statistics Canada, 2002a). More recent data have not yet been released, but if the pattern from past decades continues to hold, we cannot expect much change.

Defining Sex and Gender

What is the difference between sex and gender? Although many people use these terms interchangeably, sociologists believe that there are significant differences in their meanings. **Sex refers to the biological differences between females and males.** Our sex is the first label we receive in life and is an ascribed status. Before birth or at the time of birth we are identified as either male or female on the basis of our sex organs and genes. Despite the fact that many children do not exhibit the genitalia or chromosomes consistent with either a male or female designation, most people act as though there are only two dichotomous and "opposite" sexes. For example, when a child is born **intersexed,** that is **with either unrecognizably male or female genitalia or with both male and female genitalia**, we surgically alter the child to fit the two-sex model of reality that is currently in vogue. Within the two-sex model, males are seen as the central or standard sex, against which females, the "opposite" sex, are measured. This practice of **putting males at the centre** is known as *androcentricity.* As an illustration of the fluidity of our notions, even of the biological, in the past, Westerners had a one-sex model of humanity, the one sex being male. Females and their bodies were viewed as imperfect or flawed versions of the male. Historian Thomas Laqueur (1992:4), in a book called *Making Sex*, states that several early "scientists," such as Galen and Herophilus,

demonstrated at length that women were essentially men in whom a lack of vital heat—of perfection— had resulted in the retention, inside, of structures that in the male are visible without . . . In this world the vagina is imagined as an interior penis, the labia as foreskin, the uterus as scrotum, and the ovaries as testicles . . . for two centuries, the ovary . . . had not even a name of its own.

Scholars and lay people alike were "caught up in the female-as-male model" (see Figure 4.1) until approximately 1800, when many began to insist that there "were fundamental differences between the male and female sexes" (Laqueur, 1992:5).

Following, then, from a two-sex model, **gender refers to the culturally and socially constructed differences between females and males based on meanings, beliefs, and practices that a group or society associates with femininity or masculinity.** For many people, being *masculine* means being aggressive, independent, and not showing emotions, and being *feminine* means the opposite—being passive, dependent, and emotional. Understanding the difference between sex and gender is important, according to sociologists, because what many people think of as *sex differences*— for example, being aggressive or independent—are actually socially constructed *gender differences* based on widely held assumptions about men's and women's attributes (Gailey, 1987). In other words, males are supposed to be aggressive and independent not because they have male sex organs but because that is how people in this society think males should act. Psychologist S.L. Bem (1974) talked about masculinity and femininity being represented on two continuums. Where individuals are located on each continuum gives an indication as to their personal combination of masculine and feminine traits. Again, though, masculinity and femininity are presented as the central elements in a dichotomy instead of as simply two out of a multiplicity of possibilities for genders. For example, "trans" people are challenging widely held conceptions of gender (see Box 4.1) and queer theorists (see Chapter 6) are challenging the appropriateness of long-held binary categories to encompass and describe the fluidity of gender many people experience.

Biological and Social Bases for Gender Roles

To study gender inequality, sociologists begin with an examination of the biological and social bases for *gender*

FIGURE 4.1   The One-Sex Model

Uterus

Vagina

Source: From Making Sex: Body and Gender from the Greeks to Freud, *by Thomas Laqueur, 1992, Cambridge: Harvard University Press. Originally published in Andreas Vesalius,* De Humani Corporis Fabrica *(Basel, 1543).*

roles, which are the rights, responsibilities, expectations, and relationships of women and men in a society (Benokraitis and Feagin, 1995). Gender roles have both a biological and a social basis and, as a concept, need to be problematized in terms of power and inequality. The biological basis for gender roles is rooted in the chromosomal and hormonal differences between men and women. When a child is conceived, the mother contributes an X chromosome, and the father contributes either an X chromosome (which produces a female embryo) or a Y chromosome (which produces a male embryo). As the embryo's male or female sex glands develop, they secrete the appropriate hormones (more androgens for males, more estrogens for females), which circulate through the bloodstream, producing sexual

SOCIAL PROBLEMS AND SOCIAL POLICY

BOX 4.1   *Trans*-gressing Gender Norms

On October 15, 2002, Directors and Chairs at the University of Victoria received a memo from the Office of the President. The University of Victoria President, along with the Vice- President, Academic, and the new Dean of Graduate Studies were advising the university community that the Dean of Graduate Studies, also a tenured professor in the Department of Sociology, wished henceforth to be known as a man. The memo communicated the upper administration's "unequivocal personal support for this decision and . . . a great appreciation for his valued contributions to the university" and called for people's understanding and consideration of the wishes of the Dean to now "live as a man." Aaron (formerly Holly) Devor is the well-known Canadian author of many publications on gender and transgender issues, including the books *Gender Blending: Confronting the Limits of Duality* (1989) and *FTM: Female to Male Transsexuals in Society* (1997).

Aaron Devor's experience of "unequivocal" institutional support, economic well-being, and a high-status, high-profile position is precisely what we wish to see achieved for all "trans" people. The unfortunate reality, however, is that this experience is not at all typical among transgendered people. A recent study by "trans" activist Emilia L. Lombardi and her colleagues (2001) documents that violence and economic discrimination are more common responses to gender nonconformity. Several other studies confirm that "trans" people experience high rates of

Dr. Aaron Devor, 2003.

prejudice, marginalization, discrimination, harassment, stalking, and other violence (Appelbe, 2001; Donavon, 2001; MacDonald, 1998/2000; Nangeroni, 2001; Towle and Morgan, 2002). In addition to the external threats faced, pervasive victimization has been shown to lead to a higher incidence of depression, substance abuse, and suicide by "trans" people (Donavon, 2001; Lombardi et al., 2001; Nangeroni, 2001). As with homophobia and biphobia (see Chapter 6), it is important to remember that it is not the fact of being a transsexual or transgendered person that causes ill health and heightened risks, but rather, it is transphobia, or the hatred and fear of "trans" people, that does. Sadly, transphobia may come as much from gays and lesbians as it does from heterosexuals.

"Trans" people have begun to speak out about their experiences and the issues that they face living in a transphobic culture. As Nick Matte, a graduate student studying the history of gender and sexuality, points out,

> When we're thinking about the barriers faced by "trans" people, what's really sad is that people often have to spend so much time educating themselves and breaking down the barriers they help to create, that it's easy to forget to make time to celebrate the fact that "trans" people have already been breaking those barriers down for them/ourselves. (2003, author's files)

Recently, Tina Donavon (2001:20), a member of Senior Action in a Gay Environment (SAGE)/Queens, described a little of her experience coming out as a transgendered woman in the mid-1970s:

> I am a woman, 61 years old and transgender. I have lived the last 27 years as a woman, much to the chagrin of my parents and some friends. They did not understand the nature of my struggles since early childhood. I knew all along that I was female, not a male. When I revealed this information to my parents, my father said I was "nuts" and my mother cried. They both thought that my gender identification was a result of their failing to raise me in the correct way.

"Trans" issues have increasingly come into public focus over the last decade. Ethnographic research, largely by anthropologists, has been used to provide supposed cross-cultural "proofs" that the "Western binary gender system is neither universal nor innate" (Towle and Morgan, 2002:469). In many publications, examples of people who belong to a "third gender" are presented: the Hijras in India, the so-called Berdache[1] of North America, the female husbands of West Africa, the Xanith of the Arabian Peninsula, and the Sambia of Papua New Guinea.

While these people around the world provide interesting examples of a variety of socially constructed roles and statuses, they cannot just be slotted unproblematically into the North American context; one must carefully examine the cultural and historical contexts from which these groups spring. As anthropologists Evan B. Towle and Lynn M. Morgan (2002:490) point out,

> Invoking "third gender" examples in an oversimplified way or citing them out of context to underwrite Western social agendas is an unwitting kind of neocolonial (or at least ethnocentric) appropriation that distorts the complexity and reality of other people's lives.

The term *transgender* was originally coined by Virginia Prince in a 1970s conference presentation titled "The Transsexual and His Wife" (MacDonald, 1998/2000). We use, and have used in the past, a great many terms to refer to "trans" people: transgendered, transsexual, transvestite, butch, femme, drag king, drag queen, female to male (F to M), male to female (M to F), intersex, third gender, non-op, pre-op, post-op, androgyne, epicene, and two-spirited—to name only a few. Providing definitions of a range of "trans" experiences is beyond the scope of this feature. Moreover, it is not necessarily appropriate, given that an often common thread of "trans" experiences is precisely the challenge to identity-based categories and to how we think about identity. Political scientist Eleanor MacDonald (1998/2000:284), for example, provides this provocative notion:

> What transgender identity specifically problematizes is identity itself. Transgender identity is about identity experienced as problematic; the experience of being transgender problematizes the relationship of the self to the body, and the self to others. In doing so, it also problematizes issues of identity boundaries, stability and coherence. . . . What is radical then, to the definition of "transgender" is its origin in problem, a disjunction between one's feelings of who one is or is not, and how one is (or has once been) perceived, recognized, and understood by others.

The existence of "trans" people, "trans" bodies, and "trans" identities may be useful in understanding all gender relations, the normative and the transgressive. Towle and Morgan (2002) suggest that through an interrogation of "trans" we may be able to get at what the differences between men and women really are: Through what acts is gender identity communicated? What is the meaning, for social interactions, of failing to communicate a gender identity? and, What is the meaning of inhabiting a gendered body? David Valentine and Riki Anne Wilchins subvert the typical lines of questioning with their point that "[bodies that] are suspect . . . are not what have to be explained. Rather, the requirement that they explain themselves should itself be investigated" (in Towle and Morgan,

2002:491–492). Konnor Brett, a recent Sociology and Women's Studies graduate, adds, "I'm not sure that my transitioning broke down many aspects of the binary gender system in our society as a whole. I do know that I see my future with happiness" (2003, author's files).

The Canadian general public has responded to "trans" issues in a range of ways, from support, to confusion, to intolerance or hostility. While many people are supportive and may even constitute a "silent majority" in some sectors of the population, MacDonald (1998/2000) outlines three general responses to "trans" people that she has observed and that can present problems. One response has been hostility and/or exclusion in the form of denouncing "trans" people as dangerous to progressive enterprises, such as women's centres, for example. "Trans" people, particularly F to M, have been viewed by some as traitors or turncoats, while M to F have been treated as deceptive, as "Trojan horses," and as violators of women-only spaces. It is interesting to note both the essentialism and the sexism inherent in this response. Essentialist because "trans" people are stereotyped a certain way, using the sex they were born into; and sexist because women are often portrayed, through sexist stereotypes, as "sneaky deceivers." Further, females who transition may be seen as "switching sides," suddenly developing all the characteristics supposedly attributed to males, including a complete inability to understand women's concerns, issues, or experiences.

A second response has been to medicalize "trans" people's experiences, seemingly rendering them "apolitical." Finally, a third response has been to "celebrate trans identity as emblematic of the subversiveness of post modern theory"—where "gender doesn't [or shouldn't] matter" (MacDonald, 1998/2000:282, 285). This can create a lot of inappropriate pressure for "trans" people to think and feel and act in certain ways.

While this third response is more supportive, it does not adequately capture the complexity of lived experiences of "trans" identities. "Trans" people may "playfully or seriously" choose identities that are grounded firmly in gender-stereotypical notions of masculinity or femininity. What is sometimes overlooked is that a sense of relief and pleasure can accompany the ability to identify with a recognizable and easily understood gender, especially for those for whom a gender identity has been denied or has felt uncertain. Additionally, becoming firmly situated within a recognizable gender may be necessary from a strategic perspective, as many physicians and psychiatrists view this as the "proof" necessary to endorse a sex change or to dispense hormones.

Political scientist and activist Paisley Currah (2001:192) takes a different stance, stating that it is imperative that "trans" (and non-"trans") people push beyond the gender stereotypes that "reinforce heteronormative notions":

This young F to M couple are celebrating graduation from university. They not only have to contend with transphobia in their daily lives, but also with homophobia.

[rather] we need to give sustenance to gender-variant traditions, to preserve them, to make sure they get reproduced, not play into the larger ideological erasure of them. We need to contest, rather than support ideologies that assert that queer, gay, lesbian, bisexual, questioning, and transgender kids are pathological.

In the study about the extent to which "trans" people are at risk for violence and discrimination, Lombardi et al. (2001:99) report that "trans" youth are exposed to heightened risks of "attempted suicide, substance abuse, unsafe sexual practices, of being exposed to STDs (including HIV), of being homeless, dropping out of school, and of experiencing high levels of distress, as well as experiencing many forms of discrimination, harassment and violence." Widespread transphobia and its devastating consequences indicate that a series of policies is required to create ways to protect "trans" Canadians' fundamental human rights, such as:

- Track all incidences of violence against members of "trans" communities in order to better understand the nature of these hate crimes.

- Design and implement education for law enforcement personnel, social service workers, and other professionals who come into contact with members of "trans" communities, so that they can recognize issues and lend assistance.

- As with other "hate crimes" in Canada, ensure that penalties for hate-motivated crimes against members of "trans" communities are enhanced (e.g., made more severe). This will require the addition of gender identity and/or presentation to be added to hate crimes legislation.

- Ensure that unless it is absolutely necessary to know, "sex" should not have to be reported to bureaucracies, employers, and other officials. As with other personal information, such as age, sexual orientation, or ability, knowing someone's sex is usually unnecessary, and requiring this information could violate human rights. To require this information unnecessarily complicates the lives of "trans" people and may even set them up for negative or harmful experiences.

- Where possible, provide gender-neutral washroom spaces, either in addition to male and female washrooms, or instead of them. We often provide gender-neutral washroom space in public places already, so there is no logical reason why "trans" people should not also be afforded this measure of privacy. As the public becomes more relaxed about co-ed worlds, many public spaces, such as restaurants, are already doing away with gendered designations. (Appelbe, 2001; Devor, 2003; Lombardi et al., 2001).

8th Annual GROOVEFEST 2003-Saturday,
February 15-Vertigo Nightclub
Tickets: $9 advance/$11 at the door/
Doors open at 9 pm.

Groovefest is an annual event promoting and
facilitating the self-expression and
empowerment of individuals and communities
who do not fit dominant, imposed, standards
of beauty. An evening of high energy, fun-
filled and politically charged performances,
Groovefest sets out to challenge mainstream
beauty standards, the fashion industry,
consumerism, white supremacy, ableism,
sexism, homophobia, racism, transphobia,
ageism, classism, fatphobia and all other
forms of inequality.
    This year's Groovefest will feature a wide
variety of performances, including drag
acts, non-traditional fashion features (the
infamous "anti-fashion" show), poetry,
dance, spoken word, skits and surely a few
surprises. The evening will end with a fine
round of booty shakin' tunes provided by DJs
Mama Miche and Marlee. All proceeds go to
local groups working for social change, and
this year's beneficiaries are P.E.E.R.S and
the S.E.X.Y. Queer Youth Group. This is a
licensed event.

In addition to legislated change, measures may be taken by communities wishing to celebrate the diversity and richness of a society that is working to transcend gender norms. In Victoria, B.C., for example, several community groups, along with some university campus groups, organize an annual "Groovefest" in February, the proceeds of which go to selected not-for-profit, anti-oppression groups. Above is an excerpt from the GROOVEFEST 2003 advertisement:

While "trans" issues are often misunderstood and marginalized (even writing this feature as a "boxed item" instead of as part of the "regular" text may illustrate this fact), "trans" issues are finally coming into the mainstream in positive and empowering ways. As you read at the beginning of this box, some "trans" people are experiencing support in their workplaces. Many "trans" people experience support for their transitions through their relationships with family, friends, and peers. One "trans" person, in a relationship with another "trans" person, related that "the most common question we get asked is about family support and I have to say that both our families love and support us in all aspects" (2003, author's files). Many "trans" people also report feelings of joy in having the ability to finally feel as though they are living authentically, in ways they have chosen. As one undergraduate student recently stated:

> Before I knew about transitioning, I basically had accepted my life would be lived in a depressed state. Since my transition, I have been constantly amazed about what I was missing. I feel truly happy and balanced for the first time in my life. (2003, author's files)

These positive reports do not in any way diminish the ongoing need to be vigilant about ridding Canadian society of prejudice and discrimination against "trans" people, but they do help us to see that life as a "trans" person is not all negative and, in fact, can be cause for celebration. As one "trans" person concluded, "What you see in the media is only going to give you the miserable story" (2003, author's files). Clearly, there is much more to "trans" life than that.

Note:
[1]Use of the term "Berdache" reflects the mistaken assumptions about same-sex relations amongst Indigenous peoples made by Europeans at contact. The word "Berdache" originated as a Persian term meaning "slave youth." It later came to mean a "kept boy" in a gay relationship. Neither meaning depicts any North American Indigenous traditions or practices, nor was either term accepted as appropriate by Indigenous people. The continued widespread use of the term demonstrates, if nothing else, the pervasiveness of colonialism (Roscoe, 1995, in Goldie, 2001:10).

differentiation in the external genitalia, the internal reproductive tract, and possibly some areas of the brain. At birth, medical personnel and family members distinguish male from female infants by their *primary sex characteristics*, the genitalia used in the reproductive process. At puberty, hormonal differences in females and males produce *secondary sex characteristics*, the physical traits that, along with the reproductive organs, identify a person's sex. Females develop secondary sex characteristics such as menstruation, more prominent breasts, wider hips and narrower shoulders, and a layer of fatty tissue throughout the body. Male secondary sex characteristics include the development of larger genitals, a more muscular build, a deeper voice, more body and facial hair, and greater height. Although both males and females have androgens and estrogens, it is the relative proportion of each hormone that triggers masculine or feminine physical traits.

Is there something in the biological and genetic makeup of boys or girls that makes them physically aggressive or passive? As sociologist Judith Lorber (1994:39) notes, "When little boys run around noisily, we say 'Boys will be boys,' meaning that physical assertiveness has to be in the Y chromosome because it is manifest so early and so commonly in boys." Similarly, when we say "She throws like a girl" we mean, according to Lorber, that "she throws like a female child, a carrier of XX chromosomes." However, Lorber questions these widely held assumptions: "But are boys universally, the world over, in every social group, a vociferous, active presence? Or just where they are encouraged to use their bodies freely, to cover space, take risks, and play outdoors at all kinds of games and sports?"

According to Lorber, boys and girls who are given tennis rackets at the age of three and encouraged to become champions tend to use their bodies similarly. Even though boys gradually gain more shoulder and arm strength and are able to sustain more concentrated bursts of energy, after puberty girls acquire more stamina, flexibility, and lower-body strength. Coupled with training and physical exercise, these traits enhance, compensate for, or override different physical capabilities (Lorber, 1994). Thus, the girl who throws "like a girl" is probably a product of her culture and time: She has had more limited experience than many boys at throwing the ball and engaging in competitive games at an early age. Still, the implication that social roles "are an unproblematic reflection of biology (sex)" is analytically flawed (Marshall, 2000:24).

The social basis for gender roles is known as the gender belief system or *gender ideology*—ideas of masculinity and femininity that are held to be valid in a given society at a specific historical time (Lorber, 1994). Gender ideology is reflected in what sociologists refer to as the *gendered division of labour*—the process whereby productive tasks are separated on the basis of gender. How do people determine what constitutes "women's work" or "men's work"? Evidence from cross-cultural studies shows that social factors, more than biological factors, influence the gendered division of labour in societies. In poor agricultural societies, for example, women work in the fields and tend to their families' daily needs; men typically produce and market cash crops but spend no time on household work. In industrialized nations, an increasing proportion of women are in paid employment but still have heavy household and family responsibilities. For example, in Canada in 1998, men spent 2.7 hours per day on unpaid work while women spent 4.4 hours per day. Across cultures, women's domain is viewed as the private and domestic, and men's domain is viewed as the public, economic, and political. This difference in how labour is divided, how workers are rewarded, and what cultural value is accorded to paid vs. unpaid labour affects access to scarce resources such as wealth, power, and prestige. Given their domain, men have greater access to wealth, power, and prestige, a situation that leads to gender inequality in other areas.

To explain gender inequality, some sociologists use a *gender role approach*, focusing on how the socialization process contributes to male domination and female subordination. Other sociologists use a *structural approach*, focusing on how large-scale, interacting, and enduring social structures determine the boundaries of individual behaviour. Let's look first at how socialization can perpetuate gender stereotyping and inequality.

GENDER INEQUALITY AND SOCIALIZATION

Numerous sociological studies have found that gender-role stereotyping is one of the enduring consequences of childhood gender socialization. Socialization into appropriate "feminine" behaviour makes women less likely than men to pursue male-dominated activities, and socialization into appropriate "masculine" behaviour makes men more likely than women to pursue leadership roles in education, religion, business, politics, and other spheres of public life (Peterson and Runyan, 1993). We learn our earliest and often most long-lasting beliefs about gender roles from a variety of *agents of socialization*—people, groups, or institutions that teach us what we need to know to participate in society. Among the most significant agents of socialization are parents, peers, the education system, and the media.

SOCIAL PROBLEMS IN GLOBAL PERSPECTIVE

BOX 4.2   Female Genital Surgery or Female Genital Mutilation?

It is estimated that more than 130 million women have undergone the practice of genital cutting, with each year 2 million more women (6000 per day) joining their ranks (F.L. Gordon, 2000; Seager, 1997). The practice, variously known as female genital surgery, female genital mutilation, or female circumcision, depending, in part, on the feelings of the person describing the practice, has been performed in 30 countries worldwide for as long as 6000 years (Ward, 1999). Surgeries are typically performed on girls aged from 5 to 13.

There are at last three distinct types of surgery performed, all often confusingly referred to as "circumcision." Circumcision, the least severe and least practised, refers to the removal of the prepuce, or hood, of the clitoris. A similar practice, called "sunna," meaning "religious duty" in Arabic, refers to the removal of the sheath, or tip, of the clitoris. Excision, or clitoridectomy, practiced in approximately 80 percent of surgeries, refers to the removal of all or some of the clitoris and all or part of the inner genitals (*labia minora*). The most severe form of surgery is infibulation, which refers to the removal of the clitoris, the labia minora and most or all of the outer genitals (*labia majora*). The vulva is then fastened together through stitching or with thorns, and a reed or other small object is inserted in order to allow for urination and menstruation as the surgery heals. The girl's legs may then be bound from hip to ankle for up to 40 days to allow scar tissue to form (F.L. Gordon, 2000:270; Wood, 2001:322–323).

Surgeries are nearly always carried out by older women, in less-than-sterile surroundings, using special knives, scissors, pieces of glass, or tin or razor blades (F.L. Gordon, 2000; Wood, 2001). Further, the people performing the surgeries rarely have medical training and no anesthesia is used (Ward, 1999; Wood, 2001).

Westerners decry the custom of female genital cutting as "barbaric" and call for its immediate end. Many people within cultures who practice it criticize Westerners' approaches to the issue as "colonialism in disguise" (El Saadawi, 1980, cited in Ward, 1999:252). Those who support it say that it is a time-honoured cultural tradition that Westerners have no business involving themselves in: "Stop groping about in our panties" was a comment heard from many African women at the 1985 United Nations Decade for Women Conference in Kenya when the issue was debated (quoted in Ward, 1999:252). In contrast, many women who do not support the practice retort that "Torture is not culture" (Walker, 1993, quoted in Ward, 1999:252).

There are many reasons given for the continuation of support for female genital surgery, reasons that are viewed by some as merely a means to mask and/or justifiy patriarchal practices.

Here, Frances L. Gordon, a travel writer specializing in Africa, (2000:271) and Julia Wood, a communications scholar (2001:325), bring several such reasons to light:

- *Hygiene*: Removal of the genitals is thought to foster cleanliness.
- *Aesthetics*: Women's genitals are considered unclean and unattractive.
- *Superstition*: Some believe that a woman's genitals will continue to grow if not removed, while some believe that a woman will be unable to conceive, or if she does conceive, some believe that the resulting child will be murdered by coming into contact with the clitoris.
- *Social solidarity*: Engaging in the operation means a woman will be accepted as a fully participating member of her culture and will be able to reap the rewards of womanhood in that culture (namely marriage and children and a sense of belonging).
- *Social control of sexuality*: Operations such as this are said to lessen or completely extinguish women's ability to experience sexual pleasure or to experience orgasm; therefore, it may be less likely for her to practice infidelity. Additionally, in some countries where polygamy is practiced, it is said to result in many wives making fewer sexual demands on only one husband. Lastly, where infibulation is practised, it is clear if the woman has been sexually active previous to her marriage; thus, men can be assured of marrying virgins. This is important, as virginity "reflects the moral prestige of the girl's family, ensures a good market value for the bride and establishes the paternity of future children."

These operations often result in a variety of possible physical complications, such as hemorrhaging; scarring; painful urination, menstruation, intercourse, and childbirth; and infections and death (estimated to occur as much as 15 percent of the time); there are psychological costs reported as well; for example, depression, anxiety, and low self-esteem (F.L. Gordon, 2000:271).

It may seem clear that female genital surgery is a barbaric practice that should be halted. However, some critics of this view suggest that, rather than deflecting our attention elsewhere, we need to consider our own cultural practices that result in body modification, pain, and death. Male circumcision, while similar to female circumcision, is rarely viewed as barbaric. This practice, the removal of the sheath, or prepuce, of the penis, demonstrates no clear health or cleanliness advantages yet is often performed routinely at birth in Canada. The age at which this typically happens is what sets it apart, say some. Additionally, male circumcision does not adversely impact on men's sexual pleasure (Wood, 2001).

Increasingly, younger and younger women (mainly) are availing themselves of dieting pills, rigid exercise regimes, cosmetic surgeries, tummy tucks, breast implants, and the like, all in search of the perfect body (Boddy, 1991, in Ward, 1999; Abu-Laban et al., 2001). Girls in elementary school, as young as age 7, report being "too fat," and anorexia and bulimia, disproportionately affecting females (85 to 97 percent) are on the rise (Nelson and Robinson, 2002). The typical anorexic or bulimic is White, middle-class, and under the age of 25 (Nelson and Robinson, 2002:146). A 1990 Saskatoon study of high school girls found that 76 percent diet, 17 percent vomit, and 12 percent use diet aids (Abu-Laban et al., 2001). With the profusion of extremely thin media icons today, as compared even with 1990, it is certain these numbers would be higher today. As sociologists Adie Nelson and Barry W. Robinson (2002:146) state, "The vast majority of North American women engage, to some degree, in a regimen of self-restraint and dieting. . . . Women's concern with dieting within North America has become a 'normative obsession' and a 'cultural obsession'." Apparently today there are a number of Web sites aimed at teens that teach girls how to achieve the ultra thin "look" that is in fashion today, websites that are increasingly being blocked by parents and school districts (author's files). Moreover, we teach girls to "put on their faces" using make-up, and to wear precariously high heels and impractical, tight clothing that restricts their freedom of movement (Abu-Laban et al., 2001).

If beauty standards in Canada are narrow, they are also racialized, with Whiteness being the beauty norm (healthily tanned Whiteness, that is). We find non-White women using products that will straighten hair or lighten skin and undergoing surgery to "Westernize" their eye shape, nose shape and size, lips, body size, and so on (Abu-Laban et al., 2001:123; Nelson and Robinson, 2002:145).

Given Canadian culture's preoccupation with thinness, youthfulness, restrictive fashions and strict standards of facial beauty, can we truly say that we do not engage in harmful practices, practices that even result in death (e.g., diet pills, poisoning from breast implants, and so on)? In addition, female genital surgery was practiced in North America and Europe as well. Clitoridectomies were seen by many physicians as appropriate cures for masturbation, "nymphomania," and orgasm in women, even as late as the 20th century and "until the mid-1940s, clitoridectomies were routine for female patients in many mental hospitals" (Wood, 2001:323).

People contrasting these practices with those in countries practicing genital surgery today point out that, unlike girls in those countries, Canadian girls and women have choices about which practices they will engage in or take seriously. Given the increasingly rigid beauty standards Westerners "must" conform to and given most people's desperate desires to "fit in" and "be accepted," is it really true that we have more freedom of choice? Really? Perhaps, as some suggest, we should be turning our lens on ourselves more critically and allow female genital surgery to be dealt with by women's movements and other grassroots groups in nations that practice it. What do you think?

Gender Socialization by Parents

From birth, parents maintain gender distinctions and hierarchies between girls and boys through differential treatment. Because boys are believed to be tougher than girls, parents are more likely to bounce an infant son, to hold him up in the air, and to play with him more vigorously than they are an infant daughter (MacDonald and Parke, 1986). Parents tend to cuddle infant girls, treat them gently, and provide them with verbal stimulation through cooing, talking, and singing to them (Basow, 1992). Further, parents are more prone to reward assertiveness and accomplishments by their sons, while reacting positively to their daughters skills in interpersonal and social situations (Leaper et al.,

1998; National Public Radio, 1992). One study demonstrated that within 24 hours of birth, parents were reacting to the label of their child as male or female by describing their son as being *strong, active, hardy, alert,* and *big* and describing their daughter as being *dainty, quiet, delicate,* and *small* (Rubin et al., 1974). While this study is quite dated, recent research has supported the tendency for parents to continue this stereotypical sex-typing (Delk et al., 1986; Stern and Karracker, 1989).

Parents reinforce these gender distinctions through their selection of infants' and children's clothing. Most parents dress boys in boldly coloured "rough and tough" clothing and dress girls in softly coloured clothing encumbered with easily dirtied and torn bows, frills, and lace. Parents further reinforce gender stereotyping and gender distinctions through the toys they buy. For example, parents buy blocks and building sets, vehicles, sporting equipment, and action toys such as guns, tanks, and soldiers for boys, and they buy dolls, doll clothing, dollhouses, play cosmetics, and homemaking items such as dishes, ovens, irons, brooms, and mops for girls (Leaper, 1994). These toys and games develop different types of skills and clearly demonstrate for children what type of activities will be expected of them in the future. Moreover, "masculine" toys require little verbal interaction and promote competition and independence, while "feminine" toys promote verbal communication, interaction, and nurturance (Wood, 2001). Interestingly, children themselves show few differences in toy preference during preschool, but their parents often actively discourage interest in toys and games deemed to be appropriate for the "opposite" sex (Lytton and Romney, 1991; Wood, 2001).

Chores also reinforce gender distinctions. Most research confirms that parents use toys and chores to encourage their sons more than their daughters toward greater independence (Basow, 1992). Thus, boys frequently are assigned such maintenance chores as carrying out the garbage, cleaning up the yard, or helping dad or an older brother (a "taking care of things" orientation). Girls, on the other hand, are given domestic chores such as shopping, cooking, clearing the table, and doing laundry (a "taking care of others" orientation) (Weisner et al., 1994; Wood, 2001). When parents and others purchase gender-specific toys and give children gender-stereotypical household assignments, they send a powerful message about the gendered division of labour. In addition, in terms of preparing children for their futures, which may well include performing all activities equally dexterously, parents are not doing their children any favours. However, gender socialization varies widely, and peer group involvement is an important factor.

Peers and Gender Socialization

Peer groups are powerful socializing agents that can reinforce existing gender stereotypes and pressure individuals to engage in gender-appropriate behaviour. *Peer groups* are social groups whose members are linked by common interests and, usually, by similar age. Children are more widely accepted by their peer group when they conform to the group's notion of gender-appropriate

Take a close look at this picture. What do you notice about the two lines? Social scientists have pointed out that gender socialization occurs in many ways, including how teachers organize school activities by sex.

behaviour (Maccoby and Jacklin, 1987; Martin, 1989). Male peer groups place more pressure on boys to do "masculine" things than female peer groups place on girls to do "feminine" things (Fagot, 1984). For example, most girls today wear jeans and many play soccer and softball, but boys who wear dresses or play hopscotch with girls would be banished from most male peer groups. In a study of gendered activity with elementary school children, Thorne (1998) found three salient themes related to male–female playground interactions:

- Girls play closer to buildings than boys, where they are more closely supervised by adults, and boys control approximately 10 times more playground space than girls.
- Boys invade and interrupt girl's space and girl's games much more than the reverse.
- Girls are more often defined as contaminating than boys, as in "girl germs" or "cooties."

These themes reinforce that "the worlds of boys and girls may be separate but they are not parallel, nor are they equal" (Thorne, 1998:94).

During pre-adolescence, male peer groups also reinforce gender-appropriate emotions in boys. In a study of a Little League baseball team, for example, sociologist Gary A. Fine (1987) found that the boys were encouraged by their peers to engage in proper "masculine" behaviour—acting tough even when they were hurt or intimidated, controlling their emotions, being competitive and wanting to win, and showing group unity and loyalty. Boys who failed to display these characteristics received instantaneous negative feedback from their teammates. Boys learn the contours of masculine behaviour through sports and through membership in boys clubs and organizations. For example, a study of the inception of the Boy Scouts in the United States points out that Scout programs began in order to specifically indoctrinate young boys into stereotypical ideals of masculinity, in place of the "manliness" learned through a pioneering life in the wilderness: "The hardships and privations of pioneer life which did so much to develop sterling manhood are now but a legend in history, and we must depend on the Boy Scout Movement to produce the MEN of the future" (Beard, 1914, in Hantover, 1998:104).

Peers are important in both female's and male's development of gender identity and their aspirations for the future (Maccoby and Jacklin, 1987). Nelson and Robinson (2002:133) report that the influence of peers on children begins around age 7 or 8 and peaks between age 14 to 16. A study of Canadian teens showed that 91 percent reported that friendship was "very important" while only 65 percent rated family life equally importantly (Bibby and Posterski, 1985). Peer friendship was seen as outweighing sports, sexuality, music, partying, and family activities (Bibby and Posterski, 1992). In adolescence, peer friends assist the individual in developing his or her self-identity. Boy's culture comes to be characterized by "coolness," "autonomy," and "physicality," while girl's culture comes to be characterized by "compliance and conformity," "romance," and "domesticity" (Adler et al., 1992/1995:136). Among postsecondary students, peers play an important part in career choices and the establishment of long-term, intimate relationships (Huston, 1985; Martin, 1989). Even in kindergarten and the early grades, peers influence how and what we do in school and our perceptions of self and other.

Education and Gender Socialization

The education system is charged with the responsibility of transmitting cultural values. These values are far from gender-neutral. Like parents and peers, teachers reinforce gender distinctions by communicating to students that males and male-dominated activities are more important than females and female-dominated activities. Research on education continues to show the existence in schools of **gender bias—a situation in which favouritism is shown toward one gender.** For example, education scholars Myra Sadker and David Sadker (1994) found that teachers subtly convey the message to their students that boys (White boys, in particular) are more important than girls by devoting more time, effort, and attention to boys than to girls. In day-to-day interactions, teachers are more likely to allow boys to interrupt them and give boys more praise, criticism, and suggestions for remediation than girls. Boys are more likely to be called on in class, whether they volunteer or not. When boys make comments, teachers often follow up with additional questions or suggestions; but when girls make comments, teachers often respond with a superficial "okay" and move on to the next student. Teachers praise girls for their appearance or for having a neat paper, but boys are praised for their accomplishments. This is not to suggest that Canadian boys experience no problems in the school system, just that girl's experiences are even worse. Boys' experiences are becoming increasingly negative, an issue we will discuss more in Chapter 12.

The pervasive gender bias in the Canadian education system was recognized by the 1970 Royal Commission on the Status of Women. The main thrusts of the recommendations were the elimination of gender stereotypes in textbooks and in curricula, changing teachers' gender-stereotypical treatment of students, changing girl's feelings about mathematics, and broadening career information for females (Mackie, 1991). Despite decades of awareness and reform, studies conducted at the Ontario Institute for Studies in Education demonstrated that the self-esteem of girls aged 12 to 16 dropped significantly. It was postulated that the decrease in self-esteem was, in large part, the result of marginalization and silencing of females in co-ed classrooms (cited in Nelson and Robinson, 2002:152). One way of countering this problem has been the introduction of all-female schools. While all-female schools, like the Linden School in Toronto, Emily Murphy Junior High School in Edmonton, and St. Margaret's School for Girls in Victoria provide girls with the opportunity to learn more about women's contributions to social, political, and economic life, typically they are set up as independent or private schools with hefty tuitions attached to gender-balanced curricula (for example, $650 to $1000 per girl, per month). Therefore, whatever advantages these schools may mete out to girls in terms of maintaining high self-esteem and high academic standards are likely only to be realized by girls from wealthier families. In addition, graduates of these all-female schools will still face sexism and gender bias in their postsecondary education and in the paid labour force.

The effects of gender bias become evident when teachers take a "boys will be boys" attitude about derogatory remarks and aggressive behaviour against girls. *Sexual harassment*—**unwanted sexual advances, requests for sexual favours, or other verbal or physical conduct of a sexual nature**—is frequently overlooked by teachers and school administrators. Larkin, an education researcher, (1994:53) reports that "male students are by far the most frequent harassers of girls in schools . . . [but] according to the results of a recent survey of 4200 girls . . . three percent were harassed by their teachers. In all but one incident the teacher harasser was male." Unfortunately, media stories like the one about the Grade 1 boy who was suspended from school for kissing a female classmate on the cheek trivialize gender bias and sexual harassment, both of which create a hostile environment that makes it more difficult for many girls and young women to learn and accomplish as much as their male counterparts (see Orenstein, 1996; Sadker and Sadker, 1994).

Researchers have found that, in some schools, male students regularly refer to females as "sluts," "bitches," and "hos" without fear of reprimand from teachers, and the females' fear of reprisal keeps them from speaking out against their harassers (Orenstein, 1996). One high-school student described her experience in a shop class in this way: "The boys literally pushed me around, right into tables and chairs. They pulled my hair, made sexual comments, touched me, told sexist jokes. And the thing was that I was better in the shop class than almost any guy. This only caused the boys to get more aggressive and troublesome" (Sadker and Sadker, 1994:127). Teachers who fail to challenge or stop harassing behaviour in their classrooms are perceived by students as being unconcerned (Larkin, 1994). A survey of 4200 North American females found that 39 percent (4 in 10) experienced sexual harassment daily at school

(Mann, 1993). Moreover, the Ontario Secondary School Teacher's Federation 1994 study of sexual harassment at Ontario schools found that a disturbing 83 percent of female students had been sexually harassed in the school setting (Larkin and Staton, 1998). Harassment has the result of making girls feel ill at ease, lose confidence, exhibit reluctance to attend school or to draw attention to themselves in classrooms, and/or drop out of classes or school altogether (Larkin and Staton, 1998; Nelson and Robinson, 2002). Larkin (1994:33), citing Jacqui Halson, states that "schools help to reproduce the existing power imbalance between men and women by failing to recognize the significant impact of sexual harassment on the lives of female students and by failing to intervene." Although it may seem that boys benefit from sexual harassment and teachers' gender bias (or at least are not harmed by it), that is not the case.

Boys, too, are limited by stereotypical notions of masculinity and gender-appropriate behaviour. According to Sadker and Sadker (1994:220), boys confront the "frozen boundaries" of the male role at every turn in their school life. They are taught to "Be cool, don't show emotion, repress feelings, be aggressive, compete, and win"—the same messages that sociologist Gary Fine (1987) found Little Leaguers use to reinforce each other. Such teachings not only limit the range of emotions boys are allowed to feel but also encourage boys to see themselves—and other males—as better than girls and to distance themselves from any activity that is considered "feminine," even though it may be an activity they enjoy.

Male gender norms, which require boys to be active, aggressive, and independent, often conflict with school norms, which require students to be quiet, passive, and conforming. Many boys walk a tightrope between compliance and rebellion. They tend to receive lower grades than girls do and are more likely to drop out of school (Sadker and Sadker, 1994). Although female gender norms conflict less with school norms than male gender norms, sociologist Michelle Fine (1991) found in one study that, for many girls, the price of academic success is being compliant and muting their own voices.

Gender bias also occurs at the postsecondary level. Research consistently shows that more educational resources, ranging from athletic programs and dormitories to course offerings and career advising, are targeted primarily at men even though women constitute more than half of all Canadian college and university students. In the classroom, many professors give more attention to men than to women (Hall and Sandler, 1982; Hall, 1984). Women tend to be called on less frequently and to receive less encouragement. When they speak out in class, women are more likely to be interrupted, ignored, or devalued than men are (Fox, 1995). Women often experience a drop in self-esteem while in university or college, being negatively affected by gender bias "in terms of their self-image, aspirations, concerns and expectations" (Reynolds, 2001:247). Despite their negative experiences in academic settings, women tend to have higher grade-point averages and earn a higher percentage of baccalaureate and master's degrees than Canadian men do. Even so, women are underrepresented in fields such as economics, engineering, computer and information sciences, and physical sciences and overrepresented in the number of degrees awarded in education, psychology, and nursing and allied health fields (McAdie, 1998; Reynolds, 2001; Women's Research and Educational Institute, 1996). Some analysts attribute the underrepresentation of women in math, science, and engineering to the way these courses are taught: "The traditions are based on military applications. The programs started out in military schools and colleges" (Jane Daniels, Women in Engineering, Purdue University, quoted in Urschel, 1996:2D). Additionally, many young women lack the high-school math and science backgrounds necessary to enter these courses at the postsecondary level. Even though more women than men achieve college diplomas and undergraduate and graduate university degrees, the trend reverses when looking at doctoral (Ph.D.) degrees: Men outnumber women as recipients of degrees in all fields. In part, this can be seen as resulting from the difficulties experienced disproportionately by women as they attempt to reconcile employment and a disproportionate share of domestic responsibilities with the rigorous demands of typically full-time doctoral programs (Benoit, 2000; Husk, 1998). In part, it may also be the result of the culmination of women's low wages relative to men's and chronic underfunding of postsecondary education. Additionally, persistent cultural values and norms that suggest that education is "wasted" on women and that women's rightful sphere is the household, not higher education or the professional labour force, are to blame (Dagg and Thompson, 1988; Nelson and Robinson, 2001).

The Media and Gender Socialization

From television and radio to the Internet, from magazines and newspapers to billboards, we are relentlessly bombarded by media on a daily basis. As media are socially constructed, they reflect the realities and/or fantasies of their creators. Wood (2001) identifies three themes in contemporary media that represent gender. The first theme is the underrepresentation of women and other minority groups. The overrepresentation of able-bodied, youngish, White men in media conveys the message that they make up the majority of the population (and in Canada they do not) and, as such, that they are the cultural standard. When women and other minority groups are depicted in media, they are typically shown in ways that reinforce and perpetuate negative stereotypes about the group. The second theme is the stereotypical fashion in which males and females are presented. Males continue to be presented as competent, powerful, serious, confident, and independent, while females continue to be presented as incompetent, unintelligent, young, thin, beautiful, dependent, and passive sex objects (Wood, 2001:283–284). To redress past voids, some media have made a limited attempt to show women involved in activities outside the domestic sphere (not that these same media portray these women necessarily in a positive light); however, they have not made a corresponding attempt to show men involved in the domestic sphere. Where men are shown involved in domestic labour or childcare at all, they are typically portrayed as helpless ("hopeless"?) buffoons (Wood, 2001:284), reinforcing men's lack of "suitability" to domestic activities. The third theme is the portrayal of male–female relations along traditional lines and in ways that perpetuate and normalize violence against women (Wood, 2001:281). Communications scholar Julia T. Wood (2001:287–294) suggests there are four themes that reflect and promote gender-stereotypical, and perhaps even dangerous, relations between the sexes: (1) women's dependence and men's independence; (2) women's incompetence and men's authority; (3) women as primary caregivers and men as primary breadwinners; and, (4) women as victims and sex objects and men as aggressors.

While some critics argue that the media simply reflect existing gender roles in society, others point out that the media have a unique ability to shape ideas.

From children's cartoons to adult shows, television programs offer more male than female characters. Furthermore, the male characters act in a strikingly different manner than female ones. Male characters in both children's programs and adult programs are typically aggressive, constructive, and direct, while female characters defer to others or manipulate them by acting helpless, seductive, or deceitful (Basow, 1992). Some have argued that even educational programs, such as *Sesame Street*, perpetuate gender stereotypes because most of the characters have male names and masculine voices and participate in "boys' activities." Wood (2001:287) reports that this is no accident: "Beginning in 1991, television executives deliberately and consciously adopted a policy of having dominant male characters in all Saturday morning children's programming."

Recent studies of MTV music videos have found that these videos often show stereotyped gender roles and condone harassment of and discrimination against women. A 1992 study found most female characters were dressed in revealing clothing, made sexual advances toward men, and usually were presented as sex objects. In contrast, male characters routinely pursued fantasy adventures or engaged in aggression and violence (Seidman, 1992). Further, music-video women are shown either satisfying male sexual fantasies or being ostracized or punished for not engaging in this way. Sociologist Sut Jhally, in the documentary *Dreamworlds II* (1991), describes the fantasy world of music video as the male videomaker's and consumer's dreamworld. This "dreamworld" objectifies and dehumanizes women and denies them subjectivity, all of which puts women at risk for violence by reinforcing a ***rape culture*—the pervasive system of cultural values, attitudes, and practices that support and perpetuate sexualized violence against women.** It includes rigid gender scripts for males and females and equally rigid notions of gender-appropriate behaviours. Many music videos overtly depict male violence against women, and research by Dieter (1989) demonstrated that women who watched sexualized violence on MTV were more accepting of violence in their own intimate relationships with men than women who did not view the images (cited in Wood, 2001).

While changes have occurred in the roles men and women play in movies, most roles still embrace stereotypes. Even though there are many movie stars who are female, few notable roles exist for women, and even fewer films examine women's lives and issues from their own perspectives. (Exceptions include *Fried Green Tomatoes*, *A League of Their Own*, and *Thelma and Louise*.) Recently, boys have saved the world from an evil wizard (Harry Potter), saved the universe from destruction (*Star Wars I, The Phantom Menace*), and saved a parent from evil government agents (*Clockstoppers*). Meanwhile, girls and young women, in films such as *Clueless*, are depicted as "bimbos," shopaholics, and uninterested in school. Things may be changing somewhat: In the recently released *Scooby Doo*, the ditzy character, Daphne, is an accomplished martial artist and wins a fight with a burly wrestler, and Velma, the token "smart female," is portrayed as attractive and, in fact, even manages to hook up with a man. Like in *Harry Potter* and *The Phantom Menace*, however, even when females are portrayed positively as smart *and* attractive, they are still only supporting characters to the males who save the day. According to social psychologist Hilary Lips (1993:19), "We are surrounded with the message that masculine males can be powerful, but feminine females cannot, or that women's only effective source of feminine influence is beauty and sex appeal." Moreover, the dominant message conveyed remains that females must use their influence, however paltry, in an attempt to garner the pinnacle of feminine achievement and self-definition—an intimate relationship with a man (Nelson and Robinson, 2002).

Why is awareness of gender socialization important for understanding gender discrimination and gender inequality? Social analysts who use a gender-role approach say that because parents, peers, teachers, and the media influence our perceptions of who we are and what our aspirations should be, gender-role socialization contributes to a gendered division of labour, creates a *wage gap* between women and men workers, limits occupational and other choices for women and men, and perpetuates gendered violence and shapes our (lack of) responses to it. It is important, therefore, to keep in mind that gender is a social construction, and, as such, can be deconstructed and reconstructed. In this way, social change is possible. In the words of sociologist Judith Lorber (1986:576), "what is socially constructed can be reconstructed, and social relations can be rearranged."

However, some social analysts say that no direct evidence links gender role socialization to social inequality and that it is therefore important to use social structural analysis to examine gender inequality (see Reskin and Hartmann, 1986). In other words, these analysts believe that the decisions that people make (such as the schools they choose to attend and the occupations they choose to pursue) are linked not only to how they were socialized but also to how society is structured. We now examine structural features that contribute to gender inequality.

CONTEMPORARY GENDER INEQUALITY

How do tasks in a society get defined as either "men's work" or "women's work" and why are they differentially rewarded? Many sociologists believe that people, through various social institutions and structures, assign different roles and responsibilities to women and men based upon notions of gender appropriateness and, in the process, restrict women's opportunities. According to feminist scholars, gender inequality is maintained and reinforced through individual and institutionalized sexism. The term *individual sexism* refers to individuals' beliefs and actions that are rooted in anti-female prejudice and stereotypical beliefs. The term *institutionalized sexism* refers to the power that men have to engage in sex discrimination at the organizational and institutional levels of society. This pattern of male domination and female subordination is known as *patriarchy*—**a hierarchical system of social organization in which cultural, political, and economic structures are controlled by men.** According to some analysts, the location of women in the work force and on the economic pyramid is evidence of patriarchy (Epstein, 1988). In this section, we focus on five structural forms that contribute to contemporary gender inequality: the gendered division of labour, the wage gap, sexual harassment, the glass ceiling and the glass escalator, and the double shift.

The Gendered Division of Paid Work

Whether by choice or economic necessity, women have entered the paid labour force in unprecedented numbers in recent years. Today, Canadian women have among the highest labour force participation rates in the world (Wilson, 2001). In 1946, fewer than 20 percent of women over the age of 25 were employed in the Canadian paid labour force. This number had risen to nearly 30 percent as of 1961. Today, women represent nearly 50 percent of the total Canadian work force and nearly 60 percent of all Canadian women 25 years or older are in the paid labour force (Nelson and Robinson, 2002). Until the 1950s, these women were typically single, young, and childless. Today, however, many women with preschool children are entering the paid labour force. In fact, women with preschool children accounted for 60 percent of the increase in employed women between 1981 and 1991 (Nelson and Robinson, 2002; Wilson, 2001).

There are several reasons for these dramatic increases in women's labour force participation. Firstly, structural pressures such as inflation necessitated higher incomes generally, and the shift to a service economy from a goods-producing or manufacturing economy, with the attendant lower wages, drove the increase in dual-earner families. As well, service jobs are ones in which we disproportionately find women. Along with this, cultural values about gender, paid employment, marriage, and parenting shifted to the point where, today, women working for pay, regardless of their marital or parental status, are no longer so negatively stigmatized as they once were (Nelson and Robinson, 2002; Wilson, 2001). Even as women's labour force participation has been increasing, male participation has been gradually declining due to layoffs in the industrial sector, downsizing of business and government, and the long-term trend toward early retirement, either voluntary or involuntary (i.e., "buyouts") (Nelson and Robinson, 2002).

While many people who know these statistics are optimistic about the gains Canadian women have made in paid employment, it should be noted that women's position in the labour force is lower than men's in terms of status, opportunities, and salaries. Today, most women and men remain concentrated in occupations that are segregated by gender (see Figure 4.2). The term *gender-segregated work* refers to the extent to which men and women are concentrated in different occupations and places of work (Reskin and Padavic, 1994). For example, women are predominant in word-processing pools and childcare centres, whereas men are predominant in the construction trades. Other individuals are

FIGURE 4.2   Ten Most Common Jobs for Women and Men, 1998

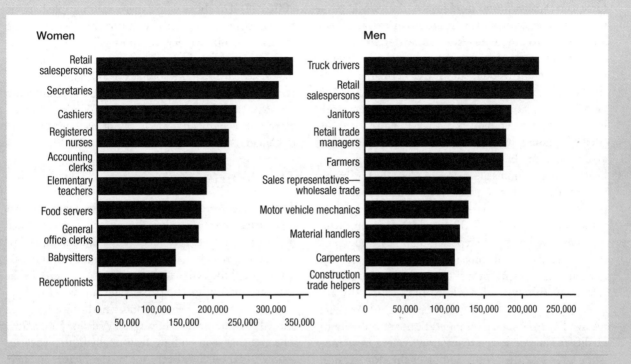

Source: "Ten Most Common Jobs for Women" and "Ten Most Common Jobs for Men," Perspectives on Labour and Income *(Summer 1998): 59, Statistics Canada (Catalogue 75-001). Reproduced by permission of the Minister of Industry.*

employed in settings where both men and women are present. In these settings, however, women are employed predominantly in clerical or other support positions, while men hold supervisory, managerial, or other professional positions. For example, despite the increasing number of women entering the legal profession, most attorneys are men, and most support-staff workers, such as legal secretaries and paralegals, are women (see Epstein, 1993; Pierce, 1995). In medicine, female doctors tend to become general practitioners or to have "family practices," wheras more male doctors tend to specialize and/or become surgeons, with the attendant higher pay and status than are allocated to general practitioners or those in family medicine.

Despite the fact that females and males are still segregated into highly gendered types of occupations, there may be some room for optimism. Occupational segregation by gender has decreased in some categories. For example, in the publication *Canadian Social Trends*, Best (1995:33) reports that the proportion of female

doctors and dentists rose to 26 percent in 1993, up from 18 percent in 1982. The latest Statistics Canada data (2001h:8) suggest that figure has risen to 53 percent today (see Chapter 10). Additionally, in 1981, 62.7 percent of the women employed full-time could be found in just three occupations, clerical, sales and service. By 1997, the percentage had declined to 52 percent (Nelson and Robinson, 2002:226). This is a significant shift; as sociologist Susannah Wilson (2001:225) reports, "the concentration of women in service and sales jobs has been a persistent aspect of the labour force since these figures were first calculated in the 1891 census."

The persisting concentration of a high proportion of employed Canadian women in only three occupations has been described as a *pink-collar ghetto*—**where the jobs primarily held by women are relatively low-paying, non-manual, and semiskilled**—such as clerical work, counter help in fast-food restaurants, medical assistance, and childcare work.

Women are overrepresented in the contingent work force as well. ***Contingent work* is part-time work, temporary work, and subcontracted work that offers advantages to employers but can be detrimental to workers' welfare.** Many employers stress that having more contingent workers and fewer permanent, full-time employees keeps corporations competitive in the global marketplace. One of the reasons contingent work is so attractive to employers is that, in addition to its "flexible" nature, it makes it possible for employers to avoid providing benefits and having to contribute to health care premiums and pension plans. While many women are found in contingent work because it often provides them greater flexibility to work around family responsibilities, in 1998, 30 percent of women who were employed part-time reported that they would prefer to be employed full-time (Statistics Canada, 1999a). Although all contingent workers experience problems related to this type of work, women especially are affected by the fact that many contingent workers receive little monetary remuneration, are unlikely to qualify for any or adequate un/employment insurance when they lose their jobs, do not qualify for pension coverage or other job-related benefits enjoyed by many full-time workers, and have difficulty finding suitable childcare arrangements (Nelson and Robinson, 2002.)

Women continue to be concentrated in jobs where they receive lower wages, less prestige, and fewer benefits, on average, than men. However, this inequity is even more compounded by racialization and (dis)ability, a situation known as *multiple jeopardy*. Multiple jeopardy often manifests as an inability to get hired or to maintain employment, to gain a promotion, and/or to obtain adequate compensation and benefits. For example, as pointed out by Nelson and Robinson (2002:228–229): the unemployment rate for First Nations people is more than double that for all Canadians; visible minority women are more likely than other Canadian women to be found in manual labour; and women with disabilities are more likely than men with disabilities to be unemployed. Following the pattern of gender disparities in income, First Nations people earn less than non–First Nations, visible minority people earn less than non–visible minorities, and people with a disability earn less than people without. Across all categories, women earn less than men. People with disabilities, visible minority people, and First Nations people all earn average annual incomes below the Canadian average (Nelson and Robinson, 2002:228). For those who experience multiple barriers to employment, it is nearly impossible to determine which particular barrier was most salient in a particular instance of discrimination. Of course, these barriers may also be made more complex by the addition of discrimination on the basis of language, sexual orientation, size, age, and foreign educational credentials that are often not recognized, or at least not accepted "on par" in Canada.

The Wage Gap

The *wage gap*—**the disparity between women's and men's earnings**—is the best-documented consequence of gender-segregated work (Reskin and Padavic, 1994). No matter what group men belong to in terms of racialization or ability, they earn more than women of that same group. A wage gap persists in Canada across full- and part-time employment and whether we measure annual income or hourly wages (Wilson, 2001:223). The fact that women have historically been a cheaper source of labour has been one of the factors in their attractiveness to employers. In 1997, women made 73 percent of men's wages for full-time, full-year work (i.e., 73 cents for each male dollar earned). This was a dramatic increase from 1967, when women made 58 percent of what men made. But in 1995, women's after-tax income was only 60 percent of men's after-tax income (Status of Women Canada, 1997). Statistics Canada notes that one-half the differential in the 1997 data can be explained by "male–female differences in labour market experience, education, and major field of study, occupation, job responsibilities, and industry" (1999a). This leaves one-half of the wage differential unexplained. Wilson (2001:224) notes "the unexplained portion is presumed to be due to discrimination."

The gendered wage gap also varies by age and marital status, with younger workers and never-married workers having lesser wage gaps. The lessened gap may be the result, for younger workers, of both males and females having a similar amount of work experience and the tendency for both sexes to be concentrated in entry-level jobs. For never-married individuals, it may be in part the result of more of a similarity in ability to take on similar kinds of work (i.e., work that involves travel, long hours, nonstandard shifts, and so on). A minimal wage gap also exists for unionized workers—

I SAID...
"YOU'VE COME A LONG WAY BABY!"...

Women   Men

EARNING POWER

Source: Gable, Regina Leader Post *84. Reprinted by permission of Brian Gable and the* Regina Leader Post.

about 30 percent of employed women and men in Canada. Unions in Canada have fought long, hard campaigns to achieve *pay equity*—**equal pay for work of equal or comparable worth**—for women, both in unions and outside unions. Interestingly, the main force driving the overall narrowing of the gendered wage gap

has been the stagnation and decline of men's wages generally (Nelson and Robinson, 2002; Roos and Reskin, 1992; Wilson, 2001).

For pay equity to occur between men and women, there has to be a broad-based commitment to *comparable worth*—**the belief that wages ought to reflect the worth of a job, not the gender or other ascribed characteristics of the worker** (Kemp, 1994). To determine the comparable worth of different kinds of jobs, researchers break a specific job into components to determine: (1) how much education, training, and skills are required; (2) how much responsibility a person in that position has for others' work; and, (3) what the working conditions are. Researchers then allocate points for each component to determine whether or not men and women are being paid equitably for their work (Lorber, 1994). For pay equity to exist, men and women in occupations that receive the same number of points must be paid the same. However, pay equity exists for very few jobs. (See Table 4.1 for a comparison of men's and women's earnings in selected occupations.)

Comparable worth is an important issue for men as well as women. Male workers in female-dominated jobs such as nursing, secretarial work, and elementary teaching pay an economic penalty for their choice of work. Additionally, if women were compensated fairly, an employer could not undercut men's wages by hiring women at a cheaper rate (Kessler-Harris, 1990).

Sexual Harassment

Millions of men never harass women in the workplace or elsewhere, but so many men do that, sadly, it is almost impossible for women to avoid the experience (Langelan, 1993). In fact, the 1993 Violence Against Women Survey, conducted by Statistics Canada, found that 87 percent of Canadian women had experienced some form of sexual harassment; just over one-half had been harassed by men they knew (Johnson, 1996). Sexual harassment is a form of intentional, institutionalized gender discrimination that includes all unwelcome sexual attention affecting an employee's job conditions or creating a hostile work environment. Sociologists Walter S. DeKeseredy and Ronald Hinch (1991:103) define it as "unsolicited, unreciprocated male behaviour that values a woman's sex role over her function as a worker." Sexual harassment includes verbal

TABLE 4.1   The Canadian Wage Gap: 25 Highest and Lowest Paid Occupations in Canada, by Gender, 1995

	Average earnings		
	Both Sexes	Men	Women
All occupations	37 556	42 488	30 130
Total—25 highest paying	80 206	86 139	58 943
Judges	126 246	128 791	117 707
Specialist physicians	123 976	137 019	86 086
General practitioners/family physicians	107 620	116 750	81 512
Dentists	102 433	109 187	71 587
Senior managers: Goods production, utilities, transportation, and construction	99 360	102 971	58 463
Senior managers: Financial, communications, carriers, other business services	99 177	104 715	71 120
Lawyers and Quebec notaries	81 617	89 353	60 930
Senior managers: Trade, broadcasting, other services	79 200	84 137	48 651
Primary production managers (except agriculture)	76 701	78 421	48 479
Securities agents, investment dealers/traders	75 911	90 391	47 323
Petroleum engineers	72 543	73 657	56 506
Chiropractors	68 808	71 032	56 764
Engineering, science, and architecture managers	68 235	69 792	53 138
University professors	68 195	72 532	55 909
Senior managers: Health, education, social and community services, membership organizations	68 187	78 012	56 190
Air pilots, flight engineers, flying instructors	67 581	68 219	43 991
Geologists, geochemists, geophysicists	66 210	68 116	51 151
Utilities managers	64 816	66 239	52 564
School principals, administrators of elementary and secondary education	64 513	66 837	60 394
Optometrists	64 419	73 920	48 337
Insurance, real estate, financial brokerage managers	64 197	73 419	46 070
Commissioned police officers	63 518	64 865	50 011
Senior government managers and officials	63 195	69 477	49 667
Supervisors, mining and quarrying	62 537	62 768	0
Information systems, data processing managers	62 387	64 999	53 140
Total—25 lowest paying occupations	17 729	20 238	16 564
Inspectors/testers, fabric, fur, leather products manufacturing	20 001	25 396	18 507
Light-duty cleaners	19 991	23 829	18 125
Early childhood educators/assistants	19 772	25 074	19 586
Pet groomers/animal care workers	19 716	24 467	17 398
Taxi/limousine drivers/chauffeurs	19 664	19 845	16 756
Visiting homemakers, housekeepers, related occupations	19 607	24 751	19 063
Hotel front-desk clerks	19 220	20 364	18 575
Cooks	19 054	20 224	17 607
Hotel mâitres d's and hosts/ hostesses	18 873	24 649	17 336
Kitchen/food-service helpers	18 799	17 320	19 697
Hairstylists and barbers	18 292	22 867	16 755
Painters, sculptors, other visual artists	18 188	20 421	14 982
Tailors, dressmakers, furriers, milliners	17 850	24 686	16 026
General farm workers	17 756	19 990	13 825

Estheticians, electrologists, related occupations	17 658	22 889	17 462
Sewing-machine operators	17 613	20 664	17 340
Cashiers	17 553	20 557	16 977
Ironing, pressing, finishing occupations	17 322	19 297	16 499
Artisans and craftpersons	16 943	20 555	13 565
Bartenders	16 740	18 899	14 940
Harvesting labourers	16 426	18 683	14 465
Service station attendants	16 203	16 520	14 947
Food-service counter attendants and food preparers	15 487	17 912	14 681
Food and beverage servers	14 891	18 192	13 861
Babysitters, nannies, and parents' helpers	12 713	15 106	12 662

Note: Although athletes were in the 25 highest paying occupations and trappers and hunters were in the 25 lowest paying occupations, their very small numbers rendered their income statistics unreliable. Hence the individuals in these occupations were excluded from this table.

Source: Adapted from Statistics Canada, 1998, The Daily (12 May); Gender in Canada, by A. Nelson and B.W. Robinson, 2002, Toronto: Prentice Hall, pp. 230–231. Reproduced by permission of the Minister of Industry.

abuse, touching, staring at or making jokes about a woman's body, demands for sexual intercourse, and even sexual assault on the job (Benokraitis and Feagin, 1995). Kemp (1994:310) distinguishes two types of sexual harassment: *quid pro quo* harassment, involving "something for something" (e.g., an explicit exchange of sex for a pay raise or better grade), or the creation of a poisoned work environment—harassment as a continuing condition of work (e.g., so-called jokes, touching, and teasing often referred to as "normal" male "on-the-job" behaviour). In a national survey of sexual harassment against employed women, 90 percent reported at least one incidence of unwanted male sexual attention in a public place which resulted in them feeling emotionally shaken and with "the nagging, gnawing sense that something horrible *could* happen" (Smith, 1993: 70).

People who are accused of sexual harassment frequently claim that their actions were merely harmless expressions of (supposedly) mutual sexual attraction. However, sexual harassment is not about attraction; it is about *abuse of power*. Sexual harassment constitutes a form of intimidation and aggression: The recipient has no choice in the encounter or has reason to fear repercussions if she or he declines. Despite the fear mongering of Hollywood movies like *Fatal Attraction* and *Disclosure*, women disproportionately experience sexual harassment at the hands of men. Some men are able to harass because they hold economic power over

women (e.g., bosses, supervisors, and colleagues who have some say over promotions and raises); others are able to harass because they hold gender-based power (e.g., power rooted in cultural patterns of male dominance and backed up by the threat of violence and the ability to rape) (Langelan, 1993). In either case, sexual harassment serves as a means of boundary heightening between men and women in the workplace. For example, sociologist Jennifer L. Pierce (1995) found that male lawyers may exaggerate the differences between women lawyers and themselves by directing unwanted sexual invitations, attention, and behaviour at women in their firms. A recent survey conducted in Saskatchewan found that 39 percent of nurses had suffered sexual harassment, often by patients, while a recent Ontario survey found that three-quarters of female family physicians had been sexually harassed by male patients (Duffy and Cohen, 2001). In the retail sales industry, where a disproportionate number of Canadian women work, a study of female retail workers and security workers employed in small outlets, mainly in Canadian malls, found that two-thirds of the retail workers reported being sexually harassed by customers (Tadic and Hughes, 1998). In an interview, one woman described her experience as follows: ". . . one guy gave me a piece of paper with his phone number on it and a condom rolled into it." Another man stared, followed her around the retail outlet and then lay on the floor in an attempt to see up her skirt (Tadic and Hughes, 1998:88). Another woman in the same study, commenting on the prevalence of unwanted touching from male customers, stated that "they'll put their arms around you or they'll put their hands on your back and rub it up and down . . . it's very uncomfortable coming into your personal space, totally unnecessary for the sales interaction" (Tadic and Hughes, 1998:88). Social scientist Jocalyn Clark (1998) conducted research in a northern British Columbia tree-planting camp, looking at health risks associated with that industry. She found that sexual harassment of female workers was central to the experience of female tree-planters, both by male co-workers and male crew supervisors. As reported by one planter:

> Certain foremen hire certain female planters based solely on the fact that they think they will be able to sleep with that person for the planting season. And when that doesn't happen, and perhaps when they see that person looking at other people, they become harder on that person and when that person shows that they obviously have no intention of sleeping with them, in some cases I've seen them just get fired. Get really dumped on, like "Plant this shit, you're a lousy planter, what the hell is wrong with you? And why don't you just leave? I'll drive you to the bus." I've seen that happen. (quoted in Clark, 1998:84)

Sexual harassment is a costly problem for women—who may lose employment opportunities, especially in today's climate where the emphasis is on "customer satisfaction"—and for their employers—who lose millions of dollars per year in low productivity, absenteeism, and employee turnover related to harassment (Basow, 1992). As one woman commented: "[with] the 'customer is always right' policy, you've got to grin and bear a lot . . ." (Tadic and Hughes, 1998:89). Sexual harassment and other forms of blatant and subtle discrimination in the workplace also contribute to the institutional barriers that limit women's opportunities to rise to the top positions in corporations and other occupational settings (see MacCorquodale and Jensen, 1993; Rosenberg et al. 1993). Sociologist Alice Abel Kemp (1994:312) theorizes that sexual harassment serves three purposes in a patriarchal society like Canada: (1) it discourages women from participating in jobs traditionally held by men; (2) it limits women to low-wage, dead-end, female-dominated jobs; and, (3) it attributes many of women's responses to harassment (like absenteeism, job turnover, and so on) to gender stereotypes of women as "uncommitted, unreliable workers."

The Glass Ceiling and the Glass Escalator

More recently, feminist researchers have used the advancement (or lack of advancement) of women into top-tier management jobs as a litmus test for how well women are faring in the labour force as a whole. They have found that women hold only a handful of top positions. Although they are inching their way up the corporate ladder, women almost always encounter barriers when they try to enter the lucrative and prestigious top positions of their occupations. This is because of what is known as the *glass ceiling*—**the invisible institutional barrier constructed by male management that prevents women from reaching top positions in major corporations and other large-scale organizations.** Among the reasons cited for this barrier are male executives who believe that male workers will not work for women supervisors, that women workers are supposed to be in support roles only, that the prestige of the profession will decrease if women are admitted, and/or that "the ideal worker is normatively masculine" (Martin, 1992:220; Benokraitis and Feagin, 1995; Nelson and Robinson, 2002).

The glass ceiling is particularly evident in the nation's 500 largest companies. In 1996, fewer than 3 percent of the 2400 people having titles such as chairman, chief executive, vice chairman, president, chief operations officer, or executive vice president, and the salary that accompanies these titles, were women. Women of colour occupy fewer than 1 percent of top management positions. According to a recent study by Catalyst (Dobrzynski, 1996), a nonprofit research group that studies women in upper-level management, 14 of the top 100 companies do not have a single woman among their top officers. Even if there are equivalent numbers of women and men in a workplace, a chilly climate may exist. The *chilly climate* is a concept used to draw attention to the fact that equality of access does not necessarily guarantee equality of treatment within any given institution. Nelson and Robinson (2002:234) explain the chilly climate using a quote from George Orwell's book *Animal Farm*, where a "funny sort of democracy" prevails, one where "all animals are equal, but some animals are more equal than others." The chilly climate can manifest as an inhospitable workplace for a person of "the wrong sex" through exclusionary, dismissive, or generally "cool" behaviours, based on cultural notions of gender-appropriate labour (Nelson and Robinson, 2002). Sociologists Susan A. McDaniel and Erica van Roosmalen, citing McKinnon, concluded after their study of female university students at one Canadian campus that sexual harassment and chilly climates affect a woman by "using her employment position to coerce her sexually, while using her sexual position to coerce her economically" (cited in Nelson and Robinson, 2002:237).

Overall, women are most likely to reach top positions in the service sector (for example, banking and diversified finance, publishing, retailing, food services, and entertainment), a sector in which they have traditionally been employed in great numbers. For example, Saskatchewan's LuAn Mitchell, voted Canada's Number One Female Entrepreneur by *Profit* and *Chatelaine* magazines and one of the 40 Leading Women Entrepreneurs in the World by the Star Group in 2001, took over her husband's family's 60-year-old meat-processing company after the death of her husband in 1998. Mitchell's Gourmet Foods brought in revenues of $268 million in 1999, after Mitchell formed an alliance with Schneider Foods, led expansion in Asia, and opened a new $45-million facility in Saskatoon (**www.profitguide.com/w100/2000/profile.asp**; **www. luanmitchell.com/news/articles/westjet_article.php**).

Women fare the worst in male-dominated businesses such as mining, crude oil, brokerages, and manufacturing. In a recent study of Canadian business students, psychologist R.J. Burke (1994) found that male students, more so than female students, had a negative attitude toward women in management roles generally. This, he said, may impact women in a variety of ways: (a) the men may, as colleagues, not endorse career-enhancing strategies for women and/or may actively promote backlash strategies; (b) the men may not mentor women and/or may serve as poor role models to other men in their workplace relationships with women; and, (c) the men may not be supportive of the career aspirations of their own female partners or spouses (Burke, 1994). In its research, Catalyst found that women who continue to bump into glass ceilings tend to leave large corporations and start their own businesses (Dobrzynski, 1996).

Unlike women who enter male-dominated occupations, men who enter female-dominated occupations are apt to find little difficulty in rising to the top of their occupation. In recent research on men working as registered nurses, elementary teachers, librarians, and social workers, sociologist Christine L. Williams (1995) found that they tended to rise in disproportionate numbers to administrative positions at the top of these occupations. Williams (1995:12) calls the upward movement of men in "women's professions" the *glass escalator effect* because, as she notes, "like being on an invisible 'up' escalator, men must struggle to remain in the lower (i.e., 'feminine') levels of their professions." Men also move into more "masculine" specialties within traditionally female-dominated occupations. Male librarians, for example, often move into high-technology computer information specialties and administration. In contrast, women in male-dominated occupations typically find they are bumping their heads on the glass ceiling and working a double shift.

The Double Shift

Although there have been dramatic changes in the participation of women in the labour force, the household division of labour by sex has remained essentially unchanged in many families. While more married women now share responsibility for earning part—or all—of the family income, many married men do not participate in routine domestic chores (Reskin and Padavic, 1994). Consequently, many employed women must deal with a double workload. In the words of sociologist Arlie Hochschild (1989), women with dual responsibilities as wage earners and unpaid household workers work "the second shift."

Not only does the relative number of hours spent on housework differ widely between women and men, but the kinds of chores men and women do also vary significantly. Women do most of the *daily* chores such as making beds and cooking and cleaning up after meals, and most of the taking care of children. Men are more likely to do chores that do not have to be done every day. For example, men typically mow the lawn, repair cars or other equipment, and do home improvements (Shelton, 1992). Although some kinds of housework can be put off, young children's needs cannot be ignored or delayed, and daily duties in families with young children consume a great deal of time and

Most working women encounter a second or even third shift when they get home from work. According to researchers, employed women still do most of the daily household chores and most of the work involved in taking care of the children. Is this photo a hopeful sign for the future?

energy. A sick child or a school event that cannot be scheduled around work causes additional stress for parents, especially mothers. Furthermore, more and more women are becoming members of "the sandwich generation." In other words, they are caught, sandwiched, between the needs of their young children and those of older relatives for whom they are often the primary caregivers. The 1996 General Social Survey reported that, amongst those employed for wages, 15 percent of women and 10 percent of men had additional responsibilities caring for someone with a long-term health issue (Nelson and Robinson, 2002:233). In an effort to keep up with family obligations while working full- or part-time, many women spend a large portion of their earnings on fees to day-care and elder-care centres, prepared foods and meals from fast-food restaurants, and laundry services and dry-cleaning (Bergmann, 1986).

When sociologists conduct research on participation in household work, both men and women state that working couples should share household responsibilities. However, when it comes down to who actually does what, most studies find that women, even those who hold full-time jobs, do most of that work. In the 1996 Census, for example, 90 percent of Canadians stated that they did some unpaid household work, but the majority of this work was done by women, in terms of both the range of tasks and the number of hours contributed (Wilson, 2001). According to Arlie Hochschild (1989), many women try to solve their time crunch by forgoing leisure activities and sleep. Additionally women become skilled multitaskers. In sociologist Melody Hessing's (1993) study of employed Canadian mothers, she found that women used a variety of strategies to cope with their double shifts. They used workday lunch hours for grocery shopping, running errands, and visiting children's schools. They worked long hours and did the housecleaning in the evenings, around food preparation, laundry, and childcare. They made several meals at once and prepared bag lunches ahead of time. As noted by Wilson (2001:234), "They rarely had the luxury of doing one job at a time." While the women in the study were able to cope, they did find this juggling act "stressful, physically exhausting and emotionally draining" (Wilson, 2001:234).

The fact that women are still disproportionately responsible for unpaid household labour and childcare, even while holding a full-time paid position, contributes to the pursuit of what has been dubbed by journalists as "the mommy track"—a less-pressured, lower-paid stream of employment, characterized by fewer opportunities for advancement than the typical "fast track" stream that males are expected to be on. While on the surface, the mommy track seems to provide a good compromise for those women (but not men?) who wish to combine family responsibilities with their career, it is significant that industry and business are not expected to accommodate the real needs of workers. As social critics Barbara Ehrenreich and Deirdre English (1995:215) point out, "Bumping women—or just fertile women, or married women, or whomever—off the fast track may sound smart . . . [but] it is the corporate culture itself that needs to slow down to a human pace. . . . Workloads that are incompatible with family life are . . . a kind of toxin—to men as well as women, and ultimately to businesses as well as families." Holding dual responsibilities, as women do, has resulted in many women having to make the difficult choice between family and the inferiorly compensated mommy track or no family and a career (the fast track). Because men do not have the same responsibilities for unpaid domestic labour and childcare, they are free to choose both family *and* a fast-track career. For example, only approximately 40 percent of top female executives have children compared with 95 percent of top male executives (Ehrenreich and English, 1995:211).

PERSPECTIVES ON GENDER INEQUALITY

Unlike functionalist and conflict perspectives, which focus on macrolevel sources of gender inequality, feminist perspectives focus on both macro structural levels and micro interactional levels. Interactionist perspectives typically focus on social constructs such as language. It is language, interactionists say, that structures our thinking and discourse about domination and subordination.

The Interactionist Perspective

Symbolic interactionists focus on the differential socialization processes that create masculinity and femininity in people. When a child is assigned a gender at birth, typically corresponding to sex, culturally appropriate gender socialization begins wholeheartedly. Children learn which attitudes, skills, behaviours, likes and dislikes, and so on are appropriate for each gender. Many people believe that socialization has changed, with fewer restrictions on the ways children are taught to act, think, and feel. It is important to recognize that many differences, where they exist at all, are class-based, with people from working classes typically enforcing more conformity to stereotypical roles. People from the middle classes often allow children more autonomy, but gender roles based on stereotypes are so entrenched and pervasive in the dominant culture that pressure to conform is enormous for most children.

Interactionists, who view society as the sum of people's interactions, view language as extremely significant in defining social realities because it provides people with shared meanings and social realities. Historically, what men have thought, written, and concluded have been the givens of our discourse (Peterson and Runyan, 1993). Today, however, English and other languages are being criticized for *linguistic sexism,* that is, for words and patterns of communication that ignore, devalue, or make sex objects of women.

Linguistic sexism, some analysts believe, perpetuates traditional gender-role stereotypes and reinforces

male dominance. These analysts note that the idea that women are secondary to men in importance is embedded in the English language: The masculine form (*he*) is used to refer to human beings generally, and words such as *chairman* and *mankind* are considered to include both men and women (Miller and Swift, 1991). When a woman enters a profession such as medicine or law, she is frequently referred to as a "female doctor" or "woman lawyer"; such terms linguistically protect these male-dominated professions from invasion by females (Lindsey, 1994).

Language can also be used to devalue women by referring to them in terms that reinforce the notion that they are sex objects. Terms such as *fox, bitch, babe,* or *doll* further devalue women by ascribing petlike, childlike, or toylike attributes to them (Adams and Ware, 1995). According to one analyst, at least 220 terms exist for sexually promiscuous women, but only 22 terms exist for sexually promiscuous men (Stanley, 1972).

Research by scholars in a variety of disciplines has demonstrated not only the importance of language in patterning our thoughts but also how gender—and the hierarchy it constructs—is built into the English language (Peterson and Runyan, 1993). According to sociologists Claire M. Renzetti and Daniel J. Curran (1995:151), "Given that women are denigrated, unequally defined, and often ignored by the English language, it serves not only to reflect their secondary status relative to men in our society, but also to reinforce it."

Linguist Deborah Tannen (1990) has examined how power differentials between women and men at home and in the workplace are reflected in their communication styles. According to Tannen (1990), men and women speak different *genderlects:* Women are socialized to speak and hear a language of intimacy and connection, while men are socialized to speak and hear a language of status and independence. For example, women's conversations tend to focus more on relationships with others and include "rapport talk." Men's conversations are more likely to convey messages about their position in workplace or social hierarchies and include "report talk." In explanation, Tannen (1990:77) states that:

For most women, the language of conversation is primarily a language of rapport: a way of establishing connections and negotiating relationships. Emphasis is placed on displaying similarities and matching experiences. . . . For most men, talk is primarily a means to preserve independence and negotiate and maintain status in a hierarchical social order. This is done by exhibiting knowledge and skill and by holding center stage through verbal performance such as story telling, joking, or imparting information.

Men's and women's communication styles also differ: Men have a more direct style of communication and are more likely to dominate conversations than women are. Men are taught to seek immediate solutions for problems, while women are taught to consider a variety of alternatives before reaching a decision. From this perspective, communication not only reflects women's and men's relative power in society but also perpetuates gender inequalities.

At the microlevel of interactions, we can see some of the ways that male dominance is perpetuated through nonverbal forms of communication such as bodily movement, posture, eye contact, use of personal space, and touching. Men typically control more space than women do, whether they are sitting or standing. Men tend to invade women's personal space by standing close to them, touching them, or staring at them. Such actions are not necessarily sexual in connotation; however, when a man nudges and fondles a flight attendant or a coworker in the office, these actions do have sexual overtones that cannot be dismissed. Recent sexual harassment cases show that women do not appreciate such acts and feel threatened by them, especially when the toucher is the employer (Lindsey, 1994:79).

Although the interactionist perspective has been criticized for ignoring the larger, structural factors that perpetuate gender inequality, it is important to note that language and communication patterns are embedded in the structure of society and pass from generation to generation through the socialization process.

The Functionalist Perspective

In focusing on macrolevel issues affecting gender inequality, functionalists frequently examine employment opportunities and the wage gap between men and women.

According to such early functionalists as Talcott Parsons (1955), gender inequality is inevitable because of the biological division of labour: Men generally are physically stronger than women and have certain abilities and interests, whereas women, as the only sex able to bear and nurse children, have their own abilities and interests. Given the biological attributes, Parsons said, men find themselves more suited to *instrumental* (goal-oriented) *tasks* and women to *expressive* (emotionally oriented) *tasks*. In the home, therefore, husbands perform such instrumental tasks as providing economic support and making the most important decisions for the family, while wives perform such expressive tasks as nurturing children and providing emotional support for all family members. The division of labour by gender ensures that important societal tasks—such as procreation and the socialization of children—are fulfilled and that the family is socially and economically stable.

According to Parsons, this division of labour continues in the workplace, where women again do expressive work and men again do instrumental work. Thus, women cluster in occupations that require expressive work, such as elementary school teaching, nursing, and secretarial work, because of their interests and abilities. Women also are concentrated in specific specialties within professions such as law and medicine because of their aptitude for expressive work and their desire to spend more time with their families than men, who are in the more lucrative specialties, are able to spend. For example, many women in law specialize in family law, and many women in medicine specialize in pediatrics (infants and children), obstetrics and gynecology (women), or family practice. In corporations, women are thought to be more adept at public relations and human resources; men are viewed as more adept at financial management. In recent years, however, critics have rejected the dichotomy between men's instrumental work and women's expressive work set forth by functionalists (see Scott, 1996). These critics have noted that the functionalist explanation of gender inequality does not take into account sex discrimination and other structural barriers that make some educational and occupational opportunities more available to men than to women. It also fails to examine the underlying power relations between women and men and does not consider the fact that society places unequal value on tasks assigned to men and women (Kemp, 1994). Functionalist theories tend to justify and perpetuate gender inequities in these ways.

Other functionalist explanations of gender inequality focus on the human capital that men and women bring to the workplace. According to human capital explanations, what individuals earn is based on choices they have made, including choices about the kinds of training and experience they accumulate. For example, human capital analysts argue that women diminish their human capital when they leave the labour force to engage in childbearing and childcare activities. While women are out of the labour force, their human capital deteriorates from nonuse. When they return to paid employment, they earn lower wages than men do because they have fewer years of work experience and "atrophied human capital," that is, because their education and training may have become obsolete (Kemp, 1994:70).

Critics of the human capital model note that it is based on the false assumption that all people, regardless of gender, racialization, or other attributes, are evaluated and paid fairly on the basis of their education, training, and other job-enhancing characteristics. It fails to acknowledge that White women and people of colour tend to be paid less even when they are employed in male-dominated occupations and take no time off for family duties (Lorber, 1994).

Conflict Perspectives

Conflict perspectives on gender inequality are based on the assumption that social life is a continuous struggle in which members of powerful groups (males, in this case) seek to maintain control of scarce resources such as social, economic, and political superiority. By dominating individual women and commanding social institutions, men maintain positions of privilege and power. However, as conflict theorists note, not all men are equally privileged: Men in the upper classes have greater economic power because they control elite positions in corporations, universities, the mass media, and government (Richardson, 1993).

Conflict theorists using a Marxist approach believe that gender inequality primarily results from capitalism and private ownership of the means of production. The gendered division of labour is seen to be inherent in capitalism and, therefore, will disappear with the demise of capitalism (Mackie, 1987). With the development of private property and inheritance based upon primogeniture, women were transformed from equal, productive members of society in hunting and gathering economies into subordinate wives (and also into

property or "chattel"). Further, with the institution of bourgeois marriage, women found it necessary to exchange their sexual and reproductive services for economic support (Mackie, 1987). As industrialization progressed and production moved further from the home, women's skills and education became increasingly separate from those required in the paid labour force. Therefore, according to conflict theorists, the subordinate position of women is the result, not of biology, as functionalists believe, but as a result of structural and historical relations (Mooney et al., 2001).

Conflict theories have been criticized for their view that gender inequality is an inherent and inevitable feature of capitalist relations and for the simplistic and androcentric view that the liberation of women was dependent on the liberation of the working class. As sociologist Rosalind Sydie (1983:216) points out, ". . . history would take care of the 'woman question'; therefore the issue [could] be ignored and the 'proper' focus of attention—class relations—be attended to."

Feminist Perspectives

Feminist perspectives in general challenge the status quo with regard to the unequal position of females in society. Feminism, however, is far from being a unified voice. Instead, it is multifaceted, critical, and activist, seeing both the scope of the problem of gender inequality, and its solutions, differently. Basing their work on a Marxist approach, *socialist feminists* state that under capitalism, men gain control over property and over women. Thus, *capitalism* exploits women in the workplace, and *patriarchy* exploits women at home (Kemp, 1994). According to this perspective, capitalists benefit from the gendered division of labour in the workplace because they can pay women lower wages and derive higher profits. Cultural ideas about the appropriateness of women in the home ensure that women return to the home after any stints in the paid labour force (for example, as a worker in the reserve army of labour required by a capitalist economy—see Chapter 2). At the same time, individual men benefit from the unpaid work women do at home by simply not having to do it and by having more leisure time. The capitalist economic system is maintained because women reproduce the next generation of workers while providing current employees (often including themselves) with food, clean clothes, and other goods and services that are necessary for those who must show up at the workplace each day (Hartmann, 1976). Sociologist Marlene Mackie (1987:40) notes that "to pay women for their efforts would mean a massive redistribution of wealth." In addition, men who labour under capitalism can feel a sense of power by having a superior social position to women and may be less apt to agitate. Marxist feminist perspectives have been criticized for their emphasis on male dominance without a corresponding analysis of how men, specifically, may be oppressed by capitalism and/or patriarchy.

Unlike socialist feminists, *radical feminists* focus exclusively on *patriarchy* as the primary source of gender inequality. From this perspective, men's oppression of women is deliberate, with ideological justification provided by other institutions such as the media and religion. The subordination of women is naturalized through the assumptions inherent in patriarchy. Radical feminism challenges patriarchy and male hegemony, seeing many traditional institutions—the nuclear family in particular—as sites of female enslavement and "domestic servitude" (Fleras, 2001:133). Radical feminists are criticized for their focus on patriarchy to the exclusion of other structures of domination (like class, racialization, and so on).

Liberal feminists believe that gender inequality is rooted in *gender-role socialization,* which perpetuates women's lack of equal rights and educational opportunities. This type of feminism arises out of classical liberal notions of individual freedoms or liberty. Women are seen to be unequal because they are not given access to the opportunities to make comparable wages and so on. The aim of this type of feminism, therefore, is to ensure that women are equally distributed in education and the paid labour force, alongside men. The system is seen as inherently sound and would be transformed with the removal of discriminatory barriers. Liberal feminism is criticized for its lack of focus on the structural roots of inequalities.

Black feminists, First Nations feminists, and other feminists "of colour" believe that Indigenous women and women of colour face heightened inequalities based on the multiplicative effect of racialization, class, and gender as simultaneous forces of oppression (Andersen and Collins, 1997). Oppressions are seen as intersecting patterns of subordination that cannot be viewed, or treated, as separate issues but rather, that must be seen as a complex whole. Solutions to gender inequality, therefore, are inextricably linked with solutions to oppression generally. Lesbians and women with a disability experience the effects of this matrix of domination as well, in our hierarchically organized society. Feminists from the margins, those who experience multilayered oppressions, have led the much-needed critique of other feminist perspectives, advancing the incisiveness of feminist perspectives overall and strengthening activism across difference.

CAN GENDER INEQUALITY BE REDUCED?

Although the rights and working conditions of women have improved during the past 30 years, much remains to be done before gender inequality is eradicated or even significantly reduced. As for how, specifically, to go about reducing gender inequality, a point that was made in previous chapters bears repeating: How people view social problems directly affects how they think the problem should be solved. Interactionists, for example, think gender inequality can be reduced only when people redefine social realities such as linguistic sexism. In their view, language should be modified so that it no longer conveys notions of male superiority and female inferiority, which are then transmitted intergenerationally through the socialization process.

Some functionalists believe that traditional gender roles should be redefined for the well-being of individuals and society, but other functionalists suggest that women should become more aware of how their human capital is diminished by decisions they make. From this perspective, to be competitive in the workplace, women must have the same educational background and qualifications for positions that men have. Some functionalists also suggest that overt sex discrimination can be reduced by enforcing existing legislation such as the *Canadian Charter of Human Rights and Freedoms* or various provincial Human Rights Codes, which forbid discrimination on the basis of sex or gender. However, this approach would not affect covert or institutionalized discrimination, which has a negative and differential impact on White, non-White, and Indigenous women.

While some conflict theorists view elimination of sex discrimination as the primary solution for gender inequality, those using a Marxist approach believe that gender equality will occur only when capitalism is abolished. Socialist feminists agree that capitalism should be eliminated and a new economy that eliminates the gendered division of labour and the wage gap between women and men should be developed. Liberal feminists say that we could reduce gender inequality by dramatically changing gender socialization and what children learn from their families, teachers, and the media about appropriate masculine and feminine attitudes and behaviour. Radical feminists suggest that gender inequality can be reduced only when patriarchy is abolished. To achieve this goal, they say that the legal system must continue to provide relief for sex discrimination, especially sexual harassment in schools and the workplace and that alternative institutions must be developed to replace existing gendered social institutions. For example, women's health care centres should replace male-dominated medicine, and childcare and elder-care centres should assume some of women's caregiving burdens. Finally, Black feminists and other feminists "from the margins" believe that equality will occur only when all women—regardless of racialization, class, gender, age, religion, sexual orientation, and ability or disability—are treated equitably (Andersen and Collins, 1997).

Clearly, many gender issues remain unresolved. As a result of technological changes and the proliferation of service jobs such as information clerk, nurses' aide, and fast-food restaurant worker, which often are equated with "women's work," gender-segregated jobs may increase rather than decrease. Moreover, if the number and quality of "men's jobs" shrink, many men at all class levels may become more resistant to women entering traditionally male-dominated occupations and professions (Reskin and Padavic, 1994). Many analysts suggest that for a significant reduction in gender inequality to occur, women have to become more involved in the political arena and take action themselves. Again, however, this view implies that the system itself is essentially sound and reform is possible using the tools that have been traditionally available. What do you think?

WHAT CAN YOU DO?

Gender inequality is a complex social problem that is rooted in structural sexism and that manifests itself every day in actions and in interpersonal interactions. In terms of proactive things that you can do, then, much depends on the situations you most often find yourself in, as well as what your interests are. Below are a few suggestions for social action that is either preventative or interventionist. What others can you think of?

- Get involved in political actions in your province by joining in protests and teach-ins and by writing letters to MLAs and the newspapers (e.g., about the recent pay equity campaign in British Columbia).

- Lobby government to restore and increase core funding for women-serving organizations like women's shelters and women's centres and sexual assault centres by writing letters to government officials linking your thoughts with your vote.

- Fundraise alone (smaller-scale effort) or with others (larger-scale effort) to support women-serving organizations in your municipality.

- Create coalitions, along with other justice-seeking groups, to raise awareness of the gender inequality issue of interest to you.

- Start or join a group aimed at effecting change on an issue of interest to you (e.g., in 2001, a group of men started the Men Against Sexualized Violence Group at the University of Victoria. They undertook the White Ribbon campaign, which involved them linking up with the National White Ribbon campaign, and they came to many classrooms to talk to their peers about the relationship of men to sexualized violence against women).

- Sign on to Internet listservs and websites of groups and organizations whose interests you share as a means of keeping up to date on the issue and informing others.

- Break the cultural taboo about wage secrecy and share information about wages as widely as possible with coworkers. Many businesses explicitly instruct employees not to discuss their wages. It is very possible that these places are paying people inequitably. You may be surprised to find where you are on the wage scale, despite what company representatives imply. If there are inequities, expose them and lobby the company to redress the situations of underpaid workers.

- When you are being told a sexist joke (or a joke that is typically inherently sexist, like the "blonde joke"), explain to the person that the joke perpetuates harmful and derogatory stereotypes about women and that you do not find the demeaning of people amusing.

- Be alert and open to hearing about (other) women's experiences with sexism or violence. Ask women you know what their experiences have been. Educate yourself about people's differing experiences—talk to males and females, White women and non-White women, lesbians, "trans" peoples, and so on. Try to hear the experience without judgment.

- Report violence, whenever you see or hear it, by calling 911. Do not get involved in a situation that is unsafe physically: Call law enforcement.

- Go to court and watch the trials of men charged with sexual assault, assaulting a women, or femicide. Critically analyze the approach of the justice system to the case. How did police handle it? How did lawyers handle it? How did the judge handle it? Write a letter to the local newspaper and/or your college/university newspaper with your analysis.

- Think about all the words you use that are gender exclusive and/or sexist. Think of words that you can use to replace them and begin practicing (don't worry about not being perfect! It takes a long time to unlearn this).

- Educate yourself and others about "trans" issues. You may even know a "trans" person and be unaware of it. Try not to assume.

- Support "trans" people when and wherever they are. Support people's inalienable right to feel comfortable in their own skin.

- Include "trans" issues whenever you talk or write about gender. In the words of renowned feminist scholar Adrienne Rich (1984), "When someone with the authority of a teacher describes the world and you are not in it, there is a moment of psychic disequilibrium, as if you looked into a mirror and saw nothing."

- Next time you, a friend, or a relative has a child, look for gender-neutral clothing, accessories, and toys and books that promote gender equality.

- Think of any gender-stereotypical assumptions you own and challenge them.

- Consumerism is power. Begin a boycott campaign against companies that use women in narrow, stereotypical, and objectified ways in advertising. Write to the company and tell it what you are doing and why and in what ways you are planning to get your boycott message out.

- Put a sign in the window of your vehicle or on your backpack stating which local company exploits its female workers and how. (Make sure you have your facts correct.)

- Write a letter to the newspaper or advertise in some other way companies that do have gender-equitable policies, wages, and so on. This demonstrates to all companies that the public is watching and does care.

- Report offences and breaches to the appropriate person or office (e.g., to police, ombuds offices, or anti-harassment offices on campuses). Be persistent. Get support. Be an advocate for people whose voices are marginalized in these systems. Help them to report and follow up, if appropriate.

- Volunteer for crisis lines, sexual assault centres, and women's shelters (men, you can volunteer in many of these places by going out and doing community education and/or fundraising, for example). It is important to demonstrate to the community that violence against women is NOT a women's issue. It is a community issue.

- If you witness sexual harassment in a public place, lend support to the person suffering and/or make it uncomfortable for the perpetrator to harass (again, do not take risks to your own safety).

- Think about ways in which your actions and words maintain current beauty standards. Think of ways to celebrate and support all women.

- Begin discussions with your family and friends about an issue of sexism that interests you. Inform people about some of the facts you have learned and explain why you feel that is unjust.

- Make music, make art, make word collages, make zines—whatever—that promotes the message that gender inequality is unjust and has got to go. Get that message out there!

SUMMARY

HOW DOES SEX DIFFER FROM GENDER?

Sex is the biological aspects of being male or female; gender is the socially constructed differences between females and males. In short, sex is what we (generally) are born with; gender is what we acquire through socialization. We currently operate under a two-sex, two-gender system that views the sexes/genders as binary opposites.

WHAT ARE THE PRIMARY SOCIALIZING AGENTS?

The key socializing agents are parents, peers, teachers and schools, and the media, all of which may reinforce gender stereotypes and gender-based inequalities as they attempt to teach culturally based gender-appropriate behaviour.

HOW ARE SEXISM AND PATRIARCHY RELATED?

Individual and institutional sexism are maintained and reinforced by patriarchy, a hierarchical system in which cultural, political, and economic structures are dominated by males.

WHAT ARE SOME OF THE PRIMARY CAUSES OF GENDER INEQUALITY?

Gender inequality results from economic, political, and educational discrimination against women as evidenced in gender-segregated work, which in turn results in a disparity—or wage gap—between women's and men's earnings. Even when women are employed in the same job as men, on average they do not receive the same (or comparable) pay.

WHAT IS THE SECOND SHIFT AND WHY IS IT A PROBLEM FOR WOMEN?

The second shift is the unpaid household work and childcare performed by employed women. Many women have a second shift because of their dual responsibilities in the workplace and at home. The typical woman in Canada who combines paid work in the labour force with parenting and housework does not have enough hours in the average day to fulfill all her responsibilities, and many men have been unwilling or unable to pick up some of the slack at home. Women, thus, employ a variety of creative strategies for coping with this problem.

HOW DO FUNCTIONALIST AND CONFLICT ANALYSTS EXPLAIN THE GENDERED DIVISION OF LABOUR?

According to functionalist analysts, women's caregiver roles in contemporary industrialized societies are crucial in ensuring that key societal tasks are fulfilled. While the husband performs the instrumental tasks of economic support and decision-making, the wife assumes the expressive tasks of providing affection and emotional support for the family. According to conflict analysts, the gendered division of labour within families and the workplace results from male control and dominance over women and resources.

WHAT ARE THE MAJOR FEMINIST PERSPECTIVES AND HOW DO THEY EXPLAIN GENDER INEQUALITY?

In liberal feminism, gender equality is connected to equality of opportunity. In radical feminism, male dominance is seen as the cause of oppression. According to socialist feminists, women's oppression results from capitalism and patriarchy and women's dual roles as paid and unpaid workers. Anti-racist feminism and other feminisms from the margins focus on matrices of oppression, linking gender inequality with other forms of oppression such as class oppression, racialization, sexual orientation or preference, ability, age, and so on.

HOW DOES SYMBOLIC INTERACTIONISM EXPLAIN GENDER INEQUALITY?

Symbolic interactionists view gender inequality as the result of faulty gender role socialization, in which language use, including body language, plays a significant role. Inequality between the sexes is seen to exist and be perpetuated through the use of gender exclusive and/or sexist language and through nonverbal actions like the male invasion of female space or males touching females more often in mixed-gender interactions.

KEY TERMS

androcentricity,   p. 74
comparable worth,   p. 91
contingent work,   p. 90
gender,   p. 74
gender bias,   p. 84
gendered division of labour,   p. 80
gender ideology,   p. 80
glass ceiling,   p. 94
intersexed,   p. 74

patriarchy,   p. 73, 88
pay equity,   p. 91
pink-collar ghetto,   p. 89
rape culture,   p. 87
sex,   p. 74
sexism,   p. 73
sexual harassment,   p. 85
wage gap,   p. 90

QUESTIONS FOR CRITICAL THINKING

1. Examine the various administrative offices and academic departments at your college or university. What is the gender breakdown of administrators, faculty, and staff in selected departments? Can you identify a gender-related pattern associated with women's and men's work at your school? What conclusions can you draw about the relationship between gender and employment, based on your observations? Are there any policies in place to counteract gendered inequities in that workplace? Do they work? Why or why not?

2. Will the increasing numbers of women in higher education, the workplace, and the military, particularly in nontraditional positions or majors, tip the balance of power between men and women and result in greater gender equality in the future? Explain why or why not.

3. What is the role of violence against women in our culture? In what ways do MTV and other music-video shows perpetuate a "rape culture" and violence against women in Canada?

4. In what ways does traditional gender socialization support capitalism?

WEBLINKS

Canadian Federation of University Women (CFUW)

www.cfuw.ca

CFUW is a nonprofit, voluntary organization of over 10 000 women graduates working to improve the socio-economic and legal situation of women. The site offers informative links, a message board and an opportunity to join.

The History of Women and Gender in Canada

www.hartford-hwp.com/archives/44/index-eb.html

Links to articles, essays, and information about the history of women and gender in Canada.

Canadian Research Institute for the Advancement of Women (CRIAW)

www.criaw-icref.ca

CRIAW is a national not-for-profit organization committed to advancing women's equality through research. The site gives links to a list of the organization's publications, conferences, and workshops, a database of feminist researchers, and other resources.

Match International Centre

www.web.net/~matchint

Match International Centre is a nongovernmental women's organization dedicated to strengthening women's movements nationally and internationally. It was created to bring to life a feminist vision of what development work can, and should, mean.

Men for Change

www.chebucto.ns.ca/CommunitySupport/Men4Change/the_group.htm

The site of Men for Change, a pro-feminist organization dedicating to promoting gender equality, offers information and links to those who wish to better understand and put an end to sexism and sexism-related violence.

National Clearinghouse on Family Violence (NCFV)

www.hc-sc.gc.ca/hppb/familyviolence

Health Canada's NCFV is a national resource centre providing information and research findings about violence within the family, including all aspects of its prevention and treatment.

Status of Women Canada

www.swc-cfc.gc.ca/direct.html

The mandate of this federal ministry is to promote gender equality and ensure that women participate fully in the economic, social, cultural, and political landscapes of Canada. The site provides links to learning resources and tools that promote women's equality.

The 3rd WWWave

www.io.com/~wwwave

Written by and aimed at middle-aged women, this site devoted to women's issues and Third Wave feminism provides information on and discussions of politics, sexuality, hobbies, and other topics.

5

INEQUALITY BASED ON AGE

A teacher saw my picture [in a newspaper article about 90-year-olds] in *USA Today* and had her class write to me. I got thirty lovely letters. . . . I've never been to the South, so I flew [to Decatur, Alabama]. . . . I answer any of their questions. Do you still have your own teeth? Do you have a boyfriend? I say, "No, but I'm looking for one who can cook. If you find somebody like that, let me know." They think it's funny.

They want to know how it feels to be ninety. I tell them I feel like myself. Don't you all feel like yourself? Okay, there's a difference. When I was your age, I loved to play basketball and climb mountains and slide down the other side. One thing I didn't want to do was make speeches. It was scary. Now I don't want to climb mountains and play basketball. I love to make speeches. So you see, when you're ninety, you'll do what you feel like doing. In a way, I'm telling them to value old age and respect it.

Hazel Wolf, age 95, in an interview with author Studs Terkel (1996:140)

As Hazel Wolf's statement indicates, how people of one age view people of another age is relative. Young people may view older people as "over the hill," while older people may consider the young as lacking experience. Throughout one's lifetime, age is a very important ascribed characteristic. Just consider how many times you have been asked, "How old are you?" Most of us answer this question in terms of *chronological age*—age based on date of birth. Although chronological age constitutes our "official" age, most of us view other people in terms of their *functional age*—observable individual attributes such as physical appearance, mobility, strength, coordination, and mental capacity that are used to assign people to age categories (McPherson, 1990:31). A wide range of physical, psychological, and intellectual factors can influence our functional age (Chudacoff, 1989). Although we may appear to be younger or older than our chronological age, there are some things that we do in life, such as driving a car or voting, that are determined by our chronological age rather than our functional age. Children—regardless of ability—are not allowed to drive and therefore eagerly look forward to the time when they will be "old enough" to drive. For the younger person, then, changes in chronological and functional age are positive. However, as some people age, they begin to lose some of the functional abilities,

such as vision or hearing, that are necessary for driving. Thus, the older person may view changes in chronological and functional age negatively.

However, unless these changes can be proven to have a direct effect on one's activities, should people be forced to follow such traditional rules as mandatory retirement at age 65? Now, in some circles, retirement at age 65 is being thought of as discrimination, or *ageism,* and against the *Charter of Rights and Freedoms.* "Mandatory retirement, where age is used to determine the person's employment status, (is) unacceptable from a human-rights perspective," stated Ontario Human Rights Commissioner Keith Norton (quoted in R. Mackie, 2002:A10). How should we deal with such questions in the future?

To help us think about these and other questions related to inequalities and aging, this chapter deals with stereotypes and inequalities through the life course, with special emphasis on the elderly; suicide and the life course; death and dying and the question of euthanasia; problems of workplace discrimination and retirement; problems of health, illness, and health care; criminal victimization; and family relationships, housing, and long-term care.

The sociological perspectives are used to help explain aging problems. The chapter concludes with a discussion of ways to reduce inequality based on age and what you can do about it.

AGEISM AS A SOCIAL PROBLEM

Ageism—**prejudice and discrimination against people on the basis of age**—is a social problem that particularly stigmatizes and marginalizes older people. Gerontologist Robert Butler (1969) introduced the term *ageism* to describe how myths and misconceptions about older people produce age-based discrimination. According to Butler, just as racism and sexism perpetuate stereotyping and discrimination against people of colour and all women, ageism perpetuates stereotyping of older people and age-based discrimination. Most research has therefore focused on the negative and differential impact ageism has on older people.

Age-Based Stereotypes

There are more stereotypes about the physical and mental abilities of older people than there are about the abilities of people in any other age category. This does not mean that children and adolescents are exempt from age-based stereotypes. Comedians often refer to very young children as "crumb crunchers," "rug rats," and "little hellions." Animated television characters such as Bart and Lisa Simpson (*The Simpsons*), Beavis and Butt-Head (MTV), and young characters in many situation comedies and movies are simply stereotypic depictions of children and young adolescents.

Older people, however, are stereotyped in numerous ways. Some stereotypes depict them as slow in their thinking and movement; as living in the past and unable to change; and as cranky, sickly, and lacking in social value (Novak, 1997:98). Other stereotypes suggest that older people are "greedy geezers," living an affluent lifestyle and ignoring the needs of future generations (Toner, 1995). When age-based stereotypes are accepted by many people, they can affect how people vote and what types of social policies legislators enact. Negative stereotypes of older people reinforce ageism and influence how younger people interact with older people.

Although most of us do not believe that we engage in stereotypical thinking about older people, researcher William C. Levin (1988) found that college students in his study evaluated people differently on the basis of their assumed age. Levin showed students three photographs of the same man, who had been made up to appear 25 in the first photo, 52 in the second, and 73 in the third. He then asked them to evaluate these (apparently different) men for employment purposes. Many students described the "73-year-old" as less competent, less intelligent, and less reliable than the "25-year-old" and the "52-year-old." Low ratings of the elderly are also given by older people. In a survey of older people, Ian D. Graham and Paul M. Baker (1989) found an inverted U-shaped curve of status ratings on a six-point scale: Older and younger people were rated lower than middle-aged people. Clearly our place in the social structure changes during our life course, and if we live long enough, any of us may become the target of stereotyping and discrimination directed at older people (Hooyman and Kiyak, 1996).

Social Inequality and the Life Course

To study age and social inequality, many sociologists and social gerontologists focus on the *life course*—the age-based categories through which people pass as they grow older. In North America, the life course tends to be divided into infancy and childhood, adolescence and young adulthood, middle age, later maturity, and old age. The field of *gerontology* examines the biological, physical, and social aspects of the aging process. We will focus primarily on **social gerontology—the study of the social (nonphysical) aspects of aging**—as we examine age classifications in Canada.

Childhood

Infants (birth to age two) and children (ages 3 to 12) are among the most powerless individuals in society. In the past, children were seen as the property of their parents, who could do with their children as they chose (Tower, 1996). Although we have a more liberal attitude today, children remain vulnerable to problems such as family instability, poverty, maltreatment by relatives and other caregivers, and sexual exploitation. The Canadian Council on Social Development reports that:

- Poor children (family incomes less than $20 000) are 1.4 times more likely to engage in aggressive behaviour than children of middle- or higher-income families;

- Poor children are 1.8 and 2.6 times more likely to exhibit delinquent behaviour than children from middle- and higher- income families, respectively;

- Serious health problems that affect a child's functioning, such as vision, hearing speech, or cognition, are 1.7 and 2.6 times more likely to be found in poor children than children in middle- and higher-income families; and

- Poor children are 1.8 times as likely to be registered in special education classes (Ross, Scott, and Smith, 2000:2).

Non-poor children have problems also. For example, the 1998–99 cycle of the *National Longitudinal Survey of Children and Youth* (see Chapter 11 for an outline of this study) found that over one-third of children aged 2 to 11 were overweight and half of these children were obese. Obesity is now estimated to be higher among children than among adults (Statistics Canada, 2002m) (see Chapter 10 for more on obesity).

Relatively high rates of single parenthood, a significant increase in the divorce rate in recent decades, differing parenting styles (see Chapter 11), and the fact that many parents work several jobs in an attempt to make ends meet have caused many children to face a complex array of problems and social relationships in their families.

Adolescence

Before the 20th century, the concept of adolescence did not exist. When children grew big enough to do adult work, they were expected to fulfill adult responsibilities such as making money to support their family (Chudacoff, 1989). Today, the line between childhood and adolescence is blurred. While some researchers define adolescence as the teenage years (ages 13 to 19), others place the lower and upper ages at 15 and 24, respectively (Corr, Nabe, and Corr, 1994).

Adolescents tread a narrow path between childhood and adulthood. They are not treated as children, but they are not afforded the full status of adulthood. Early teens are considered too young to drive, to drink alcohol, to stay out late, and to do other things that are considered to be adult behaviour by the media, particularly television and movies, and by members of some peer groups. Adolescents face an identity crisis in which they must figure out who they are and what they want to become. They also face difficult decisions pertaining to their sexuality and their relationships with people of the same sex and the opposite sex. Teen pregnancy and parenthood are major concerns for many adolescents.

Adolescents must deal with conflicting demands for money and school attendance. Most provinces have compulsory school attendance laws that require young people to attend school from about ages 6 through 16. However, some adolescents balk at this requirement; they cannot see what school is doing for them and would prefer to find employment. In fact, many teenagers who live in families that are trapped in poverty may hold jobs to supplement the family income or support themselves. On the other hand, these adolescents may not be engaged in either activity. According to the Canadian Council on Social Development, poor adolescents are 2.5 and 4.4 times more likely to be engaged in neither a school program or a job, respectively, as those in middle- or higher-income families (Ross, Scott,

and Smith, 2000:2). The resulting inactivity may leave them open to deviant behaviour.

Some social analysts suggest that we should not be surprised that individuals between the ages of 12 to 17 account for almost a third of all property crime arrests in Canada (CCJS, 1999:88). The problems of some young people may be intensified by today's media images of Canadian teenagers (see Box 5.1).

Some sociologists think that young age itself is a basis of inequality, often linked with other forms of inequality such as social class and ethnicity. Vappu Tyyska (2001:224–225) states that youth

> is a liability in societies where one's livelihood depends on the amount of wages earned. . . . The fates of adolescents and youth, more so than those of most adults in working-age groups, are tied to the level of success of those who they live with . . . At the same time, the prolonged education they are subjected to prevents them from participating in the labour force fully.

The prolonged education is shown by the increasing tendency of young people to remain in the parental home. The 2001 Census shows that 41 percent of young people aged 20 to 29 lived with their parents, a substantial increase from 33 percent in 1991 (Statistics Canada, 2002q:7). Remaining in the parental home is likely to delay what used to be called *young adulthood*.

Young Adulthood

Typically beginning in the early to mid-twenties (perhaps now in the early thirties) and lasting to about age 39, young adulthood is a period during which people acquire new roles and experience a sense of new freedom. However, many also experience problems finding their niche, particularly when it appears doubtful that they will have as high a standard of living as their parents had.

Some young adults return home or perhaps do not even leave home, prolonging the practice identified in the last section. In 1996, 50 percent of unmarried women and 60 percent of unmarried men, and 4 percent of married women and 5 percent of married men aged 20 to 34, were still living with their parents (Boyd and Norris, 1999:3). Subsequent chapters examine a variety of issues affecting young adults, including alcohol and drug abuse, divorce, and employment instability. Many of these issues also concern people older than age 40.

SOCIAL PROBLEMS IN THE MEDIA

BOX 5.1   Media Ageism: Reporting on and Preferring Age Groups

How are teenagers portrayed in the media? Although most research on media ageism focuses on portrayals of older people, activist groups such as CYRA (Canadian Youth Rights Association) have also examined media coverage of adolescents. According to CYRA's (1998) findings, the media perpetuate myths about teenagers in these ways:

- The news media seldom report stories about teenagers unless they are involved in a crime or some other "deviant" behaviour. The age of the person is often used as a hook to catch readers or viewers.

- Few news stories describe positive teenager actions, such as volunteer work.

- While media reports refer to adults as "women" or "men" and identify them by their last names, teenagers are often referred to by their first names and described as "girls" or "boys."

- Entertainment shows and movies typically depict teens as being self-centred, insensitive to the feelings of others, materialistic, sexually promiscuous, involved in alcohol and drug abuse, and prone toward harmful pranks and physical aggression.

What would constitute positive journalism about adolescents? Clearly, covering young people's positive endeavours, as well as their problematic activities, would be a start. To bring about real change in media portrayals, however, responsible journalists could focus on how problems in the society at large affect young people. For example, journalists could "publicize the enormous racial imbalances inherent in 'youth violence,' the fundamental sexism of the current debate over 'teen' pregnancy, the realities of millions of raped, beaten, and neglected children, the increasing rates of youth poverty imposed by ever-richer Canadian elites, and the futility of modern behaviour modification, laws and treatments aimed at forcing the young to 'adjust' to intolerable conditions" (Males, 1994:5). They also could look for ways to reduce or eliminate these problems.

Whether media coverage of teenagers will change is uncertain, but one thing is apparent: Many young people are "hooked" on media (Haddock, 1999). According to a recent study by the Kaiser Family Foundation, which was based on a representative sampling of 3155 individuals aged 2 through 18, "children spend so much time watching television, playing video games and the like that media use could qualify as their full-time job" (Haddock, 1999:A32). The typical young person spends more than five hours each day using media, and most of this time is spent watching television. What kinds of images do young people see of themselves when they watch television? Based on media coverage of teenagers, how do adults view today's adolescents?

Although media coverage of teenagers can be negative, as soon as teenagers turn 18 years of age, the media want to attract them. Advertisers want the 18- to 34-year-olds because the advertisers believe that, if this segment is attracted to products, they will maintain "brand loyalty." Older segments of the population, according to the advertisers, have already made up their minds.

One of the consequences of advertisers' beliefs is that television and radio networks change programs well established with the 50+ age group to appeal to younger viewers and listeners. In March, 2002, at the time when ABC was thinking of dropping *Nightline with Ted Koppel* and replacing it with David Letterman's show to attract a younger audience, the CBC announced that it would be changing well-respected programs on Radio 1 and 2, such as *This Morning* with Shelagh Rogers and *The House,* a political affairs program, for the same reason. According to Hugh Winsor (2002:A16), two-thirds of CBC's audience is over 50. Why would the CBC do this and alienate its strongest fans, especially when the CBC does not advertise products on Radio 1 and 2 and thus does not need to attract advertisers?

In addition, media portrayal of seniors is degrading. At the World Congress of Gerontology, held in Vancouver in July 2001, journalist and now Senator Laurier LaPierre said "Older people are essentially represented with ridicule" and "Older people have no life of their own beyond these media-imposed titles (bewildered grandfather or meddling mother-in-law)" (Muggeridge 2001:5). In the same article, Dolores Ewan reported on an ad from a major department store chain, which pictured the surveying of seniors. If the seniors disliked a style, that was taken as an indicator of the style being fashionable. But society does not complain about this kind of stereotyping. Ewan went on to say that if the ad had shown Blacks or Indigenous people in this light, "there would have been a hue and cry about bigotry and racism" (Muggeridge 2001:5).

What should media do about the nature of their coverage of people in different age groups? To what extent should the media, particularly public media like the CBC, organize their programming to appeal to different age groups?

Middle Age

Because life expectancy was lower in the past, the concept of middle age (age 40 to 65) did not exist until fairly recently. *Life expectancy*—the average length of time the members of a group of individuals will live—increased dramatically during the 20th century. Today, life expectancy at birth is approximately 78 years (see Chapter 10), compared to only 42 years at Confederation. Sociologists use an age pyramid to show the distribution of a given population by age and sex groupings at various points in time, though the figures no longer look like pyramids. As Figure 5.1 shows, Canada is undergoing what some social analysts refer to as the *greying of the population*, the aging of the population due to an increase in life expectancy combined with a decrease in the birth rate (Chui, 1996). The 2001 Census showed that the median (the midpoint of the population) age of Canadians is at a record high of 37.6 years (Statistics Canada, 2002q:3).

As people progress through middle age, they experience *senescence (primary aging)*, which results from molecular and cellular changes in the body. Some signs of senescence are visible (e.g., wrinkles and grey hair); others are not (e.g., arthritis or stiffness in connective tissue joints; a gradual dulling of senses such as taste, touch, and vision; and slower reflexes). Vital systems also undergo gradual change; lung capacity diminishes, and the digestive, circulatory, and reproductive systems gradually decline in efficiency (Novak, 1997:77ff.).

FIGURE 5.1   Canada's Population, 1995 and 2016

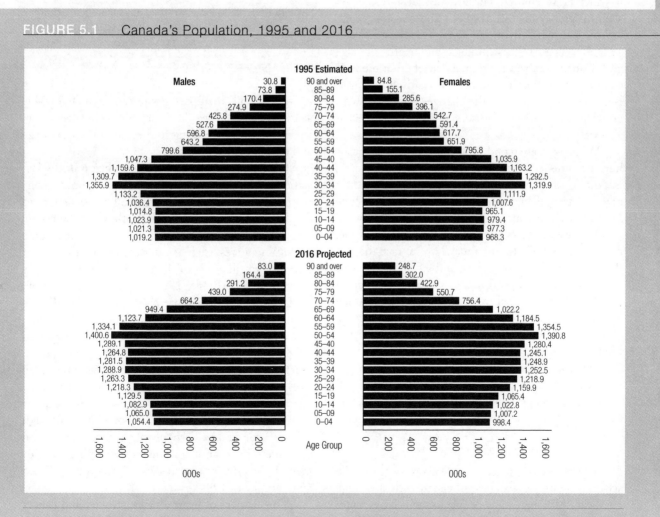

Source: "Canada's Population, 1995 and 2016," Statistics Canada, 1996, Canadian Social Trends (Autumn):3–7; Catalogue no. 11-008. Reprinted by permission.

In addition to primary aging, people experience *secondary aging,* which has to do with environmental factors and lifestyle choices. "How you age is a question of attitude and motivation. You have to stay connected and involved . . . [some] remain interested and curious, open to new challenges even as octogenarians," says Blossom Wigdor, now emeritus professor of gerontology at the University of Toronto (quoted in Kingstone, 2002:42).

Some people fight the aging process by spending billions of dollars on products such as Oil of Olay, Clairol, or Grecian Formula to hide grey hair; drugs like Viagra; and treatments like injections of Botox to eliminate wrinkles. Others have cosmetic surgery. In a recent study, one interviewee explained that she had decided to undergo liposuction (a surgical procedure in which fat is removed) because she had started to get a lot of "crepeyness" in her neck and her jowls were "coming down," owing to aging (Dull and West, 1991:57). As use of these products and treatments suggest, Canada is a youth-oriented society that tends to equate beauty, stamina, and good health with youth. Because of this, many of the changes associated with growing older are viewed as something to be avoided at all costs.

While women in middle age may believe that they have become less sexually attractive than they were, middle-aged men tend to begin to realize that their physical strength and social power over others are limited, and their occupational opportunities are limited. As if to reinforce their awareness of the passage of time, many women and also men may have to face the fact that their children have grown and left home. Any of these factors might precipitate what is often referred to as a mid-life crisis. However, for some people, middle age is a time of great contentment: Their income and prestige are at their peak, the problems of raising their children are behind them, they are content with their spouse of many years, and they may have grandchildren who give them a tie to the future. Even so, all middle-aged people know that their status will change significantly as they grow older.

Later Maturity and Old Age

Later maturity is usually considered to begin in the sixties. The major changes associated with this stage are social. Although many people in their sixties retain sufficient physical strength to be able to carry on an

Gerontologists stress that it is hard to generalize about older individuals. The stereotypes don't fit. This couple, for example, in their eighties, apparently enjoy good health—and each other.

active social life, their peer groups can shrink noticeably as friends and relatives die. Many people in later maturity find themselves caring for people of their own age and older people.

Old age is usually considered to begin in the late sixties or in the seventies. Although some people continue to work past age 70, most have left paid employment by their seventieth birthday. Problems are not just social but also increasingly biological. Some physical changes, such as arteriosclerosis (the loss of elasticity in the walls of the arteries), are potentially life-threatening (Belsky, 1990). As bones become more porous, they become more brittle; a simple fall may result in broken bones that take longer to heal than those of a younger person. Strength, mobility, and height may decline; and the abilities to see, hear, taste, touch, and smell may diminish. Because taste and smell work together to allow us to enjoy food, eating may become less pleasurable and so contribute to poor nutrition in some older adults (Belsky, 1990). Although it is not true of all elderly people, the average person over age 65 does not react as rapidly (physically or mentally) as the average person who is younger than 65 (Lefrançois, 1999).

The chances of heart attacks, strokes, and cancer increase along with the likelihood of some diseases that primarily affect the elderly. Alzheimer's, a degenerative disease that attacks the brain and severely impairs memory, thinking, and behaviour, may be the best-known example. People who have this disease have an impaired ability to function in everyday social roles; in time they cease to be able to recognize people they have always known, and they lose all sense of their own identity. Finally, they may revert to a speechless childishness, at which point others must feed them, dress them, sit them on the toilet, and lead them around by the hand. Alzheimer's and other dementias strike 8 percent of those over age 64, according to the 1991 Canadian Study of Health and Aging. Today, in Canada, there are likely over 350 000 people suffering from dementia, according to Burke and her colleagues (1997:25). Most of the people with dementia (78 percent) live in institutions (Statistics Canada, 1999b:63). In spite of promises for cures in the future, now the disease can last 8 to 20 years, ending only with death (Lefrançois, 1999).

As older people have begun to live longer, they have become an increasingly high percentage of the population. In 1998, they constituted 12 percent of the Canadian population, up 57 percent since 1981 (Statistics Canada, 1999:7). Figure 5.1 shows how the population will change from 1995 to 2016. In 2016, the largest age group in the country will be those over 50 years of age. Gerontologists have come to realize that there are significant differences among people who are now called the "young-old" (ages 65 to 74), the "middle-old" (ages 75 to 84), and the "old-old" (ages 85 and older). Although more than half of all people aged 65 and older are in the young-old category, the old-old category has grown more rapidly over the past two decades than has any other age group in Canada. In 1998, there were 380 000 people 85 years of age and older, double the numbers in 1981 (Statistics Canada, 1999a:7). As with other age categories, it is difficult to make generalizations about older people. But it is not true that old people feel lonely and lost in retirement, live in institutions, and are uniform in their health, activities, and financial situation (Novak, 1997).

As Bill Gleberzon, associate executive director of the Canadian Association for the Fifty-Plus (CARP [formerly using the term *retired persons*]), has said, "Competence, not age, should be the deciding criterion in any endeavour" (author's files). Or, to illustrate that some older persons do not perceive themselves as old,

the author's 86-year-old mother, Hilda Thompson, when asked if she had spent the money he had given her for Christmas said, "No, I'm saving it for my old age."

In some parts of the world, many older people do not have such positive feelings and they have a high rate of suicide.

Suicide and the Life Course

Around the world, older people, aged 60 and above, have a suicide rate that is three times the rate of younger people, aged 15 to 24 years of age (WHO, 2002). Is this true for Canadians as well? Figure 5.2 shows the rate of suicide for males and females over the stages of the life course in Canada. According to Langlois and Morrison (2002:21), who studied suicide rates in Canada, few major differences in these rates occur across the life course. For men, suicide rates rise steadily from the teenage years; they are highest for men aged 30 to 44; they decline slightly thereafter, levelling off again at ages 60 to 74 age group, and rise slightly again for those 75 and above. Women have far lower suicide rates at each stage—the high point coming for women aged 45 to 59, with the rate declining to a low level thereafter. These suicide rates have remained stable over the last 20 years at 14 per 100 000 population, with a high point of 18 in 1983. The authors also compared Canadian rates with those of the other industrialized countries. Among industrialized countries, Canada, with a suicide rate of 11.3 per 100 000 population, ranks in the middle of the group with countries like Australia and the Scandinavian countries; the U.S. has a slightly lower suicide rate, 10.5 per 100 000 population, than we do (Langlois and Morrison, 2002:23). Thus, it would seem that no stage of the life course is significantly more difficult than any other for Canadians and that has been true for at least the last 20 years.

Death and Dying

In previous generations, death was a common occurrence in all stages in the life course, but today most deaths occur among older people. Because of medical advances and the increase in life expectancy, death is now viewed as an event that usually occurs in old age. According to social gerontologists, the increased association of *death* with the process of *aging* has caused many people to deny the aging process and engage in

FIGURE 5.2   Canadian Suicide Rates, by Age and Sex

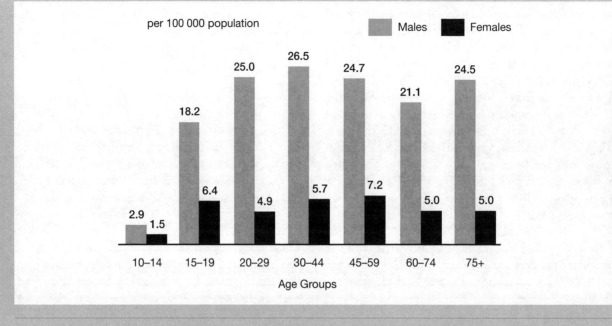

Source: "Vital Statistics Database, 1998," Statistics Canada, 2002, Canadian Social Trends *(Autumn): 21; Catalogue no. 11-008. Reprinted by permission.*

ageism as a means of denying the reality of death, particularly their own (Atchley, 2000). Euphemisms such as "pass away" or "sleep" are often used to refer to death by those who are trying to avoid its reality. Researchers have found, however, that many people do not actually fear death itself as much as they fear the possibility of pain and suffering, loss of control, and the consequences of their death for survivors (Marshall and Levy, 1990). Given a chance to choose, most people would choose a painless death over prolonged physical and mental deterioration and the prospect of being a burden on their families. Some researchers have also found that older people have less fear of death than younger people do (Gesser, Wong, and Reker, 1986, quoted in Novak, 1997:297); others have found that education and religious beliefs are important factors in how people view death and dying (Kalish, 1985).

There are three widely known frameworks for explaining how people cope with the process of dying: the stage-based approach, the dying trajectory, and the task-based approach. The *stage-based approach* was popularized by Elisabeth Kübler-Ross (1969), who proposed five stages in the dying process: (1) denial ("Not me"); (2) anger ("Why me?"); (3) bargaining and asking for divine intervention to postpone death ("Yes me, but . . ."); (4) depression and sense of loss; and, (5) acceptance. According to some social scientists (Kalish, 1985; Marshall, 1980), Kübler-Ross's study is limited because she focused primarily on the attitudes of younger people who had terminal illnesses. These scientists argue that the same stages may not apply to older people who believe that they have already lived a full life.

In contrast to Kübler-Ross's five stages, the concept of the *dying trajectory* focuses on the perceived course of dying and the expected time of death. From this perspective, not all people move toward death at the same speed and in the same way. A dying trajectory may be sudden (e.g., a heart attack) or slow (e.g., lung cancer) and is usually shaped by the condition causing death. A dying trajectory involves three phases: the *acute* phase, in which maximum anxiety or fear is expressed; the *chronic* phase, in which anxiety declines as the person confronts reality; and the *terminal* phase, in which the dying person withdraws from others (Glaser and Strauss, 1968).

The *task-based approach* suggests that daily activities can still be enjoyed during the dying process and that fulfilling certain tasks makes the process of death easier, not just on the dying person, but on everyone involved. *Physical tasks* are performed to satisfy bodily needs and to minimize physical distress. *Psychological tasks* help to maximize psychological security, autonomy, and richness of experience. *Social tasks* sustain and enhance interpersonal attachments and address the social implications of dying. *Spiritual tasks* are performed to identify, develop, or reaffirm sources of spiritual energy and to foster hope (Corr et al., 1994). Most important in any approach are the rights of the dying person and the way in which care is provided.

Technological advances in medicine have helped to focus attention on the physical process of dying and, in recent years, the needs of dying patients and their families. Many people are choosing to sign a *living will*—a document stating a person's wishes about the medical circumstances under which his or her life should be allowed to end. Some people, rejecting the idea of being kept alive by elaborate life-support systems and other forms of high-tech medicine, choose to die at home rather than in a hospital or nursing home. The hospice movement has provided additional options for caring for the terminally ill. **Hospices are organizations that provide a homelike facility or home-based care (or both) for persons who are terminally ill.** Some hospices have facilities where care is provided, but hospice is primarily a philosophy that affirms life, not death, and offers holistic and continuing care to the patient and family through a team of visiting nurses, on-call physicians, and counsellors. Home care enables many people to remain in familiar surroundings and maintain dignity and control over the dying process (Corr et al., 1994). Sophia Mumford summarizes the feeling of many older people about death:

> I'm afraid of one thing. I want my death to be dignified. My fear is that something will cause me to live past the point where my life has value. I don't want to live on. . . . From now on, if life says it's leaving, I'm not doing anything about it. If I get a bad pain and it's diagnosed as cancer, then I won't wait, I'll go. I'm ready, because I feel I've had a good life. (quoted in Terkel, 1996:429)

Because many people want a dignified death, the topic of euthanasia will likely become very prominent in the future (see Box 5.2).

PROBLEMS ASSOCIATED WITH AGING

Age stratification—the inequalities, differences, segregation, or conflict between age groups—occurs throughout the life course (McPherson, 1990:141–143). Age is a determinant of how education, jobs, and other scarce resources and opportunities are allocated in society. Age stratification can limit roles and opportunities. Many people automatically assume that at age 14 a person should be in school; that at age 30 a person should be married; and that at age 65 a person should retire from full-time employment. Such perceptions about age may create problems for people in all age categories, but the problems typically are most pronounced among older people.

Workplace Discrimination

Despite the *Canadian Charter of Rights and Freedoms*, which protects all Canadians against discrimination based on many characteristics including age, many subtle forms of age discrimination in the workplace remain. Some employers prefer younger workers to older workers, whom they believe have health problems, poor motivation, and low ability. Employers may hire younger workers because they believe that they can pay them less than older workers and make more demands on their time and energy. Older employees sometimes find that their employers have downgraded their job descriptions, failed to promote them or grant them raises, or are trying to push them out of their jobs so that cheaper workers can be hired. McMullin and Marshall (1999) found that older workers have less power and authority in the workplace just because they are thought to be old.

Despite the negative stereotypes, some employers have found it profitable to keep or hire older employees, and some older employees are able to continue working. In 1998, 6 percent of Canadians over 64 years of age had a job, mostly in agricultural and religious occupations (Statistics Canada, 1999:88). In June 2002, Ontario Human Rights Commissioner Keith Norton said that governments should ban mandatory retirement at age 65 because it discriminates against people who are capable of working and who often need the money. He went on to predict that governments will

SOCIAL PROBLEMS AND SOCIAL POLICY

BOX 5.2   Euthanasia

According to Greek etymology, *euthanasia* means, literally, a "good death," and it comes in several types. *Passive euthanasia* means withholding or ceasing treatment of someone not likely to recover from a disease or injury. *Active euthanasia* means intervening to hasten someone's terminal illness, with, for example, a lethal dose of sedatives. *Assisted suicide* means helping someone end his or her life with, for example, drugs. Since advances in medical technology have made it possible to keep people alive longer than in the past, questions are arising about the best time and method of dying.

A number of high-profile cases, such as those of Sue Rodriguez and Robert Latimer, have highlighted the problems in this area. Sue Rodriguez was a 42-year-old woman suffering from ALS (Lou Gehrig's disease) who appealed all the way to the Supreme Court of Canada to have the legal right to have someone help her commit suicide when she wanted to die. In 1993, the Supreme Court decided against her, supporting the law prohibiting assisted suicide. Sue Rodriguez actually did die with the assistance of an unidentified doctor and Svend Robinson, an NDP MP from British Columbia. Robert Latimer administered a lethal dose of carbon monoxide gas to his daughter, Tracy, who suffered from severe cerebral palsy. He was accused of second-degree homicide. After his first trial, at which he was found guilty, the judge imposed a two-year sentence. This sentence was appealed to the Saskatchewan Court of Appeal, which sentenced Latimer to the mandatory penalty for second-degree homicide, life imprisonment with no chance of parole for 10 years. Later, in 2001, the Supreme Court of Canada refused to review that sentence.

An Angus Reid poll inquired about Canadians' attitude to the Latimer case and to mercy killing. This poll indicated that Canadians were very supportive of Latimer; almost three-quarters of them said that he acted out of compassion and should have received a more lenient sentence (Sallot, 1999: A5). It also found that Canadians are quite supportive of legalizing euthanasia: 41 percent said mercy killing should not be against the law under appropriate circumstances, 38 percent said it should be illegal, but perpetrators should be treated with leniency, and 18 percent said it should be treated like any other murder (2 percent had no opinion). Notably, the young (18 to 34 years of age) were slightly less lenient than older Canadians.

Some countries are making euthanasia legal. In April 2001, the Netherlands became the first country in the world to legalize euthanasia, and later that year, Belgium did the same. In Canada, much emphasis is put on individual rights, and the *Charter of Rights and Freedoms* supports this emphasis. Should we also have a right to die when and how we want to? With the increasing cost of health care, should we ever consider rationing health care so that younger people have more access to care than older people? Do you believe that Canada should legalize euthanasia? Do you think that young people might want to euthanize older relatives to make their own lives easier? If we do legalize euthanasia, what safeguards do you think should be imposed?

come under increasing pressure to protect those who wish to continue working after 65 (Mackie, 2002:A10). Still, at some point, retirement becomes an expected part of the life course.

Retirement and Changing Roles

The *retirement principle* is the "idea that at a fixed age, regardless of mental or physical ability, a person leaves work" (Novak, 1997:192). In the past, people in many occupations and professions (including tenured faculty members at universities, police officers, and fire fighters) faced mandatory retirement at age 65 regardless of their health or desire to continue working. It was simply assumed that everyone experienced a decline in physical and mental ability at a specific age. Changes in compulsory retirement laws have led many people to view retirement less as a sign of decline than as a new-found period of leisure and opportunity for adaptation, reflection, and contribution (see Peter Hare's quote at the end of this chapter). For some, however, adapting to less income, increased dependency, and the loss of roles and activities can be very difficult.

Today, women who are over 65 are less likely to have access to pension and Canada/Quebec Pension Plan (C/QPP) income in their own name than will younger women who are currently employed. Older women are usually worse off than men, and many

Retirement is a time for leisure and reflection if it comes by choice and the individual is healthy and financially prepared. But for others, adapting to less income, increased dependency, and the loss of roles can be difficult.

women live in a state of poverty (Gee and McDaniel, 1991). Because women have worked part-time, in traditional occupations, and experienced high rates of unemployment, the income they receive from the C/QPP may not be substantial (McDonald, 2000). Moreover, many employed women—as well as many men—are losing out on traditional pension coverage because of changes in the economy and the workplace. Many unionized industrial jobs that provided pension coverage have virtually disappeared, and more women than men are employed as part-time workers, who are less likely to have pension coverage than are full-time workers. In fact, companies rarely offer pension plans or health insurance to part-time, contingent, and temporary workers.

Health, Illness, and Health Care

At age 93, Malcolm Clarke plays doubles tennis four times a week and sails his boat; he also shops and cooks for himself (Brody, 1996). Although Clarke attributes his longevity and good health to "luck," studies show that many older people are not developing the disabling diseases that were common in the past, and the vast majority function quite well. Improvement in the health

status of older people has been attributed, at least in part, to better education (knowing what to do and not do to stay healthy), nutrition, and Medicare. As a result, most seniors living at home (78 percent) report that their health is good or very good, though 82 percent have a chronic condition like arthritis or rheumatism (Statistics Canada, 1999:8–9). They tend to think of themselves as in good health, all things considered.

About 7 of every 10 deaths among older people are due to heart disease, cancer, or respiratory illness. By far, the leading killer of persons over age 65 is heart disease, the cause of 30 percent of deaths in 1996. Cancer accounted for 26 percent, respiratory illness for 11 percent, and stroke for 9 percent (Statistics Canada, 1999:58).

People aged 65 and older account for about one-third of all dollars spent on health care, and this figure is expected to rise dramatically with the aging of the Canadian population. Many believe the cost problems associated with health care will be further intensified by the *feminization of aging*—the increasing proportion of older people who are female—because women, on average, have a greater likelihood of being poor and having no spouse to care for them (Weitz, 1996). However, some researchers state that dire predictions of skyrocketing costs are greatly overstated. Robert Evans and his colleagues (2001:160) report that numerous studies show that the effects of aging on health care costs are relatively small, and some suggest the "compression of morbidity" and falling needs among the elderly. Studies in British Columbia, for example, show minimal effects of population aging on health costs. Everybody—not just the elderly—is using more complex and costly services. The claims that the aging of the population will bankrupt the system, while having intuitive appeal, serve the interests of those who provide care and who wish to privatize parts of health care (Evans, McGrail, Morgan, Barer, and Hertzman, 2001:187).

Victimization

Although older people are in fact less likely than younger people to be victims of violent crime, they fear this type of crime more than people in other age categories do. In 1997, whereas the rate of death by homicide for those aged 25 to 44 was 2.6 per 100 000, it was 1.5 for seniors; and, whereas the rate of victimization by crime was

27 percent for those aged 25 to 44, it was 6 percent for seniors (Statistics Canada, 1999:114). According to police-reported statistics in 2000, older adults had the lowest risk of being a victim of violent crime, compared with other age groups. Adults aged 65 and over reported violent crime 2.5 times less frequently than those aged 55 to 64 years, the next lowest rate (Statistics Canada, 2002i). However, older people are often the targets of other types of crime. Con artists frequently contact them by mail or telephone to perpetrate scams that often promise prizes or involve a "stockbroker" selling a "hot" stock or other commodity (Hays, 1995). In 1998, CARP (Canadian Association for the Fifty-Plus) created a National Forum on Scams and Frauds, which produced recommendations such as: providing more information to seniors, instituting cooling-off periods for contracts, and freezing assets of scam artists. The appendix to the recommendations outlined Illinois law that makes defrauding a person of $5000 or more a more serious felony if the victim is over 60 years of age (CARP, 1998). Is this a positive kind of discrimination that Canadian lawmakers should consider?

Another form of victimization is elder abuse. According to the National Clearinghouse on Family Violence (cited in Novak, 1997:282), the abuse may be physical, psychosocial, financial, and/or neglect (active or passive). E. K. Podnieks and her colleagues conducted Canada's first random sample telephone survey of elder abuse and found that, in the late 1980s, 4 percent of Canadians (about 98 000) experienced abuse after turning 65 years of age (cited in Novak, 1997). In 2000, in cases where family members were the accused, 43 percent of older men were victimized by their adult children, while older women were almost as likely to be victimized by their spouses as by their adult children (Statistics Canada, 2002i).

Victims of elder abuse may be more vulnerable to complications resulting from physical violence than younger victims, since physical injuries may worsen pre-existing health problems or inhibit an older person's ability to function independently. In 2000, according to police statistics, 37 percent of older victims suffered minor injuries and 2 percent suffered major physical injuries or death from violent crimes committed by family members; 52 percent of older adult victims suffered no physical injuries (Statistics Canada, 2002i). Many analysts believe that elder abuse is underreported because people who know of the abuse are unwilling to report it and older people who are the victims are either too ashamed or afraid to notify authorities. Although some analysts initially believed that younger people were likely to exploit older people who were psychologically and economically dependent on them, just the opposite has often proven true: Younger people are more likely to exploit elders on whom they themselves are dependent (Novak, 1997:281).

Family Problems and Social Isolation

Older people can easily become socially isolated from their families. Younger family members who once asked for advice stop asking, perhaps because they think that their older relatives are out of touch or perhaps because of some miscommunication. Sometimes, younger family members feel unduly burdened by the concerns of their elders, which don't seem truly important to them. For one reason or another, older people can come to believe (rightly or wrongly) that they are isolated from the rest of the family.

In 1996, 29 percent of people aged 65 and above lived alone vs. 9 percent of people aged 15 to 64 (Statistics Canada, 1999:31). Many older people live alone voluntarily, but others live by themselves because they are divorced, widowed, or single. The 1996 General Social Survey showed that 75 percent of Canada's widows aged 65 and older live alone (Bess, 1999:2). Living alone is not the equivalent of social isolation. Many older people have networks of family and friends with whom they engage in activities. Contrary to the myth that older people are abandoned by their families, Canadian research has shown that most seniors live in a situation called "intimacy at a distance"—families usually provide much support for their older members (C. Rosenthal, 1987). For those without children, many ties are also formed (McMullin and Marshall, 1996). Many seniors also engage in volunteer work, as shown by Peter Hare's comment on page 122 and the work of Chappell (1999). To a large degree, the extent to which they associate with others has to do with social class: People with more money are able to pursue a wider array of activities and take more trips than are those with more limited resources.

Perhaps one of the saddest developments in contemporary society is the growing number of older people who are homeless. While some older homeless

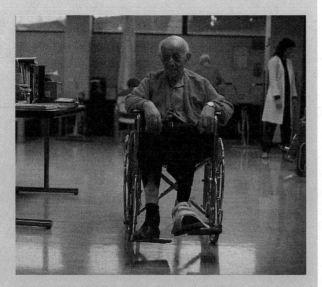

Although only about 7 percent of older people live in nursing homes or other long-term-care facilities in Canada, living in an institutional setting remains the only option for some older individuals. What alternative living arrangements can you suggest for older people in the future?

people have lived on the streets for many years, others have become homeless because they have been displaced from low-income housing such as single-room occupancy (SRO) hotels. In recent years, many SROs in cities such as Vancouver and Toronto have been replaced by high-rise office buildings, retail space, and luxury condominiums. Older people who are homeless typically lack nutritious food, appropriate clothing, adequate medical care, and a social support network. They tend to die prematurely of disease, crime victimization, accidents, and weather-related crises such as a winter blizzard, when an individual without shelter can freeze to death on a park bench. Fortunately, the picture is not this bleak for many older people who remain in residences they have occupied for many years.

Housing Patterns and Long-Term-Care Facilities

Many people mistakenly assume that most older people live in long-term-care facilities such as nursing homes. In fact, however, only about 7 percent of older people live in any kind of institution. In 1996, 93 percent lived at home in a private household (Statistics Canada,

1999b:30). More than people of any other age category, older people are likely to reside in the housing in which they have lived for a number of years and own free and clear of debt. Because of the high cost of utilities, insurance, taxes, and repairs and maintenance, older women, who are more likely to live alone than are older men (58 percent of women vs. 29 percent of men 85 years of age live alone—[Statistics Canada, 1999b:40]), are at a distinct disadvantage if they attempt to maintain their own homes.

Some low-income older people live in planned housing projects that are funded by federal and local government agencies or private organizations, such as religious groups. Older people with middle and upper incomes are more likely to live in retirement communities or in seniors' residences which provide amenities such as housekeeping, dining facilities, and transportation services. In recent years, religious organizations and for-profit corporations have developed *multilevel* facilities, which provide services ranging from independent living to skilled nursing care all at the same site.

Though only 7 percent of people aged 65 and older live in institutions, the percentage increases to almost 34 percent among people aged 85 and over (Statistics Canada, 1999b:47). Because of their greater life expectancy, higher rates of chronic illness, and higher rates of being unmarried, older women are disproportionately represented among the people who reside in institutions (Statistics Canada, 1999b:47). According to social gerontologists, the primary factors related to living in a nursing home are age (85 and over), being female, having been in the hospital recently, living in retirement housing, having no spouse at home, and having some cognitive or physical impairment that interferes with the activities of daily living (Greene and Ondrich, 1990).

While some nursing-home facilities may be excellent, others have undergone extensive media scrutiny and public criticism for violations of regulations and harmful practices such as elder abuse. As a result, many people select home care, adult day care, or assisted living for older relatives rather than institutional settings, which tend to depersonalize individuals and "reify the image of age as inevitable decline and deterioration" (Friedan, 1993:516). Home care is being seen now as a way to reduce costs in the health care system. Although home care has received increased resources in the past decade, problems of getting home care still exist (Segall and Chappell, 2000; and, see Chapter 10).

PERSPECTIVES ON AGING AND SOCIAL INEQUALITY

Although each of the major sociological perspectives focuses on different aspects of aging and social inequality, they all provide insights into how people view the aging process and how ageism contributes to social inequality in society.

The Functionalist Perspective

According to functionalists, dramatic changes in such social institutions as the family and religion have influenced how people look at the process of growing old. Given this, both the stability of society and the normal and healthy adjustment of older people require that they detach themselves from their social roles and prepare for their eventual death (Cumming and W.E. Henry, 1961). Referred to as *disengagement theory*, this theory suggests that older people want to be released from societal expectations of productivity and competitiveness. At the same time, disengagement facilitates a gradual and orderly transfer of statuses and roles from one generation to the next instead of an abrupt change, which might result in chaos. Retirement policies, then, are a means of ensuring that younger people with more up-to-date training (for example, computer skills) move into occupational roles while ensuring that older workers are recognized for years of service (Williamson, Rinehart, and Blank, 1992).

Critics of this perspective object to the assumption that disengagement is functional for society and that all older people want to disengage even when they are still productive and gain satisfaction from their work. In fact, according to some social analysts, disengagement as evidenced by early retirement policies has been dysfunctional for society. Some have suggested that C/QPP and other pension systems have been strained by the proportionately fewer workers who are paying into the plans, which must support an increasing number of retired workers. Contrary to disengagement theory, these analysts say, older people may disengage not by choice but because of a lack of opportunity for continued activity.

The Interactionist Perspective

Interactionist perspectives on aging and inequality focus on the relationship between life satisfaction and levels of activity. *The interactionist activity theory* is based on the assumption that older people who are active are happier and better adjusted than are less-active older persons. According to this theory, older people shift gears in late middle age and find meaningful substitutes for previous statuses, roles, and activities (Havighurst, Neugarten, and Tobin, 1968). Those who remain active have a higher level of life satisfaction than do those who are inactive or in ill health (Havighurst et al., 1968). In contrast to disengagement theory, activity theory suggests that older people must deny the existence of old age by maintaining middle-age lifestyles for as long as possible. But some older people are themselves critiquing this idea. According to an interview study conducted by Stephen Katz, some older people object to the idea that those preferring their inner world to being active are thought to be problem people. Katz (2000) suggests that this emphasis on activity could be transformed into a means of controlling older people.

Other interactionist perspectives focus on role and exchange theories. Role theory poses the question, What roles are available for older people? Some theorists note that industrialized, urbanized societies typically do not have roles for older people (Cowgill, 1986). Other theorists note that many older people find active roles within their own ethnic group. Although their experiences may not be valued in the larger society, they are esteemed within their ethnic subculture because they are a rich source of ethnic lore and history. According to sociologist Donald E. Gelfand (1994), older people can exchange their knowledge for deference and respect from younger people.

The Conflict Perspective

In analyzing the problems of older people in contemporary capitalistic societies, conflict theorists focus on the political economy of aging. From this perspective, class constitutes a structural barrier to older people's access to valued resources, and dominant groups attempt to maintain their own interests by perpetuating class inequalities. According to conflict theorists, aging itself is not the social problem. The problem is rooted in societal conditions that older people often face without adequate resources, such as income and housing. People who were poor and disadvantaged in their younger years become even more so in old age. However, a much smaller percentage of seniors live in a low-income situation now than as recently as two decades ago. Whereas in 1980, 34 percent of seniors had a low income (the Low Income Cut-Off [LICO] is discussed in Chapter 2), in 1997 that percentage had declined to 19 percent (Statistics Canada, 1999:100).

In the capitalist system, many older people are set apart as a group that depends on special policies and programs. Fortunately, in Canada, seniors do not have to depend on a special government program, such as the U.S. Medicare program, for health care (see Chapter 10). Canada's health program is universal. But it is under siege by those who would like to see greater privatization of services, who say among other things that seniors will bankrupt the system (Evans et al., 2001).

Conflict analysts draw attention to how class, gender, and racialization divide older people just as they do everyone else. The conflict perspective adds to our understanding of aging by focusing on how capitalism devalues older people, especially women. Critics assert, however, that this approach ignores the fact that industrialization and capitalism have been positive forces in society, greatly enhancing the longevity and quality of life for many older people.

The Feminist Perspective

Feminist theorists emphasize inequalities faced by senior women. Although women live longer than men, they are subject to higher rates of disability (see Chapter 10) and their incomes are lower. In 1997, whereas senior men's average income was $26 010, women's income was $16 070 (Statistics Canada, 1999:95). In addition, women were more likely than men (24 percent vs. 12 percent) to be in a low-income situation (Statistics Canada, 1999:100). Feminists argue that more attention should be paid to the health problems of women, as in the study done by the Ontario Women's Health Council to determine whether this difference in disability is alterable. Since later income inequality is obviously related to earlier income inequality, feminists argue that institutions that affect women earlier in the life course, such as school and employment should work to eliminate the inequality they generate.

CAN AGE-BASED INEQUALITY BE REDUCED?

As we have seen, technological innovations and advances in medicine have contributed to the steady increase in life expectancy in Canada. Advances in the diagnosis, prevention, and treatment of diseases associated with old age, such as Alzheimer's, may revolutionize people's feelings about growing older. Technology may bring about greater equality and freedom for older people (Novak, 1997:85). Home-based computer services, such as online banking and shopping, make it possible for older people to conduct their daily lives without having to leave home to obtain services. Computerized controls on appliances, lighting, and air conditioning make it possible for people with limited mobility to control their environment. Soon, sensing devices may be developed that could monitor a person's daily behaviour and report any deviation over the Internet to a concerned relative or central office. Technology also brings recreation and education into the home. For example, Senior Net is a nationwide computer network that encourages discussion of diverse topics and provides hands-on classes in computer use. Robotics and computer systems may eventually be used by frail older people who otherwise would have either to rely on family or paid caregivers to meet their needs or move to a nursing home. However, class is again a factor: While much of home care is covered by the health care system in Canada, many of the home accessibility features are paid for by users or their families.

Economic concerns loom large in the future as baby boomers (those born between 1946 and 1964) begin to retire in about 2010, bringing about a dramatic shift in the ***dependency ratio*—the number of workers necessary to support youth and those over age 64.** Instead of *five* workers supporting one retiree, *three* workers will be providing support for each retiree. Some American social analysts suggest that increased age-based inequality may bring about a "war" between the generations (Toner, 1995). Unlike in the American system, changes in the pension systems in Canada have brought about a decline in the number of low-income seniors without creating many high-income seniors (Myles, 2000:312–313) and, thus, fewer candidates for the epithet "greedy geezer." Moreover, the federal government has increased the pension contributions of current workers so that the plans will not go bankrupt. However, the wealth inequality could change in the future with the increased value of employment and personal (RRSP) retirement accounts going to the higher-income retirees. Advocates of *productive aging* suggest that instead of pitting young and old against each other, we should change our national policies and attitudes. We should encourage older people to continue or create their own roles in society, not to disengage from it. Real value should be placed on unpaid volunteer and caregiving activism, and settings should be provided in which older people can use their talents more productively (Hooyman and Kiyak, 1996).

In order to distribute time for family responsibilities and leisure more evenly throughout the life course, changes must occur in the workplace. Today, younger workers struggle to care for their families, without the support of employers in many cases, and leisure is associated with old age and "being put out to pasture." But people who have had no opportunity to engage in leisure activities earlier in their life are unlikely to suddenly become leisure-oriented. Employment, family responsibilities, and leisure must become less compartmentalized, and changes in technology and employment may make this possible. At present, however, it is difficult for most people to have *free time* and *money* at the same time.

Functionalists suggest that changes must occur in families and other social institutions if we are to resolve problems brought about by high rates of divorce, single-parent households, and cohabitation by unmarried couples, all of which tend to reduce the individual's commitment to meet the needs of other family members. These analysts argue that individuals must be socialized to care for an increasing number of living generations in their family and must be given economic incentives, such as tax breaks, for fulfilling their responsibility to children and older relatives. Because adult children may have to provide economic and emotional support for aging parents and grandparents at the same time as they are caring for their own children, more community services are needed, particularly for adult children who are "suitcase caregivers" for frail, elderly relatives living many miles away (Foreman, 1996). Communities should create or expand existing facilities such as day care centres for children and seniors, provide affordable housing, and build low-cost, community-based health facilities.

Other social analysts suggest that people need to rely more on themselves for their retirement and old age. Younger workers should be encouraged to save money for retirement in RRSPs. As conflict theorists have pointed out, however, many young people have loans to repay or do not have jobs or adequate income to meet their current economic needs, much less their future needs.

From the conflict perspective, age-based inequality is rooted in power differentials, and short of dramatic changes in the structure of political and economic power in society, the only way for older people to hold onto previous gains is through continued activism. Advocacy groups like CARP (Canadian Association for the Fifty-Plus) make presentations to government and hold forums (e.g., on scams and frauds) about policies that would benefit many older people. Nevertheless, older people as a category are devalued in a society that prizes youth over old age and in a social structure that defines productivity primarily in terms of paid employment.

According to interactionists, however, individuals who maintain strong relationships with others and remain actively involved throughout their lifetime have reason to be optimistic about life when they reach old age. An example is Peter Hare, past president of the Senior Alumni at the University of Toronto, who is doing a variety of volunteer work in his retirement:

> One topic that is important to people about to retire is the importance of continuing to be useful. I had been active in the UTAA (University of Toronto Alumni Association) and our local ratepayers association and retirement allowed me to be more active. I even added several environmental organizations. First the MetroToronto Solid Waste Environmental Assessment Program and later the RAP (clean water issues in the Toronto area). As a matter of fact, these activities increased my sense of contributing usefully to the community as I was no longer caught up in the "administrivia" of my former employment. (author's files)

WHAT CAN YOU DO?

- Study the amount of caregiving that your elderly relatives and those of your friends require.
- Volunteer for an agency that helps seniors in your neighbourhood. Helping a senior person may be as simple as listening to one on a regular basis.

- Since this chapter is also about other stages of the life course, you might also consider helping those at another stage. For example, Kids Help Phone is a national, bilingual, toll-free, 24-hour, confidential hotline that provides professional counselling, referrals, and Internet service for children and youth. It can be reached at 1-800-668-6868 or **www.kidshelp.sympatico.ca.** According to its Web site, this organization is looking for student and community ambassadors to raise funds or public awareness of its work.
- Set up a system of habits, such as exercise, recreational reading, and saving for retirement in an RRSP, to establish an activity pattern that will prepare you for later years.

- Help some seniors lobby for some improvements.
- Challenge some of the ageist stereotypes held by some young people. When one of the authors was showing a news clip about people over 80 years of age and their romantic interests, he heard sounds of disgust from the back of the classroom. You might start a discussion of ageism with questions about romantic expectations after 80. The vast majority of your age group will be there someday.
- Study the differences in problems currently faced by senior men and women. To what extent will these problems change as more women become more self-supporting?

SUMMARY

WHAT IS AGEISM AND WHY IS IT CONSIDERED A SOCIAL PROBLEM?

Ageism is prejudice and discrimination against people on the basis of age. Ageism is a social problem because it perpetuates negative stereotypes and age-based discrimination, particularly against older people.

WHAT IS THE LIFE COURSE AND WHY ARE DIFFERENT STAGES PROBLEMATIC FOR SOME PEOPLE?

The life course is generally divided into infancy and childhood, adolescence and young adulthood, middle age, later maturity, and old age. During infancy and childhood, we are dependent on other people and so relatively powerless in society. Adolescence is a stage in which we are not treated as children but nor are we afforded the full status of adulthood. In young adulthood, we acquire new roles and have a feeling of new freedom but also may have problems, ranging from alcohol and drug abuse to employment instability, that

may make life complicated. And we may continue to live at home. During middle age, we begin to show such visible signs of aging as wrinkles and grey hair, and roles begin to change in the workplace and family as children leave home. In later maturity, we increasingly find ourselves involved in caring for people of our own age and older people. Problems of older adults vary widely because of the diverse needs of the "young-old" (ages 65 to 74), the "middle-old" (ages 75 to 84), and the "old-old" (ages 85 and older).

WHAT TYPES OF PROBLEMS DO OLDER PEOPLE FACE TODAY?

Despite laws to the contrary, older workers may experience overt or covert discrimination in the workplace. Retirement brings about changing roles and a loss of status for those older people whose identity has been based primarily on their occupation. For some older people, low incomes, disease, and lack of health care or home care are problems. Older people may become the victims of scams by con artists and elder abuse by family members or nursing-home personnel. For some older people, moving into a nursing home represents a loss of autonomy.

HOW DO PEOPLE COPE WITH THE PROCESS OF DYING?

Three explanations have been given for how people cope with dying. Kübler-Ross identified five stages that people go through: (1) denial; (2) anger; (3) bargaining; (4) depression; and, (5) acceptance. However, the dying trajectory suggests that individuals do not move toward death at the same speed and in the same way. The task-based approach suggests that daily activities can still be enjoyed during the dying process and that fulfilling certain tasks makes the process of death easier, not just on the dying person, but on everyone involved.

HOW DO FUNCTIONALIST AND INTERACTIONIST EXPLANATIONS OF AGE-BASED INEQUALITY DIFFER?

According to functionalists, disengagement of older people from their jobs and other social positions may be functional for society because it allows the smooth transfer of roles from one generation to the next. However, interactionists suggest that activity is important for older people because it provides new sources of identity and satisfaction later in life.

HOW DO CONFLICT AND FEMINIST THEORISTS EXPLAIN INEQUALITY BASED ON AGE?

According to conflict theorists, aging itself is not a social problem. The problem is rooted in societal conditions that older people often face when they have inadequate resources in a capitalist society. In the capitalist system, older people are set apart as a group that depends on special policies and programs. Feminists argue that older men tend to be in a more advantageous social and economic position than older women. Since this disadvantage for women begins much earlier, institutions such as schools and businesses should work to eliminate the inequality they generate.

KEY TERMS

ageism,   p. 107
dependency ratio,   p. 121

hospice,   p. 115
social gerontology,   p. 108

QUESTIONS FOR CRITICAL THINKING

1.   If you were responsible for reducing ageism, what measures would you suggest to bring about greater equality? What resources would be required to fulfill your plan?

2.   Should retirement be compulsory for neuro-surgeons, airline pilots, police officers, firefighters, or other kinds of workers? Explain your answer.

3.   Does disengagement theory or activity theory more closely reflect how you plan to spend your later years? What other approaches to aging can you suggest?

4.   Think of synonyms, both formal and non-formal, for "senior," and look up the word *senior* in a thesaurus. How ageist are these synonyms? Make up new synonyms that are not ageist.

WEBLINKS

Health Canada Division of Aging and Seniors

www.hc-sc.gc.ca/seniors-aines

Health Canada's site for seniors provides regular updates from its Web sites to help seniors locate new services, publications, news releases, and articles.

National Children's Agenda

http://unionsociale.gc.ca/nca_e.html

This site provides a wide variety of reports and links about children and adolescents.

Canadian Centre for Activity and Aging

www.uwo.ca/actage

The Canadian Centre for Activity and Aging promotes an active and healthy lifestyle for Canadian adults.

Centre on Aging (University of Victoria)

www.coag.uvic.ca

The Centre on Aging at the University of Victoria is a multidisciplinary research centre. Other institutes that deal with seniors and/or the life course include **www.hc-sc.gc.ca/seniors-aines/seniors/english/ naca/naca.htm** (McGill University) and **www. utoronto.ca/lifecourse/** (University of Toronto).

Canadian Association of Gerontology

www.cagacg.ca

The Canadian Association of Gerontology is a national, multidisciplinary association designed to provide leadership on concerns related to aging.

6

INEQUALITY BASED ON SEXUAL ORIENTATION

The State has no business in the bedrooms of the nation.

Pierre Elliott Trudeau, Past Prime Minister of Canada, and Justice Minister in 1969

Ironically, where bisexuals are presumed to have access to heterosexual privilege, we are in fact, contending with both externalized and internalized homophobia and heterophobia, all at the same time.

Ruby Rowan, in "Sleeping With the Enemy and Liking It: Confessions of a Bisexual Feminist," 2001

I think a lot about the qualities and designs of the public spaces that I visit regularly. I want to believe that this sensitivity to my environment, verging on an obsession, is rooted in some deep well of creativity. But my narratives of design and redesign are also part of a twentieth-century Canadian fag thing. I note escape routes from possible violence. I seek out screens for privacy and to avoid more obvious forms of hostility. I covet sites in which to have fun with my friends (new and old), natural stages on which to see and be seen. I am especially interested in the places where I find new forms of communality, which often is obscured by archaic notions of community.

Gordon Brent Ingram, in Redesigning Wreck: Beach Meets Forest as Location of Male Homoerotic Culture and Placemaking in Pacific Canada, *2001*

Therefore, neither "lesbian" nor the more inclusive "queer" may be the way some choose to describe their identity or their practices, not because these terms are not plural enough to include, let's say, people of colour, but because the categories "lesbian" and "queer," when not qualified, presume a subject who is white, middle class, Euro-North American . . . in an era that demands and is engulfed by notions of globalization, categories such as "lesbian" and "queer" cannot be transposed to other nations without calling into question the very categories themselves.

Didi Khayatt, from her Addendum to Kathleen Martindale's What Makes Lesbianism Thinkable? Theorizing Lesbianism from Adrienne Rich to Queer Theory, *2001*

The opening quotations give us a sample of the diversity of issues confronted by and discussed by those interested in the question of sexual orientation in our culture and beyond. This chapter will examine many issues that face us today with regard to sexual orientation. We will look at the extent of homosexuality and bisexuality and homophobia and biphobia in Canada, beginning with the definitions of various sexual orientations.

We will try to understand how and why prejudice and discrimination against people based on sexual orientation can happen in Canadian society, a society that prides itself on it high levels of "tolerance" *and* "acceptance." We will review some of the laws regarding sexual orientation and look at hate crimes, specifically, and ways they are being dealt with. Finally, we will review several theories that pertain to sexual orientation and discrimination and consider ways we can advocate for social change

***Sexual orientation* refers to a preference for emotional–sexual relationships with individuals of the "same" sex (homosexuality), the "opposite" sex (heterosexuality), or both (bisexuality)** (Lips, 1993). The terms *homosexual* and *gay* are most often used in association with males who prefer "same"-sex relationships; the term *lesbian* is used in association with females who prefer "same"-sex relationships. Heterosexual individuals, or those who prefer "opposite"-sex relationships, are sometimes referred to as *straight* (e.g., "Have you always been straight?"). It is important to note, however, that heterosexual people are much less likely to be labelled by their sexual orientation than are people who are gay, lesbian, or bisexual, because their heterosexuality is presumed normal and is taken for granted. We will discuss this presumption of normalcy later in the chapter when we discuss heterosexual privilege. It is also important to note that although, in lay terms, we talk about the "opposite" sex, there are, biologically, physiologically, cognitively, and emotionally, very few differences between males and females. In effect, there is no such thing as an "opposite" sex. The myth of the opposite sex is one of the most persistent and foundational binaries we adhere to in our culture.

What criteria do social scientists use to classify individuals as gay, lesbian, or bisexual? In a foundational study of sexuality published in the mid-1990s, researchers at the University of Chicago established three criteria for identifying people as homosexual or bisexual: (1) *sexual attraction* to persons of one's own gender, (2) *sexual involvement* with one or more persons of one's own gender, and (3) *self-identification* as a gay man, lesbian, or bisexual (Michael et al., 1994). According to these criteria, then, engaging in a homosexual act does not necessarily classify a person as homosexual. Many participants in the Chicago study indicated that although they had *at least* one homosexual encounter when they were younger, they no longer were involved in homosexual conduct and never identified themselves as lesbians, bisexuals, or gay. In fact, self-definition plays a critical role in confounding attempts to classify people definitively. For example, many people who engage in same-sex acts, on an occasional or even regular basis, may not perceive themselves as homosexual or bisexual at all.

NATURE AND EXTENT OF INEQUALITY BASED ON SEXUAL ORIENTATION

How many homosexuals and bisexuals are there in Canada? The 2001 Canadian Census was the very first Canadian Census to ask questions specifically about same-sex couples. The Census reports that 34 200 Canadian couples, or one-half of one percent of all couples, claim same-sex common-law status (Statistics Canada, 2002v). Researchers caution, however, that these numbers may be quite low in relation to the actual number of same-sex couples in Canada—especially as they are from the first Census to explore this area—and that they should be used only as a baseline: a starting point. Indeed, researchers for Status of Women Canada Irene Demczuk, Michele Caron, Ruth Rose, and Lynne Bouchard (2002:viii) state, in the report from their recent research of Canadian lesbians, that "to this day, most lesbian couples still hide their sexual orientation and their conjugal situation, especially in the workplace, in order to protect themselves against the negative reactions of those around them." Jerome Ryckborst, a Vancouver writer, described the conflict that many gay and lesbian Canadians had to grapple with when faced with reporting, in essence, sexual orientation to the Canadian government: "It does feel risky . . . but the need for our community to grow up, stand up and be counted, outweighs the personal concerns" (Anderssen, 2002:A9). Fifty-five percent of reported same-sex couples are male and only 3 percent of these couples had children living with them. In contrast and in keeping with gender socialization norms and typical post-divorce custody arrangements in Canada, 15 percent of the 15 200 female couples had children living with them; female couples were five times more likely than male couples to have children living with them (Statistics Canada, 2002v).

While we now have a count, however inaccurate, of same-sex common-law couples in Canada, the Census has yet to count people according to their sexual orientation. Most estimates of the homosexual population state that at least 10 percent of the population engages primarily in same-sex relationships. An even higher percentage is estimated to be bisexual, as high as 25 percent of the population (Maugh, 1990; Weinberg et al., 1994). There are various reasons, mainly connected with living in a homophobic culture, for why people in Canada may keep information about their homosexuality or bisexuality unannounced.

Homosexuality has existed in most, if not all, societies throughout human history. Tolerance and acceptance of homosexuality and bisexuality exist along a continuum. Most tribal societies regard some homosexual acts as socially acceptable at least some of the time. For example, some cultures, such as the Siwans, the Azande, the Dahomy, and the !Kung of Africa and the Sambians of New Guinea regard same-sex relations as a "normal" part of maturing (Blackwood, 1986). In contrast, for most of the last two thousand years, there have been groups—sometimes entire societies—that considered homosexuality "a crime against nature," "an abomination," or "a sin" (Doyle, 1995:224). In any case, most societies have norms pertaining to *sexuality*—**attitudes, beliefs, and practices related to sexual attraction and intimate relationships with others.** The norms are based on the assumption that some forms of attraction and sexual relationships are *normal* and *appropriate* while others are *abnormal* and *inappropriate*. In many societies, including modern North American and European societies, homosexual conduct has been classified as a form of *deviance*—**a behaviour, belief, or condition that violates social norms.** This classification may make people targets of prejudice, discrimination, and even death. Extreme prejudice toward gay men and lesbians is known as *homophobia*—**the irrational and excessive fear or intolerance of homosexuals and homosexuality.** Additionally, *biphobia* **refers to fear and intolerance of bisexuals and bisexual lifestyles.** According to sociologists, homophobia and biphobia are actually *socially determined prejudices,* not medically recognized *phobias* (Lehne, 1995; Wilton, 2000). Homophobia and biphobia are intensified by the ideology of *compulsory*

TABLE 6.1   The Heterosexual Questionnaire

1. What do you think caused your heterosexuality?

2. When and how did you decide you were a heterosexual?

3. Is it possible that your heterosexuality is just a phase you may grow out of?

4. Is it possible that your heterosexuality stems from a neurotic fear of others of the same sex?

5. If you have never slept with a person of the same sex, is it possible that all you need is a good gay lover?

6. Do your parents know that you are straight? Do your friends and/or roommate(s) know? How did they react?

7. Why do you insist on flaunting your heterosexuality? Can't you just be who you are and keep it quiet?

8. Why do heterosexuals place so much emphasis on sex?

9. Why do heterosexuals feel compelled to seduce others into their lifestyle?

10. A disproportionate majority of child molesters are heterosexual. Do you consider it safe to expose children to heterosexual teachers?

11. Just what do men and women *do* in bed together? How can they truly know how to please each other, being so anatomically different?

12. With all the societal support marriage receives, the divorce rate is spiraling. Why are there so few stable relationships among heterosexuals?

13. Statistics show that lesbians have the lowest incidence of sexually transmitted diseases. Is it really safe for a woman to maintain a heterosexual lifestyle and run the risk of disease and pregnancy?

14. How can you become a whole person if you limit yourself to compulsive, exclusive, heterosexuality?

15. Considering the menace of overpopulation, how could humanity survive if everyone were heterosexual?

16. Could you trust a heterosexual therapist to be objective? Don't you feel s/he might be inclined to influence you in the direction of his/her own leanings?

17. There seem to be very few happy heterosexuals. Techniques have been developed that might enable you to change if you really want to. Have you considered trying aversion therapy?

18. Would you want your child to be heterosexual, knowing the problems that s/he would face?

Source: From "The Language of Sex: The Heterosexual Questionnaire," Changing Men (Spring 1982). Attributed to Martin Rochlin, West Hollywood, CA.

heterosexism, a belief system that offers no options for behaviour or feelings but heterosexuality and denies, denigrates, and stigmatizes any gay, lesbian, or bisexual behaviour, identity, relationships, or community. Somewhat like institutional racism and sexism, compulsory heterosexism is embedded in a society's social structure and maintained by ideologies that are rooted in religion and law (Herek, 1995). **Heterosexism is the belief that heterosexuality is the only normal, natural, and moral mode of relating, and hence is superior to homosexuality or bisexuality** (Wilton, 2000).

IDEOLOGICAL BASES OF INEQUALITY BASED ON SEXUAL ORIENTATION

Social analysts such as Bruce Bawer (1994:81), an author and cultural critic, believe that homophobia differs significantly from other forms of bigotry:

In a world of prejudice, there is no other prejudice quite like [homophobia]. Mainstream writers, politicians, and cultural leaders who hate Jews or blacks or Asians but who have long since accepted the unwritten rules that forbid public expression of those prejudices still denounce gays with impunity. For such people, gays are the Other in a way that Jews or blacks or Asians are not. After all, they can look at Jewish or black or Asian family life and see something that, in its chief components—husband, wife, children, workplace, school, house of worship—is essentially a variation of their own lives; yet when they look at gays—or, rather, at the image of gays that has been fostered both by the mainstream culture and by the gay subculture—they see creatures whose lives seem to be different from theirs in every possible way.

According to Bawer, heterosexuals cannot identify with the daily lives of lesbians and gay men, who—unlike them—exist as identifiable categories primarily because there is such strong antigay prejudice in

Canada. In fact, the stereotypical beliefs that dominant (heterosexual) group members hold about gay men and lesbians are a major impediment to achieving equal rights for gays and lesbians and reducing inequalities based on sexual orientation (Nava and Dawidoff, 1994).

Stereotypical beliefs about lesbians and gay men often equate people's sexual *orientation* with sexual *practice*. For example, all gay men and lesbians—regardless of the nature and extent of their sexual activity—are stereotyped as "sex obsessed, sexually compulsive, and sexually predatory" (Nava and Dawidoff, 1994:32). Media depictions tend to reinforce stereotypes of gay men as sexual exploiters or "limp-wristed sissies," while lesbians are "stomping macho soldiers" who hate men (Nava and Dawidoff, 1994:32; Wilton, 2000). Recently, television shows such as *Will and Grace* have sought to bring gay lifestyles into prime-time programming. Although some shows have perpetuated negative stereotypes about lesbians and gay men, others, like *Will and Grace* and *Ellen*, while it was allowed to be aired, have attempted, with limited success, to change public perceptions about issues related to sexual orientation.

Religion and Sexual Orientation

The major difference between homophobia and biphobia and other forms of discrimination such as sexism or racism is that many people believe that homosexuality or bisexuality is morally wrong. These beliefs are often, although not always, linked to religious affiliation. For example, health researcher Tamsin Wilton (2000:9) cites a strong association found by many researchers between homophobic and biphobic attitudes and strong religious beliefs. Some people use their religious affiliation as a way of reinforcing their existing prejudices against gays and lesbians while others interpret their religious doctrines as genuinely forbidding same-sex relations (Wilton, 2000:9). Most of the major religions of the world—Judaism, Christianity, Islam, and Hinduism, as well as Confucianism—have historically regarded homosexuality as a sin. Indeed, the only major world religion that does not condemn homosexuality is Buddhism (Dynes, 1990). This is not to suggest, in any way, that all, or even most, practicing religious people are homophobic, only that most of the major religions provide justifications for homophobia, should people want them. Religious fundamentalists in particular

denounce homosexual conduct as a sign of great moral decay and societal chaos. In the Judeo-Christian tradition, religious condemnation of homosexuality derives from both the Hebrew Scriptures (e.g., Genesis 19 and Leviticus 18:33) and the New Testament (e.g., Romans 1:26–27 and I Corinthians 6:9) (Kosmin and Lachman, 1993).

Since the early 1990s, same-sex marriages and the ordination of "practicing" lesbians and gay men have been vigorously debated by various religious organizations. For example, the Vatican has directed Roman Catholic bishops in Canada and elsewhere to oppose laws that protect homosexuals, promote public acceptance of homosexual conduct, or give gay relationships equal footing with traditional, heterosexual marriage. However, many Roman Catholics disagree with the directive, stating that it is based on the faulty assumption that lesbians and gay men seek to influence the sexual orientation of children or youths with whom they live or work, that gay people are erotically attracted to every person of their own gender, and that they cannot control their sexual impulses in same-sex environments (cited in Bawer, 1994). Roman Catholics are not the only religious group debating same-sex marriage and the ordination of lesbians and gay men: Recently, in Toronto, the outgoing Anglican Archbishop of Canterbury stated that, while it is permissible for homosexuals to be church members, it is not permissible for them to be ordained nor to have their unions blessed by the Church. His views are in contrast to those of his successor, who has already ordained a practicing gay priest, and of the current Anglican Bishop in Vancouver, who has been blessing the same-sex unions of his homosexual parishioners (Valpy, 2002:A8).

Episcopalians have been debating for two decades whether or not "practicing homosexuals" should be ordained. In 1996, an Episcopal bishop was accused of heresy for ordaining a gay deacon (Niebuhr, 1996; Dunlap, 1996). Other Canadian churches, like the United Church of Canada, have declared that all people, regardless of sexual orientation, are entitled to become full members of the church, including the right to become ordained ministers.

Still, increasing numbers of lesbians and gay men are carving out their own niches in religious organizations. Some gay men and lesbians have sought to bring about changes in established religious denominations; others have formed religious bodies, such as the

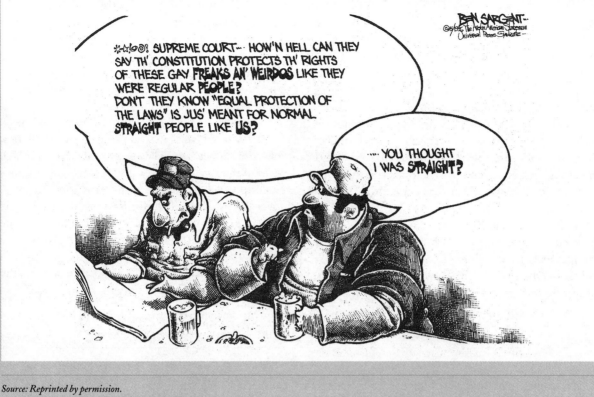

Source: Reprinted by permission.

Metropolitan Community Church, that focus on the spiritual needs of the gay community. Even so, many gay men and lesbians believe that they should not have to choose between full participation in their church and a committed same-sex relationship (Dunlap, 1996).

Law and Sexual Orientation

However divided Canadians are in their opinions of how many and what kinds of rights gays and lesbians should be afforded in Canadian society, both tolerance and acceptance of homosexual and bisexual lifestyles have increased in Canada in past decades. Canadian citizens are much more tolerant of homosexual and bisexual relations than are U.S. citizens, although the majority of people in both countries believe that, with regard to employment, there should be no discrimination on the basis of sexual orientation. In a 1996 Gallup Poll, 60 percent of Canadians said they believed that homosexuality was an acceptable alternative lifestyle compared with 44 percent of people in the U.S.

Similarly, 64 percent of Canadians believed that consensual homosexual acts between adults should be legal, while 48 percent of people in the U.S. agreed.

Over the past four decades, Canadians have witnessed, first, the decriminalization of sexual practices associated with same-sex relations; second, the inclusion of sexual orientation as a prohibited ground in human rights legislation; and, third, the enactment of federal and provincial legislation aimed at conferring rights on same-sex couples (Demczuk et al., 2002:viii). Therefore, currently in Canada, discrimination on the basis of sexual orientation is prohibited everywhere but in Nunavut. In Alberta, the provincial legislation deliberately omits sexual orientation as a prohibited ground for discrimination; however, the Supreme Court of Canada stated in an April 1998 case (*Vriend v. Alberta*) that Alberta's human rights legislation would be *interpreted* as including sexual orientation as a prohibited ground for discrimination, whether the legislation specifically stated this or not, in order to bring Alberta's legislation into line with that of the rest of the provinces and territories.

These advances have been diligently pushed for and won by gay, lesbian, bisexual, and queer advocates, mainly through successful legal challenges and not, as Demczuk et al. (2002:viii) point out, through "the expression of any political will on the part of the federal [territorial] and provincial governments to systematically eliminate discrimination."

In the late 1960s, the Canadian government debated many much-needed reforms to the Criminal Code, in order to make it more reflective of current and changing Canadian values and practices. In a 1969 omnibus bill, sexual acts that were committed between consenting adults fell within the parameters of individual freedoms, and so, many sexual practices, some believed to be associated with homosexuality—for example anal sex, or "sodomy"—were decriminalized. It still took until 1977 for the federal government to do away with the immigration regulation prohibiting homosexuals from immigrating to Canada.

> The 1969 Act . . . did not represent "a legalization of homosexuality," but rather a partial decriminalization of certain sexual practices that were not limited to homosexuals but were often associated with them. Beyond these changes to the Criminal Code, violence, discrimination in employment, police harassment and distinctions in terms of conjugality continued to exist with impunity. (Demczuk et al., 2002:6)

In the 1960s, the United Nations adopted the Universal Declaration of Human Rights. As a liberal democracy, Canada was obligated to both respect this and similar declarations and to make illegal any government acts that infringe on people's individual rights. Along with the federal government, most provinces also enacted their own human rights legislation in the late 1960s and early 1970s. When Canada repatriated its Constitution in 1982, the *Canadian Charter of Rights and Freedoms* gained ascendancy, and its Section 15 provided a vehicle for disenfranchised groups to seek remedy through court challenges. Section 15(1) of the *Charter* reads:

> Every individual is equal before and under the law and has the right to the equal protection and equal benefit of the law without discrimination and, in particular, without discrimination based on race, national or ethnic origin, colour, religion, sex, age, or mental or physical disability.

In 1977, Quebec became the first province to include sexual orientation as a prohibited ground of discrimination in its provincial human rights legislation. Ontario followed, 9 years later, but it still took 21 years, and the *Vriend* decision, for sexual orientation to be extended as a prohibited ground in all Canadian provinces and territories.

Throughout the 1980s and 1990s, through legal challenges about pensions, bereavement leaves, alimony, and various other family-law issues, individuals pushed, with varying levels of success, for recognition of same-sex couples as analogous to heterosexual couples. Governments continued to make case-by-case decisions, in several cases insisting that the decisions be non–precedent setting and that they be given more time to integrate the rights of minority groups into existing law. Finally, in the *Vriend v. Alberta* case, the Supreme Court of Canada stated:

> The need for government incrementalism was an inappropriate justification for *Charter* violations. . . . In my opinion, groups that have historically been the target of discrimination cannot be expected to wait patiently for the protection of their human dignity and equal rights while governments move toward reform one step at a time. If the infringement of the rights and freedoms of these groups is permitted to persist while governments fail to pursue equality diligently, then the guarantees of the *Charter* will be reduced to little more than empty words. (*Vriend v. Alberta* 1998. S.C.R. 493, paragraph 122, cited in Demczuk et al., 2002:17)

One year later, following a Supreme Court ruling that making distinctions between heterosexual couples and homosexual couples is unconstitutional, several provincial governments amended their Family Law Acts to include provision for same-sex couples by changing the definition of "spouse." The first to make these changes were British Columbia, Quebec, and Ontario in 1999 and Nova Scotia in 2000. For example, in Quebec, the first Canadian province to allow same-sex partners the same benefits and responsibilities as heterosexual partners, Bill 32 committed the government to making changes to 39 provincial laws, including the Quebec Pension Plan, automobile and prescription-drug insurance, legal aid, low-cost housing, child and child-care benefits, financial assistance, student assistance programs, taxation, tax credits, RSPs, employee

Same-sex couples in British Columbia, Ontario, and Quebec have challenged Canada's marriage laws. In January 2001, two same-sex couples were married in a double wedding ceremony at the Metropolitan Community Church in Toronto. To date, the Ontario government has refused to register the marriages, and neither the provincial nor the federal government has been willing to recognize their legal validity.

the law prohibiting same-sex marriages is unconstitutional. The Government of Canada was appealing the ruling but on June 17th, 2003, on the recommendation of Federal Justice Minister Martin Cauchon, Prime Minister Chrétien announced that the Federal Government would no longer engage in the legal battle and would support marriage for gays and lesbians across Canada. This marks Canada as the third country in the world to legalize same-sex marriage. The Prime Minister said that his government will:

- draft legislation aligned with the common-law definition of marriage that came into effect on June 10, 2003;
- protect faith communities from having to perform any marriage that does not conform to religious values;
- seek approval from the Supreme Court of Canada, to ensure that the marriage law complies with the *Charter*, and that it is applicable to all provinces and territories; and
- introduce the new law in Parliament's next session (September 2003) for a "free vote."

As recently as June of 1999, members of the Canadian House of Commons voted overwhelmingly to oppose same-sex marriage. However, following Chrétien's statement, and much earlier, the inclusion of sexual orientation as a protected ground in the *Canadian Charter of Rights and Freedoms*, advocates will continue to challenge all provinces to expedite marriage for gay and lesbian Canadians.

Meanwhile, attempts by same-sex couples to be viewed as analogous to heterosexual couples have inspired debate within gay and lesbian communities. Many people, citing the many, many financial, personal, and social benefits of public recognition, view inclusion as a great, progressive stride forward. Others are more wary; they propose that the inclusion of gays and lesbians in patriarchal institutions such as marriage and in other heterosexual institutions—the church, the police, the military, and so on—will increase the legitimacy of these fundamentally hierarchical models and disperse the potential for more radical social change. Still others suggest that the inclusion of homosexual couples in definitions of "family" and "marriage" and the like will act to destabilize those definitions and categories, perhaps fundamentally and radically altering

retirement plans, health insurance, and so on (Demczuk et al., 2002; Mooney et al., 2001). In British Columbia, through the Definition of Spouse Amendment, same-sex partners who have "lived and cohabitated with another person, for a period of at least two years . . . in a marriage-like relationship, including a marriage-like relationship between persons of the same gender" have all the rights and responsibilities of heterosexual couples, including the right to inherit if a partner dies without a will, the right to inherit property and pensions, and the right to apply to adopt a child together (Mooney et al., 2001:292).

Most provinces now include provisions for same-sex couples, and as of June 2003, same-sex couples can legally marry in Ontario and since July 2003, can legally marry in British Columbia. However, many advocates believe that until same-sex couples are granted the right to legally marry, across Canada, they will not be viewed by society as legitimate and will continue to be disenfranchised from some of the financial and many of the social benefits—such as holding hands in public, bringing one's spouse to the company picnic, having one's partnership recognized by one's parents as more than a "phase" one is going through, etc.—enjoyed by heterosexual spouses. In July 2002, two men who married in a church ceremony but were denied a marriage licence by the Ontario provincial government took their case to court. Three Ontario Superior Court judges ruled that

SOCIAL PROBLEMS AND SOCIAL POLICY

BOX 6.1   Coming Out: Risky Business in a Homophobic Culture

In line with most social psychological models of identity formation, psychologist Jean Baker (2001:45) states that coming out is a "complex discovery process that children or adolescents go through as they gradually recognize their homosexual identity and acknowledge it to themselves and then to others." Unlike homosexuals or even bisexuals, heterosexuals have no such process to undergo. As a member of the group that is the norm, or cultural standard, they learn from a very early age what social work researcher Janet Sawyer (1989) calls "internalized dominance." Internalized dominance refers to all the messages, overt and otherwise, that signify to White people or straight people or people with no disabilities or men that they are normal; they are the standard; they are acceptable just being who they are. They are in no way "other," as people of colour or Indigenous people are; as women are; as sexual minorities are; as people with disabilities are. One of the privileges of being part of the dominant group is the privilege of never having to consider how a fundamental aspect of your self—your sexual orientation, for example—impacts on your life. Contrast this with people who belong to a marginalized group, and it is easy to see that people in marginalized groups must, at least potentially, deal with or consider their status every day. They must consider how being openly gay or lesbian will impact their job search or apartment search or family holiday or grade in a class. Will it get them verbally or physically harassed or assaulted today?

Baker (2001:46) notes that "coming to terms with one's homosexual identity is a developmental task required of the gay child but one for which he or she receives little guidance and for which successful role models are seldom available." Taking a slightly different approach than Baker, political theorist and GLBT (gay, lesbian, bisexual, and transgender) activist Mark

Blasius (2001a:155), in a discussion of an "ethos" of gay and lesbian existence, believes that coming out is a multifaceted and lifelong process. Blasius believes that coming out, the goal of which is to live one's life as a lesbian or gay man, is not just about disclosure of one's gay or lesbian identity to one's self and others: "Rather than being an end-state in which one exists as an 'out' person, coming out is a process of becoming, a lifelong learning of how to become and of inventing the meaning of being a lesbian or a gay man in this historical moment." Coming out, thus, refers both to "an ontological recognition of the self by the self" and a "fundamental political act" (Blasius, 2001a:155).

Defining oneself as gay or lesbian can have serious consequences for youth. One survey of gay youth found that 30 percent of those identifying themselves as homosexual had attempted suicide in the past year compared with 7 percent of those identifying themselves as heterosexual (Platt, 2001, in Mooney et al., 2003). One-quarter of homosexual youth drop out of school and 40 percent report that their performance at school has been negatively affected by conflicts around sexual orientation (Mooney et al., 2003). A Calgary, Alberta, study found that gay and bisexual males were nearly 14 times more likely to have seriously attempted suicide than heterosexual males were (Mooney et al., 2003). This study also demonstrated that non-heterosexual youth of colour (lesbians, gay males, and bisexuals) were "dramatically overrepresented in the attempted-suicide statistics" (Fisher, 1999, in Mooney et al., 2003). There is evidence today that gay, lesbian, and bisexual youth are coming out at earlier ages than in the past (Baker, 2001).

What do you think should be done to decrease the numbers of suicides and attempted suicides among non-heterosexual youth?

---

them for the betterment of all persons (Blasius, 2001b; Currah, 2001; Gamson, 1996; Goldie, 2001). This debate mirrors the debate waged between those who use the term "queer" politically—as an essentialist category, to describe themselves, to be recognized and valued for who they are, and to be included as an equal with the rest of society—and those who use the term "queer" more theoretically—as a destabilizing entity, a descriptor only in that it implies non-mainstream but refuses to define, in any essential way, what "queer" is or is not. This debate will be discussed in more detail later in the chapter.

DISCRIMINATION BASED ON SEXUAL ORIENTATION

As the campaigns for equal rights and an end to anti-gay discrimination have progressed, more people have come forward to declare that they are gay, lesbian, or bisexual and to indicate their support for gay organizations. Many lesbian or gay couples have sought the statutory right to marry, to obtain custody of their children if they are divorced or separated, to adopt, and to have their property pass to one another at death—in sum, to do all the things that people in heterosexual marriages are permitted to do. However, largely because ideas about marriage and the family are at the core of many people's moral or religious objections to homosexuality, gay marriage is still among the most controversial social issues as we begin the 21st century.

Lack of Marital Rights

In Canada, many gay and lesbian couples chose to cohabit because they were prevented from entering legally recognized marital relationships. In *cohabitation*, partners live together without being legally married. Many gay men and lesbians have taken part in social or religious marriage ceremonies because their unions were not legally sanctioned by the state.

New legal changes notwithstanding, over the past decade, some provinces had given legal recognition to the concept of a ***domestic partnership***—**a partnership in which an unmarried couple lives together in a committed relationship and is granted many of the same legal rights and benefits accorded to a married couple** (Aulette, 1994). Many gay-rights advocates consider recognition of domestic partnerships a major step forward because it has meant that partners of unmarried employees are eligible for the same employment benefits—including medical plan coverage—that are offered to legal spouses (those in heterosexual marriages). In this way, domestic partnership agreements benefit all unmarried cohabiting couples, gay and straight. As discussed earlier in this chapter, gay rights advocates continue to fight for legal recognition of same-sex marriages.

Parental Rights

There could be as many as 444 000 Canadian families headed by lesbian or gay parents (Mooney et al., 2001:294). According to the most recent Census, lesbian couples are five times more likely to have children living with them than are gay male couples. Sometimes, when a gay father or lesbian mother has previously had a child with an opposite-sex partner, the other biological parent seeks custody of the child on the grounds that the lesbian or gay parent is "unfit" because of sexual orientation. In several widely publicized cases, lesbian mothers lost custody of their children when their fitness was challenged in court by ex-spouses or the children's grandparents (Gover, 1996a). Gay fathers sometimes face double jeopardy in child-custody struggles: Both their sexual orientation and the widespread belief that women make better parents may work against them (Gover, 1996a).

Parental rights are a pressing concern for gay or lesbian partners who are raising children together, particularly when only one partner is legally recognized as the parent or guardian. Many couples rely on legal documents such as special powers of attorney, wills, and guardianship agreements to protect both partners' rights, but these documents do not have the legal force of formal adoption (Bruni, 1996). As more lesbian couples choose donor insemination to become parents, issues arise about the rights of non-biological gay parents, whose claims often are the least recognized (Gover, 1996c). In recent court custody cases, the non-biological parent has had no standing, because he or she has neither biological nor legal ties to the child. Some lesbian and gay couples draft their own parenting contracts, but for the most part, these agreements are not enforceable in court and can be revoked by the biological parent at any time (Gover, 1996c). As more provinces allow unmarried partners—whether gay or straight—to adopt children, more same-sex couples will probably seek joint legal custody of their children. However, the process is extremely time consuming and expensive and involves an invasion of personal privacy (Bruni, 1996).

Many gay men and lesbians experience discrimination when they seek to become foster parents or to adopt a child. Widespread myths about the "homosexual lifestyle" lead to the notion that children living with lesbian or gay parents may witness immoral conduct or be recruited into homosexuality (Singer and Deschamps, 1994). Further, while nothing in current Canadian law prevents a gay or lesbian person from applying for custody or adoption of children, "the courts will often only take judicial notice . . . of the fact that some harm might arise from living with a homosexual parent" (Yogis et al., 1996:56). Therefore, Canadian legal decisions against homosexual parenting have been fraught with wording about protecting children from "people of abnormal tastes and proclivities" and "unnatural relationships" (cited in Mooney et al., 2001:295). In fact, research shows that children raised by lesbian or gay parents typically are well adjusted, and the parents often serve as role models for equal sharing in the family (Sullivan, 1996).

Gay rights advocates are cautiously optimistic that social norms and laws are gradually changing. They hope that in time sexual orientation alone will not be grounds for denying parental custody or visitation rights to lesbian or gay parents and that courts will rule solely on the basis of which parent can provide a better home for the child (Goldberg, 1996).

Housing Discrimination

Some lesbian and gay people are denied housing because they are gay; others are evicted from apartments where they have lived for some period of time, although reasons other than sexual orientation are usually given by landlords in order to avoid being the recipient of a human rights complaint. Even those who successfully rent or purchase property tend to remain targets of discrimination from some heterosexual residents, building managers, and custodial personnel, as Bruce Bawer (1994:254) explains:

> When two gay people decide to move in together, they commit themselves to insult and discrimination and attack. At one apartment building in which [a male partner] and I lived, the superintendent spit on me one day without provocation; at our next address, members of the building staff, not knowing that I understood Spanish, joked with one another in my presence about the maricones (faggots). Living alone, most gay people can conceal their sexuality; living together, a gay couple advertises theirs every time they step out of the house together.

Discrimination in Medical Care

Lesbians, gay men and bisexuals often receive substandard or intolerant health care because of their sexual orientation. Examples are ostracism, mistreatment of partners, breached confidence, and derogatory remarks (Spafford et al., 2002). In one study of 711 lesbian, gay, and bisexual doctors and medical students, 67 percent knew of patients who had received substandard care based on their sexual orientation and 88 percent had overheard colleagues disparage their lesbian and gay patients (cited in Spafford et al., 2002).

Another form of discrimination is based on *lack of* knowledge of sexual orientation. Studies (for example, by the American Medical Association) have found that many physicians do not ask about patients' sexual orientation, and, further, that many lesbians, gay men, and bisexuals do not tell (*JAMA,* 1996). Heterosexuality is assumed at a high medical cost to patients: When making diagnoses, physicians may overlook diseases or medical conditions that gay men or lesbians are more prone to contract. Likewise, there are diseases or conditions that lesbians and gay men are extremely unlikely to contract and are unnecessarily tested for.

Some physicians and nurses adopt a judgmental stance when dealing with gay and lesbian patients. Many current health-care providers view homosexuality as a sin, a crime, or a disease (Spafford et al., 2002). One study of 100 nurses teaching in nursing programs found that 34 percent believed that lesbians are "disgusting" and 17 percent believed that lesbians molest children (Stevens, 1992). Other physicians and nurses may provide reduced care to gays and lesbians or deny them medical care altogether (*JAMA,* 1996). For example, lesbians may be at risk for terminal breast or ovarian cancer because some doctors do not provide adequate information about the importance of early cancer detection through routine gynecological examinations and mammography screening (Gessen, 1993).

Some of the intolerance among physicians may be traced to past views in psychiatry of homosexuality as a medicalized pathology or disorder. Aversion therapy and frontal lobotomies were used in many cases to "cure" or "adjust" a non-heterosexual (Kinsman, 1996). In fact, Karlen noted that most early writing about homosexuals by medical and legal professionals was "chiefly concerned with whether the disgusting breed of perverts could be physically identified for the courts, and whether they should be held legally responsible for their acts" (cited in Kinsman, 1996:31).

Probably the most controversial topic in health care for gay men, lesbians, and bisexuals is HIV/AIDS. Although physicians, dentists, nurses, and other health professionals may learn about treating patients who are HIV-positive, many feel inadequate to deal with these patients' psychological and social needs. Since the first diagnosed case of AIDS in Canada in 1979, the numbers of those diagnosed across Canada in all risk categories (except blood product recipients) has continued to grow. By the end of 1994, 16 000 cases had been diagnosed. Different people than in the past are more at risk today. Although men who have sex with other men are still the group most at risk (by mid-1995, this group accounted for 81 percent of all diagnosed cases to date), the proportion of cases attributable to this risk factor has been dropping each year, while heterosexual contact and illicit IV drug-use are becoming increasingly high-risk factors, particularly for women (Frank, 2000). Further, the median age for HIV infection has dropped from 32 years of age prior to 1982 to 23 years of age up to 1990. In fact, in 1993,

HIV infection was the third leading cause of death for men aged 20 to 44 years (Frank, 2000).

Despite the prevalence of HIV/AIDS among gay men and bisexuals in certain age groups, many medical professionals do not inform their patients about the risks associated with various types of sexual conduct and intravenous drug use, or about measures that can be taken to prevent exposure to sexually transmitted diseases and HIV. Although HIV/AIDS has been referred to as "the gay disease," given that heterosexuals—women in particular—are so at risk, social analysts suggest that it should be viewed as *everyone's* problem.

Occupational Discrimination

Fearing that they may be stigmatized or discriminated against in the workplace, many gay and lesbian people do not reveal their sexual orientation (Woods, 1993). Their fears have some grounding in reality. Despite laws prohibiting employment discrimination on the basis of sexual orientation, openly lesbian and gay people often experience bias in hiring, retention, and promotion in both private- and public-sector employment. More than 100 major companies have stated that they do not discriminate on the basis of sexual orientation. Nevertheless, studies show that about two-thirds of gay employees in private-sector employment (e.g., small businesses and large corporations) have witnessed some type of hostility, harassment, or discrimination at their place of employment (Singer and Deschamps, 1994). Many chief executive officers are reluctant to put a lesbian or gay man at the top of the corporate hierarchy, and some employees express concern about working around gay men and lesbians (Woods, 1993). Many who do not reveal their sexual orientation to coworkers are subjected to a general disparagement of gays, as Brian, a gay executive in a large corporation, explains:

> I was in an office with the boss and another person who is my same level, and we were talking about another professional that we should probably get involved in this transaction. The person who was at the same level as me said, "Oh, he's really good, but he's a flaming faggot." What was very shocking to me was that it was an attack on this person in a professional context. You are sort of used to the way straight men sort of banter around, calling each other queer, on a social level. But it's really strange when

> they talk about it in a professional setting. But this person thought it was okay. I assume that he thought there were three straight men there, so he could still say these things that in mixed company he would never say. (quoted in Mead, 1994:40)

Although sexual harassment occurs in the workplace, supervisors frequently do not take it seriously. Because, to prove sexual harassment, victims must show that the harasser targeted a specific category of people, such as gay men, charges of harassment reflect the victim's sexual orientation. Victims of same-sex harassment may be blamed for causing the incident. Many fear they will lose their job if they file a grievance, even though gay rights advocates believe sexual orientation should be irrelevant in determining whether harassment has occurred (Gover, 1996b).

Same-sex sexual harassment and blatant discrimination in hiring and promotion are also problems in public-sector positions at the federal and provincial government levels, as well as in local law enforcement agencies. For many years, most law enforcement agencies and police departments did not employ lesbian or gay people. Today, gay and lesbian people are employed in law enforcement agencies throughout the country because of human rights policies that preclude the agencies from asking job applicants about their sexual orientation. Despite such provisions, sociologist Stephen Leinen (a former police lieutenant) found in his study of "gay cops" that many remain "totally closeted" for fear of how other police officers and gay people will treat them. The total secrecy among lesbians and gay men in many large police departments is illustrated by one gay police officer's surprise on learning that his partner, with whom he had worked for some time, also was gay: "I was deeply shocked when he told me. We had worked together for over three years and neither of us knew about the other. He said, 'How the hell could we have worked together for so long and neither one of us knew it?'" (Leinen, 1993:3)

In recent years, some gay advocates have encouraged people to "come out" (identify their sexual orientation) at work and to make the biases against people based on their sexual orientation known to the media and the general public so that demands for change will be met. As long as people remain "in the closet," the advocates argue, workplace discrimination will not be eliminated (Nava and Dawidoff, 1994).

Victimization and Hate Crimes

On November 17, 2001, Aaron Webster, a 42-year-old Vancouver resident, was viciously murdered near Second Beach in Stanley Park by a group of three or four men. While gay bashing in Vancouver, Toronto, and other large Canadian cities is well-documented, Webster's death may mark the first hate-motivated killing of a gay or lesbian person in British Columbia. While the perpetrators are still at large, homicide Detective Rob Faoro says he has been working on the case "exclusively for coming up to one year" and remains hopeful that a witness will come forward (Perelle, 2002:7). This incident echoes the brutal October 1998 murder of 21-year-old Matthew Shepard, the University of Wyoming student who was lured to the outskirts of town by two young men who then tied him to a fence, savagely beat him, and left him to die. He was killed because of his sexual orientation (matthewsplace.com, 1999).

In Canada, under the Criminal Code, hate crimes are defined as criminal acts motivated by a person's "race," religion, or ethnicity; therefore, crimes motivated by sexual orientation are not yet defined as "hate crimes." An amendment to the Criminal Code to add crimes motivated by sexual orientation to the list of hate crimes was promised by Justice Minister Anne McLellan following the 1999 gay bashing of a New Brunswick student, but the Code has not yet been amended. But, while crimes motivated by sexual orientation are not listed as "hate crimes" *per se*, there are sentencing enhancements specified in the Criminal Code, in Bill C-41 (amended in 1996), stating that where "there is evidence that the offence was motivated by bias, prejudice, or hate based on racialization, national or ethnic origin, language, colour, religion, sex, age, mental or physical disability, sexual orientation or any other similar factor," penalties in sentencing should be increased.

Before the early 1990s, few acts of violence against gays and lesbians were ever reported in the media. Indeed, hate crimes against gay men and lesbians were not acknowledged as such. Although research is finally taking place, the scope and extent of hate crimes based on sexual orientation is not known (MacMillan and Claridge, 1998), but hate crimes appear to be most prevalent where homophobic attitudes and behaviours are tolerated or at least overlooked. The Webster incident was not an isolated hate crime—there are many other incidents being reported across the country every week. This is alarming, since the B.C. Hate Crimes Team estimates that only between 5 and 10 percent of all hate crimes are actually reported to police (MacMillan and Claridge, 1998:2). The B.C. Hate Crimes Team, an initiative created by the B.C. Ministry of Attorney General in 1996, is comprised of members of the Ministry of Attorney General, Vancouver Police Department, and the RCMP. The mandate of the Hate Crimes Team is to "ensure the effective identification, investigation, and prosecution of crimes motivated by hate, bias or prejudice" (MacMillan and Claridge, 1998:7). The B.C. Hate Crimes Team reported that "based on the number of hate/bias crimes 'reported' to the police in 1997, gay males were the most victimized group in Vancouver" (MacMillan and Claridge, 1998:5). The Hate Crimes Team further reported

a tendency for hate/bias attacks to be more vicious and severe. Research has found that victims of hate-motivated crimes are four times more likely to experience assaultive behaviour, are twice as likely to receive an injury and are four times more likely to require hospitalization. . . . Assaults, such as gay bashings, are committed at night in poorly lit areas. Moreover, the initial attack generally comes from behind and the first blow is with a weapon or punch directed towards the victim's head in order to knock the victim to the ground. In such instances, it is very difficult for victims to identify or even see one or more attackers. Further, the majority of hate-motivated assaults are almost exclusively stranger on stranger events. (MacMillan and Claridge, 1998:7 and 17)

In the United States, information gathered since the passage of the 1990 Hate Crimes Statistics Act shows that more than 50 percent of all reported anti-gay harassment and violence is perpetrated by young males age 21 or under (Comstock, 1991). Further, data from Ontario show that most hate crime (95 percent) is committed by individuals who are not connected in any way to an organized hate group, despite most people's beliefs that organized hate groups such as racist groups are most often responsible for hate crime (MacMillan and Claridge, 1998:6). Clearly, stronger and more pervasive measures must be taken to eliminate homophobia, biphobia, and the associated hate crimes.

SOCIAL PROBLEMS AND SOCIAL POLICY

BOX 6.2   School's Out: Closing the Books on Homophobia

History, as taught, is devoid of gays or lesbians. Without knowing that history, it's no surprise that many consider their present-day presence strange or unnatural.

Kevin Jennings, founder of the Gay, Lesbian and Straight Education Network (in Seavor, 1996:E11)

Recently, some schools have modified their curricula to incorporate information on lesbians, gays, and bisexuals. However, journalist Dan Woog (1995), author of a book on the impact of gay and lesbian issues in schools, suggests that much remains to be done. According to Woog, within the administration of each school, there should be at least one advocate to address gay issues—a person who is available to gay, lesbian, and bisexual students; who makes sure that the school complies with its responsibility to all students; and who helps with referrals to outside support groups, counselling agencies, hot lines, and organizations for family members. Woog also suggests that schools define harassment on the basis of sexual orientation and make clear that inappropriate use of language, jokes, graffiti, and vandalism based on sexual orientation is unfair, offensive, and harmful to everyone in the school community.

In the 21st century, we are still concerned about how gay men and lesbians are treated in school. The Gay, Lesbian and Straight Education Network (GLSEN) "school climate" survey, which was conducted in 1999 among nearly 500 gay, lesbian, bisexual, and transgender students, found that 91 percent of the participants had heard words like "faggot," "dyke," or "queer" used regularly at school. Sixty-nine percent stated that they had experienced direct verbal harassment; 24 percent reported incidences of physical harassment. Are other students the primary perpetrators of prejudice and discrimination? Not necessarily. The GLSEN survey found that more than one-third of the participants had heard negative remarks about sexual orientation from faculty or staff. Judy Shepard, the mother of Matthew Shepard, a university student who was brutally murdered because of his sexual orientation, decries this type of negative behaviour among teachers, administrators, and students:

I sort of get the feeling that teachers and administrators feel that they grew up with that teasing in school, and they made it through—they treat it almost as a rite of passage. "We survived it, you survive it. This is how you grow." Oh, ignorant people! Kids have scars—from being teased because they have big ears. What kind of scars do they have from being teased because they're black, or gay? (Cullen, 1999:3)

What suggestions do you have for reducing the problems described in the GLSEN study? According to Judy Shepard, education is where change must begin first: "Kids go to school to learn how to behave in society. . . . And if we don't start doing that in the schools soon, it's harder to do as an adult" (Cullen, 1999:2). Arguing that discrimination and violence against gays must be taken seriously in any and all settings, including schools, GLSEN and other organizations conduct teacher-training workshops in an effort to make teachers and administrators more aware of this pressing problem.

Jean Baker, a psychologist and a mother of two gay sons, conducted research with school-age gays and lesbians. Through interviews with "out" students, she was able, in her book *How Homophobia Hurts Children: Nurturing Diversity at Home, at School, and in the Community,* to report a number of the suggestions the students had for creating safer climates for gay, lesbian, and bisexual students in schools. Among the actions schools can take are: (a) improving sex education to include discussions about safe gay sex; (b) having teachers, staff, or administrators start gay/straight alliance groups or clubs in schools; (c) providing sensitivity or diversity training for school personnel and students; (d) stepping up interventions against harassment based on sexual orientation; (e) openly discussing issues of homosexuality and heterosexuality in the classrooms and including gay, lesbian, and bisexual issues in the curriculum; (f) normalizing homosexuality; (g) not making heterosexist assumptions about students or their families; (h) being role models, either as gays, lesbians, or bisexuals or as those accepting of people with diverse orientations; and (i) being aware of materials and resources that students, families, and school personnel can draw upon (Baker, 2002).

What other suggestions do you have for reducing the problems described in the GLSEN study above? In what other places, besides the school system, could we introduce changes that would be beneficial in reducing homophobia?

PERSPECTIVES ON SEXUAL ORIENTATION AND SOCIAL INEQUALITY

Sexual orientation and social inequality can be understood from various perspectives. Biologists take one approach, and psychologists take another. Sociological explanations focus primarily on how sexual orientation and homophobia are associated with social learning and/or social structural factors in society. We'll look at each perspective separately.

Interactionist Perspectives

In contrast to most biological and psychological perspectives, and much like some social psychological perspectives, interactionist perspectives view heterosexual and homosexual conduct as learned behaviour and focus on the process by which individuals come to identify themselves as gay, lesbian, bisexual, or straight. According to interactionists, most people acquire the status of *heterosexual* without being consciously aware of it, because heterosexuality is the established norm and they do not have to struggle over their identity. But the same is not true of people who come to identify themselves as *homosexual* or *bisexual*. In fact, some sociologists suggest that sexual orientation is a master status for many gay men, lesbians, and bisexuals (Schur, 1965). A *master status* is the most significant status a person possesses, the one that most determines how the individual views him or herself and how he or she is treated by others. Master status based on sexual orientation is particularly significant when it is linked to other subordinate racialized/ethnic group statuses. For example, working-class gay Latinos are more hesitant than White, middle-class gay men to come out to their families because of cultural norms pertaining to *machismo* (masculinity) and the fear that relatives will withdraw the support that is essential for surviving at the subordinate end of racialized and class hierarchies (see Almaguer, 1995).

Interactionists have identified several stages in the process of accepting a lesbian, gay, or bisexual identity (Weinberg et al., 1994). First, people experience identity confusion—a situation in which they feel different from other people and struggle with admitting that they are attracted to individuals of the same sex. For example, someone who identified himself as a 14-year-

old boy posted the following note on an Internet newsgroup:

I feel like my life is over. Am I gay? God, I hope not. I walk around going, "God, I hope not." I walk around going, "Do I like him?" "Do I like her?" "How would it feel to do it with him/her?" WHY DOES THIS HAVE TO HAPPEN TO ME!! The funny thing is, I absolutely detest everything about sex with men, and relationships with men. But somehow, I feel attracted to them anyway!! (Gabriel, 1995b:1)

In the past, many gay and lesbian people had nowhere to turn in their quest for answers and support from others; today, many use the Internet and other forms of global communication to connect with others who share their concerns (Gabriel, 1995b). It is important to keep in mind, however, that in a more accepting and less-homophobic society, young people would not need to feel their lives were "over" when experiencing feelings of attraction for those of the same sex.

The second stage in establishing a lesbian or gay identity is seeking out others who are openly lesbian or gay and perhaps engaging in sexual experimentation or making other forays into the homosexual subculture. In the third stage, people attempt to integrate their self-concept and acceptance of a label such as "homosexual," "gay," or "lesbian" by pursuing a way of life that conforms to their definition of what those labels mean (Cass, 1984; Coleman, 1981/2; Ponse, 1978). Like most "stage" theories, however, not all people go through these stages. Even those who do may not go through each stage in the same way, and some may move back and forth between stages (Weinberg et al., 1994).

Studies on how people come to accept their sexual identity as gay, bisexual, or lesbian show the significance of labelling and how it can create barriers to full participation in Canadian society. However, these studies are typically based on a relatively narrow selection of people, which makes it difficult to generalize the findings to larger populations. That is, research participants who openly identify themselves as gay or bisexual may not be characteristic of the larger homosexual or bisexual population (Weinberg et al., 1994).

Functionalist and Conflict Perspectives

Unlike the interactionist approach, which focuses primarily on how individuals come to identify themselves as homosexual, bisexual, or heterosexual, functionalist perspectives focus on the relationship between social structure and sexual orientation. To functionalists, social norms and laws are established to preserve social institutions and maintain stability in society. From this perspective, then, many societies punish homosexual conduct because it violates the social norms established by those societies and thus undermines the stability of the societies. Sociologist David P. Aday, Jr., provides an overview of this perspective:

> Marriage and family are structural arrangements that contribute to the continuity of our contemporary society. . . . [Homosexuality undermines] arrangements that currently operate to replace societal members in an orderly way—that is, the arrangement has survival value. . . . If homosexual conduct were allowed to exist unchallenged and unpunished, then it might in time undermine norms and laws that underpin monogamous marital sex, at least some of which results in the production of offspring to repopulate the society. . . . The punishment of homosexual conduct, from ridicule and discrimination to imprisonment, reinforces expectations about heterosexual and marital sex and defines the boundaries of society. (Aday, 1990:25)

The functionalist perspective explains why some people do not believe homosexual conduct or marriages between lesbian or gay couples should be protected legally. It also explains why some religious and political leaders call for a renewal of "family values" in this country. But, as pointed out by political scientist and gay rights activist Andrew Sullivan (1997:147), homosexual people are part of heterosexual families too: They

> are sons and daughters, brothers and sisters, even mothers and fathers, of heterosexuals. The distinction between "families" and "homosexuals" is, to begin with, empirically false; and the stability of existing families is closely linked to how homosexuals are treated within them.

As a popular bumper sticker states, "Hate is *NOT* a family value."

Critics suggest that the functionalist approach supports the status quo and ignores a need for more current definitions of marriage and family. If marriage is understood to be the decision of two people to live together in a partnership—to be a family—then the intention

Many individuals seem to accept their identities as lesbian, gay, or bisexual in stages. Initially there is identity confusion. But seeking out others who are open about their sexual orientation and experimenting sexually can eventually lead to acceptance.

or the capacity to have children should not be a condition. These critics say that nothing but custom mandates that marital partners must be of different genders (Nava and Dawidoff, 1994).

Whereas the functionalist approach focuses on how existing social arrangements create a balance in society, the conflict approach focuses on *tensions* in society and *differences* in interests and power among opposing groups. From this perspective, people who hold the greatest power are able to have their own attitudes, beliefs, and values—about sexual orientation, in this case—represented and enforced while others are not (Aday, 1990). Therefore, norms pertaining to *compulsory heterosexuality* reflect the beliefs of dominant group members who hold high-level positions in the federal, territorial, and provincial governments and other social institutions. However, critics assert that the conflict approach fails to recognize that some people who have wealth and power are gay or lesbian yet take no action to reduce discrimination based on sexual orientation.

According to Karl Marx, conflicts over values are an essential element of social life, and less-powerful people often challenge the laws imposed on them by those in positions of power. For example, adverse decisions by provincial courts and the Supreme Court of Canada have often resulted in increased political activism by gay and lesbian rights groups. In recent years, more openly lesbian and gay people can be found in public office, as elected or appointed officials; in the medical and legal professions; as educators and business leaders; and in all walks of life. However, regardless of their location in the power structure, most gay men, lesbians, and bisexuals remain acutely aware that many social barriers have not been lifted and that major shifts in people's attitudes toward homosexuality and bisexuality are still not realized.

With rapid Internet communications, lesbians and gay men around the world keep informed about political decisions that may adversely affect them. Many coalitions have been formed to organize gay pride marches and protests around the world. For example, the International Lesbian and Gay Association reports that more than 300 lesbian and gay groups exist in more than 50 nations (Hendriks et al., 1993).

Feminist and Queer Perspectives

Feminist perspectives on sexuality have shifted considerably over the past four decades. In the late 1960s and through the 1970s, sexual orientation was mainly discussed by radical feminists who, by embracing binary and essentialist notions of males and females, claimed that women everywhere were bonded together in a sisterhood founded on their common oppression by men everywhere. As feminist writer Robin Morgan wrote in 1969, "Women have been subjugated longer than any other people on earth" (1969/1993:42). Feminist scholars Robyn Rowland and Renate Klein echoed this in 1996: "The first and fundamental theme is that women as a social group are oppressed by men as a social group and that this is the primary oppression for women" (1996:11). Along with the radical feminist theories of patriarchy came, necessarily, the analyses of compulsory heterosexuality as the cornerstone of male privilege and sexism. Feminist writer Adrienne Rich (1984), in her now famous essay, "Compulsory Heterosexuality and Lesbian Existence," pointed out that heterosexuality, far from being a "natural" inclination, was, in fact, systematically imposed upon women through various means, including violence, as well as through hegemonic notions of heterosexuality as

natural, inevitable, and universal. The radical feminist response to compulsory heterosexuality was varying degrees of separatism, at least for the short term. As theorist Chris Weedon (1999:36) points out:

> a heterosexual lifestyle was often regarded as incompatible with feminism. To relate sexually to men was to consort with the enemy. This radical version of separatism implied having nothing to do with men, the first step in the process of freeing oneself from patriarchal power structures. This process involved a decolonization of patriarchally defined female consciousness, body image and ways of living. The result, it was thought, would be the discovery of a truly woman-defined womanhood.

This is not to suggest that men, gay men in particular, are not oppressed by heterosexism or compulsory heterosexuality, but sociologist Mariana Valverde (1987/2000:257) points out, "it weighs particularly heavily on women [as] men do not need female validation for their identity."

The weight of this radical feminist perspective resulted for many heterosexual feminists in feelings of guilt and confusion, estranging some from feminism altogether and reducing many to silence on the question of sexuality (Overall, 2000; Valverde, 2000; Weedon, 1999). Recently, feminists, including radical feminists, discontented with past analyses, have again taken up the issue of sexuality, focusing on what it means to be both heterosexual and feminist. So, by the late 1980s, Valverde (1987/2000:260) made the argument that:

> Feminism asserts the right of all women to make their erotic choices, and this includes choosing men exclusively. Feminism also rejects the hierarchy of sexual practices, and so does not seek to substitute a lesbian priority for heterosexism. The goal of feminism in the area of sexuality is to establish true sexual pluralism, where no one choice is presented as "the norm."

Following on the notion of sexual pluralism, some feminist analyses focused on the possibility of being heterosexual and feminist but "conscious" of both the privileges and constraints of one's choice of heterosexuality (Overall, 1990/2000). What this question brings up is the thorny issue of privilege. Therefore, women as a group may be disenfranchised. Gay men, lesbians, and bisexuals may be disenfranchised. Men have privilege. Heterosexuals have privilege. Therefore, as sociologist Zoe Newman (2001:134) points out, "We need to map our complicity in structures of domination in order to 'move out of the subject position we claim on the margins and into the shifting and multiple subject positions of oppressed and oppressor.'" In effect, theorizing and identifying oneself as both heterosexual and feminist carries with it the discomfort of "disrupt[ing] identity posited on marginality, and reveal[ing] the coexistence of innocence and complicity" (Newman, 2001:131). Despite some heterosexual feminists' claims that their relationships with men are completely egalitarian and non-oppressive:

> it nonetheless remains *possible* for the man to take advantage of his potential power. All that stands in the way of his using that power is his own good will, while he is not similarly dependent on the woman's good will. And he still benefits, however indirectly, from male hegemony, and "even the advantages that he is in a position to refuse are waiting for him if he changes his mind." (Overall, 1990/2000:267)

Newman draws upon the work of theorist Michel Foucault (2001:134), stating that "even the act of shedding power is born of power; power circulates throughout our relations, it enables and it restricts." Contemporary feminists, then, with regard to the question of sexual orientation, have been focusing on the politics of difference. This is to say that, because of the "hierarchization of difference in heterosexist societies," homosexuality and bisexuality continue to be hotly debated political issues within feminism, as much as they are personal ones (Weedon, 1999:46).

Common ground between gay men and lesbians is discussed much more so in contemporary liberal feminist perspectives due, as Weedon (1999) points out, to the achievements of the lesbigay rights movements. For example, feminist psychologist Celia Kitzinger (1987:44) states that "the lesbian and gay man are no longer a species apart, but human beings of equal worth and dignity to heterosexuals, contributing to the rich diversity of humankind." The shift from feminist critiques of patriarchy and male power to a more inclusive politics of difference perspective accompanied the rise of postmodern thought, in particular in the form of *Queer theory*.

The quintessential feature of Queer theory is its staunch repudiation, theoretically, of any defining features, of any "normality" or "fixedness." Accepting the basic tenets of postmodern thought generally, those who subscribe to Queer theory, or to notions of "queer" in general, allow that nothing is "normal," nothing is "natural"; everything is socially constructed and, hence, arbitrary. Queer theorists view gender and sexuality as performance and refuse to hierarchize any sex above another, any gender above another, any mode of sexual expression above another (Weedon, 1999:73). Feminist psychologists Sue Wilkinson and Celia Kitzinger (1996:377) summarize one of the main thrusts of Queer theory, which is:

> . . . most popularly . . . [the] "genderfuck" . . . or "fucking with gender." The gender-fuck is supposed to "deprive the naturalizing narratives of compulsory heterosexuality of their central protagonists: 'man' and 'woman'" . . . and to illustrate the social constructedness of "sex" in all its multiple meanings.

While Queer theory seeks to subvert notions of "natural" and "normal," making any and every form of sexuality acceptable, many feminists and others find it problematic from a political or social change perspective, for a number of reasons. Queer theorists often view feminism as a "grand narrative," the assumptions and foundational propositions of which must be open to question and critique. Therefore, sexualized violence, pornography, and other heterosexually eroticized models of sexuality which are based in profoundly oppressive patriarchal relations may, within a Queer theory perspective, all be endorsed as "unimportant," "transitory," and "provisional" (Wilkinson and Kitzinger, 1996:381): "Power relations within and between heterosexuality and homosexuality become invisible, allowing for a liberalism which hides oppression" (Weedon, 1999:76).

Equally problematic is the widespread practice of gays and lesbians reclaiming the term "queer" as a means of self-identification, shifting the term from the pejorative to the celebratory. In doing this, they subvert the radical potential of the term "queer" by using it as an almost essentialist, but certainly bounded or fixed, category that has political value on the one hand but subverts the "mind fuck" potential on the other. From this perspective, then, a more radical use of the term may be for "straights" to begin to identify as "queer," thereby highlighting the multiplicity and arbitrariness of "queer." Indeed, many heterosexual people whose sexuality does not fit the norm for a variety of reasons do identify as queer. In this case, the value of queer as a destabilizing element is highlighted, rather than the term being used as simply a new category; as Newman

(2001:129) describes it, defining one's "identity as always founded on a sense of marginality." She further points out that, used in this way, "the potential of queer seems to be that we do not come together around an assumption of sameness, but around a critique of 'the normal'" (Newman, 2001:132). Sociologist Joshua Gamson (1996:396) cites queer activists Allan Bérubé and Jeffrey Escoffier saying that queer is often employed "to affirm sameness by defining a common identity on the fringes." Other critics of Queer theory note that while it may appear radical to reinterpret oneself as "queer," in terms of political activism, it is problematic. Anthropologist Max H. Kirsch (2000:97) cautions: "It is misguided as political action: it cannot generate the collective energy and organization necessary to challenge existing structures of power."

Defining oneself as queer—as "other" from a norm of heterosexuality—has concrete consequences. Some of these consequences include internalized and external oppression played out in depression, apathy, and violence. Kirsch (2000:97) notes, "We cannot simply refuse to acknowledge these facts of social life in our present society and hope that our circumstances will change." Queer theory therefore contains both the ability to be radical and destabilizing in challenging all things deemed natural or normal and, conversely, the potential to render one completely apolitical and paralyzed by apathy in the abyss of "anything goes." This is neatly summarized by political scientist Paisley Currah (2001:193–194), who also quotes feminist legal scholar Kimberlé Crenshaw, 1991:

> "At this point in history, a strong case can be made that the most critical resistance strategy for disempowered groups is to occupy and defend a politics of social location rather than to vacate and destroy it." The appropriation of queer theory's useful theoretical insights by advocates of gay rights and the rights of sexual minorities requires maintaining a delicate balance between the politics of location and the politics of deconstruction.

CAN INEQUALITIES BASED ON SEXUAL ORIENTATION BE REDUCED?

As we have emphasized in previous chapters, how people view a social problem is related to how they believe the problem should be reduced or solved. Inequality based on sexual orientation is no exception. From an interactionist perspective, homosexual conduct is learned behaviour, and people go through stages in establishing a lesbian, gay, or bisexual identity. Society should, therefore, be more tolerant of people as they come to accept their sexual identity. Legal and social barriers that prevent homosexuals and bisexuals from fully participating in society should be removed, thus making the complex psychological and social process of coming out to friends, family, and coworkers easier for those who choose to do so.

According to the functionalist perspective, social norms and laws exist to protect the family and maintain stability in society. Given this, sexual orientation becomes a social issue: Gay activists' demands for equal rights, including legal recognition of same-sex marriages, become major threats to the stability of society. With the legalization of marriage for gays and lesbians in Canada a certainty, some groups say, there will be no stopping others who wish to strike down what remains of "foundational truths once thought to be self-evident" (Thomas, 1996:A15).

Some advocates of this position believe that lesbians and gay men can change their sexual orientation:

> Homosexuals can and do change. My files bulge with stories of those who once engaged in sex with people of the same gender, but no longer do. They testify to the possibility of change for those who want to. The struggle to maintain what remains of the social fabric will ultimately determine whether we will continue to follow ancient Rome on the road to destruction, or come to our senses, turn around and re-enter a harbour of safety ordained by God for our own protection. (Thomas, 1996:A15)

Whether gay, lesbian, and bisexual individuals can or should change their sexual orientation is the subject of widespread disagreement. However, most functionalists agree that homosexuality may be dysfunctional for society if it does not contribute to society's need for new members or if it undermines social norms and laws that preserve the family unit and maintain stability in society.

Conflict theorists believe that prejudice and discrimination against lesbians, gay men, and bisexuals are embedded in the social structure of society and are reinforced by those who hold the greatest power and thus are able to perpetuate their own attitudes, beliefs, and values about what constitutes "normal" sexual conduct. From this perspective, homophobia is similar to racism, sexism, ableism, and ageism, and the overt and covert discrimination that gay men and lesbians experience is similar to the discrimination experienced by people of colour, Indigenous peoples, all women, people with disabilities, older people and children and youth. According to the conflict approach, the best way to reduce inequality based on sexual orientation is to continue to pass laws that ban all forms of discrimination against gay men, lesbians, and bisexuals or that represent barriers to their equality with heterosexuals. However, to gain equal rights, activism is necessary: People must continue to demand social change.

In the past, feminist theorists, using a radical critique of patriarchy, advocated separation of men and women. Lesbianism was promoted as the only rational and non-oppressive mode of relationship. This perspective led to deep divisiveness in the movement as heterosexual feminists had difficulties reconciling their sexual orientation with the political demands of the radical feminist separatists. More recently, feminists have approached questions of sexual orientation from the perspective of sexual pluralism, with the idea that all people, regardless of sexual orientation or gender, need to support one another to combat oppression. Therefore, according to contemporary feminists, to reduce inequality based on sexual orientation, people need to understand their commonalities in the face of oppression and also need to be clear about their varying positions of privilege in order to form alliances across location. In this way, everyone can fight against inequality based on sexual orientation as well as other inequalities by lobbying for same-sex marriages and the like.

Queer theorists believe that gender is a social construction and, thus, sexual orientation is also fluid. People use a queer perspective in one of two ways. Either they use the term "queer" as a descriptive category, or as a stand-in for the terms "gay," "lesbian," or "bisexual." This use is political in that it represents a reclaiming of a term which, in most uses, has been regarded as disparaging. However, the radical potential of "queerness" as something fluid is thus subverted. From this perspective, the category or term is a means of overcoming people's homophobia by being "out," "loud," and "proud"—by demonstrating the normalcy of being outside the "norm" and raising challenging

questions such as, Who defines what or who is normal? Using "queer" as a political category gives people something to rally around; it helps make collective action possible. Additionally, many people identify themselves as "queer" for a variety of reasons, and so it is a identity marker to use to provide common ground for all those who see themselves in opposition to "normal" sexuality, however that gets defined. Others use a queer perspective to refuse to define self or others, in this way enabling people to grapple with identity, subjectivity, and location. People may define themselves as queer but refuse to explain what makes them so, forcing people to engage with the questions about the importance of categorizing. From this perspective, by transgressing gender or sexuality norms (through cross-dressing, for example) people can flout the norms and demonstrate their arbitrariness and fluidity and, thereby, have an impact on changing or broadening norms and definitions. This is typically done on an individual basis, however, making collective actions difficult to organize.

In the 21st century, gay advocacy is perhaps the most effective means of reducing homophobia and bringing about greater equality for gay men and lesbians. In fact, it took a small riot in the United States to make the general public really aware of inequality based on sexual orientation and the need for social change. In 1969, police raided the Stonewall Inn, a bar patronized by gay men in New York City's Greenwich Village, for alleged liquor law violations. The angry response by militant gay activists caused police to stop raiding the Stonewall Inn and other gay bars and clubs on Christopher Street and ushered the Gay Liberation movement into existence (Weinberg and Williams, 1975). As recently as the 1970s in Canada, the RCMP conducted raids on bars known for or suspected of patronage by gays and lesbians, and police raids on "gay bath houses" continue today. In an article describing the outcome of a February 1981 police raid on a Toronto bath house, Todd Richmond, Features Editor of the popular Canadian website 365gay.com, wrote that while hundreds of thousands of dollars damage was done to the club and nearly 300 people were arrested, many of whom lost their jobs as a result, that raid marked:

> the watershed moment that dates the gay liberation movement in Canada. . . . The community was galvanized for the first time. The raids, and their overkill, gave the community a sense of power that

has helped lead to most of the rights enjoyed by gays and lesbians today. (Retrieved December 18, 2002, from www.365gay.com/lifestylechannel/intime/months/02-february/bath.htm)

With the emergence of HIV/AIDS as a major problem in the 1980s, and with the repatriation of the Canadian Constitution and the signing into law of the *Canadian Charter of Rights and Freedoms* in 1982, many gay advocates shifted the focus of their lobbying from human rights to the need for medical research (Shilts, 1988). Today, hundreds of organizations seek equal rights and protections for gay men, lesbians, and bisexuals; these groups represent a wide cross-section of the Canadian population. For example, groups like EGALE (Equality for Gays and Lesbians Everywhere) Canada, PFLAG (Parents and Friends of Lesbians and Gays) Canada, and the Rainbow Coalition serve the needs of all gay, lesbian, and bisexual people, whereas other groups serve a niche. These groups include: Prime-timers, specifically for older gays and lesbians; CALYPSO (Canadian Alliance Linking Young People around Sexual Orientation), for Canadian youth; Christian Lesbians, for the religiously inclined; and the Bisexual Resource Group, BiWomen of Colour, BiAdult Children of Alcoholics, and even BiStar Trekkies, which focus on the needs of some bisexual people (Gabriel, 1995a; Leland, 1995; and **www.gayscape.com**).

Despite some changes in the attitudes and laws pertaining to homosexuality, discrimination remains strong. According to a recent study, gay, lesbian, and bisexual sociologists who advocate gay rights are more likely than their heterosexual colleagues to encounter difficulty in obtaining academic positions, experience bias in the tenure and promotion process, and be excluded from social and professional networks (Taylor and Raeburn, 1995). However, not all of the study's findings were negative: For some sociologists, being involved in gay rights issues brings professional visibility, recognition, and opportunities for advancement (Taylor and Raeburn, 1995).

Gay rights advocates argue that gay men, lesbians, and bisexuals should not be the only ones responsible for reducing or eliminating inequality based on sexual orientation: It all comes down to this: Are people equal in this society by virtue of their citizenship, or not? If the answer is no, then we will be saying that equality does not exist . . . anymore but has been replaced by tiers of citizenship, and that what tier you occupy depends on whether people like you or not. And if we accept this, then we will have repudiated the constitutional principles of liberty and equality. . . . We believe that you will join in this cause because it is your cause, too, the cause of individual liberty and human equality. (Nava and Dawidoff, 1994:167)

Some analysts suggest that people in the future will ask, What was all the fuss over gay men and lesbians (or sexual orientation) about? Valverde (1998) takes the position that, 20 years in the future, it will have become as socially unacceptable to discriminate against people based on sexual orientation as today it has become to discriminate against people based on skin colour. What do you think?

WHAT CAN YOU DO?

- Reflect on the assumptions you hold about homosexuals, heterosexuals, and bisexuals, and about sexual orientation in general.
- Attend a PRIDE day or parade in your community, regardless of your sexual orientation.
- Consider voting in favour of same-sex marriages and other issues that support queer folk, in newspapers, Internet, and opinion polls.
- Do not claim heterosexual privilege. Refer to your girlfriend or boyfriend or husband or wife as your "partner" or your "spouse." Keep people guessing.
- Incorporate sexual orientation issues into your relevant research papers.
- Do not refer to gay, lesbian, or bisexual friends or colleagues as "my gay friend Kim" unless you typically refer to your straight friends as "my straight friend Lee."
- Do not assume you know someone's sexual orientation. Instead, allow people to define their gender/sexuality for you.
- Write a letter to your MP asking that he or she vote in favour of the new legislation favouring equal marriage for same-sex couples when the issue comes up in the House of Commons, and explain why he or she should do this.
- Do not treat bisexuality as an "identity of confusion" but, rather, accept it as a real and valid (and queer) identity of its own.

■ Accept public displays of affection (PDAs) between people of the same sex as natural and normal. Participate in them, to whatever degree you are comfortable (e.g., linking arms with a same-sex friend while walking down the street; hugging a same-sex friend when you meet them), in order to be in solidarity with same-sex couples and to take the heat off queer folks who are always breaking trail and feeling the brunt of it.

■ If you are heterosexual and involved in an intimate partnership with a person of the other sex, try to keep this relationship "in the closet" for one week. This could involve (a) having no physical contact with the person if anyone else (friends, family, general public) is around; (b) being careful where, or even if, you are seen together; (c) not mentioning this person and/or the relationship to anyone; and, (d) not being seen or heard talking on the phone to this person.

SUMMARY

WHAT CRITERIA DO SOCIOLOGISTS USE TO STUDY SEXUAL ORIENTATION?

Sociologists define sexual orientation as a preference for emotional–sexual relationships with persons of the "same" sex (homosexuality), the "opposite" sex (heterosexuality), or both (bisexuality). Recent studies have used three criteria for classifying people as homosexual or bisexual: (1) sexual attraction to persons of one's own gender, (2) sexual involvement with one or more persons of one's own gender; and, (3) self-identification as a gay man, lesbian, or bisexual.

HOW DO RELIGION AND LAW INFLUENCE PEOPLE'S BELIEFS ABOUT HOMOSEXUALITY?

Most major religions, with the exception of Buddhism, regard homosexuality as a sin. Contemporary religious fundamentalists denounce homosexual conduct as a sign of great moral decay and societal chaos. Throughout Canadian history, moral and religious teachings have been intertwined with laws that criminalize homosexual conduct. While many religions do not condone homosexuality, many adherents to them do.

HOW DOES COHABITATION DIFFER FROM DOMESTIC PARTNERSHIP?

In cohabitation, same-sex or opposite-sex partners live together without being legally married. Many gay or lesbian couples cohabit in this country because they could not enter into legally recognized marital relationships. This is now changing, with Ontario and British Columbia leading the way. In the past however, some provinces and territories gave legal recognition to domestic partnerships—partnerships in which an unmarried couple lives together in a committed relationship and is granted many of the same legal rights and benefits accorded to a married couple. Domestic partnership agreements benefit some couples by providing health insurance coverage and other benefits that were not previously afforded them.

WHAT TYPES OF DISCRIMINATION DO GAY AND LESBIAN PEOPLE EXPERIENCE?

Although lesbians and gay men experience discrimination in most aspects of daily life, some of the principal areas are (1) child custody and adoption, (2) housing, (3) medical care, and (4) occupations. In each of these areas, gains have been made over the past three decades. However, discrimination against lesbians, gay men, and bisexuals remains among the most blatant of all forms of prejudice and discrimination experienced by members of subordinate groups.

HOW HAVE CHANGES IN THE DEFINITION OF HATE CRIMES AFFECTED GAY MEN AND LESBIANS?

Despite sexual orientation being a "protected ground" in the *Charter* and in most provincial and territorial human rights legislation, Canada's Criminal Code legislation still does not acknowledge, specifically, crimes against people on the basis of sexual orientation to be "hate crimes." Provincial Hate Crimes Units, however, like British Columbia's, are going a long way to collect those data, perhaps influencing further and broader legislative changes in the future. Hate crimes against gays and lesbians appear to be most prevalent where homophobic attitudes are tolerated or overlooked.

HOW DO INTERACTIONISTS EXPLAIN PROBLEMS ASSOCIATED WITH SEXUAL ORIENTATION?

According to interactionists, most people acquire the status of heterosexual without being consciously aware of it. For lesbians, gay men, and bisexuals, however, sexual orientation may be a master status because it largely determines how individuals view themselves and how they are treated by others. Interactionists identify several stages in the process of accepting the identity of lesbian, gay, or bisexual: (1) experiencing identity confusion; (2) seeking out others who are openly lesbian or gay and sometimes engaging in sexual experimentation; and, (3) attempting to integrate self-concept and acceptance of a label such as "homosexual," "gay," or "lesbian."

HOW DO FUNCTIONALISTS EXPLAIN PROBLEMS ASSOCIATED WITH SEXUAL ORIENTATION?

Functionalists focus on how social norms and laws are established to preserve social institutions, such as the family, and to maintain stability in society. They also analyze reasons why societies find it necessary to punish sexual conduct that violates social norms prohibiting non-marital sex and same-sex sexual relations. According to functionalists, homosexual conduct is punished because it undermines social institutions and jeopardizes the society.

HOW DO CONFLICT THEORISTS EXPLAIN PROBLEMS ASSOCIATED WITH SEXUAL ORIENTATION?

Conflict theorists believe that the group in power imposes its own attitudes, beliefs, and values about sexual orientation on everyone else. Thus norms enforcing compulsory heterosexuality reflect the beliefs of dominant group members in the federal and state governments, the military, and other social institutions. According to conflict theorists, social change can occur only if people demand that laws be changed to bring about greater equality for gay men and lesbians.

HOW DO FEMINIST THEORISTS EXPLAIN PROBLEMS ASSOCIATED WITH SEXUAL ORIENTATION?

Like the position taken by conflict theorists, feminist theorists believe that the group in power can impose its own agenda. The group in power in this case is seen to be males, however, and notions of compulsory heterosexuality work to serve the interests of men in an unequal and gendered social system. Feminist theorists, from a radical perspective, first suggested that lesbianism was a rational, political choice, based on a critique of patriarchy. Today, many feminists reject the separatist stance of earlier writers on these issues, and instead opt for a model that values all diversity and encourages acceptance of all people, regardless of gender, sexual orientation, and so on. Therefore, homosexuals and bisexuals need to be made equal within all institutions and facets of society.

HOW DO QUEER THEORISTS EXPLAIN PROBLEMS ASSOCIATED WITH SEXUAL ORIENTATION?

Many queer theorists believe that problems associated with sexual orientation are the result of a homophobic and biphobic culture. They advocate playing with the categories, labels, definitions, and understandings of the various genders, sexes, and sexual orientations as a way of subverting consciousness. Queer theorists believe that, when people's taken-for-granted realities are disrupted, people will be enabled to see sex, gender, and sexual orientation as the social constructions they are, and thus, ease off of rigid and harmful stereotyping and actions.

HOW HAVE GAY RIGHTS ADVOCATES SOUGHT TO REDUCE INEQUALITY BASED ON SEXUAL ORIENTATION?

Beginning with the Gay Liberation movement in the 1960s, advocates have argued that lesbians and gay men are citizens and entitled to the same rights and protections that other citizens enjoy, including the right to equal employment and housing, legally sanctioned marriage, and protection from harassment and hate crimes. Some analysts suggest that future social change depends on the continued vigilance of gay, lesbian, and bisexual advocacy organizations.

KEY TERMS

biphobia,   p. 128
deviance,   p. 128
domestic partnership,   p. 134
heterosexism,   p. 129

homophobia,   p. 128
master status,   p. 140
sexuality,   p. 128
sexual orientation,   p. 127

QUESTIONS FOR CRITICAL THINKING

1.   Think of any assumptions you hold about homosexuals, bisexuals, and heterosexuals. What actions flow from your assumptions? What impact may your actions have on people whose sexual orientation/preference differs from your own?

2.   Following a Queer theory approach, critically analyze the discomfort generated by allowing or asking people to define their gender, sex, and sexual orientation for you. What assumptions are disrupted when you do this?

3.   What things can heterosexual individuals and/or couples take for granted that homosexual individuals or couples cannot?

4.   The B.C. Hate Crimes Team, created by the provincial government and including members of the RCMP, reports that gays, lesbians, and bisexuals are often reluctant to report violence that is perpetrated against them. Explain why this might be so.

WEBLINKS

BiNet Canada
www.binetcanada.org
BiNetCanada is a national volunteer organization of bisexual and sexually diverse Canadians working to raise awareness and acceptance of their issues of concern. The site gives information about regional, national, and international resources and posts up-to-date articles and press releases.

Gayscape.com
www.gayscape.com
Over 68 000 indexed sites on myriad topics of interest to gays, lesbians, and bisexuals.

Equal Marriage for Same-Sex Couples
www.samesexmarriage.ca
This site is hosted by a gay couple working to achieve the recognition in law that all people have the equal right to marry. It provides social and legal information and links to news items and articles.

Family Pride
www.familypride.ca
Family pride is a national online resource centre focusing on the social, legal, political, educational, spiritual, and psychological issues facing lesbian, gay, bisexual, and transgender parents and their families across Canada. Services include legal resources and informative literature.

Queer Culture
www.queerculture.com
This is the leading Canadian gay and lesbian culture magazine on the Internet. It links to art reviews, concerts, and club listings, offers recipes, and hosts a chat room, along with other resources.

Lesbian and Gay Immigration Task Force
www.ncf.carleton.ca/legit
The Lesbian and Gay Immigration Task Force is a national organization working toward changing Canada's discriminatory immigration laws. It offers detailed information about those laws, advice, and useful links and contacts.

Parents, Families and Friends of Lesbians and Gays
www.pflag.ca
This site offers support and information to gay, lesbian, bisexual, and transgendered persons, and to their families and friends, in order to build a more respectful and discrimination-free society. The site also provides links to other gay and lesbian organizations and a message board for discussion.

Pride Net Canada
www.pridenet.com/canada.html
The purpose of this site is to provide an intense resource centre for gays, lesbians, bisexuals, and transgenders. The information and links range from bars and restaurants to support organizations and poetry.

Pride Vision Television
www.pridevisiontv.com
PrideVision TV is the world's first GLBT television network to broadcast 24/7. The programming ranges from entertainment to current affairs and focuses on issues specifically involving the gay community.

Vancouver Island Lesbian Resources (VILR)
www.vilr.info/index2.html
VILR offers emotional support, information, Web links, message boards, and online and offline resources for lesbians from Vancouver Island seeking connection to the lesbian community.

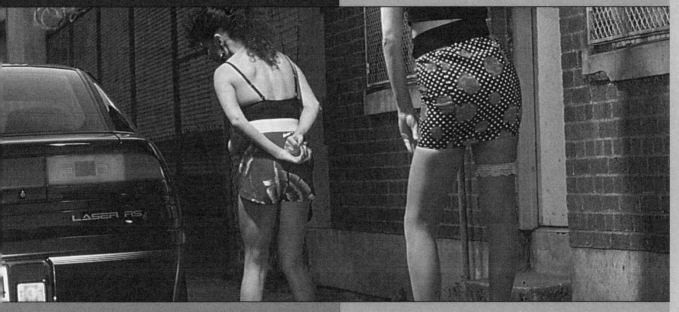

7

THE SEX INDUSTRY IN CANADA AND BEYOND

I just fell for it . . . I was in a vulnerable state, I lost my virginity to rape, and I was consistently abused by my mother. I was ashamed of myself, who I was, what I looked like and, when I met this man, he was the world to me. He said, "Oh you're so pretty" and I fell for it [and became a prostitute for him].

Female youth, Winnipeg, Manitoba (Kingsley and Mark, 2000:54)

[People] think that all prostitutes are on heroin, or they like to be beat up. The stereotype is, "oh, they all knew what they were getting into," which they don't.

Female youth, Vancouver, B.C. (Kingsley and Mark, 2000:69)

I think I would have jumped from the CN Tower a couple of times, just from being transsexual, because that's one of the things that has been so hard. Being 21, a prostitute for 10 years, being a transsexual, and just living this entire lifestyle is very hard. I've tried going home a few times, but it just doesn't work because of my sexuality. It's much easier for me to be in the city and deal with it.

Male youth, Toronto, Ontario (Kingsley and Mark, 2000:28)

I got involved in the drugs because I got I got involved with the wrong guy and eventually the drugs just took over me. I thought I would be okay, you just start [by] running drugs for people, and they started saying "why don't you just go sleep with this guy," or "why don't you just do [these] different things" . . . I got sucked into it [the sex trade].

Female youth, Mission, B.C. (Kingsley and Mark, 2000:21)

At that time [when I was working in the trade] I really wanted to die . . . I couldn't look at myself in the mirror. I couldn't accept the fact that I just thought I was a dirty bitch. Just a slut . . .

Female youth, Goose Bay, Labrador (Kingsley and Mark, 2000:31)

Know those porn star shirts that say "XXX" or "Touch This" or whatever they say . . . all I can say is that you see 15-year-olds walking around in them and I'm sorry, but the first word that comes to my mind is sex. What is this? It has a lot to do with society.

Female youth, Mission, B.C. (Kingsley and Mark, 2000:26)

A lot of our issues are the same, all the way across the country, whether we want to see it or not, and it all comes back to the same thing, that abuse in our families and our communities.

Female youth, Halifax, Nova Scotia (Kingsley and Mark, 2000:23)

There are a multitude of reasons why people enter the sex trade, and the voices of the Canadian youth quoted above speak to some of those reasons. Unlike the young men and women portrayed here, other sex-trade workers view sex work simply as a career choice—with willing buyers and sellers, a purely economic exchange—that is no more or less degrading than any other profession (Alexander, 1987; Chapkis, 1997; Doezema, 1998; Kempadoo, 1998; McWilliams, 1996). Certainly, in this country, it is a thriving multimillion-dollar industry that includes prostitution, the film and video trade, printed pornography, escort services, massage parlours, and strip and table- and lap-dancing clubs. However, prostitution and other types of sex work have always been controversial; not all social analysts even agree on whether or not the sex industry is a social problem. To better understand the controversy over prostitution, pornography, and other sex work, we will look at each of these issues and what constitutes deviant behaviour. Looking at the way these elements of the sex trade are currently organized, as well as looking into the future, nationally and globally, will help you to decide if any of the explanations provided by various sociological and feminist perspectives clarify *your* opinions.

PROSTITUTION IN HISTORICAL AND GLOBAL PERSPECTIVE

Narrowly defined, ***prostitution* is the sale of sexual services (of oneself or another) for money or goods and without emotional attachment. More broadly defined, systems of prostitution refer to any industry in which women's and/or children's—and sometimes men's—bodies are bought, sold, or traded for sexual use** (Giobbe, 1994). According to this broader definition, systems of prostitution include pornography, live sex shows, peep shows, international sexual slavery, and prostitution as more narrowly defined above. The vast majority of sex-trade workers around the globe are women and female children. Certainly, male prostitution exists, and most boys and men in the sex industry engage in sexual encounters with other males (see McNamara, 1994; Browne and Minichiello, 1995; Snell, 1995; Wolff and Geissel, 2000).

The World's Oldest Profession?

Prostitution has been referred to as the "world's oldest profession" because references to it can be found throughout recorded history. Still, over the past 4000 years, prostitution has been neither totally accepted nor completely condemned. For example, while prostitution was widely accepted in ancient Greece, where upper-class prostitutes were admired and frequently became the companions of powerful Greek citizens, the prostitutes themselves were refused the status of wife—the ultimate affirmation of legitimacy for women in Greek society—and were negatively compared with so-called virtuous women in a "bad woman–good woman" ("Madonna–Whore") dichotomy (see Bullough and Bullough, 1987; Roberts, 1992; Jolin, 1994).

In other eras, attitudes and beliefs about prostitution have ranged from generally tolerant to strongly averse. Such early Christian leaders as St. Augustine and St. Thomas Aquinas argued that prostitution was evil but encouraged tolerance toward it. According to Aquinas, prostitution served a basic need that, if unmet, would result in greater harm than prostitution itself. Later Christian leaders such as Martin Luther in 16th-century Europe believed that prostitution should be abolished on moral grounds (Otis, 1985; Jolin, 1994).

In the 19th-century feminist movement, women for the first time voiced their opinions about prostitution. Some believed that prostitution led to promiscuity and moral degeneracy in men and should therefore be eradicated. Others believed that prostitution should be legitimized as a valid expression of female sexuality outside of marriage. Recently, some advocates have suggested that prostitution should be viewed as a legitimate career choice for women (prostitute as sex worker), but others have argued that prostitution is rooted in global gender inequality (prostitute as victim of oppression). This argument will be discussed further when we examine feminist perspectives on the issue.

In terms of prostitution being Canada's oldest profession, it is not. Sociologist Dan Allman (1999) notes that, though there were some accounts of "prostitution-like" relations among Indigenous people, sex work was not actually introduced in Canada until Europeans began to settle here. Early writings about the Canadian sex trade (late 1800s to early 1900s) are limited to females who were in the public eye.

The Global Sex Industry

The past three decades have seen the industrialization, normalization, and globalization of prostitution. Although *industrialization* typically refers to the mass production of manufactured goods and services for exchange in the market, sociologist Kathleen Barry (1995:122) suggests that this term should also apply to commercialized sex manufactured within the human self. Prostitution becomes *normalized* when sex work is treated as merely a form of entertainment and there are no legal impediments to promoting it as a commodity. The *globalization* of prostitution refers to the process by which the sex industry has become increasingly global in scope (e.g., international conglomerates of hotel chains, airlines, bars, sex clubs, massage parlours, brothels, and credit card companies that have an economic interest in the global sex industry), which has occurred as people's political, economic, and cultural lives have become increasingly linked globally (Barry, 1995; Davidson, 1996). For evidence of this globalization, one has only to look at the recent increase in Canada of migrant sex workers from the former Soviet Union and Eastern Europe (see Box 7.1).

Furthermore, Internet sites, such as the World Sex Guide, post listings for hundreds of cities all over the world. Would-be travellers can simply log on, click on their destination city, and find out about specific women and agencies in the area, rates, services offered (e.g., if she allows "oral" on herself, if she will perform "oral" on you, how good it is, etc.), photos, laws of the particular jurisdiction, and so on. These kinds of services lend a whole new meaning to the Canadian advertising jingle, "Be a tourist in your own hometown," as, of course, many Canadian cities are listed, along with detailed advice and reports from businessmen, long-haul truckers, and others who travel domestically.

The United Nations estimates that, worldwide, in a $7 billion-per-year enterprise, 4 million people are

BOX 7.1 The Global Sex Trade—A Canadian Case

Many people are trafficked as domestic workers or mail-order brides. Others are trafficked for the sex trade. How many women are trafficked into Canada for involvement in the sex trade is unknown, but the demand for "exotic" and foreign-born women is well-documented. An estimated 500 000 women are trafficked for prostitution worldwide and, historically, much of this traffic has involved women from various parts of Asia. All indications are that, today, Slavic women are the main focus of traffickers, making up as many as two-thirds of women trafficked annually for the sex trade (McDonald et al., 2000:1).

The reasons for the increase in the traffic of Slavic women revolve mainly around the breakup of the Soviet Union in 1991 and the resultant economic upheaval. As Eastern Europe and the former Soviet Union struggled to make the transition from a communist economy to free-market capitalism, massive job loss and poverty ensued. Inevitably, the world over, women (and their children) have been the hardest hit by these structural economic shifts. Many women view migration to richer nations as the key to their survival or view it as a means to better their and their families' situations.

Through formal means (advertisements in local newspapers, billboards, and TV) or informal means (word of mouth by friends, relatives, and coworkers), women are recruited by sex-trade traffickers to work in Canada, the United States, Asia, and Western European countries. While some women may be aware of the working conditions and the goals of those who recruit them for the Canadian sex trade, most appear to be ill-informed, misled, or completely deceived. Sentences for traffickers are light, as well as rare, making this a lucrative industry for organized crime.

In research for the Status of Women Canada, Lynn McDonald, Brooke Moore, and Natalya Timoshkina (2000) conducted, for the first time, an exploratory study of women migrant sex workers in Toronto who had come to Canada from Eastern Europe and the former Soviet Union. Eighteen migrant sex workers, as well as service providers and other key informants such as police officers, immigration officials, and massage parlour owners, were interviewed in order to create a comprehensive picture of these women's experiences. The researchers found that trafficking networks varied in their degree of formalization, depending on size. Large-scale networks were ones with political and economic footholds in the countries of origin and destination and were "sophisticated" in terms of producing fraudulent documents and having a "substantial infrastructure" for transit routes and destination nations (McDonald et al., 2000:5). Medium-scale networks were ones that did not sell women to others but rather recruited women from one specific country to work in their own businesses in the destination country

(McDonald et al., 2000:5). The small-scale networks operated typically by fulfilling orders for one, two, or more women, perhaps from a specific region, placed by a business owner. In these operations, the traffickers recruited and then accompanied the women, ultimately delivering them to the contracting business owner (McDonald et al., 2000:5). Many women are also recruited informally, through word of mouth, by people they know who are either already here in Canada or are in the country of origin but know of contacts here.

While it would be incorrect to paint all trafficked women as innocent victims, some degree of deception is nearly always employed in recruiting them. Some women are promised legitimate employment and then forced into the sex trade, while others know they will be involved in the sex trade but are deceived about its legality in Canada, the specifics of what they are to do, the extent of their involvement, and the length of time they must be involved, as the interview comments of these Hungarian sex-trade workers in a Toronto strip-club illustrate:

I call them and I meet with them, and they said it's a babysitting job and stuff . . . and then when I come to Canada I find out here that it's not a babysitting job. And then I just find out this group in Hungary it's really organized crime. (McDonald et al., 2000:44)

The first, second, third, fourth night I didn't work at all. I said: "There is no way I'm going to dance. You can do anything with me. I'm not going to dance." On Sunday night he [owner/agent] said, "You've been here one week . . . you didn't make any money, and we are going to teach you how to make the money" . . . he sent four guys in the room so he could teach me how I have to make the money. They raped me for four days and four nights. (McDonald et al., 2000:54)

I heard that they keep the rules very strictly so I shouldn't worry about the dance. They knew I'd never danced before and that's why they said it. That nobody can ever touch me . . . always security everywhere. And so I won't have any problems with any customers, nobody can come close to me . . . The difference was that of course people tried to touch me, of course they were closer to me than I expected. There was no security where we danced. So the customers could do whatever they wanted. (McDonald et al., 2000: 44–45)

McDonald, Moore, and Timoshkina (2000) found that none of the women in their study had worked in the sex-trade industry prior to being trafficked to Canada. Many believed they were coming to Canada to become legitimate chorus line–style dancers or entertainers. Most said they were aged 18 to 26, although some may have been younger than that. All had finished high school, with half the women having postsecondary certificates, degrees, and careers in their countries of origin. Most of the women were single and one-quarter of them had children. All the women came to Canada with the idea of improving their economic situations, some having other reasons in addition, such as the actuality or the threat of war in their homeland.

What many women found was that, instead of making a great deal of money and living autonomous lives, their activities were often completely controlled; they found themselves living at places designated by the business owner or agent, being driven to and from work, working long hours, being videotaped or watched constantly, and earning just enough (if any) money to keep them perpetually engaged in the business, since against any earnings were charged creative fees for housing, food, the DJ's services, room rentals for sex with customers, fines for being late, and so on. Other women had more autonomy, earned decent money, and felt they could not make this kind of money elsewhere, so they remained tied to the industry due to lack of viable options (McDonald et al., 2000). Many of the women were brought into the country on visitor visas; when these expired, the owners or agents had that much more control over the women.

Many women are told they cannot leave the trade or the establishment because they will be arrested and deported, especially those women who are here on expired visas. Others have stayed in the work due to a (perceived) lack of options. Many women were expected to send money home to relatives or were trying to support families here and believed that they would not get comparably paid jobs due to language barriers and/or a lack of Canadian training or education:

In one day you can make $200. It's a big difference when you used to make $50 a day. It means you can work for two days, just close your eyes on everything and you can survive already. I signed up my girl for dancing classes, signed her up for music classes, and she paints too. And I became happier. I can help out my mother. (Russian massage parlour worker quoted in McDonald et al., 2000:61)

You know, I've been working in this business for several years, and I can tell you that all the girls have goals. But, for some reason, even older women who keep saying: "Oh, I'll just save some money and go to school" . . . You see, it

is so hard to get out of it, out of this business. Mainly because of the money. It's very difficult. I tried to get out three or four times. (Moldovian massage parlour worker quoted in McDonald et al., 2000:61)

The traffic of women into Canada has serious implications for the women themselves and for all Canadians. Whether or not these women choose to remain in the sex industry, they should live in conditions free from coercion, abuse, danger, and economic insecurity. How to create the conditions for women to make free choices is a matter for policymakers and others to take up. McDonald, Moore, and Timoshkina (2000:66–68) make a number of recommendations that could have implications for the Canadian Criminal Code and for Canada's immigration laws. Some of the recommendations include:

- distributing information in countries of origin and at immigration ports, in many languages, about the realities of trafficking, the legalities of sex trade in Canada, exotic dancing, and so on;

- re-evaluating visitor's visas with a view to finding ways for women whose visas expire to avoid illegal status;

- finding ways to integrate migrant women and their partners into the core Canadian economy by offering more language classes (English/French) and by expediting the process for accreditation of immigrant professionals;

- intervening in establishments where women are working in unfavourable working conditions by having health inspectors do inspections on whole workplaces, not just the kitchens;

- developing a system of regulating sex-trade businesses to ensure basic Canadian work safety rules are followed;

- having written information posted in these businesses, in many languages, about free health and social services that are available;

- funding agencies and organizations that work with people in the sex trade and mandating their access to these businesses; and

- developing and funding joint initiatives for addressing organized sex-trade trafficking.

What do you think should be done about the global sex trade? How is the global sex industry linked to the international division of labour and other forms of globalization?

trafficked every year, with anywhere from 8000 to 16 000 people, mainly women, coming into Canada. It is difficult to gain specific statistics because of the illicitness of the acts and because definitions and perceptions of "trafficking" vary. Trafficking has been defined by anti-trafficking activist Lin Lap-Chew (1999) as "all acts involved in the recruitment and transportation of a woman within and across national borders for work or services by means of violence, or threat of violence, abuse of authority or dominant position, debt bondage, deception or other forms of coercion" (in McDonald et al., 2000:8). The Solicitor General for Canada estimated that, in 1998, the money involved annually in the traffic into Canada was anywhere from $120 million (USD) to $400 million (USD).

The demand for prostitution is greatest when large numbers of men are congregated for extended periods of time in the military or on business far from home. In many countries, sex tourism began with the establishment of brothels which served foreign military bases (Seager, 1997). A connection between wartime rape and increased prostitution has been documented for the Vietnam War and, more recently, for the wars in El Salvador and Bosnia. Large populations of refugees and victims of rape and sexual violence tend to be exploited by networks of pimps and organized crime gangs such as the yakuza in Japan and other international cartels (Seager, 1997; Women's International Network, 1995).

Although recent research has indicated that the global sex industry, especially prostitution, contributes to the transmission of HIV, the virus that causes AIDS (Gil et al., 1996; Purvis, 1996), many agencies and governments have not come to grips with the problem. Moreover, the threat of HIV/AIDS may be fuelling the increased demand for younger, inexperienced sex workers as a "safe sex" strategy in the booming sex tourism business (Seager, 1997). The Japanese Foundation for AIDS Prevention, an organization affiliated with the Japanese government, launched a poster campaign featuring a grinning, middle-aged man wearing a business suit and displaying his passport, with a caption reading, "Have a nice trip! But be careful of AIDS." The Japanese government is clearly aware that many businessmen participate in sex tourism abroad (Sachs, 1994), and the poster seems to endorse this while warning them about unsafe practices. What strategies do you think these businessmen are likely to employ to avoid unsafe sex?

The picture of the global sex industry reflects the economic disparity between the poorest regions of the world—where women and children (mainly) may be bought, sold, or traded like any other commodity—and the richest regions, such as Europe and North America, where many of the global sex industry's consumers reside (see Bauerlein, 1995; Davidson, 1996).

Do the two in this photo look like mother and daughter? Actually, both are employed in a Cambodian brothel. What global social and economic factors contribute to the growing number of young girls working in the sex industry?

For example, in terms of sex tourism in the 1990s, countries that most sex tourists lived in and left from were Canada, the United States, Japan, Australia, Great Britain, France, Sweden, Germany, Norway, Saudi Arabia, China, Singapore, Malaysia, Kuwait, and Qatar. Major destinations for these tourists were Hungary, Brazil, Indonesia, Thailand, Vietnam, Kenya, Cambodia, Bangladesh, Philippines, Costa Rica, Cuba, Morocco, India, and the Dominican Republic (Seager, 1997; Ward, 1999). Additionally, as seen in Box 7.1, rich nations increasingly import the sexual services of people from poorer nations. As geographer and women's studies scholar Joni Seager (1997:115) notes: "As poverty deepens in Eastern Europe, it becomes a major source region for prostitutes; as wealth expands in China and Malaysia, men in those countries fuel an increased demand for the traffic in women and girls."

PROSTITUTION IN CANADA

Prostitution, among consenting adults, has never been illegal in Canada. However, sections 210–213 of the Canadian Criminal Code do prohibit many transactions that are quite necessary to prostitution. The activities that are illegal in Canada, relating to the sex trade are: (1) communicating in a public place for the purposes of buying or selling sexual services; (2) procuring or soliciting a person to exchange sexual services for money and living off the avails; and, (3) being involved in a common bawdy house (Millar, 2002:38; Wolff and Geissel, 2000:254). These activities are considered a threat either to public decency or to public order. Those convicted of prostitution-related offences are often fined, although jail terms are possible. For example, communicating for the purposes of prostitution carries the maximum penalty of a $2000 fine or six months in jail or both. Given the economic situation of many street prostitutes, hefty fines may ensure continued sex-trade work, and not in any way act as a deterrent. As one young Saskatoon woman explains:

> [When I was arrested for prostitution] all my friends were there and it hurt so much, it made me feel much lower . . . they [the judicial system] treat you like such a bad person or that you're a slut, tramp, or whore. You're forced to go there [the streets], you were forced into that spot and if you said no, you were beat up or something worse, you could be killed. And they make it out like you're nothing, they don't try to help you, they just charge you and send you on your merry way . . . they know where you're going off to, you have to pay off your fine. (Kingsley and Mark, 2000:27)

Federal laws on prostitution-related activities ensure that it is almost impossible to engage in the trade without breaking the law. Criminologist John Lowman (2000) reports that this fact adds to the already existing moral–political marginalization that sex-trade workers endure, increasing the risks of the work. Lowman (2000:1006) says our "system of quasi-criminalization":

1. contributes to legal structures that tend to make the prostitute responsible for her [or his] own victimization, and thus reinforces the line of argument that says that, if people choose to prostitute themselves, they deserve what they get—they are "offenders" not "victims";

2. makes prostitution part of an illicit market. As such, it is left to primitive market forces and creates an environment in which brutal forms of manager-exploitation can take root;

3. encourages the convergence of prostitution with other illicit markets, particularly the drug trade. Once the price of a habit-forming, mind-altering substance is driven up by criminal prohibition, a drug like heroin can be as demanding a "pimp" as any man; and

4. alienates persons who engage in prostitution from the protective-service potential of the police. Why would prostitutes turn to police for help when police are responsible for enforcing the laws against prostitutes? . . . Criminal law sanctions institutionalize an adversarial relationship between prostitutes and police.

This may be why, instead of going to the police when they are beaten, raped, or robbed, sex-trade workers report "bad tricks" or "bad dates" to various organizations that keep, post, and monitor Bad Date Sheets. One of the first organizations in Canada to publish a Bad Date Sheet was the Alliance for Safety of Prostitutes (ASP) in 1983. Bad Date Sheets typically report the type of offence, where the offender picked the worker up, the date and time of the offence, description of and characteristics of the offender (age, racialization/ethnicity, gender, other identifying features such as tattoos, etc.) and vehicle, the type of person victimized (e.g., woman, man, transsexual, youth), and whether the person is known to be a repeat offender or not. The sheets are then circulated monthly by street and other social service workers and posted in various agencies and places prostitutes are known to go for services (Lowman and Fraser, 1995). John Lowman and Laura Fraser's study (1995) of *Bad Trick Reports in Vancouver, B.C. 1985–1994* shows that most "bad tricks" are Caucasian males, perceived to be in their twenties and thirties, and most victims are adult females. The most common types of bad dates were physical and sexual assaults, followed by robbery and, in a quarter of the cases, a weapon was used. Lowman and Fraser (1995) encourage us to see this violence as part of a continuum of male violence against women, not as acceptable risks associated with the job.

Many Canadian youth, women, and men are involved in the Canadian sex trade, as sex workers, as "managers," or as customers, both overseas and at home. Prostitution has always been a feature of Western societies and, although some characteristics of it are changing, with increasing globalization and economic disparity between more and less industrialized nations, it certainly appears to be here to stay. How we approach the myriad issues raised by the sex trade (e.g. some of the associated dangers, like violence against sex-trade workers) will depend upon how we view it. In any case, it is interesting to note that, while in 1985, 20 percent of Canadians identified prostitution as a pressing social problem, a decade later, fewer than 1 percent of Canadians felt it was a "very serious" social problem (Bibby, 1995).

Some Characteristics of Prostitution in Canada

Clearly, not all sex-trade workers are alike: Life experiences, family backgrounds, years of formal education, locales of operation, types of customers, and methods of doing business vary widely. Even with these differences, however, sociologists have identified five levels, or tiers, of prostitution, ranging from escort workers to street prostitutes to women exchanging sex for drugs in crack houses.

Top-tier prostitutes are typically referred to as *escorts* or *call girls* and *call boys*. They are considered the upper echelon in prostitution because they tend to earn considerably higher fees and typically have more years of formal education than other prostitutes do. Many of them do not even think of themselves as prostitutes. They usually dress nicely—and often conservatively—so that they do not call undue attention to themselves at the luxury hotels, clubs, and apartment buildings they may be called to work in. Maybe most importantly, escort sex workers have more selectivity in their working conditions and customers than do other prostitutes (Chapkis, 1997; Macy, 1996). An escort worker named Terry clearly differentiates between herself and other, less fortunate workers:

> One of the reasons I think I can enjoy my work, is because I carefully screen my clients. I have no tolerance for any assholes. I'm providing a service to these men, and as far as I'm concerned, they're privileged to have it. So they have to show me the proper respect. I deserve that respect. If they don't

think so then they should keep their cock in their pants and their money in their pocket. It means that I may make less money than I might otherwise, but my safety is worth it. People in more desperate circumstances have to put up with a lot more. (Chapkis, 1997:100)

Escort prostitutes work "on call," going out to see customers who are referred to them by their escort service, pimp, or other procurers such as hotel concierges and taxi drivers who may receive a percentage of the prostitute's fees. Other escorts may "freelance," brokering their own calls and deals, advertising in local newspapers, and so on. Although their work is not as visible as that of many other sex workers, escorts generally face some of the same hazards, including abusive customers and sexually transmitted diseases.

The second tier of prostitutes is comprised of hustlers, strippers, and table dancers who engage in prostitution on the side. People in this tier work primarily out of nightclubs, bars, and strip joints. The hustlers are sometimes referred to as *bar girls* or *bar boys* because they are supposed to pressure (hustle) customers to buy drinks. Most hustlers are not paid by the bar but earn their livelihood by negotiating sexual favours with bar customers, who often are lonely and want someone to talk to as well as to have sex with (Devereaux, 1987).

The third tier is made up of *house girls* who work in brothels (houses of prostitution) run by a madam or a pimp, who collects approximately half of the fees earned by the women. Customers choose a "date" from women lined up in a parlour or receiving room. House prostitutes are not allowed to engage in "dirty hustling" (winking, running one's tongue over one's lips, or shaking a leg) or to turn down a customer (Devereaux, 1987). Operating a bawdy house or living off the avails of prostitution is illegal in Canada, and thus houses of prostitution typically operate as body-painting studios, massage parlours, or other legal businesses.

Near the bottom tier of prostitution are *streetwalkers,* who publicly solicit customers and charge by the "trick." Most street prostitutes work a specific location and many are "protected" by a pimp. Many streetwalkers derive status and some degree of protection from violent "johns" from their pimps. However, researchers have also documented the exploitative and, too often, violent nature of the pimp–prostitute relationship (B.C.

Ministry of Attorney General, 1996; Kingsley and Mark, 2000; Sexually Exploited Youth Committee of the Capital Regional District, 1997).

The very bottom tier of prostitution is occupied by women who are addicted to crack cocaine, heroin, or other drugs and who engage in drugs-for-sex exchanges (Fullilove et al., 1992; Kingsley and Mark, 2000). Researchers have found that many crack-addicted women perform unprotected oral sex on men in crack houses in exchange for hits of crack. According to one study,

> Some men will enter a crack house, purchase enough rocks for two people for several hours, and then make it clear to every woman in the house what he has in mind.... [There] seems to be an expectation [in the crack house] that if a man wants to have sex with a woman, she will not oppose the offer. The expectations are implicit. Everyone involved—the house owner, the male user/customer, and the female user/prostitute are all aware of what is expected. (Inciardi et al., 1993:74–75)

In the words of one young Winnipeg woman, "I met a bunch of guys I knew, they were always giving me rock [crack] for free, I never had to do anything, except for this one guy. Then we met these guys, [and] you had to go around the whole room to get a piece [of crack from each guy]" (Kingsley and Mark, 2000:21).

Although less research has been done on prostitution tiers with males, the tiers appear to be similar to those of females except that, with males, most customers are of the same gender as the sex worker. For example, in her report on escort services, journalist Marianna Macy (1996:249) found that some male escorts exist and "Men normally go see men." Some male prostitutes work as hustlers in bars and nightclubs, where they typically wear blue jeans, leather jackets, and boots, seeking to project a strong heterosexual image. Sexual orientation is frequently an issue with male prostitutes, some of whom do not define themselves as gay and limit the types of sexual acts they are willing to perform. Others view sex strictly as an economic exchange and define work-related sex as "not real sex" (Browne and Minichiello, 1995). Most research shows that although males are involved in the sex trade as sex workers, there are not as many boys and men as girls and women. The Department of Justice in 1993 estimated that between 10 and 33 percent of street prostitutes in Canada are male, but that at least 80 per-

cent of situations where sex is traded for money involve women as the worker (Allman, 1999). This is reinforced by the B.C. provincial study: "Sexually procured youth and adults (those who receive money for sexual services) are predominantly female. Males are less visible and tend to work primarily on a party circuit or in private residences" (B.C. Ministry of Attorney General, 1996:3).

Much research in Canada has been focused on identifying the factors that bring people into the sex trade, particularly into the relatively dangerous street prostitution tier. Recent studies of youth in the sex trade in British Columbia as well as Canada-wide studies reveal that several factors are nearly always implicated in engaging youth in the sex trade. The use of the term "youth" is not accidental, as research shows that most people (96 percent) became prostitutes before age 18 (Wolff and Geissel, 2000). One cross-provincial study, a community consultation on prostitution in British Columbia, found that the average age of entry to prostitution in that province is 14, with some beginning as early as age 8 or 9 (B.C. Ministry of Attorney General, 1996). Another study, conducted in Victoria, British Columbia's capital city, found the average age of entry to be 15.5 years, although some started as early as 11 (Sexually exploited Youth Committee of the Capital Regional District, 1997). Allman (1999) reported that approximately 10 to 12 percent of sex-trade workers were under 18 years of age, and most males in the trade admit to starting by age 16. There is evidence across Canada that males remain in the trade for much shorter durations than females, the average length of time being just over five years for men. Allman suggests that by the time males in the trade reach the age of 20 to 22, the youthful looks that attracted the customers are beginning to fade, so they move on to other things.

There is some evidence as well that males and females may enter the sex trade for slightly different reasons (Allman, 1999). Most people involved report that the money is an enticement. A 1993 Montreal study found that prostitutes were earning anywhere from $600 to $2000 per week, with females earning considerably more than males per week (maybe due to demand) (Allman, 1999). Key factors leading into the sex trade for youth are generally reported to be homelessness and/or a lack of basic necessities for survival of self or of their own children (e.g., shelter, food, clothing, etc.); emotional abuse, sexual abuse/assault and/or other physical assaults at home; the development of an alcohol and/or drug addiction; a lack of satisfactory assistance with a health/mental health issue (e.g., depression, eating disorder, bipolar disorder); a lack of life skills and employment; dropping out of school; and low self-esteem (B.C. Ministry of Attorney General, 1996; Kingsley and Mark, 2000; Sexually Exploited Youth Committee of the Capital Regional District, 1997; Wolff and Geissel, 2000). As stated by a female former street worker from Thunder Bay, Ontario, "[I wouldn't have worked in the trade if] I could have had better self-esteem, I didn't have any boundaries, and I didn't care. I didn't know my worth at that time" (Kingsley and Mark, 2000:31). One Ottawa-area study of youth sex-trade workers found that the "sex for survival" motif was more common for females than for males. Many homeless males were able to "couch surf," while females were expected to trade sex for food, shelter, or money (reported in Allman, 1999).

The presence of several or even all of these factors does not guarantee entry into the sex trade, of course. It does, however, heighten the risk of a young person having fewer choices. As stated in one recent report, "They do not move directly from a 'normal' teenage life of home, school and extra-curricular activities to being a prostitute. Long before that, most have a long history of school problems or family problems or emotional problems or all three" (Sexually Exploited Youth Committee of the Capital Regional District, 1997:4). As clearly stated by Wolff and Geissel (2000:257), "Adolescent prostitution can be viewed as a survival behaviour." On the cover of the 1997 Report of the Sexually Exploited Youth Committee of the Capital Regional District, Victoria, British Columbia, a phony employment advertisement sums up the risk factors for youth street prostitution in Canada:

```
Wanted:
Vulnerable Youth and Children
Preferably with no place to stay, no one to
protect them. Must be under 18; ages 12 to
15 preferred. Must be prepared to be all
things sexually to all people.
May be required to work on demand, day or
night. Frequent sexual, physical, verbal
assaults guaranteed. Drug addiction an occu-
pational hazard.
Pay minimal--room, board, drugs may be
included.
High management and exit fees and beatings
extracted. Equal opportunity for males and
females.Preference given to those able to
withstand abuse.
```

The Extent of Prostitution in Canada

There are no reliable estimates of the extent of prostitution in Canada, for several reasons. First, the activity is quasi-legal, and hence much activity is clandestine or otherwise hidden behind massage parlours and escort services. Second, criminal charges, which are basically our only official source for quantitative data on prostitution, almost entirely deal with street prostitution. Although this is only one component of the sex trade, it is the most visible, with 95 percent of all charges in recent years being for "communicating." Further, it is not known what proportion street prostitution makes up of all sex-trade activity. Throw into all this confusion the fact that people don't always agree on how to define certain types of sex work (i.e., is it "prostitution" or not?) and the fact that people move around, change their names and addresses, and so on. Many people drift into and out of prostitution, considering it temporary work between full-time jobs or as part-time work while attending school (Allman, 1999; Lowman, 2000; Reynolds, 1986; Potterat et al., 1990).

Prostitution and Age, Class, Racialization, and Ethnicity

Although some Canadian prostitutes are as young as 8 or 9, the vast majority is between the ages of 17 and 24. The peak earning age appears to be about 22 (Clinard and Meier, 1989; DePasquale, 1999). In contrast, the typical male customer is considerably older than the prostitute, White, and married, although some teenage and university-age males also hire prostitutes (National Victims Resource Center, 1991). Often, the age difference between teenage prostitutes and older customers is striking, as a woman forced into prostitution at age 13 by a pimp explains:

> The men who bought me—the tricks—knew I was an adolescent. Most of them were in their 50s and 60s. They had daughters and granddaughters my age. They knew a child's face when they looked into it. . . . It was even clearer that I was sexually inexperienced. So they showed me pornography to teach me and ignored my tears as they positioned my body like the women in the pictures, and used me. (Giobbe, 1993:38)

Although a small percentage of teenagers enter prostitution through coercion, most are runaways who have left home because of sexual abuse or other family problems. Some teen prostitutes are "throwaways"—thrown out of their homes by parents or other family members (Snell, 1995; Vissing, 1996). Regardless of their prior history, many teens become prostitutes because prostitution is the best—or only—job they can get.

Social class is directly linked to prostitution: Lower-income and poverty-level women and men are far more likely to become prostitutes than are more affluent people (Miller, 1986). Some people with little formal education and few job skills view prostitution as an economic necessity. As one woman stated, "I make good money [as a prostitute]. That's why I do it; if I worked at McDonald's for minimum wage, then I'd feel degraded" (quoted in McWilliams, 1996:340). However, women working for exclusive escort services are more likely to have attended college and come from the middle or upper-middle class. Racialization is also an important factor in prostitution. Sociologist Patricia Hill Collins (1991) suggests that African-American women are affected by the widespread image of Black women as sexually promiscuous. Collins traces the roots of this stereotype to the era of slavery, when Black women—and Black men and children—were at the mercy of White male slave-owners and their sexual desires. Indigenous women are affected by similar stereotyping. Historically, First Nations women have been viewed as being sexually freer than White women (Allen, 1986), a view that has, over the years, translated into the stereotype of sexual promiscuity. This

stereotype has had the effect of devaluing and even dehumanizing Indigenous women and has been used as a justification for sexualized violence against them. For example, sociologists Augie Fleras and Jean Leonard Elliott (1996:148) report on the prairie practice of "squaw hopping," the "acknowledged practice for White men to harass and sexually assault native women." According to Collins (1991:175), prostitution exists within a "complex web of political and economic relationships whereby sexuality is conceptualized along intersecting axes of race and gender." Sexually-exploited-youth advocates Cherry Kingsley and Melanie Mark (2000:28–29), in their recent national consultation of sexually exploited Indigenous youth, found Indigenous women and girls overrepresented in the visible sex trade, with Indigenous youth accounting for as much as 90 percent of the visible trade in some communities. High rates of Indigenous participation in prostitution can be attributed, in part, to many young people's experiences in foster care: "Consultations with [Indigenous] youth identified their care experiences as paving the way for their commercial sexual exploitation" (Kingsley and Mark, 2000:26). Today, prostitution remains linked to the ongoing economic, political, and social exploitation of people of colour and Indigenous people, particularly women.

A Closer Look at "Johns"

To date, no comprehensive studies have been conducted in Canada about the sex-trade customer or "john." This may be a reflection of the relative power of the john's social location in relation to the sex-trade worker's. Since both are, theoretically, equally liable for prosecution under Canada's communicating laws, we should have access to similar information about both groups. This power differential is well understood by one young Saskatoon sex-trade worker:

> They are always looking down on us and blaming us, but it's not only us. It's their husbands that are picking us up. Everybody is in denial: everybody pinpoints us, and blames us because we're the ones out on the street. But they're the ones that are picking us up and giving us money. They're always calling us little sluts and whores, but they never say anything about the johns . . . like they're picture perfect guys. (Kingsley and Mark, 2000:25)

This self-inking money stamp was made available by the Sex Workers Alliance of Vancouver, in 1999, to sex workers in the community. Its aim is to raise public awareness that money earned generated by the sex trade is an important part of the Canadian economy.

Source: Will Pritchard, Illustrator/Designer. Distributed by the Sex Workers Alliance of Vancouver © 1996, **www.walnet.org/swav/**. Reproduced with permission.

What little information is available indicates that most johns are men in their mid-20s to mid-40s (although older is common also), White, married, and gainfully employed (Brannigan et al., 1989; National Victims Resource Center, 1991). A report by the Canadian Advisory Council on the Status of Women (1984:49) notes that most observers of prostitution report that johns are "ordinary men who go to prostitutes for simple reasons," such as experiencing sexual acts they cannot have in their other relationships, experiencing sexual relationships without lasting obligations or long-term complications, engaging in "therapy" for problems like impotence, or having a good time.

A British Columbia consultation with johns that was arranged through Sexual Addicts Anonymous provided some insights into some johns' behaviour that offer a contrast to the picture of johns as ordinary, well-adjusted men. Given the nature of the group consulted, however, these men cannot be seen to be representative of all johns (B.C. Ministry of Attorney General, 1996). This consultation found that many johns reported childhood sexual abuse and believed themselves to be "addicted" to sex. The use of prostitutes resulted in the men feeling a great deal of shame, which

related to their childhood experiences and caused them to act in ways that perpetuated those feelings (engaging the services of a prostitute, for example). These johns also reported that part of the attraction to cruising for prostitutes and the use of their services was the risk of getting caught, therefore indicating that "shame the johns" campaigns may in fact work counter to the stated purpose of the campaigns. The view of the men interviewed was that stopping prostitution could only be achieved by ensuring there was a treatment component inherent in the sentencing, that punishments alone would not be successful.

In an attempt to obtain a broader picture of people who buy sexual services, the B.C. Ministry of Attorney General funded an Internet survey in 1996–1997, conducted by John Lowman, Chris Atchison, and Laura Fraser (1997). The attitudes and behaviours of 130 men worldwide who buy sex are represented in this report. As in other Canadian studies (Brannigan et al., 1989), the mean age of johns was 37, with a range from 18 to 67. Most men were married or common-law; had children; were heterosexual, White, high-school graduates; and were employed full-time. Most of the men who responded online reported that their first sexual experience was with a friend or acquaintance, not with a relative or a stranger. Twenty percent reported childhood sexual abuse. We do not have comparable figures for childhood sexual abuse for men generally.

When asked about attitudes, the men who participated in this survey believed that loneliness, sexual problems at home, the desire for specific sexual acts that partners would not perform, the desire for uncomplicated sex, and a strong male sex drive were important reasons for seeking out a prostitute. Just over one-half of the participants believed that travel to a city other than one's normal residence is important for the sex-trade transaction to occur. Most men believed female sex-trade workers are "normal," hard-working women who are "just doing another job" and provid[ing] a valuable service"; most of the participants disagreed that prostitutes are the "victims of a sexist society" (Lowman et al., 1997). When asked whether prostitution should be criminalized, unsurprisingly then, most of these men believed it should not be. The exception here was that most of these men believed that sex with children under age 13, and snuff films—films where the actor, usually the female in the film, is actually killed in front of the camera—are morally reprehensible and should be prohibited. In terms of deterrents to buying sex, nearly all the men who responded stated they would buy sex even if it was completely illegal. However, when asked which strategies would be useful in preventing men from buying sex on the street, having viable off-street options was listed, as well as the fact of their spouses finding out, public exposure or public recognition by someone they know, and fear of HIV/AIDS (Lowman et al., 1997).

PERSPECTIVES ON PROSTITUTION

Sociologists use a variety of perspectives to examine prostitution as a social problem. Functionalists focus on how deviance—including prostitution—serves important functions in society. Interactionists investigate microlevel concerns, such as how and why people become prostitutes or come to buy sexual services and how the stigmatization affects their self-esteem. Conflict perspectives seek to explain how the powerful enact their moral beliefs into law and how prostitution is related to capitalism and/or patriarchy, and feminist theorists focus on sex-trade work as gendered (and inequitable) labour.

The Functionalist Perspective

Functionalists believe that the presence of a certain amount of deviance in society contributes to its overall stability. According to early sociologist Emile Durkheim, deviance clarifies social norms and helps societies to maintain *social control*—**the systematic practices developed by social groups to encourage conformity and discourage deviance**—over people's behaviour. By punishing those who engage in deviant behaviour such as prostitution, the society reaffirms its commitment to its sexual norms and creates loyalty to the society, as people bind together to oppose the behaviour.

According to sociologist Kingsley Davis (1937), in societies (such as Canada) that have restrictive norms governing sexual conduct, prostitution will always exist, because it serves important functions. First, it provides quick, impersonal sexual gratification that does not require emotional attachment or a continuing relationship with another person (Freund et al., 1991). Second, prostitution provides a sexual outlet for men who do not have ongoing sexual relationships because they are not married or have heavy work schedules. Third, prostitution provides people with the opportunity to engage in sexual practices—multiple sex partners, fellatio (oral stimulation of the male genitalia), cunnilingus (oral stimulation of the female genitalia), anal intercourse, or sadomasochism (S&M), including the use of such devices as handcuffs, whips, and chains—that regular sex partners or spouses might view as immoral or distasteful. Fourth, prostitution protects the family as a social institution by making a distinction between "bad girls" or "bad boys"—with whom one engages in promiscuous sexual behaviour—and "good girls" and "good boys"—with whom one establishes a family. Finally, prostitution benefits the economy by providing jobs for people who have limited formal education and job skills.

The Interactionist Perspective

Why do people become prostitutes? Do some prostitutes like their work? Why do people choose to pay for sex? Interactionists investigate questions such as these by using a social–psychological framework, for example, by examining people's lived experiences. Here is an excerpt from an interview with a prostitute named Dolores:

I set my own schedule. I set my own limits and made my own rules, and I didn't have to answer to anyone. I learned a lot about myself: what I would and would not do for money, and what I was willing to do for the right amount of money. . . . I didn't have to see anyone I didn't want to see. If a man was too boring or too rough or too crude or took too much time, I didn't have to see him again. I loved it. (French, 1988:180)

Dolores's remarks suggest that some people become prostitutes because it provides them with greater autonomy and more career options than they otherwise would have. These reasons fit with sociologist Howard Becker's (1963) suggestion that entering a deviant career is similar in many ways to entering any other occupation. The primary difference is the labelling that goes with a deviant career. Public labelling of people as deviant and their acceptance or rejection of that label are crucial factors in determining whether or not a person stays in a deviant career. Some people are more willing than others to accept the label "deviant" or may believe they have no other option.

Why do men seek out prostitutes? Research by interactionists suggests that some young men seek out prostitutes to fulfill what they believe is a rite of passage from boyhood to manhood. Consider, for example, John's comments after several trips to a house of prostitution:

We went back to school, Mike and I, after going to that first whorehouse. We were probably the only two guys in the class that had done it. We were celebrities. We had crowds around us when we'd tell them all the details, how great it was, what studs we were. . . . My reaction to all this was it wasn't really very exciting. After all the talk you hear about it, all the writing, all the pictures, all the taboos about sex, I thought, "For this? This is what it was about?". . . It wasn't something bad; it just wasn't nearly as exciting as I thought it would be. But we thought, "This is a good chance to learn," so we went back several times. . . . I can remember up to eleven. . . . I always thought I'd keep count all my life; that was part of what being a man was all about. (quoted in Raphael, 1988:74–75)

Social analysts suggest that the need of men of all ages to validate their sexual prowess or reaffirm their masculinity is an important factor in their seeking out prostitutes (Raphael, 1988). Interactionist perspectives such as these highlight how people define social realities—such as the importance of sexual prowess or masculinity—in light of competing and often contradictory values they have learned through socialization.

Conflict and Feminist Perspectives

Conflict perspectives on prostitution highlight the relationship between power in society and sex work: The laws that make prostitution illegal are created by powerful dominant group members who seek to maintain cultural dominance by criminalizing sexual conduct that they consider immoral or in bad taste (Barry, 1995).

Conflict analysts using a liberal feminist framework believe that prostitution should be *decriminalized*—meaning that laws making prostitution a crime should be repealed. These analysts argue that prostitution is a ***victimless crime*—a crime that many people believe has no real victim because it involves willing participants in an economic exchange.** Therefore sex workers should not be harassed by police and the courts. According to Margo St. James, a former prostitute and founder of an activist group called COYOTE (Call Off Your Old Tired Ethics), "The profession itself is not abusive; it's the illegality; it's the humiliation and degradation that is dealt to them at the hands of the police" (quoted in McWilliams, 1996:340). In other words, prostitution is sex work in the sex industry and should be treated as a labour issue.

Conflict perspectives using Marxist feminist and radical feminist frameworks suggest that women become prostitutes because of structural factors such as economic inequality and patriarchy (Jolin, 1994). Capitalism and patriarchy foster economic inequality between women and men and force women to view their bodies as simply commodities: "When a man has bought a woman's body for his use as if it were like any other commodity . . . the sex act itself provides acknowledgment of patriarchal right. When women's bodies are on sale as commodities in the capitalist market . . . men gain public acknowledgment as women's sexual masters" (Pateman, 1994:132). Summarizing a historical feminist position, the Canadian Advisory Council on the Status of Women (1984:3) in its report on prostitution in Canada pointed out that:

Prostitution is not an exchange among equals. Men, who as a group, still hold most of the powerful positions of social, economic and political power in our society, buy services from the less powerful: women (often poor, young and under-educated women) and male and female adolescents and children. The sellers have little or no defense against the risks of physical or sexual abuse of economic exploitation . . . The buyer . . . has the money: as a group, buyers do not depend on sellers for their income, while sellers generally do depend on buyers. This economic dependence reinforces the social vulnerability that prostitutes experience.

Feminists who hold this view believe that the exploitation involved in prostitution is an extension of the kind of exploitation women experience generally, not only with regard to economic disadvantages but also with regard to cultural standards of female attractiveness, which are bound up in youthfulness, slimness, and so on. Male customers, on the other hand, like men in general in society, are not constricted by these cultural standards, as they make up the rules and have the economic means to reinforce their desires. Many feminists believe that women who are prostitutes do not understand their exploitation and need to be saved from the "false consciousness" that traps them in these degrading occupations. However, the prostitute-as-victim stance has been challenged by many people who are advocates for and/or engaged in the sex trade, including many prostitutes and other sex-trade workers who identify as feminists. These feminists have a view of prostitution as a service for which they charge a fee, much like any other service in society. The difference, about which they are fully conscious, is that they are hiring out their bodies in ways most people may find too distasteful to engage in. They do not view themselves as exploited and encourage feminists who view them as victims to, instead, respect them as self-directed, independent, hard-working women who have made the conscious choice to be involved in the sex trade; to do what they wish with their own bodies. This debate, between feminists, on prostitution, like the debate on pornography, has been going on for decades and likely will continue. As Carol Queen, a well-known writer, lecturer, sociologist, and sex-trade worker, stated:

Unfortunately, the exciting politics that promised me sexual freedom twenty-five years ago have veered toward dogma . . . Please . . . don't assume that you know what someone else's experience has been just because you can't imagine liking to do it yourself. Please don't require that all people be one certain 'politically correct' way. Please don't assume I can't make my own decisions, that my exhibitionism somehow makes me a victim . . . Don't tell me I don't have a soul (Queen, 1997:138–141).

According to Marxist feminists, the only way to eliminate prostitution is to reduce disparities in income levels between women and men and eliminate poverty. However, radical feminists believe that prostitution will not be eliminated until patriarchy is ended.

Conflict theorists and feminists, who in examining social problems focus on the interrelationship of racialization, class, and gender, suggest that criminalizing prostitution uniquely affects poor women, especially poor women of colour and Indigenous women, who are overrepresented among street prostitutes. According to these theorists, White male supremacy—which traditionally preserves the best-paying jobs for men—makes women of colour and Indigenous women particularly vulnerable to recruitment or coercion into prostitution. Kingsley and Mark (2000:14) found, in a national consultation of commercially sexually exploited Indigenous children and youth in Canada, that "for the Aboriginal (sic) youth who participated in these consultations, economic need dictated their actions . . . [their] engagement in the sex trade."

Analysts using this framework also note that discrimination in law enforcement uniquely affects women of colour and Indigenous women, as these groups are overrepresented among prostitutes in Canada. For example, law enforcement officials target street prostitutes and other sex workers, particularly when political elites decide to crack down on "deviant" behaviour such as prostitution and pornography (Barry, 1995). Lowman notes that there is a lack of political will to create safer conditions for prostitutes to ply their trade, as this would be seen as condoning prostitution, a stance Lowman (1995) calls "odd" as well as "hypocritical" given that prostitution in Canada is legal and hence already condoned. Instead, Lowman (1995) notes that crackdowns, which disproportionately affect street prostitution, occur when property-holders get up in arms about their neighbourhoods, demonstrating that "public propriety and property values heavily outweigh all other considerations."

PORNOGRAPHY

Nina Hartley (1994:176–177), founder of the Pink Ladies club, a group of women in the pornography industry, wrote of herself:

> "A feminist porno star? Right, tell me another one," I can hear some feminists saying . . . why porno? Simple—I'm an exhibitionist with a cause: to make sexually graphic (hard core) erotica, and today's porno is the only game in town. . . . As I examine my life, I uncover the myriad influences that led me to conclude that it was perfectly natural for me to choose a career in adult films. . . . I stripped once a week while getting my bachelor's degree in nursing. . . . I went into full time [adult] movie work immediately following graduation.

Pornography **is the graphic depiction of sexual behaviour through pictures and/or words—including by electronic or other data retrieval systems—in a manner that is intended to be sexually arousing.** Although Hartley claims to be a feminist porn star, many social analysts, as Hartley herself notes, believe that this is a contradiction in terms. Most of these analysts believe pornography is a pressing social problem. But what kind of social problem is it? Religious groups typically construe pornography as a social problem because they say it is obscene. On the other hand, social analysts, particularly feminists, usually frame the problem in terms of patriarchy—male oppression of women—by analyzing power differentials between the actors (Leong, 1991). Thus, the specific nature of pornography as a social problem is not clear-cut. Canadian sociologist Mariana Valverde (1985:124) discusses some of the difficulties with even defining what pornography is, saying that pornography "is a collection of images and texts, representations which have something in common." But, what is that "something"? In noting there are no concrete ways to measure what is or is not pornography, Valverde (1985:125) explains:

> Pornography is not a natural object that can be classified, like a particular species of butterfly, but rather a complex cultural *process*. . . . Pornography does not drop from heaven onto our local corner store shelves. It is first *produced* by certain people who relate to one another via the pornography industry; it is then *consumed* by customers who buy

porn in the expectation of being aroused; and finally porn derives most of its meaning and significance from the *social context* in which it exists (italics in original).

The social context in which pornography exists is all-important (Diamond, 1988; Valverde, 1985). This can be demonstrated using Valverde's example of the *Playboy* centrefold. The picture, typically of a nude, young, attractive, White woman whose genitals are featured prominently, does not have much meaning in and of itself. When viewed in a North American context of sexism, racism, ableism, ageism, and so on, however, the picture is imbued with layers of meaning. She is beautiful and helpless looking and posed in such a way as to engender a specific response (arousal) in North American men: "He will not merely glance at the photo as he would at a landscape or a family photograph; he will gaze intently, stare at, and *possess* that woman with his eyes" (Valverde, 1985:125–126). Further, the point of the picture is not to celebrate femaleness or the female body but rather, in the context of capitalism, the purpose is to use the female body for profit making. Finally, besides the feelings the picture may arouse in many men, it also heightens feelings for many women; feelings of embarrassment for the model, whose seeming naiveté is a ploy used to enhance the male viewer's pleasure in dominance. Many women may feel angry, at risk, and vulnerable. As Valverde (1985:126) concludes, "It is not the picture itself which creates these feelings. If men never raped women in real life, the same picture would not have the same power to make us feel violated." As sociologist Sara Diamond (1988:400) points out, pornography will always exist, underground or in the mainstream, until sexism is eliminated. Determining or interpreting what constitutes pornography is a difficult task.

Over time, public attitudes change regarding what should be tolerated and what should be banned because of ***obscenity***—**the legal term for pornographic materials that are offensive by generally accepted standards of decency.** Who decides what is obscene? According to what criteria? A publication is deemed to be obscene according to the Canadian Criminal Code, Section 163 (8), if its dominant characteristic is the "undue exploitation of sex" or is of "sex and any one or more of the following subjects, namely, crime, horror, cruelty, and violence" (www.safe4kids.org/law/code1.htm). The fact that pornography is criminalized, at least as it pertains to children, has in part assisted in it being constructed as deviance and as a social problem.

The Social Construction of Pornography as a Social Problem

The social construction of pornography as a social problem involves both a cognitive framework and a moral framework. The cognitive framework refers to the reality or factualness of the situation that constitutes the "problem." In regard to pornographic materials, one cognitive framework might be based on the assumption that pornography *actually affects* people's actions or attitudes; an opposing cognitive framework might be based on the assumption that pornography is a fantasy mechanism that allows people to express the forbidden without actually engaging in forbidden behaviour (Kipnis, 1996). The moral framework refers to arguments as to whether something is immoral or unjust. In the case of pornography, moral condemnation arises from the belief that graphic representations of sexuality are degrading, violent, and sinful. From this perspective, pornography is less about sex than about violating taboos in society. The moral framework often distinguishes between pornography and *erotica*—**materials that depict consensual sexual activities that are sought by and pleasurable to all parties involved**. According to sociologist Diana E. H. Russell (1993), materials can be considered erotic—rather than obscene—only if they show respect for all human beings and are free of sexism, racism, and homophobia. Contemporary erotica might include romance novels that describe two consenting adults participating in sexual intercourse (see Snitow, 1994). On the other hand, materials depicting violent assault or the sexual exploitation of children would be considered pornographic or obscene. However, the distinction appears to be highly subjective, as feminist scholar Ellen Willis (1981:222) notes: "Attempts to sort out good erotica from bad porn inevitably come down to 'What turns me on is erotic: what turns you on is pornographic.'" These are issues that the Canadian Justice system is continually called upon to

Are there any businesses like this in your community? Why do many people believe that establishments such as this not only harm individuals and their families but also the larger community?

debate but, in the words of the report of the Special Committee on Pornography and Prostitution (the Fraser Commission) (1985:7), "Activities which threaten the physical well-being of others can find no real place in civilized society."

The Nature and Extent of Pornography

As part of the multibillion-dollar sex industry, pornography is profitable to many people, including investors, filmmakers, and owners of stores that distribute such materials. *Hard-core* pornography is material that explicitly depicts sexual acts and/or genitals. In contrast, *soft-core* pornography is suggestive but does not depict actual intercourse or genitals.

Technological innovations such as digital media have greatly increased the variety of pornographic materials available as well as methods of distribution. Although some people visit live peep shows and "X-rated" adult bookstores and video arcades, sexually explicit materials are available at home or in the office through mail-order services, movies on "X-rated" cable television channels, dial-a-porn, digitized scans and striptease QuickTime movies, and private computer bulletin boards and Usenet newsgroups specializing in adult chat areas and graphics exchanges on the Internet.

Hard-core pornographic films gross over $400 million a year in the United States. It is not known how much revenue is made in Canada from the pornography industry, but it is not uncommon for a small production company that shoots, manufactures, and distributes such videos to gross more than $1 million a year in the U.S. (*New York Times*, 1993). However, "Ron," who works in the pornography industry, suggests that these profits, unsurprisingly, do not extend to most actors in the films:

> You'd have to go a long way to find an industry with worse labour practices. They work people very hard; they pay them very little, really, for what they do.... As a porn performer, you're putting up with a couple of days of hard, even abusive, behaviour that compromises your ability to do anything else in your life ever again, because the piece of evidence of your past misbehaviour continues to exist.... But after you've done porn films, you can't do anything else. You can't even do commercials.... Another thing. There's an endless appetite for new faces and new bodies, which means they work [actors] to death for about six months or a year, put out twenty to thirty videos with them. And then they can't get work any more. New ones have come along. The audience is sick of looking at the old ones and wants to see new ones. (quoted in Stoller, 1991:209–210)

According to some social analysts, pornography is a prime example of the principle of supply and demand. As long as demand remains high, pornographers will continue to market their goods and services and find new ways to use technology. According to Walter Kendrick, a scholar whose research focuses on pornography:

> Pornographers have been the most inventive and resourceful users of whatever medium comes along because they and their audience have always wanted innovations. Pornographers are excluded from the mainstream channels, so they look around for something new, and the audience has a desire to try any innovation that gives them greater realism or immediacy. (quoted in Tierney, 1994:H18)

Each new development in technology changes the meaning of pornography and brings new demands for regulation or censorship. Today, interactive media presentations and pornography on the Internet are widely believed to be a far more powerful influence on people, especially children, than the printed word is (see Box 7.2).

Research on Pornography

In June of 1983, the Department of Justice convened a seven-member committee to investigate and report on the then-current situation of pornography and prostitution in Canada. This resulted in the 1985 Fraser Commission report. The report concluded, with regard to pornography, that "there is agreement that the current situation is problematic [e.g., that current laws on availability and control are unsatisfactory], [but]...that is where consensus ends" (Special Committee on Pornography and Prostitution, 1985:5). The Committee also stated that legal reform was only part of the solution, and that social policies and actions were necessary elements of any long-term strategy. Regarding its stance on pornography generally, and informing the recommendations the Committee made, were these two points:

> In essence we see two forms of harm flowing from pornography. The first is the offence which it does to members of the public who are involuntarily subjected to it. The second is the broader social harm which it causes by undermining the right to equality which is set out in section 15 of the *Charter of Rights and Freedoms*. (Special Committee on Pornography and Prostitution, 1985:10)

Sociologists do not agree on the extent to which pornography that depicts excessive sex, violence, and the domination of one person by another affects behaviour. More than 80 percent of X-rated films reviewed in one study included scenes showing women dominated and exploited by men. The vast majority of these films portrayed physical aggression against women, and about half explicitly depicted rape (Cowan et al., 1988; Cowan and O'Brien, 1990). Explicit violence is also part of many videos in the adult section of video stores (see Duncan, 1991). Some studies have demonstrated that violent porn leads to increased aggressive attitudes toward women by men, but research has not demonstrated that attitudinal changes cause rapes or assaults on women that would otherwise have not taken place (Valverde, 1985:121). Most people therefore do not support efforts to censor adults' access to pornographic material, unless the material involves children. As Diamond (1988:396) remarks:

> The suggestion that consumers of pornographic material or other media products respond in zombie-like, imitative fashion to all-powerful images is both false and frightening.

Pornography and Age, Gender, Class, Racialization, and Ethnicity

Because viewing pornography is a secretive activity, data on the consumers of various forms are limited. Some studies have found that the typical customer of an adult bookstore is a White, relatively well-educated, married, middle-class man between the ages of 25 and 66. Other studies have found that younger and more-educated adults express more accepting attitudes toward pornography than do older, less educated adults (Lottes, 1993).

Overall, men watch more sexually explicit material and hold more favourable attitudes toward it than women do. Some analysts attribute this difference to gender-role socialization. In a society in which men are socialized to be sexual initiators and often fear rejection, pornography is satisfying because it typically shows a willing female partner. In contrast, women have been socialized to respond negatively to material showing nude bodies and male pleasure that may occur at the expense of a woman's sense of safety and dignity (see Reiss, 1986). However, in recent years, more women have become consumers of *Playgirl* magazine, erotic novels, and videos such as those by Candida Royalle, a former porn star, that are made specifically for women (see Lottes, 1993; Macy, 1996).

In general, women are more vocal than men in opposing pornography. According to sociologist Michael Kimmel (1990), men are relatively silent for several reasons: embarrassment or guilt for having enjoyed pornography; anger at women's interference in male privilege; lack of interest in what they perceive to be a non-issue; fear that speaking out will lead to questions about their masculinity; reluctance to talk openly about their sexual feelings; and confusion about "what it means to be a 'real man' in contemporary society" (Kimmel, 1987:121).

According to film scholar Laura Kipnis (1996), much of the sentiment against pornography is rooted in class-based elitism: Opposition to pornography is a form of snobbery related to maintaining class distinctions in society. From this perspective, rejecting pornography amounts to rejecting all that is vulgar, trashy, and lower class. Although Kipnis does not suggest that all consumers of pornography are lower class,

she believes that members of the upper classes typically view pornography consumers as lower-class people who may imitate the images they see. Similarly, women who appear in pornography or consume it are seen as brainwashed or unenlightened people who lack "class."

In another class analysis of pornography, philosopher Alan Soble (1986) linked men's use of pornography with their feelings of boredom and powerlessness, which are the result of capitalist work relations, the nature of labour, and the centralization of economics and politics. For these men, pornography becomes a diversion—a means of escaping from the dull, predictable world of work. Soble suggests that consumers of pornography use the material to construct fantasies and gain a sense of control; it gives men the opportunity—otherwise rarely available—to organize the world and conduct its events according to their own wishes and tastes. In Soble's eyes, pornography consumption is not an expression of men's power as much as it is an expression of their lack of power (Soble, 1986).

In other research, sociologists Alice Mayall and Diana E. H. Russell (1993) have detailed how different racialized/ethnic groups are portrayed in pornography. Examining materials in a heterosexual pornography store, the researchers found that skin colour is a highly salient issue: White women were featured in 92 percent of the pornography, perhaps because they fulfill traditional stereotypes equating female beauty with White skin and Caucasian features (Mayall and Russell, 1993).

People of colour were more likely to be found in materials featuring rape, bondage, and sadomasochism, anal sex, sex with children, and sex between women. Among women of colour, Black women were most frequently featured, followed by Asian women and Latinas. People who consume pornography have a choice of buying magazines portraying only Whites, White men with Black women, or Black men with White women. The researchers were unable to determine whether these options were based on the preferences of consumers or those of the makers of pornography (Mayall and Russell, 1993). Collins (1991) suggests that racism in pornography can be traced to the oppression of Black women in slavery: African women were depicted as animals and used as sex objects for the pleasure of White men. Others have noted that, at the same time that the White man was exploiting the Black woman, he was obsessive about protecting the White woman from the Black man (Gardner, 1994).

SOCIAL PROBLEMS AND INFORMATION TECHNOLOGY

BOX 7.2 Canada's Role in Cracking Down on Internet Child Pornography

Anonymity on the Internet makes it difficult to detect child pornography and to apprehend those who distribute or consume such materials (Simon, 1999).

Since its inception in 1989, the Internet has become the source of vast amounts of beneficial information. However, this new form of information technology has also facilitated the dissemination of child pornography. According to one legal analyst, the Internet has changed the manner in which pornography can be created, distributed, and accessed:

> Prior to the invention of the Internet, consumers and distributors of child pornography had to know each other or have connections to exchange materials. Underground networks facilitated the trade of photographs or videos through the mail or in person. Currently, however, subscribers . . . can simply download graphic images through their modems to be able to view and print images.
>
> The anonymity available on the Internet hinders the detection of child pornography. A user can create any identity and transmit a message from [Calgary] through New Zealand, and then on to Halifax, making it impossible to determine the origin. Furthermore, "anonymous remailers" enable a user to re-route outgoing messages by removing the source address, assigning an anonymous identification code number with the remailer's address, and forwarding it to the final destination. (Simon, 1999:7)

Just as the distribution of child pornography has been facilitated by the Internet, sexually explicit visual depictions of children (and adults) have become much easier to create and mass produce. Scanners, video cameras, and graphics software packages are an integral part of the production of child pornography today (Simon, 1999).

What social policy issues are raised by the increasing availability of pornographic materials? One major consideration is the use of children under the age of 18 in pornographic depictions. Another is the question of whether or not child pornography contributes to pedophilia (defined as an abnormal condition in which an adult has a sexual desire for children). Further complicating this issue is the fact that some child pornographers claim that the actors they use are over the age of 18 and simply appear to be younger or that the children shown are not actual children but rather computer-generated images—"virtual" actors.

This argument, however, is rendered irrelevant under Section 163.1 of the Canadian Criminal Code, which states that child pornography is "(a) a photographic, film, video or other visual representation, whether or not it was made by electronic or mechanical means, (i) that shows a person who is or *is depicted as being* under the age of eighteen years and is engaged in or is depicted as engaged in explicit sexual activity, or (ii) the dominant characteristic of which is the depiction, for a sexual purpose, of a sexual organ or the anal region of a person under the age of eighteen years; or (b) any written material or visual representation that advocates or counsels sexual activity with a person under the age of eighteen years that would be an offence under this Act."

In Canada, anything illegal off-line is illegal online. Many officers within Canada's police forces are gaining valuable Internet training focused specifically on the sexual exploitation of children. This training includes investigative techniques for the search and seizure of illegal computer data (**www.rcmp-grc.gc.ca/html/safe_wise_internet.htm**). Police, however, as always, are bound by the *Charter* and Canadian laws pertaining to protection of privacy issues.

Mystery hackers like "Citizen Tipster" are not so bound, or at least choose not to be. On June 29th, 2002, the *Vancouver Sun* reported on the activities of a 21-year-old Langley, B.C., computer hacker who used a computer program he wrote to monitor the private e-mails of suspected child-porn producers and child molesters worldwide. He had read hundreds of communications each day for the past three years and his tips to police resulted in the arrests of several child predators in Canada, the U.S., and Russia. His online evidence led to the arrest in 2001 of an Orange County Superior Court Judge for possession of more than 100 images of child pornography and involvement in a plot to sexually exploit young boys at a private health club. The hacker forwarded his evidence to an online organization, Predator-Hunter.com, focused on ending the exploitation of children; it, in turn, forwarded the files to the California Department of Justice. Citizen Tipster's online evidence also led to the arrest and conviction of an Alberta man who was using the Internet to sell his eight-year-old daughter for sex in 1999. Police threatened Omni-Potent (his online handle) with arrest for violations of citizen's privacy, but it took them a long time to actually find him. When they finally tracked him down, via a website, they demanded his hard-drive and all his files. In the words of 21-year-old Omni-Potent, though, "Sure, a violation of privacy you must cry, but, if you have nothing hurting kids, the future of the world, then there's no reason to worry as that is all Omni-Potent protects . . . [those] who can't protect themselves" (Dimmock, 2002:A14).

The vulnerability of children to online predators led to the introduction into the House of Commons on March 14th, 2001, of a bill to fortify existing legislation protecting children from sexual exploitation, particularly through the Internet. On June 10th, 2002, the Justice Minister and Attorney General of Canada announced that "Bill C-15A, containing tough new legislation protecting children from sexual exploitation, Internet luring and child pornography" had received royal assent. Specific to child pornography, amendments to the Criminal Code will include:

- Internet Luring and Child Pornography: It is now illegal to communicate with a child over the Internet for the purpose of committing a sexual offence against that child as well as to transmit, make available, export, and access child pornography;

- Child Sex Tourism: Amendments to the Child Sex Tourism Law (enacted in 1997) will simplify the process used to prosecute Canadians who sexually exploit children in other countries; and

- Enhanced Judicial Powers: Judges can now order both the deletion of child pornography posted on computer systems in Canada and the forfeiture of any materials and equipment used in the commission of a child pornography offence. They can keep known sex offenders away from children by using prohibition orders, long-term offender designations, and one-year peace bonds for offences relating to child pornography and the Internet (**http://canada.justice.gc.ca/en/news/nr/2002/doc_30529.html**).

Acknowledging the global scope of the issue, the Canadian Government and the RCMP are also engaged with experts from 30 other nations, through the Interpol Specialist Group on Crimes Against Children, and 24-hour law-enforcement points of contact have been established in order to facilitate co-operation and share information between countries of the G-8 (**www.rcmp-grc.gc.ca/html/safe_wise_internet.htm**). Not only is the issue global, its scope is immense because it involves the Internet. Chidley noted in 1995 that a conservative estimate of information passed on the Internet equated to approximately 300 paperback pages per second. Attempts to eliminate or censor Internet child pornography may well be futile.

Certainly many people are not happy about any movement toward censorship of the Internet. Jeffrey Shallit, a computer scientist at the University of Waterloo in Ontario, was also involved with an organization called Electronic Frontier Canada, which is focused on maintaining free speech in cyberspace. Shallit (cited in Chidley, 1995:58) and many others believe that the issue of Internet pornography has been blown way out of proportion—that it represents a minimal amount of online material. While few condone child pornography, members of online communities are nervous about where crackdowns and censorship may lead. In an open letter to the Canadian online community on the subject of "Computers and Academic Freedom," computer scientist Carl Kadie (1993) stated:

It's a tough question—how much freedom should be given up to fight serious issues like child pornography—and are these tactics working at all? Are they harming an important resource more than they are helping fight the actual problem? Are there more effective ways to deal with the problem?

Others, such as the Coalition for Lesbian and Gay Rights in Ontario (CLGRO) (1998), raise concerns about what censorship of the Internet may do to advances for people with non-heterosexual sexualities, noting that with the passage of laws, "there is no reason to believe the police and courts will suddenly become less homophobic or that serious attempts will be made to educate and empower children and youth in the area of sex or encourage the autonomy of lesbian, gay and bisexual teens." The CLGRO also points out the inconsistency in defining people 12 and under as children in the Young Offenders Act and then defining people 18 and under as children with regard to sex-related offences (CLGRO, 1998).

What social policy issues are raised by the legislation on child pornography and the Internet? Some critics argue that freedom of expression involving youthful-looking adults is limited by our laws and, therefore, our laws are unconstitutional. Other critics raise the issue of privacy, asserting that people should be able to read and view whatever they want. Suppose, they say, someone else used your computer, downloaded child pornography, and then you were accused of possessing that pornography? On the other hand, supporters of the new legislation argue that these concerns are outweighed by the necessity of protecting children from being victimized by child pornographers. What do you think?

THE FUTURE OF PORNOGRAPHY AND THE SEX INDUSTRY

Public opinion polls show that people in Canada are ambivalent about pornography and other aspects of the sex industry. While they acknowledge that the sex industry may produce goods and services that serve as a "safety valve" for some, many believe that these goods and services can be a "trigger" for others. There does seem to be a consensus regarding children and pornography: Children should be shielded from some materials. At this point, however, the consensus breaks down. Who should do the shielding (the state or families?), what materials should be banned, and what is the appropriate definition of "child" with regard to sexually explicit materials?

The controversy over sexually explicit materials is particularly strong in schools, and some school boards have banned books and audiovisual materials they consider obscene while others believe the materials to be educational and constructive to children's psycho-sexual development. For example, materials discussing or depicting homosexuality in a positive (or at least not negative) way have been banned in some schools. Many adults would also like to see children shielded from sexually explicit movies, television shows, and rock music videos—to say nothing of the sophisticated adult entertainment on child-oriented gaming platforms such as the CD-equipped Sega Genesis (Stefanac, 1993). Children also have access to sexually explicit materials on the Internet. The censorship wars—both online and in public life—continue to pose serious social policy questions.

All of the issues pertaining to pornography and censorship that we've discussed bring us to a point we've made in previous chapters: How people view social problems affects how they believe such problems should be solved. People seem to view pornography in one of four ways: liberal, religious conservative, antipornography feminist, and anticensorship feminist (Segal, 1990; Berger et al., 1991; Kinsman, 1996; Nelson and Robinson, 2002; Valverde, 1985). Each point of view espouses a different solution to the problem of pornography.

According to the *liberal* point of view, pornography may offend some people but brings harmless pleasure to others. It may even serve as a safety valve for those who have no other sexual outlet. Moreover, no scientific evidence links pornography to actual sexual violence or degradation of women. Therefore, the social problem is not really pornography but censorship—people attempting to impose their morals on others and thereby violating the *Canadian Charter of Rights and Freedoms* (Cottle et al., 1989).

In contrast, from a *religious conservative* point of view, pornography is a threat to the moral values of society, especially family values. Pornography encourages people to have sexual intercourse outside marriage and to engage in deviant sexual behaviour. Therefore, sexually explicit and violent materials should be censored to protect families and societal values.

Some feminist analysts are generally critical of pornography because it is sexist in its portrayal of women, reinforces gender scripts that emphasize male dominance and female submission, and encourages the valuing of women according to their ability to please men. However, not all feminists agree on what—if anything—should be done about pornography. *Antipornography feminists* believe that pornography is a primary source of male oppression of, and violence against, women. Viewing pornography as a form of sexual discrimination that diminishes women's opportunities in all areas of life, including employment, education, and freedom of movement, they believe it should be restricted or eliminated (see MacKinnon, 1987; Dworkin, 1988). In this view, pornography becomes a human rights issue, and antipornography feminists argue that communities should pass antipornography laws that would enable people who have been victimized by pornography to have legal recourse (see Russell, 1993).

In contrast, *anticensorship feminists* do not believe that any single factor, such as pornography, causes women's subordination. Focusing on pornography as the primary source of sexual oppression, they say, "downplays the sexism and misogyny at work within all of our most respectable social institutions and practices, whether judicial, legal, familial, occupational, religious, scientific, or cultural" (Segal, 1990:32). Therefore, pornography should not be censored because open discussions about sexuality and sexual practices promote women's sexual freedom and their right to express themselves (Willis, 1983; Kaminer, 1990). Instead, it is argued, we should have more breadth in the portrayal of women in sexually explicit materials.

In a world linked by the Internet and other rapid sources of communication, the controversy over censorship may be rapidly becoming obsolete. In such a world, whose community standards should be applied in determining whether online materials are obscene? Should we use the standards of St. John's, Newfoundland, or those of Tokyo, Japan? Should we use the standards of the community where the image is posted, or the community where it is viewed, or both? Censorship is a very complicated proposition in an increasingly global marketplace. To restrict local access to a picture, story, or idea on the Internet, access must be blocked to computer users all over the world. What are Internet service providers such as CompuServe and America Online to do? For instance, German authorities asked one U.S.-based corporation in 1996 to not let German subscribers access 200 discussion groups and picture databases that allegedly violated German pornography laws. To meet this request, CompuServe had to block worldwide access to those sites. Although the ban was only temporary, it sent shock waves throughout the community of Internet users, who became concerned that material deemed pornographic or obscene by people anywhere in the world could become unavailable everywhere. Among the materials Germany sought to ban were sexuality support groups for people with disabilities and a bulletin board for gay men and lesbians that provided a support network for gay youths (*Time*, 1996a).

In this chapter, we have focused on prostitution and materials that are defined as pornographic, obscene, and erotic. However, it is important to note that mainstream media—including magazines, movies, videos, television programming, and, specifically, music videos shown on MTV and other channels—also may contribute to negative images of women and the exploitation of children. Furthermore, the mainstream media can desensitize people to sexual assault, rape, violence, and murder through repeated exposure to depictions of women as victims and sex objects and men as aggressors, rapists, and killers. What do you think is more harmful in causing violence aimed at women and children, the sex industry or the media in general?

WHAT CAN YOU DO?

- Educate yourself about the antipornography and anticensorship debates and decide which view makes the most sense for you.
- Find out what is happening regarding youth prostitution in your area and sit on an existing committee. For example, there may be a committee to establish a "safe house" for youth desiring to leave the trade.
- If your community has a safe house, volunteer at it or help educate others about the issues faced by youth attempting to leave the sex trade.
- As many youth in prostitution come from abusive homes, get involved in child-abuse prevention programs in your area.
- Put together an education/information package, with others if you wish, to send to schools so that they may include the issue of sexual exploitation in career and personal planning curricula.
- Lobby the school district to have such information available in public schools.
- Get involved in local organizations that support making the working conditions for people in the sex industry safer (e.g., Prostitutes Empowerment and Education Resource Society–PEERS).
- Get involved in international organizations to work toward ending sexual exploitation of women and children (e.g., Global Alliance Against Trafficking in Women–GAATW).
- Volunteer to teach English or French with immigrant and refugee settlement organizations. Because cuts to funding for these programs often mean men have the first priority for language training (within certain racialized/ethnic communities and families), offer to teach women and/or youth.
- Lobby federal MPs and Provincial MLAs to have health inspectors tour entire establishments (not only kitchens) as parts of their job descriptions to ensure safer working conditions for people employed in clubs.
- Work with health care organizations to ensure that information on physical, mental, and emotional health-related issues is accurately translated into many languages and distributed in places where sex-trade workers convene.

- Write a letter to the newspaper discussing some of the issues for people in the sex trade from your point of view (e.g., Do you think prostitution or pornography should be decriminalized? Why or why not? Should johns receive counselling?)
- Lobby federal MPs and Provincial MLAs to shift the focus in prosecution from sex-trade workers onto pimps, johns, child-porn filmmakers, and so on—whomever you think should be prosecuted, if anyone.

- Work on a media awareness campaign with the goal of "deglamourizing" work in the sex trade.
- Get involved or create, with others, a public-education campaign about why young people get involved in prostitution and pornography.
- If you have been (or are) involved in the sex trade, use your knowledge to mentor others who are involved about health and safety and options.

SUMMARY

WHAT IS PROSTITUTION AND HOW HAS IT CHANGED IN RECENT YEARS?

Prostitution is the sale of sexual services (one's own or another's) for money or goods and without emotional attachment. According to some social analysts, prostitution has recently become industrialized, normalized, and globalized. The industrialization of prostitution refers to commercialized sex as a product manufactured within the human self. Normalization is the process whereby sex work comes to be treated as a form of entertainment with no legal impediments to promoting it as a commodity. The globalization of prostitution refers to the process by which the sex industry has increasingly become global in scope.

WHAT LEVELS, OR TIERS, OF PROSTITUTION HAVE SOCIOLOGISTS IDENTIFIED?

Sociologists have identified several categories: Escort prostitutes (call girls or call boys) earn higher fees and can be more selective in their working conditions and customers than other prostitutes. Hustlers (bar girls or bar boys) work out of nightclubs, bars, and strip joints, where they solicit their customers. House prostitutes (house girls) work in brothels, and a substantial portion of their earnings goes to the house madam or pimp.

Street prostitutes (streetwalkers) publicly solicit customers and charge by the "trick." At the very bottom of the tiers are those who exchange crack cocaine or other drugs for sex.

HOW DO FUNCTIONALISTS VIEW PROSTITUTION?

Functionalists point out that prostitution—like other forms of deviance—is functional for society. Prostitution continues because it provides people with (1) quick, impersonal sexual gratification without emotional attachment; (2) a sexual outlet for those who have no ongoing sexual relationships; (3) the opportunity to engage in nontraditional sexual practices; (4) protection for the family as a social institution; and, (5) jobs for people with few traditional job skills.

HOW DO INTERACTIONISTS VIEW PROSTITUTION?

Interactionists believe that prostitution—like other forms of deviance—is socially constructed. Entering a deviant career such as prostitution is like entering any other occupation, but public labelling—and the individual's acceptance or rejection of that label—determines whether a person stays in a deviant career.

HOW DO CONFLICT THEORISTS AND FEMINISTS VIEW PROSTITUTION?

There are several conflict perspectives on prostitution. Liberal feminists consider prostitution a victimless crime—involving a willing buyer and a willing seller—that should be decriminalized. Marxist feminists see prostitution as linked to the capitalist economy. Radical feminists trace the roots of prostitution to patriarchy in society. Conflict theorists who focus on the intersection of racialization/ethnicity, class, and gender believe that the criminalization of prostitution is a form of discrimination against poor women, particularly poor women of colour and Indigenous women.

DOES PORNOGRAPHY DIFFER FROM OBSCENITY AND EROTICA?

Sometimes it is difficult to distinguish among these categories, but pornography usually refers to the graphic depiction of sexual behaviour through pictures and/or words—including delivery by electronic or other data retrieval systems—in a manner that is intended to be sexually arousing. Obscenity is the legal term for pornographic materials that are offensive by generally accepted standards of decency. Erotica refers to material depicting consensual sexual activities that are sought by and pleasurable to all parties involved.

HAS PORNOGRAPHY CHANGED IN RECENT YEARS?

Yes, technological innovations have greatly increased the variety of pornographic materials available as well as their methods of distribution. According to some analysts, as long as the desire for such materials is high, the multibillion-dollar pornography industry will continue to produce and market goods and services, adapting to new technologies as they become available.

DOES RESEARCH INDICATE THAT PORNOGRAPHY CONTRIBUTES TO SEXUAL VIOLENCE?

No conclusive answer has been found to this question. Some studies have found that hard-core pornography is associated with aggression in males and sexual violence in society, but other studies have found no conclusive evidence that pornography contributes to sexual violence. However, most feminist scholars suggest that pornography exploits all women and sometimes men and children.

HOW DO PEOPLE REACT TO THE CENSORSHIP OF PORNOGRAPHY?

Reactions to the censorship of pornography are varied. People with a liberal view of pornography believe that it is a safety valve for society and that censorship—not pornography—is the social problem. Religious conservatives consider pornography a threat to moral values and encourage censorship of some materials. Antipornography feminists view pornography as a primary source of male oppression and violence against women and argue for its restriction or elimination. Anticensorship feminists believe that some pornography is bad but censorship is worse because it suppresses free speech.

KEY TERMS

erotica,   p. 167
obscenity,   p. 166
pornography,   p. 166

prostitution,   p. 152
social control,   p. 163
victimless crime,   p. 164

QUESTIONS FOR CRITICAL THINKING

1.   There have been ongoing suggestions by citizens to create "Red Light" districts in major urban centres in Canada. What arguments would you present in favour of this suggestion? What arguments would you present against it?

2.   In what ways are prostitution and pornography linked to sexism, racism, homophobia, and class-based inequality?

3.   In what ways does our general Canadian culture sustain and perpetuate an environment where commercial sexual exploitation of children and youth flourishes?

4.   Libertarian author Peter McWilliams suggests that the problem with censorship can be summed up in two words: Who decides? Who do you think should decide what materials—if any—should be censored as pornographic or obscene? Besides deciding what's acceptable and what isn't, who should decide on the punishments for violating these standards?

WEBLINKS

John Lowman's Web Site
http://mypage.uniserve.ca/~lowman
John Lowman's prostitution research: This page provides access to the results of several prostitution and related cases research projects based in B.C.

Factbook on Global Sexual Exploitation
www.globalmarch.org/virtual-library/catw/factbook/canada.htm
The Coalition Against Trafficking in Women's *Factbook* is committed to providing facts, statistics, and information on known cases of global sexual exploitation. This page focuses on trafficking and prostitution in Canada.

The Canadian Women's Health Network
www.cwhn.ca/resources/sex_trade
The Canadian Women's Health Network is an organization committed to sharing information, resources, and strategies to better women's health. This page provides information and links about child and youth trafficking and prostitution in Canada.

Criminal Code of Canada
www.safe4kids.org/law/code1.htm
This site provides definitions that illustrate what would constitute "Child Pornography," sexual exploitation and interference, children corruption, etc.

Department of Justice Canada
http://canada.justice.gc.ca/en/news/nr/2002/doc_30529.html
A link to an article entitled "Stronger Child Pornography Laws Receive Royal Assent."

Prostitution in Canada
www.walnet.org/csis/papers/sdavis.html
A link to a thesis about Canada's defective approach to prostitution and what reforms could be implemented to improve it.

8

ALCOHOL AND OTHER DRUGS

You don't know what you are talking about.

A response Kevin, 32, a former street person, received and (reported to the author) when he tried to talk with street youth who are using drugs. Kevin, who himself had contracted both HIV and Hepatitis C from a syringe used to inject drugs, added: "The city will chew you up and spit you out."

Street people are not the only people who are affected by drugs. It is estimated that over 50 000 people die annually because of tobacco, alcohol, and other drugs (Health Canada, 2002; Single, Robson, et al., 1999), and the health, economic, and social cost to Canadian society in 1992 was $18.4 billion, 2.7 percent of the gross domestic product in that year (Single et al., 1996). These costs are a combination of work-force productivity losses, transfer payments, and the costs of prevention, research, law enforcement, and health care.

In this chapter, we will examine legal drug (e.g., alcohol, tobacco, and prescription drug) use and abuse; illegal drug (e.g., marijuana, narcotics, and stimulants) use and abuse; explanations of drug abuse; drug prevention and treatment programs; and what you can do about drug abuse.

DRUG USE AND ABUSE

What is a drug? There are many answers to this question, so the definition is not always consistent or clear. For our purposes, a **drug is any substance—other than food or water—that, when taken into the body, alters its functioning in some way.** Drugs are used for either therapeutic or recreational purposes. *Therapeutic* use occurs when a person takes a drug for a specific purpose, such as reducing a fever or controlling an epileptic seizure. Sometimes, individuals who take prescription drugs for therapeutic purposes cross the line to drug abuse. *Recreational* drug use occurs when a person takes a drug for no other purpose than achieving some pleasurable feeling or psychological state. Alcohol and tobacco (nicotine) are *licit* (legal) drugs that are used for recreational purposes; heroin and cocaine are *illicit* (illegal) recreational drugs (Levinthal, 1996). Licit drugs, which include such substances as vitamins, aspirin, alcohol, tobacco, and prescription drugs, are legal to manufacture, sell, possess, and use. Illicit drugs, such as marijuana, cocaine, heroin, and LSD (lysergic acid diethylamide), are socially defined as deviant, and using them is criminal behaviour and hence a social problem.

Defining Drug Abuse

What is drug abuse? *Drug abuse* is the excessive or inappropriate use of a drug that results in some form of physical, mental, or social impairment. A more difficult question to answer is, What constitutes drug abuse? When looked at from this perspective, drug abuse has both objective and subjective components. The *objective component* is physical, psychological, or social evidence that harm has been done to individuals, families, communities, or the entire society by the use of a drug. The *subjective component* refers to people's perceptions about the consequences of using a drug and the social action they believe should be taken to remedy the problem.

Sometimes when people talk about drug abuse, the subjective component—the perception of consequences—overrides the objective component. Consider, for example, the subjective and objective components underlying our society's view of the use of marijuana. The subjective component of marijuana use is the general belief that marijuana is harmful and therefore should not be legal, even though there is little evidence that marijuana use is detrimental to health. The subjective component of alcohol use is the general belief that it is harmless and acceptable, even though there is considerable evidence that it impairs more people and produces greater costs to individuals and society than marijuana use. Thus, the use of alcohol is legal.

Drug Addiction

The term **drug addiction (or drug dependency) refers to a psychological and/or physiological need for a drug to maintain a sense of well-being and avoid withdrawal symptoms.** Drug dependency has two essential characteristics: tolerance and withdrawal. *Tolerance* **occurs when larger doses of a drug are required over time to produce the same physical or psychological effect that was originally achieved by a smaller dose.** Tolerance is a matter of degree: Some drugs produce immediate and profound levels of tolerance, whereas others produce only mild tolerance. For example, when a person first drinks a five-ounce cup of coffee, containing about 100 milligrams of caffeine, the stimulant effect is usually quite pronounced. After that person drinks the same amount of coffee over a period of several days or weeks, the effect is greatly diminished, and a second or third cup of coffee (for a total of 200 to 300 milligrams of caffeine) becomes necessary to duplicate the earlier feeling (Levinthal, 1996). **Withdrawal refers to a variety of physical and/or psychological symptoms that habitual drug users experience when they discontinue drug use.** For example, people who suddenly terminate their alcohol intake after long-term, heavy drinking experience various physical symptoms ranging from insomnia to DTs (*delirium tremens,* or mental confusion often accompanied by sweating and tremor) and psychological symptoms such as a reduced sense of self-worth.

ALCOHOL USE AND ABUSE

Much of the data in this chapter comes from the National Population Health Survey (NPHS). The NPHS was conducted by Health Canada and Statistics Canada to measure the health status of adult, non-Indigenous Canadians and to monitor changes over time (children and Indigenous people were surveyed separately). The content is multidimensional, including physical, mental, and social components, and the method is in-depth interviewing. The first wave of data collection occurred in 1994 and consisted of a sample of 17 626 Canadians; subsequent waves have been completed in 1996, 1998, and 2000.

The use of alcohol—ranging from communion wine in religious ceremonies to beer, wine, and liquor at business and social gatherings—is considered an accepted part of the dominant culture in Canada. *Alcohol* and *alcoholic beverages* are terms that refer to the three major forms in which ethyl alcohol (ethanol) is consumed: *wine,* which is made from fermentation of fruits and contains between 12 and 14 percent ethyl alcohol; *beer,* which is brewed from grains and hops and usually contains 3 to 6 percent alcohol; and *liquor,* which includes whiskey, gin, vodka, and other distilled spirits and usually contains 40 percent (80 proof) to 50 percent (100 proof) alcohol.

According to sales data in the year ending March 2002, Canadians purchased per capita 6.5 litres of spirits, 12.2 litres of wine, and 85.0 litres of beer for a total of 103.8 litres drunk per capita. This is down from 134 litres purchased per capita in 1976 (Statistics Canada, 2002c). Since some people do not drink at all, if Canada

follows the American pattern this means 10 percent of the population could account for roughly half the total alcohol consumption (Levinthal, 1996).

Many people do not think of alcohol as a drug because it can be purchased legally—and without a prescription—by adults. It is, however, a psychoactive drug that is classified as a *depressant* because it lowers the activity level of the central nervous system. The impairment of judgment and thinking associated with being drunk is the result of alcohol depressing brain functions. Alcohol also affects mood and behaviour. One to two drinks often bring a release from tensions and inhibitions. Three to four drinks affect self-control—including reaction time and coordination of hands, arms, and legs—and judgment, muddling the person's reasoning ability. Five to six drinks affect sensory perception, and the person may show signs of intoxication such as staggering, belligerence, or depression. At seven to eight drinks, the drinker is obviously intoxicated and may go into a stupor. Nine or more drinks affect vital centres, and the drinker may become comatose or even die. Of course, factors such as sex (women are more affected than men by the same amount of alcohol because they have a lower percentage of water in their bodies), body weight, physical build, and recent food and fluid consumption must be taken into account in estimating the rate of alcohol absorption in the body.

In a comprehensive discussion of the problems of drug abuse, entitled *The Dynamics of Drug Abuse,* Diana H. Fishbein and Susan E. Pease state that, although negative short-term effects of drinking are usually overcome, chronic heavy drinking or alcoholism can cause permanent damage to the brain or other parts of the body (Fishbein and Pease, 1996). Social scientists divide long-term drinking patterns into four general categories. *Social drinkers* consume alcoholic beverages primarily on social occasions; they drink occasionally or even relatively frequently. *Heavy drinkers* are more frequent drinkers who typically consume greater quantities of alcohol when they drink and are more likely to become intoxicated. *Acute alcoholics* have trouble controlling their use of alcohol and plan their schedule around drinking. *Chronic alcoholics* have lost control over their drinking and tend to engage in compulsive behaviour such as hiding liquor bottles and sneaking drinks when they are not being observed.

Alcohol Consumption and Class, Gender, and Age

Although people in all social classes consume alcohol, income and class differences are associated with alcohol use. In Canada, the relationship between income and drinking is U-shaped, with people in the highest and lowest of five relatively numerically equal income brackets reported in the NPHS (1996–97) as being the heaviest drinkers, at 4.5 and 4.1 drinks per person per week (Single, Minh, et al., 1999:43). (Note that these figures differ from the sales data reported above, possibly because they are self-reports.) In any case, affluent people typically have greater resources and more privacy than lower-income individuals have and can often protect themselves from the label "drunk" or "alcoholic." A member of the upper-middle class or upper class who drinks to excess at the country club is less visible to the public and less likely to be negatively sanctioned by law enforcement officials—unless the person drives while under the influence—than a lower-income or poverty-level person who sits on a public sidewalk drinking beer or wine.

Gender, age, and Indigenous status are also associated with drinking behaviour. More men than women drink, and men are more likely than women to be labelled as problem drinkers or alcoholics. Women who drink alcoholic beverages tend to be lighter drinkers than men. Overall, according to the NPHS (Statistics Canada, 2001b:14), 48 percent of men and 25 percent of women aged 18 and older drank at least once a week in 1998–99.

Among respondents in the 18 to 24 age category, the college/university age cohort, 46 percent of men and 25 percent of women reported drinking at least once a week in 1998–99. Seniors drank less than younger adults. Among respondents 65 or more years of age, 37 percent of the men and 19 percent of the women reported drinking at least once a week (Statistics Canada, 2001b:14). Binge drinking, at least five drinks at one sitting, is reported to be a major problem among postsecondary students. Whereas 24 percent of men and 7 percent of women aged 18 and older reported binge drinking, 44 percent of the men and 23 percent of the women aged 18 to 24 reported binge drinking at least once a month (Statistics Canada, 2001b:14).

Because the NPHS did not survey Indigenous people on reserves, it is not possible to state their drinking behaviour.

Alcohol-Related Social Problems

Alcohol consumption in Canada has been declining over the past two decades. Nevertheless, chronic alcohol abuse and alcoholism are linked to many social problems. Here we will examine health problems, workplace and driving accidents, and family problems.

According to the 1993 *General Social Survey* (GSS), nearly 1 in 10 adult Canadians (9.2 percent) reported having problems with their drinking. The most common problems affect physical health (5.1 percent) and financial position (4.7 percent). Also, 43.9 percent say they have experienced problems because of other people's drinking, such as being disturbed by loud parties (23.8 percent), being insulted or humiliated (20.9 percent), and having serious arguments (15.6 percent)(Single, Minh, et al., 1999:26). According to sociologist Eric Single and his colleagues (Single, Robson, et al., 1999), approximately 6700 people die annually as a result of alcohol-related problems.

Health Problems

Although not all heavy drinkers and chronic alcohol abusers exhibit the major health problems that are typically associated with alcoholism, their risk of them is greatly increased. For alcoholics, the long-term health effects include *nutritional deficiencies* as a result of poor eating habits. Chronic heavy drinking contributes to high caloric consumption but low nutritional intake. Alcoholism is also associated with fluctuations in blood sugar levels that can cause adult-onset diabetes. Structural loss of brain tissue may produce *alcoholic dementia*, which is characterized by difficulties in problem solving, remembering information, and organizing facts about one's identity and surroundings (Levinthal, 1996).

Chronic alcohol abuse is also linked to *cardiovascular problems* such as inflammation and enlargement of the heart muscle, poor blood circulation, reduced heart contractions, fatty accumulations in the heart and arteries, high blood pressure, and cerebrovascular disorders such as stroke (Levinthal, 1996). However, studies show that moderate alcohol consumption— such as a glass of wine a day—may improve body circulation, lower cholesterol levels, and reduce the risk of certain forms of heart disease.

Over time, chronic alcohol abuse also contributes to irreversible changes in the liver that are associated with *alcoholic cirrhosis*—a progressive development of scar tissue in the liver that chokes off blood vessels and destroys liver cells by interfering with their use of oxygen. Given all the possible health problems, perhaps it is not surprising that alcoholics typically have a shorter life expectancy—often by as much as 10 to 12 years—than nondrinkers or occasional drinkers who consume moderate amounts of alcohol.

Abuse of alcohol and other drugs by a pregnant woman can damage the fetus. The greatest risk of ***fetal alcohol syndrome (FAS)*—a condition characterized by mental retardation and craniofacial malformations that may affect the child of an alcoholic mother**—occurs during the first three months of pregnancy. Binge drinking during the third week of gestation has been linked particularly with this syndrome because that is when crucial craniofacial formation and brain growth take place in the fetus. It is estimated that approximately 100 babies per year are born in Canada with FAS and that rates are higher in remote rural and Indigenous communities (Single, Minh, et al., 1999:177). Another risk is ***fetal alcohol effects (FAE)*—a condition with some FAS characteristics that could include single birth defects, or developmental learning and behavioural disorders, that may not be noticed until months or years after the child's birth.** This condition is hard to identify, may be confused with other health problems, and must be diagnosed by physical examination and consideration of the health history. Thus, the rate of FAE could be substantially higher than FAS.

Alcohol in the Workplace

Productivity losses due to absenteeism, tardiness, and workplace accidents from alcohol use amounted to $4.1 billion, according to Single and his colleagues (1996: 247). Excessive alcohol consumption impairs the sensorimotor skills necessary to operate machinery, heavy equipment, and motor vehicles. Numerous studies have shown a relationship between alcohol—and other drugs—and many workplace injuries or fatalities (Macdonald, 1995).

Driving and Drinking

Drivers who have been drinking often do not realize how much alcohol they have consumed or what effect it has on their driving ability. As a result, many people drive dangerously even when they are not legally drunk, that is, driving with a blood alcohol level over 0.08 percent, which is referred to as *impaired driving*. Alcohol-related driving accidents occur, for example, when drivers lose control of their vehicles, fail to see a red traffic light or a car or pedestrian in the street, or miss a sharp curve in the road (Gross, 1983). According to national coroner data reported in *Canada's Drug Strategy* (*CDS*), 55.6 percent of drivers aged 26 to 35 who were killed in motor vehicle accidents in 1995 had been drinking, as had 49.1 percent of those aged 36 to 45, 30.9 percent of those aged 46 to 55, and 18.8 percent of those over 55 (Health Canada, 1998:22). Groups such as Mothers Against Drunk Driving (MADD) must continually develop new recommendations to ensure that public interest in the issue is maintained (see Box 8.1).

Family Problems

Chronic alcohol abuse or alcoholism makes it difficult for a person to maintain social relationships and have a stable family life. According to social scientist Charles F. Levinthal (1996), for every person who has a problem with alcohol, an average of at least four other people are directly affected on a daily basis. Domestic abuse and violence in families are frequently associated with heavy drinking and alcohol abuse by one or more family members. Women whose partners consume five or more drinks at one time, compared to those whose partners never drink, are at six times the risk of violence, and abused women frequently use drugs to deal with the pain (Health Canada, 1993). Growing up in a family that is affected by alcohol can have a profound impact on children. The extent to which alcohol abuse affects other family members depends on the degree of alcoholism and the type of alcoholic. Some alcoholic parents are violent and abusive; others are quiet and sullen or withdrawn. To outsiders, the family of an alcoholic may appear to be normal, but family members may feel as though they have an "elephant in the living room," as journalist Joyce Maynard (1994:80–81) explains:

> I grew up in an alcoholic household. But as difficult as it was dealing with my father's drinking, the greater pain for me was the secret keeping. Adult children of alcoholics refer to the phenomenon as "the

SOCIAL PROBLEMS IN THE MEDIA

BOX 8.1   Maintaining a Drumbeat against Drunken Driving

A selfishly drunk (BAC Blood Alcohol Concentration 240, three times the legal limit) driver took the sunshine from my life in July 1981—or was it just yesterday? That sunshine was our 19-year-old son, about to embark on his adult life: university, career, marriage. Instead, we are left with chronic emptiness: no hugs at the door on his weekends home; no daughter-in-law to love and admire; no grandchildren to be "just like so-and-so."

Helen Stauffer, former Vice President of PRIDE (People to Reduce Impaired Driving Everywhere) and its successor, MADD (Mothers Against Drunk Driving) Canada (e-mail to the author)

Like many other members of Mothers Against Drunk Driving (MADD), including Candace Lightner, who founded the organization in the United States in the early 1980s when her daughter was killed, Helen Stauffer has a personal reason for confronting the problem of drunk driving. Over the past two decades, MADD has campaigned for stricter laws against drunk driving, mounting media campaigns against driving and drinking and promoting the idea of having a designated driver. These campaigns have been very effective. The number of persons charged with impaired driving has declined since 1983 and the rate has declined from about 400 per 100 000 in 1990 to about 225 per 100 000 in 2000 (CCJS, 2001:11).

MADD is still campaigning because people are still dying and being injured because of impaired driving. MADD uses the figures from the Traffic Injury Research Foundation to state that every two days, 9 people are killed and 230 people are injured due to drinking and driving. It is the number one cause of criminal death in Canada.

MADD's latest campaign is to reduce the criminal code BAC level from 0.08 percent to 0.05 percent. Police are reluctant to charge people with a BAC lower than 0.10 percent because of measurement variation. Thus, as MADD claims, "Under Canadian law, a 200-lb. man who drinks almost 6 beers in 2 hours can drive and is not likely to be charged with impaired driving" (press release April 22, 2002, retrieved from **www.madd.ca**). The campaign to reduce the criminal code BAC led to much criticism and claims that MADD was trying to criminalize social drinking. MADD's national executive director, Andrew Murie, replied in the same press release, "A 0.05 percent BAC limit would not criminalize social drinking. What we want to stop are people who go out to drink four or five and then drive."

MADD is also concerned about the influence of beer and wine advertising (distillers have informally agreed not to advertise hard spirits). Despite the fact that the annual number of alcohol-related auto accidents in this country remains high, images and fantasies associated with drinking make it seem far more exciting, romantic, and adventurous to drink than to abstain. What further policy steps do you think MADD should take to promote its message? Do you think that alcoholic beverage manufacturers have a responsibility to inform the public about the potential consequences of their products, through health facts and graphic photos on bottles like those found on cigarette packages? Why or why not?

elephant in the living room": You have a huge, inescapable fact about your life that affects everything in your home, but nobody mentions it, although everybody's behaviour is altered to accommodate or deal with it. . . . Our family squeezed past the elephant in the living room, felt his breath on our faces, and rearranged furniture to make room for him. I hid liquor bottles if a friend was coming over. To prevent my father from driving, I even stashed away the keys to his car. But I never uttered a word, and neither did the rest of my family, about what was behind those actions. . . . It wasn't until I became an adult myself that I recognized the unhealthiness of our family's conspiracy of silence.

As Maynard suggests, family members of alcoholics frequently become *enablers*—people who adjust their behaviour to accommodate an alcoholic. Enabling often takes the form of lying to cover up the alcoholic's drinking, absenteeism from work, and/or discourteous treatment of others. Enabling leads many families to develop a pattern of **codependency—a reciprocal relationship between the alcoholic and one or more nonalcoholics who unwittingly aid and abet the alcoholic's excessive drinking and resulting behaviour**

(Jung, 1994). When codependency occurs, the spouse or another family member takes on many of the alcoholic's responsibilities and keeps the alcoholic person from experiencing the full impact of his or her actions. Children who grow up in alcoholic families tend to have higher than normal rates of hyperactivity, antisocial behaviour, low academic achievement, and cognitive impairment (Fishbein and Pease, 1996). However, although the statistical risks of becoming an alcoholic increase if one's parent has been an alcoholic, most children of alcoholics (as many as 59 percent) do not become alcoholics themselves (Sher, 1991).

TOBACCO (NICOTINE) USE AS A SOCIAL PROBLEM

The nicotine in tobacco is a toxic, dependency-producing psychoactive drug that is more addictive than heroin. It is categorized as a *stimulant* because it stimulates central nervous system receptors, activating the release of adrenaline, which raises blood pressure, speeds up the heartbeat, and gives the user a sense of alertness. Some people claim that nicotine reduces their appetite, helps them to lose weight, and produces a sense of calmness and relaxation (Akers, 1992). Perhaps these physical and psychological effects of nicotine dependency help to explain why about one in every four Canadian adults over the age of 15 (25 percent of men and 22 percent of women) smoke, according to the NPHS (Statistics Canada, 2001b:18).

Although the overall proportion of smokers in the general population has declined somewhat since the pioneering 1964 U.S. Surgeon General's warning that smoking is linked to cancer and other serious diseases, tobacco is still responsible for about 45 000 deaths per year in Canada, or five times the number of deaths from car accidents, murder, suicides, and alcohol abuse combined, according to a January 2002 advertisement from Health Canada (**www.gosmokefree.ca**). People who smoke cigarettes, cigars, or pipes have a greater likelihood of developing lung cancer and cancer of the larynx, mouth, and esophagus than nonsmokers because nicotine is ingested into the bloodstream through the lungs and soft tissues of the mouth (Akers, 1992). Furthermore, many cases of bronchitis, emphysema, ulcers, and heart and circulatory disorders can be traced to nicotine consumption. When tobacco burns, it forms carbon monoxide, which disrupts the transport of oxygen from the lungs to the rest of the body and hence contributes to cardiovascular disease (Levinthal, 1996).

Smoking typically shortens life expectancy. It is estimated that about half a pack (10 cigarettes) a day on average reduces a person's life expectancy by four years, and smoking more than two packs a day (40 cigarettes) reduces life expectancy by eight years. When a person uses both tobacco and alcohol, the cancer-causing effects of tobacco are exacerbated (Fishbein and Pease, 1996).

Even people who never light up a cigarette are harmed by *environmental tobacco smoke*—**the smoke in the air as a result of other people's tobacco smoking** (Levinthal, 1996). When someone smokes a cigarette, about 75 percent of the nicotine ends up in the air. Researchers have found that nonsmokers who carpool or work with heavy smokers are more affected by environmental smoke than nonsmokers who are only occasionally exposed to it. Therefore, smoking has been banned in many public and private facilities throughout the country.

Not surprisingly, cigarette smoking adversely affects infants and children. Infants born to women who smoke typically have lower than average birth weights and sometimes slower rates of physical and mental growth. When a pregnant woman smokes, blood vessels constrict, which reduces the amount of oxygen reaching the fetus. Carbon monoxide transmitted from the mother's blood to the fetus interferes with the distribution of oxygen that does reach the fetus (DiFranza and Lew, 1995). Children who grow up in households where one or both parents smoke are more apt to suffer from frequent ear infections, upper respiratory infections such as bronchitis and sinusitis, allergies, asthma, and other health problems than children whose parents do not smoke.

According to the NPHS, teenagers are the group most likely to start smoking: 21 percent of teens aged 12 to 17 who had been nonsmokers in 1994–95 were smokers in 1998–99 (Statistics Canada, 2001b:18).

Why do so many people use nicotine if it is so dangerous? Several reasons have been suggested. First, nicotine creates a high level of dependency, so once a person has begun to use tobacco regularly, the withdrawal symptoms may be strong enough to make the person light up another cigarette. Some researchers have found that the majority of people who smoke recognize that smoking is bad for them and would like to quit but cannot (Fishbein and Pease, 1996:213). Second, in the past, sophisticated marketing campaigns associated smoking with desirable cultural attributes such as achieving maturity, gaining wealth and happiness, or being thin and sexy. In Canada, the Tobacco Act of 1997 (amended in 1998 and 2000) prohibits cigarette manufacturers from advertising their products on radio or television or in magazines or newspapers; they are also prohibited from sponsoring sports and arts events. In addition, the manufacturers must print large health warnings and graphic antismoking pictures on cigarette packages and report marketing campaigns to the federal government. However, in January 2002, tobacco manufacturers indicated that they plan to challenge this act on constitutional grounds. Advocates of tobacco regulation are concerned that the government may have to reduce its regulations. Finally, smoking has been used by youth as a form of rebellion and method of showing solidarity with peers. Thus, many forces combine to promote the continuation of Canada's number one public health problem.

PRESCRIPTION DRUGS, OVER-THE-COUNTER DRUGS, AND CAFFEINE

When most people think of drug abuse, they picture unscrupulous drug dealers in dark alleys selling illegal drugs. But legal drugs also may be abused. Legal drugs fall into two categories: *prescription drugs,* which are dispensed only by a registered pharmacist on the authority of a licensed physician or dentist, and *over the counter (OTC) drugs,* which are available off the shelf and are restricted only by the customer's ability to pay.

Prescription Drugs

According to the NPHS, in 1998, opioid analgesics (morphine-type pain relievers) were used by 4.7 percent of Canadians aged 15 or older, antidepressants by 3.6 percent, sleeping pills by 3.5 percent, tranquillizers by 2.7 percent, steroids by 0.8 percent, and diet pills by 0.5 percent (Single, Minh et al., 1999:113). Pain medication is probably the prescription drug that is

most frequently abused. Though millions of people benefit from *narcotics*—natural or synthetic opiates such as morphine (brand names Duramorph and Roxanol), propoxyphene (Darvon), and codeine—that relieve pain, suppress coughing, control chronic diarrhea, and reduce heroin withdrawal symptoms, there are risks of short-term abuse and long-term psychological and physical dependence. Over time, users develop tolerance for the drug they are taking and must continue to increase dosages to obtain the same effect that was derived from the lower dose. Drug dependency that results from physician-supervised treatment for a recognized medical disorder is called *iatrogenic addiction.* Iatrogenic addiction is most likely to occur with long-term use and/or high dosages of a prescription drug; it most often affects people from the middle or upper class who have no previous history of drug abuse or addiction (Fishbein and Pease, 1996).

Two widely prescribed drugs that have been the subject of controversy regarding their use and abuse are methylphenidate (Ritalin) and fluoxetine (Prozac). Ritalin is a stimulant that is prescribed for children who are diagnosed with *attention-deficit hyperactivity disorder* (ADHD). According to the American Psychiatric Association, ADHD is characterized by "emotionality, behavioural hyperactivity, short attention span, distractibility, impulsiveness, and perceptual and learning disabilities" (Fishbein and Pease, 1996). Although some children are probably correctly diagnosed with this disorder, some commentators worry that Ritalin is over-prescribed in Canada. According to the continuing survey of drug use among Ontario students conducted by drug-use researchers Edward Adlaf and Angela Paglia (2001:117), 4.7 percent of Grade 7 students used the drug in 2001. Boys are more likely than girls to be diagnosed with ADHD and to use the drug. Advocates believe that children with normal to above-average intelligence who are performing poorly in school can benefit from Ritalin, which has proven to be safe for more than 40 years. But critics argue that many parents, doctors, and teachers see Ritalin as a quick fix for dealing with troublesome children and note that the drug typically is prescribed to be taken *only* during the school year (Crossette, 1996a).

One of the most abused prescription drugs for adults is Prozac, an antidepressant. Introduced in 1987 as a breakthrough medication for clinical depression, Prozac has become a cure-all for the blues, a far milder form of depression. Advocates believe that Prozac enhances the quality of life for many people, freeing them from depression and suicidal thoughts. But the long-term side effects of the drug are unknown, and there is some evidence that Prozac is associated with intense, violent suicidal thoughts in some patients. Both Prozac and Ritalin are approved by Health Canada and are considered safe and effective if taken as directed.

Over-the-Counter Drugs

A fine line exists between prescription and over-the-counter (OTC) drugs. Today, both types of drugs are advertised, in the electronic and print media, directly to the consumer, with suggestions to "ask your doctor or pharmacist about [our product] on your next visit." Some drugs are available both by prescription and over the counter, depending on their strength and dosage. For example, medication for stomach ulcers (e.g., Zantac and Tagamet) is sold over the counter in lower doses and by prescription in higher doses. Some drugs that are now sold over the counter were previously available only by prescription.

Widely used OTC drugs include analgesics, sleep aids, and cough and cold remedies. According to the NPHS, 65 percent of Canadians 12 years old and older took pain relievers; 20 percent took cold and cough remedies; and 11 percent took stomach remedies. In each case, a higher percentage of women than men took the drugs (Statistics Canada, 2001b:36). Abuse of aspirin and other analgesics can cause gastric bleeding, problems with blood clotting, complications during surgery and during labour and delivery, and Reye's syndrome (a potentially life-threatening condition that can arise when children with flu, chicken pox, or other viral infections are given aspirin). Overdoses of analgesics such as acetaminophen (e.g., Tylenol and Anacin-3), aspirin, and ibuprofen (e.g., Motrin, Advil, and Midol) have been linked to cases of attempted suicide, especially by White females between the ages of 6 and 17 years. Few of these suicide attempts have resulted in death except when the analgesics were combined with alcohol or other drugs (Levinthal, 1996). Like analgesics, sleep aids are dangerous when combined with alcohol or some cough and cold remedies because they are depressants that slow down the central nervous system. Even cough and cold medications alone

have side effects, such as drowsiness, that can be hazardous—if, for example, users attempt to drive a car or operate heavy machinery. To counteract drowsiness, some drug companies add caffeine to their products.

Caffeine

Although it is a relatively safe drug, caffeine is a dependency-producing psychoactive stimulant (Gilbert, 1986). Caffeine is an ingredient in coffee, tea, chocolate, soft drinks, and stimulants such as NoDoz and Vivarin. Coffee consumption by Canadians is higher per capita than that of either Americans or Europeans. According to Oxfam Canada, per capita we consume 402 cups per year (or 15 billion cups in total per year). Per capita, that is 77 more cups than Americans and 152 cups more than Europeans (Oxfam Canada, 2002). Most people ingest caffeine because they like the feeling of mental alertness and reduced fatigue that it produces. The extent to which caffeine actually improves human performance, however, is widely debated. Caffeine may improve concentration when a person is performing boring or repetitive tasks, but it has little effect on the performance of complex tasks such as critical thinking and decision making (Curatolo and Robertson, 1983; Dews, 1984). The short-term effects of caffeine include dilated peripheral blood vessels, constricted blood vessels in the head, and a slightly elevated heart rate (Levinthal, 1996). Long-term effects of heavy caffeine use (more than three cups of coffee or five cups of tea per day) include increased risk of heart attack and osteoporosis—the loss of bone density and increased brittleness associated with fractures and broken bones (Kiel et al., 1990).

Overall, however, the social problems associated with the abuse of caffeine and prescription and OTC drugs are relatively minor when compared with the social problems associated with illegal drugs.

ILLEGAL DRUG USE AND ABUSE

Are some drugs inherently bad and hence classified as illegal? What constitutes an illegal drug is a matter of social and legal definitions that are subject to change over time. During the 19th and early-20th centuries, people in Canada had fairly easy access to drugs that are currently illegal for general use. In the early 1800s, neither doctors nor pharmacists had to be licensed. *Patent medicines*, which sometimes contained such ingredients as opium, morphine, heroin, cocaine, and alcohol, could be purchased in stores, through mail-order advertisements, and from medicine wagons run by people who called themselves doctors and provided free entertainment to attract crowds (Young, 1961). Over time, because of the rapidly growing number of narcotics addicts, prescriptions became required for some drugs. Some forms of drug use were criminalized because of their association with specific minority groups. For example, in Canada, opium could be consumed legally in cough syrup, but smoking the same amount of opium was banned by the Opium Act of 1908 after an investigation by Mackenzie King on the use of opium. The reason for the ban was that opium smoking was a favourite pastime of the Chinese workers building railroads in Western Canada (Small, 1978). In Canada, the Division of Narcotic Control was part of the Department of Health. Its head was Col. C.H.L. Sharman, who undertook the moral entrepreneurial role against drugs in Canada that Harry Anslinger played in the United States.

The most recent legislation dealing with drugs in Canada is the Controlled Drugs and Substances Act, which came into effect in 1997. This legislation, according to *Canada's Drug Strategy* (Health Canada, 1998:10), has enforcement measures "for the interdiction and suppression of unlawful import, export, production, distribution, and possession of controlled substances and for the forfeiture of any property used or intended to be used in the commission of such offences and profits derived from such offences." Nevertheless, drugs are still widely available. Today, the most widely used illegal drugs are marijuana, stimulants such as cocaine and amphetamines, depressants such as barbiturates, narcotics such as heroin, and hallucinogens such as LSD. If drug incidents reported in the Uniform Crime Reporting Surveys are a measure of use, then the use of illegal drugs, particularly marijuana, is increasing. Whereas in 1990 the incident rate was about 225 per 100 000 population, the rate in 2000 was about 300 per 100 000 population (CCJS, 2001:11). Of course, drug incidents could also be related to different patterns of drug enforcement. Although Canada has taken a less severe approach to drugs than has the United States, emphasizing a harm-reduction rather than a punitive approach, many Canadians have reported that drugs can be harmful. About one in four people who have used illegal drugs reported that their use had harmed them during their lives (Health Canada, 1998: 24).

Marijuana

Marijuana is the most extensively used illicit drug in Canada. According to the NPHS, 7.4 percent of Canadians 15 years and older used marijuana in 1993 and a higher percentage of men than women reported using it (10 percent vs. 4.9 percent) (Single, Minh, et al., 1999:144). According to figures reported in *Canada's Drug Strategy*, about one in five people (23.9 percent) over the age of 14 has tried marijuana at least once (Health Canada, 1998:24). Students often laugh to hear that marijuana use is still considered deviant behaviour. In early 2003, the federal government was considering decriminalizing possession of small quantities of marijuana (see Box 8.2).

Although most marijuana users are between the ages of 18 and 25, use by teens between the ages of 15 and 17 is also high: in the NPHS, 25.4 percent of teens reported using it (Single, Minh, et al., 1999:144). Many teenage users report that marijuana is as easy to acquire as alcohol or cigarettes. According to one teenager, "It is so popular, so well known, it is around everywhere. Nobody is afraid of the consequences of selling it or buying it. . . . It is really easy to get" (quoted in Friend, 1996:2A). Many young people buy the drug from friends who grow their own plants.

Marijuana is ingested by smoking it, either in a hand-rolled cigarette known as a *reefer* or *joint*, or through a pipe or other smoking implement. Potent marijuana—marijuana with high levels of the plant's primary psychoactive chemical, delta-9 tetrahydrocannabinol (THC)—has existed for many years, but potency has increased in recent years because of indoor gardens. Indoor crops have levels of THC up to four times as high as plants grown outdoors and in other nations (Navarro, 1996).

Marijuana is both a central nervous system depressant and a stimulant. In low to moderate doses, the drug produces mild sedation; in high doses, it produces a sense of well-being, euphoria, and sometimes hallucinations. Marijuana slightly increases blood pressure and heart rate and greatly lowers blood glucose levels, causing extreme hunger. The human body manufactures a chemical that closely resembles THC, and specific receptors in the brain are designed to receive it. Marijuana use disrupts these receptors, impairing motor activity, concentration, and short-term memory (Cowley, 1997). As a result, complex motor tasks such as driving a car or operating heavy machinery are dangerous for a person who is under the influence of marijuana. Some studies show that heavy marijuana use can impair concentration and recall in high-school and college students (Wren, 1996). Users become apathetic and lose their motivation to perform competently or achieve long-range goals, such as completing their education. Overall, the short-term effects of marijuana are typically milder than the short-term effects of drugs such as cocaine (Fishbein and Pease, 1996).

High doses of marijuana smoked during pregnancy can disrupt the development of a fetus and result in lower-than-average birth weight, congenital abnormalities, premature delivery, and neurological disturbances (Fishbein and Pease, 1996). Furthermore, some studies have found an increased risk of cancer and other lung problems associated with inhaling, because marijuana smokers are believed to inhale more deeply than tobacco users.

Over the past decade, medical uses of marijuana have been widely debated. In 2001, Health Canada authorized the use of marijuana for medicinal purposes (see Box 8.2).

Stimulants

Cocaine and amphetamines are among the major stimulants that are abused in Canada. Cocaine is an extremely potent and dependency-producing drug derived from the small leaves of the coca plant, which grows in several Latin American countries. In the 19th century, cocaine was introduced as a local anesthetic in medical practice and a mood-enhancer in patent medicines (Akers, 1992). It was an ingredient in Coca-Cola from the 1880s to the early 1900s (Miller, 1994). Today, cocaine is the third most widely used psychoactive drug after alcohol and marijuana. Users typically sniff, or "snort," the drug into their nostrils, inject it intravenously, or smoke it in the form of crack, a potent form of cocaine that is specially processed for smoking.

According to the NPHS and reported in the *Canadian Profile*, 0.7 percent of Canadians aged 15 and older had used cocaine in 1993—slightly more males than females reported using cocaine (0.8 percent vs. 0.5 percent)—and this figure has remained relatively stationary over time (Single, Minh, et al., 1999:144). For some central-city residents living in poverty, with no hope of gainful employment, dealing cocaine is a major source of revenue and an entry point for other drug-related crime.

The effects of cocaine on the human body depend on how pure the dose is and what effect the user expects. Most cocaine users experience a powerful high, or "rush," in which blood pressure rises and heart rate and respiration increase dramatically. Reactions vary in length and intensity, depending on whether the drug is injected, smoked, or snorted. When the drug wears off, users become increasingly agitated and depressed. Some users become extremely depressed and suicidal; others develop such a powerful craving that they easily become addicted to the drug (Gawin and Ellinwood, 1988). Occasionally, cocaine use results in sudden death by triggering an irregular heart rhythm.

People who use cocaine over extended periods of time have higher rates of infection, heart disturbance, internal bleeding, hypertension, cardiac arrest, stroke, hemorrhaging, and other neurological and cardiovascular disorders than nonusers. Although these problems may develop gradually as cocaine use continues, some users experience the problems after a single dose. Intravenous cocaine users who share contaminated needles and syringes are also at risk for AIDS. The risk of contracting AIDS is especially high in crack houses, where women addicts often engage in prostitution (see Chapter 7) to acquire drugs.

Cocaine use is extremely hazardous during pregnancy. Children born to crack-addicted mothers usually suffer painful withdrawal symptoms at birth and later show deficits in cognitive skills, judgment, and behaviour controls. "Crack babies" must often be cared for at public expense in hospitals and other facilities because their mothers cannot meet their basic needs or provide nurturance. But social scientist Philippe Bourgeois suggests that blame for the problem cannot be placed on the women alone. Instead, Bourgeois blames the problem on patriarchal definitions of "family" and the dysfunctional public sector that relegates the responsibility for nurturing and supporting children almost exclusively to women. For change to occur, fathers and the larger society must share the women's burden (Bourgeois, 1995).

SOCIAL PROBLEMS AND SOCIAL POLICY

BOX 8.2 The Battle over Marijuana: Medicalization; Availability; Decriminalization; Legalization?

Victor Philippe Lucas, who runs the Vancouver Island Compassion Societies (VICS), "wants to help people stop suffering" according to an article in *The Toronto Star* (retrieved February 23, 2002 from **www.thestar.com**). But his offering of marijuana to reduce pain and to help develop people's appetite is illegal. Marijuana should be made available to people who suffer because it "increases the quality of life of the people who suffer immensely," said Alan Young, lawyer for Jim Wakeford, an AIDS victim seeking a safe and affordable supply (author's files).

As of July 30, 2001, Canada is allowing people with medical need to use marijuana. Restrictions apply to certain types of need, such as having a terminal illness with a prognosis for a remaining life span of less than 12 months; having particular diseases such as multiple sclerosis, spinal cord injury, some cancers, and HIV/AIDS; and having other serious medical conditions where conventional treatments are not relieving symptoms (Health Canada, 2001).

In addition, a doctor must declare that conventional procedures have been tried and were unsuccessful. But the question of the availability of the drug remains. People must obtain a licence to grow it for themselves, or someone else must obtain a licence to grow it for them. The problem of availability was supposed to be solved when the government began a marijuana-growing operation in a deserted mine in Flin Flon, Manitoba. However, this marijuana is not being distributed because, as Health Minister Anne McLellan revealed in May 2002, the entire crop is too impure to hand out. Instead of getting pure seeds, the seeds for growing were culled from police raids. This approach led to a huge collection of different strains of wildly varying quality. Potential recipients will still have to rely on places like Compassion clubs, such as those in Toronto and Vancouver, or local dealers to provide the drug, and both groups could be prosecuted for supplying it.

Moreover, not all doctors agree with the decision to medicalize marijuana. Both the Canadian Medical Association and the Canadian Medical Protective Association have urged physicians not to sign patients' forms, to protect the physicians against being accused of recommending an unproven treatment. In addition, Physicians for a Smoke-Free Canada say that marijuana contains many cancer-causing ingredients and more tar than tobacco and thus should not be smoked for health reasons.

Many others think the government does not go far enough to make marijuana available to the estimated thousands of sufferers who may need it. James Wakeford, a person living with AIDS, asked Health Canada to give him a safe and affordable supply of marijuana and, when it was not forthcoming, took his case to the Ontario Court of Appeal. The court rejected the appeal on a technical ground in January 2002, saying that the governmental regulations did not have an adverse effect on Wakefield's liberty, according to his lawyer Alan Young. What should be done to help those in need now?

Given the difficulties of making marijuana available to people with a medical need, the difficulties of decriminalizing or legalizing it seem overwhelming even though almost a majority of Canadians are in favour of this, and prominent associations support its decriminalization. A Leger Marketing Survey found that 46.8 percent of Canadians were in favour of a law that would allow marijuana to be sold and used legally, and the Canadian Medical Association (in spite of the reservations about medical marijuana mentioned above) and the Canadian Association of Chiefs of Police support decriminalizing the possession of marijuana for personal use (*Globe and Mail,* June 25, 2001:A4).

Advocates of *decriminalization* or *legalization* suggest that small amounts of marijuana for personal use should no longer be subject to legal control. Some U.S states have already adopted some form of decriminalization for the possession of small amounts—usually less than one ounce or so—of marijuana. In the Netherlands, it is possible to use a variety of drugs without fear of prosecution.

According to criminologist Ronald L. Akers (1992), if marijuana were treated as a legal substance, it could be subject to restrictions on advertising, content, purchase age, and other regulations for production, distribution, and sale. But Akers (1992:160) also suggests that marijuana use "has the potential to grow to the same level as tobacco and alcohol use with basically the same magnitude of threat to health and life. . . . The benefits of legalization . . . are no more certain than are the harmful consequences of legalization." And others believe that legalizing marijuana would send the wrong message about the safety of this mind-altering drug.

In more recent developments, the Ontario Superior Court ruled in January 2003 that Ottawa's rules about the medical use of marijuana were unconstitutional because users have no legal access to the drug, and thus, patients' rights ere violated. One of the consequences of this ruling is that, if the regulations are not replaced, anyone will be legally free to possess this drug. Also in January 2003, an Ontario Court judge dismissed a marijuana possession charge because an earlier ruling had meant that it is no longer illegal for any Canadian to possess marijuana. Justice Minister Martin Cauchon stated that he would introduce legislation to decriminalize possession of small amounts of marijuana in Spring 2003.

What pros and cons would you give in a debate over (a) the government guaranteeing the availability of marijuana for those with medical need, or (b) the decriminalization or legalization of marijuana?

Like cocaine, amphetamines ("uppers") stimulate the central nervous system. Amphetamines in the form of diet pills and pep formulas are legal substances when they are prescribed by a physician, but many people, believing that they cannot lose weight or have enough energy without the pills, become physically and/or psychologically dependent on them. Speed freaks—heavy users who inject massive doses of amphetamines several times a day—often do "runs," staying awake for extended periods of time, eating very little, and engaging in bizarre behaviour such as counting cornflakes in a cereal box or pasting postage stamps on the wall before "crashing" and sleeping for several days (Goode, 1989). Recent concern about amphetamine abuse has focused on a smokeable form called ICE that contains a high percentage of the pure drug and produces effects that last from 4 to 24 hours (Lauderback and Waldorf, 1993). Chronic amphetamine abuse can result in *amphetamine psychosis*, which is characterized by paranoia, hallucinations, and violent tendencies that may persist for weeks after use of the drug has been discontinued. Overdosing on amphetamines can produce coma, brain damage, and even death.

Depressants

Many people who abuse stimulants also abuse depressants—drugs, including alcohol, that depress the central nervous system and may have some pain-killing properties. The most commonly used depressants are barbiturates (e.g., Nembutal and Seconal) and anti-anxiety drugs or tranquilizers (e.g., Librium, Valium, and Miltown). Relatively low oral doses of depressants produce a relaxing and mildly disinhibiting effect; higher doses result in sedation. Users may develop both physical addiction to and psychological dependence on these depressants. Users sometimes use depressants for *potentiation*—the interaction that takes place when two drugs are mixed together to produce a far greater effect than the effect of either drug administered separately. Heroin users, for example, will sometimes combine heroin and barbiturates in hopes of prolonging their high and extending their heroin supply (Fishbein and Pease, 1996).

Recently, Rohypnol and GHB (gamma-hydroxybutyrate), also known as "Grievous Bodily Harm" or "Liquid X," have been topics of discussion on university and college campuses. Rohypnol is used as an anesthetic and sleep aid in other countries, but it is not approved

Extensive media coverage of the arrest, conviction, and incarceration of film star Robert Downey, Jr., for felony drug possession called attention to the fact that drug abuse cuts across lines of racialization, class, and gender. Do you believe that media reports about Downey's prison sentence will make young people more aware of the problems associated with illicit drug use? Or does such coverage sometimes glamorize such behaviour?

for use in Canada. Rohypnol and GHB are popular among young people because they are inexpensive ("lunch money") drugs, and they produce a "floaty" state, a mild euphoria, increased sociability, and lowered inhibitions. According to Adlaf and Paglia's (2001:155) study of Ontario students, 2.9 percent (26 000 students) and 1.2 percent (11 000 students) report having used Rohypnol and GHB, respectively. For some people, Rohypnol works like a powerful sleeping pill.

Jenny Altick was a university student when she tried the drug: "I'd just pass out. . . . it seemed like a very safe thing to take. It wasn't like acid or something that was totally chemical and bad. If you're thinking about trying coke [cocaine], you've heard how bad it is. There's that little thing in your head. But this one, no one had heard about it. It was one of those new things everyone was doing" (quoted in Bonnin, 1997:E1). For other users, however, the consequences are more dire. Rohypnol, a benzodiazepine, known colloquially as "roofies," is known as the "date rape drug" because a number of women have reported that they were raped after an acquaintance secretly slipped the drug into their drink. Victims, including men, become drowsy and pass out, not remembering what happened. The combination of alcohol and Rohypnol or GHB has also been linked to automobile accidents and deaths from overdoses, which occur because it is difficult to judge how much intoxication will result when depressants are mixed with alcohol (Bonnin, 1997). A hopeful note, according to a report in *The Economist* (June 1, 2002:76), is that a small biotechnology company, SSD, is testing a coaster that can identify these drugs when a little of the drink is dropped on it.

Narcotics

Narcotics, or opiates, are available in several forms: natural substances (e.g., opium, morphine, and codeine); opiate derivatives, which are created by making slight changes in the chemical composition of morphine (e.g., heroin and Percodan); and synthetic drugs, which produce opiate-like effects but are not chemically related to morphine (e.g., Darvon and Demerol). Because heroin is the most widely abused narcotic, we will focus primarily on its effects.

Who uses heroin? The percentage of Canadians using it is very small. The NPHS combined several drugs together to report their use. The data, reported in the *Canadian Profile,* show that 1.1 percent of Canadians aged 15 and older used heroin, speed, and/or LSD in 1994, and that a higher percentage of men than women used these drugs (1.5 percent vs. 0.7 percent) (Single, Minh, et al., 1999:144). Young people are among the heaviest users; 8.3 percent of teens aged 15 to 17 reported using one of the drugs in the previous year (Single, Minh, et al., 1999:144). Some people who try the drug have adverse side effects, such as nausea and vomiting and never use it again; others become addicted.

What effect does heroin have on the body? Most heroin users inject the drug intravenously—a practice known as *mainlining* or *shooting*—which produces a tingling sensation and feeling of euphoria that is typically followed by a state of drowsiness or lethargy. Heroin users quickly develop a tolerance for the drug and must increase the dosage continually to achieve the same effect. Heroin and other opiates are highly addictive; users experience intense cravings for the drug and have physical symptoms such as diarrhea and dehydration if the drug is withdrawn.

What are the long-term effects of heroin? Although some users experience no long-term physical problems, there are serious risks involved in use. In high doses, heroin produces extreme respiratory depression, coma, and even death. Because the potency of street heroin is unknown, overdosing is always a possibility. Street heroin also tends to be diluted with other ingredients that produce adverse reactions in some users. Shooting up with contaminated needles can lead to hepatitis or AIDS. As well, heroin use has been linked more directly to crime than have some other types of drug use. Because hard-core users have difficulty holding a job and yet need a continual supply of the drug, they often turn to robbery, burglary, shoplifting, pimping, prostitution, or working for the underground drug industry (Johnson et al., 1985).

Hallucinogens

Hallucinogens, or psychedelics, are drugs that produce illusions and hallucinations. Mescaline (peyote), lysergic acid diethylamide (LSD), phencyclidine (PCP), and MDMA (Ecstasy) produce mild to profound psychological effects, depending on the dosage. Mescaline or peyote—the earliest hallucinogen used in North America—was consumed during ancient Native American religious celebrations.

In the 1960s, LSD became a well-known hallucinogen because of Timothy Leary's widely publicized advice, "Turn on, tune in, drop out." LSD is one of the most powerful of the psychoactive drugs; a tiny dose (10 micrograms) of the odorless, tasteless, and colourless drug can produce dramatic, highly unpredictable psychological effects for up to 12 hours. These effects are often referred to as a *psychedelic trip*, and users report experiences ranging from the beautiful (a good trip) to the frightening and extremely depressing (a bad trip). Consequently, some LSD users take the drug only with the companionship of others who are familiar with the drug's effects. However, some studies have found that there is a possibility of *flashbacks* in which the user re-experiences the effects of the drug as much as a year after it was taken. Most long-term psychiatric problems associated with the drug involve people who were unaware that they had been given LSD, who showed unstable personality characteristics before taking the drug, or who experienced it under hostile or threatening circumstances (Levinthal, 1996).

Among the most recent hallucinogens are PCP ("angel dust") and MDMA (Ecstasy). PCP can be taken orally, intravenously, or by inhalation, but it is most often smoked. Initially, PCP was used as an anesthetic in surgical procedures, but it was removed from production when patients who received it showed signs of agitation, intense anxiety, hallucinations, and disorientation. Production then went underground, and PCP became a relatively inexpensive street drug that some dealers pass off as a more expensive drug, such as LSD, to unknowing customers.

In the mid-1980s, MDMA (Ecstasy) hit the street market. Manufactured in clandestine labs by inexperienced chemists, Ecstasy, or "E," is a "designer drug" that is derived from amphetamines and has hallucinogenic effects. Users claim that it produces a state of relaxation, insight, euphoria, and heightened awareness without the side effects of LSD. Ecstasy has a high abuse potential and no recognized medical use (Milkman and Sunderwirth, 1987).

Inhalants

Inhalants are products that people inhale to get high. Commonly available products that are used as inhalants include gasoline, glue, paints, cleaning fluids, and toiletries. Inhalants are often called solvents because so many of them are used as inhalants. Inhalant abuse is common because inhalants are inexpensive, easy to obtain, and fast acting. They contain poisonous chemicals that can make abusers sick, damage their nerve and brain cells, and even kill them. As with many kinds of substance abuse, precise figures about use are either unavailable or questionable. However, according to the *2001 Youth Survey* of the Addictions Foundation of

Manitoba, 2.3 percent of students in Manitoba reported using inhalants in the previous year (Manitoba Addictions Awareness Week, 2002). While inhalant abuse is found in all ethnic groups in Canada, news stories suggest it is very prevalent among Indigenous children and adolescents. A study that shows a higher prevalence of inhalant use by Indigenous than White adolescents was conducted by psychologists Barbara Gfellner and John Hundleby (1995). In a survey of students (Grades 7 to 12; N=2 353 White and 237 Indigenous adolescents in 1993) in a non-metropolitan centre in midwestern Canada, they found that a higher percentage of Indigenous than White adolescents sniffed glue (4.3 percent vs. 3.5 percent) and solvents (6.4 percent vs. 3.5 percent) in 1993 (Gfellner and Hundleby, 1995). The usual explanation for this difference is a perception of a lack of opportunities for Indigenous adolescents.

EXPLANATIONS OF DRUG ABUSE

Why do people abuse drugs? Various explanations have been given. Some focus on biological factors; others emphasize environmental influences. Social scientists believe that drug abuse is associated with continuous and cumulative influences from the time of conception throughout the life course (Fishbein and Pease, 1996). Thus, to answer the question of why people abuse drugs, we must examine the intertwining biological, psychological, and sociological factors that affect people's behaviour.

Biological Explanations

Some biological explanations of alcohol and other drug addiction focus on genetic factors. Some studies of alcoholism have found that children who have an alcoholic birth parent have a higher than normal risk of becoming alcoholics themselves, even if they are adopted at birth and reared by nonalcoholic parents. These studies suggest that the child of an alcoholic parent inherits a biological predisposition (or vulnerability) to problem drinking or alcoholism. For example, the child may inherit increased sensitivity to alcohol as indicated by impaired enzyme production, brain function, and physiological responsivity during alcohol intake. The child also may inherit cognitive or learning impairments (e.g., hyperactivity, attention deficit disorder, or language delay) or psychological features (e.g., impulsivity, sensation seeking, anxiety, or aggressiveness) that increase the risk of alcohol abuse by exaggerating the rewarding biological and psychological properties of alcohol (Fishbein and Pease, 1996).

Other biological studies focus on the relationship between the brain and drug addiction. These studies have found convincing evidence that drugs such as alcohol, heroin, and cocaine act directly on the brain mechanisms responsible for reward and punishment. As the drugs stimulate the areas of the brain that create the sensation of pleasure and suppress the perception of pain, the user receives reinforcement to engage in further drug-taking behaviour.

According to these findings, then, drugs that provide an immediate rush or intense euphoria (e.g., cocaine and heroin) are more likely to be abused than drugs that do not. Similarly, drugs that produce pleasant but rapidly dissipating effects (e.g., alcohol) tend to encourage users to take additional doses to maintain the pleasurable effects. Biological explanations provide some insights on drug abuse, but biological factors alone do not fully explain alcoholism and other drug dependency.

Psychological Explanations

Psychological explanations of drug abuse focus on either personality disorders or the effects of social learning and reinforcement on drug-taking behaviour. Some studies have found that personality disorders—antisocial personality, psychopathy, impulsivity, affective disorder, and anxiety, among others—are more common among drug abusers than among non-abusers (Shedler and Block, 1990). Hyperactivity, learning disabilities, and behavioural disorders in childhood are also associated with a greater risk of substance abuse in adolescence or young adulthood. When people have low self-esteem or lack motivation, their desire to get away from problems is intensified, and drugs often provide the most available option for escape.

Social psychologists explain drug behaviour in terms of social learning. According to *social learning theory,* drug and alcohol use and abuse are behaviours that are acquired and sustained through a learning process. Learning takes place through instrumental conditioning (positive reinforcement or punishment) and modelling (imitation) of other people's behaviour. Every person learns attitudes, orientations, and general information about drug use from family members, friends, and significant others, so he or she comes to associate positive consequences (positive reinforcement) and negative consequences (punishment) with drug use. Therefore, whether the person abstains from, takes, or abuses drugs depends on the past, present, and anticipated rewards and punishments he or she associates with abstinence, use, or abuse. In a nutshell, the more an individual defines drug behaviour as good, or at least excusable, the more that person is likely to use drugs (Akers, 1992).

The Interactionist Perspective

Like social psychologists, sociologists who use an interactionist framework believe that drug behaviour is learned behaviour that is strongly influenced by families, peers, and other people. In other words, individuals are more likely to use or abuse drugs if they have frequent, intense, and long-lasting interactions with people who use or abuse drugs. For example, some children learn to abuse alcohol or other drugs by watching their parents drink excessively or use illegal drugs. Other young people learn about drug use from their peer group. In his classic study of marijuana users, sociologist Howard S. Becker (1963) concluded that drug users not only learn how to "do" drugs from other users but also what pleasurable reactions they should expect to have from drug use.

People also are more prone to accept attitudes and behaviours favourable to drug use if they spend time with members of a ***drug subculture*—a group of people whose attitudes, beliefs, and behaviours pertaining to drug use differ significantly from those of most people in the larger society.** Over time, people in heavy-drinking or drug subcultures tend to become closer to others within their subculture and more distant from people outside the subculture. Given this, participants in hard-core drug subcultures quit taking drugs or drinking excessively only when something brings about a dramatic change in their attitudes, beliefs, and values regarding drugs. Although it is widely believed that most addicts could change their behaviour if they chose to do so, according to *labelling theory,* it is particularly difficult for individuals to discontinue alcohol and other drug abuse once they have been labelled "alcoholics" or "drug addicts." Because of the prevailing ideology that alcoholism and drug addiction are personal problems rather than social problems, individuals tend to be held solely responsible for their behaviour.

The Functionalist Perspective

Why does the level of drug abuse remain high in Canada? Functionalists point out that there is virtually no society in which people do not use drugs of some kind (Schlaadt, 1992). Drugs contribute to many rituals, like weddings and other celebrations, and some drugs, like alcohol, are often a part of daily mealtimes. Other functionalists would suggest that social institutions such as the family, education, and religion, which previously kept deviant behaviour such as excessive or illicit drug use in check, have become fragmented and somewhat disorganized. Because they have, it is now necessary to use formal mechanisms of social control to prohibit people from taking illegal drugs or driving under the influence of alcohol or other drugs. External controls in the form of law enforcement are also required to discourage people from growing, manufacturing, or importing illegal substances.

Functionalists believe that activities in society continue because they serve important societal functions. Prescription and over-the-counter drugs, for example, are functional for patients because they ease pain, cure illness, and sometimes enhance or extend life. They are functional for doctors because they provide a means for treating illness and help to justify the doctor's fee. They are functional for pharmacists because they provide a source of employment; without pills to dispense, there would be no need for pharmacists. But dysfunctions also occur with prescription drugs: Patients may experience adverse side effects or develop a psychological dependence on the drug; doctors, pharmacists, and drug companies may be sued because they manufactured, prescribed, or sold a drug that is alleged to cause bodily harm to users.

Illicit drugs also have functions and dysfunctions. On the one hand, the illicit drug trade creates and perpetuates jobs at all levels of the criminal justice system, in the federal government, in social service agencies that deal with problems of alcoholism and drug addiction, and in criminology departments. What, for example, would employees in various police services do if Canada did not have an array of illicit drugs that are defined as the "drug problem"? On the other hand, the dysfunctions of illicit drug use extend throughout society.

This man may be playing double jeopardy with his life. The purity of street drugs often is in doubt, and shooting up with contaminated needles is a significant source of new AIDS cases in Canada.

At the individual level, addictive drugs such as heroin, cocaine, and barbiturates create severe physical and mental health problems as well as economic crises for addicts, their families, and acquaintances. At the societal level, drug abuse contributes to loss of productivity, human potential and life expectancy, and money. Hundreds of millions of dollars in taxpayers' money that might be used for education or preventive health care are spent making and enforcing drug laws and dealing with drug-related crime and the spread of AIDS by addicts who shoot up with contaminated needles. Addiction to illegal drugs, the abuse of legal drugs, and the abuse of alcohol and tobacco exacerbate the loss of human potential and undermine the stability of society.

The Conflict Perspective

According to conflict theorists, people in positions of economic and political power make the sale, use, and possession of drugs abused by the poor and the powerless illegal. We mentioned earlier that opium smoking was outlawed because it was associated with the Chinese. Restricting the drugs that members of a subordinate racialized/ethnic group use is one method of suppressing the group and limiting its ability to threaten dominant group members or gain upward mobility in society (Fishbein and Pease, 1996). Those who control the nation's political and legal apparatus decide whether a drug is legal or illegal.

Conflict theorists also point out that powerful corporate interests perpetuate the use and abuse of legal drugs. Corporations that manufacture, market, and sell alcohol, tobacco, and pharmaceuticals reap huge profits from products that exact a heavy toll on the personal health and well-being of abusers, their families and communities, and the larger society. Using their wealth and political clout, elites in Canadian tobacco companies have spent years vigorously fighting measures to discourage smoking. As mentioned above, tobacco companies plan to challenge the Tobacco Act. Since sales of tobacco products are approximately $4 billion per year, tobacco companies are not likely to give up the fight.

The Feminist Perspective

Feminist theorists point out that a significant part of the explanation of drug abuse by women has to do with women's vulnerability and disadvantaged position in society. Chapter 4, "Gender Inequality," has shown many forms of inequality, such as vulnerability to sexual and spousal abuse, the wage gap and fewer promotional opportunities, and the second shift. To deal with the feelings these forms of inequality bring about, women sometimes turn to drug abuse. "Women use drugs to cope, to deal with stress, to nurture themselves, to escape from the pain of past events or of their current status, or to continue their social roles" (Harrison, 1997:230).

A feminist approach to the problem emphasizes the different types of drug abuse by males and females. Data presented above showed that males are much more likely to use alcohol and illicit drugs than females, and females are more likely to use licit, psychotherapeutic drugs than males. Several hypotheses have been suggested to account for gender differences in health behaviour. Two hypotheses that help to explain the differences in drug taking are the risk-taking behaviour of men and the willingness of women to adopt the sick role (see Chapter 10 for a discussion of the sick role). Men are socialized to take risks and women are socialized to be more cautious and take care of their health (Waldron, 1997). Thus, men would engage in risky behaviour like drinking to solve problems, and women would seek out medical help and use drugs for problems rather than engage in risky behaviour. On the other hand, the social acceptability hypothesis suggests that women are more willing than men to admit being sick, adopt a sick role, and accept medical help such as using drugs to deal with their problems (Gee and Kimball, 1987).

THE FUTURE OF ALCOHOL AND DRUG ABUSE

How to prevent abuse of alcohol and other drugs and how to treat drug-related problems after they arise are controversial issues in contemporary society. What kinds of drug abuse prevention programs are available? Will future treatment programs for alcoholics and drug addicts differ from the ones that are available today? In Canada, the federal government has developed a comprehensive strategy—*Canada's Drug Strategy* (Health Canada, 1998*)—to reduce both the supply of and demand for drugs. It consists of seven components: research/knowledge development; knowledge dissemination; prevention programming; treatment and rehabilitation; legislation, enforcement and control; national coordination; and international co-operation (Health Canada, 1998:6).

Although most of this section will deal with prevention and treatment programming, it is important to note the other aspects of the overall strategy. First, research/knowledge development comprises undertaking and supporting literature reviews, large-scale quantitative studies, and community qualitative studies. Some of the results of that work have been presented above. Second, the dissemination of knowledge is also important; the government disseminates the results of its work and that of other national and international agencies. Third, a large part of the strategy is to prevent alcohol and drug abuse, and to this end the strategy supports direct law-enforcement procedures following the Controlled Substances Act that came into effect in May 1997. In addition, Canada has ratified United Nations conventions to deal with the obvious international nature of drug smuggling. According to Single and his colleagues (1996), the law enforcement costs in 1992 were $1.8 billion. However, since government estimates of the value of the illegal drug market were $7 to $10 billion (Porteous, 1998), law enforcement to curtail the supply is not, alone, likely to be able to solve the drug problem.

Prevention Programs

Drug and alcohol prevention programs can be divided into three major categories: primary, secondary, and tertiary prevention. ***Primary prevention* refers to programs that seek to prevent drug problems before they begin.** Most primary prevention programs focus on people who have had little or no previous experience with drugs. In contrast, *secondary prevention* programs seek to limit the extent of drug abuse, prevent the spread of drug abuse to substances beyond those already experienced, and teach strategies for the responsible use of licit drugs such as alcohol (Levinthal, 1996). For example, a program directed at college students who already consume alcohol might focus on how to drink responsibly by emphasizing the dangers of drinking and driving. Finally, *tertiary prevention* programs seek to limit relapses by individuals recovering from alcoholism or drug addiction. The purpose of tertiary prevention is to ensure that people who have entered treatment for some form of drug abuse become free of drugs and remain that way.

Prevention, according to *Canada's Drug Strategy*, is best done through a combination of public awareness campaigns, educational resources, training of service providers, and community action (Health Canada, 1998:7). The programs should be part of every year's school curriculum, should involve students in planning and conducting presentations, and should present honest factual material about why people use drugs and give alternatives to their use.

Scare tactics and negative-education programs do not work; they turn students off and do not achieve their desired goal. In fact, scare tactics appear to pique some students' curiosity about drugs rather than deter their use. Objective information programs often begin in kindergarten and progress through Grade 12. Using texts, curriculum guides, videos, and other materials, teachers impart factual information about drugs to students, but as with scare tactics, students sometimes become more—instead of less—interested in drug experimentation. An 18-year-old student who smoked his first marijuana joint at age 13 explains why he thinks these programs are ineffective: "When someone tells you not to do it, that makes you want to do it even more" (Kolata, 1996a:A12).

Comprehensive programs that include school-based and peer-conducted smoking education programs for students combined with community-based smoking cessation programs for adults are more promising than single preventive strategies. Such a comprehensive program was found to be effective in an experiment in North Karelia, Finland. After a 15-year follow-up, mean lifetime cigarette consumption was 22 percent lower among program subjects than among control subjects (Vartiainen et al., 1998).

Self-esteem enhancement and affective-education programs can be effective also. They focus on the underlying emotional and attitudinal factors that are involved in drug abuse while building character through teaching positive social values and attitudes. These programs are most effective when they, too, are incorporated into more comprehensive prevention programs.

If the purpose of prevention programs is to reduce actual drug-taking behaviour, what types of programs have the greatest likelihood of success? Many social analysts suggest that family- and school-based primary and secondary prevention programs are the most effective. Previously, some prevention programs focused on high-school students, but today elementary schools are among the first lines of attack because drug-taking behaviour now starts at younger ages. Many public schools have a program known as DARE (Drug Abuse Resistance Education), which is taught by specially trained police officers who teach children how to resist drugs. Critics suggest that police officers, whom many young people view as authority figures, are not the best people to teach adolescents that drug use is not cool. Critics also note that one-shot programs that are forced on students may not prevent drug abuse. Children who have been through the DARE program are no less likely to smoke, drink, or use other drugs than children who have not been through the program (Kolata, 1996a).

Prevention programs that look hopeful for the future emphasize *life skills training*. The Life Skills Training Program developed by Gilbert Botvin at Cornell Medical School consists of a 15-session curriculum directed toward Grade 7 students. Booster sessions are offered in Grades 8 and 9. The program provides information on the short-term consequences of alcohol or other drug use and teaches participants critical-thinking skills, independent decision making, ways to reduce anxiety and resist peer pressure to take drugs, and ways of gaining a sense of personal control and self-esteem (Botvin and Tortu, 1988). Unlike programs that primarily tell students to stay off drugs, life skills training attempts to give students the tools they need to stay drug-free. Although the short-term effects of life skills programs are impressive, according to Levinthal (1996), they erode over time. Still, Levinthal believes that we can learn important lessons from prevention strategies that have failed in the past, lessons that we can use to create better approaches in the future.

Future prevention programs will be family-, school, and community-based. They will offer alternative activities and outlets to drug use. These programs—like other drug abuse prevention efforts—will take into account issues that affect people differently depending on their racialization/ethnicity, religion, or other factors. Reaching across lines of racialization, class, and gender, the next generation of drug abuse prevention programs will use cable television channels to make people aware of the effects of drugs on the human body and how to get help in dealing with alcoholism and drug addiction. The Internet will become a vital source of information. Current websites provide an array of information on drugs and offer unique features such as an online dictionary of street drug slang.

Future prevention programs provide cause for optimism, but only if social structural factors change. If illegal drugs continue to flow into Canada and television, other mass media, and advertising continue to glamorize smoking, drinking, and other drug use, the future of preventive programs is bleak. Without social change, efforts will be directed toward apprehension and incarceration of drug offenders and treatment programs for drug addicts and alcoholics, not at primary or secondary prevention strategies.

Treatment Programs

Tertiary prevention programs are programs that aim to ensure that people who have sought help for some form of drug abuse remain drug-free. It follows from the biological and social learning explanations for substance abuse and alcohol addiction that treatment must deal with the body's physiological and psychological responses. Therefore, *alcohol and drug treatment* involves the use of activities designed to eliminate physical and psychological addiction and to prevent relapse—returning to abuse and/or addiction (Fishbein and Pease, 1996). Most treatment programs are based on a medical model or therapeutic community.

The Medical Treatment Model

The *medical treatment model* considers drug abuse and alcoholism to be medical problems that must be resolved through medical treatment by medical officials. Treatment may take the form of *aversion therapy* or *behavioural conditioning*. For example, drugs such as Cyclazocine and Nalozone are given to heroin and opiate addicts to prevent the euphoric feeling that they associate with taking the drugs. Supposedly, when the pleasure is gone, the person will no longer abuse the drug. Some heroin addicts also receive methadone detoxification to alleviate withdrawal symptoms associated with stopping heroin use. Over a one- to three-week period, the patient receives decreasing doses of methadone, a synthetic opium derivative that blocks the desire for heroin but does not have its negative side effects.

Antabuse is used in the treatment of alcoholism. After the person has been detoxified and no alcohol remains in the bloodstream, Antabuse is administered along with small quantities of alcohol for several consecutive days. Because this combination produces negative effects such as nausea and vomiting, the individual eventually develops an aversion to drinking, which becomes associated with uncomfortable physical symptoms. Although the medical treatment model works for some people, it is criticized for focusing on the physiological effects of alcohol and drug dependency and not dealing with the psychological and sociological aspects of dependency.

Short- and Long-Term Services and the Therapeutic Community

According to a booklet entitled *Alcohol and Drug Treatment in Ontario: A Guide for Helping Professionals*, published by the Centre for Addiction and Mental Health, many short- and long-term services (both live-at-home and live-in) are available (at no charge, except for some specialized services) for people seeking help with addictions. (The authors acknowledge that some services may not be locally available.) Short-term services include withdrawal management (detox) services, which give people a place to stay while their bodies get rid of alcohol or drugs and adapt to a drug-free state, and services that provide a place to stay for a month and insight into leading a healthy life.

When substance abusers are perceived to have an underlying psychological problem, treatment generally involves long-term services like counselling, rehabilitation, and/or the therapeutic community. Counselling often employs rehabilitated alcoholics or addicts who encourage participants to take more responsibility for their lives so that they can function better in the community. Some counselling and rehabilitation programs take place on an outpatient basis or as day treatment; others involve residential treatment. *Outpatient programs* allow drug abusers to remain at home and continue working while attending regular group and individual meetings. *Day treatment* takes place in a hospital setting where the abuser participates in day-long treatment groups and individual counselling sessions and returns home in the evening. The *therapeutic community approach* is based on the idea that drug abuse is best treated by intensive individual and group counselling in a residential setting. Residential treatment takes place in a special house or dormitory where alcoholics or drug addicts remain for periods of time ranging from several months to more than a year while they learn to rebuild their lives without alcohol or drugs.

Perhaps the best-known nonresidential therapeutic communities are Alcoholics Anonymous (AA), founded in 1935, and its offshoot, Narcotics Anonymous (NA). Both AA and NA provide members with support in their efforts to overcome drug dependence and addiction. AA was established in 1935, in the United States, by two alcoholics who were seeking a way of returning to sober life (Fishbein and Pease, 1996). Today, the organization has more than 5100 chapters with more than 98 800 members in Canada (Fact file at **www.alcoholics-anonymous.org**). Members use only their first names to ensure anonymity, and recovering alcoholics serve as sponsors and counsellors for others. AA and NA are based on a 12-step program that requires members to acknowledge that they are alcoholics or drug addicts who must have the help of God and other people to remain sober or drug-free. Group support is central to success in these programs, as journalist Caroline Knapp (1996:253–254) explains:

> A few months after my one-year anniversary [of sobriety] I went to the meeting. . . on the ground floor of a church. . . . One person tells his or her story for the first half-hour, and then the meeting opens up, first to those in their first month of sobriety, then to those with three months or less, then six months or less, and so on. . . . At the end of the meeting there was a presentation for a young guy named John, who was celebrating one year without a drink. . . . He was so happy that evening, so grateful to get that one-year medallion, and so moved by the amount of support he'd gotten over the year, that his eyes welled up and his voice kept cracking. "I can't thank you all enough," he said, and his face was the picture of hope. . . . Then I had an image of every person in that room . . . getting into our beds clean and sober, another day without a drink behind us. It was a simple image but it filled me with a range of complicated feelings: appreciation for the simple presence of all those people; admiration for their courage and strength; a tinge of melancholy for the amount of pain it must have taken each and every one of them to put down the drink; affection for their humanity. I didn't realize until hours later that there was a name for that feeling. It's called love.

Various other types of testimonials are available at the Alcoholics Anonymous Web site: **www.alcoholics-anonymous.org/english/E_Pamphlets/ P-13_d1.html**.

Sociologists believe AA is successful because it gives former alcoholics the opportunity to be delabelled as stigmatized deviants and relabelled as former and repentant deviants. It should be kept in mind, however, that social class and personality factors affect people's ability to enter into the repentant role, which requires a public admission of guilt and repentance, and to interact successfully with others in the program (Trice and Roman, 1970).

All the approaches for reducing alcohol and drug abuse that we have discussed can help certain individuals, but none address what to do about social structural factors that contribute to the drug problem. Because drug- and alcohol-related problems and their solutions are part of deeper social issues and struggles, they cannot be dealt with in isolation, as social scientist Philippe Bourgeois (1995:319, 327) explains:

> Drugs are not the root of the problems . . . they are the expression of deeper, structural dilemmas. Self-destructive addiction is merely the medium for desperate people to internalize their frustrations, resistance, and powerlessness. . . . Instead we should

focus our ethical concerns and political energies on the contradictions posed by the persistence of inner-city poverty in the midst of extraordinary opulence. . . . The economic base of the traditional working class has eroded throughout the country. Greater proportions of the population are socially marginalized. The restructuring of the world economy by multinational corporations, finance capital, and digital electronic technology, as well as the exhaustion of social democratic models for public sector intervention [e.g., welfare programs] on behalf of the poor, has escalated inequalities around class, ethnicity, and gender. . . . There is no technocratic solution. Any long-term paths out of the quagmire will have to address the structural and political-economic roots, as well as the ideological and cultural roots of social marginalization. The first step out of the impasse, however, requires a fundamental ethical and political reevaluation of basic socioeconomic models and human values.

If Canada sets out to reduce inequalities in all areas of social life, perhaps the drug problem will be alleviated as well. What do you think it would take to make this happen?

WHAT CAN YOU DO?

- Volunteer at an agency such as Mothers Against Drunk Driving or, if a local chapter exists, Students Against Drunk Driving (SADD). If a local chapter does not exist, contact MADD at **www. madd.ca** about founding a chapter.

- Participate in or organize a committee for challenging the various kinds of drug companies and their influence on universities. In Chapter 10, reference is made to students at the University of Toronto supporting, through sponsoring an open forum, Doctors for Research Integrity. Since the influence of pharmaceutical companies on research practices is likely to be a continuing problem, much scope exists for future educational programs.

- Develop an educational program to help students stop binge drinking. Generally, the peer-initiated programs have better results. Several years ago, students at colleges in Ontario undertook a promotional campaign based on the slogan, "If you drink, don't bowl," based on the double meaning of *bowl* as a game and a place to vomit (toilet bowl). Try to devise a new catchy and effective slogan for your program. You might include some first-aid suggestions for dealing with consequences of binge drinking.

- Study the way students use prescription medicines, not only antidepressants, but also diet pills and stimulants, and study the relationship between alcohol consumption and acquaintance or date rape.

- Design a program to alert students, particularly women, to the problems of excessive body-consciousness (see also Chapter 10) as well as the need, when on dates, to use drugs with particular care.

SUMMARY

WHAT ARE THE MAJOR PATTERNS OF DRINKING?

Social scientists divide long-term drinking patterns into four categories: (1) *social drinkers* consume alcoholic beverages primarily on social occasions and may drink either occasionally or relatively frequently; (2) *heavy drinkers* are more frequent drinkers who typically consume greater quantities of alcohol when they drink and are more likely to become intoxicated; (3) *acute alcoholics* have trouble controlling their use of alcohol and plan their schedule around drinking; and, (4) *chronic alcoholics* have lost control over their drinking and tend to engage in compulsive behaviour such as hiding liquor bottles.

WHAT ARE THE MAJOR HAZARDS ASSOCIATED WITH TOBACCO USE?

Nicotine is a toxic, dependency-producing drug that is responsible for about 45 000 deaths per year in Canada. People who smoke have a greater likelihood of developing cardiovascular disease, lung cancer, and/or cancer of the larynx, mouth, and esophagus. Even those who do not smoke may be subjected to the hazard of environmental tobacco smoke—the smoke in the air as a result of other people's tobacco smoking. Infants born to women who smoke typically have lower-than-average birth weights and sometimes have slower rates of physical and mental growth.

WHAT PROBLEMS ARE ASSOCIATED WITH USE OF PRESCRIPTION AND OVER-THE-COUNTER DRUGS?

Some prescription drugs have the potential for short-term abuse and long-term psychological and physical dependence. This form of dependency is known as *iatrogenic addiction*—drug dependency that results from physician-supervised treatment for a recognized medical disorder. Over-the-counter drugs, which are widely advertised and readily available, may be dangerous when combined with alcohol or other drugs.

WHAT CATEGORIES OF PEOPLE ARE MOST LIKELY TO USE MARIJUANA?

Most marijuana users are between the ages of 18 and 25; however, use by 15- to 17-year-olds has increased in the 1990s to a level of 25 percent. More men than women smoke marijuana.

IN CANADA, WHAT ARE THE MAJOR STIMULANT DRUGS?

Cocaine and amphetamines are the major stimulant drugs abused in Canada. Cocaine is an extremely potent and dependency-producing stimulant drug. Amphetamines can be obtained legally in the form of diet pills and pep formulas when they are prescribed by a physician.

WHAT ARE DEPRESSANTS AND WHAT HEALTH-RELATED RISK DO THEY POSE?

As the name indicates, depressants depress the central nervous system; they also may have some pain-killing properties. The most common depressants are barbiturates and anti-anxiety drugs or tranquilizers. Users may develop both physical addiction and psychological dependency on these drugs. There is also the risk of *potentiation*—the drug interaction that takes place when two drugs are mixed together and the combination produces a far greater effect than that of either drug administered separately.

HOW DO BIOLOGICAL AND PSYCHOLOGICAL PERSPECTIVES VIEW ALCOHOL AND DRUG ADDICTION?

Biological explanations of alcohol and drug addiction focus on inherited biological factors and on the effects of drugs on the human brain. Psychological explanations of drug abuse focus on personality disorders and the effects of social learning and reinforcement on people's drug-taking behaviour.

HOW DO SOCIOLOGICAL PERSPECTIVES VIEW ALCOHOL AND DRUG ADDICTION?

Interactionists believe that drug use and abuse are learned behaviours that are strongly influenced by families, peers, and others who serve as role models. People are more prone to accept attitudes and behaviours that are favourable to drug use if they spend time with members of a drug subculture. Functionalists believe that drug-related problems have increased as social institutions such as the family, schools, and religious institutions have become fragmented and somewhat disorganized. However, use of alcohol and other drugs serves important functions, even though some aspects of drug use are dysfunctional for society. According to conflict theorists, people in positions of economic and political power are responsible for making the sale, use, and possession of some drugs illegal. Conflict theorists also point out that powerful corporate interests perpetuate the use and abuse of alcohol, tobacco, and other legal drugs. Feminist theorists emphasize the vulnerability and disadvantaged position of women who abuse drugs.

WHAT IS THE PURPOSE OF PREVENTION AND TREATMENT PROGRAMS?

Primary prevention programs seek to prevent drug problems before they begin. Secondary prevention programs seek to limit the extent of drug abuse, prevent the spread of drug abuse to other substances beyond the drugs already experienced, and teach strategies for the responsible use of licit drugs such as alcohol. Tertiary prevention programs seek to limit relapses by individ-

uals recovering from alcoholism or drug addiction. They may be based either on a medical model or the therapeutic community. The best-known therapeutic community is Alcoholics Anonymous (AA).

WHAT OTHER FACTORS MUST BE TAKEN INTO ACCOUNT IN EFFORTS TO REDUCE THE DRUG PROBLEM?

Alcoholism and drug abuse are intertwined with other social problems such as dramatic changes in the economic and technological bases of society, the growing gap between the rich and poor, and inequalities based on racialization/ethnicity and gender.

KEY TERMS

codependency,   p. 182
drug,   p. 178
drug addiction,   p. 178
drug dependency,   p. 178
drug subculture, p. 192
environmental tobacco smoke,   p. 183

fetal alcohol effects (FAE),   p. 181
fetal alcohol syndrome (FAS),   p. 181
primary prevention,   p. 195
tolerance,   p. 178
withdrawal,   p. 179

QUESTIONS FOR CRITICAL THINKING

1.   Does public tolerance of alcohol and tobacco lead to increased use of these drugs? Why do many people view the use of alcohol and tobacco differently from the use of illicit drugs?

2.   If stimulants, depressants, hallucinogens, and inhalants have such potentially hazardous side effects, why do so many people use these drugs? If drug enforcement policies were more stringently enforced, would there be less drug abuse in this country?

3.   As a sociologist, how would you propose to deal with the drug problem in Canada? If you were called upon to revamp existing drug laws and policies, what, if any, changes would you make in them?

4.   How have changes in technology affected the problem of alcohol and drug abuse over the past century? How have changes in the global economy affected drug-related problems in this country and others?

WEBLINKS

Alcoholics Anonymous
www.alcoholics-anonymous.org
Alcoholics Anonymous is a self-help group with chapters throughout the world to help people and their friends and relatives addicted to alcohol.

Canadian Centre on Substance Abuse
www.ccsa.ca
This nonprofit organization works to minimize the harm associated with the use of alcohol, tobacco, and other drugs. Available from the home page are links to current topics, resources, statistics, and networks.

Centre for Addiction and Mental Health
www.camh.net
The Centre for Addiction and Mental Health is a public hospital providing direct patient care for people with mental-health and addiction problems. The centre is also a research facility **www. camh.net/ research/index.html**, an education centre, **www. camh.net/ets/index.html** and a community organization providing health promotion and prevention services, and it is a collaborator with world health bodies.

Health Canada: Drug Strategy and Controlled Substances
www.hc-sc.gc.ca/hecs-sesc/hecs/dscs.htm
Health Canada's Drug Strategy and Controlled Substances Program regulates controlled substances and promotes initiatives that reduce or prevent the harm associated with these substances and alcohol. The program also provides expert advice and drug analysis services to law enforcement agencies across the country. A link is also available for tobacco control.

Medical Marijuana in Canada
www.medicalmarijuana.ca
This site presents up-to-date articles and information, links to services, and information about growers and the shipping of marijuana.

Mothers Against Drunk Driving
www.madd.ca
This site presents information about MADD and its programs, its library, and how you can help.

Narcotics Anonymous
www.na.org
Narcotics Anonymous is a world service to help people learn about and control their addiction to narcotics.

9

CRIME AND CRIMINAL JUSTICE

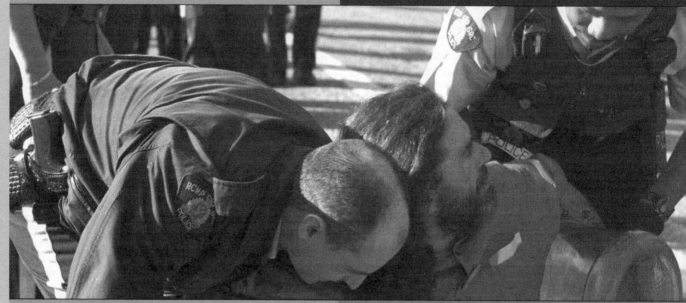

The video surveillance of public streets that the RCMP is carrying out in Kelowna is not necessary. There is no evidence that it is effective or is likely to be effective.

Privacy Commissioner George Radwanski, who has launched a lawsuit in the Supreme Court of British Columbia, believes the cameras violate the Charter's guarantee of the right to privacy (quoted in Lunman, 2002:A1)

The RCMP continually seeks to find appropriate means to ensure and increase public safety and security, be that through police or community-based initiatives.

RCMP Sergeant Paul Marsh, in reply to Privacy Commissioner George Radwanski (quoted in Lunman, 2002:A8)

The placing of cameras in what criminologists call "hot spots" (Sherman et al., 1989) is a way of deterring *routine activities crime*, **crime that occurs when a motivated offender finds a suitable target in the absence of suitable guardianship.** Some researchers suggest that crime that would be deterred by the cameras would, like street prostitution, just move to another location. What do you think? Would you feel safer with surveillance cameras around?

In this chapter you will learn about the problem of defining crime and measuring crime with official statistics or victimization surveys; the level of various kinds of crime (e.g., violent, property, and youth crime) and how the levels of some of these crimes in Canada compare to those in the United States. You will also learn about the nature of occupational and organized crime; why people commit crimes (the biological, psychological, and sociological explanations of crime); and the nature of the criminal justice system. The chapter concludes with some suggestions for ways you might help deal with the problem of crime.

CRIME AS A SOCIAL PROBLEM

Many people in Canada fear crime and are somewhat obsessed with it even though they have no direct daily exposure to criminal behaviour. Their information about crime comes from the media (Chermak, 1995) and, sometimes, from watching real-crime dramas such as *America's Most Wanted* (sightings by Canadians have led to the arrest of a couple of America's most wanted).

They are also influenced by fictionalized crime stories on television, such as *DaVinci's Inquest*. Media coverage of crime is extensive, but it has not contributed to a belief among Canadians that crime is increasing.

According to the General Social Survey of 1999, the majority of Canadians (54 percent) believe that crime levels have been stable over the last five years (Besserer and Trainor, 2000:1). With the exception of the rate of serious and violent crime, which has continued to fall during the last 10 years, crime rates have remained relatively stable over the past two decades. That is not to say that crime isn't a problem. Crime statistics tell only part of the story. Crime *is* a significant social problem because it endangers people's lives, property, and sense of well-being. In 1999, about 25 percent of Canadians over the age of 15 were victims of at least one crime, for a total of 8.3 million incidents (Besserer and Trainor, 2000:1). Since approximately $10 billion, or three cents of every tax dollar, was spent on police, courts, corrections, legal aid, and criminal prosecutions (figures for 1994–95 [CCJS, 1999:3]), individuals who are not directly victimized by crime are harmed because they have to pay taxes to fight it.

Problems with Official Statistics

Over the past two decades, sophisticated computer-based information systems have not only improved rates of detection, apprehension, and conviction of offenders but also provided immediate access to millions of bits of information about crime, suspects, and offenders (H.D. Barlow, 1996). The leading source of information on crimes reported in Canada is the *Uniform Crime Report* (*UCR*). The *UCR* was developed by Statistics Canada with the co-operation and assistance of the Canadian Association of Chiefs of Police. The survey became operational in 1962 and collects crime and traffic statistics reported by all police agencies in Canada. *UCR* data is based on reported crime substantiated by police investigation. It is made available, for use in presentations such as this chapter, by the Canadian Centre for Justice Statistics (CCJS) in its periodical *Juristat* (Logan, 2001:13). Since 1988, the *UCR* has been using an incident-based reporting system instead of an aggregate system, collecting data on each criminal event, offender, and victim. It is thus providing a more complex portrait of crime in Canada.

The crime rate reported here includes offences like homicide, assault, sexual assault, break and enter, robbery, theft, motor vehicle theft, and fraud. It does not include other violations, such as traffic and drug offences.

How accurate are these crime statistics? Any answer to this question must take into account the fact that the statistics reflect only crimes that are reported to law enforcement agencies or that police officers see occur. According to the *UCR,* overall rates of crime (number of crimes per 100 000 people), which increased from the early 1960s to 1992, have decreased annually since then. This downward trend probably reflects several factors, including increasing job opportunities and a shift in population (see Chapter 5). The percentage of the Canadian population under age 26—the age group most likely to commit crimes—began to decline in 1992.

Because the number of crimes *reported* is not necessarily the number of crimes *committed,* Statistics Canada conducts victimization surveys, most recently in the General Social Survey of 1999, surveying 26 000 randomly selected households to identify victims of personal crimes (e.g., theft of personal property, break and enter, assault, sexual assault, robbery, motor vehicle theft, and hate), and whether the crime was reported or not (see Chapter 1). These surveys indicate that the number of crimes committed is substantially higher than the number reported. However, the GSS has limitations, too:

1. Responses are based on recall, and some people don't remember specifically when a crime occurred. (They are supposed to report on the previous 12 months.)
2. For various reasons, respondents may not be truthful.
3. The surveys focus on theft and assault and do not measure workplace crimes, such as embezzlement or bribery, and organized crime.

Defining Crime and Delinquency

Crime **is behaviour that violates the criminal law and is punishable by fine, jail term, or other negative sanctions.** There are two components to every crime: the act itself, and *criminal intent*—expressed in the concept of *mens rea,* meaning "guilty mind." An individual's intent in committing a crime may range from willful conduct (hiring someone to kill one's spouse) to an unintentional act of negligence that is defined as a crime (leaving a small child unattended in a locked automobile in extremely hot weather, resulting in the child's death).

Criminal law is divided into two major categories: summary and indictable offences. *Summary offences* **are relatively minor crimes that are punishable by a fine or less than a year in jail.** Examples include public drunkenness, shoplifting, and traffic violations. *Indictable offences* **are more serious crimes, such as murder, sexual assault, or aggravated assault, that are punishable by more than a year's imprisonment or even death.** Children and adolescents (12 to 17 years of age) who commit illegal or antisocial acts usually are not charged with criminal conduct but are adjudicated as *delinquent* or *youth crime* by a juvenile court judge. However, when older juveniles are charged with violent crimes, it is becoming increasingly common to *certify* or *waive* them to adult court.

TYPES OF CRIMES

To make the study of crime—a large and complex subject—manageable, sociologists and criminologists categorize types of crime. In this section, we will look at six categories of crime: violent crime, property crime, occupational crime, corporate crime, organized crime, and youth crime.

Violent Crime

While it is well known to occur frequently in the United States, violent crime occurs much less frequently in Canada. *Violent crime* **consists of actions involving force or the threat of force against others** and includes homicide, attempted homicide, the three levels of assault and sexual assault, robbery, and other violent offences like criminal negligence causing death. Violent crimes are committed against people; nonviolent crimes are usually committed against property. People tend to fear violent crime more than other kinds of crime because victims are often physically injured or even killed and because violent crime receives the most sustained attention from law enforcement officials and the media (see Parker, 1995; Warr, 1995).

Homicide

The *UCR* defines **homicide as the unlawful, intentional killing of one person by another.** (Killing by accident, in self-defence or during wartime, is not homicide.) By this definition, murder involves not only an unlawful act but also *malice aforethought*—the *intention* of doing a wrongful act. A person who buys a gun, makes a plan to kill someone, and carries out the plan has probably committed homicide. In contrast, *manslaughter* is the unlawful, *unintentional* killing of one person by another. An intoxicated person who shoots a gun into the air probably holds no malice toward the bystander who is killed by a stray bullet. Sometimes a person's intentions are clear, but many times they are not, and the lines between intentional, unintentional, and accidental homicides are blurred.

Mass murder is the killing of four or more people at one time and in one place by the same person. Fortunately, the examples of mass murder in Canada are few. Marc Lepine's killing of 14 women in 1989 in the École Polytechnique in Montreal is an example of mass murder.

According to criminologists, mass murderers tend to kill in the areas where they live. They are likely to be male, problem drinkers, and collectors of firearms and other weapons, which they often hide (Dietz, 1986). Some recent mass murderers have been disgruntled employees or former employees who seek out supervisors and coworkers in the workplace. An example of this kind of mass murder was the 1992 killing of four faculty members by Valery Fabrikant, a professor of engineering, at Concordia University in Montreal. In the U.S., a number of these violent eruptions have occurred in post offices, hence the term "going postal."

Serial murder is the killing of three or more people over more than a month by the same person. Serial murders account for few homicides, but receive extensive media coverage. In Canada, Clifford Olson, who killed 11 boys and girls and was sentenced to life imprisonment in 1982, and Michael Wayne McGray, who pleaded guilty to 6 murders in 1998, are examples of a serial killer. The finding of many bodies at the pig farm owned by Robert Pickton in Port Coquitlam, a suburb of Vancouver, would appear to indicate another example of serial murder.

It is difficult to characterize serial killers, outside of the fact that the best known ones are White males. Some travel extensively to locate their victims; others kill near where they live. One study identified four basic types of serial killers: (1) *visionaries,* who kill because they hear a voice or have a vision that commands them to commit the murderous acts; (2) *missionaries,* who take it on themselves to rid the community or the world of what they believe is an undesirable type of person; (3) *hedonists,* who obtain personal or sexual gratification from violence; and, (4) *power/control seekers,* who achieve gratification from the complete possession of the victim (Holmes, 1988).

Nature and Extent of the Problem Statistics on homicide are among the most accurate official crime statistics available. Homicides rarely go unreported, and suspects are usually apprehended and charged. Although annual rates vary slightly, murder follows certain patterns in terms of gender, age, racialization, and region of the country. Men make up the vast majority of murder victims and offenders. Of the 542 homicides reported in 2000, three-quarters of the victims were male and 90 percent of the offenders were male (Feodorowycz, 2001:1). Males kill other males in about 90 percent of cases. Females kill 7 percent of the male victims, often because the females think they are in a life-threatening situation (Feodorowycz, 2001:1).

Age patterns are clearly evident in murder rates. Almost half of all homicide victims are 17 to 34 years of age, and 60 percent of accused murderers were 15 to 34 years of age (Fedorowycz, 2001:12). In 2000, a homicide rate of 3 per 100 000 occurred for youths aged 12 through 17, and the total number of accused decreased from the previous year, from 45 to 41 (Fedorowycz, 2001:13).

In Canada, unlike the U.S., homicide is not an urban phenomenon. In 2000, the homicide rate for the 37 percent of the population living in areas of less than 100 000 was 1.71 per 100 000, almost identical to the national rate of 1.76 per 100 000 (Feodorowycz, 2001:3). Regarding regional differences, homicide is more likely to occur in Western than Eastern Canada (Feodorowycz, 2001:3).

In the past, most murder victims knew their killers, but this pattern seems to be gradually changing somewhat. In 2000, half of all homicides were committed by an acquaintance, 32 percent by a family member, and 17 percent by a stranger (Feodorowycz, 2001:10). Among female murder victims, the pattern is more extreme. Almost 55 percent of female victims are slain by someone with whom they have had an intimate relationship, compared with only 7 percent of male victims (Feodorowycz, 2001:1)

Across the nation, firearms are used in approximately 34 percent of all murders annually—a fact that leads to ongoing political debate over gun control, especially of handguns; the percentage of homicides by firearms has increased 21 percent since 1998. In 2000, the percentage of people killed by stabbings was 28 and the percentage of people killed by beatings was 23 (Feodorowycz, 2001:1).

Social Responses to Murder Even though most murders are not random, many people have a deep and persistent fear of strangers. According to one analyst:

> We have responded [in various ways to the threat of murder]. Some of us by minimizing our time in public space for fear of encountering the random menace; many by purchasing a range of weapons, locks, bolts, alarms, and insurance; parents, by acting as virtual bodyguards for our children; governments, by dispensing crime prevention advice which promotes individual responsibility for keeping crime at bay. But has this reduced our fear? Or contributed to our greater security? Clearly not. (Stanko, 1990:viii)

Individual responses are intensified by media coverage of violent personal crimes, especially murder.

Sexual Assault

Many people think of **sexual assault** (the term "rape" is no longer used in criminal law) as a sexually motivated crime, but it is actually **an act of violence in which sex is used as a weapon against a powerless victim** (Vito and Holmes, 1994). Both men and women can be victimized by sexual assault. In Canada, it is classified into three levels:

- Level 1 includes touching, grabbing, kissing—the category of least physical harm to the victim.
- Level 2 includes assault with a weapon, threats to use a weapon, or causing bodily harm.
- Level 3, or aggravated assault, includes wounding, maiming, or endangering the life of the victim.

Date rape is forcible sexual activity that meets the legal definition of sexual assault and involves people who first meet in a social setting (Sanday, 1996). This definition is preferred by some scholars because it

encompasses dates and casual acquaintances but excludes spouses (marital rape) and relatives (incest). The phrase was coined to distinguish forced, nonconsensual sex between people who know one another from forced, nonconsensual sex between strangers—but both are against the law. Date rape is often associated with alcohol or other drug consumption (see "roofies" in Chapter 8), especially among college students. We probably know much less about the actual number of date rapes than we do about the number of stranger assaults, because victims are less likely to report sexual attacks by people they know.

On university or college campuses, date or acquaintance rape sometimes takes the form of gang or party rape. Unlike individual acquaintance rape, gang rape is used as a reinforcing mechanism for membership in a group of men (Warshaw, 1994). In fact, men who rape in groups might never commit individual rape. As they participate in gang rape, they experience a special bonding with each other and use rape to prove their sexual ability to other group members and thereby enhance their status among members.

Nature and Extent of the Problem Statistics on sexual assault are misleading at best because it is often not reported. According to the 1993 Violence Against Women Survey, which interviewed 12 300 women about their experiences of sexual and physical assault, 39 percent reported at least one incident of sexual assault since the age of 16 (CCJS, 1999:278). According to the 1999 GSS, the sexual assault rate is 21 per 1000—up from 16 per 1000 in 1993 (Besserer and Trainor, 2000:5). According to *UCR* data for 2000, sexual assault constituted less than 10 percent of violent crime. Level 1 incidents were the vast majority (98 percent) of reported sexual assault incidents. The rate of sexual assault was 78 per 100 000. The rates for all three levels have been trending down since 1993 (Logan, 2001:7). Some women may not report that they have been assaulted because they believe that nothing will be done about it. It should be noted that not only were sex offenders more likely than violent offenders overall to be incarcerated, they were more likely to be sent to prison for longer periods of time. Whereas in 1997–98, 14 percent of the violent offenders received terms exceeding one year, 37 percent of the sex offenders received terms exceeding one year (CCJS, 1999:273)

Like homicide, sexual assault follows certain patterns in terms of gender, age, racialization, and education. With the proviso that inmates of correctional institutions may not fully represent the population that commits these crimes, we can gain much information from a major inmate survey by consultant David Robinson and his colleagues (1999:275). According to the census of inmates conducted on October 5, 1996, incarcerated sexual offenders were male (99 percent), older than other violent offenders (35 vs. 31 years of age), slightly more likely to be of Indigenous status than other violent offenders (23 vs. 19 percent), and less educated (having Grade 9 or less) than the rest of the population (41 vs. 19 percent).

In most sexual assaults, according to the Violence Against Women Survey of 1993, the victim is young (18 percent for women aged 18 to 24 vs. 1 percent for women aged 45 and over. Single and separated/divorced women were six times more likely to report sexual assault than women married or living common law (CCJS, 1999:278).

Social Responses to Sexual Assault   Many sexual assaults are never reported. The extremely traumatic nature of the crime may prevent some victims from coming forward. They may believe that, if they don't think about it or talk about it, the experience will "go away." Often, the fear generated by the attack is carried over into a fear that the attacker may try to get even or attack again if the crime is reported. This is a particularly significant issue for women who are still in proximity to their attacker. Suppose the attacker is in the same college class or works at the same place as the victim. How can the woman file a report without disrupting her whole life? Many women also fear how they will be treated by the police and, in the event of a criminal trial, by prosecutors and defence attorneys. Many victims also fear publicity for themselves and their families (Sanday, 1996).

Gang Violence

Gang violence includes homicide, sexual assault, robbery, and aggravated assault. But, actually, defining a "gang" is difficult. Police define gangs so broadly—"two or more persons engaged in antisocial behaviour who form an allegiance for a common criminal purpose and who individually or collectively are creating an atmosphere of fear and intimidation within a commu-

nity" (quoted in Abbate, 1998:A10)—that to identify violence as gang violence using this definition is too inclusive. Criminologist Robert M. Gordon (2000:48) has identified six types of gangs in Vancouver:

1. youth movements, like skinheads and punks who perpetrate hate crimes;

2. youth groups, youth who hang out together in public places, like malls;

3. criminal groups, small groups who band together for a short time for illegal financial gain;

4. "wanna-be" groups, loosely structured groups, frequently substitute families, that indulge in impulsive criminal behaviour;

5. street gangs, young adults who plan criminal behaviour; and

6. criminal business organizations, older, well-established groups, sometimes with ethnic membership, like the Lotus, Flying Dragons, Hells Angels, and Bandidos.

Typically, gangs are composed primarily of young males of the same ethnicity. Some gangs are basically peer groups that hang out together, seeking a sense of belonging, like a family, but others are well organized and violent. In recent years, gang activity and gang-related violence have increased significantly not only in large metropolitan areas but also in smaller cities and suburbs. In Canada, gang-related killings tripled over the past five years, rising from 21 in 1995 to 71 in 2000. The deaths were due primarily to fighting over drug trafficking, and over half occurred in Quebec (Fedorowycz, 2001:6).

Some analysts have suggested that gang violence may be exacerbated by socialization of males for male dominance and by patriarchal social structures. Sociologist Martín Sánchez Jankowski (1991) suggests that violence attributed to gangs is often committed by gang members acting as *individuals* rather than as agents of the organization. According to Jankowski, most gang members do not like violence and fear that they may be injured or killed in violent encounters. As a result, gang members engage in collective violence only to accomplish specific objectives, such as asserting authority or punishing violations by their own members who are incompetent or who break the gang's code. Violence against other gangs occurs primarily when a gang feels threatened or needs to maintain or expand its operations in a certain area. In general, according to

Biker violence includes vandalizing clubs and killing people in their homes and cars.

Hate Crimes

Hate crimes are crimes that are motivated by the offender's hatred of certain characteristics of the victim, e.g., national or ethnic origin, language, colour, religion, gender, age, mental or physical disability, or other similar factor. In the GSS victimization survey, people were asked if the crime they reported could be a hate crime. Although no information is available about whether the incidents were performed by gangs, 4 percent of 273 000 incidents were reported as hate crimes, and the most frequently cited characteristic was the victim's ethnicity, cited by 43 percent of the victims; the culture, by 18 percent; and the gender, by 18 percent (Besserer and Trainor, 2000:180).

Social Responses to Gang Violence and Hate Crimes

For many years now, the threat of gang violence—particularly such seemingly random events as drive-by shootings—has contributed to a climate of fear in low-income and poverty-level areas of inner cities. People living in smaller cities and suburban areas have often believed that gang violence was not their problem. As gangs have spread and become increasingly violent, however, it has become apparent that no one is immune.

Intervention by law enforcement officials and the criminal justice system has had only limited success. But in the spring of 2002, "Mom" Boucher, the closest thing to a godfather in the Hells Angels in Quebec, was convicted on several counts of homicide, and police arrested 36 members of the Bandidos, the second largest biker gang.

Property Crime

***Property crime* is the taking of money or property from another without force, the threat of force, or the destruction of property.** Breaking and entering, possession of stolen goods, theft, motor vehicle theft, and fraud are examples of property crimes. According to victimization surveys, the most frequent property crime is *breaking and entering*—the unlawful or forcible entry or attempted entry of a residence or business with the intent to commit a serious crime. Breaking and entering usually involves theft—the burglar illegally enters by, for example, breaking a window or slashing a screen (forcible entry) or through an open window or unlocked door (unlawful entry). Although breaking and entering is normally a crime against property, it is more

Jankowski, collective violence is used to achieve the goals of gang membership (proving masculinity and toughness, providing excitement, and maintaining reputation), mainly when gang members are provoked by others or when they are fearful.

Sociologists Jack Levin and Jack McDevitt (1993) suggest that some gangs look for opportunities to violently attack "outgroup" members because they are seeking a thrill and view their victims as vulnerable. When violent attacks are made because of a person's racialization, religion, skin colour, disability, sexual orientation, national origin, or ancestry, they are considered to be hate crimes (see Chapter 1) and are likely performed by the "youth movements" in Robert Gordon's typology.

serious than most nonviolent crimes because it carries the possibility of violent confrontation and the psychological sense of intrusion that is associated with violent crime. To fully grasp the possibility of violent confrontation, consider the following explanations by two burglars of the pressures—both internal and external—that motivate them to commit breaking and entering:

> Usually what I'll do is a [break and enter], maybe two or three if I have to, and then this will help me get over the rough spot. . . . Once I get it straightened out, I just go with the flow . . . the only time I would go and commit a burglary is if I needed the money at that point in time. That would be strictly to pay the light bill, gas bill, rent. (Dan Whiting, quoted in Wright and Decker, 1994:37)

> You ever had an urge before? Maybe a cigarette urge or a food urge, where you eat that and you got to have more and more? That's how that crack is. You smoke it and it hits you [in the back of the throat] and you got to have more. I'll smoke that sixteenth up and get through, it's like I never had none. I got to have more. Therefore, I gots to go do another burglary and gets some more money. (Richard Jackson, quoted in Wright and Decker, 1994:39)

According to victimization surveys, the young have a higher risk of being subject to property crime than older people. Risk of victimization is also much higher for families with incomes under $15 000 living in rental property or in inner-city areas. In contrast, people who live in well-maintained residences with security systems on well-lit streets or cul-de-sacs are less likely to be victimized (Logan, 2001:1). The *UCR* does not accurately represent the number of burglaries committed because people tend to report them only when very valuable, insured goods are taken.

The most frequently reported crime is called theft $5000 & under—unlawfully taking or attempting to take property (with the exception of motor vehicles) from another person. This kind of theft includes purse snatching and pickpocketing. In 2000, 52.9 percent of the reported property crimes were theft $5000 & under; 23.4 percent were breaking and entering, 12.8 percent were motor vehicle theft, and 6.8 percent were fraud (Logan, 2001:8).

Property crimes such as this one occur far more frequently than violent crime, yet the media give far greater coverage to violence than to acts like auto burglary. Should the media's motto be "If it bleeds, it leads?" Why, or why not?

Statistics on auto theft are more accurate than those for many other crimes because insurance companies require claimants to report the theft to police. Analysts have identified four basic motives for auto theft:

1. Joyriding—the vehicle is stolen for the fun of riding around in it and perhaps showing off to friends.
2. Transportation—the vehicle is stolen for personal use.
3. The vehicle is used as an aid in the commission of another crime.
4. Profit—the vehicle is sold or taken to a "chop shop," where it is dismantled for parts, which are then sold separately (H.D. Barlow, 1996).

Shoplifting accounts for billions of dollars in losses to retail businesses each year. For some stores, the annual loss can be as high as 2 to 5 percent of the total value of inventory (Vito and Holmes, 1994). Early criminologists thought that shoplifters fell into three categories: the *snitch*—someone with no criminal record who systematically pilfers goods for personal use or to sell; the *booster* or *heel*—the professional criminal who steals goods to sell to fences (people who receive and dispose of stolen property) or pawnshops; and the *kleptomaniac*—someone who steals for reasons other than monetary gain (e.g., for sexual arousal) (Holmes, 1983). Most experts think that shoplifting is committed primarily by amateurs, across lines of racialization, class, gender, and age (H.D. Barlow, 1996).

The last type of nonviolent property crime that we will examine is *credit card fraud*—using a credit card or account number to obtain property, services, or money under false pretences. The incidence of this type of fraud has increased sharply with the increase in the availability of cards and the decrease in the use of cheques. Whereas from 1977 to 1996 the decrease in cheque fraud was 46.5 percent, the increase of credit card fraud was 143.7 percent (Janhevich, 1999:286). According to the Canadian Bankers Association, credit card frauds represented a cost of $83 million to the banks in 1996 (Janhevich, 1999:290). Despite the security measures taken by banks and other credit card issuers, credit card fraud is perpetrated in many ways. A lost or stolen wallet or purse can provide a potential offender with all the identification necessary to open up charge accounts in the victim's name and run up large bills before the individual becomes aware of what has happened. Sometimes credit cards are obtained by pickpockets, purse-snatchers, robbers, burglars, and sometimes by prostitutes who go through their customers' pockets. There are companies using the Internet to sell personal information—such as a person's Social Insurance Number and mother's maiden name—that can be used to apply for and activate some credit cards (Hansell, 1996). Credit card information can also be stolen by people who have legitimate access to personal data (e.g., airline or hotel reservationists or department or grocery store personnel) or by computer hackers.

Crime Comparisons between Canada and the United States

Canadians absorb much of their crime information from the U.S. media. It is, therefore, worthwhile to show the differences in crime rates in Canada and the U.S. so that we do not automatically assume that their crime problem is our crime problem. Over the past 20 years, Canada has had a much lower violent crime rate than the U.S. In 2000, the U.S. homicide rate was three times our rate (5.5 vs. 1.8 per 100 000); the aggravated assault rate was two times our rate (324 vs. 143 per 100 000); and the robbery rate was 1.65 times our rate. On the other hand, over the 1990s our property crime rate was higher than their rate, though it was converging toward theirs at the end of the decade. Our break-and-

enter rate in comparison to their rate was 954 vs. 728 per 100 000 and our motor vehicle theft in comparison to their rate was 515 vs. 414 per 100 000.

Sociologist Marc Ouimet (1999:403) analyzed these differences and found that they were not uniform throughout the country. For example, homicide rate differences were nine times greater in the U.S. than Canada for cities with populations of 1 million or more. Ouimet (1999:402) suggested that these differences occur because U.S. cities are much more dangerous than Canadian cities. Unlike U.S. cities, Canadian cities do not contain ghettos, where people are very poor, are disproportionately members of visible minorities, suffer many social problems, and have guns (and, see Chapter 16). Whereas two-thirds of U.S. homicides involve firearms, one-third of Canadian homicides do (Statistics Canada, 2001a). Ouimet refers to Jan van Dijk and his colleagues' international study (1990) which showed that whereas less than 5 percent of Canadian households has a gun, 29 percent of American households has a gun. Ouimet (1999:401) went on to suggest that this lack of guns might also help explain Canada's higher property crime rate. Canadian burglars might be encouraged to commit more break-and-enters than their American counterparts since they have less chance of facing an armed householder.

Another possible explanation for the different patterns could be the reporting of crimes by victims. The study by van Dijk and his colleagues (1990) shows that reporting differences are minimal. Whereas 80.6 percent of Canadian victims reported a robbery, 78.9 percent of U.S. victims did; and whereas 56.5 percent of Canadians reported a break and enter, 59.5 percent of U.S. victims did.

Occupational (White-Collar) Crime

Occupational (white-collar) crime refers to illegal activities committed by people in the course of their employment or normal business activity. When sociologist Edwin H. Sutherland (1949) first introduced the term *white-collar crime,* he was referring to such acts as employee theft, fraud (obtaining money or property under false pretences), embezzlement (theft from an employer), and soliciting bribes or kickbacks. With the advent of personal computers, some white-collar crimes have become easier to commit, and some criminals have developed new types of crime based on computer technology. One type of white-collar crime that has been in the news lately is insider trading of securities: An offender buys or sells stocks on the basis of information that isn't publicly known and that he or she obtained only as a corporate insider. A recent high-profile example of this was the case of Michael Cowpland, former president of Corel Corporation. In 1997 he sold $20.4 million worth of Corel stock a month before Corel reported a big loss. The agreement with the Ontario Securities Commission was that Cowpland's holding company was to pay a $1 million fine after pleading guilty to one count of insider trading. He did not gain a criminal record, and thus, he was not forbidden from engaging in the securities business. For individual investors, without insider knowledge, the losses from the decline in the value of Corel stock might have been in the thousands of dollars. For institutional investors, like pension funds, losses could have been much higher.

Corporate Crime

Some white-collar offenders engage in *corporate crime*—illegal acts committed by corporate employees on behalf of the corporation and with its support. Examples include antitrust violations (seeking an illegal advantage over competitors); deceptive advertising; infringements on patents, copyrights, and trademarks; unlawful labour practices involving the exploitation or surveillance of employees; price fixing; and financial fraud. These crimes arise from deliberate decisions by corporate personnel to profit at the expense of competitors, consumers, employees, and the general public. A striking Canadian example of corporate crime was the case of the gold-mining company Bre-X Minerals Ltd. A company geologist, Michael de Guzman, added gold to survey samples, making the results look like those of a great gold mine. When the adding was discovered in 1997, the company and its stock became worthless, wiping out millions of dollars from various portfolios, including pension funds, and de Guzman apparently committed suicide. A notable example of corporate crime is Nova Scotia's Westray mine, whose failure to follow good safety procedures resulted in the deaths of 26 workers in 1992. Other examples are found in the crimes of multinational companies such as Arthur Andersen—convicted in the spring of 2002 of

obstructing justice—that have consequences for the companies' branches and accounting practices in Canada.

Corporate crime has both direct and indirect economic effects. Direct economic losses from corporate crime are immense in comparison to the money lost in street property crime such as robbery, and break and enter.

The indirect costs of corporate crime include higher taxes, increased cost of goods and services, and higher insurance rates. Although personal injury and loss of life are usually associated with homicides and conventional street crimes, deaths resulting from such corporate crimes as permitting continued work in unsafe mines (e.g., the Westray mine in Nova Scotia), deliberately polluting the air and water, manufacturing defective products, or selling unsafe foods and drugs far exceed the number of homicides each year. Of course, any consideration of the indirect costs of corporate crime must include its effects on the moral climate of society (Friedrichs, 1996; Simon, 1996).

Organized Crime

Organized crime is a business operation that supplies illegal goods and services for profit. These illegal enterprises include drug trafficking, prostitution, gambling, loan sharking, money laundering, and large-scale theft such as truck hijacking (Simon, 1996). No single entity controls the entire range of corrupt and illegal enterprises (Chambliss, 1988). Instead, there are many groups—syndicated crime networks, including biker gangs—that can thrive because there is great demand for illegal goods and services. Criminologist Margaret Beare (1996) suggests that groups vary according to their dependence on organized crime. Whereas some groups are organized to carry out organized crime activities (e.g., Russian and Nigerian groups and Colombian cartels), other groups have other goals and use organized-crime activities to support them (e.g., terrorist groups and motorcycle gangs). Sometimes these groups form alliances with businesspeople, law enforcement officials, and politicians. Some law enforcement and government officials are corrupted through bribery, campaign contributions, and favours that are intended to buy them off. Known linkages between legitimate businesses and organized crime exist in banking, hotels and motels, real estate, garbage collection, vending machines, construction, delivery and long-distance hauling, garment manufacture, insurance, stocks and bonds, vacation resorts, and funeral parlours (National Council on Crime and Delinquency, 1969). Syndicated crime networks operate at all levels of society and even globally (see Box 9.1).

Youth Crime

Youth crime **involves a violation of law or the commission of a status offence by a young person 12 to 17 years of age.** Many behaviours that are identified as youth crime or juvenile delinquency are not criminal acts per se but *status offences*—acts that are illegal because of the age of the offender—such as cutting school, buying and consuming alcoholic beverages, or running away from home.

The statistics for youth crime are high. Whereas people aged 12 to 17 constitute 8 percent of the Canadian population, they account for 22 percent of all persons charged in Canada (Hendrick, 1999:88). The breakdown of their cases in 2000 showed 46 percent property cases, 22 percent violent cases, and 32 percent mischief, escape from custody, and status offences (Logan, 2001:12). Males account for 8 out of 10 cases overall, and 16- and 17-year-olds account for half of the cases (Hendrick, 1999:89). An increase in violent crime by both males and females has occurred over the last decade. Whereas the rate of violent crime by young males has increased by 25 percent, the rate by young females has increased by 61 percent, though they are responsible for only 25 percent of the total youth violent crime (Logan, 2001:12). However, in a close examination of youth crime statistics from 1977 to 1996, sociologist Peter J. Carrington (1999) questions whether there is an actual increase or whether police are making more charges

---

SOCIAL PROBLEMS IN GLOBAL PERSPECTIVE

BOX 9.1 Organized Crime: The Global Empire

Fifty people were arrested Monday in Europe and Canada in an Italian-led operation against money laundering by the Russian Mafia, Italian authorities said. Police also seized real estate, luxury cars and bank accounts for hundreds of millions of dollars, said Francesco Gratteri, the head of the police unit which led the operation.

Authorities said 20 people were arrested in Italy, 13 in France and others in Austria, Switzerland, Monte Carlo and Canada. More than half of them were Russian nationals. They have been charged with criminal association with the intent to launder money . . .

The money was allegedly coming from the Mafia's illicit activities, such as drug and arms trafficking and the smuggling of human beings, said Gratteri.

Pierluigi Vigna, Italy's anti-Mafia prosecutor, said the operation shows how deeply the Russian Mafia had infiltrated Italian and European economies. (Canadian Press, 2002)

This is one of the many reports of international organized crime, some of which involves Canada. *Money laundering* is the process of converting or cleansing money, knowing that it comes from serious crime, for the purpose of disguising its origin. Estimates of the amount of money that is laundered in Canada vary. In 1997, the RCMP estimated $5 to $10 billion, the Canadian Chiefs of Police estimated $7 to $14 billion, and Interpol estimated $17 billion (quoted in Sambugaro, 2000:10). Canada is considered a good location for money laundering because of light justice sanctions, a strong economy, closeness to the United States, many ethnic communities, and international airports. While money laundering is big business in Canada, other places, such as the Cayman Islands, the Bahamas, Liechtenstein, Panama, and Russia, are considered major havens.

Globally, seven or eight crime syndicates often operate in collusion. In addition to the Russian syndicate and the Sicilian Mafia, other organized-crime groups allegedly include the Colombian cocaine cartels, which have operations in Spain, and ethnic Chinese from East and Southeast Asia, who have overseas bases in Rotterdam and London. At a lower level, the transport and marketing of drugs and other contraband are managed by syndicates of Nigerians, Moroccans, Pakistanis, Lebanese, Albanians, and others (Viviano, 1995).

What can Canada do about global organized crime? Can any one nation or organization—such as the United Nations—reduce international money laundering and drug trafficking? What do you think?

(a drop by police in their use of discretion to charge or not charge).

Juveniles who are apprehended are processed by the youth court system, which is based on the assumption that young people can do better if they are placed in the right setting and receive guidance. Thus, of the two-thirds of cases that end in conviction, most youth dispositions are served in the community (Hendrick, 1999:90). Custody sentences are ordered in one-third of the cases with convictions (Hendrick, 1999:91). Unfortunately, most juvenile correction facilities or "training schools" hold large numbers of young people in overcrowded conditions and provide only limited counselling and educational opportunities for rehabilitation (Donziger, 1996).

WHO COMMITS CRIMES?

The most significant factor in any study of crime arrest rates is gender. Men are more likely than women to commit major property crimes (for example, robbery and theft over $5000), whereas women are more likely than men to be involved in minor property crimes (for example, theft $5000 & under and fraud) and in prostitution offences (Logan, 2001). Men have higher arrest rates than women for violent crimes such as homicide, aggravated assault, robbery, and break and enter; women are most often arrested for such nonviolent crimes as shoplifting, passing bad cheques, credit card fraud, and employee pilferage. Although a considerable number of arrests and convictions for larceny and theft occur among women, men still account for the vast majority of these arrests and convictions. Criminologists estimate that 10 percent of all homicides in this country are committed by women. Most of these are linked to domestic violence and self-defence (Harlow, 1991; Belknap, 1996).

Although there are significant gender differences in the types of crimes committed, there are also commonalities. First, for both sexes, the most common offences are impaired driving, common assault, and theft. These three categories account for about 38 percent of all arrests. Second, fraud, possession of stolen property and mischief are middle-range offences for both men and women. Third, the rate of arrests for murder, arson, and embezzlement are very low for both men and women (see for example Thomas, 2002).

Age is also an important factor in any study of those accused of a crime. The proportion of the population accused of serious crimes, such as homicide, sexual assault, and robbery, tends to peak during the teenage years or early adulthood and then decline with age. Whereas in 2000, 30.6 percent and 29.4 percent of those accused with committing offences were 18 to 24, and 25 to 34, years of age respectively, 10.2 percent and 4.5 percent were 45 to 54, and 55 or more, years of age respectively (Thomas, 2002:4). Several reasons have been advanced for age–crime patterns, including:

- differential access to legitimate or illegitimate opportunity structures at various ages; differences in social factors such as peer influences;

- physiological factors such as the effects of aging on strength, speed, and aggression; and

- building up deviant networks that make it possible for people such as fences to commit less-visible crimes (Steffensmeier and Allan, 1995).

Although individuals from all social classes commit crimes, some kinds of crimes are more associated with lower or upper socioeconomic status. People from lower socioeconomic backgrounds are more likely to be arrested for violent and property crimes; people from the upper classes generally commit white-collar or corporate crimes. Moreover, the majority of crimes committed by doctors, lawyers, accountants, and other professionals are ignored because of the prestige associated with these professions. Friends and neighbours assume that these people are law-abiding citizens, and law enforcement officials are not likely to scrutinize their behaviour (Coleman, 1995).

Having considered who commits crimes, let's look at who the victims are. Most people fear the violent stranger, but the vast majority of murders is committed by family members, friends, neighbours, or coworkers. In slightly less than half the cases, the murderers are members of the victim's family or acquaintances.

According to the GSS, little difference occurs between men and women regarding victimization for personal crimes (Besserer and Trainor, 2000:174). The young report more victimization than the older, and those earning less than $15 000 are more victimized than the more wealthy (Besserer and Trainor, 2000:1).

BIOLOGICAL AND PSYCHOLOGICAL EXPLANATIONS OF CRIME

As with other social problems, crime and delinquency have been explained in biological, psychological, and sociological terms. Most biological and psychological explanations assume that criminal behaviour is an inherent or acquired individual trait with genetic, biological, or psychological roots. Sociological perspectives, in contrast, focus on external factors.

Biological Explanations

One of the earliest biological explanations of criminality came from the *positivist school,* which created physical typologies that were used to classify and study criminals (H.D. Barlow, 1996). The biological approach of Cesare Lombroso, a 19th-century Italian physicist, is probably the best known. Lombroso suggested that some people were born criminals or *atavists*—biological throwbacks to an earlier stage of evolution—and could be recognized by their low foreheads and smaller than normal human cranial capacities. A later theory, also based on physical traits, which received some attention for a time was proposed by physician William Sheldon (1949). According to Sheldon's *somatotype theory, mesomorphs*—people who are muscular, gregarious, aggressive, and assertive—are more prone to delinquency and criminal behaviour than are *endomorphs*—people who are fat, soft, round, and extroverted—or *ectomorphs*—people who are thin, wiry, sensitive, and introverted.

Contemporary biological approaches based on genetics have attempted to link higher rates of aggression in men to levels of testosterone or chromosomal abnormality (an extra Y chromosome). But this research has produced no consistent findings, and social scientists argue that the differences in aggression may be due to gender-role socialization of men and women rather than to biological factors (Katz and Chambliss, 1995).

Other contemporary biological approaches suggest that violence is a natural and inevitable part of human behaviour that can be controlled only by social organization. Some scientists, however, say that violence is neither natural nor inevitable but the result of traumatic brain injury or some combination of brain injury and other factors. Although most people with brain injuries are not violent, injuries to certain parts of the brain or injuries in combination with an abusive childhood or psychotic symptoms (e.g., paranoia) can affect an individual's ability to conform to societal norms.

The cortex of the brain—particularly the frontal lobes—is most closely associated with violent behaviour. It is the cortex that modifies impulses, allowing us to use good judgment, make decisions, and organize behaviour; it also facilitates learning and adherence to rules of conduct (Gladwell, 1997). Using various neurological and psychiatric examinations, medical experts try to determine whether violent offenders have frontal-lobe impairment, were abused as children, or have any psychological disorders. These factors, especially in combination, make people prone to violent behaviour.

Psychological Explanations

Like biological explanations of delinquency and crime, psychological explanations focus on individual characteristics. Some researchers have used personality inventories in hopes of identifying abnormal personality traits in individuals who have committed crimes or engaged in delinquent behaviour. Other researchers have investigated the effects of social learning and positive reinforcement (e.g., rewards such as money or special attention) and negative reinforcement (e.g., the withdrawal of reward or lack of attention) on delinquent and criminal behaviour.

The most enduring psychological explanations of delinquency and crime seem to be the ones that bridge the biological explanations by linking intelligence and crime. Since the introduction of IQ (intelligence quotient) tests in the early 1900s, some analysts have suggested that people with lower intelligence scores are more likely to commit crimes than are people with higher intelligence scores. However, both the validity of IQ tests and the assertion that low intelligence causes delinquency or crime have come under great scrutiny and much criticism (see Hirschi and Hindelang, 1977).

Of course, some social analysts do acknowledge the possibility of a relationship between low intelligence and delinquency or crime. These analysts note that low intelligence may indirectly promote delinquency because it affects school performance. As mentioned above, differences are present between those who commit crimes and those who go to jail; to illustrate, the less intelligent may be more likely to become inmates. People with Grade 9 or less are greatly overrepresented in prison: Whereas 19 percent of Canada's population has Grade 9 or less, 36 percent of inmates have Grade 9 or less, according to the one-day survey of inmates in Canada's adult correctional facilities conducted by Robinson and his colleagues (1999:57).

One psychological explanation of violent crime focuses on *aggression*—behaviour intended to hurt someone, either physically or verbally—that results from frustration (Weiten and Lloyd, 1994). According to the *frustration–aggression hypothesis,* people who are frustrated in their efforts to achieve a highly desired goal become aggressive toward others (Dollard et al., 1939). The object of the aggression becomes a *scapegoat*—a **substitute for the actual source of frustration—who can be blamed, especially if that person or group is incapable of resisting the hostility or aggression.**

Explaining violence in biological and/or psychological terms suggests responses based on some type of psychiatric or other medical intervention. After all, if violent behaviour is associated with specific neurological problems, it can be diagnosed like any other neurological illness and treated with drugs, including, possibly, anticonvulsants, antidepressants, and antihypertensive medications that act on the cortex to moderate violent behaviour.

SOCIOLOGICAL EXPLANATIONS OF CRIME

Unlike biological and psychological explanations that focus on individual behaviour, sociological explanations focus on those aspects of society that may contribute to delinquent or criminal behaviour.

The Functionalist Perspective

Although there are numerous functionalist perspectives on crime and delinquency, we will focus on two: strain theory and control theory, as illustrated in social bond theory.

Functionalist explanations for why people commit crimes can be traced to Emile Durkheim, who believed that the macrolevel structure of a society produces social pressures that result in high rates of deviance and crime.

Durkheim introduced the concept of *anomie* to describe a social condition that engenders feelings of futility in people because of weak, absent, or conflicting social norms. According to Durkheim (1895/1964/, deviance and crime are most likely to occur when anomie is present in a society. On the basis of Durkheim's theory, sociologist Robert Merton (1938, 1968) developed strain theory to explain why some people conform to group norms while others do not. **Strain theory states that people feel strain when they are exposed to cultural goals that they cannot reach because they do not have access to a culturally approved means of achieving those goals.** When some people are denied legitimate access to cultural goals such as success, money, or other material possessions, they seek to acquire these things through deviant—and sometimes criminal—means. This lack of legitimate access is typical of many of Canada's inmates. According to Robinson and his colleagues, the one-day snapshot of inmates shows that inmates are much more likely to be unemployed than the general population (52 percent vs. 7 percent).

Merton identified five ways in which people respond to cultural goals: conformity, innovation, ritualism, retreatism, and rebellion (see Table 9.1).

- *Conformity* occurs when people accept the culturally approved goals and pursue them through the approved means. People who choose conformity work hard and save their money to achieve success. Someone who is blocked from achieving a high level of education or a lucrative career typically conforms by taking a lower-paying job and attending school part-time, joining the military, or trying alternative (but legal) avenues, such as playing the lottery.

- *Innovation* occurs when people accept society's goals but use illegitimate means to achieve them. Innovations for acquiring material possessions include shoplifting, theft, burglary, cheating on income taxes, embezzling money, and other kinds of occupational crime.

- *Ritualism* occurs when people give up on societal goals but still adhere to socially approved means for achieving them. People who cannot obtain expensive material possessions or wealth seek to maintain the respect of others by being "hard workers" or "good citizens" to an extreme degree.

- *Retreatism* occurs when people abandon both the approved goals and the approved means of

TABLE 9.1   Merton's Strain Theory

Mode of Adaptation	Method of Adaptation	Agrees with Cultural Goal	Follows Institutional Means
Conformity	Accepts culturally approved goals; pursues them through culturally approved means	Yes	Yes
Innovation	Accepts culturally approved goals; adopts disapproved means of achieving them	Yes	No
Ritualism	Abandons society's goals but continues to conform to approved means	No	Yes
Retreatism	Abandons both approved goals and the approved means to achieve them	No	No
Rebellion	Challenges both the approved goals and the approved means to achieve them	No—seeks to replace	No—seeks to replace

Source: Adapted from Social Theory and Social Structure, *Robert King Merton, 1968, New York: Free Press.*

achieving them. Retreatists include hard-core drug addicts and some middle- or upper-income people who reject conventional trappings of success and the means to acquire them, choosing to "drop out" instead.

■ *Rebellion* occurs when people reject both the approved goals and the approved means for achieving them and advocate an alternative set of goals and means. Rebels may use violence (such as vandalism or rioting) or nonviolent tactics (such as civil disobedience) to change society and its cultural beliefs. Or they may withdraw from mainstream society, like the Amish, to live their own life.

Another functionalist perspective—control theory—seeks to answer the question, Why do people *not* engage in deviant behaviour? According to control theory, people are constantly pulled and pushed toward deviant behaviour. Environmental factors (pulls), such as adverse living conditions, poverty, and lack of educational opportunity, draw people toward criminal behaviour while, at the same time, internal pressures (pushes) such as feelings of hostility or aggressiveness make people not want to act according to dominant values and norms (Reckless, 1967). If this is true, why doesn't everyone who is poor or has a limited education commit crimes? According to control theorists, people who do not turn to crime or delinquent behaviour have *outer containments*—supportive family and

friends, reasonable social expectations, and supervision by others—or *inner containments*—self-control, a sense of responsibility, and resistance to diversions. This lack of outer and inner containments is found among Canada's inmates. According to Robinson and his colleagues, inmates are much more likely to be unmarried than the general adult population (31 percent vs. 63 percent) (1999:57) and have high levels of crime-causing needs, like personal and emotional problems, substance abuse, and problems functioning in the community (1999:66).

The best-known control theory is **social bond theory—the proposition that criminal behaviour is most likely to occur when a person's ties to society are weakened or broken**. According to criminologist Travis Hirschi (1969), who proposed this theory, social bonding consists of (1) *attachment* to other people, (2) *commitment* to conformity, (3) *involvement* in conventional activities, and (4) *belief* in the legitimacy of conventional values and norms. When a person's social bonds are weak and when peers promote antisocial values and violent behaviour, the probability of delinquency and crime increases (Massey and Krohn, 1986).

When analyzing violent crime, some functionalists believe that a sense of anomie is the root cause. Others believe that violence increases when social institutions such as the family, schools, and religious organizations weaken and the primary mechanisms of social control in people's everyday lives become external—law enforcement and the criminal justice system. Others accept the ***subculture of violence hypo-thesis, that violence is part of the normative expectations governing everyday behaviour among young males in the lower classes*** (Wolfgang and Ferracuti, 1967). These violent subcultures are most likely to develop when young people, particularly males, have few legitimate opportunities available in their segment of society and when subcultural values accept and encourage violent behaviour.

Another functionalist perspective on violence, discussed in Chapter 1, is the *lifestyle–routine activity approach,* which holds that the patterns and timing of people's daily movements and activities as they go about obtaining the necessities of life—such as food, shelter, companionship, and entertainment—are the keys to understanding violent personal crimes and other types of crime in our society (Cohen and Felson, 1979). In other words, changes in social institutions, such as more families in which both parents (or the sole parent) work outside the home or extension of shopping hours into the night, put some people at greater risk than others of being victims of violent crime (Parker, 1995).

Functionalist explanations contribute to our understanding of crime by emphasizing that individuals who engage in such behaviour are not biologically or psychologically impaired but are responding to social and economic conditions in society. However, functionalists are not without their critics. Strain theory may point out that people from low-income and poverty-level backgrounds are prevented from achieving success goals through legitimate channels, but it is still criticized for focusing almost exclusively on crimes committed by the lower classes and ignoring crimes committed by people in the middle and upper classes. Critics of social bond theory say that it is limited in its ability to explain more serious forms of delinquency and crime (Krohn, 1995).

The Conflict Perspective

Conflict theorists explain criminal behaviour in terms of power differentials and/or economic inequality in society. One approach focuses on how authority and power relations can contribute to some people—but not others—becoming criminals. According to sociologist Austin Turk (1966, 1971), crime is not a *behaviour* but a *status* that is acquired when people with the authority to create and enforce legal rules apply those rules to others.

A second conflict approach focuses on the relationship between economic inequality and crime. Having roots in the work of Karl Marx, the *radical critical-conflict approach* argues that social institutions (such as law, politics, and education) create a super-structure that legitimizes the class structure and maintains capitalists' superior position. In fact, say these theorists, the crimes people commit are based on their class position. Thus, crimes committed by low-income people typically involve taking things by force or physical stealth, while white-collar crime usually involves nonphysical means such as paper transactions or computer fraud. Some critical theorists believe that affluent people commit crimes because they are greedy and continually want more than they have, whereas poor people commit street crimes such as robbery and theft to survive (Bonger, 1916/1969).

In sum, the conflict approach is useful for pointing out how inequalities of power, class, and racialization can contribute to criminal or delinquent behaviour. Nevertheless, critics say that conflict theorists have not shown that powerful political and economic elites manipulate law making and enforcement for their own benefit. Rather, say these critics, people of all classes share a consensus that acts such as homicide, sexual assault, and armed robbery are bad (Klockars, 1979).

The Interactionist Perspective

Interactionists emphasize that criminal behaviour is learned through everyday interaction with others. We will examine two major interactionist theories: differential association theory and labelling theory. ***Differential association theory* states that individuals have a greater tendency to deviate from societal norms when they frequently associate with people who tend toward deviance rather than conformity.** According to sociologist Edwin Sutherland (1939), who formulated this theory, people learn not only the techniques of deviant behaviour from people with whom they associate but also the motives, drives, rationalizations, and attitudes. Former gang member Nathan McCall (1994:93–94) describes such a learning process in his own life:

> Sometimes I picked up hustling ideas at the 7-Eleven, which was like a criminal union hall: Crapshooters, shoplifters, stickup men, burglars, everybody stopped

off at the store from time to time. While hanging up there one day, I ran into Holt. . . . He had a pocketful of cash, even though he had quit school and was unemployed. I asked him, "Yo, man, what you been into?" "Me and my partner kick in cribs and make a killin'. You oughta come go with us sometimes. . . ." I hooked school one day, went with them, and pulled my first B&E [breaking and entering]. . . . After I learned the ropes, Shell Shock [another gang member] and I branched out, doing B&Es on our own. We learned to get in and out of houses in no time flat.

As McCall's description indicates, criminal activity often occurs within the context of frequent, intense, and long-lasting interactions with people who violate the law. When more factors favour violating the law than not, the person is likely to become a criminal. Although differential association theory contributes to our knowledge of how deviant behaviour reflects the individual's learned techniques, values, attitudes, motives, and rationalizations, critics note that many individuals who are regularly exposed to people who break the law still conform most of the time. Many critics think that the theory does not adequately take into account possible connections between social inequality and criminal behaviour.

Labelling theory, which was mentioned briefly in Chapter 1, takes quite a different approach from differential association theory. According to *labelling theory*, delinquents and criminals are people who have been successfully labelled as such by others. No behaviour is inherently delinquent or criminal; it is defined as such by a social audience (Erikson, 1962). According to sociologist Howard Becker (1963), labelling is often done by *moral entrepreneurs*—people who use their own views of right and wrong to establish rules and label others "deviant." Furthermore, the process of labelling is directly related to the power and status of the people who do the labelling and those who are being labelled. In support of this theory, one study of juvenile offenders has found that youths from lower-income families were more likely to be arrested and indicted than were middle-class juveniles who did the same things (Sampson, 1986). Sociologists have also noted that the criminal justice system generally considers such factors as the offender's family life, educational achievement (or lack thereof), and social class in determining how to

deal with juvenile offenders. According to one study, the individuals who are most likely to be apprehended, labelled delinquent, and prosecuted are people of colour who are young, male, unemployed, and undereducated and who live in urban high-crime areas (Vito and Holmes, 1994).

Sociologist Edwin Lemert (1951) expanded labelling theory by distinguishing between primary and secondary deviance. *Primary deviance* is the initial act of rule breaking in which the individual does not internalize the delinquent or criminal self-concept. *Secondary deviance* occurs when a person who has been labelled a deviant accepts that new identity and continues the deviant behaviour. The concept of secondary deviance is important to labelling theory because it suggests that when people accept a negative label or stigma that has been applied to them, the label may actually contribute to the behaviour it was meant to control. In other words, secondary deviance occurs if a person is labelled a juvenile delinquent, accepts that label, and then continues to engage in delinquent behaviour. Labelling theory is useful for making us aware of how social control and personal identity are intertwined. Critics, however, do not think that labelling theory explains what causes the original acts that constitute primary deviance, nor do they think that it adequately explains why some people accept deviant labels and others do not (Cavender, 1995).

In 1843, Daniel M'Naughton was acquitted of attempting to kill the British prime minister and shooting an official by reason of insanity. This was the beginning of the plea of insanity, but it did not provide any clear definition or measure of irrational behaviour. Since that time, a wide variety of defences involving a loss of self-control by the accused due to medical problems have been advocated by defence attorneys. The process has been called the *medicalization of crime*, the converting of criminal behaviour to a medical condition or disease. It is parallel to the medicalization of deviance—the converting of deviance, such as alcoholism, to a medical condition. Given the current and likely future development of our understanding about the influence of biological factors on serious violent crime, questions about the definition of personal responsibility vs. medical conditions for irrational behaviour will be central to many future criminal proceedings.

Feminist Perspectives

Feminist scholarship focuses on why women commit crimes or engage in delinquent behaviour. We have already noted the differences in victimization rates for men and women. Criminologist Elizabeth Cormack (1999) reminds us that studies of offenders in prison often find that the women have experienced physical and/or sexual abuse. Scholars who use a *liberal feminist* framework believe that women's delinquency or crime is a rational response to gender discrimination in society. They attribute crimes such as prostitution and shoplifting to women's lack of educational and job opportunities and to stereotypical expectations about roles women should have in society (Daly and Chesney-Lind, 1988). Scholars who espouse *radical feminism* believe that patriarchy contributes to crimes such as prostitution, because, according to society's sexual double standard, it is acceptable for a man to pay for sex but unacceptable for a woman to accept money for such services. A third school of feminist thought, *socialist feminism,* believes that women are exploited by capitalism and patriarchy. Because most females have relatively low-wage jobs and few economic resources, crimes such as prostitution and shoplifting become a means of earning money and acquiring consumer products. Feminist scholars of colour, and other feminist scholars who wish to broaden the perspective of criminology beyond the patriarchy suggest that consideration be given to "the complex and diverse ways in which patriarchal (along with class and racialization) privilege and power invade people's subjectivities and experiences" (Cormack,1999:166).

Another approach that focuses on differences in males' and females' crime behaviour, specifically on the higher rates of male vs. female youth crime, is the Power-Control Theory of sociologist John Hagan and his colleagues (1987). This theory emphasizes the structure of the family and socialization, rating families from "unbalanced," or highly patriarchal, to "balanced," or egalitarian, in the exercise of power by husbands and wives and according to their traditional vs. egalitarian socialization of their sons and daughters. In a study in Toronto, Hagan and his colleagues found that gender differences in crime were greater in unbalanced than balanced families. Girls from families where girls were highly controlled and boys were freer committed fewer crimes relative to boys than girls from families with more egalitarian socialization (Hagan et al., 1987).

THE CRIMINAL JUSTICE SYSTEM

The term *criminal justice system* is misleading because it implies that law enforcement agencies and courts constitute one large, integrated system when actually they are a collection of somewhat interrelated, semi-autonomous bureaucracies (Sheley, 1995). The **criminal justice system is the network of organizations, including the police, courts, criminal prosecutions, and corrections, involved in law enforcement and the administration of justice** (CCJS, 1999:4). Originally, the criminal justice system was created to help solve the problem of social disorder and crime. Today, however, some social analysts wonder whether the criminal justice system is part of the problem. Most cite two reasons for concern: (1) the criminal justice system fails in its mission to prevent, control, or rehabilitate offenders; and (2) unequal justice occurs because officials discriminate against people on the basis of racialization, class, gender, age, sexual orientation, or other devalued characteristics. We'll examine both issues in greater depth. First, though, let's look at each component of the justice system, starting with the police.

The Police

The police are the most visible link in the criminal justice system because they determine how to apply the law to control crime and maintain order. The police reported 2.8 million Criminal Code incidents in 1996 and cleared, or solved, 22 percent of them with a charge (CCJS, 1999:xiii). Four factors seem to influence the occurrence of an arrest:

1. the nature of the alleged offence or problem;
2. the quality of available evidence;
3. the age, racialization, and gender of the alleged offender; and
4. the level of deference shown to police officers. (Mastrofski, 1995)

Given these factors, law enforcement officials have fairly wide *discretion*—use of personal judgment regarding whether and how to proceed in a given situation—in deciding who will be stopped and searched and which homes and businesses will be entered and for what purposes (Donziger, 1996). Sociologist Jerome Skolnick

(1975) argues that, because police officers must often make these decisions in a dangerous environment, they develop a sense of suspicion, social isolation, and solidarity.

Most officers feel that they must demand respect on the streets, but they also know that they must answer to their superiors, who expect them to handle situations "by the book."

The problem of discretion is most acute in the decision to use deadly force. Generally, deadly force is allowed only when a suspect is engaged in a felony, is fleeing the scene of a felony, or is resisting arrest and has endangered someone's life (H.D. Barlow, 1996). But police officers' lives are often on the line in confrontations with suspects, and sometimes the officers have less firepower than the individuals they are attempting to apprehend.

In Canada in June 2001, there were 57 000 police officers—184 officers per 100 000 population. This number is lower than the comparable U.S. figure of 247 per 100 000 in 1998. Among the largest Canadian metropolitan areas, Thunder Bay had 195 officers per 100 000, and Regina and Toronto had 181 per 100 000. In 1998, there were 8300 women officers, representing 15 percent of all officers. In the past, women were largely excluded from law enforcement because of stereotypical beliefs that they were not physically and psychologically strong enough for the work. The total cost of policing in 2000 was $6.8 billion (Statistics Canada, 2002n).

How can police departments become more effective in reducing crime as a social problem? According to some analysts, police departments with entrenched problems must first reform their own agencies and win the respect of the communities they serve. One way to do this is to be sure that police departments reflect the racialized and ethnic composition of these communities. It is difficult for an all-White police force to build trust in a primarily Indigenous area. In Canada in 1996, 3.0 percent of police officers were Indigenous, slightly higher than the 2.3 percent Indigenous people constitute of the Canadian population 15 years and older (Swol, 1999:23). Visible minorities do not yet appear as police officers in numbers similar to their participation in the work force. In 1996, whereas members of visible minorities composed 10 percent of the work force, they composed only 3 percent of police officers (Swol, 1999:21). When women, Indigenous peoples, and members of other visible minorities gain greater representation in police departments, a wide range of complaints against police regarding profiling, domestic violence, and violence against minorities should be reduced.

Some police departments have begun *community policing* as a way of reducing crime. Community policing involves integrating officers into the communities they serve—getting them out of their patrol cars and into a proactive role, recognizing problems and working with neighbourhood citizens to find solutions. In cities where community policing has been implemented, crime rates appear to have dropped; however, it should be noted that there has also been a general trend toward fewer crimes, especially violent crimes, in some cities where community policing is not employed (Sacco and Kennedy, 1998:356ff.).

The Courts

Criminal courts are responsible for determining the guilt or innocence of people who have been accused of committing a crime. In theory, justice is determined in an adversarial process: A prosecutor (an attorney who represents the state) argues that the accused is guilty and a defence attorney argues that the accused is innocent. In reality, judges have a great deal of discretion. Working with prosecutors, they decide who will be released, who will be held for further hearings, and—in many instances—what sentences will be imposed on people who are convicted.

Because courts have the capacity to try only a small fraction of criminal cases, an attrition process occurs. This process begins with the police, who clear about a third of all offences reported to them. The police clear a fifth of all reports with a charge. About 15 percent of the total reports result in conviction, and 4 percent of the reports result in a sentence to custody (CCJS, 1999:xiii). This attrition process has been called a "crime funnel" (Silverman et al., 1996 cited in Sacco and Kennedy, 1998:205). In 2000–01, 375 486 cases were heard in seven Canadian provinces and the Yukon, involving 816 449 charges; 61 percent of the cases resulted in a conviction (Thomas, 2002:1). Many cases are resolved by *plea bargaining*—**a process whereby the crown attorney negotiates with a defence attorney a reduced sentence in exchange for a guilty plea.** In other words, defendants (especially those who are poor and cannot afford to pay an attorney) plead guilty to a lesser crime in return for not being tried for the more serious crime for which they were arrested. As cases are sifted and sorted through the legal machinery, steady attrition occurs. At each stage, various officials determine what alternatives will be available for the cases that remain in the system (Hills, 1971).

Sometimes plea bargaining occurs to get a conviction in a high-profile case when no other avenue seems available. A notorious example was the case of the sentencing of Karla Homolka to 12 years in prison in return for her testimony and evidence (tapes missed in the search by police, recording the homicides of two girls) to convict Paul Bernardo of the girls' homicide.

Punishment and the Prisons

Punishment is any action designed to deprive a person of things of value (including liberty) because of an offence the person is thought to have committed (H.D. Barlow, 1996). Punishment is seen as serving four functions:

1. *Retribution* imposes a penalty on the offender. Retribution is based on the premise that the punishment should fit the crime: The greater the degree of social harm, the more the offender should be punished. An individual who murders, for example, should be punished more severely than one who steals an automobile.

2. *Social protection* results from restricting offenders so that they cannot continue to commit crimes.

3. *Rehabilitation* seeks to return offenders to the community as law-abiding citizens. However, the few rehabilitation programs that exist in prisons are seriously understaffed and underfunded. Often, the job skills (such as agricultural work) that are taught in prison do not transfer to the outside world, and offenders are not given help in finding work that fits the skills they might have once they are released.

4. *Deterrence* seeks to reduce criminal activity by instilling a fear of punishment. Criminologists debate, though, whether imprisonment has a deterrent effect, given that 30 to 50 percent of those who are released from prison commit further crimes.

In 1999–2000, about 31 600 people were in custody in Canada (Lommo, 2001:3). An incarceration rate of 115 per 100 000 population is not the highest rate of incarceration in relation to population in a high-income country. That distinction belongs to the U.S., which has a rate of over 600 in prison per 100 000 population. However, Canada's rate is higher than that of most European countries: England and Wales at 100, France at 95, and Germany at 90 per 100 000 population (CCJS, 1999:ix).

Jail and prison conditions often do little to rehabilitate offenders. In fact, three out of four inmates are housed in such overcrowded facilities that two people often live in a space only slightly larger than a walk-in closet. Some inmates suffer physical abuse by prison officials or other inmates.

Because of plea bargains, credit for "good time" served, and overcrowded prison conditions, most convicted criminals do not serve their full sentences. They are released on conditional sentences, including probation (close supervision of their everyday lives in lieu of serving time), parole (early release from prison), or statutory release, where inmates serve the last third of their custodial sentence in the community. About 121 000 people (79 percent of the total) are on supervision (Lommo, 2001:3). If offenders violate the conditions of their probation or parole, they may be returned to prison to serve their full sentence. Conditional sentencing can occur if several conditions are met. The judge, after imposing a term of less than two years, may order the offender to serve the prison sentence in the community, under supervision. The judge may impose further conditions, like attendance at a treatment program. If these conditions are not followed, the offender will return to court and may be sent to custody.

Recently the numbers of people sentenced to custody has declined. This is due to such factors as increased use of conditional sentences, but also to the decrease in the crime rate. Despite the decline, certain problems remain. For example, there is an overrepresentation of Indigenous people in prison. Whereas Indigenous people are 2 percent of the adult population, they are 17 percent of those admitted to custody (Lommo, 2001:8). Incarcerating Indigenous people for crimes like drunkenness, vagrancy, and so on, crimes for which Whites are less likely to be incarcerated, has been a longstanding feature of our justice system. In

Box 9.2 this fact and the overrepresentation of Black people is noted in the discussion of whether to use racialization-based statistics.

The decline in the incarceration rate also helps keep the cost of correctional services low. In 1999–2000, the cost of housing per prisoner averaged $183.66 per day in federal custody and $128.10 per day in provincial custody, or almost $2.4 billion for all correctional services per year (Lommo, 2001:14).

Restorative Justice

In Canada, Europe, Australia, and New Zealand, the concept of restorative justice comprises diverse practices, including conferencing, sentencing circles, and victim-offender mediation. **Restorative justice focuses on repairing the harm caused by crime by holding moderated meetings of crime victims, offenders, and others affected by crime, which can be used at different sites in the justice system**, for example, as a diversion from court, a pre-sentencing option, and after the release from prison.

Current applications of the idea began to emerge in the 1970s in North America, beginning with a victim–offender reconciliation program in Ontario, Canada, in 1974. A recent prominent example was the Indigenous sentencing circle created to deal with the bullying situation that resulted in the suicide death of Dawn-Marie Wesley in British Columbia (see also Chapter 12 for more on bullying). According to a report in *The National Post* by Ian Bailey (2002), the mother of Dawn-Marie hugged the girl convicted of criminally harassing her daughter and accepted her apology. The girl also received a sentence of 18 months' probation, a six-month cell-phone ban (the instrument of the harassing), and an assignment of writing a 750-word essay on bullying and doing 20 hours of community work that could include speaking about bullying.

Although sentencing circles are not common— they are primarily an Indigenous peoples' cultural practice; the concept of restorative justice is integral to many Indigenous cultures. One consisted of the participants speaking of the victim, the offender, and the nature of the tragedy over a period of five hours. The mother of the victim argued against a jail term for the offender and said she was satisfied with the sentence because it allowed her to speak to the offender in a way

that might not have been possible in a "White man's" court. She also felt that her daughter participated in the circle and was "at peace with the way it was handled." Many people are optimistic about the value of sentencing circles and satisfied with the results. However, the people who participate in circles are biased, because only those who accept responsibility for their crime are allowed to participate. Restorative justice may not work for all kinds of crime and enforcement may be a problem, but it does hold promise for youth offenders and other situations where restoration is possible.

The Death Penalty

Although in Canada capital punishment was abolished in 1976, and a 2001 Ipsos-Reid poll indicated that support for it has fallen to a low of 52 percent (Freeze, 2001:A1), the death penalty can still affect Canadians. In 2001, United States authorities wanted to extradite two Canadians to stand trial for murdering three people in the state of Washington. The Supreme Court of Canada, condemning the use of the death penalty, ruled that the two could be extradited only if the U.S. authorities would guarantee that they would not face the death penalty. The U.S. authorities did provide such assurances and the two were extradited. Americans themselves are showing less support for the death penalty, and a couple of states have halted executions because of the racist bias in death rows.

Is the solution to our "crime problem" to build more prisons and execute more people? Only about 20 percent of all crimes result in a charge, only half of these lead to a conviction, and fewer than 4 percent of convictions result in a jail term. The "lock 'em up and throw away the key" approach has little chance of succeeding. As for individuals who commit occupational and corporate crime, the percentage that enters the criminal justice system is so minimal that prison is relatively useless as a deterrent to others. Furthermore, the high rate of recidivism strongly suggests that the rehabilitative efforts of our existing correctional facilities are sadly lacking. One thing is clear: The existing criminal justice system cannot solve the crime problem.

Is equal justice under the law possible? As long as social problems exist in our society, equal justice under the law may not be possible for all people; however,

SOCIAL PROBLEMS AND SOCIAL POLICY

BOX 9.2 To Collect or Not Collect Racialization and Ethnicity Statistics

Unlike the crime statistics in the United States, those in Canada do not report on ethnic background of victim and accused. We do have information about backgrounds in the Canadian correctional system where, for example, Indigenous people (3 percent of the population) constitute 14 percent of the inmates and Blacks (2 percent of the population) constitute 6 percent of the federal inmates (Wortley, 1999:262). And the policy question is whether to include racialization/ethnicity information at other levels of the system.

Criminologist Scot Wortley (1999) presents arguments for both sides. Arguments opposed to collecting racialization/ethnicity-based data include

■ the risk of publishing inaccurate information due to the problems of official statistics and measuring racialization/ethnicity; and

■ the support provided for racist theories.

Arguments in favour of collecting the data include

■ the opportunity to **learn** whether minorities are receiving differential treatment at any level of the system (e.g., to what extent does profiling occur?);

■ the identification of crimes that are of particular concern to a minority. While it is well known that homicide is primarily an intraracial problem in the U.S., Blacks killing Blacks is also a problem for Canadians. Some Black

community leaders, like Dudley Laws in Toronto, have spoken out against publishing racialization-based crime statistics. However, in 2001, the Black Action Defence Committee, of which Laws is the executive director, launched a campaign supported by many other associations to stop the killings of Black youths by other Black youths. From 1996 to 2001, over 100 Black youths were killed by other Black youths, and the agencies were appealing to "society in general to address this very urgent problem" (*Metro Today*, August 17, 2001:9). And the killing continues. As shown in this example, members of a minority group may feel comfortable publishing data about their own group but not wish to see it compared to the data for other groups, for fear that the data will be used to label rather than address inequities faced by members of their group; and

■ a ban on such data does not prevent the spread of racist theories (racialization-based distortions are widely available, for example, on the Internet).

Do you think racialization/ethnicity-based crime statistics should be published as readily as racialization/ethnicity education and income data (see Chapters 3 and 12) or should there be no collection of this kind of data? Or should the collection be limited to certain situations? What situations would they be? Or should the decision be left with the minority group themselves? Would this last approach cause any problems?

---

that does not keep it from being a goal that citizens and the criminal justice system should strive to reach.

WHAT CAN YOU DO?

■ Seek out a community/police liaison committee in your neighbourhood and learn about local problems and what people are trying to do about them.

■ Seek out an advocacy group and participate in one of its activities. For example, in Ontario, an organization called Justice for Children and Youth challenged

the Ontario law banning squeegee kids' solicitations and various kinds of begging (e.g., while intoxicated). This organization seeks participation on its Youth Advisory Committee to help it deal with the problems of young people. It is located in Toronto (tel. 416-920-1633).

■ Organize seminars to discuss or debate ideas like the publication of racialization/ethnicity data for crime or the value of restorative justice.

■ Work with campus groups to alert female students to the problem of date rape.

SUMMARY

WHY IS IT DIFFICULT TO STUDY CRIME AND YOUTH CRIME?

Studying crime, criminals, and youth crime is difficult because it involves complex human behaviour, and many criminals and victims hide their involvement. There also are problems inherent in using official sources of data, such as the *Uniform Crime Report*, because they reflect crimes that are reported rather than crimes that are committed, and they do not provide detailed information about offenders.

HOW DOES VIOLENT CRIME DIFFER FROM PROPERTY CRIME?

Violent crime consists of actions involving force or the threat of force against others and includes homicide, sexual assault, robbery, and aggravated assault. Property crime consists of taking money or property from another without force, the threat of force, or the destruction of property.

WHY IS SEXUAL ASSAULT AS A VIOLENT CRIME NOT WELL UNDERSTOOD, AND HOW IS THIS LACK OF UNDERSTANDING REFLECTED IN OUR SOCIAL RESPONSE TO SEXUAL ASSAULT?

First, many people think that sexual assault is a sexually motivated crime, but it is actually an act of violence in which sex is used as a weapon against a powerless victim. Moreover, statistics on sexual assault are misleading at best because sexual assault is often not reported. Many reasons keep victims from coming forward. Some victims may be so traumatized that they just want to forget about it. Others fear the attacker will try to get even. Many also fear how they may be treated by the police and, in the event of a trial, by crown attorneys.

WHAT IS OCCUPATIONAL CRIME?

Occupational (white-collar) crime refers to illegal activities committed by people in the course of their employment or normal business activity. Occupational crime includes crimes such as employee theft, fraud (obtaining money or property under false pretences), embezzlement (theft from an employer), soliciting bribes or kickbacks, and insider trading of securities.

HOW DOES OCCUPATIONAL CRIME DIFFER FROM CORPORATE CRIME?

Occupational crimes are illegal activities committed by people in the course of their employment or normal business activity. Corporate crimes are illegal acts committed by corporate employees on behalf of the corporation and with its support.

WHAT IS ORGANIZED CRIME AND WHY DOES IT FLOURISH IN CANADA?

Organized crime is a business operation that supplies illegal goods and services for profit. These illegal enterprises include drug trafficking, prostitution, gambling, loan sharking, money laundering, and large-scale theft. Organized crime thrives because there is great demand for illegal goods and services.

HOW DOES YOUTH CRIME DIFFER FROM ADULT CRIME?

Youth crime refers to a violation of law or the commission of a status offence by people who are younger than a specific age. Many behaviours that are identified as juvenile delinquency are not criminal acts per se but status offences—acts that are illegal because of the age of the offender—such as cutting school or purchasing and consuming alcoholic beverages. Juvenile hearings take place in juvenile courts or before juvenile judges, whereas adult offenders are tried in criminal courts.

WHO IS MOST LIKELY TO BE ARRESTED FOR A CRIME IN CANADA?

Men are more likely to be arrested than women. Teenagers and young adults are most likely to be arrested for serious crimes such as homicide, sexual assault, and robbery. Although individuals from all social classes commit crimes, people from lower socioeconomic backgrounds are more likely to be arrested for violent and property crimes, whereas people from the upper classes generally commit white-collar or corporate crimes. Indigenous people and Blacks are overrepresented in arrest data.

HOW DO FUNCTIONALISTS EXPLAIN CRIME?

Functionalists use several theories to explain crime. According to strain theory, people are socialized to desire cultural goals, but many people do not have institutionalized means to achieve the goals and therefore engage in criminal activity. Control perspectives, such as social bond theory, suggest that delinquency and crime are most likely to occur when a person's ties to society are weakened or broken.

HOW DO CONFLICT THEORISTS EXPLAIN CRIME?

Conflict theorists explain criminal behaviour in terms of power differentials and/or economic inequality in society. One approach focuses on the relationship between authority and power and crime; another focuses on the relationship between economic inequality and crime.

HOW DO INTERACTIONISTS EXPLAIN CRIME?

Interactionists emphasize that criminal behaviour is learned through everyday interaction with others. According to differential association theory, individuals have a greater tendency to deviate from societal norms when they frequently associate with people who are more likely to deviate than conform. Labelling theory says that delinquents and criminals are those people who have been successfully labelled by others as such.

HOW DO FEMINIST THEORISTS EXPLAIN CRIME?

Feminist approaches offer several explanations of why women commit crimes: gender discrimination, patriarchy, a combination of capitalism and patriarchy, and a combination of family structure and socialization.

WHAT ARE THE COMPONENTS OF THE CRIMINAL JUSTICE SYSTEM?

The criminal justice system is a network of organizations involved in law enforcement, including the police, the courts, and the prisons. The police are the most visible link in the criminal justice system because they are responsible for initially arresting and jailing people. Criminal courts are responsible for determining the guilt or innocence of people who have been accused of committing a crime.

Imprisonment, conditional sentences, probation, and parole are mechanisms of punishment based on retribution, social protection, rehabilitation, and deterrence.

KEY TERMS

corporate crime,   p. 211
crime,   p. 204
criminal justice system,   p. 219
date rape,   p. 206
differential association theory,   p. 217
homicide,   p. 205
indictable offence,   p. 204
labelling theory,   p. 218

mass murder,   p. 205
medicalization of crime,   p. 218
occupational (white-collar) crime,   p. 210
organized crime,   p. 211
plea bargaining,   p. 220
primary deviance,   p. 218
property crime,   p. 208
punishment,   p. 221

QUESTIONS FOR CRITICAL THINKING

1.   Do you think that putting surveillance cameras in public places to monitor people and their possible deviant behaviour is a good idea? Why, or why not?

2.   How would sociologists argue with the claim that crime is committed by disturbed people?

3.   Does the functionalist, conflict, or interactionist perspective best explain why people commit corporate crimes? Organized crimes? Explain your answer.

4.   How would you reorganize the criminal justice system so that it would deal more equitably with all people in this country and prevent problems like profiling?

WEBLINKS

Centre for Restorative Justice

www.sfu.ca/crj

This site contains a variety of resources for restorative justice.

Nathanson Centre for Study of Organized Crime and Corruption

www.yorku.ca/nathanson/Links/links.htm

The Nathanson Centre for Study of Organized Crime and Corruption advances the study and discussion of this topic Canada.

National Crime Prevention Strategy

www.prevention.gc.ca/index.html

The National Crime Prevention Strategy aims to reduce crime and victimization by tackling crime before it happens. The strategy is based on the principle that the surest way to reduce crime is to focus on the factors that put individuals at risk, such as family violence, school problems, and drug abuse.

Statistics Canada

www.statcan.ca/english/Pgdb

Data at this location is devoted to a wide variety of subjects, such as the economy, the land, the people, and the form in which data about justice, crimes, and victimization is available.

Cecil E. Greek's Web Site

www.criminology.fsu.edu/cjlinks

Criminologist Cecil E. Greek has created a site with a huge set of links to crime and justice sites, primarily in the U.S., but also in Canada. These links facilitate the comparison of American and Canadian data.

10

HEALTH, ILLNESS, AND HEALTH CARE AS SOCIAL PROBLEMS

The Terry Fox Run

When you get $520 per month and pay $400 for rent, how can you live on $120?

Richard, aged 46, an engineer now on welfare, speaking of the difficulty of purchasing nutritious food on his allowance (author's files).

How many women have that amount of money lying around?

Diana Brynlee, quoted in the Globe and Mail, *March 10, 2001:A2, speaking of her ability to pay for a diagnostic test that can detect cancer early.*

I believe it is a far greater perversion of Canadian values to accept a system where money, rather than need, determines who gets access to care.

Roy Romanow, quoted in the Globe and Mail. *November 29, 2002:A1, as he delivered his report on Canada's health care system.*

Richard, quoted above, was speaking to the author at a dinner provided by Street Health, a downtown Toronto agency providing a variety of health and social services to recovering addicts and homeless and poor people. Diana Brynlee made her statement after paying to obtain a PET scan (Positron Emission Tomography takes internal pictures of people to diagnose disease). If she had not had the money to pay for it, she would have had to wait longer for a test and missed the opportunity that early diagnosis afforded. She was wondering about the consequences for people who could not afford the test. Roy Romanow disagrees with those, such as Don Mazankowski, also the author of a health care report, who think it is a perversion of Canadian values that they cannot use their own money to speed up diagnosis and treatment. Mazankowski holds that since our health care system was not designed to do all that it is doing now *(Globe and Mail,* January 9, 2002:A3), the system must diversify its revenue stream with more private options and initiatives, such as private clinics.

The health situations faced by Richard and Diana Brynlee tend to be viewed as *personal problems*, but lack of access to nutritious food and expensive diagnostic tests is also a *social problem*. For one thing, it affects many people; for another, it is a problem that cannot be reduced or eliminated without a significant social response, such as willingness to devote more money to health and social services. Despite their differing viewpoints, both Romanow and Mazankowski agree on the need for more money and/or different options for pay-

ment for the health care system. This chapter examines health, illness—including both physical and mental illness—and health care problems and current issues in providing health services in this country.

This chapter also draws attention to inequalities regarding disease and disability for people of different sex, gender, class, and racialization or ethnicity; recent problems like HIV/AIDS and obesity; mental illness as a social problem; and the crisis faced by the Canadian health care system and recommendations to improve it. The sociological perspectives are used to explain health problems, and the chapter concludes with suggestions on what you can do to improve your health and the health of others.

HEALTH AND ILLNESS AS SOCIAL PROBLEMS

According to the World Health Organization (WHO) (1946:3), *health* is a state of complete physical, mental, and social well-being. In other words, health is not only a biological issue, it is also a social issue. After all, physical and mental health are intertwined: Physical illness can cause emotional problems; mental illness can produce physical symptoms. Many people think there is a positive relationship between the amount of money a society spends on health care and the overall physical, mental, and social well-being of its people— that spending a great deal of money on health care should result in physical, mental, and social well-being. But if this were true, people in the United States would be the healthiest and most fit in the world, and they are not. While physical, mental, and social well-being are difficult to measure, **life expectancy, an estimate of the average lifetime of people born in a specific year**, is relatively easy to measure. If we use this widely accepted measure of the effectiveness of the health care system, we find the relationship between health expenditure and health of the population is not strong. The U.S. spends the equivalent of more than $4000 (OECD) (Organisation for Economic Co-operation and Development dollars, adjusted for differences in prices in different countries) per person and Canada spends less than $2500 (OECD) per person on health care each year (Canadian Institute for Health Information, 2001:Figure 64). The health service industry accounts for almost 14 percent of the gross domestic product in the U.S. and 9 percent in Canada; yet Canadians live longer. Whereas U.S. females can expect to live 79.3 years and males can expect to live 73.0 years (U.S. Bureau of the Census, 1998), Canadian females can expect to live 81.4 years and males can expect to live 75.4 years (Statistics Canada, 2001b:42).

Unfortunately, this high overall life expectancy of 78.4 years does not hold for all the members of Canadian society: A gap of 6 years exists between the life expectancy of Indigenous people and that of the general population (Frideres, 2002:155). Besides life expectancy, another widely used measure of the effectiveness of the health care system is the *infant mortality rate,* **the number of deaths of infants under 1 year of age per 1000 live births in a given year.** During the last century, Canada's infant mortality rate has decreased greatly. Recently, the infant mortality rate for Canada was 5.5 (Statistics Canada, 2001e:25). The infant mortality rate is an important indication of a society's level of preventive (prenatal) medical care, maternal nutrition, childbirth procedures, and care for infants. For all our expenditures in health care and use of high-tech equipment, however, infant mortality among Indigenous people is still high, 12.0 in 1997, or more than twice the rate for Canada as a whole (Frideres, 2002:155).

Acute and Chronic Diseases and Disability

Life expectancy in Canada and other developed nations has increased largely because vaccinations and improved nutrition, sanitation, and personal hygiene have virtually eliminated many acute diseases, including measles, polio, cholera, tetanus, typhoid, and malaria. *Acute diseases* **are illnesses that strike suddenly and cause dramatic incapacitation and sometimes death** (Weitz, 1996). Acute diseases that are still common in Canada are chicken pox and influenza. Recently, too, multi–drug-resistant strains of tuberculosis, Lyme disease, and HIV (the virus that causes AIDS)—and now SARS—have become pressing health problems, problems exacerbated by global trade, which has increased 1000 percent since World War II, and the worldwide movement of 1.5 billion airplane passengers per year (Donnelly, 2003) (See Box 10.1).

With the overall decline in death from acute illnesses in high-income nations, however, has come a corresponding increase in *chronic diseases,* **illnesses that**

are long term or lifelong and that develop gradually or are present from birth (Weitz, 1996). Chronic diseases are caused by various biological, social, and environmental factors. In Chapter 8, we discussed two of the most common sources of chronic disease and premature death: tobacco use, which increases mortality among both smokers and people who breathe the tobacco smoke of others; and alcohol abuse. According to some social analysts, we can attribute many chronic diseases in our society to the *manufacturers of illness,* groups that promote illness-causing behaviour and social conditions, such as smoking (McKinlay, 1994). The effect of chronic diseases on life expectancy varies because some chronic diseases are progressive (e.g., emphysema worsens over time), whereas others are constant (e.g., paralysis after a stroke); also, some are fatal (lung cancer), but others are not (arthritis and sinusitis). Because of the combination of longer life expectancies and the disabling consequences of some diseases, new terms have been coined—for example, "active" life or health expectancy and "disability-free" life expectancy. These terms emphasize good health rather than ill health and death. In Canada, from 1995 to 1997, *disability-free life expectancy,* **the number of years of life that can be expected to be free of activity limitation,** was 68.7 years for females and 65.5 years for males, which when subtracted from the life expectancies mentioned above indicate 12.5 years of disability for females and 9.9 years of disability for males (Statistics Canada, 2001b:42)

Some chronic diseases produce disabilities that significantly increase health care costs for individuals and for society. *Disability* can be defined in several ways. Medical professionals tend to define it in terms of organically based impairments—that is, the problem is entirely within the body (Albrecht, 1992). However, disability rights advocates believe that disability is a physical or health condition that stigmatizes or causes discrimination. Perhaps the best way to define disability is, as medical sociologist Rose Weitz (1996:428) has said, in terms of both physical and social factors: *Disability* **is a restricted or total lack of ability to perform certain activities as a result of physical or mental limitations or the interplay of these limitations, social responses, and the social environment.** In Canada in 1991, an estimated 4.2 million people, or 15.5 percent of the population, had one or more physical or mental disabilities. And many kinds of disabilities exist. Among

BOX 10.1 HIV/AIDS Worldwide

Although chronic diseases have replaced infectious diseases as the major cause of death in Canada, infectious diseases are still a problem here and a problem of epidemic proportions in the developing world. Certainly the most widely publicized of these diseases is HIV/AIDS. In Canada, 49 000 people are living with HIV/AIDS, but in the rest of the world, 42 million, including 3.2 million children, are living with HIV/AIDS. In 2002 alone, 5 million people, including 800 000 children, were newly infected with HIV (UNAIDS, 2002a). Map 10.1 shows the distribution of HIV/AIDS around the world. Note the huge number of 29.4 million people living with HIV/AIDS in Africa. Approximately 20 million people are thought to have died of AIDS, but this figure is difficult to confirm.

Map 10.1 A Global View of HIV/AIDS

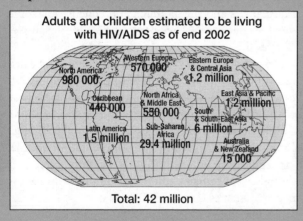

Total: 42 million

Source: World Health Organization, 2002, www.unaids.org/
worldaidsday/2002/press/EpiCoreSlides2002/EPIcore_en/Slide4.gif.
Data adapted with permission of UNAIDS.

In different parts of the world, different approaches have been taken to prevent and treat HIV/AIDS. In Canada and in the Western world generally, since the early 1980s, the approach has been an aggressive educational campaign. A dramatic example of this was the recent advertising campaign of the AIDS Committee of Toronto urging the use of condoms. These advertisements, called "Condom Country," mimicked Marlborough cigarette advertisements with pictures of rugged cowboys in a Western setting.

Action has also been vigorous in some developing countries. Thailand confronted the problem in 1991 by distributing condoms, shutting down brothels that didn't use them, and requiring radio stations to broadcast HIV/AIDS prevention information hourly. These actions have been effective. In 1990 in

Thailand, there were 215 000 new cases of HIV/AIDS; by the early 2000s, the number of new cases is expected to be down to about 90 000 (Shenon, 1996).

The story is different in India, where HIV/AIDS appeared in 1991, 10 years after it was recognized as a new disease (Altman, 1996). The number of people with HIV/AIDS is exploding in India, and the World Health Organization projects that the country will soon be the world centre of the disease, with one-quarter of all infected people (Burns, 1996). One immediate source of the problem is India's truck drivers, who often have long layovers with nothing to do, and the many prostitutes available along the roadsides, flying gaily coloured scarves to identify themselves. Drivers who pick up the disease carry it to other prostitutes in previously uninfected regions as well as home to their wives and future children. The red-light districts of Bombay, Calcutta, and New Delhi are another source of the growing epidemic. An estimated 52 percent of the brothel "cage girls" (enslaved child prostitutes who are kept in cages during the day so they don't escape) in Bombay are infected with HIV/AIDS (Burns, 1996).

Fighting HIV/AIDS in India means fighting more than the disease. It means fighting the caste system, because prostitutes and those with HIV/AIDS are discriminated against. It means fighting social taboos against talking about sex. It means fighting poverty, because prostitutes who use condoms lose clients and starve. And it means fighting the denial of the problem by political leaders; only $35 million of a five-year $100 million HIV/AIDS prevention program has been spent in four years (Burns, 1996).

In many parts of sub-Saharan Africa, the situation is even worse. While this area contains 10 percent of the world's population, it has 70 percent of its HIV/AIDS cases. All governments are undertaking prevention programs, such as the provision of drugs to rape victims and measures to prevent mother-to-child transmission of HIV/AIDS (South Africa reversed its policy of not providing drugs in April, 2002).

There is hope, however. After vigorous lobbying by HIV/AIDS activists, the United Nations, and governments of developing countries, in early 2001, five drug companies (Boehringer Ingelheim, Bristol-Myers Squibb, F. Hoffman-LaRoche, GlaxoSmithKline, and Merck) agreed to reduce the price of HIV/AIDS drugs such as antiretrovirals, and generic versions of these drugs are now being produced at costs far below Western prices (UNDP, 2001:22). In June 2001, Stephen Lewis, a former UN Ambassador for Canada, was appointed to coordinate efforts for the UN fight against HIV/AIDS in Africa, and a budget of $10 billion is being sought for the program.

How do you think Canada can best contribute to this program?

the working-age population with a disability, 52 percent are limited in mobility; 50 percent are limited in agility; 32 percent have an intellectual disability, mental health condition, or learning disability; 25 percent are limited in hearing; and 9 percent are limited in vision (Statistics Canada, 1994:ix). The number continues to increase for several reasons. First, with advances in medical technology, many people who in the past would have died from an accident or illness now survive with an impairment. Second, as people live longer, they are more likely to experience chronic diseases (such as arthritis) that may have disabling consequences (Albrecht, 1992). Third, people born with serious disabilities are more likely to survive infancy because of medical technology. (However, only a small percentage of people with a disability today were born with it; accidents, disease, and violence account for most disabilities in this country.) Many people with a chronic illness or disability will not live out the full life expectancy for people in their age category.

Sex and Gender, Class, and Indigenous Status

Chronic diseases vary substantially by major demographic variables. Non-fatal diseases or conditions are more common among females. In this chapter, much data comes from the National Population Health Survey (NPHS). The NPHS was conducted by Health Canada and Statistics Canada to measure the health status of adult, non-Indigenous Canadians and to monitor changes over time. (Children and Indigenous adults [i.e., adults with "Aboriginal status"] were surveyed separately.) The content is multidimensional, including physical, mental, and social components, and the method is in-depth interviewing. The first wave of data collection occurred in 1994–95 and consisted of a sample of 17 626 Canadians, and subsequent waves were undertaken in 1996–97 and 1998–99.

According to the 1998–99 NPHS, larger percentages of females than males aged 12 and over reported having arthritis (19 percent vs. 11 percent), high blood pressure (13 percent vs. 9 percent), migraine (13 percent vs. 4 percent), and bronchitis/emphysema (3 percent vs. 2 percent). A higher percentage of males than females reported having heart disease (5 percent vs. 4 percent) and diabetes (4 percent vs. 3 percent) (Statistics Canada, 2001b:25). A slightly higher percentage of females than

males are likely to have a disability (16 percent vs. 15 percent) (Statistics Canada, 1994:vi). The reasons for these differences could be a combination of factors that contribute to females' longer life expectancies, such as:

- consuming lower levels of drugs, tobacco, and alcohol (see Chapter 8);

- not working in hazardous occupations, like mining and construction; and

- having biological protection during the childbearing years, during which females have lower levels of heart disease, and, later, being subject to more disease.

Class, measured by income, is related to longevity. According to the National Population Health Survey, people in lower-income groups in 1994–95 had a higher mortality rate than those in upper-income groups (Statistics Canada, 1998a). Class, measured by income and education, is also related to chronic conditions. According to the same study, more people with incomes of $60 000 and above (32.9 percent) than people with incomes of less than $10 000 (15.3 percent) reported that their subjective perception of their health status was that it was excellent. As well, smaller percentages of people with university degrees than people with elementary or less education reported having heart disease (2.7 percent vs. 11.1 percent) and having functional disability (5.5 percent vs. 24.3 percent) (Segall and Chappell, 2000:162–163). The reasons for these differences are likely a combination of people with lower levels of education:

- being unable to afford nutritious food. (Richard's opening quote is telling, but evidence also comes from a study of welfare incomes and expenses in Toronto. Given the cost of housing, welfare did not cover housing and the cost of food for a single-person household, a two-parent two-child family, and a single-parent two-child family [Vozoris et al., 2002]);

- engaging in risky health behaviour like smoking, drinking, and drug use (see Chapter 8);

- working in dangerous industries; and

- living in some areas, like the North, far from medical care. (In the Yukon and NWT, in 1993, people were an average distance of 23.6 and 155.2 km from the nearest physician, and population per physician was much higher than in the 10 provinces, according to a chart from the Canadian Medical Association (Hewa, 2002:66).

Indigenous status is a very important predictor of illness, both acute and chronic. According to sociologist James Frideres (2002:156–157), Indigenous people have higher rates of infectious diseases, like TB and AIDS, than the general Canadian population; chronic conditions, like diabetes and cancer, are likewise increasing. The reasons for these differences are similar to those for class-related differences in health, including:

- high levels of poverty, with the accompanying poor housing and sanitary conditions;
- higher rates of risky health behaviour, and
- being distant from medical care in Nunavut, the Yukon and NWT.

Besides sex and gender, class, and Indigenous status, many other structural variables, like marital status, social support, and neighbourhood, and inequality of income in society, affect the health of people. Determining the relative influence of these variables and the health behaviour variables identified in Chapter 8 is not an easy task. With the comprehensive set of questions about health behaviour and social structural variables in the National Population Health Survey, it is possible to begin this analysis. Sociologists Margaret Denton and Vivienne Walters (1999) studied with the NPHS data, the relative influence of health variables—like smoking, drinking, physical activity and weight—and structural variables—like family structure, education, occupation, income, and social support—on subjective health status and functional health status data from the Health Utilities Index (in the NPHS), which inquires into vision, hearing, speech, mobility, cognition, emotion, and so on. They discovered that the social structural variables had a greater effect on health than the health variables. This finding confirms that health and illness are social problems and suggests that changing social conditions would be more helpful than health promotion in improving their health. Denton and Walters also found differences between males and females. Females' health was determined more by structural variables (e.g., being in the highest income bracket, working full-time, caring for a family, and having social support) than males' health. Regarding the influence of risky health behaviour, males' health was determined more by smoking and drinking, and females' health was determined more by exercise and weight.

For both men and women, a non-heterosexual sexual orientation can also be a factor in health, due to ignorance and discrimination on the part of doctors and other health care professionals. This issue, and related health issues for persons living with HIV/AIDS, is discussed in Chapter 6.

Obesity

A relatively new health risk—being overweight—is now affecting almost half the Canadian population. Excess weight is linked to heart disease, Type II diabetes, certain forms of cancer, and stroke. A healthy weight-range is indicated by the body mass index (BMI), which is calculated by dividing weight in kilograms (kg) by height in metres squared (m^2). A person with a BMI of less than 18.5 is considered underweight; with a BMI of 18.6 to 24.9, of normal weight; with a BMI of 25.0 to 29.9, overweight; and with a BMI of 30.0+, obese.

According to the latest report of the National Population Health Survey, in 1998–99, 3 percent of Canadians aged 15 and older were underweight; almost half were of normal weight; one-third were overweight; and 14 percent were obese. The average woman had a BMI of 24.7, and the average man, a BMI of 25.8. Men were more likely than women to be in the overweight category; however, no difference existed between the percentages of men and women in the obese category (Statistics Canada, 2001b:17). A curvilinear pattern was found for age, with middle-aged people being the most likely to be obese. A higher proportion of overweight/obese men was found in the high-income category and a lower proportion of overweight/obese women was found in the high-income category (Statistics Canada, 2001b:18). Region of the country is also important. According to André Picard, who wrote a series for the *Globe and Mail* on obesity (2001:F8), eastern provinces tend to have a higher proportion of overweight/obese people than do the western provinces and Quebec; in each province, rural people are more likely to be overweight/obese than urban people.

Obesity is not just a problem for Canadians; it is a problem worldwide. Although data are difficult to confirm, as of 2000, the World Health Organization estimates the number of obese adults to be over 300 million worldwide. And obesity is not limited to

According to a recent National Population Health Survey, one-third of Canadians aged 15 and over are overweight, and 14 percent are obese. What kinds of problems does this increasing trend present for the health care system in the fu\

Western societies. The WHO estimates that over 115 million people in developing countries also suffer from obesity-related problems (WHO, 2003). If the proportion of overweight to obese people found in Canada were true of the rest of the developed world, nearly 1 billion people would be overweight or obese.

How can we reduce the overweight/obesity problem? Besides the usual suggestions for self-help groups, increased physical activity, and better diets, suggestions now include putting health warnings, like those found on cigarette packages, on packages of junk food, as well as adding a tax to junk food to discourage consumption. Would you be discouraged from eating junk food by graphic pictures of health consequences? Would you buy as much junk food if it were taxed like cigarettes?

MENTAL ILLNESS AS A SOCIAL PROBLEM

Mental illness is a social problem because of the number of people it affects, the difficulty of defining and identifying mental disorders, and the ways in which mental illness is treated. Although most social scientists use the terms *mental illness* and *mental disorder* interchangeably, many medical professionals distinguish between a *mental disorder*—a condition that makes it difficult or impossible for a person to cope with everyday life—and *mental illness*—a condition that requires extensive treatment with medication, psychotherapy, and sometimes hospitalization.

The most widely accepted classification of mental disorders is the American Psychiatric Association's (1994) *Diagnostic and Statistical Manual of Mental Disorders IV (DSM-IV)* (see Figure 10.1). The *DSM* is now in its fourth edition, and with each revision, its list of disorders has changed and grown. Listings change partly because of new scientific findings, which permit more precise descriptions that are more useful than broad terms covering a wide range of behaviours, and partly because of changes in how we view mental disorders culturally (at one time, for example, homosexuality was considered a mental disorder). Despite these changes, some social analysts still question the extent to which mental health professionals can accurately detect and treat mental disorders.

How many people are affected by mental illness? A national study of mental illness has not been undertaken in Canada, but some indication of the extent of the problem can be found in the "Edmonton Study," an interview study of 3 258 households in Edmonton, Alberta (Bland et al., 1988). The researchers found that 21 percent of those interviewed reported mental illness in the previous year and 34 percent reported experiencing mental illness sometime in their life. While it is difficult to generalize the results from Edmonton to the rest of Canada, the results are similar to those of national mental health studies, such as that of sociologist Ronald Kessler (1994) in the United States.

Rates of mental illness are affected by gender, class, and Indigenous status. It is often thought that females have higher rates of mental illness, including depression and episodes that cause distress, than males; however, when alcohol and drug abuse are included, the

FIGURE 10.1   Mental Disorders Identified by the American Psychiatric Association

1. **Disorders first evident in infancy, childhood, or adolescence**	These disorders include mental retardation, attention-deficit hyperactivity, anorexia nervosa, bulimia nervosa, and stuttering.
2. **Organic mental disorders**	Psychological or behavioural disorders associated with dysfunctions of the brain caused by aging, disease, or brain damage.
3. **Substance-related disorders**	Disorders resulting from abuse of alcohol and/or other drugs such as barbiturates, cocaine, or amphetamines.
4. **Schizophrenia and other psychotic disorders**	Disorders with symptoms such as delusions or hallucinations.
5. **Mood disorders**	Emotional disorders such as major depression and bipolar (manic-depressive) disorder.
6. **Anxiety disorders**	Disorders characterized by anxiety that is manifest in phobias, panic attacks, or obsessive-compulsive disorder.
7. **Somatoform disorders**	Psychological problems that present themselves as symptoms of physical disease such as hypochondria.
8. **Dissociative disorders**	Problems involving a splitting or dissociation of normal consciousness such as amnesia and multiple personality.
9. **Eating or sleeping disorders**	Includes such problems as anorexia and bulimia or insomnia and other problems associated with sleep.
10. **Impulse control disorders**	Symptoms include the inability to control undesirable impulses such as kleptomania, pyromania, and pathological gambling.
11. **Personality disorders**	Maladaptive personality traits that are generally resistant to treatment such as paranoid and antisocial personality types.

Source: Adapted from **Diagnostic and Statistical Manual of Mental Disorders IV**, *by American Psychiatric Association, 1994, Washington, DC: American Psychiatric Association.*

researchers found a higher lifetime rate among males (40.7 percent vs. 26.8 percent). People in lower social classes have higher rates of mental disorders than people in upper classes. But according to sociologist Harley Dickinson (2002), this relationship could be explained by the "downward drift hypothesis"—that people with mental illnesses are unable to function properly, neither getting an education nor keeping a job. Thus, they slip into the lower classes (Dickinson, 2002:376). The Edmonton Study found that the rate of mental illness was much higher among the unemployed than the employed (60 percent vs. 34 percent). Measures of mental illness are much higher for Indigenous than non-Indigenous Canadians. Frideres (2002:157) states that, compared with the rest of the Canadian population, for Indigenous people the suicide rate is three times higher (six times for the 15 to 24 age group), the homicide rates are twice as high, and the rate of violent death is three times higher. Reasons for these differences are attributed to significant differences in living conditions, as mentioned above, and lack of opportunities.

Treatment of Mental Illness

People who seek professional help for mental illness are treated with medication and psychotherapy, to help them understand the underlying reasons for their problem. Because medication is used so routinely today, we tend to forget that institutionalization used to be the most common treatment for severe mental illness. In fact, it was the development of psychoactive drugs that made possible the deinstitutionalization movement of the 1960s.

***Deinstitutionalization* is the practice of discharging patients from mental hospitals into the community.** Although deinstitutionalization was originally devised as a solution for the problem of warehousing mentally ill patients in large, prison-like mental hospitals in the first half of the 20th century, many social scientists now view deinstitutionalization as a problem. To understand how this solution evolved into a problem, one must understand the state of mental health care in Canada during the 1950s and 1960s. The practice of *involuntary commitment* (i.e., without a patient's consent) allowed many patients to be warehoused in state mental hospitals for extended periods of time, with only minimal and sometimes abusive custodial care. According to sociologist Erving Goffman (1961), a mental hospital is a classic example of a ***total institution*—a place where people are isolated from the rest of society for a period of time and come under the complete control of the officials who run the institution.** Patients are stripped of their individual identities—or depersonalized—by being required to wear institutional clothing and follow a strict regimen of activities, meals, and sleeping hours; sometimes they are referred to impersonally, as a "CMI" (a person who is chronically mentally ill) (see Grobe, 1995). The deinstitutionalization movement sought to release patients from mental hospitals so that they could live at home and go about their daily activities. Professionals believed that the patients' mental disorders could be controlled with medication and treatment through community-based mental health services. Other advocates hoped that deinstitutionalization would remove the stigma attached to hospitalization for mental illness.

Deinstitutionalization did occur in a substantial way in Canada. Between 1960 and 1976, the number of beds in mental hospitals declined from 47 633 to 15 011, although the number of beds in psychiatric wards in general hospitals increased from 844 to 5836 (Cochrane et al., 1997:1).

Although deinstitutionalization had worthwhile goals—protection of civil rights, more humane and less costly treatment—in too many cases, it simply moved people out of mental hospitals into the streets and jails. Today, critics of deinstitutionalization argue that it exacerbated long-term problems associated with treating mental illness.

If schizophrenia and other serious mental illnesses do not lead to jail, they often result in homelessness. One study concluded that as many as 30 percent of homeless people were previously patients in mental hospitals and about 80 percent have some diagnosable mental disorder (Searight and Searight, 1988). However, it is difficult to determine which came first—the mental disorder or homelessness. If you were homeless, for instance, what are the chances that you might develop mental health problems if you tried to survive on the streets or in and out of shelters and city jails? In any case, social scientists and homeless advocates agree that most homeless shelters and other community services cannot adequately meet the needs of people known as "the homeless mentally ill" (see Torrey, 1988).

Although involuntary commitment to mental hospitals has always been controversial, it remains the primary method by which police officers, judges, social workers, and other officials deal with people—particularly the homeless—whom they have reason to believe are mentally ill and imminently dangerous to themselves and others (Monahan, 1992). However, it should be recognized that involuntary commitment is a social control mechanism, used to keep people with a history of mental illness off the streets so that they cannot engage in violent crime. It does little—if anything—

Although there are many causes of homelessness, ranging from lack of affordable housing to drug dependency, some analysts believe that the deinstitutionalization of patients from mental hospitals has significantly increased the number of people living on the streets in Canada. What other alternatives can you suggest for dealing with mental illness?

development of the system, and its current issues. We will also look at the United States's model of health care.

Development of the National Health Care System

While the idea of universal health care had been circulating for some time, and Saskatchewan had pioneered its major features, the features of the national health care system emerged with the following pieces of federal legislation and recent changes in funding:

- The Hospital Insurance and Diagnostic Service Act 1957 provided insurance for hospital and diagnostic services.

- The Medical Care Act 1966 provided insurance for medical services, to which all the provinces agreed by 1972, emphasizing five principles: universality—all Canadians should be covered; accessibility—reasonable access must be unimpeded by financial or other barriers; comprehensiveness—all medically necessary services should be guaranteed; portability—Canadians should be able to have their benefits transferable to other provinces or other countries; and public administration—the system to be operated by a public body on a non-profit basis.

- The Canada Health Act 1984 confirmed the five principles and prohibited private charges or extra billing by doctors or hospitals.

- The federal government substantially reduced its contributions to the provinces in the mid-1990s to 26 percent or less of the total cost.

- The federal government increased its contributions to the provinces in 1999, but not to the 50 percent level established at the beginning.

- A federal–provincial agreement in February 2003 saw the federal government state that it will inject almost $35 billion into the health care system over the next five years.

The many health care changes, such as reductions in the size, number, and functions of hospitals, increased use of drugs and home care, increased knowledge of health by patients and consultation of alternate health practitioners, and new technological developments for diagnosis and treatment, have brought about many issues that must be addressed.

to treat the medical and social conditions that contribute to mental disorders (Catalano and McConnell, 1996). Given this, state-run mental hospitals tend to function as revolving doors to poverty-level board-and-care homes, nursing homes, or life on the street. Patients who can pay private psychiatric facilities through private insurance coverage or Medicare are not part of this cycle (Brown, 1985).

THE "CRISIS" IN CANADIAN HEALTH CARE

We hear so often that the Canadian health care system is in a state of crisis. In this section, we will outline the

Current Issues in the Health Care System

Coverage of Care

Since much of contemporary health care is neither hospital-based nor delivered by physicians, coverage of care is an issue. With the restructuring of hospitals, closing of hospital beds, and increase of out-patient procedures, the need for home care has grown. Home care ranges from visits just after hospital discharge to long-term help in maintaining independence. Not all such care is covered by Medicare, especially the long-term general support. Although ministers of health have increased support for home care, demand seems to exceed supply. The cost of drugs can also be a problem for those in home care. During the last 25 years, the use and effectiveness of drugs has greatly increased, so that drugs now constitute double the percentage of health care costs that they did in 1975 (Canadian Institute of Health Information, 2001:Figure 69). Drugs taken outside the hospitals are not covered by Medicare. Because not everyone, especially those among the poor, has an insurance plan to cover him or her, the need for "pharmacare," or government support of drug purchases, has increased. Several provinces have created plans where citizens pay a yearly fee after which the government pays for the drugs. An example of such a program is the British Columbia plan. In 1995, the B.C. government established its reference-based program where, for each class of drugs, a low-priced (not necessary the lowest priced), effective drug is selected and the program will pay for it. If a higher-priced drug is desired, but no medical benefit is present, the individual pays the difference (Segall and Chappell, 2000:252). Needs for other kinds of care, like long-term care, palliative care, and dental care, are great and will likely increase as well as the population ages.

Accessibility

A second issue is accessibility. People complain of waiting lists for treatment. According to Statistics Canada, a significant increase in unmet health care needs occurred between 1994–95 and 2000–01. Self-reported unmet needs rose from 4.2 percent to 12.5 percent of the population—an estimated 3.2 million people. Respondents gave a variety of reasons for unmet needs,

the most prominent being waiting time. The percentage that gave waiting time as the reason rose from 23 percent in 1998–99 to 30 percent in 2000–01. The percentage who indicated availability of services as the reason remained stable at 14 percent, and those who presented personal circumstances, such as being too busy, as the reason declined somewhat (Statistics Canada, 2002b). The distance some people in Canada need to travel for medical health, especially in the North, has already been noted.

In Canada, a major factor affecting access to health care is region. Region can be defined in several ways. In Canada, provinces are frequently used as the measure for region. A better measure of region for health purposes is the "health region." In Canada, 119 health regions have been designated. The advantage of using this measure is that variation within provinces can be identified. Access to health care both between and within provinces can thus be addressed. For the past four years, *Maclean's* has been ranking health regions in Canada according to indicators such as life expectancy, low birth weight, incidence of pneumonia and flu, preventable hospital admissions, physicians and specialists per capita, and 10 other indicators. The "Fourth Annual Ranking" covers 54 of the 119 regions (those with populations over 125 000) and captures 87 percent of the national population (Hawaleshka, 2002:23). The ranking of health regions can be criticized for:

- choosing these particular indicators—no mention of cancer outcomes is made;
- weighting the indicators—outcomes have a weighting of 2 and resources a weighting of 1;
- ranking individual indicators instead of presenting actual rates (differences in ranking could reflect greatly or insignificantly different rates); and
- combining the indicators in an overall score when regions have high and low rankings for different indicators.

However, the "Fourth Annual Ranking" shows definite variation in Canada, where comprehensive health services are supposed to be accessible for all citizens. The ranking also seems to be reliable; a comparison with the "Third Annual Ranking" shows the same geographical differences in access to care (Marshall, 2001).

As expected, communities with medical schools (and thus, with teaching hospitals) appear among those with the best scores. Edmonton leads the list (as in the

"Second" and "Third" rankings), followed by Hamilton, Saskatoon, Ottawa, and Toronto. Thirteen of 15 "Communities with Medical Schools" appear in the top half of the ranking. The next group, "Other Major Communities," which includes wealthy suburbs like (a) North and West Vancouver and (b) Mississauga, Brampton, and Burlington (Ontario), demonstrates that communities close to major centres profit from the proximity of medical centres and people's ability to afford the quality services available. These two regions stood first and fourth in the ranking overall. The third group, "Largely Rural Communities," tends to fall in the lower half of the rankings, with the notable exceptions of Kelowna, B.C.; Nanaimo, B.C.; Lethbridge, Alberta; Levis, Quebec; and Moncton, New Brunswick. The top scorer in this group and the fifth overall, Kelowna, has developed programs to help residents stay healthy; for example, an outreach program teaches coronary-risk patients healthy habits, and a retirement community encourages residents to do as much as possible for themselves to prevent "learned helplessness" (Marshall, 2001).

Costs and Payment Methods

The overall costs of the health care system, and how they are paid, is increasingly an issue. While the overall costs of the health care system have risen, they have been contained: Health care costs were only 9 percent of the GDP in 1998, a figure very similar to that in the late 1980s. Although Canada has a single-payer, public method of financing health care, a private segment now exists in our system—for cosmetic surgery, dental practice, eyeglasses, drugs outside hospitals, and other out-patient aids. It amounts to 30 percent of the total health care expenditures in 1998 (Canadian Institute for Health Information, 2001:Figure 64). While this private-care figure is high relative to that of some European countries, it is well below the United States's comparable figure of 55 percent (Canadian Institute for Health Information, 2001:Figure 64).

In some countries with universal health care, people have an opportunity to pay for their own operations and thereby jump the public queue. The two-tier system of health care, with both public and private funding and delivery of health care, results in differential access—poorer access for those who cannot afford to pay. Pressure groups in the private sector are advocating that private clinics and services be made available for people who can afford to pay for them. But many others fear that allowing two tiers in the health system will reduce overall support for the public system. They believe that this is not a way that promotes equitable treatment.

Supply and Demand of Health Care Professionals

How can we ensure that we have enough health care professionals? Are health care networks an efficient operating model, and if so, how should practitioners be paid? After laying nurses off in the mid-1990s as a cost-cutting measure and after reducing positions in medical schools because of a fear of a surplus of doctors, Canada's provinces now face the looming possibility of a severe shortage of nurses and doctors. The Canadian Registered Nurses Association has suggested that we will need 60 000 nurses, about 25 percent of the current nursing labour force, and a survey by the College of Family Physicians predicts a shortage of 6000 family physicians (a shortfall of around 10 percent) by 2011, according to a report in the *Globe and Mail* (January 23, 2002:A5). Even if the need is exaggerated, many more of both professional groups will likely be needed to deal with an aging population and retirement of current professionals.

Not only is there a need for more professionals, but also their payment and organization of work is a concern. Doctors have seen their salaries fall somewhat in the last 30 years, and nurses have experienced several pay freezes in that time. Doctors are paid on a fee-for-service basis and have been criticized for "churning," or having patients return for multiple visits for a problem. They have also been criticized for trying to see too many in a single day. More imaginative methods of payment, like *roster,* or *capitation*—payment per patient in the care of a small network of doctors, nurses, and other health workers—where the incentive is to keep people well and reduce the care they require, should be offered. Local community health centres were formed in Quebec in the 1970s. In Ontario, some health centres offering a variety of health and social services exist. Recently, in Ontario, the Ministry of Health asked doctors if they would be interested in setting up family health networks consisting of at least five doctors and some nurses. The doctors would work normal hours, and a nurse triage system (organizing

SOCIAL PROBLEMS AND SOCIAL POLICY

BOX 10.2 Health Care: The American Model

The United States spends more on health care than any other high-income country, and it is well known for health care facilities like the Mayo Clinic and its many medical discoveries, such as drugs and diagnostic tools. Yet many people in the United States go without health care because it is too expensive. An estimated 44.3 million people in the United States had no health insurance in 1998—an increase of about 1 million people since 1997 (U.S. Bureau of the Census, 1999). About one-quarter of those not covered by health insurance are children.

Access to health care is often limited by racialization, class, or sex and gender. Do people have a *right* to health care? No, say some; it is unfortunate that some people suffer illness or disability, but it is not up to society to make the world a fair place (Engelhardt, 1996). On the contrary, say others; health care is a right, not a privilege or a choice, because the choice is ultimately between life and death, and every individual has inherent worth (Rawls, 1971). So far, the nays have it in the United States, but among developed nations, only the United States and the Union of South Africa stand together; all others provide universal health coverage for their citizens.

The United States, too, is concerned about containing health care costs. Several models are in place to deal with this cost. Many insurance companies have established an option known as *preferred provider organizations* (PPOs), with such names as HealthSelect (a Blue Cross/Blue Shield entity). In a PPO, doctors work out of their own offices on a fee-for-service basis, but contract with an insurance company to provide care for insured patients. The doctors agree to charge set (by the insurance company) fees for particular services; these fees may be higher or lower than those for other patients who are not covered by the PPO. This model of health care delivery shares certain commonalities with the health maintenance organization (HMO) and managed care models.

Like other private insurance plans, HMOs emerged during the Great Depression as a means of providing workers with health coverage at a reasonable rate by keeping costs down. A *health maintenance organization* **provides, for a fixed monthly fee, total heath care with an emphasis on prevention to avoid costly treatment later.** The doctors do not work on a fee-for-service basis, and patients are encouraged to get regular checkups and to practice good health habits (exercise and diet). As long as patients use only the doctors and hospitals that are affiliated with their HMO, they pay no fees, or only small co-payments, beyond their insurance premium (Anders, 1996). Believing that the HMO model could be a source of high profits because of its emphasis on prevention, many for-profit corporations moved into the HMO business in the 1980s (Anders, 1996). However, research has shown that pre-

ventive care is good for the individual's health but does not necessarily save money.

Early detection of HIV infection, diabetes, or high cholesterol, for example, often means a lifetime of costly treatments and drugs. Indeed, some health experts have suggested that for-profit HMOs are unlikely to provide top-notch early detection and prevention programs because of the costs—especially future costs—involved (Rosenthal, 1997). Some critics have even charged that some HMOs require their physicians to withhold vital information from their patients if it is going to cost the HMO money to provide the needed procedure or hospitalization (Gray, 1996). Recently, some HMOs have responded to such criticism (and threats of lawsuits) by allowing doctors and patients greater participation in the HMO's process of determining treatment.

Another approach to controlling health care costs is known as *managed care*—**a term that is used to refer to any system of cost containment that closely monitors and controls health care providers' decisions about medical procedures, diagnostic tests, and other services that should be provided to patients** (Weitz, 1996). In most managed care programs, patients choose a primary-care physician from a list of participating doctors. When patients need medical services, they first contact the primary-care physician; then, if a specialist is needed for treatment, the primary-care physician refers the patient to a specialist who participates in the program. Doctors must get approval before they perform certain procedures or admit a patient to the hospital. If they do not, the insurance company has the prerogative of not covering part of the cost.

Today, of the total U.S. health care bill, patients pay slightly less than 25 percent; insurance companies pay about 33 percent, and the government pays more than 40 percent (Pear, 1996). Although private health insurance companies were well established by the 1950s, and almost all working people and their immediate families had hospitalization insurance, those who did not work—the elderly and the poor—were often uninsured. Federal legislation extending health care coverage to the elderly and the poor was not passed until the 1960s. Two kinds of public insurance are available in the United States. Medicare is public health insurance, for people age 65 and over, that is funded by Social Security payments. Although Medicare provides coverage for many older people who otherwise would have no health insurance, there are large gaps in its coverage, and elderly near-poor individuals often find it difficult to pay the required deductibles (an initial specified amount that the patient pays before the insurance begins payments) and co-payments (shared costs). Also, Medicare provides only limited coverage for costly and sometimes long-term expenses such as post-hospital nursing services, home health care, nursing homes, and hospice services (Toner and Pear, 1995). Unlike Medicare coverage, which is based primarily on age, Medicaid provides medical, hospital, and long-term care for people who are poor *and* either aged, vision-impaired, or pregnant or have a disability. Also, whereas Medicare is funded by people's payments into the Social Security system, Medicaid is funded by the federal and state governments. As a result, many people view Medicaid as a welfare program and Medicare as an entitlement program—Medicare recipients are assumed to have earned medical coverage through years of hard work and paying into the system. Both programs are considered costly to the public because there are no incentives to keep costs down.

The United States' health care system is frequently thought of as a model of financing and delivery of care. Do you think it provides any solutions for the Canadian system?

patients according to the severity of their problems) would be available after hours, so that patients would have 24/7 coverage. In questionnaires sent to general practitioners, a small percentage of doctors responded positively, but others were not interested in changing their pattern of fee-for-service, perhaps because they were offered only $97 per person per year for the care (*Globe and Mail,* March 1, 2002:A8). The results suggest that a wider variety of options are likely needed if networks are to gain more support.

The Use of Alternative Health Care

Over the last decade, the interest in and the consultation of alternate health practitioners has increased. The NPHS has studied this behaviour asking respondents, "In the past 12 months, have you seen or talked to an alternate health care provider such as an acupuncturist, naturopath, homeopath or massage therapist about your physical, emotional or mental health?" (Millar, 2001:14). Chiropractors were not on this list, but were included by respondents to a question about contact with health care providers. Chiropractors were the most consulted alternative practitioner (Millar, 2001:14).

The researchers found an increase in the consultation of alternate health care providers over its three waves. In 1998–99, 17 percent of Canadians consulted them, up from 15 percent in 1994–95 (2001:12). Factors significantly related to consultation were sex, region, age, and experience of chronic pain:

- Women consulted them more than men (19 vs. 14 percent);

- Westerners consulted them more than Easterners (25 and 22 percent for B.C. and Alberta respectively vs. less than 10 percent for each of the Atlantic provinces);

- Working age people (25 to 64 years of age) consulted them more than younger or older people (19 vs. 11 percent); and

- People who experienced chronic pain consulted them more than those experiencing no pain (26 vs. 15 percent) (Millar, 2001:13).

In addition, those who believed in self-care and followed more proactive health behaviour like taking vitamins and avoiding foods with a high fat or sugar content and those who thought that the traditional system was not meeting their needs were more likely to consult alternative providers than others who did not report this behaviour or perception (Millar, 2001:17). Millar concluded that people were "supplementing, not rejecting, conventional health care" (2001:19) and suggested that as the population ages and more multiple chronic diseases emerge with accompanying pain that "the demand for alternate therapies could increase even further." (2001:20) Given the extensive use of alternative health providers, the willingness of some doctors to recommend their use, and willingness of some private insurance plans to pay for their use, the integration of alternate and traditional health providers is an important issue to be addressed.

Quality of Care

Two measures of our quality of care are: (a) Canadians' rating of the system; and, (b) reports of different patterns of medical practice, including different rates of procedures, such as surgical operations, that might be expected to have close-to-uniform rates across the country. Although Canadians' rating of their recent experience with doctors and general treatment by the system is high, the percentage rating the overall system excellent has declined substantially. According to the Conference Board of Canada, whereas 60 percent of the population rated the system as excellent or very good in 1991, only one-quarter rated it that highly in 2000 (Canadian Institute for Health Information, 2001:Table 6).

A study by sociologists Noralou P. Roos and L.L. Roos (1994) found these problems with medical intervention:

- physicians vary in their patterns of medical practice;
- evidence of benefit does not exist for certain procedures, such as Caesarian sections;
- a significant amount of care provided is inappropriate; and
- application of practice guidelines does not guarantee lower surgical rates.

Reports regularly appear about significant variation in surgical rates in different parts of Canada. For example, a study of data from 2000 reported:

- Hip replacements: an overall rate of 59.7 per 100 000 population, but a rate in Newfoundland of 35.5 per 100 000, and in Nova Scotia, 76.4 per 100 000;
- Knee replacements: an overall rate of 67.2 per 100 000 population, but a rate in Quebec of 34.4 per 100 000, and in Manitoba, 94.8 per 100 000; and
- Hysterectomies: an overall rate of 484 per 100 000 population, but a rate in Ontario of 476 per 100 000, and in Newfoundland, 750 per 100 000 (Statistics Canada, 2002bb).

This variation suggests the discretionary nature of medicine and that greater attention should be given to the study of the effectiveness of surgical and other procedures.

Use of Technology

Large flows of information take place among providers of traditional, alternative, and robotic care (e.g., surgical procedures at a distance). How will we integrate this information, with e-health, and with other forms of learning? Patients must be notified in advance about how their information is to be used and must give their permission. They must also have the opportunity to opt out of projects (e.g., drug promotions). Besides improved ways of maintaining connections among providers, the system needs a better means of keeping

track, across a variety of locations and data bases, of the treatment of individual patients, drugs prescribed, and so on. One controversial suggestion is that a chip be placed on the health card, so that doctors will have a record of the patient's history and thus be able to provide better care.

These are some of the major issues faced by our health care system. Not only do others exist, but more will emerge with the social and technological developments that are continuously taking place.

PERSPECTIVES ON ILLNESS AND HEALTH CARE PROBLEMS

What are the primary causes of health care problems in Canada? How can health care be improved? The answers that social scientists give to these questions depend on their theoretical framework. Analysts approaching these questions from a functionalist perspective focus on how illness affects the smooth operation of society and the functions medicine serves as a social institution. Some sociologists, using a conflict perspective, focus on how a capitalist economy affects health and health care delivery. Those who use an interactionist framework look at the social and cultural factors affecting communication between doctors and patients. Finally, feminist theorists look at inequalities of racialization, class, and sex and gender.

The Functionalist Perspective

The functionalist perspective views illness as a threat to a smoothly functioning society, which depends on all people fulfilling their appropriate social roles. According to this view, when people become ill, they cannot fulfill their everyday responsibilities to family, employer, or the larger society and instead adopt the *sick role*—patterns of behaviour expected from individuals who are ill. Sociologist Talcott Parsons (1951) identified four role expectations of the sick role:

1. Sick people are not responsible for their incapacity;
2. They are exempted from their usual role and task obligations;
3. They must want to leave the sick role and get well; and

4. They are obligated to seek and comply with the advice of a medical professional.

In other words, illness is a form of deviance that must be controlled. According to Parsons, physicians are the logical agents of social control. By certifying that a person is physically or mentally ill and by specifying how the ill person should behave, doctors use their professional authority to monitor people with illnesses, thereby granting them only a temporary reprieve from their usual social roles and responsibilities. Today, however, the dramatic increase in chronic illness and the disorganization in the delivery system for medical services mean that many people have less access to doctors, and doctors have less control over those aspects of patients' lives that can increase their chances of becoming ill. Acknowledging these major changes, sociologist Alexander Segall has modified the original conception of the sick role by identifying six expectations. The rights of sick people comprise

- making decisions about health-related matters;

- being exempt from performing usual well roles; and

- making use of social support and depending on others outside the medical profession;

  and the duties of sick people comprise

- maintaining health and managing illness;

- engaging in routine self-health management; and

- making use of available health care resources. (Segall and Chappell, 2000:2)

These changes take into account both the increase in chronic conditions and the need for a more active rather than passive role for the sick person.

Functionalists believe that the problems in Canadian health care are due to macrolevel changes, such as the development of high-tech medicine and drugs; restructuring of the system, including the reduction of the hospital sector; and increased demand for health care by consumers. As a result of these changes, the equilibrium of the system has been greatly affected, and procedures must be implemented to restore the equilibrium. Some observers, writing in a functionalist manner, state that incremental changes will solve the problems. For example, C. David Naylor, Dean of the Faculty of Medicine at the University of Toronto, suggests that incremental changes—such as strengthened home cares services, a more equitable coverage of prescription drugs, wider adoption of blended compensation mechanisms (e.g., salary, roster, and fee-for-service) for physicians, primary-care reform, integrated regional services, quality improvement initiatives, and better information-gathering—are the best ways for the health care system to "be rendered more accountable, integrated, and sustainable in the next millennium" (Naylor, 1999:24).

The Conflict Perspective

The conflict approach is based on the assumption that problems in health care delivery are rooted in the capitalist economy, which views medicine as a commodity produced and sold by the medical–industrial complex. The **medical–industrial complex encompasses both local physicians and hospitals as well as global health-related industries such as the pharmaceutical and medical supply companies that deliver health care** (Relman, 1992). Although this expression was coined to typify the U.S. health care system, it applies in part to the Canadian system also. For example, the pharmaceutical companies have been well known to put profits first, as outlined by physician Joel Lexchin (2002). Lexchin (2002:402) argues that when profit and health considerations come into conflict—in the examples of Lilly's anti-arthritis drug, benoxaprofen, and Bristol-Myers Squibb's statin drug, Pravachol (pravastatin)—then profit wins.

Another disturbing example of the influence of pharmaceutical companies is the treatment of Dr. Nancy Olivieri in 1997 because of her publishing research about the problems of a drug, deferiprone. The research was supported by the drug's manufacturer, Apotex, and Apotex threatened her with legal action because she broke a confidentiality agreement by publishing the research. Olivieri alleged that she was not supported, at first, by the Hospital for Sick Children or the University of Toronto, where she held appointments. She was ultimately supported by a report commissioned by the Canadian Association of University Teachers that stated that she "should be given redress for the unfair treatment she received" (Thompson, 2001:15) and that the "Hospital for Sick Children and the University of Toronto could and should have effectively supported Dr. Olivieri" (Thompson, 2001:14). After a five-year legal battle, a deal was announced on November 12, 2002, by Olivieri, the Hospital for Sick Children, and the University of Toronto, resolving all outstanding disputes.

Radical conflict theorists say that only when inequalities based on sex and gender, class, and racialization/ethnicity—and on occupation, neighbourhood, and region—are reduced and a system based on a different treatment model is developed will inequalities in health outcomes be reduced. For example, observers such as sociologists Pat Armstrong and Hugh Armstrong (1996:227) want to see a system that is oriented to a care model and not to a medical model like the present one. They advocate applying the four determinants of health identified in the Lalonde Report (by the then federal minister of health, Marc Lalonde [1974])—human biology, lifestyle, environment, and health care—to the provision of services: emphasizing health maintenance and promotion; improving occupational and income opportunities; and improving the physical and social environment. As long as variable societal conditions—environmental pollution, lack of affordable housing, high levels of stress associated with working conditions or unemployment, inadequate nutrition, lack of early diagnosis for diseases such as breast cancer and heart disease, and kind of available health model—affect people, health outcomes will be unequal.

Some conflict theorists also call attention to the unintended negative effects of doctors and suggest that the doctor–patient relationship should be demystified. An early theorist of the negative effects of doctors and the system was Ivan Illich, who coined the term *iatrogenesis*, **problems caused by doctors and the health care system**. These problems are of three types. *Clinical iatrogenesis* occurs when pain, sickness, and death result from medical care. The term the WHO uses for this is "medical misadventure." Although this topic is not well researched, the Canadian Institute for Health Information reported that in seven provinces, in 1995–96, the percentage of patients having misadventure as a result of hospitalization ranged from 0.2 percent in Manitoba and New Brunswick to 0.8 percent in Alberta and Nova Scotia (*Maclean's*, June 15, 1998:27). *Social iatrogenesis* occurs when the health care system creates dependency and ill health, for example by discouraging home births. *Cultural iatrogenesis* occurs when the system undermines the ability of people to care for themselves (Illich, 1975:165). Conflict theorists argue that if patients were given the information and resources they need for prevention, self-treatment, and home care, the need and demand for expensive medical care would be greatly reduced

(Stewart, 1995). And some of these theorists are doctors themselves. The Medical Reform Group is a Toronto-based voluntary association of physicians and medical students who believe that the medical profession must look to the social, economic, and political forces shaping health and health care in Canada. They believe that health care is a right and that today's health care is too hierarchical, giving too much power to doctors and not enough to patients. (The Medical Reform Group Web site is at **www.hwcn.org/link/mrg/**.)

Another group that challenges accepted thinking in the area of health is the disability rights organizations. They are especially concerned with the public's support of euthanasia, or mercy killing, of people with disabilities who cannot speak for themselves. A recent example of this is the Tracy Latimer story. Latimer was a 12-year-old girl with severe cerebral palsy. Her father asphyxiated her, was tried and convicted of her killing, and was sentenced to prison. Disability rights advocates argue that it would not be a problem to have a disability, were persons with disabilities not discriminated against and oppressed. In the United States, a rights group that campaigns against euthanasia is called Not Dead Yet (from the Monty Python film, *The Holy Grail*, in which someone about to be put on a cart of plague victims says, "I'm not dead yet"). (Its website is **www.notdeadyet.org**.)

In the past, most patients relied on doctors for heath-related information. Today, many people receive medical information from the media and the Internet. Many thousands of websites are devoted to health and medical information, ranging from potentially life-saving research in top medical journals to alternative therapies such as herbal preparations and colon irrigation (Fisher, 1996; Kolata, 1996b). Many computer bulletin boards, chat groups, and Usenet newsgroups have emerged to support people with conditions such as HIV/AIDS and multiple sclerosis (Kantrowitz, 1993). Some U.S. corporations have online ventures that offer not only research on any health care topic but also information on physicians, nurses, hospitals, HMOs, and preferred provider organizations—in the United States, fees come from the providers, not from users viewing the pages (Fisher, 1996). Because of the proliferation of medical information on the Internet, Health Canada is working to provide guidance to the consumer. Whether or not this proliferation of information helps to demystify doctor–patient relationships remains to be seen.

The Interactionist Perspective

Interactionists believe that many problems pertaining to health and illness in our society are linked to social factors that influence how people define our health care system. According to interactionists, we socially construct notions of crisis according to our desire to promote political objectives. Some provincial premiers, like Ralph Klein and Mike Harris, have described our system as being in a state of crisis. As noted at the beginning of this chapter, Don Mazankowski has declared, in a report for the Alberta government, that in its present form the system is unsustainable. On the other hand, Roy Romanow, who led a health care commission for the federal government, says that it is not in a state of crisis.

On February 5, 2003, the provincial premiers and Prime Minister Jean Chrétien (but not the territorial leaders) agreed to a new deal to pay for new programs to address some of the issues mentioned above. These new programs will include increased home care, relief from high drug costs (a form of pharmacare), and reduced waiting times for high-tech diagnostic tests, and will encourage the formation of networks or group clinics of family physicians and the creation of a database that will be able to link doctors', hospitals', and governments' databases. In addition, a health council will be created to report on how the money is spent and whether the provinces are meeting targets for the programs specified in the federal–provincial agreement. Money will also be made available to support existing services such as hospitals and more health programs for Indigenous people. Although the new federal money offered was substantial, $12 billion in new funds for the next three years and upwards of $35 million over five years, it was less than the recommendation in the final report of the Romanow Commission.

Interactionists are also interested in using telecommunications to promote health. A relatively new method being tried is Telehealth, a toll-free, confidential telecare service. For example, Telehealth Ontario, a program recently introduced in Ontario that follows models in other parts of the country, is a free, confidential telephone service anyone can call to get health advice or general health information from a registered nurse. Available 24 hours a day, 7 days a week, it provides information on symptoms, illness, medications, nutrition and health, help for teens, etc., but does not provide prescriptions or specific doctor referrals, and it is not a substitute for emergency (911) calls.

Interactionists also examine how individuals can construct their own health, to be producers rather than consumers of health. Writing in the interactionist manner, K. Green (1985) introduced the concept of self-health management, which recommends that people engage in practices to promote their own health—from following good health behaviour guidelines, to seeking alternative care, to seeking comfort from a friend. *Self-health management* **includes self-care practices, mutual aid, and membership in self-help groups** (Segall and Chappell, 2000:131). While the last two items are self-explanatory, the notion of self-care requires some expansion. This concept originated with Ivan Barofsky (1978) and has been developed by Alexander Segall (Segall and Chappell, 2000:135–138). Self-care comprises four components:

- *Regulatory* self-care consists of daily habits that affect health, like eating a balanced diet, getting rest, and exercising;
- *Preventive* self-care consists of deliberate actions taken to reduce the risk of illness, such as brushing and flossing teeth;
- *Reactive* self-care consists of determining what to do when one feels ill and may involve seeking over-the-counter remedies as well as seeking advice from friends or experts; and
- *Restorative* self-care consists of compliance with treatments and medications prescribed by professionals, or part compliance, according to self-determination.

Self-care emphasizes lay control over health decision-making and health maintenance.

The Feminist Perspective

Feminist theorists examine the extent to which women are treated in a disadvantageous manner in health or health care through processes like medicalization. *Medicalization* **is the treating of a person's condition as an illness.** This topic is of particular concern to women because many of women's natural conditions have been treated as physical or psychological illnesses. Deborah Findlay and Leslie Miller (2002) have written on the medicalization of women's bodies and women's lives. They begin by describing the rise of the medical profession, showing how healing became "men's work" and women's bodies "offered a lucrative new territory for profit-making" (2002:188). First, mothering, child rearing, and childbirth were defined as medical problems; then, disorders suffered by women—anorexia nervosa, for example—were defined as diseases. Findlay and Miller suggest that, in light of medical talk of "manopause" to typify such youth-seeking behaviour as undergoing cosmetic surgery, buying a sports car, and dating much younger women—men may now be about to experience the same process (2002:202). Another concern of feminists is the treatment of women in research studies.

Adequate funding for research on women's health issues and diseases is lacking, and women have been excluded from most experimental-drug trials, which are conducted to determine the positive and negative effects that a specific drug has on a given category of patients (Laurence and Weinhouse, 1994). Many clinical studies virtually ignore women. For example, although women are the group with the most rapidly increasing incidence of HIV/AIDS, very little HIV/AIDS research relating to women is being conducted (Nechas and Foley, 1994). Similarly, in a widely reported study on the effects of aspirin on heart disease, all of the patients were men, even though heart disease is the leading cause of death for both women and men (Steering Committee of the Physicians' Health Group Study, 1989).

The failure to include women in research contributes to their differential treatment for certain kinds of medical problems. For example, women with the same symptoms of kidney failure as men are much less likely to receive an organ transplant (Steingart et al., 1991). Similarly, far fewer women than men with an abnormal heart scan are referred for a procedure known as cardiac catheterization to remedy the problem. Without adequate studies, diseases in women may go unrecognized, be misdiagnosed, or be attributed to a nonphysical factor.

A third concern of feminists is the presence and treatment of women in the medical profession itself. It is well known that until recently it was not easy for women to enroll in medical faculties, and thus not easy to become a doctor. With the increase of women in medical schools came the corresponding increase in women in medicine and related health professions. In 2000, women made up more than half (53 percent) of all doctors and dentists in Canada, according to Statistics Canada's *Women in Canada: Work Chapter Updates* (2001h:8).

WHAT CAN YOU DO?

- Volunteer at an agency, like Street Health, that deals with people who are on welfare, are homeless, are recovering addicts, or are recently released from prison. Among the sociological insights you will get is an appreciation of how their health is affected by their social status—you may also make a difference in the life of a participant.

- Some students on your own campus may not be able to afford nutritious meals, especially at the end of term when meal cards and money run out. Students at York University organized a program called Food for Thought, a food bank for students. The bank gets funds from grants and student fees, gets workers from student volunteers, and gives unused food to community organizations (its website is **www.yorku.ca/food**). Other postsecondary schools have done the same. If your college or university has not created a food bank, you might see if such a need exists and then, if so, help to fill it.

- Participate in or organize a committee for research integrity at your college. Nancy Olivieri and David Healy—a professor whose offer of employment was originally cancelled at the University of Toronto (though later partially reinstated), possibly because of his criticism of Prozac—spoke at a fundraiser for Doctors for Research Integrity at the University of Toronto, sponsored by the Students' Administrative Council, to discuss the problems of the influence of commercial interests at universities. Since this is likely to be a continuing problem, much scope exists for future educational programs.

- Develop a self-care management program for yourself. Consider how you could make use of mutual aid and the self-help groups that are available on university and college campuses, and how you could follow the four types of self-care to maintain your health.

- Study the way women, and men too, are exploited for profit in cosmetic surgery and other health-related ways. Develop a seminar on body consciousness. You might start with the work of Tovee and associates (1997), who compare the BMIs (see above) of postsecondary female students, glamour and fashion models, and anorexic females. Fashion models (BMI=17.6) are halfway between the female students (a normal BMI=21.6) and anorexic females (BMI=14.7).

- If you plan to do research in this area in the future, apply for a grant from the recently formed Canadian Institute of Health Research. As one of its four directions, it plans to improve the health status of vulnerable populations and create institutes for specific populations, such as Indigenous peoples, and children and youth. Included in this list is the Institute of Gender and Health, which supports research about how sex and gender interact with other health factors, leading to different risk factors and interventions for women and for men. Of particular interest is research on gender inequalities.

SUMMARY

WHY ARE ILLNESS AND HEALTH CARE SOCIAL PROBLEMS?

Health care is a social issue because, according to the World Health Organization, health is a state of complete physical, mental, and social well-being. Although people in Canada pay less for health services than people in the United States, our measures of health show better outcomes than theirs. Thus, high expenditures do not translate into improved life expectancy for everyone.

HOW HAVE HEALTH CARE PROBLEMS CHANGED OVER THE LAST CENTURY?

Since acute illnesses (e.g., measles, polio) are largely under control with vaccinations and improved public health practices, most health problems today are chronic diseases (e.g., arthritis, diabetes, heart disease) or disabilities (e.g., back injuries, hearing or vision problems, brain injuries), which require long-term treatment. Medical advances mean that many people born with serious disabilities survive, as do many who would have died from acute illnesses or accidents in earlier times. As more people survive and live longer, more are likely to experience chronic illnesses and disabilities.

WHY IS OBESITY A SOCIAL PROBLEM?

Close to half of Canadians over 15 years of age are overweight/obese. Being overweight is related to a number of diseases, such as heart disease and Type II diabetes. People in rural Canada are more likely to be overweight than people in urban Canada. The problem exists worldwide, even in developing countries. Suggestions to reduce this problem are similar to those suggested to reduce smoking, such as warnings on packages and taxes on junk food.

WHY IS MENTAL ILLNESS A SOCIAL PROBLEM?

Mental illness is a social problem because of the number of people it affects, the difficulty in defining and identifying mental disorders, and the ways in which it is treated. Deinstitutionalization—discharging mental patients from hospitals into the community—was considered a solution to the problem of warehousing patients, but it has created new problems.

HOW DO SEX AND GENDER, CLASS, AND INDIGENOUS STATUS AFFECT PHYSICAL AND MENTAL HEALTH?

Men, the poor, and Indigenous people have lower life expectancies than women, the rich, and non-Indigenous people. Although women report more chronic conditions and disabilities than men, they do have higher disability-free life expectancies than men. The poor and elementary-educated report more disability and poorer health than the rich and highly educated. Although women report more mental illness than men, when addictive behaviour is included, men have higher rates of mental illness. Indigenous people have higher rates of suicide than non-Indigenous people.

WHAT ARE THE FIVE CHARACTERISTICS OF THE CANADIAN HEALTH CARE SYSTEM?

Our system is universal—covering all Canadians; accessible—unimpeded by financial and other barriers; and comprehensive—providing service on the basis of need. It is portable across provinces. Lastly, it is publicly managed and funded.

WHY IS HEALTH CARE CONSIDERED A PROBLEM?

With the restructuring and closing of hospitals and the capping of doctors' fees, waiting periods for care are longer, especially in emergency rooms. As well, many people have unmet health needs and use alternate health providers. Other components of care, like home care, pharmacare, and access to diagnostic equipment will, thanks to the recent agreement among the premiers and prime minister, become part of the system. Issues of quality of care and organization of doctors and other health professionals are more problematic.

WHAT ARE THE SOCIOLOGICAL EXPLANATIONS FOR HEALTH CARE PROBLEMS?

Functionalists consider the sick role a form of deviance that medicine as an institution controlled until recently. Some functionalists believe that the whole health system must be reorganized; others that incremental change is the best answer. Some conflict theorists believe that our health problems are rooted in capitalism and the medical–industrial complex. Some, like Ivan Illich, criticize the control of the system and would like to see people take more responsibility for their own health. Others, including some doctors, believe that only when sex and gender-, class-, and Indigenous status–based inequalities are reduced will inequalities in health care be reduced. Interactionists believe that communication problems between politicians and advocates create much of our concern about the health care system, but that these problems can be resolved through negotiation. They believe that people must become more involved in self-health management and health care reform. Feminists believe that women have been treated in a disadvantageous manner regarding their bodies and health, the distribution of money to diseases that affect them, and their participation in medical careers.

KEY TERMS

acute diseases,   p. 229
chronic diseases,   p. 229
deinstitutionalization,   p. 234
disability,   p. 229
disability-free life expectancy,   p. 229
health maintenance organization (HMO),   p. 239
iatrogenesis,   p. 243

infant mortality rate,   p. 229
life expectancy,   p. 228
managed care,   p. 239
medical–industrial complex,   p. 242
medicalization,   p. 244
self-health management,   p. 244
total institution,   p. 235

QUESTIONS FOR CRITICAL THINKING

1. Because Canadians take pride in their high level of life expectancy, they are usually surprised to learn that the infant mortality rate of Indigenous people is double the rate of Canadians generally. Why is this, and what do you think individuals can do at the community level to save these young lives?

2. In what ways are sex and gender, class, and Indigenous status intertwined with physical and mental illness? Consider causes and treatments.

3. Do you know people with mental illness? What do you think would help them function better in our society?

4. Now that our health care system will get additional funding for home care, pharmacare, better diagnostic services, and money for health care professionals, what would you propose next to reform the system?

WEBLINKS

Canadian Health Network (CHN)
www.canadian-health-network.ca
CHN is a national, nonprofit, bilingual, Web-based health information service. Its goal is to help Canadians find the information they are seeking on how to stay healthy and prevent disease. This network of health information providers includes Health Canada and national/provincial/territorial nonprofit organizations, universities, hospitals, libraries and community organizations. Links to over 10 000 resources are available, covering almost any health problem.

Commission on the Future of Health Care in Canada (The Romanow Commission)
www.hc-sc.gc.ca/english/care/romanow/index.html
Building on Values: The Future of Health Care in Canada, the final report of the Romanow Commission, is available for downloading.

Health Care Information Resources
www.hsl.mcmaster.ca/tomflem/top.html
Health Care Information Resources contains medical and health care resources for patients, family and friends, and health care workers.

Health Canada Online
www.hc-sc.gc.ca/english/
Health Canada Online provides an overview of health care in Canada, up-to-date information on health topics, headlines, governments' negotiations, information about diseases, etc., and links to frequently asked questions.

Medical Reform Group
www.hwcn.org/link/mrg/
The Medical Reform Group is an organization of physicians, medical students, and others committed to ensuring access to high-quality health care for all Canadians. Access links to a newsletter, briefs, and other like-minded health, social, and environmental organizations.

THE CHANGING FAMILY

I don't need a knight in shining armour to rescue me.

A university student (author's files)

It's difficult to expect people to live together for such a long time.

Another university student (author's files)

I was working from six-thirty in the morning to seven at night without breaks. I wasn't eating. I was irritable. I couldn't deal with anybody. I was fighting with my wife all the time. We were breaking apart. I wasn't communicating anymore. The job took control of me. I was possessed. I didn't feel patient with my daughter anymore. It was taking a big toll on me, and I didn't like it at all. I decided it wasn't worth it and the only way to stop it was to leave.

Ernie, a physical therapist, explaining that he resigned from a managerial position in a large corporation when he discovered that his job was damaging his family relationships (Gerson, 1993:145)

Since the divorce what's been hard is worrying about paying the bills—having enough money for food for my son. I don't even get to think about buying him new sneakers.

A 35-year-old secretary, who was married for 16 years and had one child (Kurz, 1995:90)

Many people today experience the problems described by these individuals: women wanting equality, worries about long-term commitment, the family–work dilemma, and economic hardship after divorce. Although most sociologists believe that the family as a social institution will endure in one form or another, they also acknowledge that family-related problems are a challenge not only to individuals but also to our entire society.

THE NATURE OF FAMILIES

What is a family? According to sociologist Robin Wolf (1996), that question generates heated debate: Some say that any definition of the family must emphasize tradition and stability; others argue that any useful definition must take into account diversity and social change. Traditionally, *family* has been defined as a group of people who are related to one another by blood, marriage, or adoption and who live together, form an economic unit, and bear and raise children (Benokraitis, 1993). Today, however, the traditional definition of family is often modified to incorporate diverse living arrangements and relationships such as single-parent households, cohabiting unmarried couples, domestic partnerships of lesbian or gay couples, and several generations of family members (grandparent, parent, and child) living under the same roof. To encompass all these arrangements, we will use the following definition as we look at family-related social problems: A *family is a relationship in which people live together with commitment, form an economic unit and care for any young, and consider the group critical to their identity* (Benokraitis, 1993; Lamanna and Riedmann, 1994).

Changing Family Structure and Patterns

The basis of the traditional family structure is *kinship*, **a social network of people based on common ancestry, marriage, or adoption.** Kinship is very important in pre-industrial societies because it serves as an efficient means of producing and distributing food and goods (clothing, materials for building shelter) and transferring property and power from one generation to the next. In many pre-industrial societies the primary kinship unit is the *extended family*, **a family unit composed of relatives in addition to parents and children, all of whom live in the same household.** Extended families typically include grandparents, uncles, aunts, or other relatives in addition to parents and children. When the growing and harvesting of crops is the basis of economic production, extended families mean that large numbers of people participate in food production, which can be essential to survival. Living together also enables family members to share other resources, such as shelter and transportation. Though extended families are not common in Canada, except in some immigrant communities, they are in some countries in Latin America, Africa, Asia, and parts of Eastern and Southern Europe (Busch, 1990).

With industrialization, other social institutions begin to fulfill kinship-system functions. The production and distribution of goods and services, for example, largely shifts to the economic sector. The form of kinship that is most typical in industrialized nations is the *nuclear family*, **a family unit composed of one or two parents and her/his/their dependent children who**

live apart from other relatives. The nuclear family in an industrialized society functions primarily to regulate sexual activity, socialize children, and provide family members with affection and companionship. Although many people view the two-parent nuclear family as the ideal family, in 2001, only 44 percent of Canadian families consisted of a married or common-law couple and one or more children aged 24 and under (Statistics Canada, 2002f:3). This is an 11 percent decrease since 1981, when 55 percent of families were two-parent, with-children households. Sociologists attribute the decrease to a greater number of births among unmarried women, a trend toward postponing or forgoing marriage and childbearing, and high rates of separation and divorce.

Are Canadian Families in Decline?

Will the family as a social institution disappear in the future? Social analysts answer this question differently, depending on whether they adopt a traditional definition of the family or a modified definition. Sociologist David Popenoe (1988, 1996) uses a traditional definition and believes that three trends mark the coming end of the traditional nuclear family:

■ The divorce rate has increased sharply (it currently is 232.5 per 100 000 people in Canada (Statistics Canada, 2002f), and parents increasingly decide to forgo marriage, so a sizable number of children are being raised in single-parent households apart from other relatives.

■ Large numbers of married women have left the role of full-time mother and housewife to go into the labour market, and not all the functions of the former role are being fulfilled.

■ The focus of many families has shifted away from childbearing to the needs of the adult members. Increasingly, even when parents have young children to raise, they break up if their psychological and self-development needs are unmet in the marriage relationship (Popenoe, 1995:16).

Some sociologists have suggested that if marriage and the family weaken enough and no satisfactory substitute for marriage emerges, industrial societies will not survive (Davis and Grossbard-Shechtman, 1985).

According to some analysts, research has shown that the structure of the family is undergoing profound changes around the world, in both rich and poor nations (see Box 11.1). These analysts say the family isn't declining, it's simply changing. From this social-change perspective, families are becoming more complex and diverse; they are not in a state of irreversible decline (Skolnick, 1991; Cherlin, 1992). In fact, according to sociologist Andrew Cherlin (1992), the family will last as a social institution precisely because it can adapt to social change and modify its form. However, Cherlin goes on to say that the best way to minimize the costs of change in the family unit is to modify the other social institutions of daily life—such as the economy and workplace.

Changing Views on Marriage and Families

The term *marriage* refers to a legally recognized and/or socially approved arrangement between two individuals that carries certain rights and obligations and usually involves sexual activity. In Canada, the only legal form of marriage is **monogamy, a marriage between one woman and one man.** The marriage rate (number of marriages per 1000 population) in Canada is about 5.0, down from 9.2 in 1972 (Milan, 2000:6).

Marriage was once a cultural imperative. There was "something wrong" with a person who didn't marry. But since the 1970s, people's attitudes toward marriage and the family have changed as other aspects of society have changed. Cultural guidelines on marriage and childbearing have grown weaker as our society has experienced a broader cultural shift toward autonomy and personal growth. In the 1970s, according to Cherlin (1992:127), "family life became a matter of personal choice in which individuals made decisions based on a calculus of self-interest and self-fulfillment. Marriage was still desirable, but no one any longer had to be married to be a proper member of society." Marriage also became much less of an economic necessity for women in the 1970s because of new job opportunities and rising incomes. Although women's wages remained low in comparison to men's during this time, their wages rose in absolute terms (Cherlin, 1992).

Still, marriage is a persistent preference for most people today. In a national survey conducted by Angus Reid, two-thirds of Canadian adults strongly agreed

SOCIAL PROBLEMS IN GLOBAL PERSPECTIVE

BOX 11.1 The Changing Family around the World

Yelena Polyakovskaya lives with her 6-month-old baby, relying on friends and babysitters to watch Aleksandr when she is at work. The father, an unmarried journalist, has never seen his child. Her 6-year-old son, Simeon, is being raised by his grandmother and great-grandmother in Kiev. Polyakovskaya says she hopes to bring him to Moscow, but cannot even afford train fare to visit him.

She loves her job covering music and ballet, but it is ill paid. In her bare one-room apartment, she sleeps on a tiny, fold-out couch next to the baby's crib. An ironing board serves as a desk. But like many women raising children alone, she said she does not want to marry again.

"My life is difficult," she said, "but God, if I had to come home from work and clean, cook and iron for a husband who keeps telling me I am doing it wrong, it would be even worse."

Yelena Polyakovskaya, age 32, a television reporter in Russia (Stanley, 1995)

Yelena Polyakovskaya is one of a growing number of women in Russia raising her family without a husband. Approximately 15 to 20 percent of Russian families are single-parent households. This is similar to Canada, but in Russia, single mothers span all social strata; in Canada, single-parent households are much more likely to be poor (Ross et al., 2000:145). In Japan, single-parenthood because of abandonment or divorce is rare, but a practice called tanshin hunin has the same effect. When middle-managers are transferred, they go without their families so that their children don't have to change schools. When possible, the fathers commute home on weekends, but the mothers are essentially single parents (O'Connell, 1994).

Increasing single-parenthood is just one worldwide trend. According to Judith Bruce, author of a report published by the Population Council, a nonprofit group in New York, "trends like unwed motherhood, rising divorce rates, smaller households and the feminization of poverty are not unique to America, but are occurring worldwide" (Lewin, 1995). Among the report's findings are the following:

- Divorce rates are rising. In many developed countries, the divorce rates doubled between 1970 and 1990; in less developed countries, about one-quarter of first marriages end by the time women are in their forties.

- Unwed motherhood is increasing virtually everywhere.

- Children in single-parent households are more likely to be poor than are children in two-parent households, especially when the parent is the mother (often termed the feminization of poverty).

Though the reason varies from country to country, more women are entering the work force and taking increasing economic responsibility for children. For example, in Bangladesh, older husbands frequently take young wives. When a husband dies, the wife must find work to support her children. In Asia, if a father who migrates for better work opportunities stops sending money, the mother must support the family herself. In sub-Saharan Africa, a woman's husband may go on to another polygamous marriage and support those children instead (Lewin, 1995).

The fact that families around the world are changing in similar ways shows that there is nothing inevitable about the form of the family or the roles of women and men even within a single society (O'Connell, 1994). The fact of so much change in the most basic unit of society also poses important questions for the 21st century. Is the basic problem really inequality between women and men? Would shared responsibilities in the home and equal opportunities in the workplace create better families? Can some general principles for social policies be developed, given vastly different societal conditions? What do you think?

---

that their families were the greatest joy in their lives (Angus Reid, 1994, cited in Milan, 2000:5). According to the 1995 General Social Survey (GSS), 98 percent of those in marriages and 96 percent of those in common-law unions feel that a long-term relationship is important for their happiness (quoted in Milan, 2000:5).

The divorce rate (number of divorces per 1000 population) in Canada during the 20th century has varied from being almost nonexistent in the early 1900s to an all-time high of 3.6 in 1987; by 2000 it had declined to 2.3 (Milan, 2000:7 and Statistics Canada, 2002f). Though many believe marriage should last "until death do us part," others feel marriage is a commitment "for as long as love allows." Through a pattern of marriage, divorce, and remarriage, many people reaffirm their belief in the institution of marriage but not to the individual they initially married. This pattern of successive marriages, in which a person has several spouses over a lifetime but is legally married to only one partner at a time, is referred to as *serial monogamy*. Some social analysts consider serial monogamy a natural adaptation to other social changes in society; others think it is detrimental to individuals and to society and serves as further evidence of the decline of the family (see Popenoe, 1996). Who is right? As with other social problems we have examined, the view of causes, effects, and possible solutions for family-related problems depends on the theoretical framework the analyst uses.

PERSPECTIVES ON FAMILY-RELATED PROBLEMS

What purposes do families serve in contemporary societies? Do families create problems for society or solve them? The latter, say functionalists, who believe that the family fulfills important functions for individuals at the microlevel and for the entire society at the macrolevel. Conflict and feminist theorists, on the other hand, consider families a primary source of inequality—and sometimes abuse and violence—in society. Taking a microlevel approach, interactionists analyze family-related social problems in terms of socialization and social interactions among family members.

The Functionalist Perspective

Functionalists emphasize the importance of the family in maintaining the stability of society and the well-being of individuals. According to Emile Durkheim, marriage is a microcosmic replica of the larger society; both marriage and society involve a mental and moral fusion of physically distinct individuals (Lehmann, 1994). Durkheim also believed that a division of labour contributed to greater efficiency in marriage and families (and in all areas of life). In his study of family life in the United States, socioloist Talcott Parsons (1955) also viewed a division of labour as important. He saw the husband in an ideal nuclear family as fulfilling an *instrumental role*—meeting the family's economic needs, making important decisions, and providing leader-

ship—and the wife as fulfilling an *expressive role*—running the household, caring for children, and meeting family members' emotional needs.

Using Durkheim's and Parsons's work as a basis for their model of the family, contemporary functionalists believe that a division of labour makes it possible for families to fulfill a number of functions that no other social institution in high-income nations can perform as efficiently and effectively:

1. Regulate sexual behaviour and reproduction: Families are expected to regulate the sexual activity of their members and thus control reproduction so that it occurs within specific boundaries. Sexual regulation of family members by the family is supposed to protect the *principle of legitimacy*—the belief that all children should have a socially and legally recognized father (Malinowski, 1964).

2. Socialize and educate children: Parents and other relatives are responsible for teaching children the values and norms of their culture.

3. Provide economic and psychological support: Families are responsible for providing for their members' physical (food, shelter) and emotional needs.

4. Provide social status: Families confer social status on their members, including *ascribed statuses* such as racialization, ethnicity, nationality, class, and religious affiliation, although some of these statuses may change later in life.

Considering their view of the family, functionalists believe that problems in the family are a social crisis. The functional family provides both social order and economic stability by providing for the survival and development of children; the physical and emotional health of adults; and the care of those who are sick, injured, elderly, and have disabilities. The family is also the front line for reinforcing society's norms and values. Functionalists consider the family to be part of the solution to many problems faced by people in contemporary societies. In this view, dysfunctions in families are problems that threaten the well-being of individuals, groups, and nations.

Functionalists believe that changes in other social institutions, such as the economy, religion, education, law, medicine, and the government, contribute to family-related problems. For example, some functionalists think that changing the law to recognize no-fault divorce contributes to higher rates of divorce and dramatically increases single-parent households, which do not provide children with the nurture and guidance they get in a two-parent home (Popenoe, 1996).

The Conflict Perspective

Most conflict analysts believe that functionalist views on family problems are idealized and inadequate. Rather than operating harmoniously and for the benefit of all members, families, these analysts say, are sources of social inequality and conflict over values, goals, and access to resources and power.

Conflict theorists who focus on class relations in capitalist economies compare family members to workers in a factory, emphasizing the inequality in each institution. Women are dominated by men in the home just as workers are dominated by managers and capitalists in factories (Engels, 1972). As wives and mothers, women contribute to capitalism by producing the next generation of workers and providing the existing labour force with food, clean clothes, and emotional support. Women's work in the family not only benefits the capitalist class, it reinforces women's subordination because the work is unpaid and often devalued. This unpaid work has received much attention in research on the family in Canada. According to Statistics Canada, in 1992 adult Canadians spent 25 billion hours on unpaid work, or 1164 hours per adult, and women spent 78 percent more time on unpaid work than men. Meal preparation and cleaning were the most time-consuming activities, but childcare and other caregiving, volunteer work, and home maintenance were also time consuming. Using the replacement-cost method of valuing work, a wage rate paid to people who do similar work, the value of unpaid work totaled about $11 000 per adult in 1992. In total, these activities were worth $235 billion, or approximately one-third of the GDP (Jackson, 1996: 29).

The Feminist Perspective

Many feminist theorists think that male dominance and female subordination began long before capitalism and the private ownership of property arose as an economic system (Mann, 1994). They see women's subordination as rooted in patriarchy, particularly in men's control over women's labour power. At the same time

that women's labour in the home is directed by men, it is undervalued, which allows men to benefit from their status as the family breadwinner (Firestone, 1970; Goode, 1982). In a more recent study, sociologist Jane Riblett Wilkie (1993) found that most men are reluctant to relinquish their status as family breadwinner. Although only 15 percent of the families in Canada are supported solely by a male breadwinner, many men continue to construct their ideal of masculinity based on this role. It is acceptable for wives to enter the paid work force if their role is simply to earn money; they should not, however, challenge the ideal roles of male breadwinner and female homemaker.

Like conflict theorists, feminist theorists argue that family problems derive from inequality—not just within the family, but in the political, social, and economic arenas of the larger society as well (Aulette, 1994). In fact, pervasive societal inequality leads to one of the most tragic family problems: wife battering. According to feminist theorists, wife battering and other forms of domestic violence may even be conscious strategies that men use to control women and perpetuate gender inequality (Kurz, 1989). Almost 55 percent of all female murder victims are killed by current or former husbands or boyfriends. In contrast, only 7 percent of all male murder victims are killed by current or former wives or girlfriends (Fedorowycz, 2001, and see Chapter 9). According to feminist theorists, family-related problems, including domestic violence and wife battering, can be solved only if all social institutions work to eliminate the subordination of women in society. Increased educational and occupational opportunities for women over the last quarter-century may be contributing to a reduction in domestic violence. From 1974 to 2000, the number of women killed by their husbands dropped 65 percent, from 16.5 to 6.3 per million couples, and the number of men killed by their wives also dropped 50 percent, from 4 to 2 per million couples (Statistics Canada, 2002i). Related to increased opportunities for women, the increase in the age of first marriage may be another contributing factor (see "Postponing Marriage," below) to the decline in violence.

The Interactionist Perspective

Some interactionists view the family communication process as integral to understanding the diverse roles that family members play; therefore these analysts examine how husbands, wives, and children act out their roles and react to the parts played by others. Although societies differ widely on the rules and norms that should shape family and kin relationships, people are socialized to accept their society's form of the family as the acceptable norm. According to sociologists Peter Berger and Hansfried Kellner (1964), marital partners develop a shared reality through their interactions with each other. Although newlyweds bring separate identities to a marriage, over time they construct a shared reality as a couple. In the process, the partners redefine their past identities to be consistent with their new realities. Interactionists say that the process of developing a shared reality is continuous and occurs not only in the family but in any group in which the couple participates together. In cases of separation and divorce, the process is reversed: Couples may start with a shared reality but once again become individuals with separate realities in the process of uncoupling their relationship.

How do interactionists explain problems in a family? Some look at the subjective meanings and interpretations people give to their everyday lives. According to sociologists Charles Jones, Lorna Marsden, and Lorne Tepperman (1990), over the past few decades, women have gained more choice and opportunities in life. Women have become more "individualized." One of the consequences of this dramatic change is that women have few role models to follow; as a result, new expectations about work and child rearing could cause problems for the family. Obviously, men would also be uncertain about how to behave with these changed expectations. According to sociologist Jessie Bernard (1982), women and men experience marriage differently. While the husband may see *his marriage* very positively, the wife may feel less positive about *her marriage*. The reverse may also be true. Evidence for the different realities of marriage comes from research that shows that husbands and wives often give very different accounts of the same event (Safilios-Rothschild, 1969).

Still other interactionists view family problems in terms of partners' unrealistic expectations about love and marriage, which can lead to marital dissatisfaction and, sometimes, divorce. These analysts note that our culture emphasizes *romantic love*—a deep and vital emotion based on significant need satisfaction, caring for and acceptance of another person, and the devel-

opment of an intimate relationship (Lamanna and Riedmann, 1994). Indeed, most couples in Canada get married because they are in love, but being a "nation of lovers" doesn't mean that men and women have the same ideas about what constitutes romantic love. According to sociologist Francesca Cancian (1990), women tend to express their feelings verbally, whereas men tend to express their love through such nonverbal actions as preparing dinner or doing household repairs. Women may not always interpret these actions as signs of love. One man complained (Rubin, 1976:146), "What does she want? Proof? She's got it, hasn't she? Would I be knocking myself out to get things for her—like to keep up this house—if I didn't love her? Why does a man do things like that if not because he loves his wife and kids? I swear, I can't figure what she wants." His wife replied, "It's not enough that he supports us and takes care of us. I appreciate that, but I want him to share things with me. I need for him to tell me his feelings."

Whatever their different viewpoints on marriage and family, most social theorists agree on one fact: Three decades ago, the nuclear family was the most common family form, and today it is only one of many patterns.

DIVERSITY IN INTIMATE RELATIONSHIPS AND FAMILIES

Greater diversity in intimate relationships and families in Canada has come about because of dramatic increases in (1) singlehood, (2) postponing marriage, (3) living together without marriage (called common-law, cohabitation, or domestic partnerships), (4) dual-earner marriages, and (5) one-parent families.

Singlehood

Although some young singles will eventually marry, 10 percent of the population will remain single for their lives. When this figure is combined with those who have been widowed, separated, or divorced, the proportion of the Canadian population that lives in one- or single-person households is 25 percent, according to the 2001 Census (Statistics Canada, 2002p:5). Some people choose singlehood over marriage because it means greater freedom from commitments to another person. Others choose it because of increased career opportunities (especially for women), the availability of sexual partners without marriage, the belief that the single lifestyle is full of excitement, or the desire for self-sufficiency and freedom to change and experiment (Stein, 1976, 1981). Though some analysts think that individuals who prefer to remain single hold more individualistic values and are less family-oriented than are people who choose to marry, sociologist Peter Stein (1981) has found otherwise: Many singles still feel a strong need for intimacy, sharing, and continuity and, as a result, develop relationships with other singles, valuing friends and personal growth more highly than marriage and children (Cargan and Melko, 1982; Alwin et al., 1985).

Some people are single not by choice but by necessity. Because of structural changes in the economy, many young working-class people cannot afford to marry and set up their own households. Indeed, some college graduates have found that they cannot earn enough money to set up households separate from those of their parents (Boyd and Norris, 1999).

Postponing Marriage

Young people today are less eager to get married than they were two decades ago; many are remaining single into their late twenties. In 1997, the average age at which men first married was 29.5 years, and the average age for women was 27.4 years (Milan, 2000:6). Although the age at which people marry for the first time has been rising steadily since the 1950s, it has accelerated since the 1970s. Between 1970 and today, the proportion of women aged 25 to 29 who have never married has tripled.

Why are more people postponing first marriages? Although some reasons are the same as those for staying single, sociologist Robin Wolf (1996) suggests four key factors: (1) economic uncertainty due to the changing job structure in Western societies; (2) women's increasing participation in the labour force; (3) the sexual revolution of the 1970s that made sexual relationships outside marriage more socially acceptable; and, (4) the rising divorce rate—young people watching their parents divorce may be less anxious to jump into marriage themselves. Other analysts suggest that a significant increase in cohabitation and domestic partnerships also contributes to the percentage of people who are counted as single or postponing marriage.

Common-law, Cohabitation, and Domestic Partnerships

The popularity of cohabitation has increased in the past two decades. **Common-law, or *cohabitation*, is two unmarried adults living together in a sexual relationship without being legally married.** According to the 2001 Census, 1.158 million couples—14 percent of all couples—were living common-law, up from 5.6 percent from 1981. Now almost 40 percent of men and women aged 30 to 39 are expected to choose common-law as their first union (Statistic Canada, 2002e:3). The proportion of cohabiting couples still varies significantly by language spoken. In Quebec, 30 percent of all couples were living common-law in 2001 (Statistics Canada, 2002p:5). This seems counter-intuitive in a predominantly Roman Catholic province. What do you think?

For some couples, cohabitation is a form of trial marriage and constitutes an intermediate stage between dating and marriage. According to anthropologist Margaret Mead (1966), dating patterns do not adequately prepare people for marriage and parenting responsibilities. Mead proposed a two-stage marriage process, each with its own ceremony and responsibilities. In the first stage, the individual marriage, two people would make a serious commitment to each other but agree not to have children during this stage. In the second stage, the parental marriage, the couple would decide to have children and to share responsibility for their upbringing. Many people today seem to be following this pattern, though without intention, and with different partners. Divorce in the first couple of years of marriage is quite common, and the break-up of a common-law relationship is even more likely. *American Demographics* editor Pamela Paul, having been through an early divorce herself, interviewed 60 other young, divorced couples and wrote a book about what she called a "starter marriage." She claimed that most of her sample had not given marriage much thought before getting married; they had developed "matrimania" due to a marriage-oriented culture (Paul, 2002).

For other couples, cohabitation is not necessarily a first step toward marriage. In one study, researchers found that slightly more than 50 percent of cohabitation relationships eventually culminated in marriage, whereas 37 percent broke up and 10 percent were still ongoing at the time of the study (London, 1991).

Does cohabitation contribute to marital success? The evidence is mixed. Some studies show that cohabitation has little or no effect on marital adjustment, emotional closeness, satisfaction, and intimacy (Watson and DeMeo, 1987). Other studies indicate that couples who cohabit first are more likely to divorce than those who do not (Bennett et al., 1988). Apparently, partners in this study who had cohabited were less satisfied with their marriage and less committed to the institution of marriage than were those who had not lived together before marrying. The researchers theorized that cohabitation may contribute to people's individualistic attitudes and values, while making them more aware that alternatives to marriage exist (Axinn and Thornton, 1992; Thomson and Colella, 1992).

Many gay and lesbian couples consider themselves married and living in a lifelong commitment. Because the law has not, historically, allowed them to marry legally, they establish *domestic partnerships* (see Chapter 6). This law, however, is changing; 260 gay marriages have occurred in Toronto since June 10, 2003 and at the time of publication. According to the 2001 Census, 34 200 couples, or 0.5 percent of all couples in Canada, are same-sex couples (Statistics Canada, 2002p:4). To make their commitment public, some couples exchange rings and vows under the auspices of churches such as the Metropolitan Community Church (the Toronto gay church). Different provinces have developed different arrangements to extend rights to domestic partners. As Canadian families continue to diversify, federal and provincial governments will have to act to ensure the protection of the rights of the members of these relationships.

Dual-Earner Marriages

More than 60 percent of all marriages in Canada are *dual-earner marriages,* **marriages in which both spouses are in the labour force.** Over half of all employed women hold full-time, year-round jobs, and in a change from the past, there are more married women with young children in the paid labour force today than ever before.

Many married women who are employed outside the household face hours of domestic work and childcare when they get home. Sociologist Arlie Hochschild

(1989) refers to the later half of women's dual workdays as the *second shift,* **—the domestic work that many employed women perform at home after completing their workday on the job.** According to Hochschild, the unpaid housework that women do on the *second shift* (see Chapter 4) amounts to an extra month of work each year. In households with small children or many children, the amount of housework increases (Hartmann, 1981). Across racialization and class lines, numerous studies confirm that domestic work remains primarily women's work (Gerstel and Gross, 1995).

In recent years, more husbands have been sharing some of the household and childcare responsibilities, especially when the wife's earnings are essential to family finances (Perry-Jenkins and Crouter, 1990). But even when husbands assume some of the household responsibilities, they typically spend much less time in these activities than do their wives (see Coverman, 1989). Women and men perform different household tasks, and the deadlines for their work vary widely.

Recurring tasks that have specific times for completion (such as bathing a child or cooking a meal) tend to be the women's responsibility, whereas men are more likely to do the periodic tasks that have no highly structured schedule (such as mowing the lawn or changing the oil in the car) (Hochschild, 1989).

Couples with more egalitarian ideas about women's and men's roles tend to share more equally in food preparation, housework, and childcare (Wright et al., 1992). An *egalitarian family* is one in which the partners share power and authority equally. As women have gained new educational and employment opportunities, a trend toward more egalitarian relationships has become evident in Canada. Some degree of economic independence makes it possible for women to delay marriage or to terminate a problematic marriage (O'Connell, 1994). For some men, the shift to a more egalitarian household occurs gradually, as the following quotation indicates:

> It was me taking the initiative, and also Connie pushing, saying, "Gee, there's so much that has to be done." At first I said, "But I'm supposed to be the breadwinner," not realizing she's also the breadwinner. I was being a little blind to what was going on, but I got tired of waiting for my wife to come home to start cooking, so one day I surprised the hell out [of] her and myself and the kids, and I had supper waiting on the table for her. (Gerson, 1993:170)

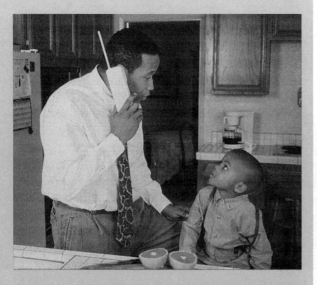

In the age of dual-earner marriages, it has become increasingly important for fathers to assume childcare and household duties. How does this photo show the competing demands faced by many employed parents?

Problems associated with providing economic support for the family and rearing children are even more pressing in many one-parent households.

Comparing Two-Parent and One-Parent Households

When the mother and father in a two-parent household truly share parenting, children have the benefit of two primary caregivers. Some researchers have found that when fathers take an active part in raising the children the effect is beneficial for all family members. Fathers find that increased contact with their children provides more opportunities for personal and emotional gratification (Coltrane, 1989).

However, living in a two-parent family does not guarantee children a happy childhood. Children whose parents argue constantly, are alcoholics, or abuse them have a worse family experience than do children in a single-parent family where there is a supportive environment. Women who are employed full-time and are single parents probably have the greatest burden of all. These women must fulfill their paid employment duties and meet the needs of their children and the household, often with little help from ex-husbands or relatives.

How prevalent are one-parent households? The past two decades have seen a significant increase in one-parent households due to divorce, death of a parent, and births outside of marriage. In 2001, lone-parent families made up 16 percent of the total families in Canada (Statistics Canada 2002p:3). Who heads most one-parent households? Today, 83 percent of all one-parent families are headed by single mothers. Men are heads of about 17 percent of one-parent families (Statistics Canada, 2002s:27); a study of one-parent households headed by fathers found that most of the men had very positive relationships with their children (Risman, 1987).

What effect does a one-parent household have on children? According to one study based on six nationally representative data sets of more than 25 000 children from various racialized and social-class backgrounds in the United States, children growing up with only one biological parent are at risk of serious problems, including poor academic achievement, dropping out of school, drug and alcohol abuse, teen pregnancy, early marriage, and divorce (McLanahan and Sandefur, 1994). Obviously, living in a one-parent family does not necessarily cause these problems. Factors such as poverty, discrimination, unsafe neighbourhoods, and high crime rates must also be considered. (See also the section below on parenting styles, for another important factor.) In fact, other researchers have found some benefits to growing up in a one-parent family (Lauer and Lauer, 1991). For example, children in one-parent families are often less pressured to conform to rigid gender roles. Rather than having chores assigned by gender, as is common in two-parent families, single-parent children typically take on a wider variety of tasks and activities. Many single-parent children also show high levels of maturity and self-sufficiency earlier because they have to help out at a younger age than do children in other families (Lauer and Lauer, 1991).

What about the fathers of children in one-parent households headed by women? Although some fathers remain involved in their children's lives, others only occasionally take their children out for recreational activities or buy them presents on birthdays and holidays. Personal choice, workplace demands on time and energy, location of the ex-wife's residence, and limitations placed on visitation by custody arrangements are all factors that affect how often absentee fathers visit their children. Increasingly, parents are receiving joint custody of their children, and it appears that joint custody can minimize the disruption of divorce in a child's life, if the ex-spouses cooperate with each other and live in relatively close geographical proximity. Ex-spouses who constantly argue or live far away from each other can create serious problems for "commuter" children, as author David Sheff (1995:64) describes:

> My son began commuting between his two homes at age 4. . . . The commuter flights . . . were the only times a parent wasn't lording over him, so he was able to order Coca-Cola, verboten [forbidden] at home. . . . But such benefits were insignificant when contrasted with his preflight nightmares about plane crashes. . . . Like so many divorcing couples, we divided the china and art and our young son. . . . For the eight years since, he has been one of the thousands of American children with two homes, two beds, two sets of clothes and toys, and two toothbrushes.

The transition from a two-parent family to a one-parent family is only one of many child-related family issues that many people today must deal with, as we discuss in the next section.

CHILD-RELATED FAMILY ISSUES

One of the major issues facing many individuals and families today is reproductive freedom, a term that implies both the desire *to have* and the desire *not to have* a child. As sociologists Leslie King and Madonna Harrington Meyer (1997:8) explain:

> The average woman is fertile, and therefore must attempt to control her reproductivity, for one-half of her life. For most women, it is the preoccupation with preventing births that consumes their health care dollars and energies; for a small minority, it is the preoccupation with achieving a birth that dominates. The ability to control fertility is, to a great extent, linked to access to various forms of reproductive health services, including contraceptives and infertility treatments.

Reproductive Freedom, Contraception, and Abortion

Reproductive freedom has been a controversial issue throughout much of Canadian history. In 1869, the Canadian government banned abortion. It was not until one hundred years later that a bill was passed making it possible, with the judgment of three doctors in a hospital that a women's life or health was in danger, for a woman to get an abortion. That bill, introduced in 1967 by then Justice Minister and future Prime Minister Pierre Elliott Trudeau with the famous expression "The state has no business in the bedrooms of the nation!" also legalized homosexuality and contraception. Earlier in the 1960s the "Pill" was introduced and public opinion about women's reproductive freedom began to change. By 1971, the "Pill" was the most popular form of contraception in Canada (Bélanger, 1998:17). Many women spend about 90 percent of their fertile years trying to avoid pregnancy (Gold and Richards, 1994).

Over the last 25 years, the methods of contraception have changed greatly. According to the General Social Survey of 1995, the use of contraceptive sterilization has doubled in that time. In 1976, whereas 30.5 percent of couples used sterilization, by 1995, 56.1 percent of couples, mostly older couples, with two or more children, were using sterilization (e.g., tubal ligation or vasectomy) (Bélanger, 1998:17). Since 1976, there has also been a decline in the use of the pill and an increase in the use of condoms. Perhaps this is because of the cost. For example, at Shoppers' Drug Mart, different types of oral contraceptives cost about $170 to $300 per year, and one dose of an after-pill to prevent pregnancy costs almost $30. Perhaps men are willing to take more responsibility for contraception and are more concerned about the spread of sexually transmitted diseases (Bélanger, 1998:19).

Although the law permitted abortion, it was not always easy to obtain one. Some provinces were not sympathetic to abortions, and some hospitals did not set up committees to judge the situations. Because he felt that women had a basic right to abortions, Dr. Henry Morgenthaler started to perform abortions in a clinic in Montreal. Since he was breaking the law, he was tried three times, but no jury would convict him. He took his case to the Supreme Court of Canada and won. The law permitting abortions under strict circumstances was declared unconstitutional in 1988. The next year, the federal government tried once again to pass an abortion bill, but it was defeated in the Senate. No provincial government has tried to pass a bill on abortion since that time, and opportunities for abortion did increase in the 1990s. However, policy on abortion has varied among the provinces:

For a number of decades, there have been intense public confrontations between abortion rights advocates and members of the anti-abortion movement. Demonstrators are a familiar sight outside abortion clinics, hospitals, and government buildings.

- Prince Edward Island refused to provide any abortion services;

- New Brunswick and Manitoba refused to fund abortions; and

- Nova Scotia and Quebec provided only partial payment for abortions.

To provide direct and immediate help, Morgentaler set up clinics in several Canadian cities, but not without a struggle: in 1992, his clinic in Toronto was bombed.

Opposition to abortion was strong into the mid-1990s. In 1994, a doctor who performed abortions, Garson Romalis, was shot in Vancouver, British Columbia. Two other anti-abortion shootings took place, one in Ontario in 1995, and one in Manitoba in 1997. While protesting at clinics has continued, no further serious attacks have occurred. This may be due to a decline in the number of abortions being performed. In 1999, 65 627 abortions were performed for women from all provinces and territories, except

Ontario, where data was not available. This is a decrease of 3.2 percent from 1998. Abortions are mostly given to young women, and the abortion rate for women in their twenties is about 27 per 1000 women. Now, there is about one abortion for every three live births in Canada (Statistics Canada, 2002t).

At the microlevel, abortion is a solution for some pregnant women and their families but a problem for others, particularly when they face religious or family opposition. At the macrolevel, abortion is both a problem and a solution when activists try to influence the making and enforcement of laws pertaining to women's reproductive rights and the control of new reproductive technologies.

Infertility and New Reproductive Technologies

Infertility is defined as an inability to conceive after a year of unprotected sexual relations. In 40 percent of

TABLE 11.1	Forms of Assisted Reproductive Technology
Name	**Description**
In vitro fertilization (IVF)	Eggs that were produced as a result of administering fertility drugs are removed from the woman's body and fertilized by sperm in a laboratory dish. The embryos that result from this process are transferred to the woman's uterus.
Micromanipulation	Viewing the process through a microscope, a specialist manipulates egg and sperm in a laboratory dish to improve the chances of a pregnancy.
Cryopreserved embryo transfer (cpe)	Embryos that were frozen after a previous assisted reproductive technology procedure are thawed and then transferred to the uterus.
Egg donation	Eggs are removed from a donor's uterus, fertilized in a laboratory dish, and transferred to an infertile woman's uterus.
Surrogacy	An embryo is implanted in the uterus of a woman who is paid to carry the fetus until birth. The egg may come from either the legal or the surrogate mother, and the sperm may come either from the legal father or a donor.

Source: "High-Tech Pregnancies Test Hope's Limit," by Trip Gabriel, 1996, New York Times (January 7):1, 10–11.

the cases, the woman is infertile, and in another 40 percent, the man is infertile; 20 percent of the time, the cause is impossible to determine (Gabriel, 1996).

Sexually transmitted diseases are a leading cause of infertility: Each year, many women become infertile as a result of a sexually transmitted disease that develops into pelvic inflammatory disease (Gold and Richards, 1994). There are also some women—both married and unmarried—who would like to have a child but cannot because of disabilities. Some analysts point out that a growing number of prospective parents delay childbearing into their thirties and forties, by which time it may be more difficult for them to conceive.

About 50 percent of infertile couples who seek treatment can be helped by conventional, low-tech treatments such as fertility drugs, artificial insemination, and surgery to unblock fallopian tubes. The other 50 percent require advanced technology, sometimes called assisted reproductive technology (ART). Many middle- and upper-income couples, for example, receive in vitro fertilization (IVF), which, according to the Infertility Awareness Association of Canada, costs a minimum of $7000 and up to $10 000 (with travel and drugs) per attempt (see Table 11.1). Despite the popularity of such treatments and the growth of fertility clinics (from 30 slightly over a decade ago to more than 300 today), only one in five couples who receive ART actually become parents (Gabriel, 1996). In Canada,

only the Ontario Hospital Insurance Plan (OHIP) will cover up to three cycles of treatment and only then if the fallopian tubes are completely blocked. Typically, very few private insurance plans will cover this procedure because it is perceived to be too expensive. (Infertility Awareness Association of Canada, 2003). For couples like Michael and Stephanie Plaut, who have spent three years and thousands of dollars trying to have a baby through IVF and other procedures, every unsuccessful attempt is traumatic. Journalist Felicia Lee (1996:A1) has documented the trauma the couple undergoes: "Michael Plaut answered the telephone. . . [and the] call confirmed his worst fear: the pregnancy test was negative. The Plauts sobbed, held each other and then had a glass of Scotch. 'It's like we're in a period of mourning,' Mrs. Plaut said. 'You just get to the point where you want this to be over.'" Couples like the Plauts who have their hopes raised by the new reproductive technologies only to find that they do not work for them often form support groups. Many couples finally decide to remain childless, but some adopt one or more children.

Adoption

Adoption is a legal process through which the rights and duties of parenting are transferred from a child's biological and/or legal parents to new legal parents. The adopted child has all the rights of a biological child. In most adoptions, a new birth certificate is issued, and the child has no further contact with the biological parents, although now agencies are arranging for people to meet their biological parents or children.

Matching children who are available for adoption with prospective adoptive parents can be difficult. The children often have specific needs, and prospective parents often specify the kind of children they want to adopt. Because many prospective parents do not want to adopt children who are non-White (most prospective parents are White), older, or have disabilities or diseases, many children available for adoption are not chosen, and instead move from foster home to foster home (Zelizer, 1985).

Prospective parents frequently want infants, but fewer infants are available for adoption than in the past because contraception and abortion are more readily available, and more unmarried teenage parents are deciding to keep their babies. Some teenagers, however, believe that adoption is the best way to solve the problem of early childbearing. Christina, one of many teenagers facing the realities of an early pregnancy and lack of resources to meet the child's needs, explained her decision this way:

> I know I can't keep my baby. I can't give it all the things a baby needs and I sure can't dump it on my parents because they can't afford to take care of their own family. I've decided to give it up for adoption. I think it's better for the baby to give it up to parents who can't have a baby themselves. I think that I'm really doing a favour to my baby, although I'm always going to wonder what it looks like and what it's doing. (Luker, 1996:163)

Because fewer infants are available for adoption, some Canadians are adopting through a private agency or from a foreign country (e.g., Romania, Russia, and China).

Parenting Style

Besides the influence of factors like low income and family structure, other factors, like the way parents treat their children, affect children's development. To study the effect of parenting styles on child development, a massive study was begun in 1994. The National Longitudinal Survey of Children and Youth (NLSCY) is a study of 23 000 families that is investigating a wide

Many parents who adopt one or more children also add to the racialized/ethnic diversity of their household. What can children and adolescents learn from growing up with others whose background is not identical to their own?

variety of variables, like income, family structure, and parenting style, on child development. Parenting style is based on responses to questions about being

- rational (e.g., How often do you think that the kind of punishment you give him/her depends on your mood?);
- responsive (e.g., How often do you praise?);
- reasoning (e.g., When your child breaks the rules... do you: (a) calmly discuss the matter? And (b) describe alternative ways of behaving . . . ?); and
- firm (e.g., When you give him/her a command to do something, what proportion of the time do you make sure that he/she has done it?).

Based on answers to questions like these, the parents are divided into four groups ranging from positive (warm and nurturing) to ineffective (very intolerant and erratic). Among the first findings the researchers made was that parenting style had more effect on behavioural problems than family structure or income. Children living with two parents with poor parenting skills were five times more likely to have such developmental problems as aggression, hyperactivity, and depression than children living with a single but effective parent; this is also a wider gap than one due to income differences (Statistics Canada, 1998b).

Teen Pregnancies and Unmarried Motherhood

The birth rate among teenagers has declined substantially over the last few decades. From the early 1970s to the 1990s, the proportion of births to teenagers declined from 11 to 6 percent of all births (Milan, 2000:7). However between 1961 and 1991, the birth rate per 1000 unmarried teenagers rose from about 11 to 19 (Belle and McQuillan, 1994:17).

Although a popular myth claims that most births to unmarried women occur in the central cities of large urban areas, the greatest proportion of unmarried women giving birth occurs in Quebec, Newfoundland, and Saskatchewan (Belle and McQuillan, 1994:17). Two of the key factors behind this statistic are poverty and lack of employment opportunity.

According to social analysts, the outcome of teen pregnancies is problematic because teenage mothers are typically unskilled at parenting, are likely to drop out of school, and have no social support other than relatives (Chase-Lansdale et al., 1992). Family support is extremely important to unmarried pregnant teens because emotional and financial support from the fathers of their children is often lacking (Nath et al., 1991). Without this support, teen mothers rely on their own mothers and grandmothers to help with child rearing. As a result, many unmarried teenage mothers do not make the same transition from the family of orientation to the family of procreation that most people make when they become parents. The *family of orientation* **is the family into which a person is born and in which early socialization takes place.** When teenage mothers and their children live with their grandmothers or other relatives, they do not establish the separate family unit known as a *family of procreation,* **—the family that married or cohabiting couples create by having or adopting children.** The picture for the children of teenage mothers without parental support is especially bleak because few of these mothers have adequate parenting skills or knowledge of child development. Children of unwed teenage mothers tend to have severely limited educational and employment opportunities and a high likelihood of living in poverty (Benokraitis, 1993). Teenagers are not the only ones having children without getting married. Since 1961 the birth rate for unmarried women between the ages of 25 to 29, and 30 to 34, has doubled. It now accounts for 27 and 15 percent respectively of births to unmarried women in 1991 (in comparison with 14 and 8 percent respectively in 1961) (Belle and McQuillan, 1994:15). Third and fourth births outside marriage are also occurring, most commonly in Quebec, Saskatchewan, and Manitoba (Belle and McQuillan, 1994:16). According to demographer Charles Westoff, these rates reflect "the declining significance of marriage as a social obligation or a social necessity for reproduction. Increasing proportions of White women who have not been married are deciding that having a child is more important than any kind of disapproval they might face" (quoted in Connell, 1995). With less of a social stigma attached to unmarried pregnancy, fewer women seem to be seeking abortion and are deciding instead to raise the child themselves whether the pregnancy was planned or not.

Same-Sex Parenting

Over the last 20 years, lesbian parenting has become a topic of public attention. Many individual accounts have appeared, discussing choosing parenthood, defining the family, raising children, reflections on identity, and lesbian parenting and the law (e.g., Arnup, 1995). However, few studies have appeared in Canada exploring these topics. The 2001 Census inquired not only about same-sex cohabitation, but also about the presence of children. More female than male same-sex couples have children (15 percent vs. 3 percent) (Statistics Canada, 2002p:4). Regarding same-sex couple interaction, a study that focuses on reproductive decision-making, mothering, and family life from the perspective of the mother was conducted by Fiona Nelson (1996). She interviewed 30 lesbian women in

Alberta cities. Fifteen women already had children from a previous heterosexual relationship and thus created blended families with their partners. Others became pregnant by means of donor insemination. One of her interesting findings was the difference in the role of the non-biological mother in the blended and donor inseminated (D.I.) families. Whereas in the D.I. family, each woman regards herself as the mother with equal division of authority and responsibilities, in the blended family, the non-biological mother is a stepparent and is rarely allowed to be a "mother" (Nelson, 1996:134). Nelson (1996:137) suggests that as more women pursue the D.I. means of family formation, it will become more visible and accepted, and "the educative effect may be such that *all* mothers will come to rethink what it means to be a mother" (emphasis in original).

Among the topics that Nelson was unable to explore was the perspectives of children. One small study from Arnup's collection reports research showing that the older children have not suffered excessively from their mother's lesbianism. They may even have grown more mature through coping with examples of homophobia (McLaughlin, 1995:249). One student wrote a letter to his teacher, who was beginning a unit on the family, complaining that as "a son of a lesbian mother, when I looked on the list for a description of my family and it wasn't there, I felt like my type of family wasn't considered 'real'." And he signed his letter "*Someone who is proud of his mom!*" (emphasis in original) (McLaughlin, 1995:248). The growing prominence of lesbian and gay parenting should lead to much rethinking of the nature of families and parenting.

In contrast to these studies of lesbian motherhood, James Miller (1996:132) presents a personal statement of his own family, which he calls an "out family" because of "its openness to homosexual membership; its opposition to *heterosexist* conformity (the prejudicial assumption of heterosexuality as normal and proper); and its overtones within the contemporary lesbian and gay movement" (emphasis in original). In a comprehensive article, Miller

- outlines various problems experienced by his children and partner;
- provides critiques of a CBC documentary about the domestic struggles of a gay father and his son, and "learning-to-read" books; and

- portrays, schematically, the relationships of family and friends in Panic Manor Family Configuration.

The book in which this article is found also provides personal voices of families of different racializations/ethnicities, stages of life cycle, region and economics, and ability and disability.

DIVORCE AND REMARRIAGE

Divorce is the legal process of dissolving a marriage, which allows former spouses to remarry if they so choose. Have you heard such statements as "Almost one out of every two marriages ends in divorce"? Statistics might initially appear to bear out this statement, but consider the following: Most sociologists use a statistic called the *refined divorce rate* to calculate the incidence of divorce. The number of divorces in a year is divided by the total number of marriages in that year. In Canada, there were 153 000 marriages and 67 000 divorces in 1997 (Statistics Canada, 2002s: 27). However, it is misleading to compare the number of marriages with the number of divorces from year to year because couples who divorce in any given year are very unlikely to have come from the group that married that year. Also, some people go through several marriages and divorces, which skews the divorce rate because the likelihood of divorce goes up with each subsequent marriage.

Why does divorce occur? A number of factors contribute to a couple's statistical likelihood of becoming divorced, including

- getting married during the teenage years (Balakrishnan et al., 1993);
- getting married after only a short acquaintanceship (Goode, 1976);
- having relatives and friends disapprove of the marriage (Goode, 1976);
- having limited economic resources and earning low wages (Spanier and Glick, 1981);
- both partners having a high-school education or less (Houseknecht et al., 1984);
- having parents who were divorced or who had unhappy marriages (Goode, 1976); and
- having children present at the beginning of the marriage (Rankin and Maneker, 1985; Morgan et al., 1988; Martin and Bumpass, 1989).

Because these factors are interrelated with such other factors as class, racialization, and age, determining the likelihood of divorce is very complicated. For example, age is intertwined with economic resources, and people from low-income families typically marry earlier than do people from more affluent families, but if divorce occurs, which factor—age or economic resources—is more closely associated with it?

Religion may affect the divorce rate of some. People who attend religious services weekly are much more likely to want to keep the family together and place more importance on home life than non-attenders, according to the 1995 GSS (Clark, 1998)

Divorce laws in Canada once required the partner seeking the divorce to prove misconduct on the part of the other spouse. Under today's *no-fault divorce laws*, however, proof of blameworthiness is no longer necessary, and most divorces are granted on the grounds of *irreconcilable differences*, which means that a breakdown has occurred in the marital relationship and neither partner is to be specifically blamed.

With or without blame, divorce usually has a dramatic economic and emotional impact on family members. An estimated 60 percent of divorcing couples have one or more children. Indeed, some children experience more than one divorce during their childhood because one or both of their parents may remarry and subsequently divorce again. Although we do not know how many Canadians have experienced multiple divorces, we do know about multiple disruptions (including death and/or remarriage of a parent) of the family and their effects on childhood happiness. The 1995 GSS asked about family disruptions and their effects on children's feelings of well-being and closeness to parents. According to Statistics Canada analyst Cara Williams (2001:3), 8 percent of Canadians (1.9 million people) aged 15 and older experienced one change in parental structure, 800 000 Canadians experienced two, and 200 000 experienced three or more. Disruptions do affect childhood happiness. Whereas 92 percent of those without disruptions reported having a happy childhood, only 50 percent of those with three or more disruptions reported having happiness (Williams, 2001:4). Those with one or more disruptions also reported being less close to their mother and father than those without disruptions (Williams, 2001:4). The topic of the consequences of divorce quickly brings out strong debate, ranging from those

like researcher Anne-Marie Ambert (1998), who say that divorce has negative effects, to those like independent researcher Judith Harris (1998), who dismiss its negative effects. Cherlin (1999) suggests that neither extreme gives a clear portrait of growing up after divorce, because his studies showed that children whose parents would later divorce already showed more emotional problems at age seven than children from families that would remain intact. Although the effects can be overstated, disruptions do tend to have negative effects on childhood happiness and on relationships with parents.

Divorce changes relationships not only for the couple and children involved but also for other relatives. Some grandparents feel that they are the big losers. Grandparents who wish to see their grandchildren have to keep in touch with the parent who has custody, but if the grandparents are in-laws, they are less likely to be welcomed and may be seen as taking the "other side" simply because they are the parents of the ex-spouse. Recently, some grandparents have sued for custody of minor grandchildren. For the most part, these suits have not been successful except when there has been some question about the emotional stability of the biological parents or the suitability of a foster-care arrangement.

Most people who divorce remarry. In 1997, in more than 34 percent of all marriages, either the bride, the groom, or both had previously been married (Milan, 2000:8). Of individuals who divorce before age 35, about half remarry within three years of their first divorce (Bumpass et al., 1990). Most divorced people marry others who have been divorced (London and Wilson, 1988), though remarriage rates vary by gender and age. At all ages, a greater proportion of men than women remarry, often relatively soon after the divorce. Among women, the older a woman is at the time of divorce, the lower her likelihood of remarrying (Wallerstein and Blakeslee, 1989). Women who have not graduated from high school and have young children tend to remarry relatively quickly. Women with a college degree and without children are less likely to remarry (Glick and Lin, 1986).

Divorce followed by remarriage often creates complex family relationships. A **blended family consists of a husband and wife or a same-sex couple, children from previous marriages, and children (if any) from the new marriage.** At least initially, stress in blended families may be fairly high because of rivalry among the children and hostilities directed toward stepparents or babies born into the family. The NLSCY found that nearly 9 percent of Canadian children under age 12 were living in a blended family. These children were more likely than children from intact families to say they lacked emotional support from their parents and to report difficulties in getting along with siblings and parents (Milan, 2000:9). In some cases, when parents divorce and marry other partners, the children become part of a *binuclear family*, living with one biological parent and a stepparent part of the time and with the other biological parent and another stepparent the rest of the time.

As Cherlin (1992) points out, the norms governing divorce and remarriage are ambiguous, so people must make decisions about family life (such as who should be invited to a birthday celebration or a wedding) on the basis of their own feelings about the people involved. But in spite of the problems, many blended families succeed.

DOMESTIC VIOLENCE

The term *domestic violence* obscures the fact that most victims of domestic violence are women and children. Women are more likely to be assaulted, injured, or raped by their male partners than by any other type of assailant. Children are extremely vulnerable to abuse and violence because of their age and economic and social dependence on their parents or other adult caregivers.

Child Abuse

In 2001, Nico Trocmé and his colleagues published the Canadian Incidence Study of Reported Child Abuse and Neglect (CIS), the first nation-wide study to examine the incidence of reported child maltreatment and the characteristics of children and families investigated by Canadian child welfare services. While most of us, when we hear the words *child abuse,* think in terms of physical injury or sexual abuse, the most frequent form of child maltreatment, according to the CIS, is *child neglect*—not meeting a child's basic needs for emotional warmth and security, adequate shelter, food, health care, education, clothing, and protection (Trocmé et al., 2001:xv). We will focus primarily on physical injury

and sexual abuse because these actions are classified as violent personal crimes.

In the past, children in Canada were considered the property of their parents and could be punished or ignored as the parents wished. Now, despite legislation protecting children, through child welfare services in the provinces and territories, many physical injuries to children are intentionally inflicted by parents and other caregivers (see Trocmé et al., 2001:4–5). Parental violence can, in fact, lead to the *battered child syndrome,* a psychological disorder in which a child experiences low self-esteem and sometimes clinical depression associated with former or current abuse by a biological or custodial parent (Kempe et al., 1962).

The CIS identified four kinds of maltreatment: physical abuse, sexual abuse, neglect, and emotional maltreatment. In 1998, 135 573 cases of maltreatment were investigated and 45 percent were substantiated (22 percent were suspected and 33 percent were unsubstantiated) (Trocmé et al., 2001:xiv). Regarding the kinds of maltreatment:

- 31 percent were physical abuse (34 percent substantiated);

- 10 percent were sexual abuse (38 percent substantiated);

- 40 percent were neglect (43 percent substantiated); and

- 19 percent were emotional maltreatment (54 percent substantiated). (Trocmé et al., 2001:xv).

The physical abuse of children in Canada is a serious social problem that remains largely hidden unless an incident results in the death or serious injury of a child. According to the CIS, some form of physical harm was found in 13 percent of the investigations, and in 3 percent the harm was sufficiently severe to require treatment (Trocmé et al., 2001:xvi). Some researchers have found that children are most likely to be assaulted in their own homes if their parents were abused, neglected, or deprived as children and if their parents are socially isolated as adults. Parents who lack a support network and suddenly face a crisis tend to make their children the targets of their frustration and sometimes their aggression (Kempe and Kempe, 1978). Other researchers have found that abusive parents characteristically feel unloved and unworthy and totally unprepared to cope with their circumstances (Tower, 1996).

The signs of physical abuse include bruises, particularly on the back of the legs, upper arms and chest, neck, head, or genitals. Fractures in infants under 12 months of age are a strong indication of abuse, as are head injuries and burns, especially cigarette burns. Most physicians and emergency room personnel are specially trained to identify signs of child abuse so that parents or guardians can be reported to the appropriate authorities. In fact, reporting of suspected child abuse has improved significantly in recent years because of increased training, awareness, and legislation, which established that reports of suspected abuse would be investigated promptly and fully. In the past, even when physicians suspected abuse, they often chose to treat the child but not to report the incident, believing that abuse would be too difficult to prove (Tower, 1996).

Besides physical harm, instances of emotional harm were noted in 24 percent of investigations, and in 15 percent of the cases, the harm was sufficiently severe to require treatment (Trocmé et al., 2001:xvii). Examples of emotional harm included changes in development (e.g., withdrawal), disruption of sleep patterns, and crying and clinging. Problems in overall functioning were also noted in 44 percent of the investigations. The five most often indicated problems were behavioural problems, depression or anxiety, negative peer involvement, irregular school attendance, and developmental delay (Trocmé et al., 2001:xxiv).

One of the most disturbing forms of maltreatment of children is sexual abuse. Unfortunately, there is a lack of consensus on how to define sexual abuse. In the CIS, sexual abuse was defined in seven categories: sexual activity attempted, sexual activity completed, touching/fondling genitals, adult exposing genitals, sexual exploitation (e.g., prostitution), sexual harassment, and voyeurism (Trocmé et al., 2001:33).

According to the CIS, the incidence of sexual abuse investigated was 2.48 per 1000 children, with 38 percent of the investigations being substantiated (Trocmé et al., 2001:33). Two-thirds of the sexual abuse cases involved female children and one-third involved males (Trocmé et al., 2001:65). Regarding the prevalence of sexual abuse, it appears that between 10 and 15 percent of girls and boys experience some form of sexual contact as children (Finkelhor, 1984). While the overall rate of investigations was similar for boys and girls at all ages, females are more likely than males to be victims of sexual abuse as well as *incest*, or sexual relations between individuals so closely related that they are forbidden to marry by law (Trocmé et al., 2001:66).

The vast majority (93 percent) of the perpetrators of maltreatment are parents and relatives (Trocmé et al., 2001:49). The alleged perpetrators of physical abuse are almost evenly divided between biological mothers (47 percent) and fathers (42 percent) and of sexual abuse are mostly male, both biological fathers (15 percent) and other relatives (28 percent) (Trocmé et al., 2001:49).

A usually less severe form of punishment, used by most parents, is spanking. Some people consider this abuse. Box 11.2 presents a discussion of this topic and reference to cases featured in the media.

Spouse Abuse

From the days of early Rome to current times, spouse abuse has been acknowledged to exist, but until recently, it was largely ignored or tolerated. Today, according to the fifth annual study of family violence in Canada, victimization reports show that 8 percent of women and 7 percent of men experienced at least one incident of spousal violence from their current or former partners between the years 1994 and 1995 (Statistics Canada, 2002i). However, the suffering and such other harmful consequences as needing medication are experienced much more strongly by the woman. Unfortunately, some of these abused women end up victims of homicide. As noted above in the section on the feminist perspective, women are more than seven times as likely as men to be killed by their spouses or intimate partners. Fortunately, a substantial decline in spousal homicide is occurring for both sexes (see above).

Social Responses to Domestic Violence

Although every few months we read in the papers about extreme domestic violence, such as a murder (of a woman) and suicide (by a man), many people who are aware of domestic abuse don't do anything about it, feeling that they do not want to become involved in a "private matter."

Historically, in Canada, an *ideology of nonintervention*—a strong reluctance on the part of outsiders to interfere in family matters—has led people and police officers to ignore or tolerate domestic violence (Lauer,

SOCIAL PROBLEMS AND SOCIAL POLICY

BOX 11.2 Should Spanking Be Permitted?

Every schoolteacher, parent or person standing in the place of a parent is justified in using force by way of correction toward a pupil or child, as the case may be, who is under his care, if the force does not exceed what is reasonable under the circumstances.

—*Criminal Code, Section 43*

In 2000, children's rights advocates appealed to the Ontario Superior Court to have this law declared unconstitutional. Judge David McCombs ruled in July 2000 that spanking does not violate the constitutional rights of children. He agreed with the advocates that corporal punishment should not involve a slap to the head or cause injury, which would be a case of child abuse, and noted that public attitudes to corporal punishment of children are changing. But he also said that parents should have a protected sphere in which to raise children and reasonable force should be used only with the best interests of the children.

When this decision was appealed to the Ontario Court of Appeal, it ruled in January 2002 that parents and teachers are free to spank children for disciplinary purposes, but only if the force they use is reasonable. The judges acknowledged that many people who were acquitted of abuse before would not be acquitted today. They also suggested such guidelines as not hitting a teenager or a child under two, not using an object such as a belt or ruler, and not hitting or slapping the head of a child (Makin, 2002:A8).

In July 2001, six children, 6 to 14 years of age, were taken from their home in Aylmer, Ontario, because their parents would not promise not to hit them with switches if they disobeyed. The parents are members of a Mennonite church whose members believe in the literal truth of the Bible, which states in the King James Version, "He that spareth his rod hateth his son: but he that loveth him chasteneth him betimes" (Proverbs 13:24). The family's pastor, Mr. Hillebrandt, indicated that following the Bible does not mean injuring the child; the children were examined for injuries, none were found. But, he does believe that corporal punishment "works in our time to do just like it's written" (quoted in Saunders, 2001:A7). Steve Bailey, the executive director of Family and Children's Services of St. Thomas and Elgin, said while they believed that spanking "per se is not child abuse . . . We would look at whether there's any use of in-animate objects such as belts or cords or sticks" (quoted in Saunders, 2001:A7). The children were originally taken into foster care and then released. In the summer of 2002, a trial took place in which the authorities sought to allow the children to remain at home, but only under a year-long supervision order which will see them subject to regular monitoring.

In their chapter "Should Johnny Be Spanked?" Tepperman and Blain (1999:33) identify some of the negative consequences of corporal punishment—from immediate depression, anxiety, lower grades, and slower physical development to crime, racism, and violence as adults. While acknowledging that though a majority of people are spanked, only a minority become abusive or criminal, they conclude that "parents should not spank their children if they want to reduce misbehaviour; it doesn't work. Alternative methods, like reasoning with the child and withholding rewards, are more successful if the parents are consistent." The National Longitudinal Study of Children and Youth also showed that aversive parenting was very often related to behavioural problems.

What do you think about the Criminal Code section? Do you think it should be repealed or amended? Do you believe in the parent's right to spank a child? What do you think about the case of the six children? Should the family be monitored for any length of time?

1995). Unfortunately, the pattern of violence that ultimately results in a homicide is eerily similar in many cases of domestic abuse, and in most of those cases, death might have been prevented by earlier intervention. Positive changes in how law enforcement officials handle domestic violence calls are now being made—changes that are long overdue.

FAMILY-RELATED PROBLEMS IN THE 21ST CENTURY

As we have seen, families and intimate relationships have changed dramatically during the 20th century.

Because of these changes, some people believe that the family as we know it is doomed; others think that returning to traditional family values can save this important social institution and create a more stable society. Another point of view, however, comes from sociologist Lillian Rubin (1994), who suggests that clinging to a traditional image of families is hypocritical in light of our society's failure to support the family, whether through family allowances or decent public-sponsored childcare facilities. Some laws even hurt children whose families do not fit the traditional model. Welfare cuts, like those by the Conservative government in Ontario in 1995, for example, affect children as well as the adults who are trying to provide for them.

For the family to remain a viable and effective social institution, a macrolevel societal commitment is needed, as sociologist Demie Kurz (1995:232) states:

> As a society we should make a commitment to helping all families—traditional nuclear families, two-parent, two-earner families, and single-parent families—and to providing adequately for their members, particularly their children. To help families we must reduce female and male poverty, making special efforts to end institutionalized discrimination against minorities. We must also promote equality between men and women in the family. This includes creating new conceptions of what it means to be a father and what it means to be a partner in a marriage and share family life and household work. It also means taking decisive steps to end violence toward women and children. While the costs of creating humane and just social policies are high, the cost of failing to promote the welfare of family members is far higher.

WHAT CAN YOU DO?

- Investigate if any shelters for women could use any help in your community. Volunteer at the shelter; help is always needed.

- Analyze who does what unpaid domestic labour in your household, or suggest that a tutorial be devoted to discussing who should do what unpaid domestic labour in a relationship.

- Find out what family concerns feminist groups on campus have and help them address them.

- Look further into the topic of Canadian parenting styles, by studying recommendations of parenting magazines and websites and thinking of new variables or situations for this research topic.

SUMMARY

WHAT IS A FAMILY?

A family is a relationship in which people live together with commitment, form an economic unit, care for any young, and consider the group critical to their identity. This definition modifies the traditional definition to account for today's greater diversity in living arrangements and relationships in families.

ARE CANADIAN FAMILIES IN DECLINE?

Not at all, say analysts who take a social change perspective. Families are becoming more complex and diverse, adapting to other changes in society. For one thing, marriage is no longer a cultural imperative; for another, many people reaffirm their belief in the institution through serial monogamy, a succession of marriages over a lifetime.

WHAT ARE THE SOCIOLOGICAL PERSPECTIVES ON FAMILY-RELATED PROBLEMS?

Functionalists believe that the family provides social order and economic stability; the family is the solution to many societal problems, and dysfunctional families threaten the well-being of individuals and the whole of society.

Conflict theorists see the family as a problem in society, not a solution; they believe that the family is a major source of inequality in society brought on by capitalism.

Feminist theorists see women's subordination as rooted in the patriarchal system, coming long before capitalism.

Interactionists view the family first in terms of socialization. Some speak of the shared reality of marriage; some view family problems in terms of the subjective meanings that people give to their everyday lives; and some cite partners' unrealistic expectations about love and marriage.

WHAT CHARACTERIZES SINGLEHOOD IN CANADA TODAY?

The proportion of the Canadian population that has never married has continued to grow since the 1960s to about 10 percent of adults. Some people remain single by choice, others by necessity; many working-class young people cannot afford to marry and set up a household.

WHY DO YOUNG PEOPLE POSTPONE MARRIAGE TODAY?

Four factors are important: Changing job structures in Canada lead to economic uncertainty; more women are in the labour force; sexual relationships outside of marriage are more socially acceptable than before; and young people observing the rising divorce rate may be cautious about jumping into marriage.

DOES COMMON-LAW OR COHABITATION USUALLY LEAD TO A SUCCESSFUL MARRIAGE? WHAT IS A DOMESTIC PARTNERSHIP?

According to one recent study, only about 50 percent of cohabiting couples marry, and evidence on the success of those marriages is mixed. Some studies show little or no effect; others show that partners who cohabit are more likely to divorce than partners who do not. A domestic partnership is a partnership in which an unmarried couple lives together in a committed relationship and is granted many of the same legal rights and benefits accorded to a married couple.

WHAT DOES RESEARCH SHOW ABOUT DUAL-EARNER MARRIAGES?

More than 60 percent of all marriages in Canada are dual-earner marriages, that is, marriages in which both spouses are in the labour force. Many women in these marriages do the domestic work at home after completing their workday jobs, though there seems to be a gradual trend toward more egalitarian division of labour.

IS A TWO-PARENT FAMILY ALWAYS PREFERABLE TO A ONE-PARENT FAMILY?

If the parents argue constantly, are alcoholics, or abuse the children, a supportive single-parent family would be preferable. However, a child growing up in a single-parent household faces serious risks that are complicated by other factors, such as poverty, discrimination, unsafe neighbourhoods, and high crime rates.

WHY IS REPRODUCTIVE FREEDOM SUCH A CONTROVERSIAL ISSUE?

Reproductive freedom implies the option to have or not to have a child. The roles that religious organizations, physicians, and society (through the legal system) should (and should not) play in controlling a woman's fertility continue to be debated. Contraception, abortion, and the new reproductive technologies all raise personal and societal issues.

WHICH IS MORE IMPORTANT, PARENTING STYLE OR INCOME?

A continuing national study has found that parenting styles ranging from positive to ineffective had more influence on behavioural problems than family income or structure.

ARE NON-MARITAL PREGNANCIES INCREASING OR DECLINING?

Births to teenagers, as a percentage of all births, have decreased over the past 30 years, but the birth rate is higher for unmarried teenagers than in the past. In addition, the proportion of births to unmarried women aged 25 to 34 has greatly increased.

ARE MEN OR WOMEN MORE LIKELY TO UNDERTAKE SAME-SEX PARENTING?

According to the 2001 Census, female same-sex couples are much more likely to have children with them than male same-sex couples. Studies of the experiences of both groups are starting to accumulate.

WHO GETS DIVORCED, AND DO MOST PEOPLE REMARRY?

Many factors affect who gets divorced (e.g., marrying during the teen years or having limited economic resources), and these factors are interrelated with class, racialization, and age, so it is very difficult to determine any kind of statistical likelihood of divorce. Most people do remarry, and divorce followed by remarriage leads to complex family relationships, such as blended families.

KEY TERMS

blended family,   p. 265
common-law and cohabitation,   p. 256
dual-earner marriages,   p. 257
extended family,   p. 250
family,   p. 250
family of orientation,   p. 263

family of procreation,   p. 263
kinship,   p. 250
monogamy,   p. 251
nuclear family,   p. 250
second shift,   p. 257

QUESTIONS FOR CRITICAL THINKING

1.   Sociologist Andrew Cherlin says that the family is a highly adaptable social institution, but we can minimize the costs of change in the family unit by modifying other social institutions of daily life, such as the economy and workplace. What specific suggestions can you give for modifications in work–family arrangements?

2.   What do you think of Margaret Mead's proposal of a two-stage marriage? What problems, such as reducing "starter marriages," might it forestall? Would it create any new ones?

3.   What suggestions can you offer to help offset the potentially detrimental effects of single-parent households, especially when the parent is a woman who is employed full-time?

4.   Why do you think a difference in the proportion of lesbian and gay couples having children exists? Do you think this will change in the future?

WEBLINKS

2001 Census: Family and Household Web Site (Statistics Canada)
www12.statcan.ca/english/census01/release/
release3.cfm
A summary of and links to a wide variety of resources, including tables and maps.

2001 Census: Family and Household Data (Statistics Canada)
www12.statcan.ca/english/census01/products/
standard/themes/ListProducts.cfm?Temporal=
2001&APATH=3&THEME=39&FREE=0
Topic-based tabulations on dozens of topics from this release of the Census.

Canadian Families Project
http://web.uvic.ca/hrd/cfp
An interdisciplinary research project, based in Victoria, B.C., studying the family in Canada

Families and Work Institute
www.familiesandwork.org
Tips for managing work and family issues.

Foundation for Equal Rights for the Family
www.ffef.ca
This organization seeks to achieve equality and recognition for same-sex family rights.

One Parent Families Association of Canada
http://hometown.aol.com/opfa222
This association offers a wide variety of resources and links for lone-parents.

Statistics Canada Web Site
www.statcan.ca/english/Pgdb
Data is available on a wide variety of subjects—such as the economy, the land, and the people—in which data about families is available.

PROBLEMS IN EDUCATION

Students should have a say in who they are [and] should not be limited by their background.

Ainsworth Morgan, a teacher at Nelson Mandela Park School, an inner-city Toronto school, who encourages students to challenge stereotypes of the "ghetto"

It's the basic tenet of the education system that you've got to try and give everyone a chance to succeed and provide them with what they need. It's why we have special education. It's why we're supposed to be there helping people succeed. And the lack of curriculum and the lack of a separate literacy test means we're setting them [students in the applied stream] up to fail right from the very beginning.

Annie Kidder, member of People for Education, quoted in the Globe and Mail (June 24, 2002)

Annie Kidder was shocked to learn that in Ontario, 70 percent of students in the vocational stream, which prepares students for the work force rather than college or university, had failed a mandatory Grade 10 literacy test for getting a high-school diploma. The students had failed a test that 80 percent of the students in the stream for college and university had passed. Devising separate streams, also known as ***tracking***—**assigning students to specific courses and educational programs on the basis of their test scores, previous grades, or both**—can have a positive effect on achievement of some students, but a negative effect on students not in the postsecondary stream, especially if they are asked to perform at the level of students in the postsecondary stream. The harm isn't intentional. The people who authorized the test want all students to perform well so that they will be able to thrive in a complex, changing environment. It is possible for inner-city students to do well with the right encouragement, like that from teachers like Ainsworth Morgan (see his story at the end of the chapter).

Canada and other industrialized nations highly value ***education***—**the social institution responsible for transmitting knowledge, skills, and cultural values in a formally organized structure.** But a wide gap exists between the ideals of Canadian education and the realities of daily life in many schools. As a result, business and political leaders, parents, teachers, and the general public tend to complain about the state of education in this country, even as many parents report

feeling relatively positive about the schools their children attend.

In this chapter you will learn about the problems of low-level literacy; educational problems of immigrants; opportunities for both high-school completion and postsecondary education available to people from differing family structures, socio-economic backgrounds, racialized/ethnic backgrounds, gender, and regions; school violence and bullying; residential schools for Indigenous children; financing for elementary, secondary, and postsecondary education and the commercialization of postsecondary education; the future of educational problems; and what you can do about them.

First, the sociological perspectives—functionalist, conflict, interactionist, and feminist—on education will be outlined to help us understand the problems and to show how educational problems are often intertwined with other problems.

PERSPECTIVES ON EDUCATION

The way a sociologist studies education depends on the theoretical perspective he or she takes. Functionalists, for example, believe that schools should promote good citizenship and upward mobility and that problems in education are related to social disorganization, rapid social change, and the organizational structure of schools. Conflict theorists believe that schools perpetuate inequality and that problems in education are the result of bias based on racialization, class, and gender. Meanwhile, interactionists focus on microlevel problems in schools, such as how communication and teachers' expectations affect students' levels of achievement and dropout rates. Lastly, feminist theorists focus on the differences of male and female performance in, and responses to, the educational system.

Functionalist Perspectives

Functionalists believe that education is one of the most important social institutions because it contributes to the smooth functioning of society and provides individuals with opportunities for personal fulfillment and upward social mobility. According to functionalists, when problems occur, they can usually be traced to the failure of

[Handwritten notes at top of page: "EDUCATION, TODAY, IS A CHOICE THAT STUDENTS MUST HAVE TO WORK AT AND WANT TO ACHIEVE. FAILURE OF STUDENTS SHOULD NOT BE ENTIRELY BLAMED ON THE INSTITUTION."]

educational institutions—schools, universities, colleges—to fulfill one of their manifest functions. *Manifest functions* **are open, stated, and intended goals or consequences of activities within an organization or institution.** While the most obvious manifest function of education is the teaching of academic subjects (reading, writing, mathematics, science, and history), education has at least five major manifest functions in society:

1. *Socialization.* From kindergarten through college, schools teach students the student role, specific academic subjects, and political socialization. In kindergarten, children learn the attitudes and behaviour generally considered appropriate for a student (Ballantine, 1997). In primary and secondary schools, ideally, students are taught specific subject matter that is appropriate to their age, skill level, and previous educational experience. At the college level, students expand their knowledge and seek out new areas of study. Throughout, students learn the democratic process.

2. *Transmission of culture:* Schools transmit cultural norms and values to each new generation and play a major role in *assimilation,* the process whereby recent immigrants learn dominant cultural values, attitudes, and behaviour so that they can be productive members of society.

3. *Social control:* Although controversy exists over whose values should be taught, schools are responsible for teaching values such as discipline, respect, obedience, punctuality, and perseverance. Schools teach conformity by encouraging young people to be good students, conscientious future workers, and law-abiding citizens.

4. *Social placement:* Schools are responsible for identifying the most qualified people to fill available positions in society. Students are often channelled into programs on the basis of their perceived individual ability and academic achievement. Graduates receive credentials generally required for entering the paid labour force.

5. *Change and innovation:* Schools are a source of change and innovation. To meet the needs of student populations at particular times, new programs—such as HIV/AIDS education, computer education, and multicultural studies—are created. University faculty members are expected to conduct research

and publish new knowledge that benefits the overall society. A major goal of change and innovation in education is to reduce social problems.

In addition to these manifest functions, education fulfills a number of *latent functions*—**hidden, unstated, and sometimes unintended consequences of activities in an organization or institution.** Consider, for example, these latent functions of education: Compulsory school attendance keeps children and teenagers off the streets (and, by implication, out of trouble) and out of the full-time job market for a number of years (controlling the flow of workers). High schools, colleges, and universities serve as matchmaking institutions where people often meet future marriage partners. By bringing people of similar ages, racialized/ethnic groups, and social-class backgrounds together, schools establish social networks.

Functionalists acknowledge many *dysfunctions* in education, but to many, one seems overriding: Our public schools are not adequately preparing students for jobs and global competition. In comparative rankings of students across countries on standardized reading, mathematics, and science tests, Canadian students were lagging. For example, in the 1996 International Mathematics and Science Study, a comprehensive study of science and math achievement by students in 41 countries, Canadian students ranked slightly above average in math and science (Bagby, 1997). Among the 9 countries that outperformed Canada in math was Singapore, where all students are tracked individually and expected to perform well, and Japan, where students used to attend regular schools for one more day than their Canadian counterparts and, in addition, may even attend cram schools (see Box 12.1). However, in the most recent international assessment sponsored by the OECD (Organisation for Economic Co-operation and Development), in 2000, Canadian students made a substantial improvement, placing sixth in mathematics and fifth in science (still behind Singapore and Japan) and second in reading (behind Finland) (Statistics Canada, 2001c). If these scores are maintained in future tests, it will show that significant change can occur in the educational system.

Other dysfunctions include our schools not preparing students for their political responsibilities as citizens of a democracy (to think and question and be well-informed). In addition, due to increasing class sizes, constantly changing curriculums, and loss of teacher-preparation time in primary and secondary public schools, actual teaching—as opposed to caretaking—is increasingly devolving onto parents and private tutors, leaving those children (predominantly lower-class) whose parents can't teach them, due to their own lack of education or lack of time, because they must work long hours, with little in the way of an education. Yet the solutions to many social problems depend to a large degree on the education system reaching those very children. In postsecondary education, the former undergraduate experience of professor/student contact is lost in class sizes of 500+ and evaluation consisting of multiple-choice questions. Moreover, tuition is skyrocketing.

SOCIAL PROBLEMS IN GLOBAL PERSPECTIVE

BOX 12.1   Change in Education in Japan: Becoming More Like Us?

Until recently, the education system was very uniform, producing children like manufactured goods.

Michiro Iida, a teacher at Shingakai Educational Institute, a nationwide chain of cram schools in Japan (WuDunn, 1996)

In Canada, education is a local enterprise. Provinces and local school districts decide on standards, set curricula, and assess—or do not assess—students' achievement. This system may seem to be just fine except that, in international math and science tests, Canada used to rank low in comparison to other modern, industrialized countries and still ranks lower than Japan and Singapore. Critics say that we need higher standards, perhaps national standards backed up by a common nationwide curriculum that culminates in standardized achievement tests.

Countries that rank highest in international pupil achievement tests have national standards. Japan, for example, boasts nearly universal literacy and high-school students who can solve complicated math problems. In Japan, at age three, sometimes earlier, children prepare for preschool entrance exams by entering the first of a series of cram schools—called *juku*. Some *juku* are national chains; others are held in small neighbourhood apartments. The best are known only by word of mouth and charge more than $9000 a year (WuDunn, 1996) but the discipline and thinking skills they teach set students on the path to a first-rate future. In Japan, the job one gets depends on the university one attended, which depends on the high school one went to, which in turn depends on one's elementary school, which, finally, depends on where one went to preschool. Thus, the sooner a child begins cramming, the better. The following excerpt describes a scene from Keiokai Educational Institute, where three- and four-year-olds sit at little desks in a 90-minute class designed to improve performance on IQ tests (WuDunn, 1996).

The children followed the teacher's instructions: first, string as many coloured beads as possible within two minutes; second, string only six beads or ten beads; third, string coloured beads without letting two beads of the same colour touch.

Then the teacher pinned pictures of fruits on the blackboard, arranging them in a line. Which fruit is in the middle? Which is second from the left? Second from the right? Then the fruits were rearranged vertically and the exercise was repeated. To a U.S. student, a cram school for 3-year-olds may sound cruel, but many students enjoy the classes. That is not to say the system is perfect: Some Japanese parents and educators feel students become "trained seals"—mechanical thinkers—and there is a movement today to nurture more individuality and independent thinking.

Another problem comes from the competition for elite schools: "Preparation for entrance exams makes students turn everyone into rivals, so they come to find pleasure in another's failure," says one Japanese headmaster. "What is most important for human society [compassion] is not nurtured in Japan" (WuDunn, 1996).

Then there are the children who cannot function in the Japanese system. These are the "school refusers"—children as young as eight or nine who will not go to school. They cannot handle the academic pressure, rigid dress and hairstyle codes, and corporal punishment during the day followed by cram school at night. Truancy is a growing problem, especially among junior high-school students (Pollack, 1996). Traditionally, truants have been considered psychologically ill and sent to strict private schools that teach discipline or to mental hospitals. With 210 beds, Tokyo Metropolitan Umegaoka Hospital is the world's largest psychiatric hospital devoted solely to treating truant students.

Today, though, the Japanese Ministry of Education acknowledges that the school system itself may play a role in the problem of truancy. In April 2002, it introduced measures to make education less pressured. Students will be encouraged to be creative and to learn independently, both for themselves and for the needs of the global economy. According to a report by foreign correspondent Geoffrey York (2002:A12), Saturday classes were eliminated, and the mathematics, science, and language programs were cut by 30 percent and replaced by field trips and general studies. Many parents and politicians, thinking that "hardship builds character," are worried that students will do less well on exams. Some wealthy parents will still send their children to *jukus* and other private schools.

Assuming that such students will get higher marks, some critics feel that the new approach will result in advantage to the middle class and the wealthy (York, 2002:A12).

Although Japan's economy did very well in the 1970s and 1980s, it was in recession during the 1990s. Although Canadians are concerned that, formerly, our students had poor results in mathematics and science, our economy has done well during the last two decades. Is it possible that a more open and flexible school system has contributed substantially to that development? Do you think that Japan's recent move is a step in the right direction even if the mathematics and science scores slide? What do you think is the best way to encourage individual creativity and prepare young people for the global economy?

Conflict Perspectives

Sociologists using a conflict framework for analyzing problems in education believe that schools—which are supposed to reduce social inequalities in society—actually perpetuate inequalities based on class, racialization, and gender (Apple, 1982). In fact, conflict theorists such as French sociologist Pierre Bourdieu argue that education *reproduces* existing class relationships (see Bourdieu and Passeron, 1990). According to Bourdieu, students have differing amounts of *cultural capital* that they learn at home and bring with them to the classroom (see Chapter 2). Children from middle- and upper-income homes have considerable cultural capital because their parents have taught them about books, art, music, and other forms of culture. According to Bourdieu, children from low-income and poverty-level families have not had the same opportunities to acquire cultural capital. Some social analysts believe it is students' cultural capital—rather than their "natural" intelligence or aptitude—that is measured on the standardized tests used for tracking. Thus, test results may unfairly limit some students' academic choices and career opportunities (Oakes, 1985).

Other sociologists using the conflict framework focus on problems associated with the hidden curriculum, a term coined by sociologist John C. Holt (1964) in his study of why children fail. The *hidden*

curriculum **refers to how certain cultural values and attitudes, such as conformity and obedience to authority, are transmitted through implied demands in the everyday rules and routines of schools** (Snyder, 1971). These conflict theorists, such as sociologists Samuel Bowles and Herbert Gintis (1976), suggest that elites use a hidden curriculum that teaches students to be obedient and patriotic—values that uphold the status quo in society and turn students into compliant workers—to manipulate the masses and maintain the elite's power in society. An update by Bowles and Gintis (2002) showing that genetic inheritance of cognitive skill explains only a small part of the persistence of status levels among families further supports this finding.

Although students from all social classes experience the hidden curriculum to some degree, working-class and poverty-level students are the most adversely affected (Ballantine, 1997). When middle-class teachers teach students from lower-class backgrounds, for example, the classrooms are very structured and the teachers have low expectations about the students' academic achievement (Alexander et al., 1987). In one study of five elementary schools with students from different class backgrounds, researchers found significant differences in how knowledge was transmitted despite similar curricula (Anyon, 1980). Schools for working-class students emphasize rules and rote memorization without much decision-making, choice, or explanation of why something is done a particular way. In contrast, schools for middle-class students stress the processes that are involved in getting the right answer. Elite schools develop students' analytical powers and critical-thinking skills, teaching them how to apply abstract principles to problem solving. Elite schools also emphasize creative activities so that students can express their own ideas and apply them to different areas of study. Compare the following comments from students in high-track and low-track classes who were asked what they learned in a particular class (Oakes, 1985:86–89):

> I want to be a lawyer and debate has taught me to dig for answers and get involved. I can express myself. —*High-track English student*

> To understand concepts and ideas and experiment with them. Also to work independently. —*High-track Science student*

> To behave in class. —*Low-track English student*

> To be a better listener in class. —*Low-track English student*

> I have learned that I should do my questions for the book when he asks me to. —*Low-track Science student*

As these comments show, the hidden curriculum teaches working-class and poverty-level students that they are expected to arrive on time, follow bureaucratic rules, take orders from others, and experience high levels of boredom without complaining (Ballantine, 1997). The limitations on what and how these students are taught mean that many of them do not get any higher education and therefore never receive the credentials to enter high-paying professions (Bowles and Gintis, 1976). Our society emphasizes *credentialism*—a process of social selection that gives class advantage and social status to people who possess academic qualifications (Collins, 1979). Credentialism is closely related to *meritocracy*—a social system in which status is acquired through individual ability and effort (Young, 1994). People who acquire the appropriate credentials for a job are assumed to have gained the position through what they know, not who they are or whom they know. According to conflict theorists, however, the hidden curriculum determines in advance that credentials, at

least at the higher levels, will stay in the hands of the elites, so Canada is not a meritocracy even if it calls itself one.

Interactionist Perspectives

Whereas functionalists examine the relationship between the functions of education and problems in schools and conflict theorists focus on how education perpetuates inequality, interactionists study classroom dynamics and how practices such as labelling affect students' self-concept and aspirations.

Interactionists believe that education is an integral part of the socialization process. Through the formal structure of schools and interpersonal relationships with peers and teachers, students develop a concept of self that lasts long beyond their schooling. Overall, social interactions in school can be either positive or negative. When students learn, develop, and function effectively, their experience is positive. For many students, however, the school environment and peer group interactions leave them discouraged and unhappy. When students who might do better with some assistance from teachers and peers are instead labelled "losers," they may come to view themselves as losers and thus set the stage for self-fulfilling prophecies. As noted in Chapter 1, *a self-fulfilling prophecy* occurs when a false definition of a situation evokes a new behaviour that makes the original false conception come true. On the other hand, the students can challenge "loser" thinking as students in a downtown Toronto school did when they criticized Ghetto Dolls for their stereotypical images (see Box 12.2).

Standardized tests can also lead to labelling, self-fulfilling prophecies, and low self-esteem.

According to interactionists, labels such as *learning disabled* stigmatize students, *marginalize* them—put them at the lower or outer limits of a group—in their interactions with parents, teachers, and other students: Such labelling leads to self-fulfilling prophecies (Carrier, 1986; Coles, 1987). To counteract this possibility, many of these students have been reintegrated into regular classes over the last decade.

At the opposite end of the spectrum, labelling students *gifted* and *talented* may also result in self-fulfilling prophecies. Students who are identified as having above-average intellectual ability, academic aptitude, creative or productive thinking, or leadership skills may

SOCIAL PROBLEMS IN THE MEDIA

BOX 12.2 Students Challenge the Ghetto Image

Shortly after teachers Ainsworth Morgan and Barbara Schwartz challenged their Grade 7 and 8 students in Nelson Mandela Park School in downtown Toronto to think about the term "ghetto" in a non-derogatory way, an article appeared in the *Toronto Star* (February 7, 2002) about a new line of dolls— Ghetto Dolls. Ghetto Dolls, appearing in different dilapidated clothes and ethnicities, were modelled after Cabbage Patch Dolls and included, in the package, a garbage can and extreme stories about surviving addicted, incarcerated, or slain parents, thus appearing to pander to stereotypes. These stories are now online at **www.ghettokidshood.com**

The G.H.E.T.T.O. Project was originally designed to help students challenge the stereotype of the ghetto by, among other things, writing acrostic poetry using the letters of ghetto, such as Great Hearts Express The Truth Openly and Giving Help Especially To Those Oppressed. As an additional component of the project, the students decided to write letters to both the *Toronto Star* and Teddi's Toys, the dolls' manufacturer, expressing their concerns about the image these toys were portraying.

Excerpts from some of the letters to the company follow. Not all responses were negative. Students envisioned parents buying a doll for their children and tried to think about how the parents could discuss the doll with their children:

I think by purchasing a doll it would be a bad influence on younger children because the stories may influence the children to do bad things . . . From my point of view I think that the dolls are not realistic. Why should the dolls have smiles if the dolls have complicated and difficult lives? . . . They're also not realistic because of their skin tones, they all have different backgrounds and they're all the same colour. —*Khadra, Grade 7*

What I think is that the Ghetto Dolls are a really good thing for kids and adults. They teach kids and show them examples (their histories) of what you are going to be if you behave like the Ghetto Dolls parents . . . Kids would talk to their parents about the Ghetto Dolls history no one would want to be like that . . . My opinion is to buy these dolls and learn something from it and then to teach your kids and they would teach their own and everybody can learn something. —*Nasim, Grade 7*

The Ghetto dolls are a good influence for children because the dolls' life is based on real life experiences that children can learn more . . . It will help your child to be prepared for what will come in the future in their lives, but there are some areas that the company could have improved on. For example, all the dolls look happy and have the same smile but they had bad lives. Their clothes are new and clean and have no sign of different backgrounds or cultures. —*Sami, Grade 8*

Both companies responded. The *Toronto Star*'s editor of the Letters to the Editor section came to the school on his day off to praise the students and to teach them about journalism. A representative of the company in Chicago replied, saying the students had addressed some important concerns and suggested that future dolls' stories might incorporate some of the students' suggestions. He also said that he would like to visit the school.

In May, the students were invited to visit the *Toronto Star* building, and afterward, almost all had decided they wanted to work for a newspaper. The guide at the *Star* suggested that some mentorships might be created with the students in the next year. In sum, Ainsworth Morgan felt that this project "helped alleviate the emphasis on stereotypical ideas and move it [the focus] toward pre-adolescents exploring and defining their identities and finding ways to approach common experiences that are challenging." He also hopes this project can be continued next year despite budget cuts.

Source: Thanks to the staff and students at Nelson Mandela Park School. A special note of thanks to Room 36, Mr. Morgan and Ms. Schwartz.

achieve at a higher level because of the label. However, this is not always the case. Girls who are identified as gifted may deny their intelligence because of cultural norms about the proper roles of women and men (see Eder, 1985; Eder and Parker, 1987). Afraid that their academic achievement will make them unpopular, high-achieving girls, and sometimes boys, can become victims of *anti-intellectualism*—hostility toward people who are assumed to have great mental ability or toward subject matter that is thought to require significant intellectual ability or knowledge (see discussion of the Horizons Program, below, which attempts to counteract this problem). White students are overrepresented in gifted-and-talented programs, whereas students of colour are underrepresented. As one social scientist puts it, if students are not given equal opportunities for gifted education, it is "a mythology that schools represent the great equalizing force in society . . . [and] . . . every child has an equal chance at success and achievement" (Sapon-Shevin, 1993:43–44).

Feminist Perspectives

Feminist theorists and researchers traditionally emphasized the extent to which girls and women were disadvantaged by receiving less attention in mathematics and science classes, as shown in a study by the American Association of University Women (1992) (see Chapter 4). Recent work has shown that it is no longer easy to show which gender is the more disadvantaged. As noted below in the section on educational opportunity, women have higher rates of educational attainment than men except at the doctoral and some professional (e.g., engineering) degree levels, and women are doing better in mathematics and science at the secondary level. As psychologist Carol Tavris (2002:B7) has said in the *Chronicle*:

> Who is having more trouble in schools: girls, more likely to be overlooked, or boys, who have more learning disabilities? Who has the greater self-esteem problem: girls, who feel insecure and fall silent, or boys, who feel insecure and brag? Who has the greater bullying problem: girls, who do it verbally, or boys, who do it physically? Who has the eating and body-image disorders: White middle-class girls, with their familiar problems of anorexia and bulimia, or teenage boys, many of whom are taking dangerous amounts of steroids and pumping themselves up to meet a cultural ideal no less damaging than gauntness is for girls?

Some feminists are studying boys and speaking up for their problems, as Carol Gilligan did by giving a keynote address at a recent international conference on educating boys. She said she had "seen some public schools switching over to single-sex classes as a way to boost concentration, reduce distractions and even enhance student performance" (Owens, 2002). Feminists have traditionally emphasized the disadvantaged situation of women and girls. In the future, we may find them not looking at men as the opposition,

To overcome gender bias in schools, some parents are now enrolling their children in same-sex schools, such as this private school that enrolls only girls.

but rather conducting programs and research to help anyone at a disadvantage, no matter which gender.

PROBLEMS IN CANADIAN EDUCATION

Although we have already identified a variety of problems in education, other issues must be addressed in planning for the future of this country. These issues include the problem of illiteracy; the impact of high rates of immigration on educational systems; racialized, class, and gender inequalities in educational opportunities; and growing concerns about violence in schools.

What Can Be Done about Illiteracy?

From time to time, reports emerge suggesting that a high percentage of Canadians are *functionally illiterate*—**unable to read and/or write at the skill necessary for carrying out everyday tasks.** To determine the extent of illiteracy in many industrialized countries, including Canada and the United States, the International Adult Literacy Survey was conducted in 1994–95. Three types of literacy were surveyed:

- Prose: understanding and responding to instructions;
- Document: understanding maps, graphs, or timetables; and
- Quantitative: calculating costs of various items.

Five levels of each type of literacy were created. For example, Level 1 of prose involved applying instructions on a medicine bottle and Level 5 involved answering a question from a personnel department in terms not used in the question. In Canada, 5660 people aged 16 to 65 were surveyed, and the majority had adequate literacy skills, measured as being at Level 3 or higher for the three types of literacy (Clark, 1996:28). Little difference was found between males and females (women scored slightly higher in prose, and men scored slightly higher in quantitative literacy). Younger people scored higher than older people (Clark, 1996:30). People who were more highly educated and people who read frequently scored predictably higher than those who did not complete high school and did not read newspapers and books (Clark, 1996:33). Another analysis of the data showed that whereas anglophones scored higher than francophones, the difference in scores was almost entirely due to education, not language differences. In Canada, until recently, anglophones tended to have higher educational attainment than francophones (Corbeil, 1998:6). Although the majority of Canadians are quite literate, a sizable proportion, one in six people, had literacy skills at Level 1. Far from reporting feelings of inadequacy, almost half the people at this level thought that their reading skills on the job were "good" or "excellent" and most thought that their skills would not limit their job opportunities (Clark, 1996:32). Perhaps, instead of "functional illiterate," a new term, such as *low-level literate,* should be used to identify **those who can maintain their current occupation but have minimal skills for adapting to a more complex occupation**. The problem is that, in a complex and rapidly changing world, Canadians need to be functioning at higher levels of literacy to adapt to new challenges. One ray of hope comes from the general increase in years of schooling, or educational attainment, among younger people. The percentage of people completing secondary school is now almost 90 percent. Thus, the proportion of people who are low-level literate might be expected to decrease in the future. Only 10 percent of secondary-school

Volunteers and trained professionals are an important link in reducing adult illiteracy. How can we make it easier for people to learn to read without experiencing embarrassment?

graduates and no university graduates function at Level 1(Clark, 1996:33).

Some critics argue that the illiteracy problem is largely an immigration problem. Recent immigrants to this country may continue to speak their own languages rather than learn English and French.

Educational Problems of Immigrants

Debates over the role of schools in educating immigrants for life in Canada are not new. In fact, high rates of immigration—along with the rapid growth of industrial capitalism—brought about the free public school movement. Many immigrants arriving in Canadian cities around the beginning of the last century spoke no English and could neither read nor write. But workers needed basic reading, writing, and arithmetic skills to get jobs in factories and offices. Initially, a Grade 8 education was considered sufficient for many jobs, but soon a high-school diploma became a prerequisite for most jobs above the level of the manual labourer. Schooling during this era was designed primarily to give people the means to become self-supporting. Educational systems were supposed to turn out workers with the knowledge and skills needed to enter the labour market and produce profits for managers and owners.

In the second half of the 20th century, this country is again experiencing high rates of immigration from many nations around the world, and many of the newcomers are school-age children (see Chapter 15). Although some of the recent groups of immigrants, including many Chinese and Asian Indians, are well educated, most have limited formal education and few job skills. Immigrant parents are likely to have either lower or higher levels of education than Canadian-born parents (Statistics Canada, 2001d) and their children likely speak neither English nor French.

How best to educate children of recent immigrants with lower levels of education and income is a pressing problem in such cities as Toronto, Vancouver, and Montreal, which have high levels of immigration.

Preliminary studies of newcomer programs show that children learn English and Canadian culture rather quickly. According to the National Longitudinal Study of Children and Youth (see Chapter 11), while children (whether or not born in Canada) of immigrant parents start school with more than 20 percent less developed reading, writing, and mathematics skills than do classmates of Canadian-born parents, by the time they are age 10 or 11, they have caught up and in some cases surpassed their classmates. Where the language spoken at home was not English or French, the children were at a greater disadvantage. But, children whose parents had more education had less of a disadvantage (Statistics Canada, 2001d).

Educational Opportunities and Ascribed Statuses

Secondary Education

We have long known that ascribed statuses—such as family structure and socioeconomic status, children's gender or racialized/ethnic status, and geographic region lived in—have a significant affect on educational outcomes. The following sections look at a variety of ascribed statuses and their influence on children's educational outcomes. The findings of the 1994 General Social Survey provide an opportunity to study the influence of family structure on the likelihood that children will complete high school. According to a study by Statistics Canada analyst Judith Frederick and sociologist Monica Boyd (1998:13), children from families living with both biological parents are more likely to complete high school than children from either blended or lone-parent families. Whereas over 80 percent of children living with both biological parents completed high school, slightly less than 70 percent of the children from blended families and slightly more than 70 percent of the children from lone-parent families completed high school. However, if the lone-parent had high-school or higher educational attainment, then the chances of the adolescents completing high school increased greatly; about 85 percent of these children completed high school, in comparison with 94 percent of the adolescents from two-parent families completing high school (Frederick and Boyd, 1998:14). Thus, whereas family structure does affect educational outcomes, parents' education appears be even more influential.

The results of an analysis by Statistics Canada analyst Patrice de Broucker and consultant Laval Lavallée (1998:13) of Canadian data from the previously noted International Adult Literacy Study also show that parents' education does count. The probability of earning a diploma or degree is highest for young adults whose parents also have postsecondary education. Whereas over 60 percent of young adults whose parents have postsecondary completion earn a diploma or degree, only about a quarter of young adults whose parents have not completed high school have postsecondary completion.

The social class of the parents is also crucial. De Broucker and Lavallée (1998:13) also discovered that the socioeconomic status (SES—composed of measures of the workers' income and education, and the percentage of women among the workers) of the parents' occupations was related to the educational attainment of the young adults. The higher the SES score of the father, the higher the child's educational level. Even fathers without high-school education but with a higher SES occupation can provide an environment and resources to help their children attain a postsecondary degree. Regarding performance in individual subjects, in an OECD study of reading, mathematics, and science, students from high SES backgrounds outperformed students from low SES backgrounds (Statistics Canada, 2001c).

As regards high-school completion, women are doing very well. According to Statistics Canada's Youth Transition survey (Statistics Canada, 2002x), only 9 percent of women dropped out of high school in 1999, as measured by the percentage of 20-year-olds who had not completed high school and were no longer in school. This is an important improvement over 1991, when 14 percent dropped out. A higher percentage of men are dropping out, 15 percent of men in 1999 in comparison to 22 percent in 1991. The results of this study also underlined the influence of family structure noted above. Although the majority of both high-school graduates and dropouts lived in a two-parent family during high school, a greater percentage of dropouts than graduates (32 percent vs. 16 percent) lived with a single parent. Dropouts were also three times as likely as graduates to have parents who had not finished high school (27 percent vs. 9 percent).

For particular subjects, like mathematics and science, a large number of past studies have shown what amounted to gender bias; girls were discouraged from doing well in these subjects or even pursuing them. Now, however, girls are now doing much better in these courses, as shown in recent national test results. According to the OECD study, in which Canadians scored very high, no significant differences between girls and boys were found in science test scores. Scores for reading were significantly higher for girls, and scores for mathematics were significantly higher for boys, but by a slimmer difference than for reading (Statistics Canada, 2001c).

Unfortunately, data on the influence of racialization/ethnicity on high-school completion are not as recent as other data seen here. A study by sociologists Jason Z. Lian and David Ralph Matthews (1998:467), using data from the 1991 Census, showed that whereas 30 percent of all Canadians had not completed high school, 60 percent of those reporting Portuguese ancestry, 44 percent of those reporting Greek, and 41 percent of those reporting Vietnamese had not completed high school. Those reporting British or French ancestry were at the overall average; 30 percent had not completed high school. Blacks were not far off that figure; 31 percent had not completed high school. A comparison of 1986 and 1996 Census data showed that the percentage of Indigenous men and women with less than high-school completion had fallen. Whereas 62 percent of men and 59 percent of women had not

completed high school in 1986, those percentages had declined to 48 and 42 respectively (Tait, 1999). But Indigenous people are still at a disadvantage, since they are still 2.6 times as likely to be without high-school completion as non-Indigenous people. In conclusion, given the present low percentage of 20-year-olds who have not graduated from high school, the 2001 Census should show much lower percentages of people from all racialized/ethnic groups who have not completed high school.

Although no clear differences are found among the large regions of Canada for completing high school, Quebec and Prince Edward Island were the provinces with the highest percentages (16 percent) of dropouts, and New Brunswick and Saskatchewan were the provinces with the lowest percentages (8 percent) of dropouts.

Postsecondary Education

Many educators had hoped that, with the expansion of the higher-education sector in the1960s and 1970s, the influence of ascribed statuses such as racialization/ethnicity, class, gender, and region would be eliminated. Indeed, a large percentage of the 1960s cohort did go to university and 19 percent of the cohort achieved a baccalaureate degree (Wanner, 1999). During the last decades of the 20th century, it was obvious that a very high percentage of women and francophones were going to university. But were class factors being reduced also? To answer this question, Wanner studied data from the 1973 Canadian Mobility Study and the 1986 and 1994 General Social Surveys. He found that in recent cohorts the influence of gender and language (francophone in Quebec) were negligible. He also found, however, that class was still a factor, though less so than previously. As noted above, parents' education is related to that of the children. If parents did not complete high school, a good chance exists that, because of lack or resources or learning environment, the children will not go on to university.

Although a relatively high percentage of Canadians have completed university, this is not true for all ethnic groups. According to the study by Lian and Matthews (1998:467), whereas in 1991, 16.7 percent of all Canadians had completed university, only 11.9 percent of Black, 4.5 percent of Portuguese, and 4.2 percent of Indigenous Canadians had completed university.

The Youth Transition Study also showed that Eastern and Central Canadians were slightly more likely to attend postsecondary school than Western Canadians, but the differences were minimal (Statistics Canada, 2002x). A more telling measure of the influence of region is commuting distance to university. It has a significant effect on university attendance. High-school students who lived beyond commuting distance of a university (beyond 80 km) were far less likely to attend university than those living within commuting distance (within 40 km). To compound the problem, commuting distance had a much greater negative impact on university access for students with lower family incomes (Statistics Canada, 2002e).

Bullying and School Violence

In the past six years, one student—Reena Virk of Victoria, B.C.—has been killed and three students—Dawn-Marie Wesley and Hamed Nastoh, also of British Columbia, and Emmet Fraslick of Halifax—have committed suicide because of bullying. But in June, 2002, two other students, David Knight and his sister Katharine Knight, in Burlington, Ontario, took a very different approach to this problem. They sued their current and former high-school principals and vice-principals for failing to protect them from a group of bullies. They are also suing the ringleaders for harassment (Malarek, 2002:A4). Because of incidents like these, bullying has become a very prominent social problem in the last few years.

Bullying is common at schools. In a Fact Sheet prepared for the National Crime Prevention Council, psychologists Debra Pepler, Wendy Craig, and Jennifer Connelly (1997:2) state that in a Canadian survey of elementary-school children, 6 percent admitted bullying others "more than once or twice" in the past six weeks and 15 percent of the children reported being victimized at the same rate. They also note that these data are similar to other surveys. As a result of its prominence, questions about bullying, defined as "when one or more people tease, hurt, or upset a weaker person on purpose," were added by drug use researchers Edward Adlaf and his colleagues (2002:46) to their continuing survey of drug use by older students in Ontario. They found for the year 2001 that 31.8 percent of students in Grades 7 through OAC (Grade 13, now abolished) reported bullying others at school and 24.6 percent reported being bullied, with 5.7 percent being bullied daily or weekly. That a higher percentage of people

report bullying than being bullied may be due to group bullying or the reluctance of people to admit being a victim. As is commonly the case, males reported both bullying and being bullied more than girls, and younger students reported both bullying and being bullied more than older students (Adlaf et al., 2002:46).

Although bullying has been prominent recently, school violence has been a concern for much longer. In his study of officials from 260 school boards and 250 police chiefs across the country, criminologist Thomas Gabor (1995) found that 80 percent of both groups felt that violence and intimidation had grown from the mid-1980s to the mid-1990s. Studying weapons use in Canadian schools, S.G. Walker (1994) found that weapons use increased from the late-1980s to the mid-1990s. Adlaf et al. (2002:43), in their study, found that 12.3 percent of the students surveyed had assaulted someone in the past year and 10.4 percent admitted carrying a weapon at school. In both cases, a higher percentage of males reported the offence, but no significant grade or age differences occurred. This study was one of the continuing biennial (since 1977) surveys of Ontario students' drug use by the now Centre for Addiction and Mental Health. Previous waves of this study of drug use had asked students in Grades 7, 9, 11, and OAC about committing assault and carrying weapons. Comparing only these grades, the researchers found that the incidence of assault peaked in 1997, with 20.4 percent of the students reporting it, and then declined to 11.5 percent in 2001; carrying weapons peaked in 1993, with 15.4 percent of the students reporting it, and then declined to 9.0 percent in 2001 (Adlaf et al., 2002:43).

Dealing with bullying and violence is a major challenge. Some places in the United States have chosen to rebuild schools. Today, some school buildings look like fortresses or prisons, with high fences, bright spotlights at night, and armed security guards. Many schools have installed metal detectors at entrances, and some schools search students for weapons, drugs, and other contraband as they enter. Consider this journalist's description of how one school district is attempting to reduce violence (Applebome, 1995a:A1):

The sprawling new brick building next to the Dallas County Probation Department has 37 surveillance cameras, six metal detectors, five full-time police officers and a security-conscious configuration based on the principles of crime prevention through environmental design. It is not the Big House. It is a schoolhouse: Dallas's $41 million state-of-the-art Townview Magnet Center.

Most educational analysts acknowledge that technology alone will not rid schools of violence and crime. In Canada, a wide variety of programs has been developed—from zero tolerance of violence (e.g., Scarborough, a former suburb of Toronto, Board of Education), to Alberta's Safe and Caring School Project, to the creation of the Canadian Safe Schools Network (CSSN), a grassroots organization dedicated to reducing youth violence and making schools and communities safer (website: **www.cssn.ca**). In September 2002, the CSSN launched the Empowered Student Partnerships (EPS) program to empower students to plan, organize, and execute safe-school programs in the Toronto area. Organizations involved include the Toronto Police Service; City Council; ProAction, a concerned business association; and the Toronto School Board. The CSSN has also created a CD-ROM of six bullying incidents and interventions, which can be viewed from the perspective of the victim, perpetrator, and bystander.

Some educators have advocated the use of school uniforms because young people are less likely to be attacked for a pair of sneakers or for jewellery or designer clothes if all students are required to dress alike (Mathis, 1996). We do not know yet whether the positive effects of school uniforms outweigh the negative consequences—such as the embarrassment of poor families who cannot purchase the uniforms (Muto, 1995; Mathis, 1996).

Ensuring safety at school for students and teachers alike is another challenge facing school districts that are burdened with shrinking budgets, decaying buildings, and heightened demands for services.

Residential Schools

Residential schools for Indigenous youth to help them assimilate into the Euro-Canadian culture began in the late 19th century and grew in number to a total of 80 schools by 1930 (Miller, 2002). By then, the Roman Catholics operated 60 percent of these schools, and the remainder was divided between the Anglican and United Churches. Generally the Indigenous students experienced more misery than benefit from poor facilities, poor teaching methods, frequent corporal punishment, and sexual abuse. In addition, Indigenous languages were forbidden in the school, Indigenous ways were disparaged, and the Euro-Canadian values were considered superior (Miller, 2002).

After many years of protest by Indigenous people and the realization that the schools were at best ineffective and at worst very damaging, in 1969 it was decided to close the residential schools. Now, Indigenous people's groups are suing the churches and government for compensation for the consequences of the maltreatment. The churches have said that settling these suits could bankrupt them. The government has made various proposals, but settling these suits will take a long time and be very costly.

PROBLEMS IN FINANCING EDUCATION

Elementary and Secondary Education

It is well known that governments have been cutting back on school budgets. Although support for elementary and secondary education in Canada is among the highest in the developed world, the contribution by governments per pupil has declined since the mid-1990s. Recently the Canadian Centre for Policy Alternatives released a study showing this decline for Ontario. The author of the study, researcher Hugh Mackenzie (2002), said that the General Legislative Grants (GLG) for 2002–03, announced by the government on May 21, 2002, were presented as providing the relief school boards needed. But an analysis of the funding announcement reveals that, when cost increases and enrollment changes are taken into account, the grants to school boards were at least $144 million short of what would be needed to avoid further cuts in programs for 2002–03. Analysis of school board funding for 2002–03 shows that funding for elementary and secondary education on a real, per-student basis has been cut by between $2.2 and $2.5 billion since 1995. Adjusting for enrollment change and cost increases, 2002–03 funding would have to be increased by at least $2.2 billion to match the 1994 level. In general, the cuts have been concentrated in large, urban public boards in southern Ontario. In 2000–01, total board operating deficits amounted to $37 million. For 2001–02, the Ontario Public School Boards Association estimates that half the boards in the province will complete the year in deficit. On a per-student basis, funding increased by $349 from 1994 before adjusting for costs. After adjusting for costs, funding per student is down by $581 from 1994.

Postsecondary Education

Like the other levels of education, the postsecondary level has seen substantial decline in governmental support. In order to make up the shortfall, universities and colleges increased tuition substantially during the 1990s. In 2001–02, undergraduate arts students paid an average of $3452 in annual tuition. This is double the average tuition of $1714 in 1991–92. Between 1990–91 and 2000–01, tuition fees of all programs rose 126.2 percent, or six times faster than the 20.6 percent increase in inflation as measured by the Consumer Price Index (Statistics Canada, 2001g). Though tuition in B.C. had not increased as much as in the other provinces by 2000–01, the province's government ended the six-year tuition freeze, and B.C. universities have increased their tuition. For example, the University of Victoria increased tuition by 30 to 60 percent in 2003 (author's files).

The provincial governments also deregulated fees for certain courses so that the universities and colleges could charge increased tuition for professional and graduate education. As a result, in 2001–02, average graduate education tuition was $4360, medicine was $6654, dentistry was $8491, and law was $4335. Although student loans were available for paying tuition and expenses, an obvious consequence was that the number of graduating students with large debts increased. Even before the most recent big hikes, students were having difficulties. According to the National Graduates Surveys of 1995 and 1997, the 1995 graduates owed more than any previous class. Nearly half the student population at colleges and universities was borrowing money. The average amount borrowed was $9600 by college students and $13 300 by university students. Because earnings did not keep pace with repayment demands, students experienced difficulties, and by 1997, 1 in 20 students had defaulted (Clark, 1998:28). Now, 5 percent of the graduating class of University of Toronto leaves school with the maximum Ontario Student Assistance Program (OSAP) debt ($28 000), according to President Robert Birgeneau (2002:5). He went on to say, "Such high debt is unacceptable in my view, and we must work with the province and our students to reduce this burden." To protest these increases in tuition, students from across the country held a National Day of Action on February 6, 2002.

A more extreme example of tuition increase is that for studying law at the University of Toronto, where the Faculty of Law plans to increase tuition to $22 000 over the next few years. In defence of the increase, Dean Ronald J. Daniels (2002:A15) wrote in the *Globe and Mail*, "We're pursuing an ideal by offering a challenging intellectual experience steeped in Canadian law and legal institutions that also takes account of broader international experience." He also said the faculty was offering expanded ranks of professors, reduced class sizes, and new courses. Finally, he noted that it was offering increased financial aid and compared the increased tuition to that at top U.S. schools, which charge $27 500 even for in-state students. The Black Law Students Association of Canada was very critical of the tuition hike and asked the Ontario Human Rights Commission to investigate the increase, saying that it would discriminate against minority and low-income students. According to the Association, the average annual income for Black families in Toronto is $25 000. Louise James, a member of the Association, quoted in the *Varsity*, the student newspaper of the University of Toronto, said that the faculty, "don't address the problem that is going to be posed by the tuition hike, in terms of attracting more students of diverse backgrounds and improving their experience at law school" (Holloway, 2002:1).

Commercialization of Postsecondary Education

Another important aspect of school financing is commercialization. The commercialization of universities and colleges takes many forms—for example, the obvious increase in corporate advertisements in washrooms and corridors and the greater numbers of soft-drink machines and fast-food franchises such as Tim Hortons. The machines are on almost every floor and the franchises are in almost every building with classrooms on campus. Another form of commercialization is the opportunity for corporations to name buildings and classrooms. Individual bricks are available for the names of individual donors. As a speaker at a retirement party for a university president suggested, "Only the doorknobs remain." As a result, the fundraising arm of universities—called by a succession of euphemisms, such as external relations, advancement, and development—has gained in importance and its vice-president is sometimes the highest-paid official at the university. These forms of commercialization are found at both colleges and universities, but a third form of commercialization is more problematic for universities.

Universities are being encouraged to form partnerships with corporations. These relationships are intended to provide research facilities and funding as government funding declines. From the access to university researchers, businesses feel they can be at the cutting-edge of their industry. The university can enhance its image if it can contribute innovative products—from drugs to software. For example, the University of Waterloo is well known for its innovative contributions to computer technology and generating of companies like OpenText. Finally, students can gain because the collaborations can help them find co-op assignments and future employment.

However, there are problems with these collaborations. For example, in Chapter 10, we have already seen an example of such conflict. Despite an agreement of confidentiality, a medical researcher, Dr. Nancy Olivieri, because of ethical concerns, published results about the harmful effects of a drug she was testing for Apotex, a pharmaceutical company. At the same time, the University of Toronto was negotiating with Apotex for a substantial grant for the university. Although the problems have been resolved now, Olivieri did not receive immediate support from the university. In their book *No Place to Learn: Why Universities Aren't Working*, political scientists Tom Pocklington and Allan Tupper (2002:148) discuss the close links between universities and corporations and conclude that universities

> may knowingly or unwittingly link themselves with corporations and thereby operate in ways contrary to other legitimate interests and groups in society. In this way, universities can seriously overextend their mandates as educational institutions. Their priorities can be badly distorted as a result.

EDUCATIONAL PROBLEMS IN THE 21ST CENTURY

Many problems remain unsolved in Canadian education. Rates of low-level literacy are worrisome, especially when many people feel complacent about their being at that level. Perhaps the best way to give the greatest number of people the opportunity to learn how to read and thus more opportunities in society is to address illiteracy at both the national and local levels.

What about the issue of Canadian students traditionally not achieving, in reading, science, and mathematics, at the levels of students in other high-income nations? Although recent results suggest that a significant improvement has been made, only when these results have been confirmed by trend data can we be confident that we are moving in the right direction.

Several years ago, the United States set national goals to be met by the year 2000:

1. All children in the United States will start school ready to learn.
2. The high-school graduation rate will be 90 percent or higher.
3. Students will leave Grades 4, 8, and 12 showing competency in challenging subject matter.
4. American students will be the best in the world in mathematics and science.
5. Every adult in the United States will be literate.
6. Schools will be free of drugs, guns, and violence.
7. Schools will promote partnerships with parents.
8. Teachers will have the means for professional development. (Kendall, 2001:267–268)

Because education is a provincial matter, Canadians do not set national educational goals. We have come very close to achieving Goal 2 and reasonably close to Goal 4. The United States is far from achieving any of the goals. Do you think it is a good idea to set goals like these? Do you think it is discouraging to set goals so lofty that they are unlikely to be met?

Some parents are avoiding the problems of school safety and quality by home schooling their children. Home schooling has become a popular option for some Canadian families, especially in the West. Home schooling occurs when a student participates in his or her schooling at home rather than attending a public, private, or other type of school (Luffman, 1998). Since the early 1990s, the numbers receiving home schooling have grown from 0.1 percent of school-aged children to over 0.4 percent—17 000 students in 1995–96. Parents who teach their children at home are generally dissatisfied with the public system or believe that parents should be the educators. The majority of home-schoolers are at the elementary level. But with the Internet providing greater access to information, and the opportunity to follow a blended approach of taking some courses at home and some at school, students may continue home schooling to higher levels. Such students can sometimes be admitted to university by passing entrance examinations, but not having a full transcript from a high school may make admission very difficult (Luffman, 1998).

Some provinces have charter schools. A charter school is an autonomous public school. The school has full authority and is freed from the bureaucracy of a larger school district. Some charter schools have a special emphasis, such as science or special education; others offer the same curricula as other public schools but in an "improved," more creative version. Some charter schools are found in Alberta. They are popular with parents, and students seem to be doing as well in these schools as students in the public system (Bosetti et al., 2000). However, many people believe charter schools create more problems than they solve because they take money away from already financially strapped, conventional public schools (Wallis, 1994).

Another approach is sending children to private schools. In 1998–99, 5.6 percent of elementary and high-school students, almost 300 000 students, went to private schools of all types (Statistics Canada, 2001f). Although private-school students tend to come from upper-income groups, they are found in all income groups, with the highest percentage, 29 percent, from households earning $50 000 to $74 000 per year. Quebec and B.C. have the highest percentages (9.2 and 8.8, respectively) of students attending these schools; very few in the Atlantic provinces attend private schools. The low rate of 4.3 percent for Ontario students was expected to rise with the introduction of a tax credit for private-school fees (deferred for a year in June 2002).

In the United States, some for-profit companies have been hired to operate public schools on a contract basis. The Edison Project took over management of schools in Boston, Massachusetts; Mount Clemens, Michigan; Sherman, Texas; and Wichita, Kansas. Initially, the project was hailed as a rousing success because academic performance improved and students received such extras as home computers. But whether improvement can be maintained is uncertain. Some argue that demands from investors for increased profits are likely to result in cost-cutting measures and lack of public accountability (Applebome, 1996). Although Canada does not yet have a privately run educational system, we do have many private tutoring services. For example, some parents hire tutors or send their children to private tutoring schools like Kumon, Oxford Learning Centre, and Sylvan Learning Center. According to sociologist Scott Davies and his colleagues (2002:37), these franchises have grown 60 percent in Ontario in the past decade and have "hundreds of sites across Canada." These franchises develop their own methods of assessment, pedagogy, and evaluation. Besides providing tutoring in mathematics and language to school-age students, they also provide tutoring in time management and preschool education. Davies et al. (2002:38) believe that private tutoring businesses and learning centres are "part of a burgeoning industry that may alter the landscape of Canadian education."

During the 21st century, we must not underestimate the importance of education as a social institution. It is a powerful and influential force that imparts the values, beliefs, and knowledge necessary for the social reproduction of individual personalities and entire cultures (Bourdieu and Passeron, 1990). But in what direction should this tremendous social force move? Some educators, parents, and political leaders believe that we should continue to focus on delivering a core curriculum and instilling discipline in students. We must also provide safety and order in our public schools (Loury, 1997).

Others argue that education must prepare students for today's high-tech living. They believe learning how to use the computer and how to access information on the Internet and the World Wide Web are perhaps the most important skills schools can teach contemporary students. Almost all Canadians, 97 percent, believe that computer technology and the Internet are key to Canada's ability to compete in the global economy in the future. Therefore, they think it is important for today's students to have access to computers and the Internet in the schools. A small percentage (less than 10 percent) feel that computers are used too much at elementary, secondary, and university levels (Ipsos-Reid, 2002). But will computers, the Internet, and the World Wide Web improve education? The Internet can make doing assignments easier for those who prefer to cut and paste information rather than think in an ordered or comprehensive manner. Here is what author Clifford Stoll (1996:E15) says about technology and learning:

> What's most important in a classroom? A good teacher interacting with motivated students. Anything that separates them—filmstrips, instructional videos, multimedia displays, e-mail, TV sets, interactive computers—is of questionable education value. . . . Yes, kids love these high-tech devices and play happily with them for hours. But just because children do something willingly doesn't mean that it engages their minds. Indeed, most software for children turns lessons into games. The popular arithmetic program Math Blaster simulates an arcade shoot-'em-down, complete with enemy flying saucers. Such instant gratification keeps the kids clicking icons while discouraging any sense of studiousness or sustained mental effort. . . . For decades, we've welcomed each new technology . . . as a way to improve teaching. Each has promised better students and easier learning. None has succeeded. Except that it is even more expensive, I suspect that classroom computing isn't much different.

The importance of a good teacher is exemplified in the philosophy and work of Ainsworth Morgan, mentioned in Box 12.2 as one of the developers of a project to challenge the ghetto image among inner-city students. He is actually a graduate of the school where he teaches, the first graduate to return to teach there in the school's 150 years. He says that his inspiration comes from his mother, who created, first, an atmosphere of respect at home, believing that "love comes later." With this inspiration, hard work, and considerable athletic ability, he obtained his bachelor's degree in the U.S. on an athletic scholarship. Then, he returned to Canada to play wide-receiver for the Toronto Argonauts and Saskatchewan Roughriders. Realizing his true calling was teaching, he then took teacher training at the University of Toronto and obtained a job

teaching science and core Grade 7 and 8 at his "alma mater."

Ainsworth's philosophy is similar to his mother's; he creates an atmosphere of respect and emphasizes, "Students should have a say in who they are" and "should not be limited by their postal code." He works closely with the students, frequently staying till six o'clock to help them with projects, like the G.H.E.T.T.O. Project. (When one of the authors visited his class at the end of the school day, he saw a student preparing to storm out of the class. After Ainsworth's quiet request for an explanation for leaving and an expression of interest in her, she returned and was still working when the author left.)

His dedication to inner-city students extends into the summer. The Horizons Project, which takes place in Upper Canada College, a private boarding and day school in Toronto, brings together urban youth who show academic potential, from situations where academic achievement is not celebrated, because local peer culture discourages it (see above the section on labelling). That potential is nurtured and celebrated in an open and caring environment. The students are taught mathematics, science, history, and language for three years beginning in Grade 6. Discovering that it is possible to do well and being supported by peers should help the youth do well in high school.

In co-operation with others, Ainsworth has developed a complex mentorship/life-skills training program and line of clothing called G.H.E.T.T.O. Movement (Gaining Higher Education To Teach Others). A portion of the profits from the clothing will go to the Pathways to Education program, an inner-city project of the Regent Park Community Health Centre to provide mentors and tutors for students, money for school supplies, and scholarships for university.

The school where Ainsworth teaches has recently been renamed after Nelson Mandela. Ainsworth has adopted an African proverb that Nelson Mandela lives by, "People are people through other people." Ainsworth Morgan's philosophy and work is a vivid example of that adage. Pursuing such an ideal and widely replicating this program would certainly help remedy some of the problems in Canadian schools.

Another excellent example of local activism in education is JUMP (Junior Undiscovered Math Prodigies), a Toronto-based charitable program founded in 1998 by mathematician and writer John Mighton and eight volunteers, which provides free tutoring, by volunteer tutors from many disciplines and backgrounds, to students having difficulty succeeding in mathematics. JUMP coordinates its program with dedicated educators at partnering elementary schools across the city, and specifically targets children and schools in low-income areas (JUMP, 2002).

Working with 11 partner schools across Toronto, JUMP recruits, trains, and schedules volunteer tutors to work with elementary-level students in need, identified and referred to the program by their teacher or school administrator. In 2002–03, JUMP has over 200 volunteer tutors working with hundreds of individual students across Toronto; a pilot program in 10 Toronto District School Board classrooms; and a pilot program with the York Detention Centre, a secure custody and detention facility located in downtown Toronto that serves youth from ages 12 to 15.

In line with the findings of accumulating research in early childhood education, JUMP believes that children, with very few exceptions, are born capable of learning anything, and that when any student fails a test, it should be seen as a failure of the education system. With its innovative teaching program and one-on-one approach, JUMP is adding to the evidence. When JUMP began, its initial four students were in remedial Grade 6 classes. This past year, having been in the program for three years, they were enrolled in academic Grade 9 math classes. In fall 2002, at Queen Victoria Public School, 30 JUMP students were given numeracy tests by a special education teacher. After five months of tutoring with JUMP, they had all advanced by one to four grade levels, with many advancing at least two grades. Similar results are being seen throughout the program, and parents and teachers are astounded at the changes they are seeing, not just in the children's math abilities, but in their overall confidence and self-esteem (JUMP, 2002). But Mighton (2002) argues that the students are not the only ones to benefit:

> Though the developed countries of the world presently have the resources to feed and educate everyone on earth, more than half the world's children still live in abject poverty. In affluent countries, violence, over-consumption, and the destruction of the environment continue at the same pace. JUMP was founded in reaction to the institutionalized apathy and ignorance that underlie these problems. if children grow up frustrated and insecure—meeting only fraction of their potential, unable to reason clearly or weigh the consequences of their actions, and having witnessed few models of effective charity, they will be easily exploited and misled by corporations and politicians seeking gain. Until educated people devote themselves to breaking this cycle of ignorance, no amount of political action is likely to improve our condition. The profound love parents feel for their children, and the money and time they lavish on their families, have not, to this day, been sufficient to change the world. Until we reach beyond our families, to children in need, we will continue to neglect the needs of the children closest to us, by passing on a world that is unfit for them to inherit.

WHAT CAN YOU DO?

- See if your college or university has a co-operative program with a local elementary or high school to provide mathematics, English, or other kinds of tutoring. If not, you might volunteer your services to a local principal or guidance counsellor.

- Find out if your student government has a program to educate students about the skyrocketing cost of tuition. You might help with the education program or organize a protest.

- Check out if your college or university has a peer-mediator program to help settle disputes or if a local, or your former, elementary or high school needs help with their programs to deal with bullying. If they do not have such programs, you might introduce them to the programs of the Canadian Safe School Network (see above) and help them organize a program.

- Familiarize yourself with the wide variety of ways in which girls and boys, and women and men, do poorly or feel at a disadvantage in schools and do some research to determine what approach can help overcome these problems.

- As a way of following all perspectives, you might consider becoming a teacher, like Ainsworth Morgan and John Mighton, to help students have a say in who they are and not be limited by their backgrounds.

SUMMARY

WHAT IS EDUCATION?

Education is the social institution responsible for transmitting knowledge, skills, and cultural values in a formally organized structure.

WHAT IS THE FUNCTIONALIST PERSPECTIVE ON EDUCATION?

Functionalists believe that education contributes to the smooth functioning of society when it fulfills its manifest functions. Education has at least five major manifest functions: socialization, transmission of culture, social control, social placement, and change and innovation. Schools also fulfill a number of latent functions—hidden, unstated, and sometimes unintended consequences of its activities—like matchmaking and networking.

WHAT IS THE CONFLICT PERSPECTIVE ON EDUCATION?

Conflict theorists believe that schools, which are supposed to reduce inequality in society, actually perpetuate inequalities based on class, racialization, and gender. The sociologist Pierre Bourdieu, for example, says that children from low-income and poverty-level families come to school with less cultural capital (values, beliefs, attitudes, and competencies in language and culture) than middle- and upper-income children. Conflict theorists also think that elites manipulate the masses and maintain their power in society through a hidden curriculum that teaches students to be obedient and patriotic and thus perpetuates the status quo in society.

WHAT IS THE INTERACTIONIST PERSPECTIVE ON EDUCATION?

Interactionists study classroom dynamics and the ways in which practices such as labelling affect students' self-concept and aspirations. If students are labelled "learning disabled," for example, the label may become a self-fulfilling prophecy, that is, an unsubstantiated or erroneous belief that results in behaviour that makes the false belief come true. A student who is erroneously labelled "learning disabled" may stop trying and teachers may lower their expectations, with the result that the student doesn't succeed in the long run.

WHAT IS THE FEMINIST PERSPECTIVE ON EDUCATION?

Feminists were traditionally concerned that girls were not getting equal attention in class with boys, especially for such courses as science and mathematics. Now, girls are performing almost as well as boys on international science and mathematics tests at the secondary level, and women are surpassing men in academic attainment at university, except for engineering and doctoral programs. As a result, some feminists are concerned that boys are at a disadvantage, with higher levels of learning disabilities, lower reading scores on the same international tests, and lower high-school completion rates than girls.

WHAT IS ILLITERACY AND WHAT CAN BE DONE ABOUT IT?

Functional illiteracy is the inability to read and/or write at the skill level necessary for carrying out everyday tasks. Today, one in six adults in Canada has low-level literacy, with higher proportions among lesser-educated and older people. Many of those with test scores at the lowest level of literacy feel that their abilities are good enough for their jobs. To be able to adapt to a modern economy it is necessary to have a high level of literacy. Perhaps with increasing percentages of people graduating from high school, there will be fewer with low-level literacy. But perhaps extra effort will be required to help people prepare to adapt.

ARE HIGH RATES OF IMMIGRATION A PROBLEM FOR CANADIAN SCHOOLS?

Though some immigrants are well educated, most have limited formal education and few job skills. Also, many immigrants are children, so schools must cope with language differences among students. Children of immigrant parents, upon entering school, are at a disadvantage, in reading, writing, and mathematics. But, with the help of a variety of programs, such children have generally overcome these problems by the end of elementary school.

HOW DO ASCRIBED STATUSES LIKE FAMILY STRUCTURE, CLASS, RACIALIZATION/ETHNICITY, GENDER, AND REGION AFFECT EDUCATIONAL OPPORTUNITIES IN SECONDARY AND POSTSECONDARY SCHOOLS?

Children from lone-parent families, from families with parents having low SES scores, from some racialized/ethnic groups (e.g., Black, Portuguese, and Indigenous), and from some provinces are less likely to graduate from high school than their classmates. Rates of high-school completion are also higher for girls than boys. As concerns postsecondary education and thus graduation, the above factors also apply, as well as how far away from college or university the students live.

HOW HAVE BULLYING AND VIOLENCE AFFECTED OUR SCHOOLS?

Suicides of students who were bullied have highlighted bullying as a significant factor at school. Among Grade 7 to OAC students in Ontario, a quarter report being bullied and almost a third report bullying someone in the past year. Regarding assault and weapon carrying, although it seems to be declining, it is still at an unacceptably high level. In Ontario, 1 in 8 report assaulting someone in the past year, and 1 in 10 report carrying a weapon to school.

WHAT IS THE CRISIS IN SCHOOL FINANCING?

Most educational funds for elementary and secondary education come from provincial and local taxes. Ontario government grants have not kept up with inflation and increasing enrollment. The per-student grant is lower now than in the mid-1990s. Government funds for postsecondary schools have also been reduced and tuition fees have been increased by over 100 percent in the past decade. Since fees for professional and graduate schools have been deregulated, some fees have skyrocketed. An extreme example is the University of Toronto Faculty of Law's plan to increase annual tuition to $22 000. As a result of past increases, some students have high levels of debt. With poor employment prospects, some students have had to default on their loans.

WHAT ARE THE MAJOR PROBLEMS IN HIGHER EDUCATION?

The soaring cost of a postsecondary education is a major problem because, say conflict theorists, it reproduces the existing class system: Those who attend university or college are stratified according to their ability to pay. Should racialization, ethnicity, and gender be taken into consideration for admissions, financial aid, scholarships, and faculty hiring?

WHAT ARE THE URGENT EDUCATIONAL PROBLEMS OF THE 21ST CENTURY?

To compete in the global economy, we must come to terms with illiteracy in our adult population and we must provide *all* children with safe, high-quality education. Some parents deal with issues of school safety and quality by home schooling their children, starting charter schools, or sending the children to private schools. Other innovative approaches are being tried by individuals and groups across the country.

KEY TERMS

education,   p. 274
functionally illiterate,   p. 280
hidden curriculum,   p. 277
latent functions,   p. 275

low-level literate,   p. 281
manifest functions,   p. 275
tracking,   p. 274

QUESTIONS FOR CRITICAL THINKING

1. Are you for or against support of schooling outside the public system (e.g., home, private, or charter schooling)? Why?

2. What would the effect be on public education if the curriculum were not subject to political agendas that can change every few years; if, for example, it were managed by an arm's length education council?

3. If you separate the caretaking function (need for childcare all day so parents can work) from the educational functions of school, what different options become possible for improving the quality of education? (For example, classes of half the size could attend school for half a day instead of a full day.) And what else in society would have to change to make this work (e.g., the length of the standard work-week, more flextime, a minimum wage that meant one income—or two half-incomes—could support a family, and so on)?

WEBLINKS

Canadian Education on the Web
www.oise.utoronto.ca/~mpress/eduweb.html
This site brings together everything about education in Canada to the Web.

Canadian Federation of Students
www.cfs-fcee.ca/pre_main.shtml
The Canadian Federation of Students represents over 450 000 students in 70 colleges and universities. Besides offering information about student concerns, like tuition hikes, it has links about health care, travel, and work abroad.

Departments of Education Across Canada
www.edu.gov.on.ca/eng/relsites/oth_prov.html
This site features education links for all the provinces and territories.

Education Index R
www.educationindex.com
Education Index R is an annotated guide to education.

Statistics Canada
www.statcan.ca/english/Pgdb
Data is available on a wide variety of subjects, such as the economy, the land, and the people, in which data about education is available.

13

PROBLEMS IN POLITICS AND THE GLOBAL ECONOMY

They did everything they could to make me forget I was human, to make me feel worthless, to make me turn my back on my principles. Though they tried to break us, we all have come out stronger, more militant and more dedicated to changing the world. When will they learn?

Liberty, a woman who was arrested and brutalized by Canadian police for her participation in the protests against the third Summit of the Americas in Quebec City—the FTAA protest (2001)

There is no activity more intrinsically globalizing than trade, no ideology less interested in nations than capitalism, no challenge to frontiers more audacious than the market. By many measures, corporations today are more central players in global affairs than nations. We call them multinational, but they are more accurately understood as transnational or post-national or anti-national. For they abjure the very idea of nations or any other parochialism that limits them in time or space. Their customers are not citizens or a particular nation or members of a parochial clan: they belong to the universal tribe of consumers defined by needs and wants that are ubiquitous, if not by nature then by cunning or advertising. A consumer is a consumer is a consumer.

Benjamin Barber, outlining his understanding of transnational corporations and their role in the world (1995)

The so-called "corporate citizen" is a super-citizen with rights that no flesh-and-blood citizen could ever dream of having. The corporate citizen never sleeps, has virtually unlimited resources, can commit horrendous crimes and never go to jail, and increasingly operates as if the other side of the citizenship coin—responsibilities—simply does not exist.

Murray Dobbin, a member of the Canadian Centre for Policy Alternatives, speaking about the myth of the good corporate citizen (1998)

The past four years have seen a wave of political organizing and militant protests. Students blockade trade meetings where politicians are bargaining their futures. In First Nations communities, from Vancouver Island to Burnt Church, New Brunswick, there is growing support for seizing back control of the forests and fisheries; people are tired of waiting for Ottawa to grant permission that the courts have already affirmed. In Toronto, the Ontario Coalition Against Poverty occupies buildings and demands the shelter that is the right of all Canadians.

Naomi Klein, talking about the grassroots protest movements that are growing in Canada (2002)

Healthy national democracies are a necessary foundation for a new global democracy. More and more people in this country feel unrepresented by the existing political system. This democracy deficit is reflected in voter turnout that declines every election: Our voter participation is now close to that in the United States. The democracy deficit is also reflected in the declining number of people who relate to political parties, and in polls that rate politicians and journalists near the bottom of the occupational respect chart. And, finally, it is reflected by the growing number of young people who are taking to the streets because they see no other way to influence government.

Judy Rebick, commenting on the increasing lack of faith Canadians have in the formal political processes (2001a)

Perhaps nothing better signifies our growing awareness of the intertwining of politics and the economy in today's global economy than the abrupt end of the World Trade Organization (WTO) meeting in Seattle, Washington, in 1999. At that time, a series of global trade talks deteriorated into confrontations between diverse protesters who demanded that large corporations and governments become more accountable for their actions and trade-talk delegates. Many of the delegates to the WTO went home frustrated after a highly unsuccessful meeting, and the world was left with a complicated set of political and economic factors to make sense of. The WTO event served to highlight some important problems that lie at the heart of the global economy and thus effect, and are affected by, Canadian politics. Among these problems are sweatshop labour conditions, child labour, and the environmental problems brought about by increased industrialization and decreased regulation (Klein, 2000).

Although there have been protests throughout Canadian history, especially during the 1930s and 1960s, the level of radical activism seen in Seattle had not been visible for many years. Some analysts believe that a new mood has arisen as more people feel a "loss of control in a world of rapid change and turbocharged global capitalism" (Elliott, 1999:37). This overall mood is leading to the development of a worldwide anti-globalization movement. Today, the Internet offers protesters and social activists a much wider audience than ever before and makes it possible to mobilize a worldwide campaign against political decisions or economic manoeuvres that are viewed as harmful to people and the environment (Elliott, 1999). This chapter will examine Canadian and global economic issues, anti-globalization movements, and Canadian politics.

THREE MAJOR MODERN ECONOMIC SYSTEMS

There are three major modern economic systems: capitalism, socialism, and mixed economies. The Canadian economy is a form of **capitalism, which is characterized by private ownership of the means of production, from which personal profits can be derived through market competition and without government intervention.** *Socialism* **is characterized by public ownership of the means of production, the pursuit of collective goals, and centralized decision-making.** Unlike capitalist economies, in which the primary motivation for economic activity is personal profit, the primary motivation in a socialist economy is the collective good of all citizens. For Karl Marx, socialism was only an intermediate stage to an ideal communist society in which the means of production and all goods would be owned by everyone. Under communism, Marx said, people would contribute according to their abilities and receive according to their needs. Moreover, government would no longer be necessary, since it existed only to serve the interests of the capitalist class.

No economy is purely capitalist or purely socialist; most are mixtures of both. A **mixed economy combines elements of both capitalism (a market economy) and socialism (a command economy).** Sweden, Great Britain, and France have an economic and political system known as *democratic socialism,* in which private ownership of some of the means of production is combined with governmental distribution of some essential goods and services and free elections. Although most industry in mixed economies is privately owned, there is considerable government involvement in setting rules, policies, and objectives. The government is also heavily involved in providing services such as health care, childcare, and transportation. Debates about problems in the Canadian economy often involve comparisons of capitalism with other types of economic systems.

There are four distinctive features of "ideal" capitalism: private ownership of the means of production, pursuit of personal profit, competition, and lack of government intervention. First, capitalism is based on the right of individuals to own various kinds of property, including those that produce income (e.g., factories and businesses). Second, capitalism is based on the belief that people should be able to maximize their individual gain through personal profit, which is supposed to benefit everyone, not just capitalists. Third, capitalism is based on competition, which is supposed to prevent excessive profits. For example, when companies are competing for customers, they must offer innovative goods and services at competitive prices. The need to do this, it is argued, prevents the market pricing of goods from spiralling out of reach of the consumer. Finally, capitalism is based on a lack of government intervention in the marketplace. According to this *laissez-faire* (meaning "leave alone") policy, also called *free enterprise*, competition in a free marketplace—not the government—should be the force that regulates prices and establishes workers' wages.

PROBLEMS IN THE GLOBAL ECONOMY

Twenty-five years ago, about one-third of the world's workers lived in countries with *centrally planned economies*—economies in which the government decides what goods will be produced and in what quantities—and another third lived in countries only weakly linked to international commerce because of protective barriers to trade and investment. Today, however, it is possible that fewer than 10 percent of the world's workers live in countries that are largely disconnected from world markets (World Bank, 1995). While the breakdown in trade barriers and the turn to economies based on the demands of the marketplace have brought new goods, capital, and ideals to many, they have also brought new fears:

> Rapid change is never easy. In rich and poor countries alike there are fears of rising insecurity, as technological change, expanding international interactions, and the decline of traditional community structures threaten jobs, wages, and support for the elderly. Nor have economic growth and rising integration solved the problem of world poverty and deprivation. Indeed, the numbers of the poor could rise still

further as the world labour force grows to a projected 3.7 billion in 30 years' time. The bulk of the more than a billion individuals living on a dollar or less a day depends on pitifully low returns to hard work. In many countries workers lack representation and they work in unhealthy, dangerous, or demeaning conditions. Meanwhile, at the end of 2002, 180 million people were unemployed worldwide, a 20 million increase from 2001 unemployment rates. The year 2003 holds no greater promise for millions more people who have given up hope of finding work. (World Bank, 1995:4; International Labour Organization, 2003)

The rapid changes in economies have raised serious concerns about the accountability of transnational corporations.

Transnational Corporations and Canada

Today, the most important corporate structure is the **transnational corporation** (**TNC**)—**a large-scale business organization that is headquartered in one country but operates in many countries, which has the legal power (separate from individual owners or shareholders) to enter into contracts, buy and sell property, and engage in other business activity.** These are different from multinational corporations, which have been around since the turn of the last century. The difference is that the **multinational corporation (MNC)—a complete corporate operation that is taken from its country of origin and integrated into its host country in order to successfully market its products in the local culture**—requires a strong host economy to survive. Transnational corporations—by design, truly global entities—prosper by serving global markets in an increasingly economically borderless world. They have advanced global capitalism in unprecedented ways (Dobbin, 2001). Some transnational corporations constitute a type of international monopoly capitalism that transcends the boundaries and legal controls of any one nation. Of the one hundred largest economies in the world, 52 percent are private corporations and not national economies (Andersson and Schemberg, 2002). The largest transnationals are headquartered in the United States, Japan, Korea, other industrializing Asian nations, and Germany. In 2001, the world's 65 000

transnationals generated over $19 trillion in sales—more than two times the world's exports for that year (Andersson and Schemberg, 2002). Examples of true transnational corporations are Asea Brown Boveri, a Swiss–Swedish engineering group, and Philips, a Dutch electronics firm. Both have 85 percent of their sales outside the country in which they are headquartered (Waters, 1995). Transnationals dominate in petrochemicals, motor vehicles, consumer electronics, tires, pharmaceuticals, tobacco, soft drinks, fast food, financial consulting, and luxury hotels (Waters, 1995). Canadian transnational corporations deal predominantly in gold and other minerals, such as nickel and copper, and oil and gas (Draffan, 2003).

Because transnational corporations are big and powerful, they play a significant role in the economies and governments of many countries. At the same time, by their very nature, they are not accountable to any government or any regulatory agency. Corporate executives often own a great number of shares in a transnational company. The shareholders in transnational corporations live throughout the world. These people have little control over where plants are located, how much money employees are paid, or how the environment is protected. As transnational corporations gain power, they increasingly determine what will be defined as news, which university departments will receive funding, what technology will be developed, and which political parities will be supported (Dobbin, 2001). Because transnationals do not depend on any one country for labour, capital, or technology, they can locate their operations in countries where political and business leaders accept their practices and few other employment opportunities exist for resident workers. For example, when Nike workers went on strike in Indonesia, Nike subcontracted to Korean entrepreneurs operating assembly plants in Vietnam. Although many workers in low-income nations earn less than a living wage from transnational corporations, the products they make are often sold for hundreds of times the cost of raw materials and labour. Managers of these plants are often also physically abusive to the women workers, and union organizing and other human rights organizing are often strongly deterred. Designer clothing and athletic shoes are two examples of products that are made under exploitative conditions (see Chapter 2). Further, the young women working in Nike factories in Indonesia and Vietnam usually go barefoot and certainly could not afford to buy the shoes they assemble (Goodman, 1996).

Still another concern is that transnational corporations foster global consumerism through advertising and the strategic placement of their business operations around the world. McDonald's golden arches and Coca-Cola signs can be seen from Confederation Square in Ottawa to Red Square in Moscow. Both companies are conquering other nations as aggressively as they have Canada. Coca-Cola has 72 000 employees worldwide on its payroll, 70 percent of whom work outside the United States; 5700 of these employees work in Canada (Hardy, 1996; Coca-Cola, 2003a, 2003b). Canada is host to many transnational corporations—primarily from the United States and some Asian countries.

While many Canadian businesses are foreign-owned, the conditions the businesses operate under are a cause of concern for many. The 2001 Canadian Democracy and Corporate Accountability Commission (CDCAC, 2002) found that 84 percent of Canadians want the government to promote international agreements to "set minimum enforceable standards for socially responsible corporate behaviour" (CDCAC, 2002: Executive Summary). Canadians across the political spectrum are expressing discomfort with transnational activities in many parts of the world, including in this country.

SOCIAL PROBLEMS IN GLOBAL PERSPECTIVE

BOX 13.1 Canada: Flirting with Disaster!

For over a decade, Canada has engaged in negotiating a collection of international trade agreements. In 1989, we signed the Free Trade Agreement (FTA). Since this time, our government has engaged in several multiyear negotiations that are designed to fully embed the nation in the global economy. Each treaty signed ties Canada's political, social, economic, and environmental well-being more closely to the interests and activities of multilateral trade organizations and transnational corporations.

Many Canadians are deeply troubled by the amount of power these agreements have given corporations and international alliances. These powers are often the same ones that have been taken away from Canadian governments and citizens. This is not a surprising response when 85 percent of our exports go south of the border to generate about $1 billion of revenue each day. It does nothing to boost confidence when people learn that the world is dominated by country-size corporations whose "central planning" capacity eclipses that of many countries or that over 350 billionaires hold a combined wealth equal to the annual income of nearly half of humanity (M. Barlow, 1996). Certainly, it is a founded fear when Canadians hear Renato Ruggerio, the Director General of the World Trade Organization (WTO), clearly state in 1996 that the WTO is being designed as "the constitution of a single world economy" (Public Citizen, 2003).

Governments and businesses justify their support of multilateral trade agreements by invoking the neoliberal rhetoric of "free market" and free enterprise. While there are clearly economic benefits to corporate involvement in the global economy, the accuracy of the notion of "free market" is questionable. A profile of the global market reveals that it is comprised of just 12 industrial sectors, and each of these sectors is controlled by 5 or fewer firms. These sectors include consumer durables, automotive, aerospace, electronic components, and steel, with oil, personal computers, and the media not far behind (Dobbin, 1998). Based on this information, it could be surmised that, rather than promoting the development of a free market, these multilateral trade agreements primarily promote and protect the interests of shareholders. Canadian policy analyst Murray Dobbin (1998) warns that this will continue to be the case if corporations are ruling the world.

An analysis of the Canadian economy shows that, for workers, multilateral trade agreements have tended to result in the loss of jobs, many in the relatively high-paying manufacturing area. Today, most new jobs are created in the service sector and are temporary, part-time, and non-unionized. As a result, Canada now has a predominantly "flexible" work force that earns smaller and smaller wages. For example, by 1999, 52 percent of Canadians were paid less than $15 per hour under the North American Free Trade Agreement (NAFTA). Further, due to NAFTA, 400 000 jobs have been lost, with re-employed workers earning an average of 77 percent of their previous wages (Steinberg, 2001). This is true in an era when dramatic cuts to social programs have helped to dismantle Canada's health care system, increased poverty for women and children, and left many sectors of society underserviced (Townson, 2003). The erosion of legislation that protects the environment and Canada's public natural resources from privatization is currently putting Canada's forests, fish, fresh water, and parks on the international auction block. Under new trade agreements, Canada is being dramatically revamped.

Many Canadians are becoming increasingly concerned that trade deals are not simply about ensuring fair trade between countries; rather, they are about securing power and profit for governments and large corporations. This becomes clear when the socioeconomic and political contexts within which multinational agreements are created, negotiated, and signed are analyzed. The Canada–U.S. Free Trade Agreement (FTA), for example, was signed when over 90 percent of trade between the two countries was tariff-free and the rest had tariffs of less than 5 percent (Dobbin, 1998). It was a decision that was strongly opposed by many Canadians. In 1999, the WTO was negotiated despite the clear protests of over 50 000 people from all walks of life, who were opposing the organization's mandate (Klein, 2002). In April 2001, the third Summit of the Americas (FTAA) was held in Quebec City—a city that had been barricaded to keep the close to 60 000 citizens expressing their criticism of the summit away from the meeting's headquarters (Editorial Collective, 2001). Dobbin (1998) states that the agreements are designed to serve the movement of capital, the removal of restrictions and regulation on that movement, the facilitation of production, and the lowering of production costs. He emphasizes that they are about the rights of capital, not people (Dobbin, 1998). Indeed, during the FTAA protest, people's everyday civil rights were violated in Quebec City and the surrounding areas. As one example, local legislators unsuccessfully attempted to pass a bylaw that would make it illegal to "wear or have [in your possession] a mask, hood, ski mask, or any other object of the same nature to cover one's face, in whole or in part" (Steinberg, 2001). These were all types of clothing protestors could wear as protection against tear gas and pepper spray. In addition, as early as January 2001, people suspected of being protest organizers were not allowed to cross the border from the U.S. into Canada (Steinberg, 2001).

One of the greatest challenges for Canadians is simply to learn about these agreements and their impacts. This is because many of the treaties are negotiated in secret caucuses; citizens are actively barred or dissuaded from stating dissent at public events; the language used to draft the agreements is often inaccessible; and, avenues for direct participation in the official process are blocked. As a clear example, the FTAA protest in Quebec City was not about the actual agreement itself but rather it was about the fact that the Canadian government would not allow its citizens access to the trade-deal documents it was discussing and signing with 33 other nations. Because trade deals impact every sphere of our daily life—from the food we eat to the clothes we wear, from the air we breathe to the health care we receive, and so on—if we are not allowed to know what our government is signing on our behalf, is democracy itself not in question?

A brief overview of the World Trade Organization and its role in the protection and perpetuation of multilateral trade agreements, such as the Free Trade Area of the Americas (FTAA) and the Multinational Agreement on Investment (MAI), demonstrate just how powerful such governing bodies are. It also shows how they will have the power to directly challenge the ability of Canadian governments and people to protect their own land, resources, and even sovereignty.

The World Trade Organization is the international body that codifies the rules upon which global trade systems of production and trade depend. It also administers dozens of trade and commerce agreements and declarations. Initiatives such as the FTAA, the MAI, and the activities of the G-8 (comprised of the seven largest economies in the world plus Russia) fall under the auspices of the WTO. The WTO was created in 1995 as a result of the Uruguay Round of negotiations of the General Agreement on Tariffs and Trade (GATT)—the body that for decades has regulated about 90 percent of global trade (Shrybman, 1999). Today, the WTO has 135 member countries and is run by its member governments. The real decision-making authority at the WTO is, however, held by the Quad (the EEU, the U.S., Japan, and Canada). "The Quad countries basically determine which issues come to the floor, and which issues do not" (Bello, in Shrybman, 1999:3). Member nations outside of the Quad, particularly those from the "Third World," complain that the issues of import to 98 percent of the WTO's members are often not meaningfully addressed. In a television interview with delegates to the WTO in Seattle, one delegate from a small nation stated clearly that the people on the streets were saying nothing that delegates from small nations inside the WTO haven't already been saying for years.

The WTO has authority and influence in part because any country found in contravention of the WTO's rulings is vulnerable to economic sanctions "too severe for even the wealthiest nation to ignore" (Shrybman, 1999:4). This is alarming when the WTO contains no minimum standards to protect the environment, labour rights, social programs, or cultural diversity and yet is used to strike down a number of key nation-state environmental, food safety, employment, and human rights laws (M. Barlow, 1996). One example is the 1999 WTO ruling that Canada unfairly subsidizes dairy products sold to the United States and New Zealand and must therefore stop its current subsidization activities, which include offering direct export subsidies for tariffs charged by other countries and quota-levies that help fund export costs. After going through the court process, Canada grudgingly complied with this ruling. The United States, on the other hand, called it a trade victory. Currently, Canada faces $35 million in sanctions from both the United States and New Zealand if it is found in contravention of the ruling one more time (IDFA, NMPF, USDEC, 2002). This ruling bolsters the evidence that the WTO is an "international bill of rights for transnational corporations" with a central goal of deregulating international trade for the benefit of these companies (Shrybman, 1999:5).

Another initiative that has a great and direct impact on Canada is the North America Free Trade Agreement (NAFTA). This agreement has grown out of the original 1989 Canada–U.S. Free Trade Agreement (FTA). It was renegotiated as the North America Free Trade Agreement in order to bring Mexico into the cross-border trade agreement. As a result of this agreement, both Canada and Mexico have increased their trade activities both with one another and with the United States. While domestic labour productivity has increased, wages and reliable employment opportunities have not (Campbell et al., 1999). This is not a surprise, however, because the Chapter 11 clause of the agreement grants corporations the authority to override existing laws that govern the behaviour of capital. Corporations are now able to effectively "sue" governments for compensation equal to the loss of profits—including *expected future profits*—if they are a result of policy change or an alteration of the original investment conditions. Typically, under Chapter 11, anything that gets in the way of the free flow of capital is referred to as a "barrier to trade," and Canada can be sued for it.

There are an increasing number of cases that have challenged Canada's ability to protect itself from transnational capital interests. A recent case involving Chapter 11 was the 1997 Ethyl Corporation case, where the corporation filed a $251 million lawsuit against Canada because a new Canadian environmental law stood in the way of potential future profit (Sforza and Vallianatos, 1997):

> Canada's decision to ban the import of the neuro-toxin and environmental pollutant MMT was challenged as "expropriation." In the middle of the NAFTA panel's deliberations, Canada threw in the towel, realizing that it was going to lose. Instead of risking a penalty in the hundreds of millions, it settled for US$19 million, apologized to Ethyl, and withdrew the import ban (Dobbin, 1998).

The impact of this case is difficult to calculate. NAFTA allows corporations to bypass democratically adopted laws and, in the case of Canada, may now be contributing to the federal government's reluctance to introduce new environmental or health-protection laws for fear that these legislations would lead to the same allegations (and hence, possible fines) of violating Chapter 11. Moreover, what are the impacts on the health and safety of the citizenry in allowing toxins that would normally be banned by the nation-state to be sold here? The Free Trade Area of the Americas (FTAA) is scheduled for completion in 2005. In 2001, Canada hosted the third Summit of the Americas, which was called to further develop the FTAA agreement. The purpose of the FTAA agreement is to extend NAFTA to the entire Western Hemisphere—a total of 34 countries.

It is clear that these global trade agreements are already profoundly affecting Canadian democracy, sovereignty, economy, and health. Certainly finding the balance between economic, social, and environmental health and prosperity is difficult. In part, this is because liberal democracies are inherently challenged by trying to balance an ideology of equality that guides democracy with the imperative of inequality that is integral to "liberal" market economies. The outcry from citizens across the globe and the discontent expressed by ministers involved in these organizations are evidence that the methods and mandates of these global treaties are not fulfilling their commitments to improve trade and *also* to improve the quality of life for the workers who participate in them.

PROBLEMS IN THE CANADIAN ECONOMY

Although an economic boom occurred late in the 20th century, corporate wealth became increasingly concentrated in Canada, as in many parts of the world. *Economic concentration* refers to the extent to which a few individuals or corporations control the vast majority of all economic resources in a country. Concentration of wealth is a social problem when it works to society's detriment, particularly when people are unable to use the democratic process to control the actions of the corporations.

Concentration of Wealth

The concentration of wealth in Canada has gone through many stages. In the earliest stage, most investment capital was individually owned. Families tended to control all the major trade and financial organizations. Canadian families like the Seagrams or the Irvings controlled whole segments of the Canadian economy.

In early monopoly capitalism, ownership and control of capital shifted from individuals to corporations. As monopoly capitalism grew, a few corporations gained control over major Canadian industries. A **monopoly exists when a single firm controls an industry and**

TABLE 13.1   Major Companies in Canada

BCE Inc. (Bell Canada Enterprise)	Telecommunications
Nortel Networks	Telecommunications
TransCanada Pipelines	Energy Equipment
Toronto Dominion Bank	Bank
CIBC (Canadian Imperial Bank of Commerce)	Bank
Royal Bank of Canada	Bank
Alcan Aluminum Ltd.	Materials
Banque de Montreal	Bank Insurance
Bank of Nova Scotia	Bank
Power Corporation of Canada	Fund Media
Celestica Inc.	Electronics
Power Financial Corp.	Finance
Seagram Co. Ltd.	Food Media
Loblaw Companies Ltd.	Retail
Bombardier Inc.	Aerospace Motorbike
Quebecor	Media Printing and Publishing Retail
Manufacturers Life Insurance Co.	Insurance Fund
Magna International	Equipment
Imasco	Conglomerate
Canadian Pacific Ltd.	Transportation
PanCanadian Energy Corp.	Energy
Thomson Corp.	Media Printing and Publishing
Petro Canada	Energy
Onex Corp.	Finance
Imperial Oil Ltd.	Energy
Hudson's Bay Co.	Retail
WestCoast Energy	Energy
Oshawa Group Ltd.	Retail
Air Canada	Air Transportation
Empire Co.	Retail
Husky Energy Inc.	Energy
Noranda Ltd.	Mining
Laidlaw Inc.	Transportation
McCain Foods Ltd.	Food
Canadian Tire Corp.	Retail
Canadian National Railway Corp.	Transportation
Teleglobe	Telecommunications
Talisman Energy	Energy

Source: Reproduced by permission of Transnationale Corporations Observatory, www.transnationale.org.

accounts for all sales in a specific market. Monopolies in Canada range from Canadian telephone and power-generating monopolies, to multitudes of marketing boards that cover dairy products, poultry, fruit, and wheat and other grains as well as Canada Post's monopoly over first-class-mail delivery.

In advanced monopoly capitalism (between 1940 and the present), ownership and control of major industrial and business sectors became increasingly concentrated. After World War II, there was a dramatic increase in *oligopoly*—**a situation in which a small number of companies or suppliers control an entire industry or service.** These large corporations use their economic resources, through campaign contributions, to lobby and influence the outcome of government decisions that affect their operations. Smaller corporations have only limited power and resources to bring about political change or keep the largest corporations from dominating the economy. In Canada, for example, Royal Trust, Canada Trust, and the Canadian Imperial Bank of Canada (CIBC) control most of the trust and custody banking activities in Canada (*Global Custodian*, 1997).

Today, mergers often occur *across* industries. In this way, corporations gain near-monopoly control over all aspects of the production and distribution of a product because they acquire both the companies that supply the raw materials and the companies that are the outlets for the product. For example, an oil company may hold leases on the land where the oil is pumped out of the ground, own the refineries that convert the oil into gasoline, and own the individual gasoline stations that sell the product to the public. Corporations that have control both within and across industries and are formed by a series of mergers and acquisitions across industries are referred to as *conglomerates*—combinations of businesses in different commercial areas, all of which are owned by one holding company. Media ownership is a case in point (see Chapter 14).

Further complicating corporate structures are *interlocking corporate directorates*—**members of the board of directors of one corporation who also sit on the board of one or more other corporations.** The problem with such interlocking directorates is that they diminish competition by producing interdependence. People serving on multiple boards are in a position to forge co-operative arrangements that benefit their corporations but not necessarily the general public. When several corporations are controlled by the same financial interests, they are more likely to co-operate with one another than to compete (Mintz and Schwartz, 1985).

The National Debt and Consumer Debt

In 1997–98, the federal government of Canada reported its first surplus ($3.5 billion) in approximately 30 years. From 2001, the country has generated a $39.7 billion surplus (Department of Finance, 2003). Since the country has been generating surplus budgets, the federal government has used them to pay down the debt. Canada is more than $536 billion in debt, and in the 2001–02 fiscal year, Canadians paid $37 billion in interest charges on this debt. It has consistently been the largest single expenditure item in the federal budget. Moreover, in the 2001–02 fiscal year, 22 cents out of every revenue dollar went toward maintaining the debt (Manley, 2001). The 2003–04 budget is the first budget in years to reflect strong public-service priorities. It has allocated a 25 percent increase in health care spending over the next three years and has also allocated more monies to childcare in Canada (Department of Finance, 2003).

While great sums of fiscal surplus go to paying down the debt, Canada also brags the fastest growing per capita Gross Domestic Product (GDP) of the leading industrial nations. This is an important point for Canadian watchdogs, such as the Canadian Centre for Policy Alternatives, who question the spending priorities of the federal government. They are concerned that the government has been paying down the fiscal debt and not sufficiently addressing the social debt. For example, researchers at the political centre point out that, while the private-sector projections of Canada's surpluses were estimated at $1.0 billion for 2002–03 and $3.1 billion for 2003–04 (Department of Finance, 2003), the authors of the Alternative Federal Budget (CCPA, 2003) forecast a combined surplus in Canada of $27.9 billion in 2002 and $40.0 billion over the last three years. The amount of projected available surplus helps government officials determine their spending priorities for the fiscal year. These watchdogs are asking why finance officials and private-sector forecasters are currently downplaying the possibility of large fiscal surpluses in Canada in an era where national unemployment rates are soaring and public social services

This photo shows an important irony in our consumer society. Just as credit cards and automated gasoline pumps make it easier for consumers to purchase gasoline, these same factors also have significant downside risks. One risk is a substantial increase in consumer debt. What are other risks affecting Canadian workers and the overall economy?

relation to their incomes" (Sullivan et al., 1989:331). Although an increase in consumer debt may benefit the Canadian and global economies, it is extremely damaging to individuals who cannot pay their bills and for those who must declare bankruptcy (Sullivan et al., 1989).

Two factors contribute to high rates of consumer debt. The first is the instability of economic life in modern society; unemployment and underemployment are commonplace. The second factor is the availability of credit and the extent to which credit-card companies and other lenders extend credit beyond people's ability to repay. Statistics Canada (1999a) shows that 68 percent of Canadian families owe an average of $55 155. Credit-card and installment debt make up $3033 of this debt, and lines of credit another $13 542. Some people run up credit-card charges that are greatly out of proportion to their income; others cannot pay off the charges they initially believed they could afford when their income is interrupted or drops due to a sudden layoff or decreased work hours. For example, Kenji Peterson (a pseudonym) ran up $20 000 in charges, a sum that was more than half his total yearly income:

> It all started when I graduated from college and took a low-paying job. . . . I didn't want to live like a student so I used credit cards to buy myself furniture and eat dinners out. I wasn't extravagant, I just didn't want to deprive myself. . . . When I got a new card with a $5000 credit limit, it felt like someone just handed me $5000. . . . The reality has been that I got in the hole financially. (Tyson, 1993:E1; cited in Ritzer, 1995:67)

Having a high level of consumer debt is a personal problem for people like Kenji Peterson, but it is also a public issue, particularly when credit-card issuers negligently give fifth, sixth, or seventh credit cards to people who are already so far in debt that they cannot pay the interest, much less the principal, on their other cards (Sullivan et al., 1989). One businessman had accumulated a total debt of $183 000 on 41 cards when he received an unsolicited application for still another card, which he accepted and quickly "maxed out" at $5000 (Ritzer, 1995).

According to sociologist George Ritzer (1995), both consumers and credit-card companies must become more responsible if consumer debt is to be reduced. Ritzer (1995:71) is particularly critical of banks and credit-card companies that entice students in high school or university to become accustomed to buying on

are being cut in efforts to reduce federal spending and to pay off the debt? Maude Barlow (1996) of the Council of Canadians states:

> Whereas in the 1960s, Canadian citizens and business contributed 50–50 to tax revenues collected, today Canadian citizens account for 92 percent of all tax revenues. Business contributes only 8 percent. As business has withdrawn its tax contribution, the Canadian government has fallen further and further into debt, as have governments all over the world.

Like the federal government, many individuals and families in this country are deeply in debt. Consumer debt is rising. What is even more worrisome to analysts is the fact that the ratio of consumer debt to income increased in the last two decades. According to a definitive study of bankruptcy, "the most distinguishing characteristic of bankrupt debtors is their high debts in credit, saying that this practice lures many people into a "lifetime of imprudence and indebtedness." He believes that the government should restrain credit-card companies by limiting the profits they can make and by restricting mail and telephone campaigns offering incentives to accept new credit cards (Ritzer, 1995). Many people are adamantly opposed to any kind of government intervention in the marketplace, whether it relates to credit cards or anything else. Interestingly, one kind of government intervention that is institutionalized in the Canadian economy is corporate welfare.

Corporate Welfare

***Corporate welfare* occurs when the government helps industries and private corporations in their economic pursuits.** Corporate welfare is not a new phenomenon in Canada. During the industrialization of Canada, corporations received government assistance in the form of public subsidies and protection from competition. To encourage westward expansion, the federal government gave large tracts of land to developers. Tariffs, patents, and trademarks from this era all continue to protect corporations from competition today.

Currently, government intervention includes billions of dollars of subsidies given to corporations in the form of conditionally repayable loans, monies intended for job-creation and job-preservation schemes, and tax breaks to corporations. The majority of financial assistance recipients are among Canada's largest and most profitable companies—those listed on the *Report on Business* 1000 and the *Financial Post* 500. For example, in 1999, the Federal government gave a $33 million "gift" to IBM Canada Ltd. under the Technology Partnerships Canada (TPC) program and a $154 million TPC loan to Pratt & Whitney. Approximately 15 percent of the $3.2 billion that Industry Canada has lent large corporations since 1982 has never been repaid and, in the past 10 years, the repayment rate went down to 2.58 percent (Canadian Taxpayers Federation, 2003)—but such gifts continue to be made. Research is showing that these governmental strategies to retain, expand, and even attract business do not actually influence a corporation's choice of location or its economic growth. This fact does not seem to influence the federal government, however; in January 2003, it legislated yet another cut in corporate income-tax rates to bring the rates down to 23 percent—rates that are just below those

in the United States. By 2004, this legislation dictates that corporate tax rates will fall below 21 percent (Department of Finance, 2003).

The fundamental problem is that, around the world, these corporate welfare programs do not actually promote economic development (Chomsky, 1996; Nader, 2000). There is growing concern that corporate welfare means that market decisions are being made by politicians and bureaucrats and not by the market; that corporate welfare creates politically driven investments, is inherently unfair, and therefore serves to undermine Canadian's confidence in our democratic institutions; and, it makes business owners and entrepreneurs focus on securing government financing (making them "grantrepreneurs") instead of developing their core competencies. In addition, at least $115 million in repayable contributions is outstanding, and the loss of loan-repayment monies is creating a higher tax burden in Canada. This means that, indirectly, individuals and small businesses are helping to recoup these losses. It is clear that, overall, most large corporations have gained much more than they have lost as a result of government involvement in the economy.

Why do we have corporate welfare programs today? Some can be traced back to the Great Depression in the 1930s, when programs were initiated to bail out companies and stabilize the Canadian economy. Some analysts say that the subsidies continue because of lobbying efforts and political contributions by organizations to governments (Tumulty, 1996). As a result, many Members of Parliament may find it more within their interests to retrench domestic spending, primarily on health care and other social programs, than to cut corporate handouts (Tumulty, 1996) (see Chapter 2 for a discussion of welfare state retrenchment).

PROBLEMS IN CANADIAN POLITICS

Social scientists distinguish between politics and government: ***Politics* is the social institution through which power is acquired and exercised by some people and groups.** The essential component of politics is *power*—the ability of people to achieve their goals despite opposition from others (see Chapter 2). People who hold positions of power achieve their goals because they have control over other people; those who lack

SOCIAL PROBLEMS AND SOCIAL POLICY

BOX 13.2 Social Problems and Social Policy: And Canadians Yelled "Shame!"

"Shame—This is Canada!" These words were scrawled across the Wall of Shame at the Summit of the Americas meeting in Quebec City (April 2001). This was one of the many recent international meetings designed to foster the fast proliferation of global trade agreements worldwide. It was also one of the many impressive sites of anti-globalization protest that are occurring around the world. The result of these protests is that today unfettered global free trade is no longer considered inevitable:

> The last decade has been marked by the explosion of free trade agreements and grassroots opposition to them . . . It is a battlefield being contested by governments and transnational corporations on one side, and organized labour, environmentalists, human rights advocates and citizens groups on the other. The rules however, are stacked in favour of governments pushing the corporate global agenda. Although, some governments in the global south also find themselves marginalized in the discussions by heavy hitters in the United States, European Union, Canada and Japan. (Corporatewatch, February, 2003)

The effectiveness of these global protests and the threat they pose to the corporate agenda make it unsurprising that mainstream media is most often disparaging and inflammatory in its treatment of protestors, referring to them as anarchists, terrorists, hoodlums, and wayward youth. The people themselves, however, identify as resistors, organizers, citizens, artists, parents, journalists, business people, students, architects, and activists.

Whatever it is called, governments and businesses now acknowledge that this is a global movement of citizens working in solidarity. Increasingly, it is a force to be reckoned with. In 1997, citizen's groups, led in Canada by the Council of Canadians, derailed the powerful and far-reaching Multilateral Agreement on Investment (MAI) negotiations, which were being carried out quietly between 29 industrialized members of the Organization of Economic Cooperation and Development (OECD). The MAI promotes the interests of international investors and applies to "all land, territory, internal water and the territorial seas of the contracting [country]" and is designed so that "all corporate behaviour is included and 'protected' from government measures" (OECD, 1997). In reference to the derailed MAI meetings, a Globe and Mail article in 1998 stated that, while high-powered politicians had reams of statistics and analysis on why a set of international investing rules would make the world a better place, "they were no match . . . for a global band of grassroots organizations, which, with little more than computers and access to the Internet, helped derail a deal" (Drohan,

1998). In 1999, in its business report, the Globe and Mail ran an article in a similar vein about the WTO:

> The activists who essentially killed the Multilateral Agreement on Investment launched a campaign yesterday to stop upcoming talks at the World Trade Organization in their tracks—the latest sign of trouble for the next round of WTO negotiations.

These were founded concerns, as more than 50 000 people gathered in Seattle to march against the WTO in 1999. It was the meeting place of riot police, the National Guard, and peaceful protestors. It marked the beginning of the global movement of citizen protest and the world's recognition of its power. In a post-WTO rally speech in Vancouver, Council of Canadians Chair Maude Barlow eloquently conveyed the point that if these trade talks and their attendant processes were truly democratic and truly what the people wanted, they would not need to be carried out behind the National Guard. The presence of barricades, riot police, and tens of thousands of protesters diminishes the claim that these trade deals are embraced by the populace (Speech, November 30, 1999, Vancouver, B.C.).

In April 2001, Canadian authorities organized the largest police deployment in Canadian history (nearly 10 000 officers and personnel, including members from the Armed Forces), costing Canadian taxpayers $100 million (Editorial Collective, 2001). This was in anticipation of the nearly 60 000 people who took to the streets of Quebec City to bring a clear "No" message to the FTAA delegates.

On July 21, 2001, an estimated 200 000 people marched along the streets of Genoa, Italy, in protest of the presidents and prime ministers of the seven richest countries in the world plus Russia (the G-8). This marked the largest mobilization to date against the globalization of capitalism. It was also the site of police brutality that culminated in the killing of Carlo Guliani and the violent raid on the Diaz school—a sleeping place for protesters (Indymedia, 2003).

In Kananaskis, Alberta, on June 26 and 27, 2002, protestors converged to register their complaints about the power of the G-8. Canadian police and army spokespeople warned that protesters and "limelight seekers" would be risking their lives if they tested security in Kananaskis. Today, the G-8 summit marks the "largest security operation in Canadian history and the most important homeland mobilization of Canadian troops since the 1970 "October Crisis" when the Trudeau government called in the War Measures Act to combat the terrorist activities of the Front de Libération du Quebec (Adelaide, 2002). In Kananaskis, the government spent $300 million on security (Hadeckel, 2002). More than 6000 Canadian Armed Forces personnel and 4500 police were deployed, a 6.5-km "no-go" zone was established around Kananaskis Village, and three antiaircraft missile batteries were set up to protect the 150-km "no-flight" zone surrounding the area. In terms of money spent, there are many other necessities that $300 million could be spent on, domestically or internationally. It was a peaceful protest of 2000 people and the anticipated terrorists did not appear.

These brief snapshots of anti-globalization protest depict a global era of extraordinary hope and optimism within a context of great suffering and desperation. Indian writer Arundati Roy (2003) states, "The corporate revolution will collapse if we refuse to buy what they are selling: their wars, their version of history." The writer urges the world's citizens to tell their own stories, "Another world is not only possible, she's on her way. And if you listen carefully on a quiet day you can hear her breathing" (Roy, 2003). This is exactly the kind of message concerned citizens are drawing hope from.

Between January 23 to 28, 2002, 3000 people gathered at the 1st World Social Forum in Puerto Alegre, Brazil. In their call to build this movement, they sent out a statement (Institute for Global Communications, 2002) proclaiming:

We are meeting in Puerto Alegre in the shadow of a global crisis. . . . We are social movements that are fighting all around the world against neo-liberal globalization, war, racism, capitalism, poverty, patriarchy and all the forms of economical, ethnical, social, political, cultural, sexual and gender discriminations and exclusions. We are all fighting for social justice, citizenship, participatory democracy, universal rights and for the right of peoples to decide their own future.

We stand for peace and international cooperation, for a sustainable society answering the needs of people for food, housing, health, education, information, water, energy, public transportation and human rights. We are in solidarity with the women engaged against social and patriarchal violence. We support the struggle of the peasants, workers, popular urban movements and all those who are urgently threatened by being deprived of homes, jobs, land and their rights.

We have demonstrated in millions to say that another world is possible.

This has never been more true and more urgent . . .

This meeting marks the first global gathering of people in protest to share stories and tactics for disrupting the current economic order and to develop their visions for the future. The numbers of people involved in this movement are growing and so too are their skills and their commitments to creative, positive, and peaceful protest.

Naomi Klein (2002), Canadian journalist and author, has noted that this movement is one full of celebration, subversive humour, a refusal to engage in classic power struggles, and a commitment to challenge structures of power centralization:

Even the heavy-handed security measures have been co-opted by activists into part of the message: The fences that surround the summits become metaphors for an economic model that exiles billions to poverty and exclusion. Confrontations are staged at the fence—but not only the ones involving sticks and bricks: Tear-gas canisters have been flicked back with hockey sticks, water cannons have been irreverently challenged with toy water pistols and buzzing helicopters have been mocked with swarms of paper airplanes. During the summit of the Americas in Quebec City, a group of activists built a medieval-style wooden catapult, wheeled it up to the three-metre-high fence that enclosed the downtown and lofted teddy bears over the top. In Prague, during a meeting of the World Bank and the International Monetary Fund, the Italian direct-action group, the Tute Bianche, decided not to confront the black-clad riot police dressed in similarly threatening ski masks and bandanas; instead, they marched to the police line in white jumpsuits stuffed with rubber tires and Styrofoam padding. In a standoff between Darth Vader and an army of Michelin Men, the police couldn't win. Meanwhile, in another part of the city, the steep hillside leading up to the conference centre was scaled by a band of "pink fairies" dressed in burlesque wigs, silver-and-pink evening wear and platform shoes (Klein, 2002:xxv–xxvi).

This is a movement with heart, humour, and hope. It is being lead by young people primarily, and mentored along by those who have lived through wars, embargoes, sanctions, discrimination, and patriarchal rule—those who have long lived with oppression and who understand, first hand, the importance of working in solidarity to make lasting change. Globalization has not only made commerce everyone's business, it has made informed citizen participation everyone's responsibility. The result is a diverse, intelligent, and highly determined movement of global citizens who know they must stick together in the fight for their lives and for the life of this planet.

power carry out the wishes of others. Powerful people get others to acquiesce to their demands by using persuasion, authority, or force.

Canadian politics are complex, laden with political tensions and the conflicting interests—both current and historical—of many groups. Certainly, First Nations and *Charter* groups (English and French) have engaged in intense negotiations about politics and power with one another for hundreds of years. As a result, many of the defining historical events that have occurred over that last 400 to 500 years in Canada still have contemporary currency. For example, the 1763 Seven Years War ended with France's surrender of its land in North America to Britain and led to Britain becoming the controlling force in North America at that time. The 1775 War of Independence resulted in the 13 North American colonies winning their independence from Britain and the recognition of the United States as an independent country. The 1867 move to confederation of "British North America" by the British colonies— British Columbia, Newfoundland, Nova Scotia, New Brunswick, Prince Edward Island, and the Province of Canada—resulted in the formation of the country of Canada (National Library of Canada, 2001). These battles and governmental activities have helped to shape the current political framework in Canada. One characteristic of Canada is its long history of *Charter* groups finding ways to work with each other across great geographical, cultural, and linguistic differences.

These same historical events have also informed the longstanding power-dynamics that exist between Canada and the United States. Today, the United States stands as the world's only superpower. It is our closest neighbour, a military ally, and Canada's largest market for imports and exports. Another part of Canada's political history that still impacts the social fabric of our country today is the genocidal practices carried out by Canada's governments and churches against Indigenous people. These practices were expressed through the creation of residential schools, missionaries, a democratic system that prohibited participation by Indigenous communities, and treaties that forced Indigenous peoples to leave their original territories and to move onto smaller and less resource-rich tracts of land (Henry et al., 2000).

Canada is a country that encompasses 10 million square kilometres of land, making it the second-largest country in the world. It is bordered by both the Pacific and the Atlantic oceans and has a population of over 31 million. The country's geography, reputation for a high standard of living, and relatively strong economy make Canada an attractive immigration destination (Statistics Canada, 2002o; UN Human Development Index, 1995). The reliance of Canada on a diverse immigrant population, the historical tensions between the three major interest groups, and the new forces and constraints placed on Canada by globalization, trade, and international relations make the Canadian political economy a complex one to understand and a challenge to govern (Jackson and Jackson, 1996).

In contemporary societies, the primary political system is *government*—**a formal organization that has legal and political authority to regulate relationships among people in a society and between the society and others outside its borders.** The government (sometimes called the state) includes all levels of bureaucratized political activity such as executive, central, and local administrations; the legislature; the courts; and the armed forces and police (Perdue, 1993).

Canada is a parliamentary *democracy,* **a political system in which the people hold the ruling power, either directly or through elected representatives.** In a direct participatory democracy, citizens meet regularly to debate and decide issues of the day. While ancient Athens was a direct democracy, and many small Canadian communities rely heavily on town meetings as a method of decision making, Canada has never functioned as a direct democracy. Rather, a system was created by the founders of the Canadian nation-state whereby political decisions were made by representatives of the people. Canada has a system of a *fusion of powers*, whereby the government and Members of Parliament are made up of the same people. Importantly, however, the executive may hold office and retain power only so long as it holds the support of the majority of the legislative branch.

In countries that have some form of representative democracy, such as in Canada, citizens elect representatives who are responsible for conveying the concerns and interests of those they represent. If these representatives are not responsive to the wishes of the people, voters can unseat them through elections. This is not to say that representative democracy is equally accessible to all people in a nation. In Canada, at the time of confederation (1867), the vote was extended to all adult male British subjects and forbidden to Indigenous men living on reserves. Indigenous and

Inuit peoples, who have lived in North America for thousands of years, were thereby systematically barred from participating in the democratic process of the day. It was not until 1950 that the Inuit women and men won the right to vote in federal elections, and not until 1960 that Indigenous people on reserves won the same federal rights. This meant "native people had no say over the future of the land that they had lived on for thousands of years" (National Library of Canada, 2001). For over 50 years after Confederation, all women were barred from direct participation in the political system; they were not allowed to vote until 1918, and could not be elected to the House of Commons until 1919. In Quebec, women did not win full democratic voting and parliamentary rights on a provincial level until 1940 (National Library of Canada, 2001). Today, 95 seats out of 405, or 23.4 percent of the seats in the Senate and House of Commons, are held by women. Democratic participation is, at least theoretically, available to all Canadian citizens age 18 and older. Structural racism and sexism (discussed in Chapters 3 and 4) inhibit full participation, however. Who is granted the right to participate in democratic processes and the conditions of their involvement directly influences the priorities of the country.

Unfortunately, the democratic deficit—in particular, voter apathy—threatens to undermine the principles upon which our democracy is based. We will discuss this briefly below.

Representation in Canadian Politics

The Canadian voting system is based on one of eight types of democratic voting systems, the "winner-take-all," or "first-past-the-post," system. The candidate who receives the highest number of votes wins the seat. Candidates often win a seat with much less than 50 percent of the popular vote. For example, in the 2000 federal election, the Liberal party won 40 percent of the popular vote and gained 57 percent of the seats, and the Progressive Conservatives won 12 percent of the vote and gained 4 percent of the seats (Fair Vote Canada, 2001). The need for democratic reform has been a longstanding concern in Canada, as we are one of the last democratic countries to still use the "first-past-the-post" system (Milner, 1999). In 1979, the Pepin-Robarts Commission suggested that Canada

move more toward a semi-proportional voting system, and in 1997 the Privy Council called for proportional representation in Parliament and the Senate. Today, there are various grassroots organizations, such as Fair Vote Canada, Mouvement pour une Démocratie Nouvelle (in Quebec), Fair Voting B.C., and Every Vote Counts (in Prince Edward Island) that are currently working for electoral reform (Law Commission of Canada, 2002).

Among developed nations, Canada has one of the lowest percentages of voting-age citizens who actually vote. What causes voter apathy? Research suggests that young people do not vote because they believe that existing political parties and government generally do not adequately reflect their needs and values (Fair Vote Canada, 2001; Law Commission of Canada, 2002). In terms of other segments of the general population, the Law Commission of Canada offers these thoughts:

> Some suggest that the political system no longer reflects the diversity of Canadian society. Others suggest that citizens' sense of disempowerment is related to the emergence of the "global economy," which has undermined the role of national governments. The impact of technology is yet another factor that is cited for the change in the way Canadians relate to each other and to their government.

Whatever the reasons, the Canadian public is clearly frustrated with the government and its institutions. This raises important questions about how democracy functions in Canada.

While voter apathy is one problem, so is the problem of representation in Canadian politics today. One issue of growing concern is the gender gap in Canadian voter turnout. The **gender gap—the difference between the number of votes from women and men received by a candidate for public office**—is rooted in how women and men view economic and social issues, such as health care, welfare reform, abortion, childcare, and education, and what they believe the nation's priorities should be. However, it is also a result of the voting system itself, in that women (and minority groups) typically do not see people "like themselves" presented as candidates:

> In fact, the lowest levels of women and minority representation are found in democratic countries using

Typically during Canadian elections (especially at the federal level), a high percentage of the population chooses not to vote. Could voter apathy be linked to the low racialized/ethnic and gender representation in our political system?

the first-past-the-post system. Neither women, nor minorities, are regionally based groups, and therefore do not benefit from regional concentration approaches to voting. In the first-past-the-post "winner take all" system, political parties aim to maximize their chances of success by running the safest possible candidate in each riding. Women and minority candidates are often seen as controversial and are therefore not readily nominated. (Law Commission of Canada, 2002)

Since the 2000 federal election, voter apathy, the increase in the gender gap, and an unrepresentational voting system are all receiving more attention. There are citizens who hope to implement a new voting system by the time of the next federal election, in order to create a more representational democracy.

Government by Special-Interest Groups

What happens when *special-interest groups*—political coalitions composed of individuals or groups sharing a specific interest they wish to protect or advance with the help of the political system—have a major influence on how the government is run? Some special-interest groups exert their influence on single issues, such as abortion, the 2010 Olympic Bid, or the media. For example, Canada's broadcasting industry contributed almost $1 million in donations to federal political parties during the year 2000. Three of the top 20 donors to the Liberal Party of Canada in 2000 were broadcasters—each dependant on the federal government for a broadcasting licence. This raises troubling questions about Canada's media and the growing conflict between their traditional duty to inform Canadians about national political affairs and their increasingly significant role as financial supporters and beneficiaries of the governing party. Funds tend to come from organizations or corporations that represent particular occupations or industries. The second-largest political contributors in the last federal election were businesses and commercial organizations—they accounted for 22.8 percent of political contributions in that election. The structure of political contributions in Canada enables funders—for example, industry-based corporations—to make contributions to candidates who have a history of protecting their interests. An example of this is the logging industry, which benefits from corporate welfare in the form of stumpage fees and other subsidized operating expenses. These special-interest activities have the potential to threaten the integrity and efficacy of the democratic process in Canada.

Government by Bureaucracy

Special-interest groups wield tremendous political power, but so does the federal bureaucracy. The federal bureaucracy, or **permanent government, refers to the top-tier civil service bureaucrats who have a strong power base and play a major role in developing and implementing government policies and procedures.** The federal government played a relatively limited role in everyday life in the 19th century, but its role grew during the Great Depression in the 1930s. When faced with high rates of unemployment and persistent poverty, individuals and big business demanded that the government do something. Public welfare was instituted, security markets were regulated, and programs for labour–management relations were set in place. With better technology and demands that the government "do something" about the problems facing society, government has continued to grow.

Sociologists point out that bureaucratic power in any sphere tends to take on a life of its own over time. The government bureaucracy is able to perpetuate itself and expand because many of its employees possess highly specialized knowledge and skills and cannot easily be replaced. As the issues facing Canada have grown in number and complexity, offices and agencies have been established to create rules, policies, and procedures for dealing with such things as nuclear power, environmental protection, and drug safety. Today, public policy

is increasingly made by agencies rather than by elected officials. These agencies receive little direction from Parliament or the prime minister. While their actions are subject to challenge in the courts, most agencies are highly autonomous.

The federal budget is the central ingredient in the bureaucracy. Preparing the annual federal budget is a major undertaking for the prime minister and the minister of finance, one of the most influential ministers in Ottawa. Getting the budget approved by Parliament is a monumental task. However, even with the highly publicized wrangling over the budget by the Members of Parliament, it usually changes little from its original draft. As powerful as the federal bureaucracy has become, it is not immune to special-interest groups, as such groups can help a ministry secure more operating money. The close relationship between politics, power, and economy is one that Canadian's are paying closer attention to in this age of globalization and democratic change.

PERSPECTIVES ON THE POLITICAL ECONOMY

Politics and the economy are so intertwined in Canada that many social scientists speak of the two as a single entity, the *political economy*. At issue for most social scientists is whether political and economic power are concentrated in the hands of the few or distributed among the many in this country. Functionalists adopt a pluralistic model of power, while conflict theorists adopt an elitist model. Symbolic interactionists focus on the microlevel patterns of people's relationships with one another, and feminists adopt a holistic analysis of power inequalities in society.

The Functionalist Perspective

Pluralism is rooted in the functionalist perspective, which assumes that people generally agree on the most important societal concerns—freedom and security—and that government fulfills important functions in these two regards that no other institution can. According to the early functionalists, government serves to socialize people to be good citizens, to regulate the economy so that it operates effectively, and to provide necessary services for citizens (Durkheim, 1893/1933). Contemporary functionalists identify four similar functions:

A government maintains law and order, plans society and coordinates other institutions, meets social needs, and handles international relations, including warfare.

But what happens when people do not agree on specific issues or concerns? Functionalists say that divergent viewpoints lead to political pluralism; that is, when competing interests or viewpoints arise, government arbitrates. Thus, according to the ***pluralist model,*** **power is widely dispersed throughout many competing interest groups in our political system** (Dahl, 1961). In the pluralist model, (1) political leaders make decisions on behalf of the people through a process of bargaining, accommodation, and compromise; (2) leadership groups (such as business, labour, law, and consumer organizations) serve as watchdogs to protect ordinary people from the abuses of any one group; (3) ordinary people influence public policy through voting and participating in special-interest or lobby groups; (4) power is widely dispersed in society (the same groups aren't equally influential in all arenas); and, (5) public policy reflects a balance among competing interest groups, not the majority group's view (Dye, 2000).

How might a social analyst who uses a functionalist framework address problems in politics and the economy? Such an analyst might begin by saying that since dysfunctions are inevitable in any social institution, it is important to sort out and remedy the specific elements of the system that create the problems. It should not be necessary to restructure or replace the entire system. Consider, for example, government regulations: Some regulations are considered to be good, and some are considered to be bad. The trick, functionalists say, is to keep the good ones and get rid of the bad (Barlett and Steele, 1996). Too often, the Canadian government moves between two extremes: overregulation of business and society, or seeking to end most, if not all, regulation. This perspective is based on the belief that a certain amount of government intervention in the economy is appropriate but that too much—or the wrong kind—is detrimental.

The Conflict Perspective

Most conflict theorists believe democracy is an ideal, not a reality, in our society today. This is because the government primarily benefits the wealthy and the politically powerful, especially business elites. In fact, according to conflict theorists, economic and political elites use the powers of the government to impose their will on the masses. According to the ***elite model,*** **power in political systems is concentrated in the hands of a small group, whereas the masses are relatively powerless.** In the elite model, (1) elites possess the greatest wealth, education, status, and other resources and make the most important decisions in society; (2) elites generally agree on the basic values and goals for the society; (3) power is highly concentrated at the top of a pyramid-shaped social hierarchy, and those at the top set public policy for everyone; (4) public policy reflects the values and preferences of the elite, not of ordinary people; and, (5) elites use the media to shape the political attitudes of ordinary people (Dye, 2000).

According to sociologist C. Wright Mills (1959a), there is a hierarchical structure of power. The rulers are the ***power elite,*** **which at the top is composed of business leaders, the executive branch of the federal government, and the "top brass" of the military.** The corporate rich—the highest-paid CEOs of major corporations—are the most powerful because they have the unique ability to parlay their vast economic resources into political power. The next most powerful level is occupied by Members of Parliament, special-interest groups, and local opinion leaders. The lowest (and widest) level of the pyramid is occupied by ordinary people, the unorganized masses who are relatively powerless and vulnerable to economic and political exploitation.

Individuals who comprise the power elite have similar class backgrounds and interests and interact on a regular basis. Through a revolving door of influence, they tend to shift back and forth between and among the business, government, and military sectors. For example, it is not unusual for people who have served in the prime minister's Cabinet to become directors of major corporations that do business with the government, for powerful businesspeople to serve in Parliament, or for former military leaders to become important businesspeople. Through such political and economic alliances, people in the power elite can influence many important decisions, including how federal tax money will be spent and to whom lucrative subsidies and government contracts are awarded.

In his analysis of the political economy, sociologist G. William Domhoff (1978) speaks of a *ruling class,* which is made up of the *corporate rich*—a relatively fixed group of privileged people who wield power over political processes and serve capitalist interests. The corporate rich influence the political process in three ways: (1) by financing campaigns of candidates who favour their causes; (2) by using loophole contributions to obtain favours, tax breaks, and favourable regulatory rulings; and, (3) by gaining appointment to governmental advisory committees, national commissions, and other governmental positions. For example, some members of the ruling class influence international politics through their involvement in banking, business services, and law firms that have a strong interest in overseas sales, investments, or raw materials extraction (Domhoff, 1990).

Some analysts who take a conflict perspective say that the only way to overcome problems in politics and the economy is to change the entire system. Our present system exploits the poor, people of colour, women, gays and lesbians, people with disabilities, and others who are disenfranchised from the political and economic mainstream of society.

Other conflict theorists think that we can solve many problems by curbing the abuses of capitalism and the market economy and thereby reducing the power of political and economic elites. Political scientist Benjamin R. Barber (1996:242) believes that we cannot rely on the capitalist (market) economy to look after common interests:

> It is the job of civil society and democratic government and not of the market to look after common interests and make sure that those who profit from the common planet pay its common proprietors their fair share. When governments abdicate in favour of markets, they are declaring *nolo contendere* [no contest] in an arena in which they are supposed to be primary challengers, bartering away the rights of their people along the way.
>
> Markets simply are not designed to do the things democratic polities do. They enjoin private rather than public modes of discourse, allowing us as consumers to speak via our currencies of consumption to producers of material goods, but ignoring us as citizens speaking to one another about such things as the social consequences of our private market choices. They advance individualistic rather than social goals. Having created the conditions that make markets possible, democracies must also do all the things that markets undo or cannot do. They must educate citizens so that they can use their markets wisely and contain market abuses well.

The Symbolic Interactionist Perspective

Symbolic interactionism focuses on the micro-, or small-scale, interactions that occur between individuals in specific settings. This perspective views society as a dynamic process that is continually being created through human interaction and negotiation. As a result, humans develop subjective interpretations of the physical world at the same time that they are socialized to integrate into society. Symbolic interactionism is particularly interested in how members of society socialize one another and how people utilize shared symbols—objects, words, sounds, and events—to construct social reality and express their experiences of it.

With a focus on the subjective meanings that people attach to their own and other people's behaviour and the processes people engage in to construct and agree upon various definitions of realty, researchers ask very specific questions about human activity. In terms of the political economy, people using this perspective will want to study the interactions that occur between people within democratic processes and business negotiations. How do people experience and interpret laws, fiscal priorities, and budget cuts? How do these societal activities influence people's relationship to and involvement in the democratic process? How do people reach agreements about the role politicians should take in addressing the issues of dissatisfied constituents, and what should citizens do if they are not satisfied with what is happening in their communities? Clearly, it is important to consider the opinions of a diverse range of people in order to build a complete picture of society. People from different racialized/ethnic, gender, and social-class groups, and of different sexual orientations, to name just a few variables, experience the world in dramatically different ways. Their perspectives are essential to the project of understanding the microlevel patterns of human interactions in society.

One question that symbolic interactionists like to ask is, What happens when a network of people come together to challenge the status quo? This explains the fascination with the forces that shaped the "Battle in Seattle" (a popular media phrase for the 1999 anti-WTO protests in Seattle). Why did anti-globalization protestors gather in Seattle; why did people develop and utilize the protest strategies they did during the marches; and, what shaped the interactions between police and civilians during the protests? While the meaning each individual and small group attributes to the experience is important, so too are the ways in which symbols are used. Symbolic interactionists may focus their attention on ways that mainstream media reporters framed the protestors as dangerous and anarchistic. They may also do a comparative analysis of the contents of protestors' accounts of police confrontations and the official reports of the same incidents given by police chiefs and elected officials.

Feminist Perspectives

"Black women, be ready. White women, get ready. Red women, stay ready . . ." (Honey, in Brodribb, 1999:13). Feminist theoretical perspectives are as diverse as the women who develop them. While feminism as a whole has advanced women's rights and institutional accountability in Canada, there is a wealth of diverse approaches that are responsible for these successes. A close-up look at feminist engagements with the political economy show that liberal, materialist, multicultural, radical, and ecological feminists are among those most concerned with addressing issues of the political economy.

Liberal feminists, for example, work to ensure that women have the rights and abilities to participate fully in political and economic spheres of social life. Securing women's right to vote in Canada, pushing for pay equity, equal opportunity legislation, and universal daycare, and supporting women in business are some of the liberal-feminist initiatives. Their work from the 1960s to the mid-1980s dramatically increased the rights of and opportunities available to women in Canada (Elliott and Mandell, 2001).

Materialist feminists are concerned with class inequity and the widening gaps between different groups' control over resources, participation in the production of knowledge, and control of power globally. This perspective maintains that social life is inextricably linked to the "materiality of meaning, identity, the body, state, or nation" (Hennessy and Ingraham, 1997:1). Central commitments are to analyze, challenge, and work to change business practices, globalization initiatives, and development programs that continue to exploit women's productive and reproductive labour.

Multicultural feminists maintain that global survival depends on meaningful exchanges of knowledge, under-

standing, and solidarity between peoples across the globe. Multicultural feminists focus on the experiences of African, Asian, Middle-Eastern, Latin American, and Caribbean women in Canada and around the world. Institutional, interpersonal, and internalized racism and their impacts on the lives of people such as foreign domestic and sweatshop factory workers and immigrant and refugee women and their communities are a primary concern for these feminists.

Radical feminists see women's personal experiences as political and focus on developing strategies of resistance (Elliott and Mandell, 2001:34). This perspective critiques patriarchy and masculinist practices that construct women as passive and submissive. Radical feminists engage in actions such as the fight for the rights and freedoms of women and children who are trafficked in the global sex trade (Kempadoo, 1998) (see Chapter 7).

Ecological feminists draw feminist, ecological, and materialist perspectives together in order to build an understanding of how political and economic activities such as free trade agreements, transnational corporations, and war impact women, the natural environment, and the quality of life of people, animals, and the earth (Sturgeon, 1997).

These feminists represent perspectives that, when brought together, can be used to build a holistic understanding of the matrices of oppression that shape our current historical moment. Feminists have impacted theoretical and practical approaches to the political economy in many significant ways in Canada. While women today have many rights and freedoms that women in Confederate Canada did not, feminists point out that some of the advances women have made are still legally tenuous and in times of backlash are slowly revoked. It may come as no surprise then, that in 2003, Canadian women and children are the poorest they have been in 20 years (Townson, 2003).

PROBLEMS IN POLITICS AND THE ECONOMY IN THE 21ST CENTURY

What will Canadian politics and the economy be like as we progress through the 21st century? There is no single vision, of course, but many social analysts think that digital democracy—the use of information technologies such as the Internet and the World Wide Web—will dramatically change not only economic relationships but also the way in which politics and government are conducted. For example, digital democracy can inform people about political candidates and issues. Volunteers use e-mail and websites to encourage people to go to the polls and vote for their candidate. These tools also can be used to send messages to voters who indicate an interest in a specific topic.

The World Wide Web, cable access channels, and other new information technologies have radically democratized access to political information. However, critics point out that there are some major problems with trying to maintain a pluralist democracy through digital democracy:

> The ultimate threats to [Canadian] democracy in the digital age are not the rise of splinter groups, or new tycoons, or government-imposed limits on speech. The dangers are more subtle and insidious. One is the lack of a common starting point for discussion . . . The other danger is that leadership as we knew it will disappear as politicians become all too connected to the voters. . . . What if our [leaders] become nothing more than the sum of our whims and misinformation? The "netizens" of the future will have to take their jobs seriously. Are we ready for this much democracy? Let's hope so. (Fineman, 1997:52)

Is it possible that the Canadian economy and democratic politics will become obsolete in the face of the global economy and digitized democracy? Despite digital democracy and the transnational nature of politics and the economy, scholars such as Paul Kennedy (1993:134) argue that individual nations will remain the primary locus of identity for most people. Regardless of who their employers are and what they do for a living, individuals pay taxes to a specific government, are subject to its laws, serve in its armed forces, and can travel internationally only by having its passport. Therefore, as new challenges arise, most people in democracies will turn to their own governments and demand solutions.

WHAT CAN YOU DO?

There are many things that individuals can do on their own and in groups to address the important economic and political issues we face as Canadians in a global economy:

- Remember that your consumer habits are a way of registering votes in the global economy—make informed decisions.
- Learn more about globalization and how it affects you.
- Find out what these are—NAFTA, MAI, WTO, FTAA, CUSFTA, GATT, NORAD, NATO, OAS—and how their mandates are impacting you in your daily life.
- Find out about anti-sweatshop campaigns and make informed consumer decisions that reflect your knowledge.
- Organize a non-sweatshop fashion show or "anti-fashion" show or another kind of awareness-raising event at your university or in your community.
- Learn about the local, provincial, and federal political leaders in your area and what they, and their parties, stand for.
- Send letters, faxes, e-mails, and other creative messages to corporations and governments to tell them what you think about current issues and what you want them to do about it.
- Vote in elections and get your friends to vote as well.
- Demand that there be political representatives running in your area that reflect your political concerns.
- If you invest, or know people who do, research companies that invest in things that reflect your politics.
- Explore what kinds of alternative actions you can take if your concerns and priorities are not being addressed.

SUMMARY

WHAT KIND OF ECONOMIC SYSTEM DOES CANADA HAVE?

Canada has a capitalist economy. Ideally, capitalism is characterized by private ownership of the means of production, pursuit of personal profit, competition, and lack of government intervention.

WHAT ARE MULTINATIONAL CORPORATIONS?

Multinational corporations have been around since the turn of the last century. A multinational corporation is a complete corporate operation that is taken from its country of origin and integrated into its host country in order to successfully market its products in the local culture. These operations require a strong host economy to survive.

WHAT ARE TRANSNATIONAL CORPORATIONS, AND WHY DO THEY POSE SOCIAL PROBLEMS?

Transnational corporations are large-scale business organizations headquartered in one country but operating in many countries. Many transnationals lack accountability to any government or regulatory agency. They are not dependent on any one country for labour, capital, or technology. They can play important roles in the economies and governments of countries that need them as employers and accept their practices.

WHY IS THE NATIONAL DEBT A SERIOUS PROBLEM? HOW IS CONSUMER DEBT A PUBLIC ISSUE?

When we increase the national debt, we are borrowing from future generations, leaving them with a social debt of higher taxes, fewer benefits, and a lower rate of economic growth. Consumer debt becomes a public issue when people cannot repay their credit-card loans.

WHAT IS CORPORATE WELFARE?

Corporate welfare occurs when the government helps industries and private corporations in their economic pursuits. Many subsidies that were originally put in place to help stabilize the economy continue unnecessarily because of lobbying by special-interest groups and business campaign contributions.

WHY IS VOTER APATHY A PROBLEM? WHAT IS THE GENDER GAP?

Voter apathy undermines the basis on which representative democracy is built; if large numbers of people don't vote, the interests of only a few are represented. The gender gap is the difference between an electoral candidate's number of votes from women and men. More than ever today, women and men seem to view economic and social issues differently.

WHAT IS THE FUNCTIONALIST–PLURALIST MODEL OF THE POLITICAL ECONOMY?

The functionalists use a pluralist model, believing that power is widely dispersed through many competing interest groups in our political system. Functionalists therefore believe that problems can be solved by identifying dysfunctional elements and correcting them.

WHAT DO CONFLICT THEORISTS SAY ABOUT POWER ELITES?

Conflict theorists use an elite model, believing that power in political systems is concentrated in the hands of a small group, whereas the masses are relatively powerless. Sociologist C. Wright Mills used the term *power elite* to describe this small group composed of business leaders, the executive branch of the federal government, and the "top brass" of the military.

WHAT ASPECT OF THE POLITICAL ECONOMY DO SYMBOLIC INTERACTIONISTS FOCUS ON?

Symbolic interactionists focus on the micro-, or small-scale, interactions that occur between individuals in specific settings. They want to know how humans are socialized, how we develop subjective interpretations of the political economy, and how we find ways to function within it. Specific attention is paid to how people utilize shared symbols—objects, words, sounds, and events—to build, challenge, and change political and economic activities.

WHAT IS A FEMINIST APPROACH TO GLOBALIZATION?

Feminists are concerned with political, economic, gendered, racialized/ethnic, and sexual power inequalities in the world. Global capitalism is seen as a force that threatens the health and well-being of people and the planet. Feminists are theoretically and socially committed to protecting and improving the rights, freedoms, and opportunities of women across the globe.

KEY TERMS

capitalism,   p. 296
corporate welfare,   p. 304
democracy,   p. 307
elite model,   p. 311
gender gap,   p. 308
government,   p. 307
interlocking corporate directorates,   p. 302
mixed economy,   p. 296
monopoly,   p. 301

multinational corporation (MNC),   p. 297
oligopoly,   p. 302
permanent government,   p. 310
pluralist model,   p. 310
politics,   p. 304
power elite,   p. 311
socialism,   p. 296
transnational corporation (TNC),   p. 297

QUESTIONS FOR CRITICAL THINKING

1.   Imagine that you are given unlimited funds and resources to reverse the trend in voter apathy. What would you do at the local level? What would you do at the provincial and national levels? Why is this not done, do you think?

2.   How would you respond to this Canadian Gallup Poll survey question: "Do you think that the government is run by a few big interests looking out for themselves or that it is run for the benefit of all the people?" Please explain your answer.

3.   Do you favour or oppose sociologist George Ritzer's proposal that the government restrain credit-card companies? What do you think about his idea of limiting profit and restricting incentives for accepting new credit cards? What would you propose as other means of reducing consumer debt?

4.   How do you think globalization will affect democratic practices in Canada in the next 10 years?

WEBLINKS

LabourWatch

www.labourwatch.com

This is a site is designed to help employees find neutral information about their rights and responsibilities and employers to better understand the law.

"Finding Information about Organizations"

www.upei.ca/library/html/canpolorg.html

From the University of Prince Edward Island's Political Studies Department, a web page providing useful links to many other web pages of political and governmental information.

Canadian Taxpayers Federation (CTF)

www.taxpayer.com/studies/federal.htm

"The CTF is a nonprofit, nonpartisan organization acting as a watchdog on government spending and taxation. This URL links to the federal archives page, with literature and information in PDF format.

CorpWatch

www.corpwatch.org/home.html

"Corp Watch, Holding Corporations Accountable" provides in-depth information related to corporate globalization.

Worldwatch Institute

www.worldwatch.org

This site is a source of information on the interactions among key environmental, social, and economic trends. The institute's work focuses on interdisciplinary research, and the site offers accessible literature and articles.

Transnationale.org

www.transnationale.org/anglais

This site lists more than 21 000 national and international brands and provides answers to the questions, Who owns these brands? Where and how were the goods actually manufactured? The site also gives links and highlights related current affairs.

Straight Goods

www.straightgoods.com

Straight Goods, an independent Canadian online source of news, acts as a watchdog for citizens by providing investigative reports, news, and forums and untangling controversial issues to help consumers make up their own mind and protect their rights.

Maple Leaf Web

www.mapleleafweb.com

This nonprofit, nonpartisan Canadian political education site located at the University of Lethbridge provides articles and background information on Canadian political events and institutions.

Sweatshop Watch

www.sweatshopwatch.org

A coalition of labour, community, and civil rights organizations and individuals that serves low-wage garments workers, Sweatshop Watch is dedicated to putting an end to the exploitation that occurs in sweatshops. The site offers information, links, and ways to get involved.

14
PROBLEMS IN THE MEDIA

Our children are born into homes in which the dominant story tellers are not those who have something to tell but a small group of global conglomerates that have something to sell. Channels multiply but communication technologies converge and media merge. With every merger, staffs shrink and creative opportunities diminish. Cross-media conglomeration reduces competition and denies entry to newcomers. Fewer sources fill more outlets more of the time with ever more standardized fare. Alternative perspectives vanish from the mainstream. Media coalesce into a seamless, pervasive, and increasingly homogenized cultural environment that has drifted out of democratic reach. Even fund-starved public television is fighting for its life.

George Gerber speaking about the relationship between the democratization of communication and the empowerment of individuals as a prerequisite of democracy (in Sridhara, 2003)

It is our TV viewing that shapes our understanding of the world and ourselves. However, it is saturated with U.S. influence and media imperialism. How much television has affected [Canadian] culture and sovereignty is yet to be seen. Only time will tell.

Catherine Woods discussing the role of media in identity construction in Canada (1998)

I've had more than one recent column sliced and diced. I can only assume it was done to remove opinions that did not correspond with those of the new owners. They didn't. And I admit I've also done some self-censoring too, steering clear of certain subjects on which I know the owners have taken a stand for me . . . Why shouldn't freedom of the press, as legendary press critic A.J. Liebling once put it, be "guaranteed only to those who own one?" Because, quite simply, real democracy depends on the free flow of ideas, on debate and disagreement. And newspapers are the best forum for those debates. Which is why we need to consider the real impact of concentrating so much newspaper ownership in so few hands.

Stephen Kimber, Director of the School of Journalism at the University of King's College, describes why he finally quit his job as columnist with the Daily News *after 16 years (2002)*

The notion that the Internet would "set us free," and permit anyone to communicate effectively, hence undermining the monopoly power of the corporate media giants, has not transpired. Although the Internet offers extraordinary promise in many regards, it alone cannot slay the power of the media giants. Indeed, no commercially viable media content site has been launched on the Internet, and it would be difficult to find an investor willing to bankroll any additional attempts. To the extent the Internet becomes part of the commercially viable media system, it looks to be under the thumb of the usual corporate suspects.

Robert W. McChesney, professor and acting editor of Monthly Review, *in his speech to UNESCO about concerns for the future of global media (2001)*

The media play a vital role in the daily lives of Canadians. Whether we realize their existence or try to ignore their influence, various forms of the media are with us constantly. In this chapter we will look at the role the media plays in contemporary society. In particular, we explore the relationship between media and democracy in Canada. The impact of globalization on media ownership is also reflected upon, as is the importance of critical engagement with media in the 21st century.

What constitutes the media? *Media* is the plural of *medium,* which refers to any device that transmits a message. The media include newspapers, magazines, television, and movies, among other things. When sociologists refer to the media (or mass media), however, they are usually speaking of the **media industries— major businesses that own, or own interests in, radio and television production and broadcasting; motion pictures, movie theatres, and music companies; news- paper, periodical (magazine), and book publishing; and Internet services and content providers, and that influence people and cultures worldwide.** Recent estimates show that the average person in North America spends more than one-half of her or his waking hours in some media-related activity. Indeed, today, many people spend more time in media-related activities than they do in any other single endeavour, including sleeping, working, eating, or talking with friends and family (Biagi, 1998).

Is this time well spent? Most analysts and media scholars agree that the media industries that emerged in the 20th century are one of the most significant social institutions at work in Canada and in many other nations. The media facilitate human communication and provide news and entertainment to their consumers. Therefore, the corporations who own and control media content and distribution have a powerful influence on all the social institutions, including education, health care delivery, religion, families, and politics. Some aspects of this influence are positive, but other aspects may be negative. Some critics who are concerned about possible negative influences note that we are experiencing a media glut and increased commercialization of all aspects of life (Biagi, 1998). For example, commercialization of the Internet and the rise of the World Wide Web in the 1990s have magnified the amount of media messages and products that confront people who use computers and online services (McChesney, 1999). Other critics question the effects of contemporary media ownership on Canadian democracy (McChesney, 1999; Hackett et al., 2000). In our current Canadian cultural context, democracy, consumption, and the media have become inextricably linked. Today, radio, television, newspapers, and the Internet are the main sources of news and entertainment for most people. As a result, it is important to know who owns media, to assess the quality of the information that is disseminated through them, and to understand the roles media play in shaping (and creating) public opinion (Biagi, 1998; McChesney, 1999).

THE POLITICAL ECONOMY OF MEDIA INDUSTRIES

Twenty years ago, about 50 firms dominated the global media market. Today, there are fewer than 10 (Guma, 2001:1). In that time, media ownership has become increasingly concentrated. Today, a few companies own a large percentage of television and radio stations, film studios, and publishing houses. Those few companies and their monopolistic control over media content, production, and distribution have come to be known as Big Media. Many factors have led to the development of Big Media—one of them is the evolution of media-related technology. Technology, in the form of motion pictures, radio, and television, increased competition and broadened media markets during the 20th century. Prior to this time, newspapers and books had been the primary means of disseminating information and entertainment to large numbers of people. The companies involved in producing these forms of media were usually small and focused on a single output. For example, companies whose only business was news-

papers produced newspapers, and books were published by companies that dealt just in books (Biagi, 1998). There were challenges faced by these first industries. At least two factors limited market demands for the information and entertainment provided by the newspaper and publishing industries: the length of time it took to get the product to consumers and the consumer's own literacy. Radio, on the other hand, offered consumers, from coast to coast, immediate access to information and entertainment. In Canada, the first broadcasting licence was issued in 1919, and by 1922, radio had become a competitor to the newspaper and publishing industries. Simply by turning a knob, consumers could listen to the latest news (sometimes even as it happened!), hear the latest song, laugh with their favourite comedian, or thrill to the adventures of their favourite detective. Consumers and corporate executives alike felt that radio's dominance in the media industries could not be shaken. In 1952, however, a new cable television technology took hold in Canada. By 1958, the Canadian Broadcasting Corporation's (CBC's) microwave network extended from Victoria, B.C., to Sydney, Nova Scotia, making it the longest television network in the world (Canadian Museum of Civilization, 2003). Television's domination in the media world had begun. Television had all the advantages of radio and one more: moving images. Now consumers could not only listen to the world around them, they could watch it.

Media Ownership and Control

Technology has played a significant role in the development of media industries as well as in the changes that have occurred within these industries.

Consider, for a moment, the effects that fibre-optic cable, broadcast satellites, and computers have had on media industries. The introduction of cable television, for example, brought about a significant shift in media ownership. The development of more sophisticated space satellites in the 1970s made it possible for cable television systems to become interconnected throughout North America. Satellites also contributed to the success of cable networks such as Shaw Cable, Rogers Communications, and COGECO, to which consumers pay a monthly fee for viewing rights. Having a variety of cable channels to watch increased the number of cable TV subscribers, resulted in more broadcast stations being built, and inspired the creation of additional cable channels. At the same time, the dramatic increase in cable television viewers drastically reduced the audience-share previously held by the original television networks. This evolution of technology and business strategies within the media industry has been characterized by a trend where a few megacorporations own increasing proportions of the media businesses and where companies own more than one form of media business (Biagi, 1998).

In Canada, the years between 1983 and 1992 saw the total number of control companies in the media industry shrink from 46 to 20 (Hoynes, 2002:1). In the television industry, for example, a few megacorporations gained a great deal of control over all aspects of the television industry. As a result, functions ranging from program production to distribution to the audience fell under Big Media control. As businesses with a goal of generating profit, these corporations also consolidated their holdings in other sectors of the media—ranging from film and music production to books and magazine publishing. They also acquired interests in technologies such as computers and direct broadcasting from satellite (Budd et al., 1999). The biggest media merger in Canada occurred in 2000, when Conrad Black sold 17 percent of his newspapers and Internet properties to Izzy Asper, the owner and CEO of CanWest. Asper's empire is Canada's largest integrated media company. It includes the Global television network, Fox Sports, DejaView, Prime TV, and Fireworks Entertainment, as well as many of the major and minor Canadian dailies and radio stations (CanWest Global, 2003). In the United States, America Online (AOL) and Time Warner agreed to enter into the largest media merger to date. Why would the largest worldwide media company, Time Warner, agree to join AOL? The answer lies in access to the Internet, which is central to the contemporary music, publishing, and television industries (Hansell, 2000). Through the merger, AOL's 22 million subscribers (as of January 2000) were linked to Time Warner's cable television systems, which have about 13 million customers. Since the merger, AOL-TW has been affected by a slowdown in advertising spending and consumer growth and, in 2003, carried a debt of $26 billion (Kapadia, 2003). Analysts describe these types of mergers in the media industries as *convergence,* meaning that a consolidation or amalgamation of the communications, computer, and electronics

industries has occurred. Convergence in the media industry has led to media concentration (Rosenwein, 2000). ***Media concentration* refers to the tendency of the media industries to cluster together in groups with the goal of enhancing profitability** (Biagi, 1998). Figure 14.1 shows some of the top media industries in Canada.

As this definition suggests, profit is the driving force in media concentration. According to media scholar Shirley Biagi (1998:263), "Media companies are owned by people who want to make money." Since profits in this sector are high compared with profits in the manufacturing sector, businesspeople view investments in the media industries positively—although the losses experienced by AOL-TW do raise questions about what kinds of mergers are most profitable. Thus far, corporate megamergers have led to the following changes in the media industries (Biagi, 1998):

1. *Concentration of ownership within one industry:* For example, as this book goes to press, the three biggest newspaper chains own 25 percent of all the daily newspapers in Canada. In some provinces, media concentration is above the national average. As examples, all of the daily newspapers in New Brunswick are owned by the Irving family; one company owns all the daily papers in Saskatchewan, Prince Edward Island, and Newfoundland; and in Quebec, only one small independent paper has survived (Press Campaigns, 2003). Concentration occurs in part because small presses and independent media sources are not able to access the advertising revenue and large audiences that large corporations can. As a result, many small Canadian presses are closing. This is also true of Canadian television, where 60 percent of the market is reached by only 5 corporations. In 2003, 3 companies controlled 68 per cent of the cable television market and 10 companies controlled 55 per cent of the revenue from the radio industry (Biagi, 1998; McChesney, 1999; Press Campaigns, 2003).

2. *Cross-media ownership:* Cross-media ownership occurs when media companies own more than one type of media property. Today, a single giant media corporation may own newspapers, magazines, and radio and television stations. Even among smaller media corporations, cross-media ownership is common. The Canadian company Rogers

FIGURE 14.1   Canadian Media Ownership in 2001

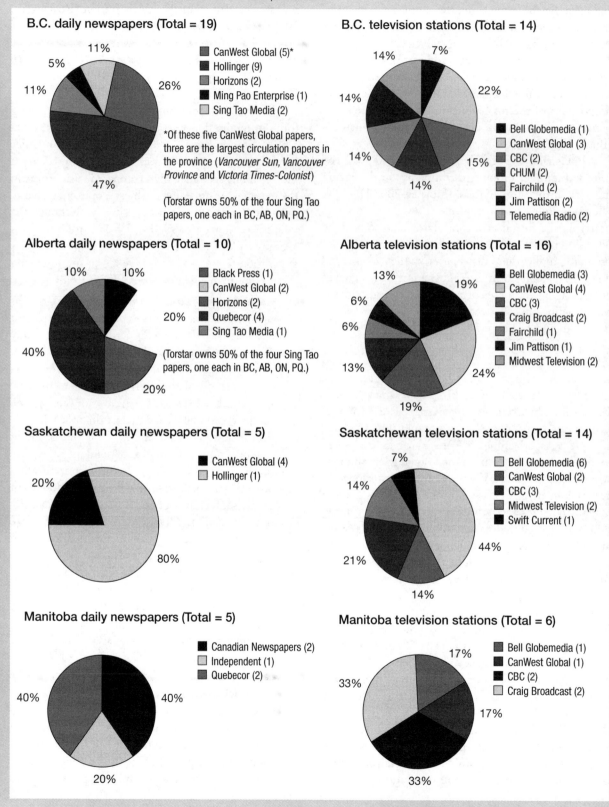

B.C. daily newspapers (Total = 19)

11%
5%
11%
26%
47%

- CanWest Global (5)*
- Hollinger (9)
- Horizons (2)
- Ming Pao Enterprise (1)
- Sing Tao Media (2)

*Of these five CanWest Global papers, three are the largest circulation papers in the province (*Vancouver Sun, Vancouver Province* and *Victoria Times-Colonist*)

(Torstar owns 50% of the four Sing Tao papers, one each in BC, AB, ON, PQ.)

B.C. television stations (Total = 14)

14%
7%
22%
14%
14%
15%
14%

- Bell Globemedia (1)
- CanWest Global (3)
- CBC (2)
- CHUM (2)
- Fairchild (2)
- Jim Pattison (2)
- Telemedia Radio (2)

Alberta daily newspapers (Total = 10)

10%
10%
20%
40%
20%

- Black Press (1)
- CanWest Global (2)
- Horizons (2)
- Quebecor (4)
- Sing Tao Media (1)

(Torstar owns 50% of the four Sing Tao papers, one each in BC, AB, ON, PQ.)

Alberta television stations (Total = 16)

13%
19%
6%
6%
13%
24%
19%

- Bell Globemedia (3)
- CanWest Global (4)
- CBC (3)
- Craig Broadcast (2)
- Fairchild (1)
- Jim Pattison (1)
- Midwest Television (2)

Saskatchewan daily newspapers (Total = 5)

20%
80%

- CanWest Global (4)
- Hollinger (1)

Saskatchewan television stations (Total = 14)

7%
14%
21%
14%
44%

- Bell Globemedia (6)
- CanWest Global (2)
- CBC (3)
- Midwest Television (2)
- Swift Current (1)

Manitoba daily newspapers (Total = 5)

40%
40%
20%

- Canadian Newspapers (2)
- Independent (1)
- Quebecor (2)

Manitoba television stations (Total = 6)

17%
33%
17%
33%
33%

- Bell Globemedia (1)
- CanWest Global (1)
- CBC (2)
- Craig Broadcast (2)

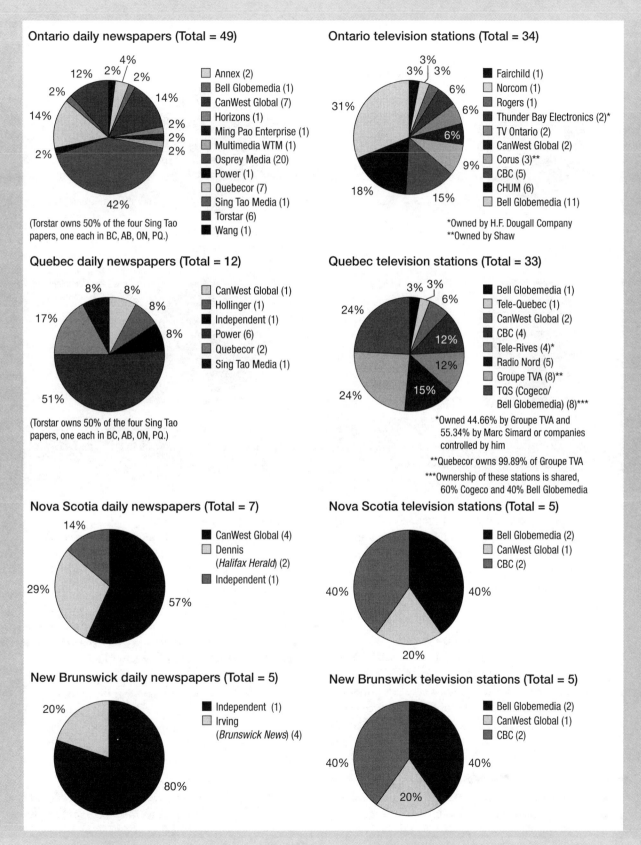

Ontario daily newspapers (Total = 49)

4%, 2%, 2%, 12%, 2%, 14%, 2%, 14%, 14%, 2%, 2%, 2%, 2%, 42%

- Annex (2)
- Bell Globemedia (1)
- CanWest Global (7)
- Horizons (1)
- Ming Pao Enterprise (1)
- Multimedia WTM (1)
- Osprey Media (20)
- Power (1)
- Quebecor (7)
- Sing Tao Media (1)
- Torstar (6)
- Wang (1)

(Torstar owns 50% of the four Sing Tao papers, one each in BC, AB, ON, PQ.)

Ontario television stations (Total = 34)

3%, 3%, 3%, 6%, 6%, 6%, 31%, 9%, 18%, 15%

- Fairchild (1)
- Norcom (1)
- Rogers (1)
- Thunder Bay Electronics (2)*
- TV Ontario (2)
- CanWest Global (2)
- Corus (3)**
- CBC (5)
- CHUM (6)
- Bell Globemedia (11)

*Owned by H.F. Dougall Company
**Owned by Shaw

Quebec daily newspapers (Total = 12)

8%, 8%, 8%, 8%, 17%, 51%

- CanWest Global (1)
- Hollinger (1)
- Independent (1)
- Power (6)
- Quebecor (2)
- Sing Tao Media (1)

(Torstar owns 50% of the four Sing Tao papers, one each in BC, AB, ON, PQ.)

Quebec television stations (Total = 33)

3%, 3%, 6%, 24%, 12%, 12%, 24%, 15%

- Bell Globemedia (1)
- Tele-Quebec (1)
- CanWest Global (2)
- CBC (4)
- Tele-Rives (4)*
- Radio Nord (5)
- Groupe TVA (8)**
- TQS (Cogeco/
  Bell Globemedia) (8)***

*Owned 44.66% by Groupe TVA and
55.34% by Marc Simard or companies
controlled by him

**Quebecor owns 99.89% of Groupe TVA

***Ownership of these stations is shared,
60% Cogeco and 40% Bell Globemedia

Nova Scotia daily newspapers (Total = 7)

14%, 29%, 57%

- CanWest Global (4)
- Dennis
  (*Halifax Herald*) (2)
- Independent (1)

Nova Scotia television stations (Total = 5)

40%, 40%, 20%

- Bell Globemedia (2)
- CanWest Global (1)
- CBC (2)

New Brunswick daily newspapers (Total = 5)

20%, 80%

- Independent (1)
- Irving
  (*Brunswick News*) (4)

New Brunswick television stations (Total = 5)

40%, 40%, 20%

- Bell Globemedia (2)
- CanWest Global (1)
- CBC (2)

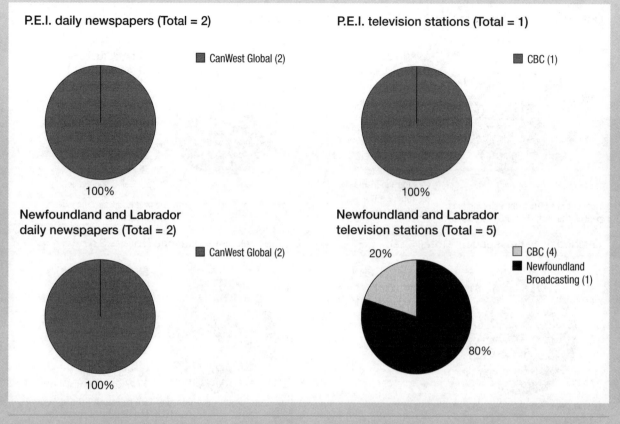

P.E.I. daily newspapers (Total = 2)

■ CanWest Global (2)

100%

P.E.I. television stations (Total = 1)

■ CBC (1)

100%

Newfoundland and Labrador daily newspapers (Total = 2)

■ CanWest Global (2)

100%

Newfoundland and Labrador television stations (Total = 5)

20%

□ CBC (4)
■ Newfoundland Broadcasting (1)

80%

Source: From "Media Ownership Study," UBC Thunderbird Journalism Review Online, **www.journalism.ubc.ca/thunderbird/2001-02/december/all-media.html**. *Reproduced with permission.*

Communications, for example, has over 3 million cable subscribers. This communications company owns 20 video stores, the Home Shopping Network, one-third of the shares of AT&T Canada, the Viewers Choice cable service, the Rogers-Cantel cellular phone network, the YTV network, 10 radio stations, and 1 television station, as well as Maclean-Hunter and *Maclean's* magazine (Rogers Communication, 2003). Clearly, cross-media ownership has a particularly serious impact in geographical areas where people have access to media owned by only one source. For example, a strike at Irving Oil may receive biased coverage by the majority of media sources that are owned by Irving in the province.

3. *Conglomerate ownership:* Conglomerates occur when a single corporation owns companies that operate in different business sectors. Universal/Seagram is

a conglomerate created by the acquisition of MCA/Universal by Seagram, the Canadian liquor company (*Brill's Content,* 2000). Seagram Company owns theme parks, concert halls, motion picture production companies, movie theatres, and retail stores such as Spencer Gifts (Budd et al., 1999).

4. *Vertical integration:* Vertical integration occurs when the corporations that make the media content also control the distribution channels. CanWest, for example, owns CanWest Entertainment Inc., which is one of Canada's largest integrated production, distribution, and financing companies of television programs and motion pictures. The film and television production companies it owns (CanWest Entertainment, Fireworks Television, and Fireworks Pictures) supply programming to its television networks (Global Television Network, Prime TV, and CHECK television). CanWest also

partnered with Samuel Goldwyn Films and Stratosphere Releasing, forming IDP Distribution, in order to market and distribute feature films in North America (CanWest Entertainment, 2003; Brill's Content, 2000; Rosenwein, 2000).

Supporters of convergence believe that much can be gained by these corporate strategies; they speak of synergy. The term *synergy* is often used to describe the process used in capitalizing on a product to make all the profit possible. Media analysts believe that synergy is created, for example, when a corporation acquires ownership of both a production studio and a television network. Theoretically, the products made by one branch of the company may be distributed and sold by the other branch of the company in a more efficient and profitable manner than if separate companies were involved. Shaw Cable, the second largest cable television operation in Canada, is a good example of synergy. Corus Entertainment, Shaw's media arm, owns 49 radio stations, television services, Nelvana Limited (an international producer and distributor of children's programming and products), and the television networks YTV, Country Music Television, Premium Pay TV Services, Videon Cable, and WTN (CBC, 2003). This network allows for the programs and products generated by one branch of the company to be promoted through others in an efficient and cost-effective manner.

Most people in the media industries do not see consolidation as a problem. Supporters claim that concentration in media ownership ensures that Canadian voices are able to compete with those promoted by companies from the United States and by the international media market. The executive vice-president of CanWest Global, Ken Goldstein, claims Canadian companies could not successfully compete against the more powerful media conglomerates from the United States if they were prevented from consolidating resources. Goldstein stated in a CBC interview, "You would not have a true viable independent media without it" (CBC, 2002). However, some media executives have acknowledged that the close link between their sectors may lead to conflicts of interest or accusations of collusion. Michael Eisner, chairman of Disney, has stated that he believes ABC News (which is owned by Disney) should not cover Disney: "I think it's inappropriate for Disney to be covered by Disney. . . . By

and large, the way you avoid conflict of interest is to, as best you can, not cover yourself" (Rosenwein, 2000:94). However, according to the media magazine *Brill's Content*, Eisner's comments were made only days before ABC News killed a story about Disney's unintentionally hiring convicted pedophiles to work at its theme parks (Rosenwein, 2000).

Problems Associated with Convergence

Concentration and conglomeration are profitable for investors and media executives. These processes don't only involve the amalgamation of businesses, they also involve initiatives designed to streamline media systems. Strategies to increase profits include asking journalists to report on several separate stories each day as opposed to developing one or two well-researched stories. These stories are then distributed throughout the same conglomerates' different media outlets. Many people watching these trends are concerned about the effects this is having on the quality and integrity of journalism in Canada (Lill, 2001). Many analysts indicate that convergence has reduced the amount of *message pluralism*, the "broad and diverse representation of opinion and culture," available to the Canadian public (Biagi, 1998:265). This is also a concern when the bias of the small community of media owners influences the nation's media content. As one media scholar has noted:

> Media fare is even more closely linked to the needs and concerns of a handful of enormous and powerful corporations, with annual revenues approaching the [Gross Domestic Product] of a small nation. These firms are run by wealthy managers and billionaires with clear stakes in the outcome of the most fundamental political issues, and their interests are often distinct from those of the vast majority of humanity. By any known theory of democracy, such a concentration of economic, cultural, and political power into so few hands— and mostly unaccountable hands at that—is absurd and unacceptable. On the other hand, media fare is subjected to an ever-greater commercialization as the dominant firms use their market power to squeeze the greatest possible profit from their products (McChesney, 1999:29–30).

As this statement suggests, other industries have used convergence in the media industries to increase their own market shares. Advertising agencies have found that convergence has allowed them to perfect the process of branding. Molson Canadian has launched the ad campaign "I Am Canadian" in order to promote a "good-living" lifestyle that is characterized by drinking Molson Canadian beer and expressing one's patriotism about Canada. There are many Canadians who, possibly in search of a Canadian identity, are inspired to buy "I Am Canadian" paraphernalia, consume "Bubba-sized" beer and register their patriotic sentiments on the IAM.CA website. The Molson Canadian ad states:

> I'm not a lumberjack or a fur trader. I don't live in an igloo or eat blubber or own a dog sled. And I don't know Jimmy, Sally, or Suzy from Canada, although I'm certain they're really, really nice. I have a prime minister, not a president. I speak English and French, not American. And I pronounce it about, not aboot. I can proudly sew my country's flag on my backpack. I believe in peacekeeping, not policing. Diversity, not assimilation. And that the beaver is a truly proud and noble animal. A toque is a hat, a chesterfield is a couch. And it is pronounced zed, not zee, zed. Canada is the second largest landmass, the first nation of hockey and the best part of North America. My name is Joe, and I am Canadian!" (www.IAM.CA, 2003).

Commercialization and branding have already found their way to the Internet, which, even as it is hailed as a new source of news and entertainment that is relatively free from corporate constraints, has experienced criticism similar to the criticism levelled at more established forms of media.

Convergence and the loss of truly open democratic debate are two of the reoccurring criticisms levied against mainstream media houses today. There are five primary areas where media are accused of failing to facilitate democratic exchanges in society. Analysts believe that convergence has created conditions that are leading to: (1) the decline of journalism as a public service profession; (2) constant pressure for all journalistic endeavors to be immediately profitable; (3) a significant decrease in the quantity and quality of international news available to Canadian audiences; (4) the quashing of public debate about the power of the media industries and how they deal with important social issues; and, (5) a dramatic increase in the influence of powerful Ottawa lobbyists who represent the interests of the media conglomerates (McChesney, 1999; Phillips, 1999). Because the reach of the media industries is worldwide, these concerns are not limited to Canada.

GLOBAL MEDIA ISSUES

To understand the effect transnational media corporations may have on other nations of the world, consider this: Six major media conglomerates—AOL Time Warner, Sony, Viacom, Disney, Bertelsmann, and News Corporation—control most of the publishing, recording, television, film, and mega–theme park business in the high-income nations of the world (McChesney, 1999).

Perhaps it should not be surprising that advertising by transnational corporations has fueled the rise of commercial television—and consequently, the profitability of media conglomerates—around the world. For example, more than half of the advertising on the ABN-CNBC Asia network (which is co-owned by Dow Jones and General Electric) is for transnational corporations, most of which are U.S.-based businesses (McChesney, 1999). As international agreements over trade, such as NAFTA (the North American Free Trade Agreement) and GATT (the General Agreement on Tariffs and Trade) have come into effect, companies in fields such as oil production, aerospace engineering, and agribusiness have used transnational media corporations to improve their communication base and extend their international operations (Schiller, 1996). All in all, the global economy has proved profitable for media conglomerates (see Chapter 13 for more discussion on trade).

While Canada is not involved in producing, distributing, and controlling media transnationally to the same degree that the major U.S.-based media companies are, Canada still plays a role internationally. For example, as of January 2003, the Hollinger Corporation owned the Telegraph Group Limited (with over 25 media productions) in the United Kingdom, the Chicago Group (with over 70 publications) and the Community Newspaper Group (with approximately 30 newspapers) in the United States, and 6 major newspapers in Israel (Hollinger, 2003). CanWest owned Fireworks Pictures based out of Los Angeles, and Fireworks International,

Do you see the Starbucks coffee on the table? That distinctive cup did not get into the second Austin Powers film accidentally. Corporations such as Starbucks pay millions of dollars for "product placements" in the media so that consumers will be constantly reminded to buy their brand. How is branding such as this changing films and the Internet?

which is a worldwide TV-program distributor based in London, England. It also owned radio broadcasting interests in New Zealand and television broadcasting interests in Australia, New Zealand, and Ireland. It operates with a budget of almost $2 billion per year (CanWest Global, 2003).

There is growing concern about the amount of control a few media giants have over the world's information. Some have predicted that a very few major media conglomerates will soon control approximately 90 percent of all global information (Kilbourne, 1999). These same few media companies are rapidly gaining the ownership and control of both the hardware and software that will make it possible for them to fully control messages and images appearing in any format (Schiller, 1996; Kilbourne, 1999). This fact may be particularly alarming to those who are already critical of how the media giants depict other nations.

While global media industries obviously provide news and entertainment to people who otherwise might not know what is going on in the world, according to media critic Robert McChesney (1999), they also contribute to the development of "neoliberal" democracies in those nations in which people have the formal right to vote but where the wealthy actually hold political and economic power:

> The global commercial media system is *radical*, in the sense that it will respect no tradition or custom, on balance, if it stands in the way of significantly increased profits. But it ultimately is politically *conservative*, because the media giants are significant beneficiaries of the current global social structure, and any upheaval in property or social relations, particularly to the extent it reduced the power of business and lessened inequality, would possibly—no, probably—jeopardize their positions (McChesney, 1999:100).

Many critics also worry that the North American–based media giants undermine traditional cultural values and beliefs in other nations, replacing them with North American values—particularly those that support materialism and consumerism. Some call this media imperialism, which occurs when one society's media dominates another country's culture (Knight, 1998:110). Globally, the major transnational agencies control over 90 percent of the sources of televised images, while 45 percent of developing countries have no television producers of their own. U.S. media critic Jean Kilbourne (1999:55) states, "Today we export a popular culture that promotes escapism, consumerism, violence and greed." The countries that import media portrayals of Western culture do not have the means to depict values, activities, or perspectives indigenous to their own country in a way that rivals the ability of the United States.

In Canada, there is a great deal of intra-national legislation that is dedicated to protecting the cultural, linguistic, and political differences between English- and French-speaking Canada. The management, editorial priorities, and communications culture of the mass media in French- and English-speaking Canada are characteristically different in some important ways. Internationally, legislation is focused on limiting the percentage of media programming that is imported into Canada, particularly from the United States (Siegel, 1996). The historical idea that broadcasting should be a public service created to reflect public, and not private, interests resulted in the creation of the Canadian Broadcasting Corporation (CBC), Le Societé Radio-Canada (SRC), and the Canadian Radio-Television

BOX 14.1   This Is What Democracy Looks Like

"Most of what has been written is so inaccurate that I can't decide if the reporters in question should be charged with conspiracy or simply incompetence," stated one observer after the 1999 protest against the World Trade Organization (WTO) in Seattle, Washington (Donahue, 2000). Official media houses reported that violent protestors and "anarchists" had taken to the streets, breaking windows, spraying graffiti on stores such as Starbucks, Nike, and McDonalds, and engaging in confrontational behaviour with police as they progressed through Seattle's downtown. In contrast, many of the 50 000 who attended the protest did so in a spirit of peaceful protest against the World Trade Organization and the impacts of globalization. Many of these people have stories to tell about their experiences at the "Battle in Seattle" that differ from those covered by mainstream media.

Critical analysis of media coverage of the "Battle in Seattle" makes explicit the relationships between media, government, and big business. The close links between these three social institutions calls into question the role media plays in maintaining the status quo and therefore the degree to which "objectivity" in mainstream reporting is currently being compromised. *Globe and Mail* reporter Barry McKenna (1999:A9) wrote, the morning the WTO summit began, that "Nine of the thirteen companies that contributed more than $150 000 to the Seattle organizing committee are high-technology companies." Companies such as these are forecasted to generate trillions of dollars in annual revenue in the next decade. They are the same companies that make up the new global media system and that work in tandem with the five or six super-ad agencies that control the $350 billion global advertising industry. Together they dominate global trade. In the lead-up to the WTO, these corporations actively lobbied the WTO for tax-free e-commerce regulations to be passed. During the WTO, they dictated to the media houses they own what spin North American reporters should take on reporting the events surrounding the WTO meeting and protests (Gutstein, 2000).

Events like the anti-WTO protests demonstrate how media concentration is impacting democratic processes around the globe. Without a voice in the mainstream media, protesters' analyses of and experiences at the WTO were hard for many Canadians to access—unless they were aware of alternative media houses, which carry stories such as those about the "Battle in Seattle" told by anti-WTO protestors. Alternative media radio and television programs and zines, and film and video collectives as well, are responsible for the creation of media pieces such as the collaboration of over 100 media activists to make the Indy.media documentary *This Is What Democracy Looks Like.*

These alternative media sources are typically run by volunteers and organized around a commitment to model a democratic media process where a diversity of opinion is expressed and the mainstream is intelligently criticized. For example, the volunteers who run *Adbusters* state on their homepage, "We want folks to get mad about corporate disinformation, injustices in the global economy, and any industry that pollutes our physical or mental commons." This declaration clearly marks this organization's bias about media concentration, which is at odds with the bias of the mainstream media, and invites people to engage with *Adbusters* in a debate about the role of media in the political economy.

As a result of the structure of media in Canada, people who wanted to learn about the common person's experience on the streets of Seattle turned to alternative media sources. Instead of articles discussing the importance of multilateral agreements or the property costs incurred by "anarchistic" protestors, these sites tended to carry critiques of the global political economy and the institutional measures set in place to protect it. During the WTO protests, web-based sites gave eye-witness reports that challenged official statements made by police, politicians, and other authorities in the mainstream media. For example, many reported on alternative media sites that the police initiated violent attacks against protestors four hours before any vandalism occurred (Donahue, 2000). In other stories, people wrote that police violence may have started because the riot squads began to feel intimidated by the unified and committed presence of the nonviolent protesters and set about to undermine it. On the Internet, people like Matt Guynn, a non-violence trainer and eyewitness, distributed accounts, such as this one, about police violence:

> In one scene I witnessed this morning, police who had been standing behind a blockade line began marching in lock-step toward the line (of protesters), swinging their batons forward, and when they reached the line they began striking the nonviolent, seated protesters repeatedly in the back. Then they ripped off the protesters' gas masks, and sprayed pepper spray at point-blank range into their eyes repeatedly. After spraying, they rubbed the protesters' eyes and pushed their fingers around on their lips to aggravate the effect of the spray. And after all this, they began striking them again with batons (in Donahue, 2000).

Eyewitnesses who had been attacked by police with pepper spray and tear gas returned to their communities to suffer the chemical impacts of these attacks and to share stories about what really happened on the streets at the WTO (author's files). Many families and friends were shocked to learn that the footage shown on television and in national newspapers was almost completely at odds with what the vast majority of protestors reported seeing and experiencing. The discrepancies between the official and unofficial stories were so dramatic that a new era of distrust in the mass media began.

Increasingly, Canadians are becoming aware of the five basic filters that are used in the media to manage social debate and to "manufacture consent." The first filter is media ownership. Currently, media concentration, which leads to a decrease in the diversity of voices represented through mainstream media, is of grave concern for many Canadians. Media activists and organizations such as MediaWatch, based at Simon Fraser University in British Columbia, focus their efforts on identifying the blind spots (stories and points of view not covered in the mainstream media) that are the result of media concentration, conglomerate ownership, and other institutional bias. These blindspots contribute to fewer and fewer points of view being meaningfully covered in the media. The second filter is advertising, as it tends not to challenge, criticize, or offer alternative approaches to capitalism or the doctrines of elite social rule in general. Clothing, car, cosmetic, and beer advertisements, for example, consistently reinforce messages that encourage people to consume and to conform to idealized societal norms. The third filter is the sources of news. In North America, the trend is that fewer agencies are generating and monitoring media activity. The Canadian Press, Reuters, and Associated Press are three of the main sources of media in Canada. "Flak" is the fourth filter. Within democratic societies where the ideal of "one voice, one vote" is upheld, media watchdogs serve the role of ensuring that the media production and distribution industries are performing in a democratically appropriate way. In Canada, however, most widely disseminated "flak" is generated by right-wing media watchdogs and industry groups, such as the Fraser Institute and the Canadian Association of Broadcasters. The final filter within North American propaganda production is the "official enemy." Identifying and fighting against an enemy or enemies helps to maintain domestic social discipline and conservative or neoconservative hegemony. "Enemies" inside Canada include protesters, immigrants, the poor, and people with disabilities, as well as racialized/ethnic, sexual, and religious minorities. International enemies in the post-Soviet world include the Arab world, Afghanistan, the Iraqis, and "terrorists" in general. Understanding the existence and the function of these five filters enables people who are media-literate to become informed consumers of media in Canada.

Having an awareness of the presence and the function of these filters is one way of making sense of how media is managed. The anti-WTO protests blew the cover off media bias for many Canadians and revealed the dramatic effects media concentration is having on the ability of North Americans to engage in democratic exchanges of mass communication.

and Telecommunications Commission (CRTC). Within this country, a primary challenge is to maintain control over Canadian ownership of, and content within, the mass media. The CRTC has slowly been changing these protective legislations. Currently, foreign companies are prevented from owning more than 46.7 percent of Canadian media distribution companies. In 2002, however, lobbying pressure by the Canadian CEOs of CanWest, Rogers, and Shaw further challenged the existing legislation that prevents foreign media-ownership in Canada (Standing Committee on Canadian Heritage, 2002). It is worth noting that corporations involved in these negotiations are also some of the biggest contributors to the federal liberal government.

The social, cultural, and political impacts of the media have also been experienced by Indigenous communities within Canada. John Amagoalik, President of the Inuit Tapirisat of Canada, describes the impact of the Canadian government's 1972 decision to bring television into communities in the far North in which the population numbered just over 500 people:

> When television first came, the effect of the television on the community was very drastic. People no longer visited their neighbours. Children did not play outside and the interactive activities of the community in general were broken down. The home and the family was the last refuge of the Inuktitut language, and television, by coming into the home, was invading this last refuge." (in *Magic in the Sky*. Dir. Peter Raymont, 1981)

As Kilbourne and other media scholars point out, for the first time in history, people are hearing most stories about life, not from their parents, schools, churches, or friends, but from transnational media conglomerates that have something to sell. If it is true that the media are a crucial influence in shaping and creating global cultural perceptions, then all of us must give careful consideration to the images and information offered to us. Of particular significance is how the news is framed. ***Framing* refers to how news content, and the accompanying visual images, are linked together to create certain audience perceptions and give specific impressions to viewers and readers.** When framing occurs in a news story, some analysts use the term "spin," because the process often involves "spinning" information so as to present it from a particular (and different) angle, or point of view. Critics point out that once a frame is established; journalists must adhere to it. The danger is that media coverage falling outside of the frame is not covered by mainstream media. In Canada, media bias is a growing concern for professional journalists. In January, 2002, the Canadian Association of Journalists (CAJ) and the Quebec Federation of Professional Journalists (FPJQ), responded to patterns of censorship within major Canadian newspaper chains as well as the erosion of editorial independence in major urban dailies by calling for a parliamentary inquiry into the effects of media concentration in Canada.

Media bias, in the form of *structural media bias*, refers to the areas of life and work that are not covered in the media. This distorts how people view the world and can significantly influence the priorities people develop. In the 1990s, the face of national news changed in Canada. Hollinger Press changed its reporting priorities and cut regular columns on the environment, social affairs, education, and health issues and replaced them with entire sections on business affairs. Consequently, today, Canadians are presented with extensive information on stock markets and business concerns while the environment, health, education, and social affairs are treated as "special interest" pieces (M. Barlow, 1996). This structural bias results in media coverage that suggests to Canadians that national and international business interests are now the most pressing concerns of the 21st century, while other issues, such as the environment or culture, are only intermittently important.

POTENTIAL MEDIA EFFECTS

Today, as we have said, the global media industries are the primary source of news and entertainment for many people. Although these industries may have greater influence over some people than over others, media analysts suggest that all of us are more profoundly—and often negatively—influenced by media messages than we realize. The portrayal of aggression and violence and the presentation of ethnic, class, and gender stereotypes are two examples of negative media influences.

Aggression, Violence, and the Media

A number of media analysts assert that the need of media industries to capture public interest and thus increase the size of their markets has contributed to the use of violence or incidences of violence as a means of selling newspapers, television programs, movies, heavy metal and rap music, and other media-related commodities (see Chapter 1 for more discussion). A Canadian study also reports that television violence affects children of varying age groups differently, and with children between the ages of 10 and 17 spending the majority of their time watching TV and listening to music, the overall impacts must be considered (Children Now, 1999). A comprehensive economic analysis of television programming led one researcher to conclude that violent fare emerges as a logical extension of commercial broadcasting. While television executives claim their programs reflect audience desires, they do so in a commercially exploitable manner (Hamilton, 1998). In other words, when audiences say they want to see justice triumph, television executives make sure justice does triumph in their programs, but only after several violent fights or shootings that hold viewers in their seats even during commercials.

What effect does the depiction of violence have on audiences? There is no definitive answer to this question. Most scholars do not believe that the media *cause* aggressive behaviour in people (Freedman, 2002). Although there have been some studies that have shown a relationship between at least short-term aggressive behaviour and media depictions of violence, other studies have suggested that media may actually prevent acts of violence by providing people with an outlet for pent-up feelings and emotions. According to the *cathartic effect hypothesis,* television shows, videos, motion pictures, and other forms of media offer people a vicarious outlet for feelings of aggression and thus may reduce the amount of violence engaged in by the media consumer. Believing that current research does not support this hypothesis, other analysts have suggested that continual depictions of violence tend to desensitize viewers and create values that contribute to aggressive behaviours and feelings of fear and frustration (Gerbner, 1995). These analysts point out that depictions of violence do not require the use of language; thus, global audiences are drawn to violence, as it needs no translation. Over time, however, desensitization makes it necessary for films and television programming to become even more violent in order to maintain the potential audience's attention. This theory may help to explain the recent popularity of animal documentaries showing "kill sequences" and blood fights among animals (McElvogue, 1997). At a minimum, constant exposure to violence-laden media content may contribute to an individual's feelings of fear and a need for greater security and protection in everyday life.

According to Kilbourne, one of the many ways in which the media perpetuate violence against women is through advertising. Kilbourne (1999) analyzed tens of thousands of advertisements to determine what effect they might have on viewers. She found that "the poses and postures of advertising are often borrowed from pornography, as are many of the themes, such as bondage, sadomasochism, and the sexual exploitation of children" (Kilbourne, 1999:271). She points out that advertisements showing women as dead or in the process of being killed are particularly popular themes among perfume advertisers. Advertising in other nations can be even more explicit than what is allowed in Canada. An Italian version of *Vogue* showed a man aiming a gun at a nude woman who was wrapped in plastic and had a leather briefcase covering her face (Kilbourne, 1999).

Media advertising also tends to treat women as sexual objects. In order to sell products, advertisements frequently show women in compromised positions or as the victims of rape or other violence and thus contribute to the ongoing subordination of women. Such depictions may also normalize the idea that forcing sex

on a woman is acceptable, as Kilbourne (1999:273) points out:

> Men are also encouraged [by advertisements] to never take no for an answer. Ad after ad implies that girls and women don't really mean "no" when they say it, that women are only teasing when they resist men's advances. "NO" says an ad showing a man leaning over a woman against a wall. Is she screaming or laughing? Oh, it's an ad for deodorant and the second word, in very small print, is "sweat." Sometimes it's "all in good fun," as in the ad for Possession shirts and shorts featuring a man ripping the clothes off a woman who seems to be having a good time. And sometimes it is more sinister. A perfume ad running in several teen magazines features a very young woman, with eyes blackened by makeup or perhaps something else, and the copy, "Apply generously to your neck so he can smell the scent as you shake your head 'no.'" In other words, he'll understand that we don't really mean it and he can respond to the scent like any other animal.

As studies continue on the relationship between violence in the media and in everyday life, we will no doubt learn more about the causes and consequences of extensive media violence in society (see Chapter 4 for more discussion).

Perpetuation of Racialized, Ethnic, and Gender Stereotypes in the Media

Although a growing number of media consumers are not members of the dominant racialized/ethnic groups or of the privileged classes, some media may reinforce existing racialized/ethnic and gender stereotypes and even create new ones. As defined previously, a stereotype is an overgeneralization about the appearance, behaviour, or other characteristics of all members of a group.

Racialization and Ethnic Stereotyping

Numerous media scholars have documented the long history of stereotyping Indigenous people, Black Canadians, Asian Canadians and Indo-Canadians in film, television programming, and other media forms (Fleras and Kunz, 2001; King-Irani, 2002). More recently, studies have examined the effects of stereotyping on perceptions about Middle Eastern and Arab Canadians (Fleras and Kunz, 2001; King-Irani, 2002). No matter which racialized or ethnic group is depicted, stereotyping often involves one or more of the following:

1. Perpetuating images that appear to be positive in nature and thus flattering to members of a specific racialized or ethnic group. For example, some stereotypes attribute superior traits, such as being "naturally" better at activities such as music and sports, or mathematics and science, to members of one racialized or ethnic category. In the case of Asian Canadians, the term "the model minority" is used to praise the achievements of Vietnamese Canadians, Japanese Canadians, Korean Canadians, Chinese Canadians, and others. However, this stereotype is also used to question why some people have been able to achieve the "American Dream" while others have not (see Chapter 3).

2. Exaggerating the physical appearance of subordinate group members or suggesting that all people in a specific category "look alike."

3. Creating racialized or ethnic characters who have undesirable, and stereotypical, attributes, ranging from laziness and unwillingness to work to lack of intelligence or so-called lower-class attitudes and behaviour.

4. Using statements and visual images that link subordinate racialized or ethnic group members to illegal actions, such as gang or organized-crime activity, prostitution, drug dealing, or other deviant sexual or criminal conduct.

Many questions about intent and impact are raised by studying racialized/ethnic stereotyping in Canadian media. Important questions to ask are, Why do media makers and producers create and distribute stereotypical depictions of people? What kinds of long-term negative effects will these images have on populations, particularly on children? Perhaps as media industries and those who use them to advertise their goods begin to view non-White racialized/ethnic groups around the globe as viable consumers of their products, greater concern will be shown over the harmful impact of stereotypical images. In 2001, 18.4 per cent of Canadians were foreign-born—the highest percentage in 70 years. In fact, this is a great deal of buying power that is being stereotyped and discriminated against in the mainstream media.

Gender Stereotyping

According to scholars who have conducted studies of gender stereotypes in the contemporary media, such stereotyping may result, at least in part, from the under-representation of women as producers, directors, and executives in the largest media industries. It is also a result of some ideologies and practices that uphold gender inequality within Western culture. Regardless of the cause, some studies of female roles in television programs and films have shown the following:

1. *The intertwining of gender and age bias:* Gender-specific age bias is apparent in the casting of many female characters. Older men and significantly younger women are often cast in leading roles in films, causing some women to ask, "Where are the roles for older women in Hollywood?"

2. *The perpetuation of traditional roles for women and the maintenance of cultural stereotypes of femininity:* Female characters who do not live up to the gendered expectations associated with femininity are overtly or subtly punished for their conduct.

3. *Impulsive conduct by women holding professional positions:* When television shows portray professional women, they are often shown engaging in compulsive behaviour. A recent example is *Ally McBeal*, the television show about a law firm in which the lead character, Ally McBeal (played by Calista Flockhart), has a variety of impulsive sexual encounters, including one with a male stranger in a car wash and another with a female in her law firm. She also engages in other impulsive, and socially unacceptable, behaviours. Do these portrayals normalize actions previously seen as deviant or do they cast the character (and arguably then, all women) in a negative light?

4. *Women in positions of power abusing their positions:* Prior to the 1990s, most female characters were depicted in lower-status occupations or in roles that were clearly subordinate to those of men. Although recently, more female characters on prime-time television shows have been lawyers or judges, these characters are often shown as "seducers, harassers, and wimps in black robes" (Goodman, 1999:AR 47). Again, the *Ally McBeal* show provides numerous examples.

5. *Women overwhelmed by their work:* In the PBS television program *Judging Amy*, the young family

Even when women are shown in professional careers in a television series, their characters are sometimes depicted as "bimbos" who wear extremely short skirts and engage in impulsive behaviour that would not be typical of a "real life" professional. An example is Ally McBeal (right), a lawyer on the hit show by the same name, who often engages in bizarre behaviour in the law firm or in the middle of a courtroom trial.

court judge makes important decisions regarding child custody, foster care, and other family-related situations but appears overwhelmed by her case-load, her aggressive mother, and even her child's kindergarten teacher (Goodman, 1999).

Although the depiction of women characters in television programs, films, and other forms of media has improved significantly in recent decades, much remains to be done. Progress must still be made if women are to be shown in the wide diversity of occupations and endeavours which real-life women participate in on a daily basis.

PERSPECTIVES ON MEDIA-RELATED PROBLEMS

Just as they do in regard to other social issues, inter-actionist, functionalist, conflict, and feminist approaches to media-related problems start with differing assumptions about these problems.

The Interactionist Perspective

Perhaps the earliest interactionist theory concerning the media's effect on individuals and groups was the *hypodermic needle theory*, which suggested that audiences were made up of passive individuals who were equally susceptible to the messages of the media. However, a World War II study of military personnel who were shown movies designed to portray the enemy as evil and to increase morale among soldiers concluded that most of the subjects showed little change in their morale level, although the movies did influence their views of the "enemies" as "evil". Based on these findings, researchers suggested an alternative explanation: the theory of limited effects. The **theory of limited effects states that the media have a minimal effect on the attitudes and perceptions of individuals.** According to this theory, people may not always be selective about what they watch or read, but they gather different messages from the media, and many people carefully evaluate the information they gain. This theory notes that when people are interested and informed about an issue, they are less likely to be influenced by what members of the media report. Those who are poorly informed or have no personal information about a particular topic or issue are more likely to be affected by what other people, including reporters and journalists, say about the social concern.

A similar theory, known as *use and gratification theory*, suggests that people are active audience partic-ipants who make conscious decisions about what they will watch, listen to, read, and surf on the Internet. However, this theory assumes that people using differ-ent media have specific wishes or desires and will choose media sources that gratify their desires. In other words, people use the media to entertain and inform them-selves but are aware of the limitations the media have in their coverage of topics and the forms of entertainment.

Another interactionist theory, mentioned in Chapter 8, is *social learning theory*, **which is based on**

SOCIAL PROBLEMS IN THE MEDIA

BOX 14.2 How You Can Tell When the Media Poor-Bash

Sometimes poor-bashing is obvious. Calling people on welfare names like "cheats" or "criminally inclined opportunists" is blatant poor-bashing. But subtle poor-bashing can be just as devastating. You must read or listen critically to make sure you're not being taken in by it.

When Newfoundland anti-poverty activist Bev Brown gives workshops on poverty and the media, she asks these questions about media coverage of poverty issues:

What's left out of the story?

Issues usually left out of articles about welfare and UI are the high unemployment rate, the poor quality of jobs that are available (when they are), an explanation of who benefits from poverty, information about the laws that cause poverty (like low welfare rates and minimum wages), and information about who has the funds or could create the jobs or pay the wages to reduce poverty.

Who is speaking?

Do poor people or groups that represent poor people have any voice in the story? Do we hear directly from people in poverty or only from people who work for agencies or charities or from researchers who theorize about them?

Is the story based on false assumptions?

Is it assumed that jobs are available when they aren't? That welfare is generous? That people on welfare are lazy? That welfare is easily available? That people on welfare and EI don't have to look for work? That single moms aren't productive? That people have to be forced to look for work? That training programs will create enough jobs for all who need them?

What are the subtle messages of the story?

Does it suggest—without clearly stating it—that people who have paid work are better than people who have unpaid work (child care, for example)? Does it imply that people on welfare prefer this to a range of other options?

Does the story use facts, or gossip and insinuation?

Are the sources named? Are the sources right-wing think-tanks that have a vested interest in policies that cut the taxes and reduce the wages that their member corporations pay? Are the sources "authorities" that promote the typical stereotypes about people on welfare or EI? Would a similar standard of accuracy apply when reporting about a person or a group with a lot of power?

Does the story use the social policy newspeak words?

Does it use words or phrases like "dependent," "incentive," "disincentive," and others . . . that blame the poor and take the pressure off the rich?

Brown recommends these supplementary questions:

1. Does the story ask how to end poverty, or does it merely expose the suffering of poor individuals?

2. Does it ask who benefits from poverty?

3. Does it investigate what laws cause poverty instead of focusing on individual characteristics of poor people?

4. Does it deal with the morality of poverty in the midst of great wealth?

5. If a publication includes stories advising upper-income people how to use RRSPs, does it also print stories advising poor people how to use welfare and EI? If there are stories about welfare fraud, are there any about tax fraud, or corporate fraud?

6. Does the story assume charity is the only way to deal with poverty?

A final test: How would it sound if the statements about poor people were made about women or people of colour? Would it be okay to say that women are "criminally inclined opportunists"? That would be sexist. Would it be okay to say that people of colour are "criminally inclined opportunists"? No, that would be racist. Then it's poor-bashing to say that people on welfare are "criminally inclined opportunists."

Source: Poor-Bashing: The Politics of Exclusion, *by Jean Swanson, 2001, Toronto: Between the Lines, 191–92. Reprinted by permission of Between the Lines Publishing.*

the assumption that people are likely to act out the behaviour they see in role models and media sources. To support this theory, social psychologist Albert Bandura (1977) conducted a series of experiments on aggression in children. For the experiment, children were divided into four groups. One group watched a film of a man attacking and beating a large, inflatable doll and being rewarded for his behaviour. The second group saw a similar film, except in this version the man was punished for attacking the doll. The third group was shown a version in which the man was neither rewarded nor punished for his behaviour. The final group was not shown any film. Prior to the experiment, researchers believed that the children who saw the man rewarded for hitting the doll would be the most likely to show aggressive behaviour toward the doll. However, this did not prove to be true. Regardless of which version of the film they saw, children who were prone to aggression before the film tended to act aggressively toward the doll but other children did not. As a result, the researchers concluded that many factors other than the media influenced aggressive behaviour in children, including their relationship with their parents, how much formal education their parents possessed, and the personality of the children.

More recent theories have sought to explain the effects of media on individuals by emphasizing the part that viewers, listeners, and readers play in shaping the media. According to the *audience relations approach*, people use their own cultural understandings to interpret what they hear and see in the media. Factors involved in the audience relations approach include how much previous knowledge individuals have about a topic and the availability of other sources of information. This viewpoint is somewhat in keeping with functionalist approaches, which highlight the important contemporary functions of the media.

The Functionalist Perspective

Functionalist approaches to examining the media often focus on the functional—and sometimes dysfunctional—effects the media have on society. Functionalists point out that the media serve several important functions in contemporary societies. First, the media provide news and information, including warnings about potential disasters, such as an approaching hurricane. Second, the media facilitate public discourse regarding social issues and policies, such as welfare reform. Third, the media pass on cultural traditions and historical perspectives, particularly to recent immigrants and children (Lasswell, 1969). Fourth, the media are a source of entertainment, providing people with leisure-time activities (Biagi, 1998). Finally, the media confer status on individuals and organizations by frequently reporting on their actions or showing their faces and mentioning their names. According to sociologist Joshua Gamson, becoming a media celebrity is a means of gaining power, privilege, and mobility. "Audiences recognize this when they seek brushes with it and when they fantasize about the freedom of fame and its riches and about the distinction of popularity and attention" (Gamson, 1994:186).

As Gamson notes, some people become celebrities *because* the media confers that status on them. In other words, as the popular saying goes, "Some people are famous for being famous." As a recent Canadian example, a Torontonian became possibly the most well-known lawyer in North America for a short while when he sued Starbucks Coffee Company for $1.5 million because of damage to his penis—an injury he received from getting it caught in a toilet seat in the washroom of one of Starbucks' coffee shops. Reporters and producers from across North America deluged the man with requests for interviews. In Toronto, the media focused so heavily on this story that only the World Trade Organization talks and protests in Seattle were covered more heavily (Associated Press, 1999; Hackett et al., 1999). According to the functionalist approach, the media are dysfunctional when they contribute to a reduction in social stability or weaken other social institutions, such as the family, education, politics, and religion. For example, television has brought about significant changes in family interaction patterns, as one media scholar explains:

> The most pervasive effect of television—aside from its content—may be its very existence, its readily available, commanding, and often addictive presence in our homes, its ability to reduce hundreds of millions of citizens to passive spectators for major portions of their waking hours. Television minimizes interactions between persons within families and communities. One writer I know only half-jokingly claims, "I watch television as a way of getting to know my husband and children." Another associate, who spent years in Western agrarian regions, relates how a farmer once told her: "Folks used to get together a lot. Now with television, we see less of each other" (Parenti, 1998:188).

When dysfunctions occur, they should be addressed in ways that benefit individuals, families, and the larger society. While the media has changed how people interact with one another, it may have also profoundly influenced the ways in which individuals react to events in their personal and community-based lives. There are other functionalist approaches, however, which suggest that individuals and families are responsible for social change in regard to the media. Analysts who favour this approach believe that rather than changing the nature of television programming, parents should monitor their children's television-watching habits and schools should offer media education for parents and children to make them aware of the classic persuasion and propaganda techniques often used in programming and advertising (Minow and LaMay, 1999).

The Conflict Perspective

Conflict theorists typically link the media industries with the capitalist economy. From this approach, members of the capitalist class own and control the media, which, along with other dominant social institutions, instruct people in the values, beliefs, and attitudes that they should have (Curran et al., 1982). All of these efforts to maintain the status quo and the privileged position of the power elites within it are achieved through *hegemony*—**the use of the media and other cultural institutions to represent the interests, values, and understandings of the capitalist class and other powerful groups as natural and universal** (Knight, 1998:106). According to this perspective, the *process of legitimization* takes place as media consumers are continually provided with information that supports the validity of existing class relations. As a result, members of the working class are lulled into a sense of complacency in which they focus more on entertainment and consumption than on questioning existing economic and social relations. This perspective is sometimes referred to as *hegemony theory*—**the view that the media are instruments of social control and are used by members of the ruling classes to create "false consciousness" in the working classes.** Edward S. Herman and Noam Chomsky, in their book *Manufacturing Consent* (1988) and the 1993 National Film Board film of the same title, discuss this concept at length. One of the major points in this work is that people from the ruling classes need not be involved together in any kind of conspiracy to hoodwink the masses. Rather, the fact that their interests are the same dictates what they should do.

Although there are various conflict approaches, most view ownership and economic control of the media as a key factor in determining what kinds of messages are disseminated around the globe. Media analysts such as Michael Parenti (1998:149) believe that media bias is inevitable as transnational media industries become concentrated in the hands of a few megacorporations:

Media bias usually does not occur in random fashion; rather, it moves in the same overall direction again and again, favouring management over labour, corporations over corporate critics, affluent whites over inner-city poor, officialdom over protestors, the two-party monopoly over leftist third parties, privatization and free-market "reforms" over public-sector development . . . domination of the Third World over revolutionary or populist social change, investor globalization over nation-state democracy, national security policy over critics of that policy, and conservative commentators and columnists . . . over progressive or populist ones.

According to Parenti, the built-in biases of the media reflect the dominant ideology that supports the privileged position of members of the capitalist class.

There are a number of ways in which media manipulation occurs: (1) sponsors control broadcasting decisions; (2) information may be suppressed by omitting certain details of a story or the entire story, particularly if the story may have a negative effect on a person or organization to whom members of the media feel beholden; (3) a story may be attacked or the reporting may not present a balanced view of the diverse viewpoints involved; (4) negative labels that subsume a large number of people, for example, "Islamic terrorists" or "inner-city gangs," may be used; and, (5) stories may be framed to convey positive or negative connotations through the use of visual effects, placement, and other means. Like other conflict theorists, Parenti (1998:157) believes that the media tell people what to think before they have had a chance to think about an issue for themselves: "When we understand that news selectivity is likely to favour those who have power, position, and wealth, we move from a liberal complaint about the press's sloppy performance to a radical analysis of how the media serve the ruling circles all too well with much skill and craft." Viewing media activities in Canada from these perspectives inspires one to learn more about the relationship between media, social control, and the economy in the new millennium.

In an era marked by increased concentration of all forms of media, including the Internet and the World Wide Web, conflict perspectives on media ownership and control raise important questions. Although people engaged in political critique and social activism, such as members of environmental or women's movements, have been able to marshal the media on their behalf, the media often implicitly support the status quo. This is because of their corporate interests and their need to maintain and enhance advertising revenues.

Feminist Perspectives

Beginning in the late 1960s, Second Wave feminist media scholarship focused on the role of visual representation in women's oppression. Studying media texts that range from television and movies to radio, feminists have critiqued male domination in the media and its role in reinforcing gender stereotypes that sustain socially endorsed and oppressive views of gender:

> Media has consistently misrepresented the goals, activities, and members of the women's movement. Because most editors and media executives are men, they have not experienced the daily frustrations women face in a society where they lack equal rights, opportunities, and status equal to those of men. (Wood, 2001:295)

Second Wave feminists radicalized Canadian's understanding of the problem of women's devaluation (be it individualistic, psychological, sociocultural, biologistic, or economic) and the ways traditional relationships between men and women are used to normalize such things as violence against women in the media. Both feminists and conflict theorists are concerned about the role media has in shaping people's values, beliefs, and attitudes. They are also critical of the role the mass media play in supporting and perpetuating hierarchies of oppression.

Feminists maintain that meaning is mediated, and therefore, they examine both media texts and the ways in which they are produced (Reinharz, 1992:145). As a result, how media present women's roles in both the "public" and "private" spheres of life and the discords that exist between represented and lived experiences are important. Viewing women as agents, feminists also study the ways in which women and girls are receptive to (or rejecting of) the media and the ways these individuals interpret and consume media images. The goal is to challenge male dominance in the media and the devalued status of women in media and society. To this end, women involved in alternative feminist media (i.e., feminist film, documentaries, publishing houses, and art) utilize the media as a political tool by articulating their own perspectives and demands and representing and re-representing themselves. In the 22 years that the women's arm of the National Film Board, Studio D, was in operation, it actively supported the creation of films by, for, and about women (Shannon, 1997).

Today, feminist analysis of the media is complexified by the work of multicultural feminists, queer feminists, Marxist feminists, anti-racist feminists, "Third World" feminists, and other Third Wave feminists. Feminists today understand that the matrices of oppression are interconnected and, therefore, theory and lived experience cannot be separated (see Chapters 2 and 3 for more discussion). Now, feminists study the impact of gender as well as class, racialization/ethnicity, sexual orientation, age, national origin, and physical and mental ability in their analysis of the roles mass media play in shaping the life-conditions and life-choices of people in media texts and in real life.

Theoretically and methodologically, feminists of all persuasions analyze the activities and impacts of the mass media on the institutional, organizational, and individual levels (Valdivia, 1995). Institutional analysis is concerned with studying the norms and values that govern the media as an institution and subsequently the smaller institutional entities, such as the press, that comprise the whole. Analysis on an organizational level is concerned with studying the conventions and practices that govern each institution. Finally, individual-level analysis is concerned with the ways in which individuals participate in accepting, challenging, and reproducing societal norms and values. The activities of individuals within the media institution and the ways they function within established practices that are shaped by institutional norms and values are studied. Constructions of femininity and the impacts of the media on men, women, and "trans" people are considered important because all groups are negatively impacted by gendered discourse in the media.

Regardless of which theoretical perspective on the media industries most closely resembles our own thinking, each of us should take a closer look at the ideas, images, and advertisements that bombard us daily. We can learn a great deal from reflecting upon the ways images are produced and the role media play in maintaining oppressive hierarchies that are all too readily accepted as a satisfactory status quo. While most of us may believe that we are not affected by the constant

Around the globe, U.S. media conglomerates influence local cultures through continual marketing of films, television programming, and other media. This moviegoer in Beijing, China, is purchasing tickets for the movie Titanic. According to media sources, the film was a gigantic box-office success in Beijing and other cities worldwide.

stream of advertisements that we encounter, we should realize, as Kilbourne (1999:27) states, "The fact is that much of advertising's power comes from this belief that advertising does not affect us. The most effective kind of propaganda is that which is not recognized as propaganda." Although individuals alone cannot solve the problems associated with the media industries, they can become more aware of the pervasive impact of television, films, newspapers, the Internet, and other forms of mass communication.

THE MEDIA IN THE 21ST CENTURY

Problems associated with the media will continue well into this century, and many of the issues will probably become even more complex. For example, it has been suggested that the Internet and e-commerce will affect all aspects of life, particularly in high-income nations such as Canada. Some analysts have suggested that Canadian cities will lose more of their tax base to untaxed Internet commerce, bringing about a need to restructure relations between cities, states, and the federal government (Friedman, 2000a). Indeed, the ability of a single government to control the activities of transnational media industries may be weakened as globalization continues to occur. Thus, according to journalist Thomas L. Friedman (2000a:A31), a world of global communications means that many issues that were once considered the domain of individual nations and governments will have to be viewed from a new perspective:

> Issues such as freedom of speech and libel are going to have to be rethought as the Internet makes everyone a potential publisher in cyberspace—but with no censor or editor in charge. Privacy protection is going to have to be rethought in a world where for $39 Web sites will search out anyone's assets and home address for you. And our safety nets are going to have to be rethought in a world in which access to the Internet is going to be viewed as a human right, essential for basic survival—especially as governments move more services to the Web.

In the years to come, new communication technologies will undoubtedly continue to change our lives. While new forms of media offer many potential benefits, they also raise serious concerns about social life as many of us know it.

WHAT CAN YOU DO?

- Become media-literate by learning about who owns your local media and identifying their political and economic interests.
- Critically analyze advertisements and think about how they affect you and your friends.
- Think critically about everything you see, hear, or read (including this textbook) in the media.
- Find out about current events by accessing both alternative and mainstream media sources in order to see the spin different media give an issue and if the issue is even covered.
- Contact your local, provincial, and national newspapers and state that you want journalists to dig deeper and to seek out more-diverse viewpoints before they write—insist that their employers support this type of journalism.

- Actively learn about the impacts of "cross-ownership" of broadcast and newspaper holdings (where one company owns both radio or television stations and newspapers) and media concentration in your life.

- Insist on diversity in the media you consume, so that media owners, journalists, reporters and stories reflect the diversity of your community and province.
- Check out alternative Canadian media activist associations that might be of interest to you (see the Web Links section of this chapter, below).

SUMMARY

WHAT ARE THE MEDIA INDUSTRIES? HOW MUCH TIME DO INDIVIDUALS SPEND IN MEDIA-RELATED ACTIVITIES?

According to social scientists, the media industries are media businesses that influence people and cultures worldwide and own interests in radio and television production and broadcasting; motion pictures, movie theatres, and music companies; newspaper, periodical (magazine), and book publishing; and Internet services and content providers. Today, many people spend more time in media-related activities than they do in any other single endeavour, including sleeping, working, eating, or talking with friends and family; therefore, some analysts believe the media have a major influence on how people think, feel, and act.

WHAT PART DOES TECHNOLOGY PLAY IN HOW VARIOUS MEDIA INDUSTRIES CHANGE OVER TIME?

For many years, newspapers were the primary source of news. However, new technologies brought about radio as the media phenomenon of the 1920s and television as the phenomenon of the 1950s. With the introduction of new communications technologies such as computers, fibre-optic cable, and broadcast satellites, the media industries continue to change rapidly.

HOW HAS MEDIA OWNERSHIP CHANGED?

Although there once were a variety of independent companies that produced books, records, television programs, and films, there are now large corporate conglomerates that own more than one form of the media business.

WHAT IS CONVERGENCE? HOW DOES IT RELATE TO MEDIA CONCENTRATION?

Convergence refers to a melding of the communications, computer, and electronics industries that gives a few huge corporations control over an increasing proportion of all media sources. Convergence contributes to greater concentration in the media. Media concentration refers to the tendency of the media industries to cluster together in groups.

WHAT FORMS MAY MEDIA CONCENTRATION TAKE?

Media concentration may take place in several forms: (1) within one industry (such as newspaper chains); (2) cross-media ownership, in which media companies own more than one type of media property (such as newspaper chains and television stations); (3) conglomerate ownership, in which corporations own media properties but also own other businesses; and, (4) vertical integration, in which the corporations that make the media content also control the distribution channels (such as film and television production companies, television networks, and movie theatres).

WHY DO SOME PEOPLE FAVOUR MEDIA CONVERGENCE WHEREAS OTHERS DO NOT?

Supporters believe that much can be gained from the synergy created by media convergence because it makes it possible to take a media brand and capitalize on it. This process is clearly profitable for investors and media executives; however, media critics believe convergence limits the news and entertainment that the public receives by reducing message pluralism. Other problems include: (1) the decline of journalism as a public service profession; (2) constant pressure for all journalistic endeavours to be immediately profitable; (3) a significant decrease in the quantity and quality of international news available to North American audiences; (4) the quashing of public debate about the power of the media industries and how they deal with important social issues; and, (5) a dramatic increase in the influence of powerful Ottawa lobbyists representing the interests of the media giants.

WHAT POTENTIAL PROBLEMS ARE ASSOCIATED WITH GLOBAL MEDIA CONCENTRATION?

A few large media conglomerates are rapidly gaining control over most of the publishing, recording, television, film, and mega–theme park business worldwide. One major problem is the extent to which a few media giants have almost complete control over the world's information. Some people in other nations have been critical of how the media conglomerates depict nations around the globe and the influence, often negative, that they have on the politics and culture of other nations.

WHAT IS FRAMING AND HOW DOES IT AFFECT MEDIA COVERAGE?

Framing refers to how news content and its accompanying visual images are linked together to create certain audience perceptions and give specific impressions to viewers and readers. This process of "spinning" information provides audiences with a particular angle, which usually is favourable to the media and the interests they favour while minimizing or eliminating coverage of other issues and concerns.

WHY ARE SOME MEDIA CRITICS CONCERNED ABOUT DEPICTIONS OF VIOLENCE IN THE MEDIA?

Although most scholars do not believe that the media *cause* aggressive behaviour in people, a number of media analysts assert that the media's need to capture public interest has contributed to the gratuitous use of violence as a means of selling newspapers, television programming, movie tickets, heavy metal and rap music, and other media-related commodities. According to a recent study, violent television shows make up 60 percent of all television programming. Some studies have shown a relationship between short-term aggressive behaviour and media depictions of violence; however, others have suggested that the media may prevent acts of violence by providing people with an outlet for pent-up feelings and emotions.

WHAT FORMS OF MEDIA COMMUNICATION TYPICALLY SHOW VIOLENCE AGAINST WOMEN?

According to media scholar Jean Kilbourne, advertising, which often uses sexually violent images and themes such as bondage, sadomasochism, and the sexual exploitation of children to sell products, is one of the ways in which the media perpetuate violence against women. The media also contribute to the view of women as sexual objects that do not need to be taken seriously.

WHAT IS A STEREOTYPE AND HOW MAY THE MEDIA PERPETUATE STEREOTYPES ABOUT RACIALIZED AND ETHNIC GROUPS?

A stereotype is an overgeneralization about the appearance, behaviour, or other characteristics of all members of a group. The media may perpetuate stereotypes by casting some groups as having superior traits such as being "naturally" better at music and sports or mathematics and science and then using the "model minority" image to question why some people succeed while others do not. Other media stereotyping includes exaggerating people's physical appearance, suggesting that all people in a specific category "look alike," creating racialized/ethnic characters who have undesirable attributes, and using statements and visual images that continually link subordinate ethnic group members to illegal actions.

WHY IS GENDER STEREOTYPING PERVASIVE IN THE MEDIA? WHAT MAJOR FORMS DOES THIS PROBLEM TAKE?

Underrepresentation of women as producers, directors, and executives in the largest media industries may be a factor in the more limited range of roles available to women in television programs and films. First, gender-specific age bias is apparent in the casting of many female characters. Second, television shows and films often perpetuate traditional roles for women and maintain cultural stereotypes of femininity.

HOW DO INTERACTIONISTS EXPLAIN THE INFLUENCE OF THE MEDIA ON INDIVIDUALS?

According to the theory of limited effects, the media have a minimal effect on individuals' attitudes and perceptions. The use and gratification theory suggests that people are active audience participants who make conscious decisions about what they will watch, listen to, read, and surf on the Internet. However, social learning theory is based on the assumption that people are likely to act out the behaviour they see in role models and media sources. The audience relations approach states that people interpret what they hear and see in the media by using their own cultural understandings as a mental filtering device.

HOW DO FUNCTIONALIST AND CONFLICT PERSPECTIVES ON THE MEDIA DIFFER?

According to some functionalist analysts, the media fulfill several important functions in contemporary societies, including providing news and information, facilitating public discourse on social issues and policies, passing on cultural traditions and historical perspectives, and entertaining people. In contrast, conflict theorists assert that members of the capitalist class (either intentionally or unintentionally) use the media to provide information that supports the validity of existing class relations. Hegemony theory states that the media are an instrument of social control that is used by members of the ruling classes to create false consciousness in the working classes.

WHAT DOES THE FEMINIST PERSPECTIVE SAY ABOUT THE RELATIONSHIP BETWEEN TEXTUAL OR VISUAL REPRESENTATIONS OF WOMEN'S LIVES IN MEDIA AND THE REAL LIVED EXPERIENCES OF WOMEN?

Mass media in Canada has consistently represented women and men in traditional gender roles and relationships of power inequity that undermine efforts to challenge and change oppressive values, beliefs, and attitudes. Contemporary feminists are particularly articulate in their criticism of the discords between reality presented in the media and lived reality. These theorists and activists understand how gender, class, racialization, ethnicity, sexual orientation, age, national origin, and physical ability act together to shape the life-conditions and life-choices of people in media texts and in real life—realities are seldom depicted with accuracy in the mass media.

KEY TERMS

framing,   p. 330
hegemony,   p. 336
hegemony theory,   p. 336
media concentration,   p. 321

media industries,   p. 319
social learning theory,   p. 333–334
theory of limited effects,   p. 333

QUESTIONS FOR CRITICAL THINKING

1.   Why might media concentration be a potentially greater social problem than concentration in other industries?

2.   Sociologist Graham Knight (1998) has said, "In order to be successful, hegemony must incorporate a range of different viewpoints." Explain why this might be so.

3.   Is continued consolidation in the media a serious threat to democracy? Please explain.

4.   Do media "manufacture consent"?

5.   Should we be concerned about the ability of some companies to "buy" political influence? Why or why not?

WEBLINKS

Rabble
www.rabble.ca
Rabble is a Canadian online publication built by progressive journalists, writers, artists, and activists across the country and aligned with human rights, social justice, and democracy movements around the world. It includes news stories, in-depth features, interviews, and commentaries; publishes columns from progressive voices in the mainstream media; reprints articles from Canada's best independent magazines; and offers discussion groups and event listings.

MediaChannel
www.mediachannel.org
This nonprofit, public-interest site offers special reports and thematic features designed to inspire discussion and citizen engagement.

Open Democracy
www.opendemocracy.net
This information site is dedicated to covering global political, social, and cultural issues.

Campaign for Press and Broadcasting Freedom
www.presscampaign.org
At this site you'll find a campaign for freedom of the press and against the concentration of media ownership and media propagation of ideologically biased information.

The Canadian Association of Journalists (CAJ)
www.caj.ca
The CAJ is the national voice of Canadian journalists. It is a nonprofit corporation that promotes investigative and independent media coverage.

Canadian Women in Communication
www.cwc-afc.com/home.cfm
Canadian Women in Communications, an organization designed to help women succeed in the business environment, focuses on sectors of the communication industry. The site offers professional development information and information on conferences and other events.

Diversity in the Media

www.media-awareness.ca/english/issues/
stereotyping/ethnics_and_minorities/index.cfm
Offering commentary and research about media
stereotyping, this web page examines the
representation of ethnic and visible minorities in the
media industry.

Independent Media Center

www.indymedia.org
This is a coalition of independent media
organizations and journalists that offer grassroots,
noncorporate media coverage.

Adbusters

www.adbusters.org
A network of artists, writers, educators, and students
raise their voices about the invasion of the
environment by commercial forces; corporate
disinformation; injustices in the global economy; and
other similar issues.

Newswatch Canada

http://newswatch.cprost.sfu.ca
In this project by students, researchers, and
journalists, the research focuses on significant but
underreported news stories.

Media Awareness

www.media-awareness.ca
This site offers resources—including reports and
articles—and support for parents and teachers
interested in media and information literacy for
young people.

15

POPULATION AND THE ENVIRONMENTAL CRISIS

You see, there are only nine cabins in the steamer launch which comes from Dhaka to Patuakhali. In the nine cabins only 18 people can travel. The ticket is expensive, so only the rich people travel in the cabins. The rest of the common passengers travel in the deck. The latrine facility [restroom] is provided only for the cabin passengers. But sometimes the passengers from the deck want to use the latrines. The cabin passengers allow them to use the latrine because they are afraid that if the poor deck passengers get angry then they might go down and make a hole in the launch. Then the launch will sink; they will die no doubt but the rich cabin passengers will not survive either. So, my dear sisters, do not give birth to more children as they cause a problem for the cabin passengers.

Writer Farida Ahkter recalls the story she heard one family-planning officer tell a group of poor and illiterate women in a remote village in Bangladesh (The Ecologist, *1993:143)*

Johannesburg [the World Summit on Sustainable Development, August, 2002] aims to put equal emphasis on the twin aspirations of sustainable development . . . to show that we take this challenge seriously and ultimately to exercise greater responsibility, for one another as well as for the earth on which our progress and well-being depend.

UN Secretary General Kofi Annan writing about challenges for the World Summit and humanity (2002)

It's a great day today: I am passing Kyoto.

Canadian Prime Minister, Jean Chrétien, on December 10, 2002, speaking after Parliament voted to ratify the Kyoto Protocol

Global population-control policies are the subject of international controversy. Although some people believe that government policies are essential for curbing overpopulation, others argue that government policies are a means by which dominant group members decide "*who* will be born, *how* many will be born, and of *what* race, class, sex and 'quality' they will be" (*The Ecologist*, 1993:143). On the other hand, the concern of *sustainable development*—**meeting the needs of the present generations without compromising the ability of future generations to meet their needs**, as pursued by Kofi Annan and the United Nations, should contribute to both the development of people and the preservation of the environment. The Kyoto Protocol,

an important step to reduce greenhouse emissions and preserve the environment, has been ratified by the Canadian Parliament and is close to overall ratification.

In this chapter, you will learn about the causes of population growth—fertility, mortality, and migration; the impact of population growth and the consequences for world hunger; suggestions for controlling population growth; immigration and its consequences; environmental degradation and various kinds of pollution, such as air and water pollution and including global warming; problems of soil erosion, deforestation, and solid and toxic wastes; and how sociologists study these problems using the functionalist, conflict, interactionist, and feminist perspectives. We will also discuss what the earth's population and the environment will be like in the future, and what you can do about it.

GLOBAL POPULATION PROBLEMS

During the past 50 years, the world's population has more than doubled, growing from 2.5 billion in 1950 to over 6 billion today. At this rate, the world population will double again in the next 50 years. Even today, more than 1 billion of the world's people do not have enough food and lack basic health care (Hauchler and Kennedy, 1994). Will the earth's resources be able to support such a population? This is an urgent question and one for which we need answers.

Population Growth

Growth rates vary among nations; high-income nations (for example, Canada and the United States) have a lower population growth rate than low-income nations, especially those in Africa, Asia, and Latin America. A *population* is all the people living in a specified geographic area. In some nations, the population growth rate is negative; that is, fewer people are added to the population through birth and immigration than are lost through death and emigration. Current estimates suggest that countries such as Italy, Romania, Russia, and Spain will shrink in population over the next 50 years (Sanger, 2000).

***Demography* is the study of the size, composition, and distribution of populations.** Global population changes are important because they have a powerful influence on social, economic, and political structures both within societies and between societies. For example, the population growth imbalance between high-income and middle- and low-income nations is a potential source of global conflict, particularly if world hunger and environmental destruction increase. Three primary factors affect the rate of population growth in any nation or area: fertility (births), mortality (deaths), and migration (movement between geographic areas). We'll look at each in turn.

Fertility

Fertility **refers to the number of children born to an individual or a population.** The most basic measure of fertility is the *crude birth rate*—the number of live births per 1000 people in a population in a given year. In 2000, there were 380 000 live births in Canada, yielding a crude birth rate of 10.8 per 1000 (Statistics Canada, 2001e:25). The crude birth rate is used to gauge fertility because it is based on the entire population and does not take into account the variables that affect fertility, such as age, marital status, and racialization/ethnicity.

The level of fertility in a society is associated with social, as well as biological, factors. For example, countries that have high rates of infant and child mortality often have high birth rates. By having many children, parents in these nations are more likely to see a few of them survive to adulthood. In nations without social security systems to provide old-age insurance, parents may view children as an "insurance plan" for their old age. In patriarchal societies, having many children—especially sons—is proof of manliness. Finally, in cultures in which religion dictates that children are God-given and family planning is forbidden because it "interferes with God's will," many more children are usually born (Hauchler and Kennedy, 1994).

Although men are obviously important in the reproductive process, the measure of fertility focuses on women because pregnancy and childbirth are more easily quantified than biological fatherhood. One factor in determining how many children will be born in a given year is the number of women of childbearing age (usually between the ages of 15 and 45) who live in the society. Other biological factors that affect fertility include the general health and nutrition level of women of childbearing age. However, on the basis of biological capability alone, most women could produce 20 or more children during their childbearing years. In industrialized nations, therefore, many people limit their biological capabilities by practicing abstinence, refraining from sexual intercourse before a certain age, using contraceptives, being sterilized, or having one or more abortions over the course of their reproductive years. Fertility rates also are affected by the number of partners available for sex and/or marriage, the number of women of childbearing age in the work force, and government policies regarding families. China, for example, had a one-child policy, so abortion or sterilization can be required by the government when there is an unauthorized pregnancy (Mosher, 1994).

Mortality

Birth rates are one factor in population growth; another is a decline in *mortality*—**the number of deaths that occur in a specific population.** The simplest measure of mortality is the *crude death rate*—the number of deaths per 1000 people in a population in a given year. In 2000, there were 200 000 deaths in the Canadian population, yielding a crude death rate of 7.5 per 1000 (Statistics Canada, 2001e:25). In many nations, mortality rates have declined dramatically as diseases such as malaria, polio, cholera, tetanus, typhoid, and measles have been virtually eliminated by vaccinations and improved sanitation and personal hygiene (Weeks, 1998).

In addition to measuring the crude death rate, demographers often measure the *infant mortality rate*—the number of deaths of infants under one year of age per 1000 live births in a given year. In general, infant mortality has declined worldwide over the past two decades because many major childhood and communicable diseases are now under control. Still, infant mortality rates vary widely between nations. In high-income nations, the average was 6 deaths per 1000 live births in 1997 (Japan had a low of 4 deaths per 1000 live births), in sharp contrast to about 72 deaths per 1000 live births in southern Asia and about 105 deaths per 1000 live births in sub-Saharan Africa (UNDP, 1999).

In any nation, the infant mortality rate is an important reflection of a society's level of preventive (prenatal) medical care, maternal nutrition, childbirth procedures, and neonatal care for infants. In Canada, differential levels of access to these services are reflected in the gap between infant mortality rates for Indigenous and non-

Indigenous people. As we saw in Chapter 10, in 1997, for example, mortality for Indigenous infants was 12.0 deaths per 1000 live births (Frideres, 2002:155), compared to 5.5 per 1000 live births for the total Canadian population (Statistics Canada, 2001e:25).

Demographers also study *life expectancy*, the estimated average lifetime of people born in a specific year. For example, in 1998, the life expectancy at birth for a person born in Canada was 78.4 years, compared to 80.0 years in Japan and less than 50.0 years in the African nations of Burundi, Chad, Rwanda, and Uganda (Statistics Canada, 2001b:42; U.S. Bureau of the Census, 1998). In fact, the estimated life expectancy for people in Uganda and Zambia has dropped significantly over the past two decades. In Uganda, life expectancy has dropped from 48 to 43 years for women and from 45 to 41 years for men (United Nations, 1995). Life expectancy varies not only by nation but also by sex. Females born in Canada now have a life expectancy of about 81 years, whereas males born now have a life expectancy of about 75 years. Life expectancy also varies by racialization and ethnicity. Indigenous people have a life expectancy that is 6 years less than non-Indigenous people (Frideres, 2002:155).

Migration

Migration **is the movement of people from one geographic area to another for the purpose of changing residency.** Migration takes two forms: *immigration*—the movement of people *into* a geographic area to take up residency—and *emigration*—the movement of people *out of* a geographic area to take up residency elsewhere. Today, more than 23 million people live outside their countries of origin (Kane, 1995).

In the mid-1990s, about 250 000 people were entering Canada each year, but this number has decreased to 200 000 and will likely decrease further because of more restrictive immigration policies and stricter enforcement. This is still a large number of people for a country the size of Canada. The number is about equal to the natural increase (births minus deaths) in the country (Bourne and Rose, 2001:110). However, it should be noted that official immigration statistics do not reflect the actual number of immigrants who arrive in this country. Canadian immigration authorities record only legal immigration based on entry visas and change-of-immigration-status forms. Some people who enter the country as temporary visitors, coming

for pleasure or business, as students, or as temporary workers or trainees, do not leave when their stated purpose has been achieved and their permits expire.

Approximately 20 000 refugees are also admitted to this country annually as permanent residents. According to the 1951 United Nations Convention on Refugees, the term *refugee* applies solely to those who leave their countries because of persecution for reasons of racialization, religion, nationality, membership in a particular social group, or political opinion (Kane, 1995). People who leave home to escape famine or to improve their economic position, for example, do not officially qualify as refugees.

Although some immigrants enter illegally, it is impossible to estimate their number or how many are still in Canada, since many come to Canada to gain access into the United States. Occasionally we learn of large numbers of illegal immigrants because of problems with the boats that were transporting them.

To determine the effects of immigration and emigration, demographers compute the *crude net migration rate*—the net number of migrants (total immigrants minus total emigrants) per 1000 people in a population in a given year. Currently, the net migration rate in Canada is about 5.6 per 1000 population (Statistics Canada, 2001e:25).

Many nations face the challenges and opportunities offered by the migration of people worldwide (see Box 15.1).

The Impact of Population Growth

What is the effect of population growth on a society? Population growth affects ***population composition***—**the biological and social characteristics of a population, including such attributes as age, sex, racialization, marital status, education, occupation, income, and size of household.** In Canada, for example, the age distribution of the population is associated with the demand for community resources such as elementary and secondary schools, libraries, health care and recreational facilities, employment opportunities, and age-appropriate housing.

What are the effects of rapid population growth on individuals? According to Population Action International's *Human Suffering Index* (HSI), the countries that have the highest rates of growth also

SOCIAL PROBLEMS IN GLOBAL PERSPECTIVE

BOX 15.1   Challenges and Opportunities Presented by Worldwide Migration

These countries in Europe will face the wall. They either bring in migrants, or they are going to decline in size. The model that the United States has—and Canada and Australia—is increasingly becoming attractive to some of the thinkers in those countries.

Joseph Chamie, director of the United Nations population division (Crossette, 2000:WK1)

For years, many nations have had strictly limited immigration. Canada had limited immigration, especially of non-Whites; for example, there was a head tax on Chinese between 1885 and 1923; the *Chinese Immigration Act* of 1923 banned almost all Chinese; and refugees, notably Jews before and during WWII, have been refused entry. However, with the introduction of the point system in 1967, nationality and racialization/ethnicity were removed from the selection process. Now, according to the 2001 Census, the proportion of Canada's population that was born outside the country has reached its highest level in 70 years (Statistics Canada, 2003). On Census Day, 2001, 5.4 million people, or 18.4 percent of the total population, were born outside Canada and, now, the "People's Republic of China was the leading country of birth among individuals who immigrated to Canada in the 1990s" (Statistics Canada, 2003). And the three largest visible minority groups in 2001, Chinese, South Asians, and Blacks, accounted for two-thirds of the visible minority population (Statistics Canada, 2003).

According to the United Nations, because of the inequality between the rich and the poor in the world, numerous countries can expect large migrations. More than 900 000 Turkish "guest workers" have moved to Germany and the Scandinavian countries to work; nearly 3 million Mexicans live in the United States; and more than 1 million immigrants work in Saudi Arabia (Kane, 1995; U.S. Bureau of the Census, 1998). Migrants follow the flow of jobs, and in countries with severely shrunken labour forces and increasing ranks of older retirees, immigrants may be part of the solution to population concerns rather than part of the "problem," as they have been perceived to be in the past.

Today, many European countries (as well as Canada, the United States, and Japan) are faced with populations that will soon have more older people and fewer babies than ever

before. If these nations want to maintain the social services and economic structures that many residents have become accustomed to, it will be necessary for them to "lower their borders" and accept a change in the racialized/ethnic composition of their populations (Crossette, 2000). According to some demographers, Italy will have to add about 9 million immigrants by 2025, at a rate of about 300 000 a year, to maintain its population at its 1995 level; Germany will need to import an additional 14 million people, or 500 000 a year; and France will need to add 2 million. Overall, the European Union will need to allow the immigration of about 35 million people to maintain the population at the level of the 1990s (Crossette, 2000). By comparison, Canada will need to admit 250 000 immigrants per year after 2020 just to prevent population decline (Bourne and Rose, 2001:117).

As the pressure from overpopulation builds in some nations, and given that Canada, the United States, and some European countries have increasingly "aging" populations, demographers believe that the flow of migrant workers will increase dramatically around the world. Many challenges remain, however.

Policies and programs to overcome hurdles like language barriers are scant in much of Europe because cultural homogeneity has been deeply valued, citizenship has often been defined ethnically or linguistically, and the naturalization process that has made Americans out of millions of foreigners does not exist. (Crossette, 2000:WK4)

In some European nations, cultural homogeneity has led to anti-immigration sentiment and hate crimes perpetrated against people on the basis of perceptions about their racialization, ethnicity, or nationality. In Scandinavia and Central and Eastern Europe, racist violence has erupted on various occasions against non-Europeans.

While some nations continue to look to the past to determine what should be done about immigration in the future, spokespersons for organizations such as the United Nations believe that political leaders and citizens must acknowledge that their countries face either a declining population or a future that is built by immigrants (Crossette, 2000). What other issues are important to consider regarding global migration?

have the most human suffering. For example, 20 of the 27 countries listed in the "extreme human suffering" category are in Africa, the fastest-growing region in the world (*Human Suffering Index*, 1992). The HSI also shows that while many people in poverty-stricken regions die from hunger and malnutrition each year, people in the high-income nations spend billions of dollars annually on diet products and exercise gear because they think they are overfed and overweight.

What are the consequences of global population growth? Not all social analysts agree on the answer to this question. As you will discover in the sections that follow, some analysts warn that the earth is a finite system that cannot support its rapidly growing population. Others believe that capitalism—if freed from government intervention—could develop innovative solutions to such problems as hunger and pollution. Still others argue that capitalism is part of the problem, not part of the solution.

The Malthusian Perspective

Rapid population growth and overpopulation are not new problems. Causes and solutions have been debated for nearly two centuries. In 1798, for example, Thomas Malthus, an English clergyman and economist, published *An Essay on Population*. Malthus (1798/1965) argued that the global population, if left unchecked, would exceed the available food supply. The population would increase in a geometric (exponential) progression (2, 4, 8, 16, . . .), but the food supply would increase only by an arithmetic progression (1, 2, 3, 4, . . .). Thus, the population would surpass the food supply, ending population growth and perhaps eliminating the world population (Weeks, 1998). Disaster, according to Malthus, could be averted only by positive checks (e.g., famine, disease, and war) or preventive checks (e.g., sexual abstinence before marriage and postponement of marriage for as long as possible) to limit people's fertility.

The Neo-Malthusian Perspective

Today, *neo-Malthusians* (or "new Malthusians") speak of the "population explosion" and "population bomb" to emphasize the urgent need to reduce global population growth. Among the best known neo-Malthusians are biologists Paul Ehrlich and Anne H. Ehrlich, who believe that world population growth is following the

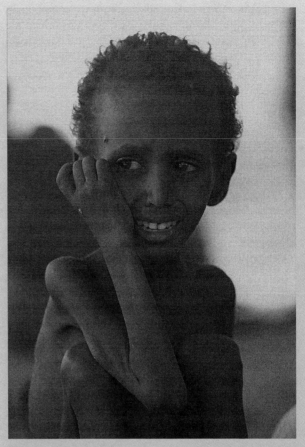

Starving children in nations such as Somalia raise important questions about Malthusian and neo-Malthusian perspectives. *Is world hunger primarily a consequence of overpopulation or are other political and economic factors also important?*

exponential growth pattern that Malthus described (Ehrlich and Ehrlich, 1991:15):

> Exponential growth occurs in populations because children . . . remain in the population and themselves have children. A key feature of exponential growth is that it often seems to start slow and finish fast. A classic example . . . is the pond weed that doubles each day . . . to cover the entire pond in thirty days. The question is, how much of the pond will be covered in twenty-nine days? The answer, of course, is that just half of the pond will be covered in twenty-nine days. The weed will then double once more and cover the entire pond the next day. As this example indicates, exponential growth contains the potential for big surprises.

To neo-Malthusians, the earth is a dying planet with too many people in relation to the available food supply. Overpopulation and rapid population growth exacerbate global environmental problems ranging from global warming and rainforest destruction to famine and epidemics such as AIDS.

Demographic Transition Theory

According to **demographic transition theory, societies move from high birth and death rates to relatively low birth and death rates as a result of technological development.** The demographic transition takes place in four stages. The *preindustrial stage* is characterized by little population growth: High birth rates are offset by high death rates. This period is followed by the *transitional* or *early industrial stage,* which is characterized by significant population growth as the birth rate remains high but the death rate declines because of new technologies that improve health, sanitation, and nutrition. Today, large parts of Africa, Asia, and Latin America are in this second stage. The third stage is *advanced industrialization and urbanization*: The birth rate declines as people control their fertility with various forms of contraception, and the death rate declines as medicine and other health care technologies control acute and chronic diseases. Finally, in the *postindustrial stage*, the population grows very slowly, if at all. In this stage, a decreasing birth rate is coupled with a stable death rate.

Proponents of demographic transition theory believe that technology can overcome the dire predictions of Malthus and the neo-Malthusians. Critics point out that not all nations go through all the stages or in the manner outlined. They think that demographic transition theory explains development in Western societies but not necessarily in others. As an example they cite China, which was in the process of significantly reducing its birth rate but only because of the government's mandated one-child-per-family policy, not because of technological advances or urbanization (Weeks, 1998).

World Hunger

Food shortages, chronic hunger, and malnutrition are the consequences of rapid population growth, particularly in low-income nations. Approximately 800 million people in the world experience *chronic malnourishment*—inadequate food to provide the minimum energy necessary for doing light work over a period of time (FAO, 1995). Chronic malnourishment contributes to childhood health problems such as anemia (a blood condition that produces weakness and a lack of energy and can result in child mortality or impaired mental functioning), stunting (impaired physical growth or development), and being underweight (United Nations, 1995). In pregnant women, malnutrition increases the risk of anemia, infection, birth complications, and lack of breast milk (see Figure 15.1). In contrast, improvements in nutrition significantly reduce health risks and the spread of some communicable illnesses (Hauchler and Kennedy, 1994).

What efforts are being made to reduce global food shortages and world hunger? Organizations such as the United Nations, the World Health Organization, and the International Red Cross have programs in place, but the most far-reaching initiatives are known as the green revolution and the biotechnological revolution.

The Green Revolution

The *green revolution* refers to dramatic increases in agricultural production that have been made possible by high-yield "miracle" crops, pesticides, fertilizers, and good farm management. In the 1940s, researchers at the International Maize and Wheat Improvement Center started the green revolution by developing high-yield varieties of wheat, which increased world grain production. The new dwarf-type wheat, which produces more stalks, has dramatically increased the wheat yield in countries such as India and Pakistan since the 1960s. Researchers have also developed a high-yield dwarf rice with twice as many grains per plant, greatly improving the rice output in India, Pakistan, the Philippines, Indonesia, and Vietnam (Weeks, 1998).

How successful has the green revolution been in reducing world hunger? During the 1970s, the green revolution helped to increase the global food supply at a somewhat faster pace than the global population grew, but in the 1980s and 1990s, agricultural production slowed considerably. Also, while the new miracle crops have increased food production in Latin America and Asia, they have not really benefited Africa (Kennedy, 1993).

They have not done so for several reasons. For one thing, the fertilizers, pesticides, and irrigation systems

FIGURE 15.1   The Circle of Malnutrition

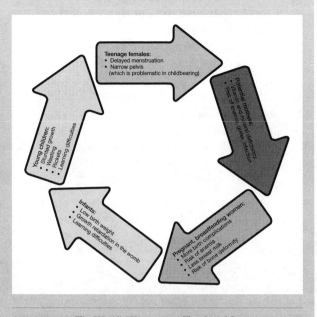

Teenage females:
• Delayed menstruation
• Narrow pelvis
 (which is problematic in childbearing)

Potential mothers:
• Vitamin and mineral deficiency
• Risk of anemia, spread infection

Pregnant, breastfeeding women:
• More birth complications
• Risk of anemia
• Less breast milk
• Risk of bone deformity

Infants:
• Low birth weight
• Growth retardation in the womb
• Learning difficulties

Young children:
• Stunted growth
• Wasting
• Rickets
• Learning difficulties

Source: Based on **The World's Women 1995: Trends and Statistics,** *United Nations, 1995, New York: United Nations.*

needed to produce these new crops are very costly and beyond the budgets of most middle- and low-income nations. Furthermore, the fertilizers and pesticides often constitute health hazards and become a source of surface water and groundwater pollution (Weeks, 1998). Moreover, for the green revolution to eliminate hunger and malnutrition, the social organization of life in many middle- and low-income nations would have to change significantly. People would have to adopt the Western methods of farming on which the green revolution was built, and they would have to be willing to produce a single crop in very high volume. But reliance on a single crop can lead to nutritional deficiencies if other varieties of food are not available. Even with these drawbacks, however, the green revolution continues. Researchers recently developed high-yield sorghum, yams, and other crops that can be grown successfully in the nations of Africa where some of the greatest food shortages exist (Weeks, 1998).

The Biotechnological Revolution

A second approach to reducing global food shortages, known as the *biotechnological revolution*, encompasses any technique for improving plants or animals or using microorganisms in innovative ways. Developing pest-resistant crops, thus reducing the need for pesticides, is one technique. Using growth hormone to increase milk output in cows is another technique. Scientists are also exploring ways to genetically alter the reproductive cells of fish, poultry, sheep, and pigs to speed up conventional breeding times (Kennedy, 1993). Scientists have already genetically altered microorganisms in several ways. Soon, for example, it should be possible to spray frost-sensitive plants, such as strawberries, with a strain of bacteria that will protect the plants against up to 95 percent of frost damage.

Some scientists believe that the biotechnological revolution can close the gap between worldwide food production and rapid population growth, but the new technology is not without problems. First, giving growth hormones to animals can make their meat unfit for human consumption. Hogs that get growth hormones are prone to gastric ulcers, arthritis, dermatitis, and other diseases (Kennedy, 1993). Second, the cost of biotechnological innovations is beyond the budgets of most middle- and low-income nations. Third, the new biotechnologies are developed for use with conventional (Western) farming methods (Hauchler and Kennedy, 1994). Fourth, genetic erosion (by breeding or gene manipulation) may eventually make the people of the world reliant on only a few varieties of plants and animals for their entire food supply and thus vulnerable to famine as the result of a single pest or disease. Finally, environmental accidents, such as the unintentional release of genetically manipulated microorganisms, pose a potential hazard.

Increasing the food supply is one way of coping with a rapidly growing world population, but hardly the only way. Some people believe that we can forestall the problem by controlling fertility.

CONTROLLING FERTILITY

The global population increase in the 20th century has been unprecedented. As Table 15.1 shows, the global population has increased by a factor of four. And an additional 3 billion young people will soon enter their reproductive years (United Nations, 1995). Although demographers know that limiting fertility is the best way to slow down population growth, they also know that the issue is fraught with controversy. Consider the

TABLE 15.1   The Measure of the 20th Century

Item	Increase Factor, 1890s to 1990s
World population	4
Urban proportion of world population	3
Total world urban population	13
World economy	14
Industrial output	40
Energy use	16
Coal production	7
Air pollution	≈5
Carbon dioxide emissions	17
Sulfur dioxide emissions	13
Lead emissions to the atmosphere	≈8
Water use	9
Marine fish catch	35
Cattle population	4
Pig population	9
Horse population	1.1
Blue whale population (Southern Ocean only)	0.0025 (99.75% decrease)
Fin whale population	0.03 (97% decrease)
Bird and mammal species	0.99 (1% decrease)
Irrigated area	5
Forest area	0.8 (20% decrease)
Cropland	2

Note: Some of the numbers are more trustworthy than others. Comments on their reliability appear in the source from which they are all drawn.

Source: *From* **Something New Under The Sun: An Environmental History of the Twentieth-Century World**, *by J.R. McNeill, 2000, New York: Norton. Copyright © 2000 by J.R. McNeill. Used by permission of W.W. Norton & Company, Inc.*

three preconditions that demographer Ansley Coale (1973) believes are necessary before there can be a sustained decline in a society's fertility:

1. *People must accept calculated choice as a valid element in marital fertility.* If people believe a supernatural power controls human reproduction, it is unlikely that they will risk offending that deity by trying to limit fertility. On the other hand, the more worldly-wise people are, the more likely they are to believe they have the right to control reproduction.

2. *People must see advantages to reduced fertility.* People must have some reason to want to limit fertility. In some places, children become workers for the family and support parents in their old age. Without incentives to reduce fertility, natural attraction could lead to unprotected sexual intercourse and perhaps numerous children.

3. *People must know about and master effective techniques of birth control.* The means for limiting family size must be available, and people must know how to use them successfully.

Although Coale believes that all three preconditions must be met to limit fertility effectively, most government policies in the developing world focus only on the third: family planning measures (Weeks, 1998).

Family Planning

Family planning programs in the developing world provide birth control information, contraceptive devices, sometimes sterilization and abortion procedures, and health services. The earliest programs were based on the assumption that women have large families because they do not know how to prevent pregnancy or they lack access to birth control devices. Though we know today that women may have large families for many other reasons, most programs are still based on this assumption. Such programs do little, for example, to reduce a couple's desire to have children; and they ignore the reality that, in some middle- and low-income nations, women are not free to make their own decisions about reproduction. There is overwhelming evidence that women want only the number of children that they can care for adequately (United Nations, 1995).

Some critics of family planning programs argue that most policies are developed by political leaders in high-income nations who are motivated by racialization and class issues rather than by a genuine concern about world hunger or overpopulation. They say that high-income nations—such as England, France, and the United States—encourage births among middle- and upper-income women in their own countries but advocate depopulation policies in low-income regions such as sub-Saharan Africa (O'Connell, 1994). For example, the French government is promoting larger families because of a rapidly aging population, a low fertility rate, and a national concern that the country is losing its identity because of high immigration rates (Weeks, 1998).

Some analysts believe that China's one-child policy devalued female infants. What long-term effects might such a policy have on the sex ratio (number of males in relation to number of females) in that country? Could this influence the number of females and males available for marriage and parenting in the future?

Zero Population Growth

With **zero population growth, there is a totally stable population, one that neither grows nor decreases from year to year because births, deaths, and migration are in perfect balance** (Weeks, 1998). For example, the population growth rate would be zero if a nation had no immigration or emigration and the birth rate and the death rate were the same (Ehrlich and Ehrlich, 1991).

Canada is nearing zero population growth because of several factors:

1. A high proportion of women and men in the labour force find satisfaction and rewards outside of family life;

2. Birth control is inexpensive and readily available;

3. The trend is toward later marriage (see Chapter 11);

4. The cost of raising a child from birth to adulthood is rising rapidly; and

5. Schools and public service campaigns make teenagers more aware of how to control fertility (United Nations, 1995).

Near-zero population growth is one characteristic of the Canadian population; another is a rapidly changing population.

IMMIGRATION AND ITS CONSEQUENCES

High rates of immigration are changing the composition of the Canadian population. Today, according to the 2001 Census, over 5.4 million people—or 18 percent of the total Canadian population—have come here from other nations. In fact, most Canadians are immigrants or first-generation descendents of immigrants. On a global basis, immigration and internal migration are causing urban populations to grow faster than the total population (see Map 15.1, and note that, according to the 2001 Census, about 80 percent of Canada's population is now urban; see also Map 16.1 for recent growth in urban centres). Because most cities do not have the capacity to deal with existing residents, much less with significant increases in the number of those residents—especially those with limited education and economic resources—immigration and internal migration often lead to patterns of urban squalor and high levels of stress in daily living.

What are the consequences of today's high rate of immigration to Canada as a whole? Not all social analysts agree on the answer to this question. Some believe that immigrants cost taxpayers millions of dollars each year in adjustment and education (teaching English or French as a second language) costs. But we also know that immigrants contribute as workers and consumers to the economy. American economist James P. Smith sums this up for the U.S. (Pear, 1997:1, 15):

> It's true that some Americans are now paying more taxes because of immigration, and native-born Americans without a high school education have seen their wages fall slightly because of the competition sparked by lower-skilled, newly arrived immigrants. But the vast majority of Americans are enjoying a healthier economy as a result of the increased supply of labour and lower prices that result from immigration.

Richard Florida (2002:T8), a professor of regional development at Carnegie Mellon University, goes further, to suggest that major cities' and Canada's economic future depends on immigration, which helps to create and nourish a Creative Class (see also Chapter 16).

However, although the economic future depends in part on immigrants, recent immigrants do not seem to be

MAP 15.1   Urban Population as a Percentage of Total National Population

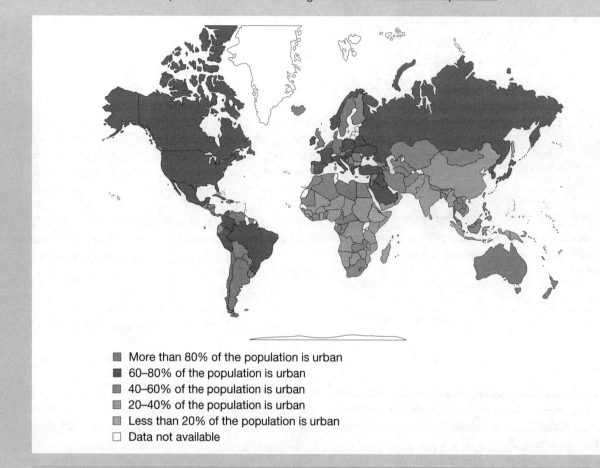

■ More than 80% of the population is urban
■ 60–80% of the population is urban
■ 40–60% of the population is urban
■ 20–40% of the population is urban
■ Less than 20% of the population is urban
□ Data not available

Source: From **Statistical Abstract of the United States, 1998** *(118th ed.), U.S. Bureau of the Census, 1998, Washington, DC: U.S. Government Printing Office.*

sharing in the opportunities as quickly as did their predecessors. According to sociologists Abdolmohammed Kazemipur and Shiva S. Halli (2001:235), recent immigrants have a poorer economic record, including lower salaries and more unemployment, than previous cohorts, and it is not because they do not have good education or language skills. In addition, since it is the immigrant men who are likely to have the jobs, immigrant women are unlikely to get an appropriate return on their education (Kazemipur and Halli 2001:236).

Besides being undesirable, stemming the flow of immigrants appears to be a virtually impossible task for any one nation. Another problem too large for solution by an individual nation is environmental degradation.

ENVIRONMENTAL PROBLEMS

Although it is popularly believed that most environmental problems arise from rapid growth in middle- and low-income nations, this is not entirely the case. Many scientists believe that high-income nations present a much greater threat to the earth's ecosystems (Ehrlich and Ehrlich, 1991). An *ecosystem* is "all the populations of plants and animal species that live and interact in a given area at a particular time, as well as the chemical and physical factors that make up the nonliving environment" (Cable and Cable, 1995:124). Thus, an ocean is an ecosystem; a tropical rainforest is an ecosystem; and, on a much smaller scale, a house on a lot is an ecosystem. When all of the earth's ecosystems are put together, they make up the *biosphere*.

Ecosystems do not have an infinite ability to support either population growth or environmental depletion or destruction. In fact, some scientists believe that many of the world's ecosystems have already exceeded their *carrying capacity*—the maximum population that an ecosystem can support without eventually being degraded or destroyed (Cable and Cable, 1995). According to Ehrlich and Ehrlich (1991), a baby born in a country like the U.S., and to a lesser extent Canada, will have 2 times the destructive impact on the earth's ecosystems and services as a baby born in Sweden; 100 times the impact of a baby born in Bangladesh or Kenya; and over 200 times the impact of a baby born in Chad, Rwanda, Haiti, or Nepal. How did the Ehrlichs reach such a conclusion? They developed a formula for determining the impact that human beings have on their environment: $I = P \times A \times T$, or Impact = Population × Affluence × Technology. Thus the size of the population, its level of affluence, and the technology available in the society are major contributing factors to **environmental degradation— disruptions to the environment that have negative consequences for ecosystems** (Cable and Cable, 1995). Environmental degradation involves both removing natural resources from the environment and adding to environmental problems through pollution.

In Canada, environmental degradation increases as people try to maintain the high levels of wealth and material comfort to which they have become accustomed. They consume the earth's resources and pollute its environment with automobiles, airplanes, speedboats, computers, television sets and VCRs, year-round air conditioning and heating, and other amenities that are far beyond the grasp of most of the world's people. Although these products are made possible by high levels of industrial production and economic growth, economic growth often depletes and destroys the environment.

Economic Growth and Environmental Degradation

During most of the 20th century, economic growth in Canada and the world was based on increased output in the manufacturing sector (see Table 15.1 for the increase in industrial output in the 20th century). The environment is affected at all phases of the manufacturing process, from mining and transportation to manufacturing and waste disposal. Industrial production involves extracting raw materials—natural resources—from the environment, usually through mining. Mining depletes mineral resources and fossil fuel reserves—coal, oil, and natural gas. Mining also disturbs ecosystems; this is particularly true of surface mining, which strips bare the land, destroying natural vegetation and wildlife habitats. Other problems typically follow, including erosion of the land by wind and water and runoff of acids, silt, and toxic substances into nearby surface water and groundwater; this leads to the pollution of rivers and streams with toxic compounds that kill fish and other aquatic life (Cable and Cable, 1995).

Table 15.1 provides some indication of the enormous effects humanity's activity has had on our planet during the last 100 years. This chart ignores huge expansions that took place after 1900, like automobiles—in Canada, from zero to 14 million (see Chapter 16)—and huge declines of special interest to Canadians, like the 99 percent decrease in the cod fishery, which has not returned to 1980s levels despite more than a 10-year moratorium on fishing and may never return.

The environmental impact of mining doesn't stop when the raw materials have been mined. Now the raw materials must be transported to a plant or factory, where workers will transform them into manufactured products. Transporting requires the use of energy—particularly the burning of fossil fuels—which contributes to air pollution because motor vehicles produce carbon monoxide, nitrogen oxides, and photochemical pollutants. Each of these pollutants is associated with various illnesses, including heart and respiratory disease and cancer. The manufacturing process further depletes the supply of fossil fuels and contributes to air pollution. (See Table 15.1 for the amount of various kinds of pollution produced in the 20th century.) People who work in or live near facilities that pollute the environment are often harmed by the solid or toxic wastes resulting from the manufacturing process.

Many analysts believe that we cannot continue this pattern of environmental degradation. They believe future economic development—in Canada and globally—will require drastic changes in the structure of industry, especially in the energy, transportation, chemical, and agricultural sectors of the economy. If we don't make changes, environmental degradation—of our air, water, soil, and forests—constitutes a major threat to the well-being of all human beings and eco-systems on the earth.

Air Pollution and Smog

Nature performs many *ecosystem services*—valuable, practical functions that help to preserve ecosystems. For example, if the atmosphere is not overburdened, it can maintain a proper balance between carbon dioxide and oxygen, as well as provide ozone for protection against ultraviolet radiation (see Table 15.2). However, air pollution interferes with many ecosystem services. The carbon dioxide that pollutes the air we breathe keeps the sun's heat from radiating back into space, thereby causing the earth to heat up (the greenhouse effect, discussed in the next section). Other air pollutants deplete the upper atmosphere ozone that shields the earth from ultraviolet radiation. The ozone layer, located 30 miles above our planet's surface, protects us from the sun's ultraviolet rays (Petersen, 1994). Without ozone protection, these rays can kill the organic life that produces food and oxygen and thus make life unsustainable.

The drastic increase in air pollution during the 20th century has placed an undue burden on the atmosphere's ecosystem services (Stevens, 1997). Beginning with the Industrial Revolution in the late 19th and early 20th centuries, more and more pollutants have been emitted into the atmosphere by households, industries, and automobile traffic. Though these three sources have become more fuel-efficient, constantly increasing amounts of carbon dioxide, carbon monoxide, nitrogen oxide, and sulfur oxide, as well as such heavy metals as lead, zinc, and copper still pollute our air (Hauchler and Kennedy, 1994). Today, 85 percent of the air pollution in urban areas can be attributed to the internal combustion engine used in automobiles and other vehicles, like Sports Utility Vehicles (SUVs) (U.S. Bureau of the Census, 1998).

Air pollution affects all life and ecosystems on the planet. Air pollution in the form of acid rain destroys forests, streams and lakes, and other ecosystems. ***Acid rain* is rainfall containing large concentrations of sulfuric and nitric acids (primarily from the burning of fuel and car and truck exhausts).** Canadian efforts to reduce acid rain from the United States have been blocked by the automobile industry; companies that mine, haul, and sell high-sulphur coal; and coal miners. Fortunately, new industries are less dependent on burning coal than are older factories in the industrial northeast and midwest states (Petersen, 1994).

The word "smog" is a combination of the words "smoke" and "fog," Smog is the most visible form of air pollution. According to the North American

TABLE 15.2	What the Natural World Does for Us (If We Don't Mess It Up Too Much)
Food production	Produces fish, game, and crops—even without our help.
Raw materials	Produces (without our help) the raw materials from which humans create things.
Genetic resources	On its own, creates the ability for crops, vegetation, and animals to survive.
Pollination	Without our help, plants and animals naturally reproduce.
Biological control	Somehow, most species of plants and animals survive for millions of years without our help.
Climate regulation	Unless we mess it up, nature has created an ozone layer that protects all plant and animal life from the sun's ultra-violet radiation.
Water regulation	If we don't mess with it, the world's water supply keeps reproducing and distributing itself.
Gas regulation	If we don't mess it up too badly, nature keeps carbon dioxide and oxygen in balance—a balance necessary for life.
Recreation	Just think of the wonderful sights and recreation that nature has created.

Source: From "How Much Is Nature Worth? For You, $33 Trillion," William K. Stevens, 1997, New York Times *(May 20): B7, B9.*

Commission for Environmental Cooperation (CEC) (2001), Ontario is the most polluted area in Canada and the fifth most polluted area in North America, after Ohio, Texas, Michigan, and Indiana. Since the Atlantic provinces, followed by British Columbia and Alberta, are among the cleanest of 63 North American areas studied, and Quebec is 24th, this discussion will concentrate on Ontario. Ontario has half of the top 10 polluters in Canada, such as Ontario Power Generation's Nanticoke Generating Station and the Inco Ltd. Copper Cliff Smelter Complex (North American CEC, 2001).

To monitor air pollution in Ontario, the Air Quality Index (AQI) was devised to measure ground level ozone, nitrogen dioxide, carbon monoxide, sulphur dioxide, sulphur compounds, and suspended particles. An AQI of 50+ may cause eye irritation, breathing difficulties, and even lung damage to those physically active. Since the inception of the AQI in 1993, the number of smog alerts has been growing. In 2001 in southern Ontario, 33 smog alerts were made, and in 2002, up to mid-August, 21 smog alerts were made (quoted in Spears and Brennan, 2002:A18). And smog is not limited to Southern Ontario. Smog can be so bad in the summer in Vancouver that it can eliminate Mt. Baker from view when the polluted air is trapped against the mountains.

Showing relationships between long-term exposure to air pollution and mortality has been difficult because of a wide variety of confounding variables and the problems of measuring air pollution consistently. A Toronto Public Health publication by research consultant Ronald Macfarlane and his colleagues (2000:5) states that air polution in Toronto is linked to about 1000 early deaths, and 5500 hospital visits are linked to heart and lung diseases every year, based on 1995 data. But this is only one centre. A study that followed 1.2 million adults in more than 150 cities in the United States since 1982 confirmed the health hazards of air pollutants. The results of this study, by economist C. Arden Pope III and colleagues (2002), among whom were Canadian colleagues, showed fine particulate and sulphur oxide were associated with all-cause lung cancer and cardiopulmonary mortality. Furthermore, it they showed that elevations in the amount of pollutants were associated with definite percentage increases in mortality. Long-term exposure to combustion-caused air pollution is thus a risk factor for mortality from lung cancer and heart disease.

Air pollution is a pressing problem in many nations, but nowhere more so than in Mexico City, where daylight hours often look like they do in this photo. How is air pollution related to people's health and life expectancy?

In the past, air pollution in middle- and low-income nations was attributed primarily to the fight for survival and economic development, whereas most air pollution in high-income nations was attributed to relatively luxurious lifestyles. However, distinctions between air pollution in high-income and middle- and low-income nations are growing weaker, even though Western industrial nations account for about 68 percent of the carbon monoxide in the atmosphere (World Resources Institute, 1992). Automobile ownership, once considered a luxury, is rising rapidly in urban centres in middle-income nations such as Mexico, Brazil, Taiwan, Indonesia, and China (Bradsher, 1997). In 1997, for example, São Paulo, Brazil, had approximately 4.5 million cars on its streets (Bradsher, 1997). That is about one-third of all the cars, almost 14 million, in Canada (Kremarik, 2000:18). Mexico City, known as the smog capital of the world, has only 37 days a year when the air quality measures as "satisfactory" (S.L. Walker, 1994). Affluent Mexican residents buy bottled oxygen at the drug store; the less affluent buy quick shots of oxygen at street-corner kiosks (Cleeland, 1991). Cities such as Bombay, Shanghai, and Jakarta have also seen a significant increase in the number of automobiles, bringing a corresponding rise in air pollution and traffic problems (Bradsher, 1997). In the summer of 2002, southern and lower eastern Asia was suffering from a "brown cloud," a three-kilometre-thick haze, from combustion of wood and fossil fuels.

But there are some hopeful signs that we are curbing fossil fuel pollution. In Canada, antipollution laws have brought about changes in how automobiles are made and the fuels they consume. Cars are now equipped with catalytic converters and other antipollution devices, and leaded gasoline (a major offender) has been phased out. However, while some middle-income nations are requiring antipollution devices on new vehicles, many leaded-gas-burning cars—often used cars from Canada and the United States—are still a significant source of air pollution.

The Greenhouse Effect

Emissions from traffic and industry not only add to general air pollution but also contribute to the enhanced *greenhouse effect*—**an environmental condition caused by excessive quantities of carbon dioxide, methane, and nitrous oxide in the atmosphere.** When carbon dioxide molecules build up in the earth's atmosphere, they act like the glass roof of a greenhouse, allowing sunlight to reach the earth's surface but preventing the escape of infrared radiation back into space. The radiation that cannot escape is reradiated as heat, causing the earth's surface temperature to rise (Weiner, 1990). Scientists believe that the earth will have a temperature increase of from 1.5 to as much as 5 degrees over the next hundred years. In fact, if current rates of emission into the atmosphere remain unchanged, temperature increases might eventually bring about catastrophic consequences.

One consequence could be significant changes in weather patterns and climate. Changes in weather patterns could bring increased evaporation, creating new deserts and decreasing regional water reserves. Changes in air circulation and climatic conditions could also result in more frequent and intense storms, hurricanes, flooding, and droughts. Vegetation zones could shift, and forests in the northern hemisphere might die off (see Map 15.2 for the possible consequences of climate change in different parts of Canada).

Not all scientists believe that the greenhouse effect exists or that its effects will be this disastrous (Lomborg, 2001; and see the interactionist perspective below). However, studies show a marked retreat of glaciers and the beginning of a shift in vegetation, and one possible cause is the greenhouse effect (Hauchler and Kennedy,

1994). To reduce greenhouse gases, the Kyoto Protocol was developed (see Box 15.2).

Depletion of the Ozone Layer

There is some indication that the ozone layer of the atmosphere has been endangered by air pollution. In 1992, a hole the size of North America was reported in the ozone layer over Antarctica, and scientists have concluded that the ozone layer has been thinning out at a rate of 6 percent a year in the 1990s (Hauchler and Kennedy, 1994). Ozone is vital to life on earth because it is the only gas in the atmosphere that can absorb the sun's dangerous ultraviolet radiation. A thinning ozone layer increases risk of skin cancer, damages marine life, and lowers crop yields. It is important to note that the ozone shrinkage that scientists are currently measuring is the result of emissions in the early 1980s. Thus, the emissions we produce today will exert their destructive effects in the future (Hauchler and Kennedy, 1994). Although past damage cannot be undone, as a result of the Montreal Protocol, many countries, hoping to control damage to this delicate ecosystem in the future, are now phasing out products that contain CFCs, which damage the ozone layer and do not break down quickly.

Toxic Air Pollutants

Toxic air pollutants refer to a wide variety of chemicals found in the air in low but sufficient concentrations to be associated with a lifetime cancer risk greater than one in a million. A study commissioned by Toronto Public Health assessed the potential for exposure to 10 key carcinogens, including asbestos, benzene, and polycyclic aromatic hydrocarbons (PAHs), in Toronto workplaces and environments. The results showed that Toronto residents are routinely exposed to a variety of carcinogenic chemicals in the environment and "many of these people are exposed to additional and even higher levels of carcinogens at work" (Basrur, 2002:iii). The report also recommends finding ways to determine people's actual exposure to these chemicals and reduce the releasing of them.

Problems with Water, Soil, and Forests

Water, soil, and forests (vegetation) are interdependent, crucial resources that face increasing degradation or destruction because of pollution. As a result of climate

MAP 15.2   Climate Change across the Country

Sea levels on the northern coast of BRITISH COLUMBIA could rise up to 30 cm by 2050. The Fraser River Delta is expected to experience flooding. Warmer ocean temperatures will send salmon further north in search of colder water. Inland, melting permafrost and glaciers will increase the risk of landslides in mountain regions.

Permafrost is melting in Canada's NORTH, putting transportation routes and buildings at risk. The Arctic sea ice cover is thinning and summer cover has shrunk by some 15%. Shorter ice seasons mean less feeding time for polar bears, who become 10 kg lighter for every week earlier they are forced to stop hunting, impairing cub survival. An increase in summer insects is threatening caribou and reindeer populations.

Climate Change ACROSS the COUNTRY...

The North

West Coast

Expect more severe weather-related events such as heat waves, floods, and winter storms in QUEBEC. Water levels in the St. Lawrence River are projected to be about 1.25 metres lower. In 1988–1991, a 30 cm drop resulted in a 15% decrease in tonnage handled by the Port of Montréal.

Overall crop yields on the PRAIRIES are expected to fall as drought offsets a longer growing season. Northward expansion of agriculture may offset some of this loss. Drier weather could also make crops more vulnerable to pests and disease. Forest zones could shift north, and longer, warmer, and drier fire seasons would lead to more frequent forest fires.

Prairies

Quebec

Atlantic

Ontario

SOUTHERN ONTARIO will see shorter winters but an increase in hot, humid days in summer, with more smog; Toronto could experience 50 days every year with temperatures above 30°C instead of the current 10 days. Water levels in the Great Lakes are projected to be lower; for every centimetre below average water levels, ships have to reduce their cargoes by 50–100 tonnes. Reduced water availability would affect hydro-electricity generation. Farmers would have a longer growing season, particularly in NORTHERN ONTARIO, but there are also expected to be more pests, floods, and droughts. There would also be increases in the frequency of forest fires.

Rising sea levels – as much as 70 cm on the Atlantic coast of Nova Scotia by 2100 – and more intense and more frequent storms would lead to flooding, coastal erosion, and harm to animal and plant life in the ATLANTIC PROVINCES. Many plants are already flowering earlier each spring, making them more vulnerable to late frosts.

Visit www.climatechange.gc.ca for more info.

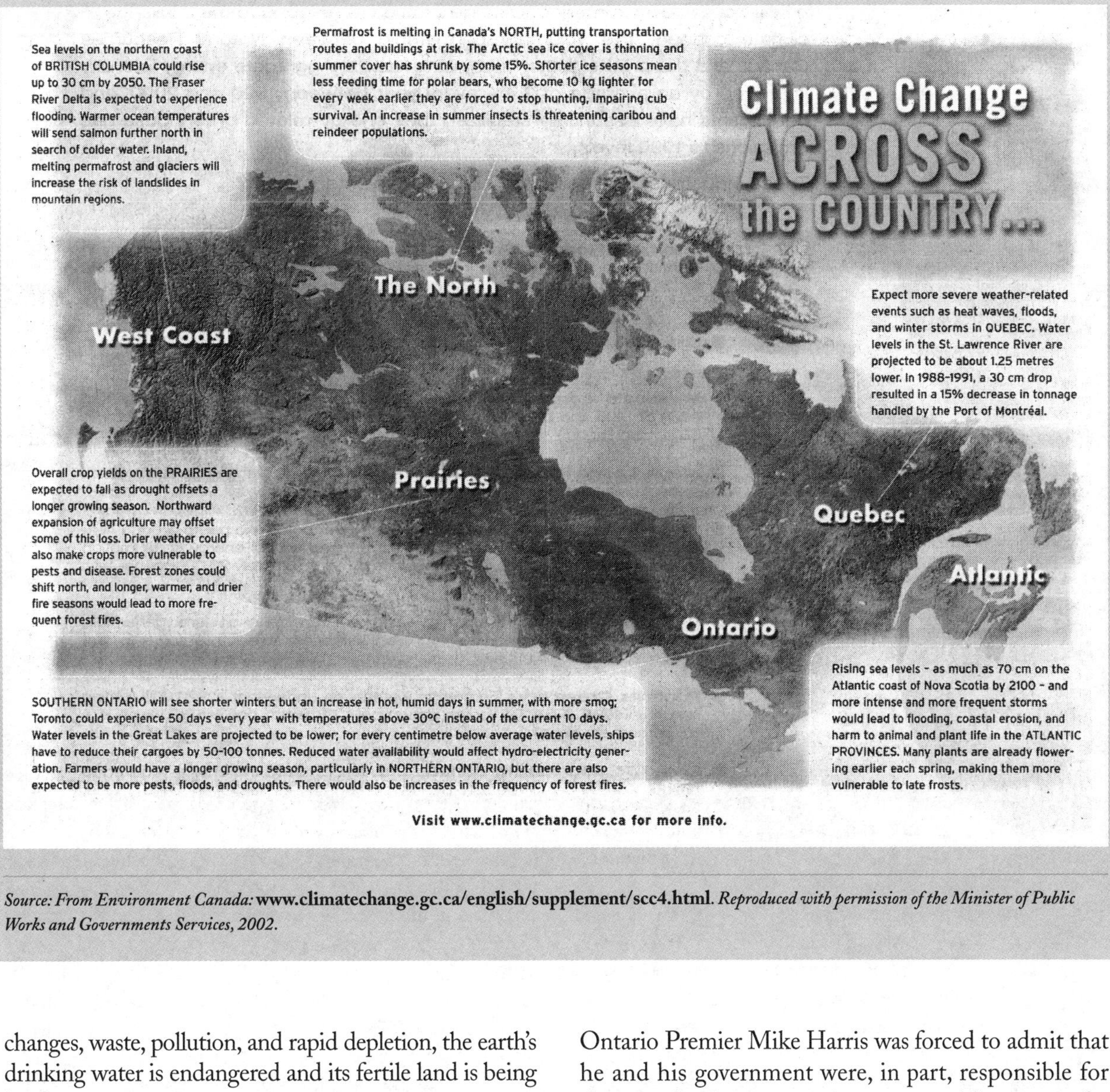

Source: From Environment Canada: **www.climatechange.gc.ca/english/supplement/scc4.html**. *Reproduced with permission of the Minister of Public Works and Governments Services, 2002.*

changes, waste, pollution, and rapid depletion, the earth's drinking water is endangered and its fertile land is being lost.

Water Shortages and Pollution

Water depletion and pollution are serious problems. A recent, shocking example occurred in 2000 in the small town of Walkerton, in southern Ontario. Seven people died and about 2300 became ill as a result of e-coli contamination in the water. The primary source of the contamination was manure that had been spread on a farm near a major well. This well was not monitored appropriately by the water utility operators. In the end,

Ontario Premier Mike Harris was forced to admit that he and his government were, in part, responsible for the tragedy: Despite ongoing strong public support for environmental protection, they had slashed funding for environmental programs (along with funding for welfare, education, and health); at the same time, they had devolved responsibility in many areas—including water testing and manure management—to the municipalities, which had neither the money nor the knowledge needed to handle these responsibilities.

Obviously, such problems are not limited to Canada. Although approximately 70 percent of the earth's surface is covered by water, most water is not

SOCIAL PROBLEMS AND SOCIAL POLICY

BOX 15.2   The Ratification of the Kyoto Protocol

The problem of global warming has the highest profile of any of the environmental problems we face. According to most scientists, a major contributor to global warming is our fossil fuel, or CO_2, emissions. In an attempt to reduce CO_2 emissions, 150 nations met in Kyoto, Japan, in 1997 and agreed to a plan, called the Kyoto Protocol, to reduce the amount of emissions expected in the year 2012 by 20 to 30 percent. This reduction required the industrialized countries to reduce their emissions to about 6 percent below their 1990 level. (The non-industrialized countries were not required to reduce their CO_2 emissions in this round, the belief being that the faster they industrialized, the faster their rates of emissions would decline, as the industrialized world's CO_2 emissions have over the last 50 years.)

After the general agreement, individual nations still had to ratify the protocol. Since the agreement, Japan and the 15 European Union countries have ratified it and the United States has said it will not ratify it. On December 10, 2002, the Canadian Parliament voted to ratify the protocol. The federal budget, tabled on February 18, 2003, allocated $2 billion to meeting Canada's commitments under the protocol. Technically, we have until 2008, when the first cutbacks are supposed to take place. Although the vast majority of Canadians (93 percent, according to a Decima Research Inc. poll reported in the *Globe and Mail* [Middlestaedt, 2001: A4]) believe the government should do more to reduce pollution that causes climate change, many business people, the premier of Alberta, and some outside commentators, like Bjorn Lomborg, have publicly opposed ratification in favour of other methods. The business people are concerned about the cost of reducing emissions, especially when their principal competitors in the U.S. will not have these costs. The premier of Alberta is concerned because the province is an energy-producer, and with this production comes CO_2 emissions. The Alberta oil company Syncrude is one of the chief sources of CO_2 in Canada. Alberta claims that it is not opposed to taking action on climate change, just to this protocol. Estimates of the costs of ratifying Kyoto range from the Alberta government estimate of $30 to $40 billion and the loss of 450 000 jobs to the federal government estimate of $300 million to $3 billion, or a 0.5 percent reduction in the expected growth of 31 percent in GDP by 2010. As part of the strategy to keep costs low, the federal government (a) has sought a reduction in the 6 percent below the 1990 standard to 3.5 percent; (b) has sought consideration for producing and exporting emission free hydroelectricity; (c) has offered to cap, at $15 a tonne, the cost of greenhouse gas emissions to corporations; and, (d) is expecting to buy emission credits from industries and areas (e.g., Eastern Europe) that surpass their reduction goals. The selling of emission credits is often considered to be a licence to pollute, but it makes sense from an economic point of view of rewarding the reducers and increasing costs to the lesser reducers.

Although the Kyoto Protocol is not a perfect document, and although the case against fossil fuels is not fully confirmed, in the past, we have acted against chlorofluorocarbons (CFCs), which we believed caused the depletion of the ozone layer, without fully confirmed knowledge. In 1987, 49 countries signed the Montreal Protocol to cut CFC production and consumption by 50 percent by the year 2000 (Harper, 2001:131). As a result of this protocol, world CFC production has been reduced greatly, from over 1 000 000 Ozone Depleting Tonnes in 1986 to less than 150 000 Ozone Depleting Tonnes in 1999 (Sheehan, 2002:55). Thus, we have proved that joint action without complete knowledge of the causes of a problem can reduce a major pollutant. Likewise, taking action against the possibility that emissions are contributing to global warming and all its consequences would also seem to be worthwhile. Another reason suggested for ratifying this protocol is that it is the only internationally agreed-upon framework for action. Success with this measure may lead to other worthwhile international frameworks on the environment and other social problems.

Now that the Canadian Parliament has ratified the Kyoto Protocol, what can you do to help reduce CO_2 emissions?

drinkable: 97 percent is saltwater, 2 percent is in ice caps and glaciers, and most of the remaining 1 percent is so far underground that it is beyond human reach (Petersen, 1994). The primary sources of water for use and consumption are rainfall, streams, lakes, rivers, and aquifers (accessible underground water supplies).

Canada is often thought to be a source of limitless fresh water, but, according to the Water Quickfacts website of Environment Canada (2002), we have only 7 percent of the world's renewable, or flowing, freshwater, as opposed to the stationary freshwater in lakes; moreover 60 percent of our fresh water runs north.

Because of the current rate of world population growth and existing climatic conditions, water scarcity is increasing throughout the world. According to the *UN World Water Development Report*, the first global assessment of the world's fresh water supply, about 7 billion people, two-thirds of the world's population in the middle of this century, will likely face water scarcity. Areas that already experience water shortages, like India, Pakistan, the Middle East, and sub-Saharan Africa, will experience the most severe problems (UNEP, 2003).

Where does the water go? The largest amount (about 70 percent) is used for crop irrigation; in some African and Asian countries, as much as 85 percent of the available water is used in agriculture. The second largest use of water is in industry (23 to 25 percent). Industrial use of water depends on the level of development in a country and the structure of its economy. For example, high-income nations use as much as 60 percent of their water for industry, whereas a middle- or low-income nation may use less than 10 percent. A mere 8 percent of all available water is used for domestic or private household use. Over the past 100 years, global use of water has gone from 1000 to 2000 litres per day (Lomborg, 2001:151), with affluent people in high-income nations using far more water than do families living in African villages, where water must often be carried several kilometres (about 2 to 5 litres is the physical minimum needed per person per day). Medical analysts believe that about 80 percent of all illnesses in developing nations are partly due to insufficient water supplies (Petersen, 1994). According to the *UN World Water Development Report*, about 6000 people die daily due to water-borne diseases (UNEP, 2003). Overall, water pollution has killed tens of millions of people in the 20th century, making it humanity's most costly pollution problem (McNeill, 2000:147).

Water pollution seriously diminishes the available supply of water. Water may be polluted in a variety of ways. Most often, though, the cause is unpurified or insufficiently treated sewage from households and industry discharged into groundwater, or surface water, or pesticides and mineral fertilizers leached from farmland (Hauchler and Kennedy, 1994). The pollutants range from nitrates and phosphates to metals, salts, and disease-causing microorganisms.

The paper-manufacturing industry is a major water polluter. Dioxin and other chlorinated organic compounds used in manufacturing paper products are

In our delicate ecosystem, water pollution has a disastrous effect on all forms of life—not just on human life. What measures might we implement to reduce water pollution like this?

emitted into the streams below paper mills. People can become seriously ill from drinking the polluted water or eating contaminated fish. Environmental activists believe that paper mills should be required to convert to totally closed systems in which there are no chemical discharges into nearby water. Mills in Canada and Europe are required to use closed systems (Cushman, 1997). But not all water pollution comes from industry. Agriculture, especially as practiced by transnational corporations that are engaged in agribusiness, also pollutes water. Fertilizers and pesticides containing hazardous toxic chemicals that seriously impair water quality are used extensively and often leach into water supplies.

Soil Depletion and Desertification

About 11 percent of the earth's surface is used for growing crops, 32 percent is forest, and 24 percent is used to graze animals. Each year, however, many acres of usable land are lost through erosion and contamination. *Deforestation*—excessive removal of trees—usually results in serious erosion. Since the 1992 Earth Summit in Rio de Janeiro, high-income nations have made an effort to protect forests. Unfortunately, prior industrialization in Canada and other high-income nations has already taken a serious toll on forests, and the pattern is continuing in some middle- and low-income nations as they become more industrialized. In Canada, especially in the Pacific Northwest, logging is an issue. Environmentalists say that logging, besides destroying old-growth forests, increases landslides, floods, and changes in rivers and streams, which devastate fish stocks (Goldberg, 1997). Furthermore, when road building, which is necessary to get to the trees in the forest, is combined with cutting all the timber in an area (clear-cutting), the damage is even greater. More water flows down slopes, and when roads wash out, rocks and soil fall onto lower slopes and into streambeds (Goldberg, 1997).

Today, many regions are losing an increasing amount of useable land as a result of **desertification— the process by which usable land is turned into desert because of overgrazing, harmful agricultural practices, or deforestation.** It is estimated that desertification destroys as many as 15 million acres of land a year. An additional 50 million acres of crop and pasture land become inefficient each year because of excessive application of herbicides and pesticides, insufficient crop rotation, and intensified agricultural production (UNEP, 1992).

In Canada's prairies, according to the North American Commission for Environmental Cooperation (2002), in the mid-1990s, soil loss through erosion is thought to have been about 177 million tones annually, despite successful efforts to reduce loss by the planting of winter cover crops and windbreaks. Although soil erosion has declined, more soil is being lost than is being regenerated naturally, because heavy use of chemical fertilizers has harmed soil structure.

Although desertification takes place in both high-income and middle- and low-income nations, its effects are particularly devastating in middle- and low-income nations. When a country is already hard hit by rapid population growth, virtually any loss of land or crops is potentially devastating to large numbers of people (UNEP, 1992). The United Nations and other international organizations have therefore tried to make protection of the environment an integral part of all economic development policy. However, environmental protection specialists say that, to translate policy into action, conservation programs must be supported by the people, and the major sources of the problem— population and poverty—must also be addressed (UNEP, 1992).

Solid, Toxic, and Nuclear Wastes

Even with a rapidly growing world population and ongoing economic development in industrialized nations, the planet might be able to sustain life for a long time if it weren't for all the solid and toxic chemical waste that is dumped into the environment.

Solid Waste

In Canada and some other high-income nations, people consume a vast array of products and—in these *disposable societies*—throw away huge quantities of paper, plastic, metal, and other materials. *Solid waste* is any and all unwanted and discarded materials that are not liquids or gases. For example, in 2000, each person in Canada disposed of about 0.75 tonnes of waste (Statistics Canada, 2002k), of which only 30 percent was recycled—reused resources that would otherwise be discarded. In comparison, earth sciences reporter Alanna Mitchell (2000:F4) found that the Dutch recycle 91 percent of their glass, 70 percent of their paper and cartons, 86 percent of their car wrecks, and 50 percent of their packaging.

Toxic Waste

At the same time that technology has brought about improvements in the quality and length of life, it has created the potential for new disasters. One source of a potential disaster is *toxic waste*, the hazardous chemical by-products of industrial processes. Perhaps the most widely known U.S. case of toxic waste is Love Canal. In the late 1970s, residents of Niagara Falls, New York, learned that their children were attending a school that had been built on top of a toxic landfill (Gibbs, 1982). After large numbers of children became ill and the smell and appearance of the chemicals permeated the entire area, many people mobilized against Hooker Chemical Company, which had dumped tons of chemicals there (Gibbs, 1982). Eventually, the federal government bought many of the houses, moved the residents out, and removed as much of the toxic waste as possible. Today, families again live in the area, but they have a highly visible neighbour: a 16-hectacre grassy landfill, 9.14 metres high at the centre, with a 2.4-metre-high chainlink fence surrounding it. The landfill contains 20 000 tonnes of toxic chemical waste and the remains of 239 contaminated houses (Hoffman, 1994). A lesser-known Canadian example of chemical discharge, by Uniroyal Chemical, permanently contaminated the water supply with a "toxic soup of cancer-causing chemicals" in Elmira, Ontario. In 1989, the Ontario Ministry of the Environment ordered Uniroyal to cease the discharge and clean up the local environment (Cameron, 1995:298).

Today, government regulates the disposal of toxic wastes, but some hazardous wastes are not covered by regulations, and some corporations avoid the regulations by locating their factories in other countries (see also Chapters 2 and 13). In addition, there is often nowhere to safely dispose of the chemicals. Many people take a "not in my backyard" attitude toward toxic chemical waste dumps (Dunlap, 1992; Freudenberg and Steinsapir, 1992).

According to a report by the North American Commission for Environmental Cooperation, Canada is now a dumping ground for hazardous waste. Representatives from three environmental groups—the Texas Center for Policy Studies, the Canadian Institute for Environmental Law and Policy, and La Neta: Proyecto Emisiones—prepared a joint report that they presented at the CEC's North American Symposium on Understanding the Linkages Between Trade and Environment, in October 2000. Their findings (North American CEC, 2002) were disturbing:

- Exports of hazardous waste from the United States to Canada grew by nearly 400 percent between 1994 and 1999, with Quebec and Ontario receiving the bulk of it. In 1999, Quebec disposed of more than 333 000 tonnes of American toxic waste and Ontario more than 325 000 tonnes.

- The largest increase in American waste exports to Canada occurred in 1994, the year that the U.S. adopted tough new laws for treatment and disposal. In that year alone, Ontario's share of U.S. toxic waste surged by 414 percent.

Nuclear Waste

Nuclear, or radioactive, wastes are the most dangerous of all toxic wastes. Radioactive waste in Canada comes primarily from nuclear power plants, which provide enough electricity in Canada to power 6 million homes (Canadian Nuclear Association, 2002). In addition, small amounts of waste are by-products of certain medical procedures. According to the *Harper's* Index, citing an Organization for Economic Co-operation and Development Report, Canada generates more grams of nuclear waste per capita than either Britain or the U.S. (50 vs. 15 and 7 respectively) (*Harper's*, 2002). Nuclear waste remains deadly for prolonged periods of time. For example, uranium waste from nuclear power plants (an estimated 50 000 tonnes by the early 2000s) will remain dangerously radioactive for the next 10 000 years, and plutonium waste for the next 240 000 years (Petersen, 1994). Although there are many problems with nuclear power, some environmentalists are reconsidering its value, because it does have the advantage of not producing any CO_2 emissions.

Technological Disasters

Technological disasters, such as the 1986 meltdown and radiation leak at the Chernobyl nuclear power plant in the Ukraine, have increased global awareness of the problems associated with radioactive waste. However, despite the disaster, the former Soviet Union was still using 19 similar reactors in 1994 (Petersen, 1994). Sociologist Kai T. Erikson (1991:15) sees the world facing a new species of trouble today:

> [Environmental problems] contaminate rather than merely damage . . . they pollute, befoul, taint, rather than just create wreckage . . . they penetrate human tissue indirectly rather than just wound the surfaces by assaults of a more straightforward kind. . . . And the evidence is growing that they scare human beings in new and special ways, that they elicit an uncanny fear in us.

The chaos that Erikson (1994:141) describes is the result of *technological disasters*—"meaning everything that can go wrong when systems fail, humans err, designs prove faulty, engines misfire, and so on." Chernobyl, Love Canal, and Elmira were technological disasters, as were radiation leakage at the Three Mile Island nuclear power plant in Pennsylvania in 1979 and the leakage of lethal gases at the pesticide plant in Bhopal, India, which killed over 3000 people in 1984. In the worst-case scenario, technological disasters kill tens of thousands of people; in the best-case scenario, they place tremendous stress on the world's ecosystems and greatly diminish the quality of life for everyone.

PERSPECTIVES ON POPULATION AND THE ENVIRONMENT

As sociologists have examined how human behaviour affects population and environmental problems, the subdiscipline of environmental sociology has emerged. According to Cable and Cable (1995:5), "*environmental sociology* examines people's beliefs about their environment, their behaviour toward it, and the ways in which the structure of society influences them and contributes to the persistent abuse of the environment." Like all sociologists, environmental sociologists—as well as demographers—approach their study from one or another perspective.

The Functionalist Perspective

Some functionalists focus on the relationship between social structure, technological change, and environmental problems. On the one hand, they say, technological innovation serves important functions in society. For example, automation and mass production have made a wide array of goods—from automobiles and computers to McDonald's burgers—available to many people. On the other hand, technological innovation has latent dysfunctions; automation and mass production, for example, create air pollution, overuse and depletion of natural resources, and excessive solid waste. From this point of view, some environmental problems are the price a society pays for technological progress. If this is true, the best way to alleviate the problem is to develop new technologies. This is what happened, some functionalists note, when the catalytic converter and other antipollution devices were developed for automobiles.

Other functionalists take a neo-Malthusian perspective and believe that to reduce food shortages and environmental problems, population must be controlled. In other words, the more people there are alive, the greater are the overuse of finite resources and degradation of soil, water, and land.

No matter which view functionalist environmental sociologists take, they believe that solutions to overpopulation and environmental degradation lie in social institutions such as education, the government, and even business. Educators can encourage population control by teaching people about the limits to agriculture and the difficulty of feeding rapidly increasing populations. Government leaders and international organizations such as the United Nations can co-operate to find far-reaching and innovative solutions and develop understandings about more equitable use of the world's resources (Ehrlich and Ehrlich, 1991). Unfortunately, international co-operation does not always occur. In July 2002, the U.S. decided to withhold a contribution of $34 million (USD) from the UN's Family and Population Fund, which supports family planning and reproductive-health programs in 142 countries. Some U.S. Republicans believed that the money was used to support abortions and sterilizations in China. The UN claims it does not support abortion in China or anywhere.

A central concept for the functionalist perspective on the environment is sustainable development, integrating development with environment protection. Business can be helpful by becoming "greener"—applying environmentally friendly principles to its buildings and operations, putting gardens on plant roofs, using alternative energy sources to coal and oil, and cutting waste. Business can also develop environmentally friendly products like cars powered by a hybrid of gasoline-powered engines and electric motors (e.g., Toyota's Prius) and solar- and wind-powered devices. These are example of products that contribute to sustainable development, which the Johannesburg World Summit is promoting.

The Conflict Perspective

Analysts using a conflict framework believe that population and environmental problems have less to do with overpopulation and shortages of resources than with power differentials in societies and in the larger global economy. For example, early conflict theorists, such as Karl Marx and Friedrich Engels (1848/1976), did not think that the food supply was threatened by overpopulation because agricultural technology (even in their era) could meet the food needs of the growing world population, if it were not for poverty. According to Marx and Engels (1848/1976), poverty exists because workers are exploited by capitalists. They argued, for example, that poverty existed in England because the capitalists skimmed off some of the workers' wages as profits. Thus, the labour of the working classes was used by capitalists to earn profits, which, in turn, were used to purchase machinery that could replace the workers rather than supply food. From this classical Marxist point of view, population growth is encouraged by capitalists who use unemployed workers (the industrial reserve army) to keep other workers from demanding higher wages or better working conditions.

According to contemporary conflict theorists, corporations and the government are the two main power institutions in society. As a result, when economic decisions made by members of the capitalist class and elite political leaders lead to environmental problems, the costs are externalized, or passed along to the people (Cable and Cable, 1995:13):

> [The externalization of environmental costs of production] . . . means that the costs of production's negative impact on the environment (for example, the expense of cleaning polluted water to make it suitable for drinking) are not included in the price of the product. The company neither pays for the privilege of polluting the water nor cleans it; it saves the cost of proper waste disposal and makes environmentally conscious competition impossible. Not even the consumer of the product pays the environmental costs of production directly. Rather, the public at large essentially subsidizes the company, by either paying for the cleanup of the environment or enduring degraded environmental quality.

Another conflict approach uses an *environmental justice framework*, examining how racialization and class intersect in the struggle for scarce environmental resources. Of particular interest to these theorists is *environmental racism*—the belief that a disproportionate number of hazardous facilities are placed in areas populated primarily by poor people and people of colour (Bullard and Wright, 1992). Hazardous facilities include waste disposal and treatment plants and chemical plants (Schneider, 1993). A 1987 study by the U.S. Commission for Racial Justice concluded, "Race was the most potent variable in predicting the location of uncontrolled (abandoned) and commercial toxic waste sites in the United States" (Bullard and Wright, 1992:41). A possible example of environmental racism occurred in Halifax, Nova Scotia in 2002. According to *Maclean's* magazine, a proposal to build a water treatment plant to prevent the dumping of sewage into the ocean elicited a complaint to the Nova Scotia

Human Rights Commission stating that the placement of the plant discriminates on the basis of class and colour against the local population, which includes a large Black population. According to local authorities, repositioning the plant would cost $11 million and the concerns about noise and odour are misplaced, as the plant is built to a state-of-the-art design (DeMont, 2002).

The Interactionist Perspective

Since interactionists take a microlevel approach, viewing society as the sum of all people's interactions, they look at environmental problems in terms of individuals. Specifically, they think environmental problems are exacerbated by people's subjective assessment of reality. They point out that children in North American societies are often taught core values that can be detrimental to the environment. Consider the following widely held beliefs (Cable and Cable, 1995:11–12):

- *A free-market system provides the greatest good for the greatest number of people:* Economic decision making works best in private hands.
- *The natural world is inexhaustible:* There will always be more natural resources.
- *Faith in technology:* Any challenge can be met through technology.
- *The growth ethic*: Growth equals progress; bigger is better.
- *Materialism*: Success can be measured in terms of consumption.
- *Individualism*: Individual rights and personal achievement are most important.
- *An anthropocentric worldview*: Human beings are at the centre of the world, and humans are superior to other species. Standing *apart from* nature rather than recognizing that we are *part of* nature, we attempt to conquer and subdue the environment.

In schools and families across Canada, teachers and parents are actively challenging many of these beliefs, and many children and teenagers today are much more aware of environmental issues and sustainable development principles than, arguably, most adults. However slowly, as people become aware of the effects of environmental degradation, concern for the environment is emerging as a core value in Canada and elsewhere. According to sociologist Alan Scott (1990), quality-of-life issues, such as concern for the environment, have become an impetus for new social movements. In the 21st century, we may see the rise of global environmental movements.

To try to understand how environmental issues arise, become of widespread concern, and lead to movements, some theorists employ a social constructionist approach. According to sociologist John A. Hannigan (1995), environmental claims-makers assemble, present, and contest the claims they make about various environmental problems. To gain public attention and support, the claims must be newsworthy, have scientific credibility, and get past various interests. It is helpful to have

- supporters who span science and media, such as David Suzuki, the award-winning scientist (the UN Environmental Medal and many honourary degrees), host of the CBC program, *The Nature of Things*, and author of many books concerned with the environment;

- incentives for change, such as better health; and

- sustaining support by major international organizations, such as the United Nations. (Hannigan, 1995)

Having institutional support can lead to the creation of international protocols, like the Kyoto Protocol for global warming (see Box 15.2), though it cannot guarantee full international co-operation.

Although few would argue that the concerns raised by environmentalists are groundless, some feel the dangers may be exaggerated. For example, in *The Skeptical Environmentalist* (2001), Bjorn Lomborg, an associate professor of statistics in Denmark and former member of Greenpeace, challenges claims about natural resources running out, a growing population depleting the food supply, the relative value of the Kyoto Protocol vs. helping "Third World" countries develop, and great quantities of species becoming extinct (Harvard University entomologist E.O. Wilson, in contrast, suggests 50 percent of species will be extinct by the end of the century). Though Lomborg is not an environmental researcher, he has been concerned about the environment for a long time and is a former member of Greenpeace (2000:xix). Lomborg and his work were severely criticized in *Scientific American* (January, 2002), and he was not given an opportunity to respond. (His response does appear on his website: **www.lomborg.org**.) If some claims of environmental degradation were to turn out to have been exaggerated

for effect, would that undermine the environmental movement? Which picture, a scientifically accurate or a dramatically exaggerated one, will better solve environmental problems?

The social construction approach also helps us understand people's accounts of the estimation of environmental risk and their response to different kinds of communication. McMaster University researchers John Eyles and his colleagues (1993) studied the effects of the tire fire in 1990 in Hagersville, Ontario—a fire broke out on a site on which 13 to 14 million tires were located and burned for 17 days before being extinguished. When the fire broke out, 300 households were evacuated. Eyles and his colleagues conducted in-depth interviews among a small sample of those who experienced the evacuation and were helped by local groups. The researchers found (1993: 287) that although the effects of the fire were short-lived, many residents had anxieties about future problems such as their children's health, toxic water runoff, and the value of their property. Eyles et al. (1993:287) also found that the authorities did not do a good job of communicating with people about the evacuation, the de-evacuation, the clean up, and compensation for loss. Since perceived risk is increased when the threat is uncontrollable, involuntary, and problematic for future generations, the researchers "conclude that the nature of the message is as important as information itself" (Eyles et al., 1993: 288). For the authorities to communicate better with people, they must "recognize and cater to ways in which lay publics act, think and talk" (Eyles et al., 1993:288).

Feminist Perspectives

Two strands of feminist theorizing in population and the environment are *women's agency* and *ecofeminism*. Regarding overpopulation, the relationship between women's literacy and fertility is well established. Higher-educated women have fewer children not only in developed countries, but also in developing countries. While the fertility rate in India is over 3.0, the rate in Kerala, a state in which women are well educated and participate in the labour force, is below replacement level at 1.7 (Sen, 1999:199). Thus, encouraging women's education and participation in the labour force would contribute to both women's well-being and the reduction of fertility rates.

The term *ecofeminism* was coined by French writer Francoise d'Eaubonne, who thought that men's oppression of women and of the environment were two components of the same phenomenon (Eckersley, 2001). Ecofeminists believe that women are more nurturing, co-operative, and conservation-minded than men and point to the term "Mother Nature" to support the general acceptance of women as being closer to nature. The viewpoint that women have a unique capacity to construct a new approach to the environment and the viewpoint is combined with activism (Mies and Shiva, 1993). Women have the opportunity to take on a bigger share of social and environmental decision-making. Equally, men could assume a bigger share of domestic, social, and environmental responsibility as part of a more equitable division of labour in the home and community. These goals should be part of a much broader ecofeminist protest against what British ecofeminist Mary Mellor (1997) has called "*parasitical transcendence.*" This concept draws attention to the gross asymmetries in the size of the ecological and social "footprints" left behind by certain classes, social groups, and nations relative to others. It argues that any form of "parasitism" (living off the back of others, benefiting from the unacknowledged work, social marginalization, or suffering of others) or transcendence (attempting to deny and live beyond our human biological and ecological means) cannot be supportable (Mellor, 1997). Sociologist Melody Hessing (1995:254) also believes in expanding the issues to include reviews of taxation of child-support payments, assessment of habitat loss for endangered species, and reduction of poverty for sole-support mothers. This scenario would "increase values of life support, caring, co-operation, and well-being."

POPULATION AND THE ENVIRONMENT IN THE FUTURE

The problems we have considered in this chapter include some of the greatest challenges that humans face in the 21st century. Global overpopulation and environmental depletion and devastation have irreversible consequences, and actions taken—or not taken—today will be with us far into the future. Futurists believe that we must use a wide-angle lens to examine population and environmental concerns (Peterson, 1994). We must see the world and our role in it in a much different way than we did in the past. We must understand that environmental issues are *security* issues—as much so as a terrorist threat or a missile or bomb (Peterson, 1994). Once we understand that, we will think of environmental problems in a completely different light. For example, to eliminate the global threats posed by overpopulation and environmental degradation, all societies can make the following changes (based on Petersen, 1994:109):

- Reduce the use of energy.
- Shift from fossil fuels to solar-based energy systems or other energy-efficient systems such as water power, wind power, or geothermal energy.
- Develop new transportation networks and city designs that reduce automobile use.
- Work for redistribution of land and wealth so that the poor will not be exploited by increasing concentration of farming.• Push for equality between women and men in all nations, emphasizing literacy training, educational opportunities, and health care (including reproduction and contraception information) for women.
- Effect a rapid transition to smaller families.
- Co-operate internationally to reduce the consumption of resources by the wealthy nations and bring higher living standards to poorer nations.

Are these changes likely to occur? Probably not, if people in high- and middle-income nations adhere to their current belief systems. Some social analysts think that it will take a threatening event—a drastic change in the earth's weather patterns or a sudden increase in natural disasters—to capture the attention of enough of the earth's people and convince political leaders that a serious change in direction is required if the planet is to continue to support human life (Petersen, 1994). We can only hope that people will not wait until it's too late.

WHAT CAN YOU DO?

For this cause, there is no shortage of opportunities to do something. Here are a few places to start:

- Visit the Youth website from the federal government, which describes just about every opportunity imaginable, at **www.ec.gc.ca/ youth/index_e.html**.

At this site, one is invited to apply for a Youth Round Table on the Environment (for youth up to 26 years of age) to increase involvement in Environment Canada program and policy development and act as an advisor to the minister. Links are available to environmental jobs and internships and community volunteer efforts, such as monitoring plant and frog populations in your area. You can find out about events and conferences such as the yearly Sustainable Campuses Conference for groups promoting environmentally friendly and sustainable campuses. There are also links to issues like Sustaining the Environment, where you find more opportunities to learn about sustainable development and what you can do to contribute to it. You will find an EnviroZine to read, and a mailing list to join to learn what is new. Finally, it is possible to contact the ministry with questions and concerns. This site provides a great range of possibilities for participation.

- Reduce energy consumption (e.g., by driving less, having a fuel-efficient car, not idling the car engine, and, at home, reducing heating fuel use through proper insulation, lowering water and air heating, etc.); reduce waste (e.g., recycling, and composting); and reduce consumption—you know what we mean.

- Lobby Members of Parliament, by yourself or with others, to encourage them to take action to promote a sustainable environment.

- Join with others to change energy use (e.g., urge people idling their cars to stop, as students in Mississauga, Ontario, are doing as part of an environmental internship program with City Council and their Environmental Studies Program at University of Toronto).

SUMMARY

WHAT IS THE GLOBAL POPULATION AND WHY IS POPULATION GROWTH A PROBLEM?

The world's population is more than 6 billion in 2003; it doubled in the last 50 years and, if this trend continues, will double again in the next 50 years. Can the earth's resources support this rapid population growth?

WHAT ARE THE PRIMARY FACTORS THAT AFFECT POPULATION GROWTH?

Three factors affect population growth: fertility, the actual number of children born to an individual or population; mortality, the number of deaths that occur in a specific population; and migration, the movement of people from one geographic area to another for the purpose of changing residency.

HOW DOES POPULATION GROWTH AFFECT A SOCIETY?

Population growth affects population composition—the biological and social characteristics of a population, including such attributes as age, sex, racialization, marital status, education, occupation, income, and size of household. In Canada, for example, the age distribution of the population affects the need for schools, employment opportunities, health care, and age-appropriate housing.

WHAT ARE THE MAJOR THEORETICAL PERSPECTIVES ON OVERPOPULATION?

According to the Malthusian perspective, population expands geometrically while the food supply increases arithmetically; disaster can be averted through positive checks (e.g., famine, disease, war) or preventive checks (e.g., sexual abstinence, delayed marriage). The neo-Malthusians believe that the earth is a ticking bomb because population problems exacerbate environmental problems. The third perspective is more hopeful. According to demographic transition theory, societies move from high birth and death rates to low birth and death rates as a result of technological development. However, critics say that demographic transition theory applies chiefly to Western societies.

WHAT SOLUTIONS DO WE HAVE TO WORLD HUNGER?

Two of the most far-reaching initiatives are the green revolution (the growing of high-yield "miracle" crops) and the biotechnological revolution, which involves "improving" plants or animals or using microorganisms in innovative ways. However, some social analysts believe that the solution is not to produce more food but to control fertility.

HOW IS IMMIGRATION CHANGING THE POPULATION COMPOSITION OF CANADA?

Today, the proportion of Canadian immigrants in the population is about 18 percent. If immigration continues at the present rate, it will account for half of the expected population growth in the next 50 years. (Canada is otherwise below zero population growth—a stable population.) Immigration could lead to higher taxes, but it also brings substantial economic and cultural benefits.

WHAT IS ENVIRONMENTAL DEGRADATION AND WHAT ARE ITS CAUSES?

Environmental degradation is caused by disruptions to the environment that have negative consequences for ecosystems. Human beings, particularly as they pursue economic development and growth, cause environmental degradation.

WHAT IS THE MAJOR SOURCE OF AIR POLLUTION AND WHAT ARE ITS EFFECTS?

The major source is fossil fuel pollution, especially from vehicles but somewhat from industry. One of the most serious consequences of air pollution is the greenhouse effect, an environmental condition caused by excessive quantities of carbon dioxide, methane, and nitrous oxide in the atmosphere, leading to global warming. Another is depletion of the ozone layer, the part of the earth's atmosphere that absorbs dangerous ultraviolet radiation from the sun. Although restrictions on the use of CFCs may prevent serious depletion, the already present CFCs will continue to adversely affect the ozone layer.

WHAT WATER, SOIL, AND FOREST PROBLEMS DO WE FACE?

Water is increasingly scarce throughout the world, and water pollution further diminishes the available water supply. About 177 million tonnes of soil are lost each year on the Canadian prairies. However, desertification is greatest in middle- and low-income nations.

WHY ARE SOLID, TOXIC, AND NUCLEAR WASTES A PROBLEM?

High-income nations are running out of space for the amount of solid waste produced by their "disposable societies." Toxic waste (hazardous chemical by-products of industry) causes death and disease if it is not disposed of properly. Canada has become a significant importer of toxic waste. Nuclear, or radioactive, waste is a problem because of the length of time it remains deadly.

WHAT IS THE FUNCTIONALIST PERSPECTIVE ON POPULATION AND THE ENVIRONMENT?

On the subject of the environment, functionalists say that the latent dysfunctions of technology cause problems but that new technologies can solve these problems. Most functionalists take a neo-Malthusian perspective on population but believe that social institutions, especially education and the government, can co-operate to solve population and environmental problems.

WHAT IS THE CONFLICT PERSPECTIVE ON POPULATION AND THE ENVIRONMENT?

In the classical Marxist view, there would be enough food for all people if poverty were alleviated, and poverty exists because capitalists skim workers' wages for profits. Contemporary conflict theorists believe that the two main power institutions in society—corporations and the government—make economic decisions that result in environmental problems.

WHAT IS THE INTERACTIONIST PERSPECTIVE ON POPULATION AND ENVIRONMENT?

Interactionists see population and environment problems in microlevel—individual—terms. Through socialization, children learn core values that are often detrimental to the environment. However, increasingly, concern for the environment is becoming a core value in North America. Social constructionists, without denying that an environmental problem may exist, show how environmental claims-makers assemble, present, and contest the claims they make about various environmental problems. Sometimes scary scenarios are created and those who challenge this definition of reality can be dismissed as Pollyannas. Social contructionists can also help us understand people's estimation of environmental risk.

WHAT IS THE FEMINIST PERSPECTIVE ON POPULATION AND THE ENVIRONMENT?

Feminists emphasize the importance of promoting women's literacy and participation in the labour force to help control fertility. Ecofeminism emphasizes that the patriarchy is the root cause of the oppression of women and of nature. Living off the backs of others and living beyond ecological means are both unsupportable.

KEY TERMS

acid rain,   pp. 356
demographic transition theory,   p. 350
demography,   p. 345
desertification,   p. 362
environmental degradation,   p. 355
environmental racism,   p. 365
fertility,   p. 346

greenhouse effect,   p. 358
migration,   p. 347
mortality,   p. 346
population composition,   p. 347
sustainable development,   p. 345
zero population growth,   p. 353

QUESTIONS FOR CRITICAL THINKING

1.   Which perspective on population growth do you favour—neo-Malthusian or demographic transition theory—and why?

2.   If you had to focus on a single aspect of environmental degradation—air pollution; water, soil, or forest problems; or, solid, toxic, or nuclear waste disposal—which would it be, and why? What would you do to make people aware of the seriousness of the problem? What new solutions could you propose?

3.   Explore how people use the term *sustainable development*. Do you think this is a good term for the effort to help a variety of institutions become more protective of the environment?

4.   Is it possible to have development without environmental degradation?

WEBLINKS

Environment Canada

www.ec.gc.ca/envhome.html

Visit this site for a general introduction to environmental problems, to find out what Environment Canada does, and to find out what you can do to help the environment.

Environmental Defence Canada

www.edcanada.org

This organization hosts information-awareness programs and watches for air, food, and pollution.

World Population Data Sheet

www.prb.org/Template.cfm?Section=PRB&
template=/Content/ContentGroups/Datasheets/
wpds2002/2002_World_Population_Data_
Sheet.htm

Here is information on population projections, including lists of the world's largest countries now and in 2050.

United Nations Environment Programme (UNEP)

www.unep.net

The UNEP provides a wide variety of information accessed from thematic portals dealing with climate change, fresh water, and socio-economic topics and regional portals for the Arctic, Latin America, and Europe (with more to come).

World Wildlife Fund (WWF)

www.panda.org

The WWF's site provides regional and country-specific conservation program information, information on WWF strategy and partnerships, news, fact sheets and other publications, a photo gallery, and activist information.

Worldwatch Institute

www.worldwatch.org

Worldwatch works to inform policy makers and the public about emerging global problems and trends and the complex links between the world economy and its environmental support systems.

16
URBAN PROBLEMS

Eighty percent of Canadians now live in urban centres.

Canadian Census, 2001

Given the already established centrality of cities to the current and future prosperity of the country, then all great social policy questions of the day—education, health, poverty, housing and immigration—become urban policy questions.

Meric S. Gertler, Goldring Chair in Canadian Studies at the University of Toronto (2001:128)

People are noticing that our quality of municipal services has been falling for the last decade. And we have got to reverse that trend if we are going to be competitive.

Jack Layton, former president of the Federation of Canadian Municipalities (Moloney, 2002:A9)

A vibrant city depends on communities of mixed incomes and uses.

Pam McConnell, Toronto City Councillor (statement to author)

Cities are obviously important to Canada. But over the last decade, the increased services our cities have had to provide—as a result of provincial downloading of hundreds of millions of dollars in new responsibilities with no increase in taxing powers—have put overwhelming strains on their capacity to provide support for Canada's new economy. Can Canadian cities recover from this situation?

In this chapter, we examine some of the most pressing urban problems in Canada and the rest of the world. You will learn about the growth of cities in Canada over the last 100 years; urban problems, such as fiscal crises, health care, housing (and homelessness), and spatial separation of the poor and visible minorities; the great growth of global cities and the formation of megalopolises; how sociological perspectives, functionalist, conflict, interactionist, and feminist, help us understand these problems; and future urban problems and what you can do about them.

CHANGES IN CANADIAN CITIES

Urban problems in Canada are closely associated with the profound socioeconomic, political, and spatial changes that have taken place since the Industrial Revolution. One hundred years ago, many people (about two thirds of Canadians) lived in rural areas. Early in the 21st century, about 80 percent of the Canadian population lives in urban areas, and many of these people live in cities that did not exist 200 years ago (Statistics Canada, 2002r).

Early Urban Growth and Social Problems

Industrialization and urbanization bring about profound changes in societies and frequently spawn new social problems, such as housing shortages, overcrowding, unsanitary living and working conditions, environmental pollution, and crime (see Chapter 1). By definition, a city involves population density. According to sociologists, a *city* is a relatively dense and permanent settlement of people who secure their livelihood primarily through non-agricultural activities (Weeks, 1998). Although cities existed long before the Industrial Revolution, the birth of the factory system brought about rapid *urbanization*, which we defined in Chapter 1 as the process by which an increasing proportion of a population lives in cities rather than in rural areas. Canada industrialized after World War I, and the shift toward urban living is shown in home-ownership rates. Today, two-thirds of Canadian households own their homes, but in 1931, although over three-quarters of rural families owned their own home, less than half of urban families did (Kremarik, 2000:18).

At the beginning of the 20th century, towns and cities were small with very few commercial buildings over five stories. People lived close to their place of work or, where streetcars existed, close to public transit lines. Slums did exist, populated by poor workers and recent immigrants. Urban congestion and poor sanitation resulted in epidemics that spread beyond the slums. In 1914, following a typhoid epidemic, Montreal introduced a water filtration plant and Toronto built a sewage treatment plant at the same time (Kremarik, 2000:18). After WWI, a boom in housing occurred, but that came to an end with the Great Depression in the 1930s and this situation continued until after WWII.

Contemporary Urban Growth

The growth of suburbs and outlying areas after WWII forever changed the nature of city life in this country. Suburban areas existed immediately adjacent to many central cities in the 1920s, but after the late 1940s, these communities began to grow in earnest because of the automobile and families wanting their own homes in which to bring up what is now called the "baby boom" generation. They were referred to as "bedroom communities" because most of the residents were there on nights and weekends but went into the central city for jobs, entertainment, and major shopping. Most suburban dwellers drove to work each day, except where public transit was convenient, establishing a pattern that would result, decades later, in traffic congestion and air pollution, problems that have drastically worsened in the past decade.

To reduce the housing shortage, the federal government subsidized what became a mass exodus from the central city to outlying suburbs. The federal government established the Central (now Canada) Mortgage and Housing Corporation to grant and insure mortgages. Between 1945 and 1951, the CMHC was responsible for the construction of half a million houses (Kremarik, 2000:19). Other factors also contributed to the postwar suburban boom, including the availability of inexpensive land, low-cost mass construction methods for building tract houses, new federally and provincially financed highway systems, inexpensive gasoline, and consumers' pent-up demands, after the depression and war, for single-family homes on individually owned lots. By 1971, 60 percent of Canadian households owned their own home, and although they had their dream, more than half had a mortgage (Kremarik, 2000:19).

Although early suburbanization provided many families with affordable housing, good schools and parks, and other amenities not found in the central city, the shift away from central cities set up an economic division of interests between cities and suburbs that remains in place even today (Flanagan, 1995). While many people in the suburbs still rely on the central city for employment, entertainment, or other services, they pay taxes to their local governments and school districts. As a result, suburban police and fire departments, schools, libraries, and recreational facilities are usually well funded and well staffed, with up-to-date equipment. Suburbs also have newer infrastructures (such as roads, sewers, and water treatment plants) and money to maintain them. In contrast, many central cities have aging, dilapidated schools and lack funds for essential government services (see Chapter 12).

Today, edge cities are springing up beyond the central cities and existing suburbs. An *edge city* is a **middle- to upper-middle-class area that has complete living, working, shopping, and leisure activities so that it is not dependent on the central city or other suburbs** (Garreau, 1991). Map 16.1, presenting the Canadian population change between the 1996 and 2001 Censuses, shows examples of edge cities around Toronto, Montreal, Vancouver, and from Calgary to Edmonton. These four areas grew 7.6 percent, compared with virtually no growth (0.5 percent) in the rest of the country. In 2001, 51 percent of Canada's population lived in these four areas (Statistics Canada, 2002r).

Edge cities begin as residential areas; then retail establishments and office parks move into the adjacent area, creating an unincorporated edge city. Automobiles are the primary source of transportation in many edge cities, and pedestrian traffic is discouraged—and even dangerous—because streets are laid out to facilitate high-volume automobile traffic, not walkers or bicyclists. Edge cities may not have a governing body, so they drain taxes from central cities and older suburbs. Many businesses and industries move their physical plants—and tax dollars—to these areas because land is cheaper, workers are better educated, and utility rates and property taxes are lower than those in the city. As a result, many jobs move away from poor, visible minority racialized/ethnic workers in central cities, creating structural unemployment.

Over time, large-scale metropolitan growth produces a *megalopolis*—**a continuous concentration of two or more cities and their suburbs that have grown until they form an interconnected urban area.** The East Coast of the United States, for example, is a megalopolis, with Boston, Providence, Hartford, and their suburbs merging into New York City and its suburbs, which in turn, merge southward into Newark, Philadelphia, Baltimore, and Washington, D.C., and their suburbs. It is almost impossible to tell where one metropolitan area ends and another begins. When metropolitan areas merge into a megalopolis, there are big population changes that can bring about or exacerbate social problems and inequalities based on

MAP 16.1   Canada's Population Change, 1996 to 2001, by 2001 Census Division

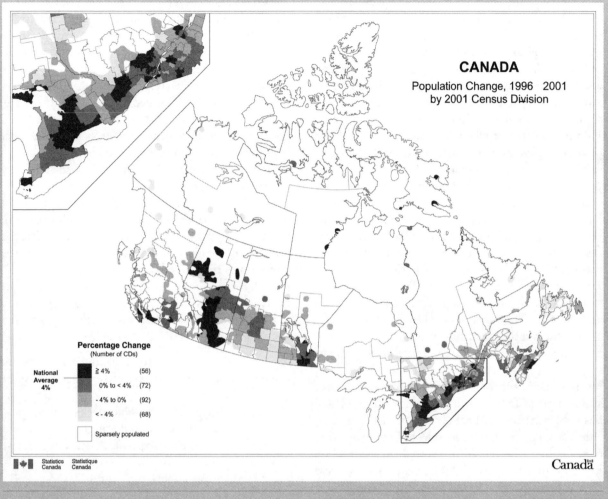

Source: Adapted from map produced by the Geography Division, Statistics Canada, 2002, from **http://geodepot.statcan.ca/Diss/Highlights/Maps_e.pdf**. Reproduced with permission.

racialization, class, and gender. In Map 16.1, the beginning of megalopolises can be seen in the west, Surrey-Delta-Vancouver and in the centre, Hamilton-Toronto-Oshawa. In the future, that concentration could extend to Montreal and beyond.

URBAN PROBLEMS IN CANADA

While we have traditionally thought that Canadian cities did not have the magnitude of the problems of poverty, crime, racism, homelessness, drug abuse, and inadequate school systems that cities in the United States experience because of years of neglect and deterioration, now "the rebirth of American cities is putting Canada's urban landscapes to shame" according to David Crombie (2001:A15), Toronto's former mayor. Intertwined with and exacerbating these problems in many older central cities are periodic fiscal crises.

Fiscal Crisis in Cities

It has traditionally been thought that Canadian cities were in better fiscal shape than U.S. cities. No major

Canadian city went into financial default like Cleveland in 1978 or to the edge of collapse like New York in 1975. Nor did our cities experience the flight to the suburbs or the major *deindustrialization*—**the process by which capital is diverted from investment in basic industries (in the form of economic resources, plants, and equipment) to business practices such as mergers and acquisitions and foreign investment**—that left so many blighted areas in the centres of U.S. cities. However, today the tables have turned. Federal and provincial government cutbacks have left Canadian cities, with their limited sources of revenue—primarily property taxes—in desperate financial straits. Out of every $1.00 of taxes collected, $0.07 goes to municipalities, and the federal and provincial governments receive $0.51 and $0.42, respectively (Moloney, 2002:A9). In the Toronto Dominion Bank's recent report, *A Choice Between Investing in Canada's Cities or Disinvesting in Canada's Future* (2002), the bank calls for the revitalization of cities and notes that, between 1995 and 2001, local government revenues increased by 14 percent and the federal and provincial government revenues increased by 38 percent and 30 percent respectively. U.S. cities, with additional sources of revenue such as income and sales taxes and greater support from federal and state governments and business, are spending more per person than Canadian cities. Jack Layton, former president of the Federation of Canadian Municipalities, stated that Canadian municipalities spend $785 (USD) per person, whereas their U.S. counterparts spend $1652 (USD) per person (Moloney, 2002:A9). Many groups, like the TD Bank, the Prime Minister's Task Force on Urban Issues, and the Conference Board of Canada, have called for a revitalization of Canadian cities with the help of more stable and ongoing revenue and business partnerships (see Box 16.2 on page 387 for more discussion about saving our cities).

One plan to help the cities is to build homes on sites of abandoned factories. In Toronto, Massey-Ferguson, a major maker of farm machinery, and Inglis, a maker of stoves, closed their factories and left land vacant for a decade. Now, houses are being built on the land, and condominium lofts are being built in the 120-year-old Massey-Ferguson headquarters. The first residents came in five years ago, and now there are a dozen condominium complexes and hundreds of houses, which will be home to over 5000 people. City

planners say that this community, called King West Village, is a good example of the kind of redevelopment that they want to promote. With projects like this, planners hope to house up to a million more residents over the next 30 years (Immem, 2002:A10).

To what extent are cities' financial problems brought on by suburbanites? On the one hand, city governments bear the economic burden for the municipal services (e.g., street maintenance, fire and police departments) and amenities (e.g., parks and other recreational facilities) that are used by suburban residents. On the other hand, suburban dwellers frequently believe that they do their fair share to finance necessary services. Consider the following recent editorial; it is from a U.S. paper but could just as well have been written by a person who lives in Coquitlam, for example, and works in Vancouver. In this editorial, the writer states that although he and his family live in a suburban community outside the taxing authority of the city of Austin, Texas, they contribute significantly to the central city's sales tax, which helps to pay for the city's transit system (Barry, 1997:A13).

> You hear a lot of demonizing of suburban dwellers. . . . We use the city streets but don't pay for them; we work in town but pay property taxes to some other entity. . . . Of all the suburban-bashing mantras, the one that irks me most is the one that says we don't pay taxes. . . . We're still paying Austin taxes, and we still support Austin businesses. . . . Practically everything we buy, we buy in Austin. My sport utility vehicle and [my wife's] car were bought at Austin dealerships. . . . Although there's a grocery store two minutes from the house, we still do much of our grocery shopping in Austin. I eat at least five meals a week at Austin restaurants. . . . We gas up from Austin dealer's pumps. We buy clothes at Austin clothiers. We shop at Austin malls. My barber is in Austin, as is [my wife's] beauty shop of choice. . . . Ninety percent of the [metropolitan transit authority] sales tax may be collected in Austin, but a lot of it is collected from people like us. . . . Austin is a city in a region, not a fortress. We're friends, neighbors and coworkers, not barbarians at the gate.

According to this point of view, cities benefit more from suburban residents than critics think. Still, the federal government programs that subsidized private housing and contributed to the mass exodus to the suburbs after World War II, combined with years of government neglect, have greatly intensified urban problems.

The Crisis in Urban Health Care

As Meric Gertler (2001) indicates in the opening quote, most of our social problems are urban problems. This is also true for health care. Although *Maclean's* magazine's Fourth Annual Ranking of Canadian health centres found that most of the major cities (except Montreal) ranked in the top 10 regions, they were helped by having medical schools in their area (Hawaleshka, 2002:24; and see Chapter 10). However, overall scores may mask some problems, particularly with disadvantaged populations. We also know from Chapter 10 that disadvantaged people have greater rates of disease, disability, and death. A study of hospital use in a downtown neighbourhood in Toronto showed that, while those from poor neighbourhoods were not discriminated against regarding admission, they had high admission and readmission rates (Glazier et al., 2000). As a result, the costs of care are about 50 percent greater for poor than for wealthy neighbourhoods. These added costs put greater burdens on hospital emergency, admitting, billing, and discharge departments (Glazier et al., 20001:272). The authors conclude (2000:272) that "Canadian policy makers should take account of the income levels of the neighbourhood when deciding on resource allocation for public health, ambulatory care, community services and hospitals." If hospitals in downtown neighbourhoods do not get additional resources, they will not be able to continue to provide appropriate help to the often disadvantaged people they serve.

The growing homeless population in major urban areas has simply added to the cost of providing health care.

Housing Problems

Many regions in Canada lack affordable housing for low-income individuals and families (see Chapter 2). Over the last 10 years, there has been a significant increase in homelessness, especially among families with children. Each year, we are made aware of the plight of homeless people through extensive media coverage during the Christmas holiday season and after winter deaths on the street. During the rest of the year, many people view the homeless with less compassion (see Box 16.1).

The Housing Shortage

Recent information shows that two-thirds of Canadian households own their homes (Statistics Canada, 2002j). And since the rent for a two-bedroom apartment in a major city like Toronto equals the costs of carrying a median-priced townhouse of $185 000, a good chance exists that the percentage of households that realize their dream of owning their home will increase. But housing is still an income issue, because only 40 percent of people in the lowest income quintile (see Chapter 2) own their homes. In addition, although 86 percent of Canadian households are suitably housed (measured by the homes not needing major repairs and being large enough for their needs), 20 percent of those in the lowest income quintile and 23 percent of female lone-parents are not suitably housed (Statistics Canada, 2002j).

Although Canadian cities do not have the blighted neighbourhoods and abandoned buildings found in U.S. cities, they do have pockets of poverty. With the reduction in the building of social housing due to government cutbacks, a big increase has occurred in the percentage of people paying 50 percent or more of their income on rent. According to the Federation of Canadian Municipalities, the completion of social housing units went from a high point of 19 621 in 1992 to 1439 in 1998 (Layton, 2000:212). In 1991, according to the Federation of Canadian Municipalities, 16 percent of Canadians, over half a million people, were paying 50 percent or more of their income for rent; by 1996, 21.6 percent were (Layton, 2000:210).

Governments are beginning, again, to realize the importance of social housing; in spring 2002, the federal government created a $680 million national program to build 27 000 affordable apartments and townhouses across Canada. This program requires matching grants from the provinces. In Ontario, the Harris government withdrew from social housing in 1998, but in 2002, the Eves government endorsed the federal plan. However, when building will commence is uncertain.

Meanwhile, whereas 8 percent of those Canadians in the highest income quintile live in unsuitable housing, 20 percent of those in the lowest income quintile

SOCIAL PROBLEMS IN THE MEDIA

BOX 16.1 Homelessness and the Holidays and Deaths

The charity of the holiday season is traditional—and welcome. The problem is that so much is seasonal. . . . Come January, when people go back to their normal routines, the hunger and homelessness recognized in the holiday season will remain. It would be nice if most of the spirit of giving remained, too.

From a Los Angeles Times *editorial, December 25, 1988*

Not only does charity toward the homeless wax and wane during the year, so does media coverage. Around Christmastime, the press appears at homeless shelters to interview "Jimmy G." and "Sherry P.," and their stories are all the more poignant because, by now, in all parts of the country, the weather is pretty raw.

Research shows that the media, especially newspapers, give steady, fairly minimal coverage to the homeless until late fall, when the amount increases. Coverage peaks in December (at Christmas), and then in January again diminishes until it returns to its standard plateau in April (Bunis et al., 1996; Snow and Anderson, 1991). Why does this happen?

For one thing, homeless people are human-interest stories for the holiday season. For another thing, people are in a giving mood during the holidays, so if the media make us aware of the plight of the homeless, we are likely to help. One billboard poster, for example, showed a drawing of Jesus above the head, "How can you worship a homeless man on Sunday and ignore one on Monday?"

It is true that an important function of the media is to make the public aware of social problems. Sociologists, though, dig deeper. Why do the media increase coverage at *this* time of year—during the holidays? Part of the explanation may come from sociologist Lewis A. Coser (1969:104), who says "we have only so much emotional energy and yet we live in a world filled with inhumanity and suffering." Thus, sympathy for the afflicted in a society fluctuates over time. Otherwise, we would be emotionally overwhelmed.

Another reason points to the holidays as the time that most people express sympathy for the homeless: Holidays are times of ritual, opportunities to affirm shared values. But, of course, the values that are affirmed by any particular holiday ritual derive from the culture. In North America, where individualism is highly valued but people believe, at the same time, that they are responsive to social problems, the holidays function to reassert community solidarity by redistributing goods in the community (Barnett, 1954).

Along these same lines, Thomas J. Scheff (1977:71–73), sees sympathy as a catharsis (emotional release) for guilt:

Insofar as Americans have imbibed this heady drink of socially induced ambition, they tend to ignore or slight the precepts of brotherhood, kindness, and cooperation in favor of those related to attaining individual success. However, many persons experience a sharp conflict of values because, though the ideals of brotherhood and kindness are relegated to a secondary place, they retain their normative quality. Therefore, widespread feelings of guilt develop into this clash of divergent social norms and furnish some of the motivation for Christmas charity (Bunis et al., 1996).

Not only are the media selective during the year, they have been selective over the decades. Computer searches of Canadian newspapers of the 1960s, 1970s, and early 1980s found no mention of homelessness (Layton, 2000:3). But the Toronto media started to pay attention to deaths from exposure beginning with the death of Drina Joubert, a homeless woman in Toronto, in 1986. Other deaths, like that of Eugene Upper in 1996 and Linda Houston in 1997, also attracted attention. In his book *Homelessness,* Jack Layton mentions how Linda Houston's death in North York (a former suburb of Toronto) was especially poignant. The then-mayor of North York, Mel Lastman, had recently said, during a debate for the position of mayor of the newly amalgamated city of Toronto, that there were no homeless people in North York. When Lastman became mayor of Toronto, he said that he was so shaken by the news of Houston's death that he would make homelessness his first priority. As his first act as mayor, he created the Mayor's Homelessness Action Task Force (Layton, 2000:27). (The findings and recommendations of this task force are found in the next section.) In this case, the media reports precipitated political action. Two more deaths during December 2001 brought forth more media stories. For example, an article in the *Globe and Mail* stated that, from May 1999 to the end of 2001, Toronto witnessed the deaths of 102 street people (Priest, 2001:A18). However, this time, no significant political action occurred.

What have you observed in the media's coverage of social problems, particularly homelessness? Does the concept of "charity as catharsis," or of the media as agents of social change, make sense to you?

In an effort to replace substandard housing and build lower-cost housing for poor and lower-income families, groups such as Habitat for Humanity continually build houses in communities across the country. Would you be willing to volunteer to build low-income housing for others like these volunteers are doing?

live in unsuitable housing (Statistics Canada, 2002j). One of the ways in which unsuitable housing is created is by landlords who let their properties become substandard through years of neglect. Abandoned buildings can increase fear and isolation in the residents of adjoining properties. The empty buildings may become hiding places for drug dealers or even fugitives, and some are dangerous places for children to play. In some cities, however, *urban squatters*—people who occupy land or property without any legal title to it—have moved into abandoned apartment buildings and fixed them up. As people take up unofficial residence in the buildings, they create a sense of community by watching out for each other's possessions.

Some cities are encouraging developers to create housing on these sites, as in the Toronto example mentioned earlier. But, this kind of housing is not likely to help the homeless or the people who need subsidized housing.

Many of the most successful recent initiatives for replacing substandard housing and building lower-cost housing for poor and lower-income families have come from community groups and volunteer organizations. One of the best known of these, in the U.S., is Habitat for Humanity, which has received extensive press coverage because of former U.S. President Jimmy Carter's participation. This organization also operates in Canada and, according to its fundraising letter, its volunteers built homes for 85 families in 2001 and propose building 100 homes in 2002.

Perhaps the Pruitt-Igoe project in St. Louis is the all-time worst example of public housing projects. Built as a monolithic highrise, the building immediately had structural problems, high rates of crime, inadequate maintenance, and poor management. Pruitt-Igoe received media attention and was the subject of sociological research, but finding a solution to the building's many problems was virtually impossible, and it was demolished in the 1970s. Although little highrise social housing has been built in Canada, St. Jamestown, in Toronto, is a similar project. It was developed in the 1960s by the private sector and consists of 18 highrise apartment buildings with 7000 units for 12 000 people. It is one of the most densely populated residential areas in Canada (cited in Hulchanski, 1990:16). While it is still standing, this now somewhat shabby development never became the model neighbourhood its proponents claimed it would become.

But another large development *has* become a neighbourhood. The St. Lawrence Neighbourhood in downtown Toronto is a good example of a large development that is socially mixed. This neighbourhood was conceived in the mid-1970s, with first occupancy in mid-1979. Although it is a large development of 3500 units, it has become a neighbourhood because people who wanted to live there were involved in the planning. St Lawrence was begun, planned, and implemented by the municipal government (the former City of Toronto) in co-operation with other levels of government, the private sector, and community organizations (such as housing co-operatives and nonprofit societies) (Hulchanski, 1990:4). The neighbourhood is

- socially mixed, including people of different ages, income, and household size (Hulchanski, 1990:13);
- tenure mixed, including 39 percent condominium apartments, 30 percent nonprofit co-operatives and nonprofit rentals, 27 percent municipal nonprofit rental and 4 percent ownership of townhouses (Hulchanski, 1990:15); and
- 57 percent non-market, or social, housing (Hulchanski, 1990:3).

"St. Lawrence demonstrates that public planning of large development projects in an open and democratic fashion can be successful and that desirable high density socially mixed neighbourhoods can be developed by a municipality." (Hulchanski, 1990:17)

Since the 1970s, some middle- and upper-middle-class families and developers have re-entered central city areas and gentrified properties. **Gentrification is the process by which people renovate or restore properties in central cities.** Some people view gentrification as the way to revitalize the central city. Others think that it further depletes the stock of affordable housing for the poor and pushes low-income people out of an area where they had previously lived (Palen and London, 1984; Flanagan, 1995; and see below, "The Spatial Separation of the Poor and Visible Minorities").

Homelessness

The worst outcome of the housing shortage has been a significant increase in the number of homeless people in Canada. Accurate data about the actual number of homeless people in Canada is unavailable. It is extremely difficult to count the number of homeless people because most avoid interviews with census-takers and social scientists. The 2001 Census did try to identify one group of homeless people by counting those in shelters for persons lacking a fixed address. On May 14, 2001, 14 145 people were counted in such shelters (Statistics Canada, 2002u). This count does not identify all the homeless people, since many others may have been in other accommodations or on the street. A more comprehensive study of the number of homeless people in a major metropolitan area, Toronto, is found in the *The Report of the Mayor's Homelessness Action Task Force* (sometimes called the Golden Report, after its head, Anne Golden) (and see Box 16.1 for the origin of this task force). The researchers found that:

- The fastest-growing groups of homeless people using hostels are youth under 18 and families with children. Families were 46 percent of the people using Toronto hostels in 1996.

- Nearly 26 000 different people used hostels in that year. There were about 3200 on any given night in 1996, and the number was much higher in the winter. (Now an estimated 6000 people seek emergency shelter each night in Toronto.)

- There were 5300 children living in hostels in 1996.

- Between 30 percent and 35 percent of homeless people are living with mental illness. The estimates are higher for some groups. For example, 75 percent of homeless single women have mental illness.

- 4400 people (17 percent of hostel users in 1996) stayed in the hostel system for a year or more. This group of "chronic hostel users" takes up about 46 percent of the beds and services.

- 170 000 different people used shelters between 1988 and 1996.

- At least 47 percent of hostel users come from outside Toronto. (Golden et al., 1999:4)

According to social scientists, studies that focus exclusively on personal problems of the homeless, such as mental illness or substance abuse, may result in *specialism*—the assumption that individual characteristics of poor people cause their homeless condition and that, therefore, the only way to alleviate homelessness is to cure the individual's personal problems (Wagner, 1993). This approach downplays the significance of structural factors such as the unavailability of low-income housing and mental-health care, which are the most important determinants of homelessness.

Realizing the importance of structural change, Golden and her colleagues made many recommendations to deal with the problem of homelessness, including:

- a shelter allowance for the working poor;

- supportive housing for people with mental illness and/or addictions;

- new affordable housing;

- a plan to preserve existing housing;

- incentives for prevention including preparing people to leave hostels and providing follow-up support after leaving;

- service planning for key subgroups, such as youth and families; and

- a homeless services information system with a database of services and a 24-hour information telephone line (Golden et al, 1999:8–10).

In late 1999, the *Let's Build* program was launched in Toronto to help create some affordable housing. In 2002, 304 housing units in six projects are underway, and it is anticipated that, with the help of other programs, 700 to 1000 units a year could be generated (Guslits, 2002:24).

Because of the lack of affordable housing in major Canadian cities, homeless people rely on homeless shelters for food and protection at night, or resort to constructing their own form of shelter in unused city lots or buildings. In 2002, this tent city erected by a number of homeless people in Toronto was ordered destroyed and its residents evicted without notice.

Spatial Separation of the Poor and Visible Minorities

Although it is generally acknowledged that Canada does not have the segregation of poor—especially racialized poor—and non-poor found in the U.S., the increasing immigration of racialized/ethnic minorities to our cities leaves open the possibility that the U.S. segregation problems could occur here. Residential segregation in the U.S., according to sociologists Douglas S. Massey and Nancy Denton, is associated with many other problems.

To determine the extent of spatial separation of poor and visible minorities in Canada, sociologists Eric Fong and Kumiko Shibuya (2000) studied 22 Canadian cities using the 1991 Census. Three determinants of spatial separation are:

■ Economic: separation by peoples' economic resources;

■ Racialization and ethnicity: separation by racialized/ethnic group; and

■ Uneven development: separation by capitalist investment in areas where profit is maximized.

Two ways of gaining profit are to open up unused land (e.g., new suburbs or former factory lands) and to redevelop valuable land (e.g., gentrification of existing housing). These two ways attract residents with resources and can either leave poor in the area or shift them to neglected neighbourhoods. Thus, uneven development can lead to group differentiation and stratification. In the U.S., profit was more likely to be made in the suburbs than in the city because the U.S. governments were less involved in land management, and services like health and education were more locally determined than is the case in Canada.

Using the LICO (low-income cut-off, see Chapter 2), to distinguish poor from non-poor and an index of dissimilarity, Fong and Shibuya (2000:449) found that economic separation does not play a strong role in spatial separation of poor and non-poor. There are no extensive areas of blight, decay, or housing abandonment in Canadian cities similar to those found in the U.S. In addition, because of a more progressive housing and taxation policy than that found in the U.S., Canadian governments contribute to preventing the separation of various groups. Nevertheless, racialized and ethnic separation does occur for some groups. There is a high degree of separation of Blacks and a moderate separation of poor Asians from the non-poor population. To a lesser extent and outside Quebec, poor French-speaking people are separated from non-poor.

Since the 1991 Census, used by Fong and Shibuya, figures from the 1996 Census showed that the poor population of metropolitan areas was growing at a much greater rate than the population as a whole. Whereas the metropolitan population grew by 6.9 percent, the poor population in the same areas grew by 33.8 percent (Lee, 2000). Moreover, the poor population tended to be in the centre of the cities. For example, the percentage of poor in the centre of Toronto was 27.5 (Lee, 2000:91). In 2000, the Canadian Council for Social Development (CCSD) and the United Way of Greater Toronto (UWGT) wrote a report to identify the current problems. Among their key findings were:

■ Income gaps also grew in the 1990s between the poor and non-poor neighbourhoods in the city. The median income in Toronto's 12 poorest neighbourhoods fell from $43 600 in 1990 to $36 800 in 1999 (in 1999 constant dollars), or a loss of $6800 in real income in the decade;

- The rate of poverty for all persons in Toronto rose from 22.6 percent in 1995 to 23.3 percent in 1999—a 0.7 percent increase. By comparison, poverty grew by 1.9 percent within the 12 neighbourhoods with the highest rates of poverty; and

- Although there are some very distressed neighbourhoods in Toronto and pockets of poverty where more than one-third of the population is poor, poverty is still quite widely dispersed across the city. In both 1995 and 1999, the 12 lowest-income neighbourhoods contained about 13 percent of the city's population, but over 18 percent of the population living in poverty. These bottom 12 neighbourhoods had poverty rates of 29 percent or higher in 1999, but another 72 neighbourhoods had poverty rates between 12 percent and 29 percent (CCSD and UNGT, 2000).

New data from the 2001 Census show that the proportion of visible minorities has grown in Canadian cities. Table 16.1 shows the growth in the proportion of visible minorities in the Census Metropolitan Areas (CMAs) in Canada from 1991 to 2001. At the top of the list, visible minorities constitute 36.9 percent and 36.8 percent of the populations of Vancouver and Toronto respectively. And in just about every other major CMA the proportion of visible minorities has grown substantially. However, the proportion of visible minorities in a CMA does not indicate the extent of segregation in that area. The 2001 Census release does provide maps of the major CMAs showing the concentration of visible minorities by individual census tracts. It is not possible to include maps for every major city in Canada in this textbook, but you can see the concentration of visible minorities in the CMAs by going to the website: **http://geodepot.statcan.ca/Diss/Maps/ThematicMaps/Ethnocultural_e.cfm**. According to these maps, the concentration of visible minorities seems greater in Montreal than in Toronto or Vancouver, where they are more evenly distributed. This segregation may help account for the findings of a report that shows that, in Montreal, Blacks had a higher unemployment rate than in the rest of Canada (26.5 vs. 19.3 percent) and a much higher rate than non-Blacks (26.5 vs. 9.9 percent) (Solyom, 2001:A14).

The separation of the poor and non-poor also appears to be increasing to an even higher degree around the world.

TABLE 16.1   Proportion of Visible Minorities, Census Metropolitan Areas, 2001, 1996, and 1991

	2001	1996 %	1991
Canada	**13.4**	**11.2**	**9.4**
Vancouver	36.9	31.1	24.0
Toronto	36.8	31.6	25.8
Abbotsford	17.8	12.9	10.6
Calgary	17.5	15.6	13.7
Edmonton	14.6	13.5	12.7
Ottawa-Hull[1]	14.1	11.7	10.2
Ontario part	17.3	14.5	12.3
Quebec part	4.3	3.1	3.7
Montreal	13.6	12.2	11.0
Windsor	12.9	9.8	8.9
Winnipeg	12.5	11.1	10.5
Kitchener	10.7	8.9	8.4
Hamilton	9.8	7.9	7.1
London	9.0	7.4	6.6
Victoria	8.9	7.6	7.1
Halifax	7.0	6.6	6.2
Oshawa	7.0	6.0	5.9
Saskatoon	5.6	5.2	4.7
Regina	5.2	5.4	5.1
Kingston	4.7	4.5	4.0
St. Catharines–Niagara	4.5	3.7	3.3
Saint John	2.6	2.1	2.3
Sherbrooke	2.6	2.1	2.3
Thunder Bay	2.2	2.1	2.1
Greater Sudbury	2.0	1.7	2.0
Quebec	1.6	1.5	1.4
St. John's	1.4	1.4	1.4
Trois-Rivières	0.9	0.9	0.8
Chicoutimi-Jonquière[2]	0.6	0.4	0.5

[1]Now known as Ottawa-Gatineau
[2]Now known as Saguenay

Source: Adapted from Canada's Ethnocultural Portrait: The Changing Mosaic, 2001 Census (Analysis Series), *Statistics Canada, p. 59 (Catalogue no. 96F0030XIE2001008). Reproduced with permission.*

PROBLEMS IN
GLOBAL CITIES

Although people have lived in cities for thousands of years, the time is rapidly approaching when more people worldwide will live in or near a city than live in a rural area. In 1900, only 1 person out of 10 lived in a city; by 2005, 1 person out of 2 will live in a city (Crossette, 1996c). Moreover, two-thirds of the world's expected population of 8 to 9 billion people will live in cities by 2025 (Crossette, 1996c). Of all the middle- and low-income regions, Latin America is becoming the most urbanized: Four megacities—Mexico City (20 million), Buenos Aires (12 million), Lima (7 million), and Santiago (5 million)—already contain more than half of the Latin America's population and continue to grow rapidly. By 2010, Rio de Janeiro and São Paulo are expected to have a combined population of about 40 million people living in a 350-mile-long megalopolis (Petersen, 1994). By 2015, no European or U.S. city will be among the 10 most populous in the world (see Table 16.2).

Rapid global population growth is producing a wide variety of urban problems, including overcrowding, environmental pollution, and the disappearance of farmland. In fact, many cities in middle- and low-income nations are quickly reaching the point at which food, housing, and basic public services are available to only a limited segment of the population (Crossette, 1996c). With urban populations growing at a rate of 170 000 people a day in 1996, cities such as Cairo, Lagos, Dhaka, Beijing, and São Paulo are likely to soon have acute water shortages; Mexico City is already experiencing a chronic water shortage (*New York Times*, 1996).

Natural increases in population (higher birth rates than death rates) account for two-thirds of new urban growth, and rural-to-urban migration accounts for the rest. Some people move from rural areas to urban areas because they have been displaced from their land. Others move because they are looking for a better life. No matter what the reason, migration has caused rapid growth in cities in sub-Saharan Africa, India, Algeria, and Egypt. At the same time that the population is growing rapidly, the amount of farmland available for growing crops to feed people is decreasing. In Egypt, for example, land that was previously used for growing crops is now used for petroleum refineries, food-processing plants, and other factories (Kaplan, 1996). Some analysts believe that the United Nations should encourage governments to concentrate on rural development; otherwise, acute food shortages brought about by unchecked rural-to-urban migration may lead to riots (Kaplan, 1996).

As global urbanization has increased over the past three decades, differences in urban areas based on economic development at the national level have become apparent. According to sociologist Immanuel Wallerstein

TABLE 16.2   Populations of the World's 10 Largest Cities

(In Millions, Estimated)			
1996		**2015**	
Tokyo, Japan	26.8	Tokyo, Japan	28.7
São Paulo, Brazil	16.4	Bombay, India	27.4
New York City, U.S.A.	16.3	Lagos, Nigeria	24.4
Mexico City, Mexico	15.6	Shanghai, China	23.4
Bombay, India	15.1	Jakarta, Indonesia	21.2
Shanghai, China	15.1	São Paulo, Brazil	20.8
Los Angeles, U.S.A.	12.4	Karachi, Pakistan	20.6
Beijing, China	12.4	Beijing, China	19.4
Calcutta, India	11.7	Dhaka, Bangladesh	19.0
Seoul, South Korea	11.6	Mexico City, Mexico	18.8

Source: "The Megacity Summit," New York Times, 1996 (April 8):A14.

(1984), nations occupy one of three positions in the global economy: core, semi-peripheral, and peripheral. *Core nations* **are dominant capitalist centres characterized by high levels of industrialization and urbanization.** The United States, Japan, and Germany, among others, are core nations. Some cities in core nations are referred to as *global cities*—interconnected urban areas that are centres of political, economic, and cultural activity. New York, Tokyo, and London are generally considered the largest global cities. They are also considered postindustrial cities because their economic base has shifted largely from heavy manufacturing to information technologies and services such as accounting, marketing, finance, mergers and acquisitions, telecommunications, and other highly specialized fields (Friedmann, 1995). Global cities are the sites of new and innovative product development and marketing, and they often are the "command posts" for the world economy (Sassen, 1995). But economic prosperity is not shared equally by all people in the core nation global cities. Growing numbers of poor people work in low-wage service sector jobs or in assembly production, in which they are paid by the item (piecework) for what they produce but they have no employment benefits or job security. Sometimes the living conditions of these workers more closely resemble the living conditions of workers in semiperipheral nations than those of middle-class workers in their own country.

Most African countries and many countries in South America and the Caribbean are *peripheral nations*—**nations that depend on core nations for capital, have little or no industrialization (other than what may be brought in by core nations), and have uneven patterns of urbanization.** According to Wallerstein (1984), the wealthy in peripheral nations support the exploitation of poor workers by core nation capitalists in return for maintaining their own wealth and position. Poverty is thus perpetuated, and the problems worsen because of the unprecedented population growth in these countries.

Between the core and the peripheral nations are the *semiperipheral nations*, **which are more developed than peripheral nations but less developed than core nations.** Only two global cities are located in semi-peripheral nations: São Paulo, Brazil, the centre of the Brazilian economy, and Singapore, the economic centre for a multicountry region in Southeast Asia (Friedmann, 1995). Like peripheral nations, semiperipheral nations—

Overcrowded living conditions are a way of life for people residing in this area of Bombay. How will rapid population growth in the future affect urban areas in global cities?

such as India, Iran, and Mexico—are confronted with unprecedented population growth. In addition, a steady flow of rural migrants to large cities is creating enormous urban problems. Semiperipheral nations exploit peripheral nations, just as the core nations exploit both the semiperipheral and the peripheral nations.

According to Wallerstein, it is very difficult—if not impossible—for peripheral and semiperipheral nations to ever occupy anything but their marginal positions in the classlike structure of the world economy because of their exploitation by the core nations (Wallerstein, 1984). Capital investment by core nations results in uneven economic growth, and in the process, the disparity between the rich and the poor in the major cities increases. Such economic disparity and urban growth is obvious at the U.S.–Mexican border, where transnational corporations have built *maquiladora plants*, factories where goods are assembled by low-wage workers—on the Mexican side—to keep production costs down. The demand for workers in these plants has caused thousands of people to move from the rural areas of Mexico to urban areas along the border in hope of earning higher wages. The influx has pushed already overcrowded cities far beyond their capacity. Because their wages are low and affordable housing is nonexistent, many people live in central city slums or at the edge of cities in *shantytowns*, where houses are made from discarded materials. Squatters are the most rapidly growing segment of the population in many Mexican cities (Flanagan, 1995).

Social analysts are just beginning to develop comprehensive perspectives on the position of cities in the contemporary world economy, and not all analysts agree with Wallerstein's hierarchy (1984). However, most scholars acknowledge that nations throughout the world are influenced by a relatively small number of cities (e.g., New York) as well as by transnational corporations that have brought about a shift from an international to a more global economy (see Knox and Taylor, 1995; Wilson, 1997). In middle- and low-income nations, all social problems are "incubated and magnified in cities" (Crossette, 1996c:A3).

PERSPECTIVES ON URBAN PROBLEMS

Throughout the 20th century, sociologists have analyzed urban problems to determine the causes and consequences of rapid industrialization and urbanization for people's daily lives and the structure of society. The conclusions they reach about the underlying problems and possible solutions depend on the framework they apply.

The Functionalist Perspective

In examining urban problems, most functionalists focus on three processes that have contributed to social disorganization and the disruption of social institutions. First, mass migration from rural areas to urban areas during the industrializing of Canada contributed to social disorganization by weakening personal ties in family, religion, education, and other institutions. Second, large-scale immigration in the late 19th and early 20th centuries was more than most cities could absorb, and many individuals were never fully assimilated into the cultural mainstream. With larger numbers of strangers living close together in central cities, symptoms of social disorganization, such as high rates of crime, mental illness, and suicide, grew more pronounced. According to Durkheim (1893/1933), urban life changes people's relationships. Rural areas are characterized by *mechanical solidarity*—**social bonds based on shared religious beliefs and a simple division**

of labour—but these bonds are changed with urbanization. Urban areas are characterized by *organic solidarity*—**social bonds based on interdependence and an elaborate division of labour (specialization).** Although Durkheim was optimistic that urbanization could be positive, he also thought that some things were lost in the process. Third, mass suburbanization created additional social disorganization, and many central cities in the U.S., though less so in Canada, have been unable to reach an equilibrium since the mass exodus to the suburbs following World War II. According to urban ecologist Amos Hawley (1950, 1981), new technologies, such as commuter railways and automobiles, have led to the decentralization of city life and the movement of industry from the central city to the suburbs, with disastrous results for some people. Although urbanization, mass immigration, and suburbanization have had functional consequences—including citizenship, job opportunities, and home ownership—for many people, they have also created problems, particularly for people who are left behind in rapidly declining parts of central cities and people who experience discrimination.

Besides emphasizing processes, functionalists also emphasize systems. Sociologist Talcott Parsons (1966:28) identified four systems that interact with each other: the cultural system, social system, personality system, and behavioural organism. William Michelson (1976:24) has drawn attention to a fifth system, the environmental system, in particular the human-made physical, or built, environment, most fully illustrated by the urban environment. He suggested that the effects of the phenomena in the built environment on the other systems, and vice versa, should be studied. Michelson also developed the concept of *congruence* to indicate that some states of variables in one system may coexist with some states of variables in another system better than with others. Mismatches of states of variables constitute incongruence. An example of incongruence is the building of economically efficient highrise subsidized housing for families with small children, like the Pruitt-Igoe project in St. Louis mentioned above; mothers living in such projects are not able to follow their children to other floors and ground level to supervise or protect them (Michelson, 1976:26). Highrise public housing has also had problems with property damage and bullying because of lack of supervision.

The Conflict Perspective

Conflict analysts do not believe that cities grow or decline by chance. Members of the capitalist class and political elites make far-reaching decisions about land use and urban development that benefit some people at the expense of others (Castells, 1977; Feagin and Parker, 1990). According to conflict theorists, the upper classes have successfully maintained class-based and sometimes racialized segregation (in the United States) through political control and legal strategies such as municipal incorporation, defensive annexation, restrictive covenants, and zoning regulations (Feagin and Parker, 1990; Higley, 1995). But where do these practices leave everyone else? Marx suggested that cities are the arenas in which the intertwined processes of class conflict and capital accumulation take place; class consciousness and worker revolt are more likely to develop when workers are concentrated in urban areas (Flanagan, 1995).

Contemporary conflict theorists Joe R. Feagin and Robert Parker (1990) speak of a *political economy model*, believing that both economic and political factors affect patterns of urban growth and decline. Urban growth, they say, is influenced by capital investment decisions, power and resource inequality, class and class conflict, and government subsidy programs. Members of the capitalist class choose corporate locations, decide on sites for shopping centres and factories, and spread the population that can afford to purchase homes into sprawling suburbs located exactly where the capitalists think they should be located (Feagin and Parker, 1990). In this view, a few hundred financial institutions and developers finance and construct most major and many smaller urban development projects, including skyscrapers, shopping malls, and suburban housing projects. These decision makers can make housing more affordable or totally unaffordable for many people. Ultimately, their motivation rests not in benefiting the community, but rather in making a profit, and the cities they produce reflect this mindset (Feagin and Parker, 1990).

The concept of *uneven development*—the tendency of some neighbourhoods, cities, or regions to grow and prosper while others stagnate and decline—is a byproduct of the political economy model of urban development (Perry and Watkins, 1977). Conflict theorists argue that uneven development reflects inequalities of wealth and power in society. Uneven development not only affects areas in decline but also produces external costs that are paid by the entire community. Among these costs are increased pollution, traffic congestion, and rising rates of crime and violence. According to sociologist Mark Gottdiener (1985:214), these costs are "intrinsic to the very core of capitalism, and those who profit the most from development are not called upon to remedy its side effects." One advantage of the political economy framework is that it can be used to study cities in middle- and low-income nations as well as high-income nations (see Jaffee, 1990; Knox and Taylor, 1995; Wilson, 1997).

Uneven development does not occur in the same way in Canadian cities as it does in U. S. cities. Canadian city governments are more actively involved in land-use management and are committed more strongly than American city governments to public services, including transit, parks, and libraries. Canadian cities also are characterized by more equal distribution of public services than the more politically fragmented American cities (Ley and Bourne, 1993). Thus, the land and property values in the Canadian central city remain highly competitive despite a substantial rate of suburban development.

This difference in uneven development does not mean that corporate capitalism does not have an effect on major cities in Canada. For example, Gertler (2001:123) notes that Toronto's share of the top 500 Canadian firms declined from 40 percent to 35 percent from 1989 to 1999 (pre– and post–North American Free Trade Agreement) due primarily to a decline in foreign-based Canadian subsidiaries, from 105 to 85. He suggests that a worldwide concentration of corporate control is likely occurring. However, since then, Toronto's share of headquarters of Canadian firms has increased slightly, from 89 to 91. Other centres, like Calgary, Vancouver, and Ottawa, have seen substantial growth in headquarters placement from both Canadian and foreign firms (Gertler, 2001:123). This movement could have harmful effects for workers and their families and merchants in the older downtowns of Toronto and Montreal unless other projects, like in-fill housing (for example, the King West Village mentioned earlier) is developed to fill the void of the former headquarters.

SOCIAL PROBLEMS AND SOCIAL POLICY

BOX 16.2   Saving Our Cities

A wide variety of policies are being recommended to save Canadian cities. Implicitly following a functional perspective, some politicians and advocates have recommended amalgamation of cities and their suburbs and edge cities, or at least, regional thinking. Rob MacIssac (2002:T3), mayor of Burlington, part of the "905" (named after the telephone exchange) edge city of Toronto and a member of the Ontario government's Smart Growth Panel, states that "we need to be thinking about the connectedness of the entire Golden Horseshoe from Oshawa to Barrie to St. Catharines—one continuous area with its own economy." He says that infrastructure to deal with such problems as pollution, congestion, and land use must be planned and maintained over 25- or 50-year horizons, and politicians must be willing to cut services or raise taxes or user fees. He concludes that, because Ontario's and Canada's futures are depending on it, we should "insist on the creation of a city-region we deserve" (MacIssac, 2002:T3). However, MacIssac does acknowledge that co-operation between cities and edge cities is difficult, because the main city's politicians do not always think about the region and edge cities' politicians fear being taken over by the main city (MacIssac, 2002:T3).

Second, implicitly following a conflict perspective, many politicians and advocates would like to see a redistribution of income among the federal, provincial, and municipal governments. Gaining income primarily from property taxes, cities gain less than 10 percent of the taxes raised in Canada, and property taxes have increased less than other forms of taxes during the 1990s. Thus, advocates would like to see a more definite revenue stream, perhaps coming from a tax source like the GST or a percentage of federal and provincial taxes. Recently, some federal cabinet ministers, such as David Collenette (2002:T3), have suggested that "the federal government has an obligation to relieve urban congestion, to remove impediments to trade and productivity, to ensure air and water quality to improve the health of Canadians, and to help provide shelter for those less fortunate." However, Collenette did go on to state that "there can be no issuing of blank cheques," implying that no new sources of income will be designated for cities. A key problem is that, in Canada, cities are the responsibilities of provinces, so the federal government has to work with the provincial governments to provide help for the cities. For the federal government to be able to fund cities separately, a fundamental change in the nature of Canadian federalism would be needed.

Third, implicitly following the interactionist perspective, some advocates recommend promoting the creativity and dynamism of the city by attracting creative people. Richard Florida has written about the importance of the availability of technology, talent, and tolerance to attract creative people to promote economic development. It is not usually possible for cities to grow just with technology and world class universities, as London, Ontario, a smaller city, has. Cities also have to be sufficiently tolerant and open-minded to attract and retain top creative talent (Florida, 2002:T8).

Besides being tolerant and open to diversity, cities should welcome immigrants, build participatory features like bike paths and waterfronts, and cut back on big generic shopping malls. Creating comprehensive transit plans—including express bus service around the city, new or shoulder bus lanes for highways, and expanded park and ride lots, as recently recommended by the Central Ontario Smart Growth Panel (Brennan, 2002:A1)—would also help people mix and participate in city life. Such plans could have very beneficial results, but they can also be stalled by lack of resources and political will.

Obviously, many major proposals as well as proposals to encourage individual participation exist to help us save our cities. What do you think should be done and how can you see yourself contributing?

The Interactionist Perspective

Interactionists examine urban problems from the standpoint of people's *experience* of urban life and how they subjectively define the reality of city living. How does city life affect the people who live in a city? According to early German sociologist Georg Simmel (1950), urban life is so highly stimulating that people have no choice but to become somewhat insensitive to events and individuals around them. Urban residents generally avoid emotional involvement with one another and try to ignore the events—including, possibly, violence and crime—that take place nearby. They are wary of other people, looking at others as strangers; some people act reserved to cloak deeper feelings of distrust or dislike toward others. At the same time, Simmel thought that urban living could be liberating because it gives people opportunities for individualism and autonomy (Flanagan, 1995).

On the basis of Simmel's observations of social relations in the city, early University of Chicago sociologist Louis Wirth (1938) suggested that urbanism is a "way of life" that increases the incidence of both social and personality disorders in individuals. *Urbanism* refers to the distinctive social and psychological patterns of life that are typically found in the city. According to Wirth, the size, density, and heterogeneity of urban populations result in an elaborate division of labour and in spatial segregation of people by racialization/ethnicity, social class, religion, and/or lifestyle. The division of labour and spatial segregation produce feelings of alienation, powerlessness, and loneliness.

In contrast to Wirth's gloomy analysis of urban life, sociologist Herbert Gans (1962/1982) believed that not everyone experiences the city in the same way. On the basis of research in the West End of Boston in the late 1950s, Gans concluded that many residents develop strong loyalties and a sense of community in central city areas that outsiders often view negatively. According to Gans, in large urban areas, personal behaviour is shaped by the type of neighbourhood a person lives in. For example, *cosmopolites*—students, artists, writers, musicians, entertainers, and professionals—view the city as a place where they can be close to cultural facilities and people with whom they share common interests. *Unmarried people* and *childless couples* live in the city because they want to be close to work and entertainment. *Ethnic villagers* live in ethnically segregated neighbourhoods because they feel most comfortable within their own group. The *deprived* and the *trapped* live in the city because they believe they have no other alternatives. Gans concluded that the city is a pleasure and a challenge for some urban dwellers and an urban nightmare for others.

According to interactionists, the deprived and the trapped contribute to a social construction of reality that stereotypes city dwellers as poor, down-and-out, and sometimes dangerous, whereas most city dwellers are not this way at all. Because of the U.S. movies and television shows seen by Canadians, and, particularly, because of extensive media coverage of crime or racialized unrest in the largest metropolitan areas of the U.S., which presents a very negative image of cities, an anti-urban bias remains strong among many nonurban dwellers.

On the other hand, Richard Florida, a professor of regional development, like Gans, believes that cities can be pleasurable and tolerant, and thus attract the kind of creative people (what he calls the Creative Class) that will hold the key to Canada's economic future. He compiled, with Canadian collaborator Meric Gertler, a Bohemian Index, a measure of talent that looks at Canadian cities' per capita population of artists, poets, novelists, and various entertainers using the 1996 Census. Florida and Gertler concluded that Vancouver had 12.85 bohemians per 1000 population and, slightly behind it, Toronto had 12 bohemians per 1000 (or about 50 000 people). In comparison with American cities, the two Canadian cities rank below but close to San Francisco, New York, Los Angeles, Seattle, and Washington (Florida, 2002:T8).

Finally, cities are also known for problems of loneliness and alienation. Some interactionists propose that people who live in large metropolitan areas develop subcultural ties to help them feel a sense of community and identity. A *subculture* **is a group of people who share a distinctive set of cultural beliefs and behaviors that set them apart from the larger society.** Joining an interest group—from bowling with friends from the office to volunteering in a literacy program—is one way of feeling connected. Ethnic neighbourhoods are an example of subcultures; some are tightly knit, whereas others have little influence on residents' daily lives. Interactionists note that members of subcultures, especially those based on racialization, ethnicity, or religion, sometimes come into conflict with each other. These conflicts can result in verbal exchanges, hate crimes, or other physical violence, or they can cause the individuals to withdraw almost entirely from the larger community and become more intensely involved with the subculture. (See Chapter 12, Box 12.2, to discover how some teachers and students are challenging subcultural stereotypes.)

The Feminist Perspective

In the same way that great social policy issues are urban policy issues, feminist analyses are germane to virtually every aspect of city life. Many of these analyses have been dealt with in other chapters; here are just a couple of examples of feminism's application to urban problems. Some feminist theorists emphasize the occupational opportunities, freedom, convenience, and stimulation for women present in cities but not available in smaller centres or suburbs—Betty Freidan (1963) and, more recently, Margrit Eichler (1995) have been very critical of the lack of stimulation and the oppressiveness of dealing with life in a low-density suburb. In cities, women have the chance to participate in a variety of occupations, and they are very well represented in the (usually lowly paid) jobs that constitute the Bohemian Index (e.g., artists and entertainers). Moreover, in cities, women do not have to worry about what the neighbours will think of their behaviour. They can choose to interact with their neighbours, or not. Lastly, women who live in a city instead of a suburb and have the dual roles of worker and mother will usually have a shorter commute to their jobs and more locally available services. Thus, they may feel less stress in fulfilling their responsibilities and have more time for themselves. On the other hand, some feminists have been so concerned about the threats to women at night in cities that they have organized "Take Back the Night" marches in most major cities.

URBAN PROBLEMS IN THE FUTURE

In a best-case scenario, Canada would convert to regional governments to provide water, wastewater (sewage), transportation, schools, parks, hospitals, and other public services. In this scenario, revenues would be shared among central cities, affluent suburbs, and edge cities, since everyone would benefit from the improved quality of life. Cities would get a permanent source of taxation, besides property taxes; and, they would create a tolerant and creative climate (see Box 16.2). As we wait and hope for solutions to the problems of urbanization at the macrolevel, we can, meanwhile—as citizens, neighbours, tenants, property owners, workers, employers, and users of public and private services throughout the city—exercise some degree of control over the quality of life in our own communities. There is increasing impetus to take control because one thing is certain: As the world population continues to grow in this century, urban problems will intensify, and this will affect us all.

WHAT CAN YOU DO?

- Many downtown agencies would be eager to have your help, as a facilitator for programs, newsletter helper, advocacy worker, even computer room supervisor. Just call one and volunteer.

- If you live in a city, you might join your local residents' association. These associations are always looking for volunteer help for committees: to undertake liaison with the police, to have representatives for every street in the area, to keep track of problems like drug dealing and prostitution, and to undertake social projects. Be aware that some of the members of some of these groups are more concerned with enhancing the value of their properties than with solving social problems in the area and may seek to reduce local shelters and social agencies. For an example of the concerns and activities of a residents' association, visit Cabbagetown South in Toronto (website: **www.CabbagetownSouth.ca** [the "Members Area" requires a password]).

- If you are searching for a place to live and like the idea of working with your neighbours, try cooperative housing. You will gain a great experience working with others.

- Join a group lobbying for the homeless. Public Interest Research Groups are found on many university and college campuses, and they sometimes, like the Ontario Public Interest Research Group in Toronto, support action to help the homeless. In Toronto, some students have joined a tent city, created in a public garden in the wintertime, to show solidarity with the homeless.

- Participate in irregular programs to plant trees or clean up your neighbourhood.

- Sit in on a city council meeting so you can learn more about the activities and governance of a city and meet other interested citizens.

- Keep in mind that NIMBY (Not In My Back Yard) ideas can emerge anywhere. Confront those ideas in your neighbourhood.

- Participate in the "Take Back the Night" march that occurs annually in most cities in the fall.

SUMMARY

HOW DID URBANIZATION COME ABOUT?

Urbanization—the process by which an increasing proportion of a population lives in cities rather than rural areas—began with industrialization. Before the Industrial Revolution, most people lived in sparsely populated rural areas, where they farmed. Industrialization led to the growth of cities; and urbanization brought about profound changes in societies and spawned new social problems such as housing shortages, overcrowding, unsanitary conditions, environmental pollution, and crime.

HOW DID MASS SUBURBANIZATION OCCUR AND WHAT WERE THE RESULTS?

Mass suburbanization began with government efforts to correct the housing shortage that followed World War II. The Central (now Canada) Mortgage and Housing Corporation, by granting mortgages, contributed to the building of half a million homes between 1946 and 1951. Other factors included the availability of inexpensive land, low-cost mass construction methods, new federally financed highway systems, inexpensive gasoline, and consumer demand for single-family homes on individually owned lots. Mass suburbanization brought about a dramatic shift in the distribution of the Canadian population and set up an ongoing economic division of interests between cities and suburbs.

WHY ARE MANY CITIES IN FISCAL CRISIS?

Large numbers of middle- and upper-income people have moved out of the central cities to the suburbs, and more recently, many retail businesses and corporations have also moved to the suburbs or moved their operations abroad. The shrinking central cities have been left with greatly reduced sources of revenue. Many of the remaining central city residents are poor, unemployed, or older people living on fixed incomes, who cannot afford to pay higher taxes. At the same time, city governments must still provide city services for them. Moreover, suburbanites who regularly use city services do not pay taxes to the city to keep up these services.

WHY IS THERE A HOUSING SHORTAGE IN CANADA AND WHAT IS BEING DONE ABOUT IT?

A major reason for the housing shortage is that Canada has yet to find a way to provide safe, livable, low-income housing. In addition, as part of governmental cutbacks in the mid-1990s, the federal and provincial governments stopped building social housing. Some non-governmental groups have been doing good work. One of the most successful initiatives for creating affordable housing is the volunteer organization Habitat for Humanity.

HOW GREAT A PROBLEM IS HOMELESSNESS? ARE THERE ANY SOLUTIONS?

Accurate data on the actual number of the homeless are extremely difficult to get because homeless people avoid interviews with census takers and social researchers. The Golden Report showed that the fastest-growing segment of the homeless population is families and children. Most experts agree that any long-term, successful solution to homelessness must take structural factors into account, especially low-income housing and mental-health care.

DOES RESIDENTIAL RACIALIZED OR ETHNIC SEGREGATION EXIST?

Spatial separation of the poor and non-poor is greater than separation of racialized/ethnic groups. While, in contrast to in U.S. cities, there are no extensive areas of blight, decay, or abandoned housing in Canadian cities, there are pockets of poor racialized/ethnic groups coexisting beside upscale neighbourhoods.

WHAT ARE THE MAJOR PROBLEMS IN GLOBAL CITIES?

By 2005, one out of every two people in the world will live in a city. Increasing population accounts for two-thirds of the new urban growth, and rural-to-urban migration accounts for the rest. Rapid urban growth brings a wide variety of problems, including overcrowding, environmental pollution, and the disappearance of farmland. The exploitation of semiperipheral nations by core nations and of peripheral nations by both semiperipheral and core nations serves to increase the urban problems in these nations. Core nations are dominant capitalist centres characterized by high levels of industrialization and urbanization. Peripheral nations depend on core nations for capital, have little or no industrialization (other than what is brought in by core nations), and have uneven patterns of urbanization. Semiperipheral nations are more developed than peripheral nations but less developed than core nations.

WHAT IS THE FUNCTIONALIST PERSPECTIVE ON URBAN PROBLEMS?

Functionalists believe that today's urban problems are the result of mass migration from rural areas during the Industrial Revolution, large-scale immigration in the late 19th and early 20th centuries, and mass suburbanization. One solution is to create regional governments.

WHAT IS THE CONFLICT PERSPECTIVE ON URBAN PROBLEMS?

Conflict theorists believe that cities grow or decline according to decisions made by capitalists and the political elite. In other words, these theorists use a political economy model. Urban problems can be reduced through political activism and organized resistance to oppressive conditions.

WHAT IS THE INTERACTIONIST PERSPECTIVE ON URBAN PROBLEMS?

Interactionists look at how people subjectively experience urban life. According to German sociologist Georg Simmel, urban life is so stimulating that people have no choice but to become somewhat insensitive to people and events around them. On the other hand, urban living gives people opportunities for individualism and autonomy. Sociologist Louis Wirth expanded on Simmel's ideas, saying that urbanism produces feelings of alienation and powerlessness. Herbert Gans concluded from his research that city life is a pleasure for some and a nightmare for others. Commenting on Toronto and Vancouver, Richard Florida states these cities have a high rate of Creative Class people because of the stimulation and tolerance in these cities, and this is a key to a bright economic future. A way to avoid the nightmare of alienation is to develop subcultural ties.

WHAT IS THE FEMINIST PERSPECTIVE ON URBAN PROBLEMS?

Feminist theorists emphasize the occupational opportunities, the freedom from scrutiny, and the convenience of short distances between work and home that allows fulfillment of multiple roles for women.

KEY TERMS

core nations,   p. 384
deindustrialization,   p. 376
edge city,   p. 374
gentrification,   p. 380
mechanical solidarity,   p. 385

megalopolis,   p. 374
organic solidarity,   p. 385
peripheral nations,   p. 384
semiperipheral nations,   p. 384
subculture,   p. 388

QUESTIONS FOR CRITICAL THINKING

1. Where do you live—in the core central city, an edge city, a suburb, or a megalopolis? What examples from your everyday life can you give that relate to the problems described in this chapter? Which sociological perspective do you think best explains the urban problems you observe?

2. The government has so far failed to provide adequate low-income and poverty-level housing. What new initiatives can you suggest?

3. The 2001 Census releases have included maps of the distribution of visible minorities in the Census Metropolitan Areas. They are available at **http://geodepot. statcan.ca/Diss/Maps/ThematicMaps/Ethnocultural_ e.cfm**. Study the map of your area and compare it to maps of other cities. How segregated are racialized/ethnic groups? What do you think can be done to ensure that Canadian cities do not have the segregation that causes so many problems in the U.S.?

WEBLINKS

2001 Census: Ethnocultural Portrait of Canada

www12.statcan.ca/english/census01/release/ release5.cfm

This site introduces two 2001 Census releases, our ethnocultural portrait and information about immigration and citizenship, both with discussion, tables, and maps.

2001 Census: Where We Live

www12.statcan.ca/english/census01/release/ pop_dwell.cfm

Where We Live, the first of the 2001 Census releases, shows the general population increase and the extent of urbanization in Canada, with discussion, tables, and maps.

Statistics Canada: Community Profiles, 2001

www12.statcan.ca/english/Profil01/ PlaceSearchForm1.cfm

Informative profiles of Canada's communities.

Teaching and Learning About Canada

www.canadainfolink.ca/cities.htm

This site provides information about the 30 largest metropolitan/urban centres in Canada based on the 2001 Census data, with links to cities and provinces.

Urban Alliance on Race Relations (UARR)

www.tgmag.ca/magic/uarr.html

The UARR organizes workshops, seminars, and conferences and publishes reports, builds alliances, etc., to promote understanding around anti-racist issues.

Urbanization in Asia

www.prb.org/Template.cfm?Section= PRB&template=/ContentManagement/ ContentDisplay.cfm&ContentID=3931

This site presents a discussion of urbanization in Asia by Terry McGee, a professor of geography at the University of British Columbia. A highlight is a comparison of Seoul, South Korea, and Dhaka, Bangladesh.

17

GLOBAL SOCIAL PROBLEMS

OUR COMMON HUMANITY— ADDRESSING WAR AND TERRORISM

Beware the leader who bangs the drums of war in order to whip the citizenry into a patriotic fervor, for patriotism is indeed a double-edged sword. It both emboldens the blood, just as it narrows the mind. And when the drums of war have reached a fever pitch and the blood boils with hate and the mind has closed, the leader will have no need in seizing the rights of the citizenry. Rather, the citizenry, infused with fear and blinded by patriotism, will offer up all of their rights unto the leader and gladly so . . .

A famous quote about the drawbacks of patriotism that is credited by many to Gaius Julius Caesar

Our response involves far more than instant retaliation and isolated strikes. Americans should not expect one battle, but a lengthy campaign, unlike any other we have ever seen. It may include dramatic strikes, visible on TV, and covert operations, secret even in success. We will starve terrorists of funding, turn them one against another, drive them from place to place, until there is no refuge or no rest. And we will pursue nations that provide aid or safe haven to terrorism. Every nation, in every region, now has a decision to make. Either you are with us, or you are with the terrorists. From this day forward, any nation that continues to harbor or support terrorism will be regarded by the United States as a hostile regime. . . . The course of this conflict is not known, yet its outcome is certain. Freedom and fear, justice and cruelty, have always been at war, and we know that God is not neutral between them. Fellow citizens, we'll meet violence with patient justice—assured of the rightness of our cause and confident of the victories to come. In all that lies before us, may God grant us wisdom, and may He watch over the United States of America.

President George W. Bush, outlining his declaration of war against terrorism in his address to a Joint Session of Congress and the American People in Washington, D.C., on September 20, 2001

Naturally the common people don't want war . . . That is understood. But, after all, it is the leaders of the country who determine the policy and it is always a simple matter to drag the people along, whether it is a democracy, or a fascist dictatorship, or a parliament, or a communist dictatorship. Voice or no voice, the people can always be brought to the bidding of the leaders. That is easy. All you have to do is tell them they are being attacked, and denounce the peacemakers for lack of patriotism and exposing the country to danger. It works the same in any country.

Hermann Goering, president of the Reichstag, Nazi Party, and Luftwaffe Commander in Chief, testifying at the Nuremberg Trials in 1946 (in Gilbert, 1995)

Deep down we must have a real affection for each other, a clear realization or recognition of our shared human status. At the same time, we must openly accept all ideologies and systems as means of solving humanity's problems. One country, one nation, one ideology, one system is not sufficient. It is helpful to have a variety of different approaches on the basis of a deep feeling of the basic sameness of humanity. We can then make a joint effort to solve the problems of the whole of humankind. The problems human society is facing in terms of economic development, the crisis of energy, the tension between the poor and the rich nations, and many geopolitical problems can be solved if we understand each other's fundamental humanity, respect each other's rights, share each other's problems and sufferings, and then make a joint effort to address them.

His Holiness the Dalai Lama, speaking about pathways to peace (1991:13)

With the collapse of the former Soviet Union and the end of the Cold War between the United States and the former Soviet bloc in the 1980s, prospects for world peace were bright. This hope was challenged in 2001 by the United States' declaration of sustained war against nations that harbour terrorism. The war is mandated to expand anywhere in the world and will be fought with the participation of several other allied nations, including Canada. In 2003, the threat of imminent war has been made real by the United States, which maintains that the Iraqi government, with its nuclear capacities and potential for terrorist activity, poses a threat to the world. Citizens across the globe fear this could mark the beginning of World War III. In addition to an impending world war, there is national conflict in Sierra Leone and state-vs.-state conflicts in China, Tibet, and North Korea. Many countries possess nuclear and chemical weaponry that is capable of destroying all life on the planet (Daley, 1997). The importance of peaceful resolutions to armed conflict has never been greater.

The 20th century saw the development of advanced technologies that provided new potential for wars that could be far more deadly than those in the past. These technologies are now defining what war looks like. Long-range, hypersonic munitions that strike from the air have made it unnecessary to send aircraft and soldiers into the theatre of war (Friedman and Friedman, 1996).

Moreover, the stockpile of nuclear weapons from the arms race between the former Soviet Union and the West has vastly increased the potential for waging war on a massive scale.

> In olden times when there was a war, it was a human-to-human confrontation. The victor in battle would directly see the blood and suffering of the defeated enemy. Nowadays, it is much more terrifying because a man in an office can push a button and kill millions of people and never see the human tragedy he has created. The mechanization of war, the mechanization of human conflict, poses an increasing threat to peace. (Dalai Lama, 1991:6)

However, as the capability of waging mechanized war is increasing, so too is global resistance to it. As social analyst and critic Barbara Ehrenreich (1997:239) has said: "If the twentieth century brought the steady advance of war and war-related enterprises, it also brought the beginnings of organized resistance to war . . . in the situation where everyone is expected to participate in one way or another, and where anyone can become a victim whether they participate or not, opposition to the institution of war itself could at last develop." This chapter will examine some of the characteristics of war and terrorism and look at Canada's role in past and upcoming conflicts. We will examine some of the consequences of war—even before it happens, in Canada's case—and look at possible explanations for seeing war as a solution to global conflicts. Finally, we will look at resistance and prospects for peace and discuss the roles and effectiveness of citizen's groups in opposing war.

WAR AS A SOCIAL PROBLEM

What is war? Most people think of war as armed conflict between two countries or two factions within a country, such as the historical 1775 American invasion of the St. Lawrence region of Quebec or the Korean War of 1950. But social scientists define war more broadly, including not only declared wars between nations or parties but also undeclared wars, civil and guerrilla wars, covert operations, and some forms of terrorism (Wright, 1964). To social scientists, *general warfare* refers to violent armed conflict between nations, whereas *regional warfare* refers to conflict between rival factions located within a specific geographic area. Social scientists also say that societies that are prepared at all times for war possess a **war system**—**components of social institutions (e.g., the economy, government, and education) and cultural beliefs and practices that promote the development of warriors, weapons, and war as a normal part of the society and its foreign policy** (Cancian and Gibson, 1990).

How, then, do social scientists define *peace*? Sociologists Francesca M. Cancian and James William Gibson (1990) believe that peace is a less clearly defined concept than war. Cancian and Gibson note that people generally agree that peace is highly desirable, but they often have different ideas of what constitutes peace. Some equate peace with harmonious relations in a world where there is no bloodshed between groups; but sometimes nations equate peace with prevailing in battle (Gibson and Cancian, 1990). Despite the problems associated with distinguishing between war and peace, we can conclude that both consist of actions and beliefs held by people like ourselves and that these actions and beliefs have serious consequences for individuals, groups, and nations.

The Characteristics of War

First and foremost, war is an institution that involves *violence*—behaviour intended to bring pain, physical injury, psychological stress, and/or death to people or to harm or destroy property (Sullivan, 1997). Violence occurs on both micro and macro levels. As we have seen, violence is a component of many social problems, including violent crime and domestic violence. Both of these are forms of *interpersonal violence* and typically involve a relatively small number of people who are responding to a particular situation or who are pursuing their own personal goals. In contrast, war is a form of **collective violence** that **involves organized violence by people seeking to promote their cause or resist social policies or practices that they consider oppressive** (Sullivan, 1997).

War is an abstract concept for many Canadians. It is less abstract for those who have experienced combat, or who are friends and family members of people who have experienced it, or who are survivors of war. Early in Canada's history, during the fighting of civil wars and rebellions, war was much less abstract: It took place at home or close to home. But in the 20th century, military action was transformed: Wars were now fought on foreign soil and vastly more Canadian military personnel were sent into combat. In World War I, for example, Canada, with its a population of 8 million people, sent 418 000 of them overseas to fight. In World War II, Canada entered the war with an entirely Canadian command and forces. At that time, Canada had a population of 12 million people, and 1.1 million of them got into uniform (Veteran Affairs Canada, 2002; Ehrenreich, 1997).

The two world wars were different from each other in a very significant way. In World War I, killing civilians was considered unduly violent, but in World War II civilians were killed intentionally. The targeting of civilians during World War II added a new dimension to war (Hynes, 1997). This is how Ehrenreich (1997:206–207) describes the shift to civilians as the targets of war-related violence:

> By World War II, the destruction (and exploitation) of civilians was deliberate policy on all sides. The British used air power to "de-house" the German population; the U.S. bombed the civilian populations of Hiroshima, Nagasaki, and Dresden; the Germans and Japanese destroyed cities and exploited defeated populations as slave labour. . . . Air power made the mass bombings of civilians possible, but it was the huge involvement of civilians in the industrial side of war that made it seem strategically necessary. . . . In this situation, there were no "innocent" civilians, except possibly children, and the war took on a genocidal character unknown to the more gentlemanly conflict of [World War I].

One of the most significant characteristics of war is its persistence. Following World War II, Canada emerged as a leading "middle power"—assuming the role of peacekeeper and negotiator in international disputes. This was a natural extension for Canada, as the protocol from 1909 to 1946 was that the Prime Minister was to serve as the Canadian Secretary of State for External Affairs. Canadian prime ministers have maintained that tradition and have endeavoured to remain prominent in international affairs, taking part in visits from foreign heads of state, world tours, treaty negotiations, and other activities (National Library of Canada, 2003). Today, some view Canada as a "moral superpower"—one that exercises a "soft power" when it comes to world affairs. Since 1956, Canada has sent peacekeeping forces into operations around the world. Soldiers, police, and civilians have all played prominent roles in separating armies and in the resolution of conflicts in places such as Cypress, the Middle East, Haiti, Bosnia, Cambodia, El Salvador, and Angola. In 2002, Canadian peacekeepers were serving in 14 operations in Europe, Asia, Africa, South America, and the Middle East. However, more than 100 Canadians have been killed while on peacekeeping duties around the world, and operations in both Somalia and Rwanda have led to a crisis of confidence in the Canadian military's peacekeeping efforts (McCluskey, 2002). Diplomatically, Canada seems to now be having trouble maintaining its role as peacekeeper in the world as well as keeping the peace with the United States, our closest neighbour and primary trading partner.

According to Ehrenreich (1997), the end of World War II was marked by the United States government's declaration of itself as the "leader of the free world." The ideology supporting this pronouncement gave the nation's political and economic leaders the impetus to perpetuate the U.S.'s position as a world military superpower. Since that time, the American Congress has established defence spending as a national priority, and the U.S. *military–industrial complex*—**a term referring to the interdependence of the military establishment and private military contractors**—that had emerged during World War II became a massive industrial infrastructure that today produces an array of war-related goods, such as uniforms, tanks, airplanes, and warships. This military–industrial complex flourished during the 1950s, when the international arms race brought about what became known as the *Cold War*—a conflict between nations based on military preparedness and the threat of war but not actual warfare. Between 1950 and the mid-1990s, the U.S. government responded to the perceived "Soviet threat" by spending approximately $10.2 trillion (USD) for its arms buildup. In 1991 alone, the defence industry received more than $121 billion (USD) in government contracts, giving some corporations a virtual monopoly over an entire market in which there was only one buyer (the U.S. government) and very few (if any) competitors.

The Consequences of War

The direct effects of war are loss of human life and serious physical and psychological harm to survivors. It is impossible to determine how many human lives have been lost in wars throughout human history. Were we to attempt to do so, we would need a more precise definition of what constitutes war, and we would have to assume that there would always be survivors available to count the dead (Hynes, 1997).

Despite these difficulties, social analyst Ruth Sivard (1991, 1993) has tackled the problem in a limited way. She has determined that 589 wars have been fought by 142 countries since 1500 and that approximately 142 million lives have been lost. But according to Sivard, more lives were lost in wars during the 20th century than in all of the other centuries combined. World War I took the lives of approximately 8 million combatants and 1 million civilians. The toll was even higher in World War II: More than 50 million people (17 million combatants and 35 million civilians) lost their lives. Over 1.5 million Canadians fought in World War I, World War II, and the Korean War—and, of that number, 110 000 people lost their lives (Veteran Affairs Canada, 1999).

The consequences of all these wars, however, pale when compared to the consequences of an all-out nuclear war. The devastation would be beyond description. Although the development of nuclear weapons may have contributed to peace among the major world powers since the late 1940s, we can see the potentially destructive effects of nuclear war in the U.S. attacks on Hiroshima and Nagasaki, Japan. On August 6, 1945, a U.S. aircraft dropped a 1.5-kiloton atomic bomb on Hiroshima. Three days later, the U.S. dropped a second bomb on Nagasaki. These bombs killed 200 000 people, either instantly or over the next few months as a result of the deadly radiation that rained on the city (Erikson, 1994). One of the few accounts about the morning of August 6 in Hiroshima is given by Hara in the 1975 UNESCO Messenger:

A little after 8 o'clock, the bomb exploded. . . . [there was a] . . . terrible burst, nobody succeeded in giving an explanation to what had happened: the only certainty, they were persons—thousand of persons burnt—that were along the river that crosses Hiroshima were looking for a shelter and for water to drink. The scenery became even more terrible the immediately following mornings, when columns of wheelbarrows took away hundreds of dead bodies: women, men, old men and children indiscriminately, everybody burnt, disfigured and crippled. Some days after, the situation became uncontrollable, the corpses were too many and nobody succeeded in taking them away. The persons died one after the other and nobody came to take the dead bodies away. With the upset air, the alive lived among the corpses. All the ruins in the principal roads were seen in that moment. An empty and gray space extended under a leaden sky. (in Spoto, 2003)

Today, some nuclear warheads held by governments throughout the world are more than 4000 times as powerful as the bombs that were dropped on Japan. In fact, scientists estimate that a nuclear war would kill more than 160 million people outright and that more than 1 billion people would die in the first few hours as a result of radiation poisoning, environmental contamination and destruction, and massive social unrest (Friedman and Friedman, 1996).

The capacity to obliterate the world many times over exists. There are five declared nuclear powers in the world: the United States, Britain, France, Russia and China. Each country has signed onto the 1970 Nuclear Non-Proliferation Treaty (NPT), while the three new nuclear states—Pakistan, Israel, and India—have not. The Non-Proliferation Treaty is a landmark international treaty whose objective is to prevent the spread of nuclear weapons and weapons technology, to promote co-operation in the peaceful uses of nuclear energy, and to further the goal of achieving nuclear disarmament and general and complete disarmament. The NPT represents the only binding commitment in a multilateral treaty to the goal of disarmament by the nuclear-weapon states (United Nations, 2003b). According to the United States, countries thought to be developing nuclear power, even as signatories of the NPT, are Libya, North Korea, Iran, and Iraq (BBC, 2000). While it is difficult to know if nations are developing and stockpiling nuclear weapons, it is common knowledge that, from the 1940s until the early 1990s, when 154 nations signed the Comprehensive Test Ban Treaty, nuclear weapons continued to be tested in all environments—underground, underwater, and in the atmosphere—and in test sites around the world.

According to Greenpeace (1996), since July 16, 1945, there have been 2044 tests worldwide, the equivalent of one test occurring somewhere in the world every nine days for the last 50 years.

It is estimated that the total yield of all the atmospheric nuclear weapons tests conducted is 438 megatons. That's equivalent to 29 200 Hiroshima size bombs. In the 36 years between 1945 and 1980 when atmospheric testing was being conducted this would have been equivalent to exploding a Hiroshima size bomb in the atmosphere every 11 hours. (Greenpeace, 1996)

The former Soviet Union and the United States have also engaged in a program of "Peaceful Nuclear Explosions" (PNEs). These PNEs serve a variety of official purposes, including: deep seismic sounding; creating underground storage cavities; helping to extract gas and oil; extinguishing burning gas or oil wells; and, creating reservoirs. Regardless of their "peaceful" applications, radioactive seepage from these test explosions has left large tracts of land uninhabitable and the health and livelihood of people—particularly marginalized populations who, not accidentally, tend to live near test sites—in miserable conditions. Three types of military activities are responsible for the contamination of many sites around the world, including the Arctic. Russia and the United States are primarily responsible for nuclear activity in Russia, which includes nuclear testing; naval accidents involving nuclear-armed/powered vessels; and the intentional dumping of radioactive materials into the ocean in the Arctic. Together, these activities "raise the spectre of radioactive contamination of the North and, as such, represent a particularly serious threat to the health and welfare of the states and the peoples in the region" (Gizewski, 1994:2).

The use of supercomputers and advanced technology has created a new era of military activity. Military technology is rapidly evolving, and often the danger of handling new weapons as well as deploying them is largely unknown. Technology has also impacted military strategy. Today, military strategy calls for deploying bombs and long-range missiles to eliminate the enemy's weapon production plants and supply centres. Because these plants are located in major cities, civilians are more likely to be killed than they were in the past. And whereas Europe was the primary battleground for most wars from 1500 through World War II,

middle- and low-income nations, with their growing populations, are now the primary sites. Using Iraq as a contemporary example, 11.3 of the 23.6 million people in Iraq, or close to half of the population, are children under the age of 18 years (Bellamy, 2003). With each successive war, more civilians are killed. What justifications are sufficient to support a war in which the death toll is almost certain to include millions of children?

The trend toward more civilian casualties that began in World War II has continued in subsequent wars, including the Vietnam War and the Gulf War (Ehrenreich, 1997). Some analysts believe that civilians accounted for 75 percent of all war-related deaths in the 1980s and nearly 90 percent in the 1990s (Renner, 1993). Other social analysts disagree. In their recent book *The Future of War* (1996), George Friedman and Meredith Friedman argue that the use of precision-guided munitions ("smart weapons") in Desert Storm (another name for the Gulf War) made it possible for the United States to strike particular parts of particular buildings without striking noncombatants, hence keeping the civilian death count low. However, a demographer employed by the U.S. Bureau of the Census has calculated that 40 000 Iraqi soldiers were killed during the war but more than 80 000 Iraqi civilians, mostly women and children, were killed in air strikes—13 000 in precision bombing and 70 000 as a result of disease associated with the systematic destruction of water purification and sewage treatment systems in their country (Colhoun, 1992). Moreover, many hospitals were damaged or destroyed. In some cases, when nearby power plants were hit, hospitals could no longer operate basic equipment or provide emergency medical care to people injured by bombs (Burleigh, 1991).

Patriotism, even when temporary, is another consequence of war. In this way, war can be seen as functional because it provides an external enemy for people to hate. During the Gulf War, and again today, the Iraqi leader Saddam Hussein is being framed as the enemy (Bush, 2001; Ehrenreich, 1997). Today, mass media technology, used by global networks such as CNN, enables countries to broadcast their coverage of war across the globe. During the Gulf War, coverage such as this created what Ehrenreich (1997) calls nationalistic fetishism in the United States. Boy scouts, sports teams, and public employees decorated their communities with yellow ribbons and wove flags with the message "SUPPORT OUR TROOPS." At the same time, "dissenters (and those deemed to look like Iraqis) were in some cases attacked or threatened with attack" (Enrenreich, 1997:223). Racist attacks against Sikh- and Muslim Canadians also occurred in Canada after the September 11, 2001, bombing of the World Trade Center in New York. A dysfunctional aspect of war is that the enemy is dehumanized—that is, seen as an object to obliterate rather than as another human being. Also, according to sociologist Tamotsu Shibutani (1970), prolonged conflicts such as wars tend to be turned into a struggle between good and evil; one's own side is, of course, righteous and just, while the other side has no redeeming social or moral value.

In 2002, Veteran Affairs Canada provided benefits to 14 clients who served in WWI, 314 405 who served in WWII, and 16 327 who served in the Korean War (Veteran Affairs Canada, 2002). Many of these veterans were totally disabled. Of those who received benefits from World War II, 33 845 are women. Not all injuries sustained in wars are physical. We have no accurate count of the soldiers and civilians—of all nations involved—who experience psychological trauma that affects them the remainder of their lives. One psychological disorder that is getting a great deal of attention currently is known as post-traumatic stress disorder (PTSD). Symptoms include difficulty sleeping and concentrating; anxiety; and recurring flashbacks or nightmares, many of which are triggered by loud, sudden noises such as thunder, automobiles backfiring, or other things that sound like gunshots or explosions. When some stimulus triggers a flashback, the individual re-experiences the horror of some deeply traumatic wartime event. High rates of drug abuse and suicide among war veterans are attributed to PTSD.

Civilians in Canada have shown evidence of high levels of PTSD from participating in military operations; for example, medical staff and war correspondents suffer from the effects of witnessing death and destruction. Many of the artists commissioned to paint the WWI and II canvasses also suffered deep depression and other emotional side-effects upon returning from the wars (Abbott, 2000). PTSD, however, is most documented among war vets and peacekeepers. In Canada, 20 percent of peacekeeping troops are believed to have the symptoms. Consider, for example, the psychological effects experienced by General Romeo Dallaire, the UN Commander in Rwanda who left that country, shaken and suicidal, to go on indefinite sick leave:

> It took nearly two years . . . of . . . not being able to cope; not being able to hide it; not being able to forget it or to put it in, keep it in a drawer . . . I became suicidal because there was no other solution. You couldn't live with the pain and the sounds and the smell and the sights. I couldn't sleep. I couldn't stand the loudness of silence. . . . And sometimes I wish I had lost a leg instead of having all those brain cells screwed up. You lose a leg, it's obvious; you've got therapy, all kinds of stuff. You lose your marbles; very very difficult to explain, very difficult to gain that support that you need. But those who don't recognize it and don't go to get the help are going to be at risk to themselves and to us (CBC TV, 1999).

Roberta Abbott (2000), student of the Norman Paterson School of International Affairs, wonders, if we were made more aware of the inevitable psychological distress that results from combat and its far-reaching consequences, would we Canadians be less inclined to accept constructed images of the enemy? Such an awareness might force us to confront the reality behind words like "peacekeeping" and "humanitarian intervention" and to take a more careful approach to it.

While we cannot put a price tag on loss of life, physical disability, or psychological trauma associated with war, we know that the direct economic costs of war are astronomical. Consider, for example, the cost of 40 F-117A stealth fighters deployed with laser-guided bombs during the Gulf War—over $4 billion (USD). These fighters, which are capable of penetrating enemy air defences without being seen by radar or infrared or acoustical sensors, destroyed critical Iraqi air-defence command posts and communication centres (Friedman and Friedman, 1996). We have no way of knowing the exact dollar amount of the property damage inflicted on Iraqi buildings, power plants, and communications centres, but we do know that the cost for the F-117A stealth fighters is only a minuscule part of the United States's approximately $250 billion annual defence budget. To put defence and war-related expenditures in perspective, 20 years ago, one analyst calculated that a single aircraft carrier would build 12 000 high schools and the cost of developing one new bomber would pay the annual salaries of 250 000 teachers to staff the schools (de Silva, 1980).

Today, more middle- and low-income nations are involved in defence buildups than in the past. In 1995, the nations of the world spent about $689 billion (USD) on their militaries (U.S. Bureau of the Census, 1998). About 15 percent of the total amount was spent by middle- and low-income nations. Canada's military spending is estimated to be more than $12.3 billion for 2002–03, making Canada the sixth highest military spender within NATO, and the sixteenth highest in the world. The February 2003 federal government budget added an additional $800 million per year of new military funding beginning in 2003–04; $325 million in contingency reserve funds to be allocated between 2002 and 2004; and $50 million in the next year for unforeseen domestic security needs (Department of Finance, 2003). The United States, in contrast, spends about $400 billion (USD) per year on defence; $100 billion (USD) of that is spent on acquiring weapons (CATO Institute, 2003).

War on Ecology

Ecological and human health is an important aspect of military activity. Human bodies and landscapes reveal a great deal about the long-term effects of violence, toxicity, and invasions. As images of ecological devastation and human suffering around the world are depicted in mainstream media, such as on CNN, it is becoming more and more difficult to ignore these issues. People are also recognizing that, in this global era, citizens and their economies, health, and environments are interconnected. In a recent brief to the International Peace Bureau (IPB) in Geneva, Disarmament Coordinator for the Bureau David Hay-Edie (2002:2) advised:

> Some of the major threats to human security come from the deterioration of the physical environment. Air and water pollution, the depletion of underground water tables, deforestation, desertification, loss of biodiversity, and above all climate change, are having profound effects on many societies today. . . . Military activities place a number of stresses on the physical environment, but their contribution to overall environmental deterioration has not received its share of attention.

To illustrate Hay-Edie's concerns: The world's military forces are responsible for more than two-thirds of the chlorofluorocarbon-113 released into the ozone layer. The Pentagon generates five times more toxins than the five major U.S. chemical companies combined, and the U.S. military is the largest single source of U.S. environmental pollution (Olson and Elder, 1992). If this is true of the United States, then the impact of other militaries around the world can be estimated in relative terms. The cost to clean up military-related sites, for example, is thought to be more than $500 billion (Hay-Edie, 2002:2). What is the cost in Canada? Each additional war, terrorist attack, military training manoeuvre, and peacetime nuclear test adds to this social and ecological debt.

The impact of specific conflicts and wars must be considered. The use of chemical and biological warfare—such as scorched-earth tactics, "Agent Orange," and other toxic materials felt to be linked to the Gulf War "syndrome"—are all examples of the long-term impacts these weapons have. In Vietnam, for example, about one-third of the country was rendered a wasteland by military activity. It will take many generations to repair these agricultural areas. In the Gulf War, 4 to 8 million barrels of oil spilled into the sea, damaging 740 kilometres of coastline—creating an inestimable loss for generations to come. Air attacks in Kuwait and during the NATO military action in Kosovo and the Federal Republic of Yugoslavia have destroyed oil refineries and caused the leakage of oil products and chemicals into lands, rivers, lakes, and oceans (Hay-Edie, 2002). These actions devastate the integrity of drinking water, arable land, yards, school grounds, and public parks, as well as natural habitats and ecological reserves.

As humans and the earth are connected, toxic attacks on the earth are equally damaging to humans. One particularly potent hazard to human and ecological health is depleted uranium—a waste product that arises during the production of enriched uranium for nuclear weapons and reactors. It is a very dense material that has the capability of slicing through heavily armoured vehicles. Seventy percent of the uranium burns on impact, turning into a fine ceramic dust of depleted uranium oxide particles that get distributed across great distances by wind and water activity. One of the most devastating aspects about this compound is that it has a radioactive half-life of 4.5 billion years. Environmental educator Guy Dauncey (2003:1) states:

This means that the cities, battlefields, and locations where depleted uranium is used will be radioactive and remain radioactive for the next 4.5 billion years. . . . That's as long as the Earth has existed. That's twice as long as the entire evolution of life on Earth. Seventy times longer than the time since the dinosaurs became extinct.

Depleted uranium was used by the U.S. army in Iraq, in Kosovo, and in Afghanistan. Even though the United Nations wants a worldwide ban on it, reports indicate that the U.S. is currently using it in its war against Iraq (Dauncey, 2003:1).

Chemical and biological warfare is becoming commonplace in the "theatre of war." Many Canadian, British, and U.S. troops returned from the Gulf War with a mysterious set of health problems that have become known as the Gulf War Illnesses (GWI). Medical research now shows, however, that it is actually three illnesses that function either alone or together to create this highly infectious disease. Eighty percent of people are affected by the first of these syndromes, which is caused by a marked depression of cell-mediated immunity. The second of the Gulf War syndromes is associated with organophosphate toxicity. In addition to the symptoms of the first group, group two suffers from tightness in the chest, coughing, dyspnea, and pulmonary edema, bizarre behaviour, sweating, salivation, and blurred and/or dark vision. The third Gulf War illness is related to wearing petrochemical-soaked clothing for three days as the result of the explosions of oil wells by Allied missiles. H.H. Fudenberg (1995), in his studies of the Gulf War Illnesses, has found that some of the compounds thought to be responsible for the syndrome include anthrax, insecticides commonly used in the United States, as well as an insecticide used in Northern England for "dipping" sheep to protect against insect infestation. Some expressions of the Gulf War syndrome seem identical to the "sheepherders syndrome" found in people who use this chemical in their sheep husbandry practices. There have been some suggestions that GWI victims share some symptoms that are found in laboratory animals tested for certain kinds of chemical reactivity (Fudenberg, 1995).

The Gulf War syndrome is highly infectious. Veterans, medical staff, and other personnel with the illness have become unknowing vectors of it. As a result, 80 percent of spouses, 60 percent of children, and 40 percent of dogs and cats living in the same household as type I and II GWI develop the same symptoms 6 to 18 months after they are exposed to the affected person. The veteran is usually a parent, sibling, or spouse (Fudenberg, 1995).

There are several reasons why the military continues to contribute to the devastation of human and ecological health. One is an antiquated notion of maintaining national security through traditional military methods. In a global age characterized by interdependence as well as by the ability to end life on earth with the "flick of a switch," old techniques of arms build-up and confrontation are no longer appropriate. There is also an underlying ideological view of the earth as an infinite resource that allows for incredible assaults against ecological integrity to occur without significant thought about the qualitative and quantitative results of these actions. Finally, there is a refusal to see the military as a money-making "industry" and an unwillingness to submit armed forces to levels of transparency and accountability that are required of other governmental or civil-society actors. But the increasingly widespread evidence of the profound impacts landmines, nuclear testing, and other invasive military techniques have on the environment is beginning to change this (Hay-Edie, 2002). Rosalie Bertlee, winner of the IPB's Sean MacBride Peace Prize in 2001, insists that we must set up a co-operative, not a dominant, relationship with the earth—this is in part because ultimately the gift of life is the legacy we pass on to our children and the generations to follow (International Peace Bureau, 2001).

GLOBAL TERRORISM

Terrorism **is the use of calculated, unlawful physical force or threats of violence against a government, organization, or individual to gain some political, religious, economic, or social objective.** Terrorists, however, are often difficult to conclusively identify, because those who are perceived as terrorists in one country may be perceived as freedom fighters by another. There are some things that are relatively easy to agree upon however, such as identification of and assessment of terrorist tactics. Typically, these include bombing, kidnapping, hostage taking, hijacking, assassination, and extortion (Vetter and Perlstein, 1991).

War and terrorism keep some people's lives in a constant state of turmoil. Can you imagine what life must be like for this Chechen refugee who is shown here holding her baby as she returns home to Chechnya in the aftermath of Russian forces pounding Grozny, the Chechen capital?

Although terrorists sometimes attack government officials and members of the military, they more often target civilians as a way of pressuring the government.

Collective violence and terrorism share certain commonalities with war. Both terrorism and war pose major threats to world stability and domestic safety. Terrorism and war also extract a massive toll on individuals and societies by producing rampant fear, widespread loss of human life, and extensive destruction of property.

One form of terrorism—political terrorism—is actually considered a form of unconventional warfare. Political terrorism uses intimidation, coercion, threats of harm, and other violent attempts to bring about a significant change in or overthrow of an existing government. There are three types of political terrorism: revolutionary terrorism, repressive terrorism, and state-sponsored terrorism.

Revolutionary terrorism **refers to acts of violence against civilians that are carried out by internal enemies of the government who want to bring about political change.** Some groups believe that if they perpetrate enough random terrorist acts, they will achieve a political goal. In Lebanon and Jordan, for example,

members of revolutionary movements engage in terrorist activities such as car bombings and assassinations of leading officials. On occasion, they are also the victims of such actions. For example, a car bomb in 1994 killed one of the officials of the Party of God, a militant Shiite group battling Israeli troops in southern Lebanon. At the time of the killing, the Party of God was suspected in the kidnappings of U.S. citizens (including a newspaper correspondent) who were living in Lebanon (*New York Times*, 1994a). In Jordan, members of a militant Muslim movement were accused of bombing two theatres that showed adult films and attempting to bomb a supermarket that sold alcohol. Pornography and alcohol are forbidden by Islam and thus represent a decadence that the Muslim movement adamantly opposes (*New York Times*, 1994b). In 1995, the Aum Shinri Kyo (Japanese for "sublime truth") religious sect allegedly set off a nerve-gas attack in a Tokyo subway, killing more than 10 people, making thousands more ill, and raising the spectre of a new and even deadlier form of terrorism (WuDunn, 1995). In some circumstances, revolutionary terrorists receive economic help from other governments that support their objectives (Vetter and Perlstein, 1991).

Unlike revolutionary terrorism, *repressive terrorism* **is conducted by a government against its own citizens for the purpose of protecting an existing political order.** Repressive terrorism has taken place in many countries around the world, including Haiti, the People's Republic of China, and Cambodia, where the Pol Pot regime killed more than 1 million people in the four years between 1975 and 1979. In 1975, for example, Cambodia's Khmer Rouge, a Communist faction, forced the evacuation of all city dwellers to the countryside, where many died of disease or starvation. Teachers, civil servants, Buddhist monks, and other "enemies of the revolution" were killed in mass executions (Mydans, 1997). In *Children of Cambodia's Killing Fields* (Pran, 1997), Teeda Butt Mam states that everyone was a potential victim: the rebellious, the kind-hearted, the brave, the clever, the individual; the person who wore glasses; the literate, the popular, the complaining, the lazy; the one with talent, the one who had trouble getting along with others, the one with soft hands. After a Vietnamese invasion in 1979, the Khmer Rouge were driven into the mountains and jungles, where they tried to regain power through guerrilla warfare (Mydans, in Pran, 1997).

In the third type of political terrorism, *state-sponsored terrorism,* **a government provides financial resources, weapons, and training for terrorists who conduct their activities in other nations.** In Libya, for example, Colonel Muammar Qaddafi has provided money and training for terrorist groups such as the Arab National Youth Organization, which was responsible for skyjacking a Lufthansa airplane over Turkey and forcing the Bonn government to free the surviving members of Black September, the terrorist group responsible for killing Israeli Olympic athletes in the 1970s (Parry, 1976). Other countries that have been charged with using terrorism as a form of surrogate warfare include Iran, Syria, Yugoslavia, Bulgaria, Israel, and the United States (Vetter and Perlstein, 1991). The United States conducted surrogate warfare when it supported the Contras, who waged war against the Sandinista government of Nicaragua, until the Sandinistas were defeated in a 1990 election (Vetter and Perlstein, 1991).

Terrorism also occurs intra-nationally. Domestic terrorism is sometimes referred to as "home-grown terrorism" by the media because the perpetrator is usually a resident of the country in which the incident occurs or has other strong ties to the country, such as relatives or acquaintances who live there. Like international terrorism, domestic terrorism typically is used to reach some political goal. The most famous example of Canadian domestic terrorism involves the Front de Liberation du Quebec (FLQ), which sought to turn Quebec into an independent state. In the late 1960s, the group set off several bombs, and in the 1970s, they kidnapped British Trade Commissioner James Cross and Quebec's Liberal Labour and Immigration minister, Pierre Laporte. Prime Minister Pierre Trudeau invoked the War Measures Act in response to the kidnappings. The night after the War Measures Act was proclaimed, Laporte's body was found in the trunk of an abandoned car. Eventually, Cross was freed by his captors, who were given free passage to Cuba in exchange for his life (NFB, 1973; Zolf, 2003). There have been no similar incidents of domestic terrorism in Canada since that time.

How widespread is terrorism? In 1995, terrorist attacks killed 311 people worldwide, and in 1996, 296 people. Most of these deaths occurred in Sri Lanka as a result of activities of the Tamil Tigers. While terrorism has always been considered a serious problem

and threat, it has not been a priority on the world agenda. On September 11, 2001, however, the face of terrorism changed when the largest terrorist onslaught ever waged occurred, against the United States. Hijackers caused the crash of four American Airlines jets, killing 3173 people, including the hijackers. Shortly before 8:45 a.m. EDT on September 11th, the first two airliners flew into the World Trade Center's twin towers. A third airliner later slammed into the Pentagon building, and a fourth crashed outside Pittsburgh (Crary and Schwartz, 2001). The immediate response of the United States government to the attacks was to unofficially declare that the country was now at war, although it did not know against whom (Crary and Schwartz, 2001). Nine days later, this declaration was made official. The United States later drew upon evidence, such as a videotape released on December 13, 2001, that has footage of Osama Bin Laden commenting on the hijackings and his surprise about how great the impact of the incident was, to deduce that Bin Laden—formerly funded by the CIA for 10 years—was the man behind the atrocities. While the United States has gathered an incredible volume of information to indicate that he is indeed the man responsible, there are many, like Canadian economist Tom Naylor (2002), who believe that the evidence is still not convincing. Naylor claims that while Bin Laden is a troublemaker, he is not powerful enough to have coordinated the September 11th hijackings. Nor has Bin Laden ever claimed responsibility for the attacks. The United States government's declaration has brought Canada and many NATO allies into the "war on terrorism." The United States has declared that its targets are any nation that provides sanctuary, weapons, money, and intelligence to aid suspected terrorists as well as those nations that are suspected of terrorist activities themselves. Those who do not declare themselves allies of the United States are considered to be enemies (Bush, 2001).

CANADA, POLITICS, AND TERRORISM

Canada was quick to show its support to the United States in the form of infrastructural, citizen, and military support; freezing the assets of suspected terrorists; and working with the United States to improve security along the 8850-kilometre Canada–U.S. border (Council on Foreign Relations, 2003). Canada also supported the NATO decision to invoke Article V of the NATO charter, which declares an armed attack against any member of the council is considered "an attack against them all." In October 2001, Canadian Prime Minister Jean Chrétien launched Operation Apollo, committing Canadian forces to the U.S.–led war in Afghanistan. Canada established an organization called the Canadian Joint Task Force South West Asia and sent approximately 3000 Canadian forces to assist the war effort. As of January 2002, we had also provided a forward headquarters co-located with the U.S. Central Command in Tampa, Florida; five ships; one CC-150 Polaris aircraft; two CP-140 Aurora aircraft; a component of the JTF-2; and three CC-130 Hercules transport aircrafts (*Wednesday Report*, 2002; Council on Foreign Relations, 2003). In February 2003, Canada declared that it would dispatch a 2000-person battle group and a brigade headquarters to join the Kabul-based 22-nation International Security Assistance Force for one year of peacekeeping duties in Afghanistan (Ljunngren, 2003).

Sociologists critically analyze the motives and actions of people and their governments in times of war or anticipated war. They ask questions such as, Why is Canada participating in the war on terrorism in the ways it is and how are these actions affecting people in Canada? Historically, wars and periods of national crisis have resulted in serious and unjustified losses of civil rights for many, and especially for immigrants, refugees, and people of colour. This is because war is not simply a fight for justice; rather, war is an institution that shapes the economic, environmental, civic, ideological, and political activities and practices of civilians and governments. For example, immediately after the shock of the September 11th terrorist attack, the federal government passed Bill C-36, an Anti-Terrorism Act. This Anti-Terrorism Act is a key component of the Government of Canada's Anti-Terrorism Plan, which has four objectives:

1. Stop terrorists from getting into Canada and protect Canadians from terrorist acts;
2. Bring forward tools to identify, prosecute, convict, and punish terrorists;
3. Prevent the Canada–U.S. border from being held hostage by terrorists and impacting on the Canadian economy; and

4. Work with the international community to bring terrorists to justice and address the root causes of such hatred (Department of Justice, 2001).

The bill was passed in haste and within a panicked civic environment. It comes under the Criminal Code and is linked to at least 12 United Nations Anti-Terrorism Conventions. Unlike the War Measures Act, Bill C-36 is not emergency legislation. It has changed, forever, laws and conduct under the Criminal Code, the Official Secrets Act, the Privacy Act, and the Canada Evidence Act.

The government maintains that this Act ensures that Canadian values of respect and fairness are preserved and "rigorous safeguards ensure that the fundamental rights and freedoms of Canadians are upheld" (Department of Justice, 2001). The Canadian Centre for Policy Alternatives (CCPA), in a Brief to the House of Commons Justice Committee, challenged this proclamation. The following are the aspects of the bill that the CCPA (2003b) identified as posing the greatest potential for civil liberties violations or for rendering our justice system and government more secretive and less accountable:

- the definition of "terrorist activity," which could encompass legitimate protest and dissent;
- the process whereby organizations are put on a public "terrorist" list without procedural protections;
- the vague definitions of the new terrorist offences of "participating, facilitating, instructing and harbouring," offences that carry substantial penalties;
- intrusive new investigative procedures, including a new investigatory hearing that removes the right to silence;
- important changes to the Privacy Act and the Access to Information Act that would prohibit the disclosure of information to Canadians; and
- the creation of new layers of scrutiny for charities that will significantly hamper their legitimate operations.

Bill C-36 is not the only controversial bill. Other bills that have been ratified recently include the new Citizenship of Canada Act (Bill C-18—replacing the 1977 Citizenship Act), the Immigration and Refugee Protection Act (Bill C-11), and the Public Safety Act (Bill C-42).

Bill C-42 raises anxieties about the need to balance fundamental rights with security interests. Of particular concern is a provision that allows the Minister of Defence to declare certain areas—even in major cities—security zones, thereby curtailing the right of peaceful assembly and protest (Canadian Human Rights Commission, 2003). Given the extent of legitimate and peaceful protest against the G-8 and various trade acts, many people see this bill as being more about trade than about "security" per se. The Ontario Council of Agencies Serving Immigrants (OCASI) is concerned that Bill C-18 will create a two-tiered approach to citizenship in Canada—the implications of which are immensely disturbing. For example, a child born outside of Canada to a first-generation Canadian (even if the mother has lived all but the first couple of months of her life in Canada) does not have the right to citizenship and may even become stateless. There are no citizenship restrictions faced by a Canadian-born mother who lives outside of the country but gives birth in Canada (Casipullai, 2003). The bill also gives broad powers to Cabinet to refuse citizenship to a person who has "demonstrated a flagrant and serious disregard for the principles and values underlying a free and democratic society" (in Casipullai, 2003). The act does not clearly outline the aforementioned "principles" and "values" but rather leaves it up to the interpretation of cabinet ministers and other individuals in a given historical moment. The possibility of an abuse of power and a decision to refuse citizenship within this framework is real. The revocation of citizenship is yet another potential for the violation of human rights as is the policy that evidence used against an individual in an immigration process may not be disclosed to the person in question, giving a person no way of addressing, or even knowing about, allegations against them (in Casipullai, 2003).

The impact of these bills is already being felt by many people, most significantly, those involved in immigration processes, those who belong to "visible minorities," and those citizens who are the victims of racialized or ethnic profiling. Some critics say that these are all cases of scapegoating—a process where people blame visible "others" for a perceived threat. The implementation of tighter immigration laws, legislation such as that discussed above, and cases of civilian hostility against people most easily identified as immigrants and refugees are all aspects of this larger movement of "nationalist protectionism." Many point out, however, that these attitudes are not new. Rather, feelings of vulnerability to attack lead people to create a hostile climate where underlying attitudes of suspicion, discrimination, and intolerance gain strength and even become institutionalized as new legislation and policies (Choudry, 2001). Recalling the internment of Japanese Canadians and German Canadians during World War II provides easy examples.

Ethnic or racialized profiling is a controversial policing technique that involves identifying and pursuing suspects on the basis of their ethnicity or racialization. It is becoming increasingly common practice amongst Canada–U.S. immigration officers in a post–9/11 world. While proponents of ethnic/racialized profiling say that it can provide a government with a tool for risk analysis, they acknowledge that it inevitably involves injustices (Gillis, 2001). The result is that a person fitting the profile for a "high-risk" group—these days, a person from any of Afghanistan, Algeria, Bahrain, Djibouti, Egypt, Eritrea, Indonesia, Iran, Iraq, Jordan, Kuwait, Lebanon, Libya, Malaysia, Morocco, Oman, Pakistan, Qatar, Saudi Arabia, Somalia, Sudan, Syria, Tunisia, Turkey, the United Arab Emirates, and Yemen—may be searched, fingerprinted, photographed, registered, detained, and even deported. As the criterion for this invasive treatment is a person's ethnicity or racialization, authorities assume that all people from certain ethnic/racialized groups have the potential to be affiliated with terrorists from their country (or region) of origin—or of ancestral origin— and could therefore pose a threat to national security. For example, on September 26, 2002, a Syrian-born Canadian engineer, on his way home to Montreal from Zurich, landed at Kennedy Airport in New York. U.S. authorities suspected that he had ties to a terrorist organization and deported him to Syria without first consulting Canadian officials. Canada's Foreign Affairs Department protested his deportation, saying they had no information that the man was a security threat, but to no avail; he remains in jail in Syria (*Migration News*, 2002). In another case, one of Canada's most celebrated writers, Indian-born Canadian Rohinton Mistry, was given such humiliating and traumatic treatment by U.S. border officials that he cancelled the second half of his U.S. book tour (Gillis, 2001). Situations like these abound and, since 9/11, many groups have reported an upsurge of hostility and aggression.

Ethnic/racialized profiling is a procedural practice that affects Canadians of all walks of life. Andrew Telegdi (2002), Minster of Parliament for Kitchener–Waterloo, addressed Parliament in November, 2002:

> We are a nation of immigrants who come from all over the world . . . Fifty-two members of the House were not born in Canada . . . There are members of Parliament who originally came from some of those [targeted] countries. . . . Under these procedures they too are subjected to being registered and having their fingerprints taken . . . I understand that in the context of 9/11 we do look at the world in a different fashion but practices such as ethnic profiling do not work. They require a great deal of resources and they are not effective.

Ethnic/racialized profiling, in fact, exacerbates the racism found throughout Canada by giving people formal, or state-sanctioned, justifications for their dislikes. Today, the subjective character of immigration practices and the vulnerability of immigrants is a great concern for Canada. Clearly, the numerous changes that have been made to the immigration and citizenship acts in Canada contain potential threats to present and future citizens' civil liberties. While this is true, mechanisms of appeal, such as the Refugee Appeal Division (RAD) of Bill C-18, have not yet been implemented even though all other aspects of the bill have been. The result is that those people denied refugee status by the Immigration and Refugee Board of Canada still do not have a means of recourse (Neve, 2003). This is particularly important for those individuals seeking asylum in Canada who face harsh penalties in their countries of origin.

The Canada Race Relations Foundation (CRRF) has tried to put current legislative activities into a historical context. It has drawn the country's attention to the injustices suffered by the Japanese Canadian community during World War II and attempted to draw parallels to the current "backlash" being visited today upon Muslim and Arab Canadians in a post 9/11 world. "We have witnessed grave injustices that befell a community and, from this, have a clearer understanding of what can arise in response to increased security concerns in a society that has not yet stripped itself of racism" (CRRF, 2001). Indeed, Indigenous people and other non-White Canadian citizens have always faced, and continue to face, "racial"

profiling, not only in war times, but also in everyday life. "Racial" profiling accompanies racist attitudes and structures. This is not a new phenomenon, although a broader awareness does seem new. In this current historical moment, Canadians are actively engaged in shaping the face of Canadian politics. In this global age, people understand that all things are connected—including the causes and effects of war and terrorism on national and international levels.

SUPERPOWERS AND WAR TODAY

Today, the United States is engaged in a full-blown effort to unleash its second war against Iraq. People and their governments around the whole world are refusing to accept the U.S. justifications for an attack on Iraq. The events surrounding this war and their long-term implications mark a turning point in international politics; shifts in the acceptance of superpower military might; and, the power of people around the globe to make their votes for peace heard.

The United States government has been targeting Iraq since the end of the Gulf War in 1991. In 2002, the Bush administration regards Iraq as a member of the "Axis of Evil." By September 2002, the president had won authorization from the U.S. Congress and sought support from the United Nations Security Council to initiate a U.S.-led war for "regime change" in Iraq (Global Policy Forum, 2003). The United States, however, has not received easy support from NATO members. In the lead-up to the current threat of war, major Canadian newspapers carried a statement by Prime Minister Jean Chrétien, "Canada will not support an attack on Iraq if the issue of UN weapons inspectors is used as the justification" (Ljunggren, 2003). Chrétien, British Prime Minister Tony Blair, and French President Jacques Chirac stated that they were "of the view that we have to have a direct connection because what has been agreed upon is a fight against terrorism" (Ljunggren, 2001). This statement reflects an international statement that there is very little evidence to support U.S. allegations that Iraq is guilty of terrorist activities that threaten U.S. or international safety. It is this point that is currently being debated in the United Nations. In 2002, England decided to fully support the United States (against the urging of its

SOCIAL PROBLEMS IN THE MEDIA

BOX 17.1   The First Casualty of War Is Truth

On October 1, 2001, Sunera Thobani, a professor of women's studies at the University of British Columbia and ex-President of the National Action Committee on the Status of Women, addressed the Women's Resistance—From Victimization to Criminalization conference in Ottawa. In her address, Thobani spoke out in opposition to colonialism and imperialism. She criticized the United States government's foreign policy and its declaration of a unilateral war against terrorism. In her speech, Thobani (2001a) spoke about military violence and focused her comments on the current U.S.–led buildup to an attack on Iraq, referring to it as another form of patriarchal and racist violence:

> The women's movement, we have to stand up to this. There is no option. There's no option for us, we have to fight back against this militarization, we have to break the support that is being built in our countries for this kind of attack. We have to recognize that the fight is for control of the vast oil and gas resources in central Asia, for which Afghanistan is a key, strategic point! . . . There's nothing new about this, this is more of the same, this is more of the same that we have been now fighting for, for so many decades. . . .

While the 500 people attending Thobani's talk gave her a standing ovation, much of the mainstream media published statements of outrage against her.

Newspaper, television, and radio reports asked how this "Tanzanian-born immigrant" dared to speak out against the U.S. government's response to the September 11, 2001, terrorist attacks. British Columbia Premier Gordon Campbell called Thobani's speech "hateful" and an editorial in the right-leaning *National Post* said Thobani "condensed her febrile misandry and vicious anti-war hatred into a spit ball aimed squarely at the memory of those who died on Sept. 11" (in Mick, 2001). Yet others maintained that she was wrong to criticize the Canadian government's position, particularly at a women's conference that had received funding of $80 000 from the federal government (O'Neill, 2001, McElroy, 2001).

Journalists such as Terry O'Neill (2001) of the right-wing magazine *Report* wrote that it is "ironic" that at "one of those all-too-frequent feminist conferences about the alleged evils of the patriarchy," one of Canada's leading multiculturalists had revealed herself to be "ungrateful" and a "first-class hater of the very country that so warmly welcomed her." O'Neill continued, "Ultimately, Ms. Thobani has made it clear that the hotbed from which multiculturalism grows is a noxious mixture of bitterness and envy. . . . At a time when, as President Bush said, you're either with freedom or with the terrorists, it is clear Sunera Thobani has made her choice."

There were also citizens who wrote editorials to mainstream newspapers in Canada to express their contempt for Sunera Thobani's position. On Saturday, October 13, 2001, the *Vancouver Sun* ran a story with the headline "Thobani's views bring call to halt support for UBC." The article profiled a letter Charles Huntzinger, president and CEO of Imperial Parking, had written to the *Vancouver Sun*. In the letter, Huntzinger accused Thobani of being "anti-American" and called on alumni of the University of British Columbia to withhold contributions to the university for as long as Sunera Thobani is employed there. Huntzinger wrote:

> Obviously in free societies like Canada and the United States, people like Thobani have the right to free speech, even if they are apologists for terrorist murderers. However, Canadians have the right to show their displeasure towards her attitudes. . . . The idea that such a terrorist sympathizer is teaching your children is a scary picture of the future. . . .

There was also an unnamed B.C. resident who filed a "hate crimes" complaint with the RCMP against Thobani, accusing her of inciting hatred against Americans.

The same type of coverage was given in the United States. On October 16, 2001, journalist Wendy McElroy gave this report on the FOX News Channel:

> On October 1st, the Tanzanian-born Thobani grabbed headlines by denouncing the "bloodthirsty" U.S. government as "the most dangerous global force" with a "foreign policy . . . soaked in blood." Thobani labeled the War as "patriarchal racist violence" conducted to colonize coloured people. In response to these remarks, Canadian authorities are now investigating Thobani for hate speech. Under Section 319(1) of Canada's Criminal Code, she faces a jail sentence if convicted of inciting public hatred of an "identifiable group"—in this case, Americans—that is likely to lead to a breach of the peace.

McElroy (2001) mused that prosecuting Thobani under hate speech laws has a morbid justice about it, "feminists and the Left have championed these sorts of laws to stifle 'offensive' words and attitudes toward minorities and women. But stifling anyone's speech cannot be tolerated by a free society." McElroy concluded her article with the statement that Thobani has been spreading "intolerance at tax-payer expense since at least as early as 1993" and that as president of Canada's

National Action Committee on the Status of Women, "she became notorious for driving the white leadership out of power and for shifting the focus of Canadian feminism away from women and on to race."

Thobani's comments challenged many aspects of the status quo, including the assumption of White hegemony. In a fashion typical of backlash, those people who felt that their privilege was being challenged were quick to fight back. While most called upon the media or the criminal justice system to punish Thobani for her statements, members of government criticized each other for letting Thobani speak. Opposition MPs chastised Canadian Secretary of State Hedy Fry and indicated that the government should fire her for failing to renounce Thobani's statements at the conference itself (O'Neill, 2001; McElroy, 2001). Chuck Strahl, deputy leader of the Tory–Democratic Representative coalition said, "[Fry] should apologize to Canadians and our American cousins for not condemning these comments and [immediately] walking out on this insulting inflammatory speech." Fry responded to these allegations by saying that, while she defended the freedom of speech within Canada, she did not applaud Thobani's speech, and immediately left the event after Thobani spoke (O'Neil, 2001). The political environment was becoming hostile of dissident voices and those who did not move to quickly quell them.

The heat was also felt at the University of British Columbia, which, as an institution of higher education, is a place mandated to foster critical engagements with society. Barry McBride, academic vice-president of UBC, drew upon the notion of academic freedom in his interviews with reporters. "I'm not here to judge on the content . . . but to defend [Thobani] as an academic and her . . . academic freedom" (in McElroy, 2001). Tineke Hellwig, chair of UBC's women studies program, told the media, "It's essential that people see different sides to an issue," and Thobani (2001b) herself told FOX's McElroy, "They are trying to silence dissent in this country."

Thobani was not alone in her statements about silencing dissent in Canada. New Zealand academic Aziz Choudry observed, in his November 21, 2001, article titled "Canada's Dirty War Over Words," that backlash to Thobani's words was extraordinary in the sense that many others have made similar points. He pointed out, however, that it demonstrates the strength of racist ideology which lies just under Canada's liberal façade:

> Sunera Thobani is a woman of colour living in a society founded on the attempted extermination of Indigenous Peoples and maintained by denial of that genocide. For speaking the truth about U.S. foreign policy she has been variously attacked as a nutty professor, an ungrateful immigrant, a brown bitch and a terrorist sympathizer or a combination thereof.

Forms of social difference, freedom of expression, and the right of association of oppressed groups are all constituent aspects of an unshakable democratic nation. Choudry (2001) warns that approaches to national security that include attacking the democratic rights of such groups threaten the foundations of democracy. In the month following Thobani's speech, journalists and public figures critical of the United States were "censored, reprimanded and, in some cases, fired for offering anything other than wholehearted support of the United States government and whatever course of action George W. Bush deems fit to follow" (Coady, 2001). Canadian journalist Judy Rebick (2001b), a White woman and leader of the National Action Committee before Sunera Thobani took over the post, stated in her CBC.ca column, that the ferocity of the attack on Thobani smacks of a new kind of McCarthyism. The reality is that an overwhelming number of Canadians—and many, many Americans—share Thobani's critiques of the foreign policy of the current U.S. government.

Many Canadians are neither "with" the United States nor "with" the terrorists; rather, they are working to create tolerant, intelligent, and long-term solutions to global conflicts—as are many Americans. Sunera Thobani is one woman who "refused to play the submissive role expected from immigrant women of colour" and who "defied the agreed-upon rules of debate set by the ruling elite" (Rebick, 2001b). Thobani's insights, the outcry produced by mainstream media, and the myriad critical analyses generated by academics, activists, and everyday citizens alike raise questions about the way wars are created and support for them generated in Canada and around the world. When the first casualties of war are truth telling and support for diversity in Canada, this gives us, as citizens, a great deal to think about.

populace), while France and Germany are amongst veto nations in NATO that are refusing to be directed by the United States. Canada, on the other hand, has engaged in a diplomatic tightrope act. On one hand, government officials maintain that it is important to send a clear message of allegiance to the United States while maintaining its policy to not attack Iraq for the reasons presented by the United States.

Tens of thousands of protesters are shown here, marching in an anti-war protest in downtown Toronto on a bitterly cold day in February 2003. Such protests took place around the world in the weeks leading up to the invasion of Iraq by forces from the United States, Great Britain, and several other nations.

On February 24, 2003, France, Russia, and Germany directly challenged the United States by presenting to the UN Security Council a very detailed plan for Iraq's disarmament. The plan proposed to strengthen the weapon inspections as an alternative to war (UN Security Council, 2003). The United States was reluctant to comply and pursued a unilateral attack on Iraq. This would mark a new era of international politics where the alliances of the European nations are no longer of import to the United States. This action may have created a fissure in the United Nations, which was founded in 1945 to:

> Maintain international peace and security; to develop friendly relations among nations; to cooperate in solving international economic, social, cultural and humanitarian problems and in promoting respect for human rights and fundamental freedoms; and to be a centre for harmonizing the actions of nations in attaining these ends. (UN Security Council, 2003)

The UN serves as a global governing body. It is an international agency intended to enforce international accountability to global conventions. These commitments are designed to protect and improve the quality of life for people across the globe. Undermining the UN could have dramatic and long-term global implications for humans and their environments (CBC, 2003).

Experts around the world have been busy developing theories about the United States' determination to wage a war on Iraq, as such an act could bring about global instability. Many assert that Hussein is not a threat to U.S. security:

> Ever since he lost the Persian Gulf war a dozen years ago, Saddam Hussein has been caged up within the boundaries of Iraq, a loathed pariah within the international community. The 65-year-old brutal tyrant is still being punished by economic sanctions imposed by the United Nations. He has been unable to take punitive action against the rebellious Kurds in the North because of the U.S. "no fly zone." He is not overtly threatening any of his neighbours. And certainly, he presents no threat to the people of the United States. (Kelber, 2002:1)

Critical textual analysis of the Bush administration's public declarations indicate that there at least five potential reasons why the U.S. is committed to waging a war against Iraq: (1) geo-political interests in oil; (2) the protection of Israeli interests; (3) the prevention of an economically and politically integrated Arab region that would undermine U.S. economic supremacy; (4) the encouragement of a "clash of civilizations" (some believe this could set a process in motion that will eventually allow the U.S. to establish complete global hegemony); and, (5) political re-election for the Bush government (Center for Cooperative Research, 2003; Bertrand, 2003:Laxer, 2002; Kelber, 2002). Whatever the reason, it is clear that citizens around the world do not want war. (See Box 17.2 for an account of global resistance to the war in 2003).

EXPLANATIONS OF WAR AND TERRORISM

What causes collective violence such as war and terrorism? Can war and acts of terrorism be reduced? Despite centuries of war and terrorism, we still know little about the origins of violence or how to reduce such acts (Turpin and Kurtz, 1997). In Chapter 9, we discussed biological, psychological, and sociological explanations for violence. We will now examine sociological approaches as they relate to war and terrorism.

Sociological explanations for war and terrorism use a functionalist, conflict, interactionist, or feminist

---

SOCIAL PROBLEMS IN GLOBAL PERSPECTIVE

BOX 17.2   The Largest Day of Demonstration the World Has Ever Seen

Incredible numbers of people across the globe do not support the war the U.S. is waging against Iraq and its leader Saddam Hussein. In addition, people internationally are not convinced that the reasons to wage war are sufficient to throw the whole world order into potential disarray. Globalization has shown people that economies, as well as health and peace, require international co-operation. Globalization has, therefore, created a global movement of citizens dedicated to making the world a safer, saner place to live.

February 15, 2003, marked what people are calling the largest day of demonstration the world has ever seen. The day of protest began in New Zealand. In the end, approximately 10 million peace protesters had registered their votes—people across the globe said "NO" to war (CBC, 2003). There were 1.5 million or more each in London and Rome; 1 million in Barcelona and the same in Madrid; in New York City, 500 000 people took over 20 city blocks, as they did in Berlin, to give their message. Melbourne and Athens each drew 200 000 protesters, and 100 000 walked to avert war in each of Dublin, Belgium, Paris, Sweden, Jakarta, and San Francisco. The numbers are adding up: 80 000 in Amsterdam; 60 000 each in Oslo and Seville; 50 000 each in Montevideo, Brussels, and Toronto, as well as in the 20-block march to the UN Headquarters. If the message wasn't clear enough, 40 000 people sent it from Thessaloniki, Greece, and 35 000 from Stockholm; 30 000 from São Paulo, and Bern, and Glasgow. In Japan, 25 000 marched, sending a message from those who have lived through the horrors of nuclear bombs. There were 20 000 protesters in the cities of Copenhagen, Vancouver, Budapest, Vienna, Sydney, Montreal,

and Irunea, Basque Country. Fifteen thousand marchers walked along streets and avenues in Buenos Aires, Rio de Janeiro, Helsinki and Austria.

Crowds of 10 000 marched against the United States' initiative in the cities of Johannesburg, Auckland, and Beirut; 5000 in Cape Town, Canberra, Quebec City, Victoria, B.C., and Ottawa. The cold was no deterrent for the 3000 in Edmonton or those who gathered in the Ukraine. The heat did not stop 2000 protestors in Dhaka, Bangladesh, or the delegation of 2000 Israelis and Palestinians who marched together in Tel Aviv to protest the possibility of war. Nine hundred Puerto Ricans chanted anti-war slogans, as did 600 people from Hong Kong. In divided Cyprus, about 500 Greeks and Turks braved heavy rain together to briefly block a British air-base runway. In Moscow, 300 people marched to the U.S. Embassy, and 250 Iqaluit residents in Nunavut created symbols of peace, visible by air, on the ice using their brightly clothed bodies. In the Bosnian city of Mostar, about 100 Muslims and Croats united for an anti-war protest—the first cross-community action in seven years (CNN, 2003; Indymedia, 2003; Kairos, 2003; CBSnews.com, 2003).

The picture is clear; people do not want war. While reflecting upon the magnitude of this movement, it is helpful to ask, What do protests for peace of this size teach us about the global community? What does it reveal about the dynamics of power between citizens and their governments as well as between governments involved in global governing systems, such as the United Nations? When people know that together they can change the course of world politics, what will happen next?

perspective, or a combination of approaches. We'll look at all four, starting with the functionalist.

The Functionalist Perspective

Some functionalist explanations focus on the relationship between social disorganization and warfare or terrorism. According to these explanations, disorganization in social institutions, for example, the government, contributes to overall political instability. Militia members believe that governments no longer serve the purposes for which they were intended, namely, to protect the individual's rights and freedom. In their eyes, governments have become dysfunctional. Some militia groups engage in acts of terrorism to undermine a particular government in the hope that it will change radically or be abolished.

Other functionalists focus on the functions that war serves. Looked at from this perspective, war can settle disputes between nations. However, in the age of nuclear weaponry, many nations seek other means to deal with their disagreements. Among these means are *economic sanctions*, or cutting off all trade. Thus, Canada has imposed economic sanctions, rather than engaging in war or military action, against countries engaging in terrorism, environmental violations, abuse of workers' rights, regional strife, drug trafficking, human and political rights abuses, and nuclear proliferation (Myers, 1997). However, some political analysts argue that Canada is cutting off its nose to spite its face when it imposes economic sanctions against other governments. This is because economic sanctions are dysfunctional for another social institution—the economy. Also, even though Canada has used sanctions against other nations from its earliest days, corporations are concerned that the sanctions deny them access to the world's markets and the profits in those markets (Myers, 1997).

Some functionalists believe that we will always have wars because of other important functions that they serve in societies. First, war demonstrates that one nation or group has power over another. Historically, conquering forces acquire the "spoils of war," including more territory and material possessions. Second, war functions as a means of punishment in much the same manner that the Canadian government uses sanctions to force other nations to comply with our viewpoint on certain issues. Third, war is a way to disseminate ideologies, usually political or religious. For example, under the slogan "making the world safe for democracy," the United States has fought its largest wars in defence of a democratic form of government (Crossette, 1997). Canada explains its involvement in contemporary conflicts using the same ideological commitment to the protection and strengthening of democracy in the world. But there is more to democracy than one may think. Larry Diamond, a scholar who has examined new democracies in nations outside North America, explains (cited in Crossette, 1997:E3):

> Political freedom has deteriorated in several of the longest-surviving democracies of the developing world, including India, Sri Lanka, Colombia, and Venezuela. . . . It isn't enough to have elections. . . . Democracy is not something that is simply present or absent. It's not like a light switch that you flip on or off. It emerges in different fragments in different sequences in different countries and in different historical periods.

Finally, many functionalists point out the economic function of war: War benefits society because it stimulates the economy through increased war-related production and provides jobs for civilians who otherwise might not be able to find employment. Conflict analysts also see an economic side to war, but they are not so optimistic.

Conflict and Interactionist Perspectives

Conflict theorists view war from the standpoint of how militarism and aggressive preparedness for war contribute to the economic well-being of some, but not all, people in a society. According to sociologist Cynthia Enloe (1987:527), people who consider capitalism the moving force behind the military's influence "believe that government officials enhance the status, resources, and authority of the military in order to protect the interests of private enterprises at home and overseas." In other words, the origins of war can be traced to corporate boardrooms, not to governmental war rooms. Those who view war from this standpoint note that workers and business owners alike come to rely on military spending for jobs.

A second conflict explanation focuses on the role of the nation and its inclination toward coercion in response to perceived threats. From this perspective, nations inevitably use force to ensure compliance within their societies and to protect themselves from outside attacks.

A third conflict explanation is based on patriarchy and the relationship between militarism and masculinity. Across cultures and over time, the military has been a male institution, and the "meanings attached to masculinity appear to be so firmly linked to compliance with military roles that it is often impossible to disentangle the two" (Enloe, 1987:531).

Interactionists would call this last perspective the *social construction of masculinity*. That is, certain assumptions, teachings, and expectations that serve as the standard for appropriate male behaviour—in this case, values of dominance, power, aggression, and violence—are created and re-created, presumably through gender socialization, and particularly in military training. Historically, the development of manhood and male superiority has been linked to militarism and combat—the ultimate test of a man's masculinity (Enloe, 1987; Cock, 1994). This is also a perspective held by some feminists who have focused a great deal of attention on the relationships between patriarchy and military violence.

Feminist Perspectives

Feminist scholarship on war has proliferated since the late 1980s. Women are the targets of massacres in wars, the victims of systematic rape during warfare, and the largest percentage of the population that is forced to flee war-torn areas. Women are also increasingly participating as soldiers in the military and are continuing to work together internationally for peace (Goldstein, 2001:1). While war and gender are connected, feminists take many theoretical and political approaches to understanding issues of women and war. As a result, a cohesive "feminist theory" of war does not exist; rather, a "polyphonic chorus of female voices" comprises current scholarship and political debate about women and war (J. Elshtain, in Goldstein, 2001:2).

Most feminists share a concern with changing "masculinism" in both scholarship and political–military practice, where masculinism is defined as an ideology justifying male domination. Within this framework, women are seen as a disadvantaged class, unjustly dominated and exploited by men. In addition to their substantive objections to arguments of biological determinism, some feminists challenge the methods of knowledge generation that they see as based on masculine qualities—such as objectivity, control, and theoretical parsimony (especially binary dualisms)—at the expense of detailed knowledge about complex social relationships (Goldstein, 2001).

Liberal feminists, with their emphasis of classical individual rights to full participation in all social and political roles, maintain that women should also be able to assume war roles without facing discrimination. They argue that women equal men in ability and that the gendering of war reflects male discrimination against women (i.e., sexism). Furthermore, the exclusion of women from positions of power in international relations is unfair and prevents women from contributing fully to society (Goldstein, 2001). Liberal feminist scholars often include women as subjects of study—female state leaders, female soldiers, and other women operating outside the traditional gender roles in international relations. This brand of feminism pays homage to women who succeeded in nontraditional positions, despite the obstacles they faced in a sexist society (Goldstein, 2001).

Materialist feminists draw upon a Marxist approach to class differences and their role in the perpetuation of power inequalities in and between societies. To this end, materialist feminists have studied the construction of productive and reproductive roles of women and men beginning in horticultural societies and progressing through to post-capitalist economies (Mies, 1986). Through paying particular attention to the links between economies and warfare, these feminists have come to challenge the construction of gender roles in general, and those concerning violence and aggression in particular. Research by materialist feminists shows that the claims that gender roles are genetically determined, natural, difficult to change, and adaptive in an evolutionary sense are easily proven false (Mies, 1986; Goldstein, 2001). While war has existed, perhaps, as long as humans have, an explanation for the roots of war is often sought. Anthropologists, for example, have turned to an evolutionary model to explain the origins of war. Such scholars have tended to argue, for example, that in early societies, man-the-hunter used his tools to protect woman-the-gatherer. With the advent of agricultural economies, men began to engage in larger-scale conflicts in order to protect accumulated wealth, land, and community and, finally, in capitalist societies, men engaged in large, often international modes of warfare (Mies, 1986). The underlying argument is that males have an evolutionary predisposition to wage war. Materialist feminists show that man-the-hunter actually used violence to control his own communities and that warfare across the ages is more often linked to battles for control over resources and power than it is about adaptive protection and preservation tactics (Meis, 1986).

Multicultural feminism theorizes about war and peace from the perspective of "Third World" and Indigenous women. It is a perspective that shows how globalization and colonization remain rooted together. It also demonstrates that there will be no true and sustainable social justice, no anti-racism, feminist emancipation, or liberation of any kind for anybody until Indigenous people have self-determination and the fundamental divide between the North and the South, between "Third World" people and those in the West, is ended (Thobani, 2001a).

Ecofeminism brings together theories of feminism, environmentalism, and movements for social justice and equality under one theoretical perspective. Ecofeminists begin with critiques of the 17th-century philosopher of science, Francis Bacon, who cast nature as female and who used explicit sexual metaphors to demonstrate the requisite relations of domination and seduction that were to replace an earlier attitude of wonder and contemplation (Merchant, 1983; Sturgeon, 1997). Ecofeminists argue that all forms of oppression are deeply connected, although they pay particular attention to the types of violence that are created by patriarchal systems of rule and anthropocentrism, which permit people to exploit the natural world based on an ideology of human supremacy.

War is seen as an extension of the aggressive and exploitative relationships embodied in sexism, racism, and the "rape" of the environment. Ecofeminism influenced the character of women's peace movements in the 1980s and 1990s, and of the Greens political parties in Europe (Mies, 1986; Goldstein, 2001; Sturgeon, 2001). These feminists trace war to an "ideology of control" that gives rise to various forms of oppression; ecofeminism sees the problem of war in very broad terms, connecting peace to a deep restructuring of society (Goldstein, 2001).

WAR AND TERRORISM IN THE 21ST CENTURY

What will happen during the 21st century? How will nations deal with the proliferation of arms and nuclear weapons? Will some of the missiles and warheads fall into the hands of terrorists? What should be done with the masses of nuclear waste being produced? No easy answers are forthcoming, as Ehrenreich explains (1997:239):

> War . . . is a more formidable adversary than it has ever been. . . . war has dug itself into economic systems, where it offers a livelihood to millions. . . . It has lodged in our souls as a kind of religion, a quick tonic for political malaise and a bracing antidote to the moral torpor of consumerist, market-driven cultures. In addition, our incestuous fixation on combat with our own kind has left us ill-prepared to face many of the larger perils of the situation in which we find ourselves: the possibility of drastic climatic changes, the depletion of natural resources, the relentless predations of the microbial world. The wealth that flows ceaselessly to the project of war is wealth lost, for the most part, to the battle against these threats.

Ehrenreich, like most other social analysts, is not totally pessimistic about the future. She believes that human resistance to war can provide a means to spare this nation and the world from future calamities.

The anti-war movements of the late 20th and early 21st century show that "the passions we bring to war can be brought just as well to the struggle *against* war" (Ehrenreich, 1997). But, she notes, people must be willing to educate, inspire, and rally others to the cause. Like other forms of warfare, the people fighting for peace must be willing to continue the struggle even when the odds seem hopeless. Ehrenreich's point is supported by Gibson and Cancian (1990:9), who believe that making peace can be more difficult than making war:

> Making peace requires democratic relationships: soldiers who refuse to fight in a war they do not support; citizens who claim the right to participate in making decisions instead of accepting rule by elites who make decisions in secret; newspaper reporters, magazine editors, movie makers, and others in the mass media who question the necessity of casting

another nation as an "enemy" and instead look for ways to communicate with other human beings who are potentially our friends.

Why do we end our discussion of social problems with war and terrorism? They are the ultimate category of social problems. When class, racialization, ethnicity, or any of the other dominant/subordinate categories discussed in this book escalate to a level of "doing something about it" regardless of the consequences, terrorism or war may be the result. Redressing inequality is an admirable goal, but perhaps the goal should be the one stated by Tim O'Brien, who wrote about his tour of duty in Vietnam (quoted in Hynes, 1997:283–284):

> I would wish this book could take the form of a plea for everlasting peace, a plea from one who knows, from one who's been there and come back, an old soldier looking back at a dying war. . . . That would be good. It would be fine to integrate it all to persuade my younger brother and perhaps some others to say "No" to wars and other battles.

The international society—the community of all the nations of the world—must work to alleviate inequalities and create a better—peaceful—world for future generations. What role will you and I play during the 21st century? Will we be part of the problem or part of the solution? The answer is up to us: each of us individually and us collectively.

WHAT CAN YOU DO?

- Check in with your local anti-war action groups to see what rallies and actions are happening in your area. Participate in them!
- Call and fax your MLAs, MPs, and Senators DAILY—several time a day if possible—to express your opposition to current military activities, including sanctions, questionable peacekeeping missions, anti-terrorist initiatives, and invasions. See Canadaonline (**http://canadaonline.about. com/library/elections/blelmlalist.htm**) for a comprehensive list of MLAs and MPs.
- Write a letter to the editor of your local newspaper saying why you oppose a particular military initiative. Your letter should be from one to three paragraphs long. You can find out where to send your letter by looking on the Letters to the Editor page of your local newspaper.
- E-mail a friend and ask her or him to join you in opposing war. Send this list of things you can do to stop war to a friend along with a copy of information about current conflicts you wish to oppose.
- Distribute flyers about why people should stop war before it starts. Good, heavily trafficked locations include: bus stops, subway stations, grocery stores, college and university campuses, libraries, and churches, among other sites. Looks for sample flyers on the Internet.
- Organize a weekly vigil against current wars and conflicts at your Parliament buildings, the office of an MLA or MP who supports the war, City Hall, or another public place.
- Call a press conference where local community leaders, religious leaders, veterans, politicians, and others can speak out against war. Once you have some community leaders who are willing to speak out against war, determine the time and location of the press conference, send a news release to local media outlets, and then follow up with a phone call to tell editors and reporters what you are doing.
- Connect with the local peace group in your community. They will have many other ideas for how you can work to stop war.
- Speak out against racist and anti-immigrant attacks. Ensure that the needs of victims (and those at risk for attack) are front and centre.
- Circulate the criticisms of Bill C-42, Bill C-36, Bill C-18, and Bill C-11 that have been raised by many community groups. Find out about these bills from government, social justice organizations, and alternative media sources, and conduct your own critical analysis.
- Work with Canadian and U.S. immigrant and refugee-rights groups, such as the Canadian Council for Refugees (**www.web.net/~ccr**) or the Lesbian and Gay Immigration Task Force (**www. ncf.carleton.ca/legit**) to ensure that no new draconian legislation or regulations get introduced.
- Subscribe to local, regional, or national organizations that are addressing the effects of military activity on the health of humans and their environments.

SUMMARY

HOW DO SOCIAL SCIENTISTS DEFINE WAR?

Social scientists define war broadly. The term *war* includes armed conflict between two countries, undeclared wars, civil and guerrilla wars, covert operations, and some forms of terrorism. War is a form of collective violence that involves organized violence by people seeking to promote their cause or resist social policies or practices that they consider oppressive.

WHAT ARE THE CONSEQUENCES OF WAR?

The most direct effect of war is loss of human life. In World War I and before, it was mostly military personnel who lost their lives, but in World War II and thereafter, war was waged against civilians. If a nuclear war took place, the devastation would be beyond description. Other consequences for both military personnel and civilians are physical and psychological damage, including post-traumatic stress syndrome. Finally, the economic costs of war and war preparedness are astronomical.

HOW IMPORTANT IS MILITARY TECHNOLOGY TO WINNING A WAR?

Military technology is a dominant factor, as military history shows. In the 14th century, smaller European and Western armies defeated bigger armies by using the newly discovered black powder. Today, precision-guided munitions render old technologies obsolete and global warfare possible. But wars can be won on the basis of factors other than military technology, too, as the U.S. experience in Vietnam shows.

HOW DOES WAR AFFECT HUMAN AND ECOLOGICAL HEALTH?

The impacts of military activity in times of war and peace are often left out of mainstream debates about war. The effects, however, include both visible and invisible reminders of the impact military activity has on people and environments. Some examples of this are the effects of depleted uranium on human and ecological life and the Gulf War Illnesses.

WHAT IS TERRORISM?

Terrorism is the use of calculated unlawful physical force or threats of violence against a government, organization, or individual to gain some political, religious, economic, or social objective. Tactics include bombing, kidnapping, hostage taking, hijacking, assassination, and extortion.

WHAT ARE THE THREE TYPES OF POLITICAL TERRORISM?

Revolutionary terrorism involves acts of violence against civilians that are carried out by internal enemies of the government who want to bring about political change. Repressive terrorism is terrorism conducted by a government against its own citizens for the purpose of protecting an existing political order. In state-sponsored terrorism, a government provides financial resources, weapons, and training for terrorists who conduct their activities in other nations.

WHAT IS THE STATE OF TERRORISM IN THIS CURRENT HISTORICAL MOMENT AND WHO IS RESPONSIBLE?

Until 2001, incidents of terrorism globally tended to be considered more of a regional problem as opposed to a global threat. This changed however, in September 2001, when terrorist hijackings of American Airlines jets killed over 3000 people in New York, NY, and Washington, DC. The government of the United States reacted to the terrorist attacks by declaring a "war on terrorism." This "war" is being fought by NATO members and is targeted at any nation that is suspected of terrorist activities or of acting as a surrogate nation to terrorist activities. This U.S.-led war on terrorism is changing the face of international politics as well as inspiring unprecedented civic movements across the globe to put an end to war.

WHAT IS THE FUNCTIONALIST PERSPECTIVE ON WAR AND TERRORISM?

Some functionalists focus on the relationship between social disorganization and warfare or terrorism. Examining the growth of militias, they note that disorganization in social institutions contributes to overall political instability. Other functionalists say that war serves certain functions: War settles disputes; demonstrates that one nation or group has power over another; punishes; is one way to disseminate religious and political ideologies; and, finally, stimulates the economy.

WHAT ARE THE CONFLICT AND INTERACTIONIST PERSPECTIVES ON WAR AND TERRORISM?

Some conflict theorists say that militarism and preparedness for war contribute to the economic well-being of some—not all—people. Another conflict perspective says that nations inevitably use force to ensure compliance within their society and to protect themselves from outside attacks. A third conflict perspective is based in patriarchy: Across cultures and over time, the military has been a male institution; it is almost impossible to untangle masculinity from militarism. Interactionists call this last perspective the *social construction of masculinity*—the connection between manhood and militarism is historically created and recreated through gender socialization.

WHAT ARE FEMINIST PERSPECTIVES ON WAR?

Feminist scholarship focuses on the links between war and gender. There is no such thing as a cohesive "feminist theory" of war. There are many thoughts that feminist scholars do agree upon, including constructions of masculinism, which is an ideology that justifies male domination. Liberal feminists focus on issues of women's equality with men and therefore work for women's rights to participate fully in all aspects of war. Materialist feminists analyze the relationship between economics, patriarchy, and power on a world-scale and how this affects the life-conditions of women in times of peace and conflict. Multicultural feminism theorizes from the perspective of "Third World" and Indigenous women and demonstrate how globalization and colonization remain rooted together. Ecofeminists take a holistic approach to war and maintain that ideologies of control over nature mirror patriarchal ideologies of men's control over women, and anthropocentric attitudes of human's dominion over the earth.

KEY TERMS

collective violence,   p. 395
military–industrial complex,   p. 396
repressive terrorism,   p. 402
revolutionary terrorism,   p. 402

state-sponsored terrorism,   p. 403
terrorism,   p. 401
war system,   p. 395

QUESTIONS FOR CRITICAL THINKING

1.   In World War II and every war since, more civilians than military personnel have died. Given the military technology available, how can we safeguard civilians?

2.   What impacts does the U.S.-led war on terrorism seem to have on Canada and the rest of the world today?

3.   Consider the question posed in the last paragraph of this chapter: What can you yourself do to make the world a better—peaceful—place in the 21st century?

4.   Considering the massive resistance against war in Iraq, why had it gone ahead anyway?

WEBLINKS

Center for Cooperative Research

www.cooperativeresearch.org/home.htm
A web-based alternative news site and co-operative research project designed to encourage critical public awareness.

Global Policy Forum

www.globalpolicy.org
This international forum for information and discussion of global policy issues focuses on the UN Security Council, international justice, and global social and economic policy. The site offers documents and publications on these issues.

Women Waging Peace

www.womenwagingpeace.net
This international network of women activists and researchers works for participation of women and inclusion of their perspectives in conflict transformation and peace processes.

Canada Online

http://canadaonline.about.com
A handy primer on Canadian government, with useful links to elected officials and government departments and ministries.

Wage Peace

www.wage-peace.org
This site provides resources for Alberta-wide antiwar activism, including listings of antiwar events and groups in Calgary.

National Network to End the War against Iraq

www.endthewar.org
This is a U.S.-led coalition of peace and justice organizations fighting together to put an end to the war and sanctions against Iraq.

Why War?

www.why-war.com
This U.S. site is committed to the education of the general population on all relevant issues pertaining to the war in Iraq.

Z Communications

www.zmag.org
This site provides links to ZNet, Z Magazine, Z Media institute, and Z videos, all committed to offering information and material encouraging critical thinking on political, economic, social, and cultural issues.

Alternet

www.alternet.org
This alternative online magazine publishes current investigative news stories on the environment, technology, health issues, and cultural trends and hosts a huge database.

Eco-Compass

www.islandpress.org/eco-compass
Information to help solve environmental problems can be found at Eco-Compass, an Internet guide to environmental information.

18

CAN SOCIAL PROBLEMS BE SOLVED?

The ____ Hotel here is a favorite watering hole of the well-heeled and is known for its fantastic views of the city. . . . Just across the street in ____ Park, homeless people, more concentrated here than in most parts of the city, spend the day sipping from half-empty juice boxes and picking through the garbage discarded by children using the playground. . . . The gap between rich and poor . . . is widening, spurred by economic and social change.

Stephanie Strom (2000:A1)

Does this scenario describe Vancouver? Regina? Montreal? Another large urban centre in Canada? No, this is a reporter's description of what's going on in Tokyo, Japan, as the 21st century begins. Although the similarity of patterns associated with such social problems as poverty and homelessness in Canada and Japan leaves us concerned about their persistence, we are also hopeful that we may be able to find ways to reduce or alleviate some of these problems—across cities, provinces, and nations—in the 21st century. However, as social analysts have said, solving social problems is a far more complex undertaking than simply identifying them and pinpointing their social locations:

> Identifying social problems and calling for action are quite different matters from actually designing and implementing programs to solve them. Calling attention to the problem, for example, can often be accomplished relatively quickly and easily. Trying to actually carry out a solution, by contrast, involves innumerable obstacles, delays, and frustrations, and demands immense dedication and perseverance. (Weinberg et al., 1981:6)

Perhaps the first obstacle that we face in trying to solve social problems is the difference between ideal solutions and "do-able" solutions. As sociologists Martin S. Weinberg, Earl Rubington, and Sue Kiefer Hammersmith (1981:6) have stated, "There is usually considerable conflict between what the *ideal* solution would be and what a *workable* solution might be." Sometimes, for example, the ideal solution to a problem entails high costs that governments may be unwilling to pay. Sometimes there is little or no agreement about what the problem *is* and what efforts should be made to reduce or eliminate it. After all, the people and organizations involved in the problem-defining stage of a social problem generally are not the same people and organizations involved in the problem-solving stage. Social problems are often identified and defined by political or social activists, journalists, social scientists, and religious leaders. In contrast, the problem-solving stage usually involves elected officials and/or people working in agencies and governmental bureaucracies. Moreover, sometimes a proposed solution to a problem only gives rise to a whole new set of unforeseen problems (Weinberg et al., 1981). In this chapter, we will review microlevel, mid-range, and macrolevel approaches for dealing with social problems and reiterate a pressing question: What are you willing to do to reduce or eliminate social problems?

A REVIEW OF MAJOR SOCIAL THEORIES ON SOCIAL PROBLEMS

The underlying theoretical assumptions that we hold regarding social problems often have a profound influence on what we feel may be the best solution for a specific problem. Do we believe society is based on stability, or conflict? Is conflict good for society or bad for society? Each of the four sociological perspectives summarized below suggests ways in which social problems may be reduced. In doing so, they produce divergent views on social changes that might reduce or eliminate social problems.

According to the functionalist perspective, a society is a stable, orderly system that is composed of a number of interrelated parts, each of which performs a function that contributes to the overall stability of the society. From the functionalist perspective, social problems arise when social institutions do not fulfill the functions they are supposed to or when dysfunctions (undesirable consequences of an activity or social process that inhibit a society's ability to adapt or adjust) occur. Dysfunctions create social disorganization, which in turn causes a breakdown in the traditional values and norms that serve as social control mechanisms. As shown in Table 18.1, the social disorganization approach of functionalists traces the causes of social problems to any social change that leaves existing rules inadequate for current conditions. In societies undergoing social change—for example, retrenchment of social programs, high rates of immigration, rapid changes in technology, and increasingly

TABLE 18.1   Perceived Problems and Possible Solutions

Perspective	Causes	Possible Solutions
Functionalist:		
Social disorganization	Social change; inadequacy of existing social rules	Development and implementation of social rules that are explicit, workable, and consistent
Conflict:		
Value conflict	Conflict between different groups' values; economic, social, and cultural diversity	Group action involving confrontation of opponents for lasting changes in policy or legislation
Critical-conflict (Marxist)	Relations of domination and subordination are reinforced by the global capitalist economy and political leaders who put other priorities ahead of the good of the people	Changing the nature of society, particularly inequalities that grow more pronounced as the wealthy grow richer and the poor worldwide become increasingly impoverished
Interactionist:		
Deviant behaviour	Inappropriate socialization within primary groups	Resocialize or rehabilitate individuals so that they will conform
Labelling	How people label behaviour, how they respond to it, and the consequences of their responses	Changing the definitions through discriminalization; limit labelling
Feminist:		
Interlocking oppressions	Patriarchy, capitalism, and other hierarchical systems that cause competition between groups and place value on one group over another	Consider the ways that oppressions are interconnected; educate oneself and others about inequities; change one's own behaviours; join with others to create models of change and visions of co-operative society; help to alleviate the suffering of individuals and groups who experience discrimination while simultaneously working to make broadbased and foundational social and political change.

Source: Based on **The Solution of Social Problems: Five Perspectives** *(2nd ed.), Martin S. Weinberg, Earl Rubington, and Sue Kiefer Hammersmith, 1981, New York: Oxford University Press; and* **Social Problems: A Critical-Conflict Perspective** *(5th ed.), Joe R. Feagin and Clairece Booher Feagin, 1997, Upper Saddle River, NJ: Prentice Hall.*

complex patterns of social life—social disorganization produces stress at the individual level and inefficiency and confusion at the institutional and societal levels (Weinberg et al., 1981). Thus, the functionalist approach to reducing social problems has as central factors the prevention of rapid social changes, the maintenance of the status quo, and the restoration of order.

In contrast, the conflict perspective assumes that conflict is natural and inevitable in society. Value conflict approaches focus on conflict between the values held by members of divergent groups. These approaches also highlight the ways in which cultural, economic, and social diversity may contribute to misunderstandings and problems. According to Marxist, or critical-conflict, theorists, groups are engaged in a continuous struggle for control of scarce resources. As a result of

the unjust use of political, economic, or social power, certain groups of people are privileged while others are disadvantaged. Thus, for critical-conflict theorists, social problems arise out of major contradictions that are inherent in the ways in which societies are organized. When this approach is used, the root causes of social problems—capitalism and spending priorities that place corporate tax breaks and military spending ahead of social services, for example—must be radically altered or eliminated altogether. Focusing on the political economy, one critical-conflict approach states that the capitalist economy, which is now global, maintains and reinforces domination and subordination in social relations. This approach also examines how political leaders may put their own interests ahead of any common good that might exist (Feagin and Feagin, 1997). Clearly, any solutions to social problems proposed by this approach would require radical changes in society and thus are not always viewed positively in societies in which economic prosperity based on individual attributes rather than collective activities is considered a mark of personal and social achievement. This is particularly problematic, conflict theorists point out, when elites maintain power through hegemony. Change can only be achieved, then, through counter-hegemonic means.

Operating at the microlevel, the interactionist perspective focuses on how people act toward one another and make sense of their daily lives. From this perspective, society is the sum of the interactions of individuals and groups. Thus, interactionists often study social problems by analyzing the process whereby a behaviour is defined as a social problem and how individuals and groups then come to engage in activities that a significant number of people view as major social concerns. Interactionist theories of deviance note that inadequate socialization or interacting with the "wrong" people may contribute to deviant behaviour and crime and, hence, to some social problems. Similarly, interactionists who use the labelling framework for their analysis of social problems study how people label behaviour, how they respond to people engaged in such behaviour, and the consequences of their responses (Weinberg et al., 1981).

Feminist theorists concentrate analyses at both macro and micro levels of interaction. Social problems are therefore examined on the basis of power in individual relations and in ideologies and structures, in particular looking at gender as a key component. Society is seen as a matrix of oppression, organized according to specific relations of domination–subordination. Sexism, along with other forms of oppression, such as classism, homophobia, bi-phobia or transphobia, racism, ableism, and so on, are examined in terms of the ways they privilege and disadvantage whole groups of people as well as the ways that these forms of oppression work in tandem to reinforce a paradigm of oppression, competition, and hierarchy. Feminist theorists who look at social problems look at the roles people play in resisting and/or perpetuating oppressions and at the locations or standpoints people come from. The inequalities and harm stemming from interlocking systems of oppression and domination are viewed as central to social problems. The solutions for reducing or eliminating social problems are, therefore, multifaceted: Pivotal is the push for a paradigm shift that holds the values of cooperation, diversity, and power sharing in highest regard; also key is changing the unequal dynamics embedded in current racialized/ethnic, class, and gender relations and in relationships between individuals that get played out within these contexts. Paradigm shifts require dramatic changes in the ways we view society and the ways we interact with one another, individually and collectively. Further, paradigm shifts require us to retrain ourselves so that our behaviours fall into line with our new ways of thinking. This takes a great deal of commitment and hard work and is one of our challenges in the new millennium.

SOCIAL CHANGE AND REDUCING SOCIAL PROBLEMS

It should be clear from what has been said in the preceding section that the concept of social change is important to our discussion of reducing social problems. **Social change is the alteration, modification, or transformation of public policy, culture, or social institutions over time** (Kendall, 2000). Notice that this definition states that social change occurs "over time." Thus social change has a temporal dimension. Some efforts to deal with social problems are *short-term* strategies, whereas others are *middle-term* remedies, and still others constitute *long-term* efforts to alleviate the root causes of a social problem. In other words, efforts to alleviate individual unemployment or reduce unemployment rates in a community have a different temporal dimension than efforts to change the political economy in such a manner that high levels of employment and greater wage equity are brought about throughout a nation or nations. Clearly, efforts to alleviate individual unemployment are a short-term solution to the problem of unemployment, while efforts to reduce unemployment in a community or to change the entire political economy are middle-term and long-term solutions, respectively. Sometimes discussions of social change sound idealistic or utopian because they are middle-term or long-term strategies that attempt to target the root causes of a social problem. For most social problems, however, a combination of strategies is required to eliminate, or even reduce, social problems.

MICROLEVEL ATTEMPTS TO SOLVE SOCIAL PROBLEMS

In Chapter 1, we described sociologist C. Wright Mills' (1959b) belief that we should apply the sociological imagination to gain a better understanding of social problems. According to Mills, the sociological imagination is the ability to see the relationship between individual experiences and the larger society. For Mills, social problems cannot be *solved* at the individual level because they are more than personal troubles or private problems. However, sometimes social institutions cannot deal with a problem effectively and political and business leaders are unwilling, or unable, to allocate the resources necessary to reduce a problem. In these situations, we typically begin to deal with the problem in an individualized way.

Seeking Individual Solutions to Personal Problems

Microlevel solutions to social problems focus on how individuals operate within small groups to try to remedy a problem that affects them, their family, or friends. Usually, when individuals have personal problems, they turn to their *primary groups*, **small, less specialized groups in which members engage in face-to-face, emotion-based interactions over an extended period of time** (Kendall, 2000). Primary groups include one's family, close friends, and other peers with whom one routinely shares the more personal experiences in life.

How can participation in primary groups help us to reduce personal problems? According to sociologists, members of our primary groups usually support us even when others do not. For example, some analysts believe that we have many more people who are without a domicile (technically homeless) than current statistics suggest, but whenever possible, these people live with relatives or friends, many of whom may already live in overcrowded and sometimes substandard housing. Many people who seek individualized solutions to personal troubles believe the situation will be temporary. However, if the problem is widespread or embedded in the larger society, it may stretch out for months or years without resolution. At best, individualized efforts to reduce a problem are short-term measures that some refer to as a "Band-Aid approach" to a problem because these efforts

Microlevel attempts to solve social problems often focus on how individuals operating within small groups can try to remedy a problem that affects them. An example is how people use their extended families as a source of economic, social, and spiritual support in "tough times." Here, several generations of one family live under the same roof in an effort to minimize housing expenses.

do not eliminate the causes of the problem, they merely ameliorate the effects of it for a few, for a while.

Some microlevel approaches to reducing social problems focus on how individuals can do something about the problems they face. For example, a person who is unemployed or among the "working poor" because of low wages, seasonal employment, or other factors may be urged to get more education or training and work experience in order to find a "better" job and have the opportunity for upward mobility. Individuals who appear to have eliminated problems in their own lives through such efforts are applauded for their "determination," and they are often held up (sometimes unwillingly or unknowingly) as examples that others are supposed to follow.

Limitations of the Microlevel Solutions Approach

While certainly individuals must be responsible for their own behaviour, and they must make decisions that help solve their own problems, there are serious limitations to the notion that social problems can be solved one person at a time. When we focus on individualistic solutions to reducing social problems, we are not taking into account the fact that secondary groups and societal institutions play a significant part in creating, maintaining, and exacerbating many social problems. ***Secondary groups* are larger, more specialized groups in which members engage in impersonal, goal-oriented relationships for a limited period of time** (Kendall, 2000). Without the involvement of these large-scale organizations, which include government agencies and transnational corporations, it is virtually impossible to reduce large-scale social problems. Consider, for example, the problem of air pollution. According to scholars Mike Budd, Steve Craig, and Clay Steinman (1999:169–170):

> Sport utility vehicles, for example, pollute the air and add to global warming far more than the cars they displaced on the nation's roads. Indeed, if a legal loophole did not consider them "light trucks" instead of cars, the environmental damage they cause would keep them off the road altogether. Light trucks, which also include pickup trucks and minivans, are the fastest-growing source of global warming gasses . . . contributing nearly twice as much per vehicle as cars, according to a study by the Environmental Protection Agency.

Thus, while individually we can stay inside all the time so that we do not inhale polluted air, this individual solution does not solve the problem of air pollution and does not address the role of others (vehicle manufacturers, gasoline producers, and consumers, among others) in the creation of air pollution. In other words, In other words, the impact of personal choices alone in reducing some national and global problems can be limited. Even if one person decides to give up a sport utility vehicle or to stay inside all day when cities have smog alert days, the environment continues to be contaminated and the air quality for future generations becomes more and more questionable. On the other hand, suppose a group of people banded together in a grassroots effort to deal with a social problem: What effect might their efforts have on reducing or eliminating it?

MID-RANGE ATTEMPTS TO SOLVE SOCIAL PROBLEMS

Mid-range solutions to social problems focus on how secondary groups and formal organizations can deal with problems or assist individuals in overcoming problems such as drug addiction or domestic violence. Some groups help people cope with their own problems, and some groups attempt to bring about community change.

Groups That Help People Cope with Their Problems

Most mid-range solutions to social problems are based on two assumptions: (1) some social problems can best be reduced by reaching one person at a time; and, (2) prevention and intervention are most effective at the personal and community levels. Groups that attempt to reduce a social problem by helping individuals cope with it, or eliminate it from their own lives, are commonplace in our society. Among the best known are Alcoholics Anonymous (AA) and Narcotics Anonymous (NA); however, a broad range of "self-help" organizations exists in most Canadian communities. Typically, self-help groups bring together individuals who have experienced the same problem and have the same goals. For example, a shared goal may be quitting a particular behaviour that has caused the problem, which can be anything from abuse of alcohol, tobacco, and other drugs to overeating, gambling, and chronic worrying. Volunteers who have had similar problems (and believe they are on the road to overcoming them) often act as role models for newer members. For example, AA and NA are operated by recovered alcoholics and/or other recovered substance abusers who try to provide new members with the support they need to overcome alcohol addiction or drug dependency. According to some analysts, AA is a subculture with distinct rules and values that alcoholics learn through their face-to-face encounters with other AA members (Maxwell, 1981). Social interaction is viewed as central for individual success in the programs. Confessing one's behavioural problems to others in an organizational setting is believed to have therapeutic value to those who are seeking help.

Like other mid-range approaches, organizations such as AA and NA may bring changes in the individual's life; however, they usually do not systematically address the structural factors (such as unemployment, work-related stress, and aggressive advertising campaigns) that may contribute to the problems. For example, AA typically does not lobby for more stringent laws pertaining to drunk driving or the ready sale and consumption of alcoholic beverages. In British Columbia, for example, recent legal changes have made the purchase of alcohol easier by expanding the hours it can be made available to consumers and expanding the kinds of outlets it can be sold at. As a result, larger societal intervention is necessary to reduce the problems that contribute to individual behaviours.

Grassroots Groups That Work for Community-Based Change

Some grassroots organizations focus on bringing about a change that may reduce or eliminate a social problem in a specific community or region. *Grassroots groups are organizations started by ordinary people who work in concert to deal with a perceived problem in their neighbourhood, city, province or territory, or nation.* Using this approach, people learn how to empower themselves against local, provincial, territorial, and national government officials; corporate executives; and media figures who determine what constitutes the news in their area:

> By their nature, grassroots groups emerge to challenge individuals, corporations, government agencies, academia, or a combination of these when people discover they share a grievance. In their search for redress, they have encountered unresponsive, negative public agencies, self-serving private businesses, or recalcitrant individuals and groups. The answer for them is to select specific issues and find like-minded others. (Adams, 1991:9)

A central concern of those who attempt to reduce a social problem through grassroots groups is the extent to which other people are apathetic about the problem. Some analysts suggest that, even when people are aware of problems, they do not think that they can do anything to change them or they do not know how to work with other people to alleviate them:

> The biggest problem . . . is not those issues that bombard us daily, from homelessness and failing schools to environmental devastation and the federal deficit. Underlying each is a deeper crisis. Some see that deeper problem in the form of obstacles that block problem solving: the tightening concentration of wealth, the influence of money in politics, discrimination, and bureaucratic rigidity, to name a few. These are powerful barriers. But for us the crisis is deeper still. The crisis is that *we as a people don't know how to come together to solve these problems.* We lack the capacities to address the issues or remove the obstacles that stand in the way of public deliberation. Too many [people] feel powerless. (Lappé and Du Bois, 1994:9)

According to social analysts, more community dialogue is needed on social issues, and more people need to become involved in grassroots social movements. A *social movement* is an organized group that acts collectively to promote or resist change through collective action (Goldberg, 1991). Because social movements when they begin are not institutionalized and are outside the political mainstream, they empower outsiders by offering them an opportunity to have their voices heard (Kendall, 2000).

An example of a mid-range group is Pollution Probe, a Canadian environmental organization, whose purposes, according to its website (**www.pollution probe.org**), are to

- define environmental problems through research;
- promote understanding through education; and
- press for practical solutions through advocacy.

The organization has four major programs:

1. An air program to promote tougher controls on urban smog;
2. A water program to ensure safe, clean drinking water and to help develop a global water ethic;
3. An energy conservation program; and
4. An indoor air quality program.

Pollution Probe has worked to protect the environment since 1969, when a few University of Toronto students began working with faculty members, such as Donald Chant, then chair of the Department of Zoology. Early concerns were dangers of pesticides for birds, high levels of phosphates in detergents for fresh water lakes, and smog in cities. To help deal with these concerns, Pollution Probe undertook a variety of programs. For example, in 1970, a community development project was devised to send people to different parts of southern Ontario's cottage country to encourage summer camp participants, cottage association members, and townspeople to look into problems of water pollution and waste management in their area. Over its 30-year history, Pollution Probe has had a wide variety of accomplishments, including limiting the phosphate content of detergents, encouraging roadside recycling, helping to launch the Coalition Against Acid Rain, helping develop an Ontario act that guarantees the right of residents to participate in environmental decisions, and being instrumental in the passage of an act for mandatory emissions testing of vehicles in Ontario. Although the Ontario Government has not always agreed with the ideas and methods of Pollution Probe, on the occasion of Pollution Probe's 30th anniversary celebration, in 1999, then Minister of the Environment Tony Clement said:

> But trust is exactly what Pollution Probe has earned. It's trust that has enabled you to be at the centre of the environmental debate all these years. And it's trust that will ensure your continued role in protecting and improving our air, water and land.

Pollution Probe has an enviable combination of accomplishments and trust that should ensure its continued effectiveness.

Many social movements, such as Mothers Against Drunk Driving (MADD), begin as community-based grassroots efforts (see Chapter 8, Box 8.1). Over time, many mid-range organizations evolve into national organizations; however, their organization and focus often change in the process (Adams, 1991). Table 18.2 provides examples of activist organizations that seek to reduce specific social problems in communities.

Grassroots organizations and other local structures are crucial to national social movements because national social movements must recruit members and gain the economic resources that are necessary for nationwide or global social activism. Numerous sociological studies have shown that the local level constitutes a necessary microfoundation for larger-scale social movement activism. In Fact, Bob Ratner (1997:275), a UBC sociologist, notes that the politics of new social movements have prompted

> a shift from national politics to local grassroots action and the formation of a vast and profound solidarity grounded in the validity of communal experience. Such movements, as they multiply and spread, represent a different sort of globalization, one tantamount to a "globalization from below."

TABLE 18.2   Selected Organizations That Seek to Reduce a Social Problem

Category	Organization	Web Site Address
Environment:	Earth First	www.efmedia.org
	Greenpeace	www.greenpeace.ca
	Sierra Club	www.sierraclub.org
	Student Environmental Action Coalition	www.seac.org
	Western Canada Wilderness Committee	www.wildernesscommittee.org
Driving while drinking:	Mothers Against Drunk Driving	www.madd.ca
Wages and working conditions:	Canadian Labour Congress	http://clc-ctc.ca
	Industrial Workers of the World	http://iww.org
Poverty, hunger, and homelessness:	Canadian Association of Food Banks	www.cafb-acba.ca
	National Anti-Poverty Organization	www.napo-onap.ca
	Poverty Net	www.povnet.org
	Raising the Roof (Homelessness)	www.raisingtheroof.org
Violence and war:	Food Not Bombs	www.webcom.com/~peace/ PEACETREE/stuff/stuff/HOMEPAGE.html
	Peace and anti war	www.wagepeace.org www.acp-cpa.ca/CPAmainEnglish.htm
	Canadian Peace Alliance	www.peace.ca/canadianpeacealliance.htm
	The Nonviolence Web	www.nonviolence.org

Note: Web addresses often change. Those given here were accurate at the time of publication.

To understand how grassroots organizations aid national social movements, consider the problem of environmental degradation. Leaders of national environmental organizations often participate in local or regional rallies, protests, and letter-writing or e-mail campaigns, particularly when politicians are making decisions that environmentalists believe will have a negative effect on the environment. By working with local and regional activists and seeking to influence local and regional power structures—city councils, provincial and territorial planning commissions, and legislatures—national organizations assert the need for their existence and attempt to garner additional supporters and revenue for their efforts nationwide or around the globe. By intertwining local, regional, and national organizational structures, these groups create a powerful voice for social change regarding some issue. In this sense then, many social movement groups participate in what the well-known Canadian sociologist William Carroll (1997:29) has defined as counter-hegemonic practice—"a coherent practical and ethical alternative" to prevailing hegemony. The danger of creating counter-hegemonies is one that social movement groups need to be aware of; by defining a group's issues as "the" issues of the day, thereby relegating other group's issues to the back burner, a group risks the possibility of creating new injustices (Carroll, 1997). As discussed above, however, a paradigm shift that moves people away from notions and practices of competition is one way of ensuring this does not happen. If social movements are truly counter-hegemonic, then they leave us with a "hopeful prognosis for social and political transformation" (Carroll, 1997:25).

Limitations of the Mid-Level Solutions Approach

Although local efforts to reduce social problems affecting individuals and collectivities in a specific city or region bring about many improvements, they typically lack the sustained capacity to produce the larger, systemic changes, at national or international levels, that are necessary to actually reduce or eliminate the problem (see Box 18.1).

Many people involved in mid-range organizations see themselves as local activists. Some display bumper stickers saying, "Think globally, act locally" (Shaw, 1999). Many activists believe that, in the absence of any sustained national agenda, national problems such as poverty, low wages, and lack of affordable housing can be reduced by community-based organizations; but some analysts believe that local activists must demand large-scale political and economic support to bring about necessary changes.

Those working in grassroots organizations may be fighting a losing battle, because further funding cuts can only diminish their future efforts. Accordingly, some grassroots activists have changed their motto to "Think locally and act globally" (Brecher and Costello, 1998) and now work at the macrolevel, attempting to educate national leaders and corporate executives about the part that governments and transnational corporations must play if social problems are to be reduced or solved.

MACROLEVEL ATTEMPTS TO SOLVE SOCIAL PROBLEMS

Macrolevel solutions to social problems focus on how large-scale social institutions such as the government and the media may be persuaded to become involved in remedying social problems. Sometimes individuals who view themselves as individually powerless bind together in organizations to make demands on those who make decisions at the national or global level. As one social analyst explains:

> Most individuals are largely powerless in the face of economic forces beyond their control. But because millions of other people are affected in the same way, they have a chance to influence their conditions through collective action. To do so, people must grasp that the common interest is also their own personal interest. This happens whenever individuals join a movement, a union, a party, or any organization pursuing a common goal. It happens when people push for a social objective—say universal health care or human rights—which benefits them by benefiting all those similarly situated. It underlies the development of an environmental movement which seeks to preserve the environment on which all depend (Brecher and Costello, 1998:107).

BOX 18.1   The Lysistrata Project

I am positive. If we douse ourselves in perfume but ignore them when they pine—if we cook there'll be no resisting us. If we truly shut them out, it will drive them mad. They will miss us! Not just our husbands and boyfriends, but all of our fathers, brothers, sons and male friends! Our men will do whatever it takes to get back with us. The longer we neglect them on account of the war, the more desperate they'll be to end it.

Lysistrata, planning a sex strike to end the Peloponnesian War (Aristophanes, 2003)

Approximately 2400 years ago, Aristophanes wrote a play, *Lysistrata*, about a group of women, led by Lysistrata, who, in protest against the 28-year-old Peloponnesian War, withheld sex from their husbands until the men laid down their swords. In early 2003, the Lysistrata Project—to have coordinated readings of the play—was conceived by Sharron Bower and Kathy Blume, who were frustrated that, "We could do nothing but sit and watch in horror as the Bush Administration drove us toward a unilateral attack on Iraq" (Greene, 2003). So they decided to e-mail "all [their] friends and put up a website. The response has been enormous." Blume added, "Many people have e-mailed us to say they now feel empowered to do something, and foster dialogue in their own communities about the dangers of this war." (The website is **www.lysistrataproject.com**.)

The Lysistrata Project took off via the Internet. Over 900 play readings in over 50 countries were planned for March 3, 2003. Countries participating included Russia, China, Thailand, Greece, and Iceland. Many famous actors volunteered to participate, including F. Murray Abraham, Kevin Bacon, and Julie Christie in New York and Los Angeles, and David Hare and Vanessa Redgrave in London. In Canada, at least 37 readings took place, with some in almost every province, and many in locations in British Columbia and Ontario. Any money raised was to be donated to humanitarian charities in the Middle East. In some cases, the readings were accompanied by presentations by various peace groups. For example, in one location in Toronto, besides having a reading of the play, the organizers of the production planned to have presentations from the Council of Canadians, Ploughshares, Artists Who Oppose War, the Humanist Delegation from the United Nations, and the Voice of Women for Peace.

The web has been harnessed for peace demonstrations (see Chapter 17), but this is the first worldwide theatre event for peace. At the time of writing, it is hoped that this event leads to the coordination of presentations for peace, leading to worldwide Teach-Ins, the programs that were so effective at educating people and developing protest during the Vietnam War.

For example, when Canadian workers organize to support the rights of workers in low-income nations and are able to bring about changes that keep them from competing with these workers, they not only help workers abroad, they also help themselves (Brecher and Costello, 1998).

Working through Special-Interest Groups for Political Change

At the national level, those seeking macrolevel solutions to social problems may become members of a *special-interest group*—a political coalition composed of individuals or groups sharing a specific interest they **wish to protect or advance with the help of the political system** (Greenberg and Page, 1993). Examples of special-interest groups include the Canadian Labour Congress, the Reform Party, and REAL Women. In the United States, **special-interest groups that fund campaigns to help elect (or defeat) candidates based on their positions on specific issues are known as** *political action committees* **(PACs).**

Through special-interest groups, which are sometimes called *pressure groups* or *lobbies*, people seek to change social situations by exerting pressure on political leaders. These groups may be categorized on the basis of four factors:

1. *Issues:* Some groups focus on *single issues*, such as abortion, gun control, or teaching acceptance for

family diversity in Canadian schools; others focus on *multiple issues,* such as equal access to education, employment, and health care (Ash, 1972; Gamson, 1990).

2. *View of the present system of wealth and power:* Some groups make *radical demands* that would involve the end of patriarchy, capitalism, governmental bureaucracy, or other existing power structures; others do not attack the legitimacy of the present system of wealth and power but insist on specific social reforms (Ash, 1972; Gamson, 1990).

3. *Beliefs about elites:* Some groups want to *influence* elites or incorporate movement leaders into the elite; others want to *replace* existing elites with persons whom they believe share their own interests and concerns (Ash, 1972; Gamson, 1990).

4. In recent decades, many special-interest groups have been single-issue groups that focus on electing and supporting politicians who support their views. There may be more than one single-interest group working to reduce or eliminate a specific social problem. Usually, however, these groups do not agree on the nature and extent of the problem or on proposed solutions for the problem. For this reason, competing single-interest groups may aggressively place their demands in front of elected officials and bureaucratic policy-makers (see Chapter 13).

Working through National Social Movements to Reduce Problems

Collective behaviour and national social movements are significant ways in which people seek to resolve social problems. **Collective behaviour is voluntary, often spontaneous activity that is engaged in by a large number of people and typically violates dominant group norms and values** (Kendall, 2000). Public demonstrations and riots are examples of collective behaviour. Since the civil rights movement in the U.S. in the 1960s, one popular form of public demonstration has been *civil disobedience*—**nonviolent action that seeks to change a policy or law by refusing to comply with it** (Kendall, 2000). People often use civil disobedience in the form of sit-ins, marches, boycotts, and strikes to bring about change. When people refuse to abide by a

Collective behaviour is a powerful form of social protest against perceived injustices. Numerous protests have been staged in Canada against environmental degradation caused by logging, pollution, hunting, and other activities. Why do sociologists refer to this form of protest as emancipatory politics rather than life politics?

policy or law and challenge authorities to do something about it, they are demanding social change with some sense of urgency. Protestors at the WTO protest used civil disobedience strategies by sitting on the street, linking arms together, and chanting over and over the words "non-violent protest" in response to the advancing lines of the National Guard in full riot gear.

Groups that engage in activities that they hope will achieve specific political goals are sometimes referred to as *protest crowds*. For example, in Victoria, B.C., on February 23, 2002, thousands of demonstrators blocked traffic in the downtown core for an entire afternoon as they marched to the parliament buildings in a extensively organized and festive "Provincial Day of Action" against the budget-cutting measures of the newly elected government of Gordon Campbell and the B.C. Liberals. The protest included members of a huge range of groups: seniors, union activists, students, firefighters, hospital employees, teachers, children, Indigenous groups, environmentalists, religious leaders, peace activists, and others joined together in one of the largest and most multi-stakeholdered demonstrations ever to take place in the province. It was reminiscent of the scope of the WTO protest that preceded it by a little more than one year.

Other protests have been organized, for example, in resistance to the recent B.C. government referendum on treaty issues. Organizations that help organize these protests are usually said to be engaged in emancipatory politics rather than in life politics. *Emancipatory politics* involve "liberating people from adverse constraints on their life chances through the reduction or elimination of exploitation, inequality, and oppression, and through the promotion of justice, equality, and participation" (Buechler, 2000:150).

Unlike emancipatory politics, *life politics* involves lifestyles, particularly those issues and social problems pertaining to the self, sexuality, reproduction, and the human body. The women's movement is an example of the life politics approach, which is often expressed as the "personal is political" (Buechler, 2000:150). However, life politics also reaches outward to look at global concerns, such as ecological survival and nuclear devastation (Buechler, 2000).

What types of national and international social movements may be used to reduce social problems? National social movements may be divided into five major categories: reform, revolutionary, religious, alternative, and resistance movements. *Reform movements* seek to improve society by changing some specific aspect of the social structure. Environmental groups and disability rights groups are examples of groups that seek to change (reform) some specific aspect of the social structure. Reform movements typically seek to bring about change by working within the existing organizational structures of society, whereas *revolutionary movements* seek to bring about a total change in society. Examples of revolutionary movements include utopian groups and radical terrorist groups that use fear tactics to intimidate and gain—at least briefly—concessions from those with whom they disagree ideologically. Some radical terrorists may kill people in their pursuit of a society that more closely conforms to their worldview.

Religious movements (also referred to as *expressive movements*) seek to rejuvenate people through inner change. Because they emphasize inner change, religious movements are often linked to local and regional organizations that seek to bring about changes in the individual's life. National religious movements often attempt to persuade political officials to enact laws that will reduce or eliminate what they perceive to be a social problem. For example, some national religious movements view abortion as a social problem and thus lobby

Religious movements are one kind of national social movement. Religious movements, such as the Promise Keepers (shown here), seek to renovate or renew people through "inner change." What are the strengths of this approach in bringing about personal change and reducing social problems? What are the limitations?

for a ban on abortions. In contrast, *alternative movements* seek limited change in some aspects of people's behaviour. Currently, alternative movements include a variety of so-called New Age movements that emphasize such things as the development of a collective spiritual consciousness.

Finally, *resistance movements* seek to prevent change or to undo change that has already occurred. In public debates over social policies, most social movements advocating change face resistance from reactive movements, which hold opposing viewpoints and want social policy to reflect their own beliefs and values. Examples of resistance movements include groups opposing same-sex marriage initiatives for gay or lesbian couples; anti-abortion groups, such as "Operation Rescue," which seek to close abortion clinics and make abortion illegal; and anti-immigrant groups seeking to close Canadian borders to outsiders or place harsher demands on immigrant workers.

Can national activism and social movements bring about the changes that are necessary to reduce social problems? Some analysts believe that certain social problems can be reduced through sustained efforts by organizations committed to change. An example of national social movements is the Council of Canadians.

The council was formed in 1985 by Maude Barlow and associates and has become Canada's pre-eminent citizen watchdog organization. According to its website (**www.canadians.org**):

> Strictly non-partisan, the Council lobbies Members of Parliament, conducts research, and runs national campaigns aimed at putting some of the country's most important issues into the spotlight: safeguarding our social programs, promoting economic justice, renewing our democracy, asserting Canadian sovereignty, advancing alternatives to corporate-style free trade, and preserving our environment.

The Council of Canadians is sustained by volunteers and financed by its members, who now number over 100 000 in over 70 chapters across the country. Past campaigns include combating bank mergers, control of newspapers by conglomerates, and changes in public pensions. Current issues include energy deregulation, sustainable development, media concentration, health care, and water.

A major successful campaign was the fight against MAI (Multilateral Agreement on Investments) in 1998. The Council of Canadians called it a charter of rights and freedoms for global corporations. As part of the campaign to free up the movement of capital and protect investors, the MAI was criticized for wanting standardized national policies that could potentially erode environmental legislation, culture, and sovereignty and bring in a two-tiered health system. The council sent a letter to Prime Minister Chretien, supported by prominent Canadians such as Carol Shields, David Suzuki, Judy Rebick, and Buzz Hargrove, emphasizing five principles that should govern all international trade and investment agreements. The principles were

1. Upholding the rights of citizens;
2. Protecting the common good;
3. Promoting the development of sustainable communities;
4. Guaranteeing the sovereignty of democratically elected governments over corporations; and
5. Ensuring effective citizen participation in the development of trade and investment policies. (Council of Canadians, 1999)

The Council of Canadians called on Canada to pull out of negotiations. MAI was defeated because, in 1998, France, and later Australia, also concerned about the MAI's encroachment on their national sovereignty, pulled out of the negotiations.

What about global activism? Once again, we turn to the environmental movement for an example. According to Jared Diamond (2000), a physiology professor and director of World Wildlife Fund, some transnational corporations are becoming aware that they have a responsibility for the environment. Diamond believes that a new attitude has taken hold of corporations such as Chevron and Home Depot, both of which now claim to realize that it is better to have a clean operation than to have costly industrial disasters. Of course, consumers have also demanded that corporations become more accountable for their actions: "Behind this trend lies consumers' growing awareness of the risks that environmental problems pose for the health, economies, and political stability of their own world and their children's world" (Diamond, 2000:A31). For example, growing consumer awareness has led some companies that buy and retail forest products to no longer sell wood products from environmentally sensitive areas of the world and instead give preference to certified wood—that is, lumber that has been derived from forests where guidelines for environmentally sound logging practices have been met (Diamond, 2000). Consumer power should not be underestimated when it comes to impacting corporations' profits.

According to some analysts, what is needed is the "globalization from below" mentioned above (Brecher and Costello, 1998). In other words, people cannot rely on corporations to solve environmental problems. Indeed, it is necessary to develop a human agenda that will offset the corporate agenda that has produced many of the problems in the first place. Social activists Jeremy Brecher and Tim Costello (1998) suggest these criteria for any proposed human agenda:

- It should improve the lives of the great majority of the world's people over the long run.

- It should correspond to widely held common interests and should integrate the interests of people around the world.

- It should provide handles for action at a variety of levels.

- It should include elements that can be at least partially implemented independently but that are compatible or mutually reinforcing.

- It should make it easier, not harder, to solve social problems such as protection of the environment and reduction of war.
- It should grow organically out of social movements and coalitions that have developed in response to the needs of diverse peoples.

Based on these guidelines, the only way that a major global social problem, such as environmental degradation or world poverty, can be reduced is through a drastic redirection of our energies, as Brecher and Costello (1998:184) explain:

> The energies now directed to the race to the bottom need to be redirected to the rebuilding of the global economy on a humanly and environmentally sound basis. Such an approach requires limits to growth—in some spheres, sharp reductions—in the material demands that human society places on the environment. It requires reduced energy and resource use; less toxic production and products; shorter individual worktime; and less production for war. But it requires vast growth in education, health care, human caring, recycling, rebuilding an ecologically sound production and consumption system, and time available for self-development, community life, and democratic participation.

Do you believe such human co-operation is possible? Will it be possible for a new generation of political leaders to separate *politics* from *policy* and focus on discovering the best courses of action for Canada and the world? Where do ideas regarding possible social policies come from? Some of the ideas and policies of tomorrow are being developed today in public policy organizations and think tanks like the right-wing Fraser Institute or the left-leaning Canadian Centre for Policy Alternatives. If, as some analysts believe, these think tanks are increasingly setting the Canadian government's agenda, how much do we know about these groups, their spokespersons, and the causes they advocate?

Perhaps gaining more information about the current state of Canadian and global affairs is the first step toward individual efforts to be part of the solution rather than part of the problem in the future. Can the media, particularly the Internet, be part of our education, or is the media part of the problem (see Box 18.2)?

Limitations of the Macrolevel Solution Approach

As C. Wright Mills stated, social problems by definition cannot be resolved without organizational initiatives that bring about social change. Thus, macrolevel approaches are necessary for reducing or eliminating many social problems. However, some analysts believe that macrolevel approaches may overemphasize structural barriers in society and give people the impression that these barriers are insurmountable walls that preclude social change. Macrolevel approaches may also de-emphasize the importance of individual responsibility. Reducing the availability of a particular drug, for example, does not resolve the problem of the individual drug-abuser who still needs a means to eliminate the addiction in her or his personal life. Similarly, macrolevel approaches usually do not allow for the possibility of positive communication and the kind of *human co-operation* that transcends national boundaries (Brecher and Costello, 1998). Experience, however, has shown us that positive communication and global cooperation are possible.

At the beginning of the 21st century, journalist Thomas L. Friedman (2000b:A23) used the events surrounding the turn of the century as an example of how human beings can transcend threats of terrorism, fear of computer failures, and the general apprehension associated with a change from one century to the next:

> Best of all, the Y2K computer bug didn't lead to a global meltdown—not because it was a false alarm, but because countries and companies got informed early and mobilized to defeat it, each in [their] own way. "We leveraged the resources of the whole planet to smash an incredibly powerful problem," said one IBM exec. Who knows, maybe it will inspire us to do the same for the environment, for poverty, for AIDS. Why not?

A similar idea was suggested by sociologist Immanuel Wallerstein, a former president of the International Sociological Association:

> We live in an imperfect world, one that will always be imperfect and therefore always harbor injustice. But we are far from helpless before this reality. We can make the world less unjust; we can make it more beautiful; we can increase our cognition of it. We

SOCIAL PROBLEMS IN THE MEDIA

BOX 18.2 Mobilizing for Change through the Echo Effect

Jeff Cohen, executive director of the media watchdog group Fairness and Accuracy in Reporting (FAIR), was speaking on the radio about journalism's "echo effect." This phrase refers to a story appearing in one news outlet that then reaches a far broader audience as it is discussed, featured, and "echoed" through other media sources. Cohen noted that news stories of interest to conservatives readily enter the national public debate by echoing through such sources as radio talk shows, televised discussions by Beltway pundits, and the writings of syndicated columnists. By contrast, a front-page exposé or newspaper series on corporate wrongdoing or a similar story that advances a progressive agenda is unlikely to be echoed; such stories then quickly pass from public consciousness.

Activist Randy Shaw (1999:252), discussing his frustration with how little play certain kinds of social problems get in the media, particularly when activists cannot count on the "echo effect" working for their concerns

According to activist Randy Shaw (1999), most national campaigns for social and economic justice require continuing media coverage by mainstream reporters and alternative media sources. However, Shaw believes that the media are, at best, a limited source for mobilizing people because, today, (1) fewer people closely follow national news than in the past; and (2) those who do follow the news may get their information from a wide variety of sources, including network programming, cable news shows, radio, and the Internet. Among the people it is most important to mobilize are students and people under the age of 30; however, individuals in these categories are increasingly hard to reach through traditional media sources.

Why are the mainstream media usually reluctant to carry information about some social problems? Shaw (1999:253) believes that the media have a vested interest in news decisions: "Media dependent on advertising dollars cannot afford to use their news and editorial bureaus to build campaigns in favour of policies that their advertisers likely oppose." Some national activists have worked with public-relations firms to get out the word on their cause and create the desired echo effect. Shaw gives the example of Thuygen Nguyen's 1997 report on Nike's abusive labour practices in Vietnam:

There had been little publicity about such abuses until Thuygen Nguyen visited the Vietnam plants and wrote a shocking report for his group, Vietnam Labor Watch. Thuygen sent a press release about his report throughout the national media but received no response. He then contacted Global Exchange, which put . . . Communication Works to work. Communication Works took Nguyen's previously ignored report of Nike's Vietnam labor abuses and created a packed New York City press conference that brought widespread national media coverage. The Vietnam Labor Watch findings subsequently echoed through editorial columns, sports pages, and a series of strips in *Doonesbury*. Media stories about the anti-Nike campaign invariably cite Nguyen's report and the story is likely to echo for years after its release. Yet without the intervention of Communication Works Nguyen's pathbreaking report would likely have remained unknown. (Shaw, 1999:265)

Will the Internet open up new possibilities for activists to get information to those they would like to mobilize? Clearly, given the number of websites now open, a large number of individuals and organizations believe that this may be the case. Many sites serve as national mobilizing vehicles for groups seeking avenues to foster social change. Through news groups, bulletin boards, and other vehicles, people are able to learn from each other and share information about social problems. They are also able to join in collective action or encourage others to take some specific action. However, in the United States, a 1998 nationwide survey found that only 7 percent of all Internet users had tried contacting an elected official online or expressed an opinion on a political survey (Shaw, 1999). Although this percentage has increased somewhat in recent years, it is still a very low proportion of users. Perhaps most of those who are able to afford personal computers and access to the Internet consider themselves part of the mainstream and have little interest in bringing about social change. It is also possible that younger activists who do not read newspapers also do not follow news online. Shaw (1999:287) concludes that, for whatever reason, "the prospect of the Internet becoming the voice of new broad-based national movements . . . remains to be realized."

Do you follow the news about social issues? If so, do you get your information primarily from television, radio, the Internet, or other sources? Based on the information you receive from various media sources, are you motivated to participate in organizations or actions that endeavour to bring about social change?

need but to construct it, and in order to construct it we need but to reason with each other and struggle to obtain from each other the special knowledge that each of us has been able to seize. We can labour in the vineyards and bring forth fruit, if only we try. (Wallerstein, 1999:250)

As we conclude this book and our time together, won't you join sociologists, social activists, and others who seek to face up to one of the greatest challenges of the 21st century: bringing peace, justice, and greater social equality to all the world's people?

SUMMARY

WHY IS IT DIFFICULT TO REDUCE OR ELIMINATE SOCIAL PROBLEMS?

According to social scientists, reducing or solving social problems is more complex than simply identifying such problems and pinpointing their social locations, because many obstacles, delays, and frustrations confront those who attempt to bring about social changes that may alleviate the problems. Solving a problem may entail prohibitive costs or may give rise to a whole new set of problems.

WHAT IS THE PRIMARY FOCUS OF FUNCTIONALIST, CONFLICT, INTERACTIONIST, AND FEMINIST APPROACHES TO SOLVING SOCIAL PROBLEMS?

From the functionalist perspective, social problems arise when social institutions do not fulfill the functions they are supposed to or when dysfunctions occur; therefore, social institutions need to be made more effective and social change needs to be managed carefully. According to critical-conflict theorists, social problems arise out of the major contradictions inherent in the way societies are organized (particularly such factors as capitalism). Consequently, attempting to solve social problems requires major changes in the political economy. Interactionists focus on how certain behaviour comes to be defined as a social problem and why some individuals and groups engage in that behavior. To reduce problems entails more adequate socialization of people as well as a better understanding of how labelling affects people's behaviour. Feminists focus on structures

and relationships that create a matrix of oppression. Gender, racialization/ethnicity, sexual orientation, age, ability, and so on are viewed as interlocking sites of domination and subordination that privilege some while disadvantaging others. Reduction and elimination of social problems requires both individual-level shifts in beliefs, values, and behaviours and macro paradigm shifts that will bring about broad-based social change.

WHAT IS SOCIAL CHANGE AND WHY IS IT IMPORTANT IN REDUCING SOCIAL PROBLEMS?

Social change refers to the alteration, modification, or transformation of public policy, culture, or social institutions over time. Social change is important in reducing social problems because a combination of strategies, some previously untried, are usually required to reduce major social problems.

WHAT ARE MICROLEVEL SOLUTIONS TO SOCIAL PROBLEMS? WHAT ARE THE LIMITATIONS OF THIS APPROACH?

Microlevel solutions to social problems focus on how individuals operate within small groups to try to remedy a problem that affects them, their family, or friends. Most people turn to their primary groups to help them deal with a problem. However, solving social problems one person at a time does not take into account the fact that secondary groups and societal institutions play a significant part in creating, maintaining, and exacerbating many social problems.

WHAT ARE MID-RANGE ATTEMPTS TO DEAL WITH SOCIAL PROBLEMS? WHAT ARE THE LIMITATIONS OF THIS APPROACH?

Mid-range attempts to deal with social problems focus on how secondary groups and formal organizations deal with problems or seek to assist individuals in overcoming problems, such as addiction to drugs or alcohol. Grassroots groups often work to change a perceived wrong in their neighbourhood, city, province or territory, or nation. Although local efforts to reduce problems affecting individuals and collectivities in a specific city or region have brought about many improvements in the social life of individuals and small groups, they usually lack the sustained capacity to produce the larger systemic changes needed at the national or international levels to reduce or eliminate the problems.

WHAT ARE MACROLEVEL ATTEMPTS TO DEAL WITH SOCIAL PROBLEMS? WHAT ARE THE LIMITATIONS OF THIS APPROACH?

Macrolevel solutions to social problems focus on how large-scale social institutions such as the government and the media may become involved in remedying social problems. Some people work through social movements, others through special-interest groups, and still others through various forms of collective behaviour. While macrolevel approaches are necessary for reducing or eliminating many social problems, some analysts believe that these approaches may overemphasize structural barriers in society and give people the impression that these barriers constitute insurmountable walls that preclude social change. Macrolevel approaches may also de-emphasize the importance of individual responsibility.

WHAT ARE THREE KEY FACTORS THAT CAN BE USED TO DIFFERENTIATE SPECIAL-INTEREST GROUPS?

The three factors by which special-interest groups may be categorized are: (1) issues (single-issue vs. multiple demands); (2) view of the present system of wealth and power (positive vs. negative); and (3) beliefs about elites (whether to try to influence elites or seek to replace them).

WHAT IS COLLECTIVE BEHAVIOUR? HOW DOES CIVIL DISOBEDIENCE OCCUR?

Collective behaviour is voluntary, often spontaneous activity that is engaged in by a large number of people and may violate dominant-group norms and values. As a form of collective behaviour, civil disobedience refers to nonviolent action that seeks to change a policy or law by refusing to comply with it. Many WTO protestors engaged in this form of direct action by linking arms, sitting in the streets, and chanting "non-violent protest" over and over again in the face of advancing lines of the armed National Guard.

HOW DOES EMANCIPATORY POLITICS DIFFER FROM LIFE POLITICS?

Emancipatory politics involves the liberation of people from adverse conditions by reducing or eliminating exploitation, inequality, and oppression, or through the promotion of justice, equality, and participation. In contrast, life politics involves lifestyles, particularly those issues and social problems pertaining to the self, sexuality, reproduction, and the human body. Life politics also reaches outward to look at global concerns, such as ecological survival and nuclear devastation.

WHAT ARE THE KEY CHARACTERISTICS OF THE FIVE MAJOR CATEGORIES OF NATIONAL SOCIAL MOVEMENTS?

National social movements are divided into five major categories: reform, revolutionary, religious, alternative, and resistance movements. Reform movements seek to improve society by changing some specific aspect of the social structure. Revolutionary movements seek to bring about a total change in society. Religious movements seek to renovate or renew people through "inner change." Alternative movements seek limited change in some aspects of people's behaviour and currently include a variety of so-called New Age movements. Resistance movements seek to prevent change or undo change that has already occurred.

WHAT IS A HUMAN AGENDA? WHAT MIGHT BE THE MAJOR CRITERIA FOR SUCH AN AGENDA?

According to some analysts, we need to develop a human agenda that focuses on the needs of people and offsets the corporate agenda that is currently taking precedence over other issues and concerns. Social activists Jeremy Brecher and Tim Costello suggest that any proposed human agenda should: (1) improve the lives of the great majority of the world's people; (2) correspond to widely held common interests as well as integrate the interests of people worldwide; (3) provide handles for action at a variety of levels; (4) include elements that can be implemented independently, at least in part, but that are compatible or mutually reinforcing; (5) make it easier to solve social problems such as environmental protection; and, (6) grow out of social movements and coalitions that have developed in response to the needs of diverse peoples.

KEY TERMS

civil disobedience,   p. 432
collective behaviour,   p. 432
grassroots groups,   p. 428
political action committee (PAC),   p. 431
primary groups,   p. 426

secondary groups,   p. 427
social change,   p. 425
social movement,   p. 428
special-interest group,   p. 431

QUESTIONS FOR CRITICAL THINKING

1.   What is most useful about applying a sociological perspective to the study of social problems? What is least useful about a sociological approach? How can you contribute to a better understanding of the causes, effects, and possible solutions to social problems?

2.   Do you believe that corporations can be trusted to "do the right thing" when it comes to reducing or eliminating existing social problems? Is good corporate citizenship a possibility in the global economy today? Why, or why not?

3.   Suppose that you were given the economic resources and political clout to reduce a major social problem. Which problem would you choose? What steps would you take to alleviate this problem? How would you measure your success or failure in reducing or eliminating the problem?

4.   Do governments at all levels in Canada listen to their constituents about social issues? What evidence can you find to support that they do or do not? Why is the situation the way it is?

GLOSSARY

absolute poverty a condition that exists when people do not have the means to secure the most basic necessities of life (food, clothing, and shelter).

acid rain rainfall containing large concentrations of sulfuric and nitric acids (primarily from the burning of fuel and car and truck exhausts).

acute diseases illnesses that strike suddenly and cause dramatic incapacitation and sometimes death.

ageism prejudice and discrimination against people on the basis of age.

amalgamation a process in which the cultural attributes of diverse racialized or ethnic groups are blended together to form a new society incorporating the unique contributions of each group.

androcentricity putting males at the centre.

Anglo-conformity model a pattern of assimilation whereby members of subordinate racialized/ethnic groups are expected to conform to the culture of the dominant (white) Anglo-Saxon population.

anti-Semitism prejudice and discriminatory behaviour directed at Jews.

assimilation the process by which members of subordinate racialized and ethnic groups become absorbed into the dominant culture.

biphobia fear and intolerance of bisexuals and bisexual lifestyles.

blaming the victim a practice used by people who view a social problem as emanating from within the individual who exhibits the problem.

blended family a family that consists of a husband and wife, or a same-sex couple, children from previous marriages, and children (if any) from the new marriage.

capitalism an economic system characterized by private ownership of the means of production, from which personal profits can be derived through market competition and without government intervention.

chronic diseases illnesses that are long-term or lifelong and that develop gradually or are present from birth.

civil disobedience nonviolent action that seeks to change a policy or law by refusing to comply with it.

class system a system of social inequality based on the ownership and control of resources and on the type of work people do.

codependency a reciprocal relationship between the alcoholic and one or more nonalcoholics who unwittingly aid and abet the alcoholic's excessive drinking and resulting behaviour.

collective behaviour voluntary, often spontaneous activity that is engaged in by a large number of people and typically violates dominant group norms and values.

collective violence organized violence by people seeking to promote their cause or resist social policies or practices that they consider oppressive.

common law, or cohabitation, two adults living together in a sexual relationship without being legally married.

comparable worth the belief that wages ought to reflect the worth of a job, not the gender or other ascribed characteristics of the worker.

conflict perspective a framework for viewing society that is based on the assumption that groups in society are engaged in a continuous power struggle for control of scarce resources.

contingent work part-time work, temporary work, and subcontracted work that offers advantages to employers but can be detrimental to workers' welfare.

core nations dominant capitalist centres characterized by high levels of industrialization and urbanization.

corporate crime illegal acts committed by corporate employees on behalf of the corporation and with its support.

corporate welfare a phenomenon that occurs when the government helps industries and private corporations in their economic pursuits.

crime a behaviour that violates criminal law and is punishable by a fine, a jail term, or other negative sanctions.

criminal justice system the network of organizations, including the police, courts, criminal prosecutions, and corrections, involved in law enforcement and the administration of justice.

437

cultural capital social assets, such as values, beliefs, attitudes, and competencies in language and culture, that are learned at home and required for success and social advancement.

date rape forcible sexual activity that meets the legal definition of sexual assault and involves people who first meet in a social setting.

deindustrialization the process by which capital is diverted from investment in basic industries (in the form of economic resources, plants, and equipment) to business practices such as mergers and acquisitions and foreign investment.

deinstitutionalization the practice of discharging patients from mental hospitals into the community.

democracy a political system in which the people hold the ruling power either directly or through elected representatives.

demographic transition theory the theory that societies move from high birth and death rates to relatively low birth and death rates as a result of technological development.

demography the study of the size, composition, and distribution of populations.

dependency ratio the number of workers necessary to support youth and those over age 64.

desertification the process by which usable land is turned into desert because of overgrazing, harmful agricultural practices, or deforestation.

deviance a behaviour, belief, or condition that violates social norms.

differential association theory the belief that individuals have a greater tendency to deviate from societal norms when they frequently associate with people who tend toward deviance rather than conformity.

disability a restricted or total lack of ability to perform certain activities as a result of physical or mental limitations or the interplay of these limitations, social responses, and the social environment.

disability-free life expectancy the number of years of life that can be expected to be free of activity limitation.

discrimination actions or practices of dominant group members (or their representatives) that have a harmful impact on members of subordinate groups.

domestic partnership a partnership in which an unmarried couple lives together in a committed relationship and is granted many of the same legal rights and benefits accorded to a married couple.

dominant group the group whose members are disproportionately at the top of the hierarchy, "with maximal access to society's power resources, particularly political authority and control of the means of economic production" (Marger, 1999: 273). (see also **majority group**, below)

drug any substance—other than food or water—that, when taken into the body, alters its functioning in some way.

drug addiction (or drug dependency) a psychological and/or physiological need for a drug to maintain a sense of well-being and avoid withdrawal symptoms.

drug subculture a group of people whose attitudes, beliefs, and behaviours pertaining to drug use differ significantly from those of most people in the larger society.

dual-earner marriages marriages in which both spouses are in the labour force.

edge city a middle- to upper-middle-class area that has complete living, working, shopping, and leisure activities so that it is not dependent on the central city or other suburbs.

education the social institution responsible for transmitting knowledge, skills, and cultural values in a formally organized structure.

elite model a view of society in which power in political systems is concentrated in the hands of a small group, whereas the masses are relatively powerless.

environmental degradation disruptions to the environment that have negative consequences for ecosystems.

environmental racism the belief that a disproportionate number of hazardous facilities are placed in areas populated primarily by poor people and people of colour.

environmental tobacco smoke the smoke in the air as a result of other people's tobacco smoking.

erotica materials that depict consensual sexual activities that are sought by and pleasurable to all parties involved.

ethnic group a category of people who are distinguished, by others or by themselves, on the basis of cultural or nationality characteristics. These can include language, country of origin, and adherence to culture.

ethnic pluralism the coexistence of diverse racialized/ethnic groups with separate identities and cultures within a society.

ethnocentrism the assumption that one's own group and way of life are superior to all others.

extended family a family unit composed of relatives in addition to parents and children, all of whom live in the same household.

family a relationship in which people live together with commitment, form an economic unit and care for any young, and consider the group critical to their identity.

family of orientation the family into which a person is born and in which early socialization takes place.

family of procreation the family that married or cohabiting couples create by having or adopting children.

feminization of poverty the trend whereby women are disproportionately represented among individuals living in poverty.

fertility the number of children born to an individual or a population.

fetal alcohol effects (FAE) a condition with some FAS characteristics that could include single birth defects, or developmental learning and behavioural disorders, that may not be noticed until months or years after the child's birth.

fetal alcohol syndrome (FAS) a condition characterized by mental retardation and craniofacial malformations that may affect the child of an alcoholic mother.

field research the study of social life in its natural setting: observing and interviewing people where they live, work, and play.

framing the manner in which news content, and the accompanying visual images, are linked together to create certain audience perceptions and give specific impressions to viewers and readers.

functionalist perspective a framework for viewing society as a stable, orderly system composed of a number of interrelated parts, each of which performs a function that contributes to the overall stability of society.

functionally illiterate being unable to read and/or write at the skill level necessary for carrying out everyday tasks.

gender culturally and socially constructed differences between females and males that are based on meanings, beliefs, and practices that a group or society associates with femininity or masculinity.

gender bias a situation in which favouritism is shown toward one gender.

gender gap the difference between the number of votes from women and men received by a candidate for public office.

gender ideology ideas of masculinity and femininity that are held to be valid in a given society at a specific historical time.

gendered division of labour the process whereby productive tasks are separated on the basis on gender.

gendered racism the interactive effect of racism and sexism in exploiting Indigenous and visible minority women.

genocide the deliberate, systematic killing of an entire people or nation.

gentrification the process by which people renovate or restore properties in central cities.

glass ceiling the invisible institutional barrier constructed by male management that prevents women from reaching top positions in major corporations and other large-scale organizations.

government a formal organization that has legal and political authority to regulate relationships among people in a society and between the society and others outside its borders.

grassroots groups organizations started by ordinary people who work in concert to change a perceived problem in their neighbourhood, city, province or territory, or nation.

greenhouse effect an environmental condition caused by excessive quantities of carbon dioxide, methane, and nitrous oxide in the atmosphere.

hate crime an act of violence motivated by prejudice against people on the basis of racialized identity, ethnicity, religion, gender, or sexual orientation. This can include the dissemination of materials intended to incite hatred.

health maintenance organization (HMO) an organization that provides, for a fixed monthly fee, total health care with an emphasis on prevention to avoid costly treatment later.

hegemony the use of the media and other cultural institutions to represent the interests, values, and understandings of the capitalist class and other powerful groups as natural and universal.

hegemony theory the view that the media are instruments of social control and are used by members of the ruling classes to create "false consciousness" in the working classes.

heterosexism the belief that heterosexuality is the only normal, natural, and moral mode of relating, and hence is superior to homosexuality or bisexuality.

hidden curriculum how certain cultural values and attitudes, such as conformity and obedience to authority, are transmitted through implied demands in the everyday rules and routines of schools.

high-income nations countries with highly industrialized economies; technologically advanced industrial, administrative, and service occupations; and relatively high levels of national and per capita (per person) income.

homicide the unlawful, intentional killing of one person by another

homophobia the irrational and excessive fear or intolerance of homosexuals and homosexuality.

hospice an organization that provides a homelike facility or home-based care (or both) for people who are terminally ill.

iatrogenesis problems caused by doctors and the health care system.

income the economic gain derived from wages, salaries, income transfers (governmental aid, such as income assistance [welfare], or ownership of property).

indictable offence a more serious crime, such as murder, rape, or aggravated assault, that is punishable by more than a year's imprisonment or even death.

individual discrimination one-on-one acts by members of the dominant group that harm members of the subordinate group or their property.

industrialization the process by which societies are transformed from a dependence on agriculture and handmade products to an emphasis on manufacturing and related industries.

infant mortality rate the number of deaths of infants under one year of age per 1000 live births in a given year.

institutional discrimination the day-to-day practices of organizations and institutions that have a harmful impact on members of subordinate groups.

interactionist perspective a framework that views society as the sum of the interactions of individuals and groups.

interlocking corporate directorates members of the board of directors of one corporation who also sit on the board of one or more other corporations.

internal colonialism a process that occurs when members of a racialized/ethnic group are conquered or colonized and forcibly placed under the economic and political control of the dominant group.

internalized dominance all the ways that white people learn they are normal, feel included, and do not think of themselves as "other" or "different."

intersectionality when people experience oppression in more than one aspect of their lives (e.g., sexism plus racism plus homophobia), the resulting oppression is greater than the sum of these oppressions.

intersexed having either unrecognizably male or female genitalia, or having both male and female genitalia

kinship a social network of people based on common ancestry, marriage, or adoption.

labelling theory the proposition that delinquents and criminals are those people who have been successfully labelled as such by others.

latent functions hidden, unstated, and sometimes unintended consequences of activities in an organization or institution.

life chances the extent to which individuals have access to important societal resources such as food, clothing, shelter, education, and health care.

life expectancy an estimate of the average lifetime of people born in a specific year.

lifestyle–routine activity approach the belief that the patterns and timing of people's daily movements and activities as they go about obtaining the necessities of life—such as food, shelter, companionship, and entertainment—are the keys to understanding violent personal crimes and other types of crime in our society.

low-income nations are primarily countries with agrarian economies, little industrialization, and low levels of national and personal income.

low-level literate those who can maintain their current occupation but have minimal skills for adapting to a more complex occupation.

macrolevel analysis focuses on social processes occurring at the societal level, especially in large-scale organizations and major social institutions such as politics, government, and the economy.

majority (or dominant) group a group that is advantaged and has superior resources and rights in a society.

managed care any system of cost containment that closely monitors and controls health care providers' decisions about medical procedures, diagnostic tests, and other services that should be provided to patients.

manifest functions open, stated, and intended goals or consequences of activities within an organization or institution.

mass murder the killing of four or more people at one time and in one place by the same person.

master status the most significant status a person possesses because it largely determines how individuals view themselves and how they are treated by others.

mechanical solidarity social bonds based on shared religious beliefs and a simple division of labour.

media concentration the tendency of the media industries to cluster together in groups with the goal of enhancing profitability.

media industries major businesses that own, or own interests in, radio and television production and broadcasting; motion pictures, movie theatres, and music companies; newspaper, periodical (magazine), and book publishing; and Internet services and content providers, and that influence people and cultures worldwide.

medical-industrial complex encompasses both local physicians and hospitals as well as global health-related industries such as the pharmaceutical and medical supply companies that deliver health care.

medicalization the treating of a person's condition as an illness.

medicalization of crime the converting of criminal behaviour to a medical condition or disease.

megalopolis a continuous concentration of two or more cities and their suburbs that have grown until they form an interconnected urban area.

meritocracy a nation where the best person can rise to the top in any situation, despite his or her antecedents.

microlevel analysis focuses on small-group relations and social interaction among individuals.

middle-income nations countries undergoing transformation from agrarian to industrial economies.

migration the movement of people from one geographic area to another for the purpose of changing residency.

military-industrial complex the interdependence of the military establishment and private military contractors.

minority (or subordinate) group a group whose members, because of physical or cultural characteristics, are disadvantaged and subjected to negative discriminatory treatment by the majority group and regard themselves as objects of collective discrimination.

mixed economy an economic system that combines elements of both capitalism (a market economy) and socialism (a command economy).

monogamy a marriage between one woman and one man.

monopoly a situation that exists when a single firm controls an industry and accounts for all sales in a specific market.

mortality the number of deaths that occur in a specific population.

multinational corporation (MNC) a complete corporate operation that is taken from its country of origin and integrated into its host country in order to successfully market its products in the local culture.

norms established rules of behaviour or standards of conduct.

nuclear family a family unit composed of one or two parents and her/his/their dependent children who live apart from other relatives.

obscenity the legal term for pornographic materials that are offensive by generally accepted standards of decency.

occupational (white-collar) crime illegal activities committed by people in the course of their employment or normal business activity.

oligopoly a situation in which a small number of companies or suppliers control an entire industry or service.

organic solidarity social bonds based on interdependence and an elaborate division of labour (specialization).

organized crime a business operation that supplies illegal goods and services for profit.

patriarchy a hierarchical system of social organization in which cultural, political, and economic structures are controlled by men.

pay equity equal pay for work of equal or comparable worth

peripheral nations nations that depend on core nations for capital, have little or no industrialization (other than what may be brought in by core nations), and have uneven patterns of urbanization.

permanent government the top-tier civil service bureaucrats who have a strong power base and play a major role in developing and implementing government policies and procedures.

perspective an overall approach or viewpoint toward some subject.

pink-collar ghetto where the jobs primarily held by women are relatively low-paying, non-manual, semiskilled.

plea bargaining a process whereby the crown attorney negotiates with a defence attorney a reduced sentence in exchange for a guilty plea.

pluralist model the view that power is widely dispersed throughout many competing interest groups in our political system.

political action committees (PACs) special-interest groups that fund campaigns to help elect (or defeat) candidates based on their positions on specific issues.

politics the social institution through which power is acquired and exercised by some people and groups.

population composition the biological and social characteristics of a population, including such attributes as age, sex, racialization, marital status, education, occupation, income, and size of household.

pornography the graphic depiction of sexual behaviour though pictures and/or words—including by electronic or other data retrieval systems—in a manner that is intended to be sexually arousing.

poverty rate the proportion of the population whose income falls below the government's official poverty line—the level of income below which a family of a given size is considered to be poor.

power the ability of people to achieve their goals despite opposition from others.

power elite the rulers of society, which at the top is composed of business leaders, the executive branch of the federal government, and the "top brass" of the military.

prejudice a negative attitude about people based on such characteristics as racialization, gender, age, religion, or sexual orientation.

prestige the respect, esteem, or regard accorded to an individual or group by others.

primary deviance the initial act of rule breaking.

primary groups small, less-specialized groups (see **secondary groups**) in which members engage in face-to-face, emotion-based interactions over an extended period of time.

primary prevention programs that seek to prevent drug problems before they begin.

property crime the taking of money or property from another without force, the threat of force, or the destruction of property.

prostitution the sale of sexual services (of oneself or another) for money or goods and without emotional attachment.

punishment any action designed to deprive a person of things of value (including liberty) because of an offence the person is thought to have committed.

racialized group a category of people who have been singled out, by others or themselves, as inferior or superior, on the basis of subjectively selected physical characteristics such as skin colour, hair texture, and eye shape.

racism a set of attitudes, beliefs, and practices used to justify the superior treatment of one racialized or ethnic group and the inferior treatment of another racialized or ethnic group.

rape culture the pervasive system of cultural values, attitudes, and practices that support and perpetuate sexualized violence against women

relative poverty a condition that exists when people may be able to afford basic necessities, such as food, clothing, and shelter, but cannot maintain an average standard of living in comparison to that of other members of their society or group.

repressive terrorism terrorism conducted by a government against its own citizens for the purpose of protecting an existing political order.

restorative justice the focus on repairing the harm caused by crime by holding moderated meetings of crime victims, offenders, and others affected by crime; restorative justice practices can be used at different sites in the justice system.

revolutionary terrorism acts of violence against civilians that are carried out by internal enemies of the government who want to bring about political change.

routine activities crime crime that occurs when a motivated offender finds a suitable target in the absence of suitable guardianship.

scapegoat a person or group that is blamed for some problem causing frustration and is therefore subjected to hostility or aggression by others.

second shift the domestic work that many employed women perform at home after completing their workday on the job.

secondary analysis of existing data a research method in which investigators analyze data that originally were collected by others for some other purpose.

secondary deviance the process that occurs when a person who has been labelled a deviant accepts that new identity and continues the deviant behaviour.

secondary groups larger, more-specialized groups (see **primary groups**) in which members engage in impersonal, goal-oriented relationships for a limited period of time.

segregation the spatial and social separation of categories of people by racialization, ethnicity, class, gender, religion, or other social characteristics.

self-fulfilling prophecy the process by which a false definition of a situation results in new behaviour that makes the original false conception become true.

self-health management includes self-care practices, mutual aid, and membership in self-help groups.

semiperipheral nations nations that are more developed than peripheral nations but less developed than core nations.

serial murder the killing of three or more people over more than a month by the same person.

sex the biological differences between females and males.

sexism the subordination of one sex, female, based on the assumed superiority of the other sex, male.

sexual assault an act of violence in which sex is used as a weapon against a powerless victim.

sexual harassment unwanted sexual advances, requests for sexual favours, or other verbal or physical conduct of a sexual nature.

sexual orientation a preference for emotional–sexual relationships with individuals of the "same" sex (homosexuality), the "opposite" sex (heterosexuality), or both (bisexuality).

sexuality attitudes, beliefs, and practices related to sexual attraction and intimate relationships with others.

situational approach the belief that violence results from a specific interaction process, termed a "situational transaction."

social bond theory the proposition that criminal behaviour is most likely to occur when a person's ties to society are weakened or broken.

social change the alteration, modification, or transformation of public policy, culture, or social institutions over time.

social construct a classification of people based on social and political values—rather than a biological given.

social control the systematic practices developed by social groups to encourage conformity and discourage deviance.

social disorganization the conditions in society that undermine the ability of traditional social institutions to govern human behaviour.

social gerontology the study of the social (nonphysical) aspects of aging.

social learning theory a theory that is based on the assumption that people are likely to act out the behaviour they see in role models and media sources.

social movement an organized group that acts collectively to promote or resist change through collective action.

social problem a social condition (such as poverty) or a pattern of behaviour (such as violence against women) that people believe warrants public concern and collective action to bring about change.

social stratification the hierarchical arrangement of large social groups on the basis of their control over basic resources.

socialism an economic system characterized by public ownership of the means of production, the pursuit of collective goals, and centralized decision-making.

society a large number of individuals who share the same geographical territory and are subject to the same political authority and dominant cultural expectations.

sociological imagination the ability to see the relationship between individual experiences and the larger society in which they are contextualized.

sociology the academic and scholarly discipline that engages in systematic study of human society and social interactions.

special-interest group a political coalition composed of individuals or groups sharing a specific interest they wish to protect or advance with the help of the political system.

state-sponsored terrorism political terrorism resulting from a government providing financial resources, weapons, and training for terrorists who conduct their activities in other nations.

stereotypes overgeneralizations about the appearance, behaviour, or other characteristics of all members of a group.

strain theory the proposition that people feel strain when they are exposed to cultural goals that they cannot reach because they do not have access to culturally approved means of achieving those goals.

subculture a group of people who share a distinctive set of cultural beliefs and behaviours that set them apart from the larger society.

subculture of violence hypothesis the hypothesis that violence is part of the normative expectations governing everyday behaviour among young males in the lower classes.

subordinate group a group whose members, in relation to the dominant group (or groups), do not occupy positions of power (see also **minority group**, above).

summary offence a relatively minor crime that is punishable by a fine or less than a year in jail.

survey research a poll in which researchers ask the research participants a series of questions about a specific topic and record their responses.

sustainable development meeting the needs of the present generations without compromising the ability of future generations to meet their needs.

terrorism the use of calculated, unlawful physical force or threats of violence against a government, organization, or individual to gain some political, religious, economic, or social objective.

theory a set of logically related statements that attempt to describe, explain, or predict social events.

theory of limited effects a theory that states that the media have a minimal effect on the attitudes and perceptions of individuals.

theory of racial formation a theory that states that the government substantially defines racialized and ethnic relations.

tolerance a condition that occurs when larger doses of a drug are required over time to produce the same physical or psychological effect that was originally achieved by a smaller dose.

total institution a place where people are isolated from the rest of society for a period of time and come under the complete control of the officials who run the institution.

tracking assigning students to specific courses and educational programs on the basis of their test scores, previous grades, or both.

transnational corporation (TNC) a large-scale business organization that is headquartered in one country but operates in many countries, which has the legal power (separate from individual owners or shareholders) to enter into contracts, buy and sell property, and engage in other business activity.

urbanization the process by which an increasing proportion of a population lives in cities rather than in rural areas.

values collective ideas about what is right or wrong, good or bad, and desirable or undesirable in a specific society.

victimless crime a crime that many people believe has no real victim because it involves willing participants in an economic exchange.

violence the use of physical force to cause pain, injury, or death or damage to property.

violent crime actions involving force or the threat of force against others.

wage gap the disparity between women's and men's earnings.

war system components of social institutions (e.g., the economy, government, and education) and cultural beliefs and practices that promote the development of warriors, weapons, and war as a normal part of the society and its foreign policy.

wealth the value of all economic assets, including income and savings, personal property, and income-producing property, minus one's liabilities or debts.

welfare state a nation in which the government intervenes in the welfare of its citizens through various social policies, programs, standards, and regulations.

withdrawal a variety of physical and/or psychological symptoms that habitual drug users experience when they discontinue drug use.

youth crime a violation of law or the commission of a status offence by a young person 12 to 17 years of age.

zero population growth a situation in which a population is totally stable, neither growing nor decreasing from year to year because births, deaths, and migration are in perfect balance.

Abbate, Gay. 1998. "Gangs Small But Growing Roots: Police Hope to Arrest Development." *Globe and Mail.* (November 20):A10.

Abbott, Roberta. 2000. "From Shell Shock to Post-Traumatic Stress Disorder: What Are We Asking of Our Armed Forces Personnel?" Presented at the Third Annual Graduate Student Symposium Conference of Defence Associations Institute (November 3–4).

Abella, Irving. 1989. *A Coat of Many Colours: Two Centuries of Jewish Life in Canada.* Toronto: Lester and Orpen Dennys.

Abella, Irving, and Harold Troper. 1991. *None Is Too Many: Canada and the Jews in Europe 1933–1948* (3rd ed.). Toronto: Lester and Orpen Dennys.

Abu-Laban, Sharon McIrvin, and Susan A. McDaniel. 2001. "Beauty, Status, and Aging." In Nancy Mandell (Ed.), *Feminist Issues: Race, Class, and Sexuality* (3rd ed.). Toronto: Pearson, pp. 108–133.

Adams, Karen L., and Norma C. Ware. 1995. "Sexism and the English Language: The Linguistic Implications of Being a Woman." In Jo Freeman (Ed.), *Women: A Feminist Perspective* (5th ed.). Mountain View, CA: Mayfield Publishing, pp. 331–346.

Adams, Tom. 1991. *Grass Roots: How Ordinary People Are Changing America.* New York: Citadel Press.

Aday, David P., Jr. 1990. *Social Control at the Margins: Toward a General Understanding of Deviance.* Belmont, CA: Wadsworth.

Addiction Research Foundation (ARF). 2000. *Alcohol and Drug Treatment in Ontario: A Guide for Helping Professionals.* Toronto: Centre for Addiction and Mental Health.

Adelaide, David. 2002. "G-8 Security Operation—The Stifling and Criminalizing of Dissent." World Socialist Web site (June 27). Retrieved from **www.wsws.org/articles/2002/jun2002/g8-j27.shtml**

Adlaf, Edward M., and Angela Paglia. 2001. *Drug Use Among Ontario Students 1977–2001.* Toronto: Centre for Addiction and Mental Health.

Adlaf, Edward M., Angela Paglia, and Joseph H. Beitchman. 2002. *The Mental Health and Well-Being of Ontario Students 1991–2001: Findings from the OSDUS.* Toronto: Centre for Addiction and Mental Health.

Adler, Patricia A., Steven J. Kless, and Peter Adler. 1995. "Socialization to Gender Roles: Popularity Amongst Elementary School Boys and Girls." In E.D. Nelson and B.W. Robinson (Eds.), *Gender in the 1990s: Images, Realities and Issues.* Toronto: Nelson, pp. 119–141.

Advocates for Community Based Training and Education for Women (ACTEW). 1998. "ACTEW's Top 8 Reasons Why Workfare Won't Work." In Luciana Ricciutelli, June Larkin, and Eimear O'Neill (Eds.), *Confronting the Cuts: A Sourcebook for Women in Ontario.* Toronto: Inanna, pp. 96–97.

Akers, Ronald L. 1992. *Drugs, Alcohol, and Society: Social Structure, Process, and Policy.* Belmont, CA: Wadsworth.

Albrecht, Gary L. 1992. *The Disability Business: Rehabilitation in America.* Newbury Park, CA: Sage.

Alexander, Karl L., Doris Entwisle, and Maxine Thompson. 1987. "School Performance, Status Relations, and the Structure of Sentiment: Bringing the Teacher Back In." *American Sociological Review,* 52:665–682.

Alexander, Priscilla. 1987. "Prostitution: A Difficult Issue for Feminists?" In Frederique Delacoste and Priscilla Alexander (Eds.), *Sex Work: Writings by Women in the Sex Industry.* San Francisco: Cleis Press, pp. 184–214.

Alfred, Taiaiake. 1999. *Peace, Power, Righteousness: An Indigenous Manifesto.* Don Mills, ON: Oxford University Press.

Allen, Paula Gunn. 1986. *The Sacred Hoop: Recovering the Feminine in American Indian Traditions.* Boston: Beacon Press.

Allman, Dan. 1999. *M is for Mutual, A is for Acts: Male Sex Work and AIDS in Canada.* Co-published with Health Canada; AIDS Vancouver; The HIV, Social, Behavioural, and Epidemiological Studies Unit, Faculty of Medicine, University of Toronto; and the Sex Workers Alliance of Vancouver [online]. Retrieved from **www.walnet.org/members/dan_allman/mutualacts/index.html**

Allport, Gordon. 1958. *The Nature of Prejudice* (abridged ed.). New York: Doubleday/Anchor.

Almaguer, Tomás. 1995. "Chicano Men: A Cartography of Homosexual Identity and Behavior." In Michael S. Kimmel and Michael A. Messner (Eds.), *Men's Lives* (3rd ed.). Boston: Allyn and Bacon, pp. 418–431.

Altman, Lawrence K. 1996. "India Quickly Leads in H.I.V. Cases, AIDS Meeting Hears." *New York Times* (July 8):A8.

Alvi, Shahid, Walter DeKeseredy, and Desmond Ellis. 2000. *Contemporary Social Problems in North American Society.* Don Mills, ON: Addison-Wesley.

Alwin, Duane, Philip Converse, and Steven Martin. 1985. "Living Arrangements and Social Integration." *Journal of Marriage and the Family*, 47:319–334.

Ambert, Anne-Marie. 1998. *Divorce: Facts, Figures, and Consequences.* Ottawa: Vanier Institute of the Family.

American Association of University Women (AAUW). 1992. *The AAUW Report: How Schools Short-Change Girls.* Washington, DC: The AAUW Educational Foundation and National Educational Association.

American Psychiatric Association. 1994. *Diagnostic and Statistical Manual of Mental Disorders IV.* Washington, DC: American Psychiatric Association.

Amott, Teresa, and Julie Matthaei. 1991. *Race, Gender, and Work: A Multicultural Economic History of Women in the United States.* Boston: South End Press.

Anders, George. 1996. *Health against Wealth: HMOs and the Breakdown of Medical Trust.* Boston: Houghton Mifflin.

Andersen, Margaret L., and Patricia Hill Collins (Eds.). 1997. *Race, Class, and Gender: An Anthology* (3rd ed.). Belmont, CA: Wadsworth.

Anderssen, Erin. 2002. "Same-Sex Census Numbers Due Today." *Globe and Mail* (October 22):A9.

Andersson, Thomas, and Georgina Schemberg. 2003. "Transnational Corporations and Export Competitiveness: A Summary and Comment." (February 8). Retrieved from **www.iked.org/pdf/UNCTAD.pdf**

Annan, Kofi. 2002. "Beyond the Horizon." *Time* (August 26):46–47.

Anyon, Jean. 1980. "Social Class and the Hidden Curriculum of Work." *Journal of Education*, 162:67–92.

Appelbe, Alison. 2001. "Culture War: Trans-Sexual Fights for Right to Counsel Rape Victims." *CNS News* (April 17). Retrieved from **www.cnsnews.com/culture/archive/200104/CUL20010417c.html**

Apple, Michael W. 1982. *Education and Power: Reproduction and Contradiction in Education.* London: Routledge & Kegan Paul.

Applebome, Peter. 1995. "For the Ultimate Safe School, Official Eyes Turn to Dallas." *New York Times* (September 20): A1, B8.

Applebome, Peter. 1996. "Grading For-Profit Schools: So Far, So Good." *New York Times* (June 26):A1, A13.

Aristophanes. 2003. *Lysistrata.* Adapted by Adam Webster (orig. published in 1996). Retrieved March 2, 2003, from **www.lysistrataproject.com**

Armstrong, Pat, and Hugh Armstrong. 1996. *Wasting Away: The Undermining of Canadian Health Care.* Don Mills, ON: Oxford University Press.

Arnup, Katherine (Ed.). 1995. *Lesbian Parenting: Living with Pride and Prejudice.* Charlettetown, PEI: gynergy books.

Ash, Roberta. 1972. *Social Movements in America.* Chicago: Markham.

Associated Press. 1999. "Crushed Cock Earns Cash." (December 2). Retrieved from **www.geocities.com/athens/thebes/9940/taboo/sexnews.html**

Atchley, Robert C. 2000. *Social Forces and Aging: An Introduction to Social Gerontology* (9th ed.). Belmont, CA: Wadsworth.

Aulette, Judy Root. 1994. *Changing Families.* Belmont, CA: Wadsworth.

Axinn, William G., and Arland Thornton. 1992. "The Relationship between Cohabitation and Divorce: Selectivity or Casual Influence?" *Demography*, 29(3):357–374.

Bagby, Meredith (Ed.). 1997. *Annual Report of the United States of America 1997.* New York: McGraw-Hill.

Bailey, Ian. 2002. "Dead Girl's Mother Hugs Bullying B.C. Teenager." *National Post* [online] (May 15).

Baker, Jean M. 2002. *How Homophobia Hurts Children: Nurturing Diversity at Home, at School, and in the Community.* London: Harrington Park Press.

Balakrishnan, T.R., Evelyn Lapiere-Adamoyk, and Karol J. Krotk. 1993. *Family and Childbearing in Canada: A Demographic Analysis.* Toronto: University of Toronto Press.

Ballantine, Jeanne H. 1997. *The Sociology of Education: A Systematic Analysis* (4th ed.). Englewood Cliffs, NJ: Prentice-Hall.

Bandura, Albert. 1973. *Aggression: A Social Learning Analysis.* Englewood Cliffs, NJ: Prentice-Hall.

Bandura, Albert, and R. H. Walters. 1977. *Social Learning Theory.* Englewood Cliffs, NJ: Prentice Hall.

Bane, Mary Jo, and David T. Ellwood. 1994. *Welfare Realities: From Rhetoric to Reform.* Cambridge, MA: Harvard University Press.

Bannerji, Himani. 1995. *Thinking Through: Essays on Feminism, Marxism and Anti-Racism.* Toronto: Women's Press.

Barber, Benjamin. 1995. *Jihad vs. McWorld.* Toronto: Random House.

Barber, Benjamin R. 1996. *Jihad vs. McWorld: How Globalism and Tribalism Are Reshaping the World.* New York: Ballantine Books.

Barlett, Donald L., and James B. Steele. 1996. *America: Who Stole the Dream?* Kansas City, KS: Andrews and McMeel.

Barlow, Hugh D. 1996. *Introduction to Criminology* (7th ed.). New York: HarperCollins.

Barlow, Maude. 1996. "Globalization and the Dismantling of Canadian Democracy, Values and Society." PCD Forum, Article # 17 (March 10). **http://iisd1.iisd.ca/pcdf**

Barnett, James H. 1954. *The American Christmas: A Study in National Culture.* New York: Macmillan.

Barofsky, I. 1978. "Compliance, Adherence and the Therapeutic Alliance: Steps in the Development of Self-Care." *Social Science and Medicine*, 12:369–376.

Barrett, Stanley R. 1991. "White Supremists and Neo-Fascists: Laboratories for the Analysis of Racism in Wider Society." In Ormond McKague (Ed.), *Racism in Canada*. Saskatoon: Fifth House, pp. 85–99.

Barry, Kathleen. 1995. *The Prostitution of Sexuality*. New York: New York University Press.

Barry, Tom. 1997. "'Burb-arians Pay Share of Austin's Sales Tax." *Austin American-Statesman* (May 27):A13.

Basow, Susan A. 1992. *Gender Stereotypes and Roles* (3rd ed.). Pacific Grove, CA: Brooks/Cole.

Basrur, Sheila V. 2002. *Ten Key Carcinogens in Toronto Workplaces and Environment: Assessing the Potential for Exposure*. Toronto: Toronto Public Health.

Bauerlein, Monika. 1995. "The Borderless Bordello." *Utne Reader* (November–December):30–32.

Bawer, Bruce. 1994. *A Place at the Table: The Gay Individual in American Society*. New York: Touchstone.

Beare, Margaret E. 1996. *Criminal Conspiracies*. Scarborough, ON: Nelson.

Becker, Howard S. 1963. *Outsiders: Studies in the Sociology of Deviance*. New York: Free Press.

Bedard, Gabriel. 2000. "Deconstructing Whiteness: Pedagogical Implications for Anti-Racism Education." In George J. Sefa-Dei and Agnes Calliste (Eds.), *Power, Knowledge and Anti-Racism Edication: A Critical Reader*. Halifax: Fernwood, pp. 41–56.

Beeghley, Leonard. 1989. *The Structure of Social Stratification in the United States*. Boston: Allyn and Bacon.

Bélanger, Alain. 1998. "Trends in Contraceptive Sterilization." *Canadian Social Trends*, (Autumn):16–19.

Belknap, Joanne. 1996. *The Invisible Woman: Gender, Crime, and Justice*. Belmont, CA: Wadsworth.

Bellamy, Carol. 2003. UNICEF Briefing on Iraq at the Palais, Geneva (January 28). Retrieved from **www.unicef. org/ newsline/2003/03bn01iraq.htm**

Belle, Marilyn, and Kevin McQuillan. 1994. "Births Outside Marriage: A Growing Alternative." *Canadian Social Trends*, (Summer):14–17.

Belsky, Janet. 1990. *The Psychology of Aging: Theory, Research, and Interventions* (2nd ed.). Pacific Grove, CA: Brooks/Cole.

Bem, S.L. 1974. "The Measurement of Psychological Androgyny." *Journal of Consulting and Clinical Psychology*, 42:155–162.

Bennett, Niel G., Ann Klimas Blanc, and David E. Bloom. 1988. "Commitment and the Modern Union: Assessing the Link between Premarital Cohabitation and Subsequent Marital Stability." *American Sociological Review*, 53:127–138.

Benoit, Cecilia M. 2000. *Women, Work, and Social Rights: Canada in Historical and Comparative Perspective*. Scarborough, ON: Prentice Hall/Allyn and Bacon.

Benokraitis, Nijole V. 1993. *Marriage and Families: Changes, Choices, and Constraints*. Englewood Cliffs, NJ: Prentice-Hall.

Benokraitis, Nijole V., and Joe R. Feagin. 1995. *Modern Sexism: Blatant, Subtle, and Covert Discrimination*. Englewood Cliffs, NJ: Prentice-Hall.

Berger, Peter. 1963. *Invitation to Sociology: A Humanistic Perspective*. New York: Anchor.

Berger, Peter, and Hansfried Kellner. 1964. "Marriage and the Construction of Reality." *Diogenes*, 46:1–32.

Berger, Peter, and Thomas Luckmann. 1967. *The Social Construction of Reality: A Treatise in the Sociology of Knowledge*. Garden City, NY: Anchor Books.

Berger, Ronald J., Patricia Searles, and Charles E. Cottle. 1991. *Feminism and Pornography*. Westport, CT: Praeger.

Bergmann, Barbara R. 1986. *The Economic Emergence of Women*. New York: Basic Books.

Bernard, Jessie. 1982. *The Future of Marriage*. New Haven, CT: Yale University Press.

Bertrand, Serzge Capt. 2003. "Fighting Islamist Terrorism: An Indirect Strategic." Approach. *Canadian Military Journal* [online], 3(4/Winter). Retrieved from **www.journal. forces. gc.ca/engraph/v3n4_terror1_e.asp**

Bess, Irwin. 1999. "Widows Living Alone." *Canadian Social Trends*, (Summer):2–5.

Besserer, Sandra, and Catherine Trainor. 2000. "Criminal Victimization in Canada, 1999." *Juristat*, 20(10).

Best, P. 1995. "Women, Men and Work." *Canadian Social Trends*, 36(Spring):30–33.

Biagi, Shirley. 1998. *Media Impact: An Introduction to Mass Media* (3rd. ed.). Belmont, CA: Wadsworth.

Bibby, Reginald. 1995. *The Bibby Report: Social Trends Canadian Style*. Toronto: Stoddart.

Bibby, Reginald W., and Donald C. Posterski. 1985. *The Emerging Generation: An Inside Look at Canada's Teenagers*. Toronto: Irwin.

Bibby, Reginald W., and Donald C. Posterski. 1992. *Teen Trends Canadian Style*. Toronto: Stoddart.

Birgeneau, Robert J. 2002. "The Noise about Rising Tuition." *The University of Toronto Magazine*, (Spring).

Bishop, Anne. 2002. *Becoming an Ally: Breaking the Cycle of Oppression in People* (2nd ed.). Halifax: Fernwood.

Blackwood, E. 1986. "Breaking the Mirror: The Social Construction of Lesbianism and the Anthropological Discourse on Homosexuality." In *The Many Faces of Homosexuality: Anthropological Approaches to Homosexual Behavior*. New York: Harrington Park Press, pp. 1–17.

Bland, R.C., H. Orn, and S.C. Newman. 1988. "Lifetime Prevalence of Psychiatric Disorder in Edmonton, Alberta." *Acta Psychiatrica Scandinavia*, 77(Suppl. 338):24–32.

Blasius, Mark. 2001a. "An Ethos of Lesbian and Gay Existence." In Mark Blasius (Ed.), *Sexual Identities—Queer Politics*. Princeton, NJ: Princeton University Press, pp. 143–177.

Blasius, Mark. 2001b. "Sexual Identities, Queer Politics, and the Status of Knowledge." In Mark Blasius (Ed.), *Sexual Identities—Queer Politics*. Princeton, NJ: Princeton University Press, pp. 3–19.

Blauner, Robert. 1972. *Racial Oppression in America*. New York: Harper & Row.

Bluestone, Barry, and Bennett Harrison. 1982. *The Deindustrialization of America: Plant Closings, Community Abandonment, and the Dismantling of Basic Industry*. New York: Basic Books.

Bonacich, Edna. 1972. "A Theory of Ethnic Antagonism: The Split Labor Market." *American Sociological Review*, 37:547–549.

Bonacich, Edna. 1976. "Advanced Capitalism and Black–White Relations in the United States: A Split Labor Market Interpretation." *American Sociological Review*, 41:34–51.

Bonger, Willem. 1969. *Criminality and Economic Conditions* (abridged ed.). Bloomington, IN: Indiana University Press (orig. published in 1916).

Bonnin, Julie. 1997. "Knockout Drugs." *Austin American-Statesman* (February 2):E1, E12.

Bosetti, Lynn, et al. 2000. *Canadian Charter Schools at the Crossroads: Executive Summary*. Kelowna, BC: Society for the Advancement of Excellence in Education.

Botvin, Gilbert, and Stephanie Tortu. 1988. "Preventing Adolescent Substance Abuse through Life Skills Training." In Richard M. Price, Emory L. Cowen, Raymond P. Lorion, and Julia Ramos-McKay (Eds.), *Fourteen Ounces of Prevention: A Casebook for Practitioners*. Washington, DC: American Psychological Association, pp. 98–110.

Botvin, Gilbert, and Stephanie Tortu. 1988. "Preventing Adolescent Substance Abuse through Life Skills Training." In Richard M. Price, Emory L. Cowan, Raymond P. Lorion, and Julia Ramos-Mckay (Eds.), *Fourteen Ounces of Prevention: A Casebook for Practitioners*. Washington, DC: American Psychological Association, pp. 98–110.

Bourdieu, Pierre, and Jean-Claude Passeron. 1990. *Reproduction in Education, Society, and Culture*. Newbury Park, CA: Sage.

Bourgeois, Philippe. 1995. *In Search of Respect: Selling Crack in el Barrio*. New York: Cambridge University Press.

Bourne, Larry S., and Damian Rose. 2001. "The Changing Face of Canada: The Uneven Geographies of Population and Social Change." *Canadian Geographer*, 45(1):105–119.

Bowles, Samuel, and Herbert Gintis. 1976. *Schooling in Capitalist America: Education and the Contradictions of Economic Life*. New York: Basic Books.

Bowles, Samuel, and Herbert Gintis. 2002. "Schooling in Capitalist America Revisited." *Sociology of Education*, 75(1):1–18.

Boyd, Monica, and Doug Norris. 1999. "The Crowded Nest: Young Adults at Home." *Canadian Social Trends*, (Spring): 2–5.

Bradsher, Keith. 1997. "In the Biggest, Booming Cities, a Car Population Problem." *New York Times* (May 11):E4.

Brannigan, Augustine, Louis Knafla, and Christopher Levy. 1989. *Street Prostitution: Assessing the Impact of the Law—Calgary, Regina, Winnipeg*. Ottawa: Department of Justice Canada.

Brecher, Jeremy, and Tim Costello. 1998. *Global Village or Global Pillage: Economic Reconstruction From the Bottom Up* (2nd ed.). Cambridge, MA: South End Press.

Brennan, Richard. 2002. "Leave the Car, Take the Bus." *Toronto Star* (August 15):A1.

Brill's Content. 2000. "Big Media Road Map" (January):99–102.

British Broadcasting Corporation (BBC). 2000. "The World's Nuclear Arsenal." (May 2).

British Columbia (B.C.) Ministry of Attorney General. 1996. *Community Consultation on Prostitution in British Columbia: Overview of Results*. Victoria, BC: Ministry of Attorney General, Government of British Columbia.

Brodribb, Somer. 1999. "Introduction." In Somer Brodribb (Ed.), *Reclaiming the Future: Women's Strategies for the 21st Century*. Charlottetown, PEI: gynergy books, pp. 13–22.

Brody, Jane E. 1996. "Good Habits Outweigh Genes as Key to a Healthy Old Age." *New York Times* (February 28):B9.

Brown, Phil. 1985. *The Transfer of Care: Psychiatric Deinstitutionalization and Its Aftermath*. Boston: Routledge & Kegan Paul.

Browne, Jan, and Victor Minichiello. 1995. "The Social Meanings Behind Male Sex Work: Implications for Sexual Interactions." *British Journal of Sociology*, 46(4):598–623.

Bruni, Frank. 1996. "Gay Couples Cheer Adoption Ruling, Saying It Lets Law Reflect Reality." *New York Times* (November 5):16.

Budd, Mike, Steve Craig, and Clay Steinman. 1999. *Consuming Environments: Television and Commercial Culture*. New Brunswick, NJ: Rutgers University Press.

Buechler, Steven M. 2000. *Social Movements in Advanced Capitalism: The Political Economy and Cultural Construction of Social Activism*. New York: Oxford University Press.

Bullard, Robert D., and Beverly H. Wright. 1992. "The Quest for Environmental Equity: Mobilizing the African-American Community for Social Change." In Riley E. Dunlap and Angela G. Mertig (Eds.), *American Environmentalism: The U.S. Environmental Movement, 1970–1990*. New York: Taylor & Francis, pp. 39–50.

Bullough, Vern, and Bonnie Bullough. 1987. *Women and Prostitution: A Social History*. Buffalo, NY: Prometheus.

Bumpass, Larry, James E. Sweet, and Teresa Castro Martin. 1990. "Changing Patterns of Remarriage." *Journal of Marriage and the Family*, 52:747–756.

Bunis, William K., Angela Yancik, and David Snow. 1996. "The Cultural Patterning of Sympathy toward the Homeless and Other Victims of Misfortune." *Social Problems* (November):387–402.

Burke, Mary Anne, Joan Lindsay, Ian McDonald, and Gerry Hill. 1997. "Dementia among Seniors." *Canadian Social Trends*, (Summer):24–27.

Burke, R.J. 1994. "Canadian Business Students' Attitudes toward Women as Managers." *Psychological Reports*, 75:1123–1129.

Burleigh, Nina. 1991. "Watching Children Starve to Death." *Time* (June 10):56–58.

Burns, John F. 1996. "Denial and Taboo Blinding India to the Horror of Its AIDS Scourge." *New York Times* (September 22):A1.

Busch, Ruth C. 1990. *Family Systems: Comparative Study of the Family.* New York: P. Lang.

Bush, George W. 2001. Address to a Joint Session of Congress and the American People. Washington, DC. (September 20). Retrieved from **www.whitehouse.gov/news/releases/2001/09/20010920-8.html**

Butler, Robert N. 1969. "Ageism: Another Form of Bigotry." *The Gerontologist*, 9:243–246.

Cable, Sherry, and Charles Cable. 1995. *Environmental Problems, Grassroots Solutions: The Politics of Grassroots Environmental Conflict.* New York: St. Martin's Press.

Cambell, Bruce, Maria Teresa Gutierrez Haces, Andrew Jackson, and Mehrene Larudee. 1999. *Pulling Apart: The Deterioration of Employment and Income in North America Under Free Trade.* Ottawa: Canadian Centre for Policy Alternatives.

Cameron, David. 1995. "The Making of a Polluter: A Social History of Uniroyal Chemical in Elmira." In Michael D. Mehta and Eric Ouellet (Eds.), *Environmental Sociology Theory and Practice.* North York, ON: Captus Press, pp. 297–320.

Canadian Advisory Council on the Status of Women. 1984. *Prostitution in Canada.* Ottawa: Canadian Advisory Council on the Status of Women.

Canadian Association of Food Banks (CAFB). 2002. *Hunger-Count 2002—Eating Their Words: Government Failure on Food Security.* Prepared by Beth Wilson and Emily Tsoa. (October). Toronto: Canadian Association of Food Banks.

Canadian Broadcasting Corporation (CBC). 1999. "Alberta Shooting Renews Gun Debate." (April 30). **http://cbc.ca/news**

Canadian Broadcasting Corporation (CBC). 2002. "Media Ownership." (November 27). Retrieved from **www.cbc.ca/stories/2002/11/27/media_ownership021127**

Canadian Broadcasting Corporation (CBC). 2003. "A Deathly Silence." *Witness* (February 6, 9 p.m. EST).

Canadian Centre for Justice Statistics (CCJS) (Ed.). 1999. *The Juristat Reader: A Statistical Overview of the Canadian Justice System.* Toronto: Thompson.

Canadian Centre for Justice Statistics (CCJS). 2001. "Canadian Crime Statistics, 2000." *Juristat*, 21(8).

Canadian Centre for Policy Alternatives (CCPA). 2002a. "Alternative Federal Budget 2003–04." Retrieved from **www.policyalternatives.ca**

Canadian Council for Policy Alternatives (CCPA). 2003b. "CCPA Analysis of Bill C-36: An Act to Combat Terrorism." (February 12). Retrieved from **www.policyalternatives.ca/publications/c-36.html**

Canadian Council on Social Development (CCSD) and the United Way of Greater Toronto (UWGT). 2000. *A Decade of Decline.* Retrieved from **www.uwgt.org/who_we_help/Decade_in_Decline/Poverty_Report.htm#key_findings**

Canadian Democracy and Corporate Accountability Commission (CDCAC). 2002. "Executive Summary." In *The New Balance Sheet: Corporate Profits and Responsibility in the 21st Century.* Retrieved from **www.corporate-accountability.ca**

Canadian Human Rights Commission. 2003. *Annual Report 2001: The Health of Human Rights in Canada.* Retrieved from **www.chrc-ccdp.ca/ar-ra/RapportAnnuel2001/AR01RA/annualReport_1_rapportAnnuel.asp?l=e**

Canadian Institute of Health Information. 2001. *Health Care in Canada 2001.* Retrieved January 15, 2003, from **http://secure.cihi.ca/cihiweb/dispPage.jsp?cw_page=AR_43_E&cw_topic=43**

Canadian Labour Congress. 2002. "Analysis of UI Coverage for Women" and "The UI Fact Book." (July 2). Retrieved from **www.clc-ctc.ca/web/english/en_index.htm**

Canadian Museum of Civilization, 2003. Retrieved from **www.civilization.ca**

Canadian Nuclear Association. 2002. Retrieved July 30, 2002, from **www.cna.ca**

Canadian Press. 2002. "Fifty People Arrested in Europe and Canada in Anti Money-Laundering Operation." (June 10). Retrieved June 15, 2002, from **www.canada.com/search/site/story.asp?id=DAA8BD19-BECF-4B9E-8083-D3E784E89179**

Canadian Race Relations Foundation (CRRF). 2001. "Canadian Race Relations Foundation Urges Balance in Anti-Terrorism Act; Provisions on Hate Crime Lauded, But Revisions to Bill Still Needed." (November 19). Retrieved from **www.crr.ca/en/MediaCentre/NewsReleases/eMedCen_NewsRel20011119.htm**

Canadian Youth Rights Association (CYRA). 1998. "Media Ageism." Retrieved November 11, 1999, from **www.cyra.org/media/shtml**

Canadian Taxpayers Federation. 2003. Retrieved from **www.taxpayer.com**

Cancian, Francesca M. 1990. "The Feminization of Love." In C. Carlson (Ed.), *Perspectives on the Family: History, Class, and Feminism.* Belmont, CA: Wadsworth, pp. 171–185.

Cancian, Francesca M., and James William Gibson. 1990. *Making War, Making Peace: The Social Foundations of Violent Conflict.* Belmont, CA: Wadsworth.

CanWest Entertainment. 2003. (January 14). Retrieved from **www.canwestglobal.com**

CanWest Global Communications. 2003. "Fast Facts." Retrieved from **www.canwestglobal.com/fastfacts.html**

Capponi, Pat. 1999. *The War at Home: An Intimate Portrait of Canada's Poor.* Toronto: Viking/Penguin.

Cargan, Leonard, and Matthew Melko. 1982. *Singles: Myths and Realities.* Newbury Park, CA: Sage.

Carmichael, Stokely, and Charles V. Hamilton. 1967. *Black Power: The Politics of Liberation in America.* New York: Vintage.

CARP. 1998. *CARP's National Forum on Scams and Frauds.* Toronto: CARP.

Carrier, James G. 1986. *Social Class and the Construction of Inequality in American Education.* New York: Greenwood Press.

Carrington, Peter J. 1999. "Trends in Youth Crime in Canada: 1977–1996." *Canadian Journal of Criminology,* 41(1):1–32.

Carroll, William K. 1997. "Social Movements and Counter-hegemony: Canadian Contexts and Social Theories." In William K. Carroll (Ed.), *Organizing Dissent: Contemporary Social Movements in Theory and Practice.* Toronto: Garamond Press, pp. 3–38.

Casipullai, Amy. 2003. *Bill C-18* (Citizenship Bill). Ontario Council of Agencies Serving Immigrants (OCASI). Retrieved from **www.ocasi.org/sys/anno_detail. asp?AnnoID=70**

Cass, Vivien C. 1984. "Homosexual Identity Formation: Testing a Theoretical Model." *Journal of Sex Research,* 20:143–167.

Castells, Manuel. 1977. *The Urban Question.* London: Edward Arnold.

Catalano, Ralph A., and William McConnell. 1996. "A Time-Series Test of the Quarantine Theory of Involuntary Commitment." *Journal of Health and Social Behavior,* 37:381–387.

CATO Institute. 2003. "China's Military Modernization Poses Little Threat to U.S. Interests: U.S. Defense Spending Dwarfs China and Supports the Most Advanced Military in the World." (January 23). Retrieved from **www.cato. org/new/01-03/01-23-03r.html**

Cavender, Gray. 1995. "Alternative Approaches: Labeling and Critical Perspectives." In Joseph F. Sheley (Ed.), *Criminology: A Contemporary Handbook* (2nd ed.). Belmont, CA: Wadsworth, pp. 349–367.

CBC TV. 1999. *Peacekeeping: The Invisible Wounds.*

CBSNews.com. 2003. "Massive Anti-War Outpouring." (Feb. 15). Retrieved from **www.cbsnews.com/stories/2003/02/ 16/iraq/main540782.shtml**

Center for Cooperative Research. 2003. "Bush's So-called Evidence." (February 25). Retrieved from **www.cooperativeresearch.org/home.htm**

Chambliss, William J. 1988. *Exploring Criminology.* New York: Macmillan.

Chapkis, Wendy. 1997. *Live Sex Acts: Women Performing Erotic Labour.* New York: Routledge.

Chappell, Neena L. 1999. *Volunteering and Healthy Aging: What We Know.* Report for Volunteer Canada, Ottawa: Manulife Financial and Health Canada.

Chase-Lansdale, P. Lindsay, Jeanne Brooks-Gunn, and Roberta L. Palkoff. 1992. "Research and Programs for Adolescent Mothers: Missing Links and Future Promises." *Family Relations,* 40(4):396–403.

Cherlin, Andrew J. 1992. *Marriage, Divorce, and Remarriage* (rev. and enlarged ed.). Cambridge, MA: Harvard University Press.

Cherlin, Andrew J. 1999. "Going to Extremes: Family Structure, Children's Well-Being, and Social Science." *Demography,* 36(4):421–428.

Chermak, Steven M. 1995. *Victims in the News: Crime and the American News Media.* Boulder, CO: Westview.

Chidley, Joe. 1995. "Red Light District. . . From S & M to Bestiality, Porn Flourishes on the Internet." *Maclean's* (May 22):58.

Children Now. 1999. "Children Now Annual Report 1999 Highlights." Retrieved from **www.childrennow.org/ annual-reports/annual- report-1999.htm**

Chomsky, Noam. 1996. *Class Warfare: Interview with David Barsamian.* Monroe, ME: Common Courage Press.

Choudry, Aziz. 2001. "Canada's Dirty War Over Words." *ZMag* (November 21). Retrieved from **www.zmag.org/ sustainers/content/2001-11/21choudry.cfm**

Chudacoff, Howard P. 1989. *How Old Are You? Age Consciousness in American Culture.* Princeton, NJ: Princeton University Press.

Chui, Tina. 1996. "Canada's Population: Charting into the 21st century." *Canadian Social Trends,* (Autumn): 3–7.

Clark, Jocalyn. 1998. "The More Lady You Are, the More They Treat You Like a Lady: Sexual Harassment and Health Risk for Young Women in a Male-Dominated Work Setting." *Canadian Women's Studies,* 18(1):82–85.

Clark, Warren. 1996. "Adult Literacy in Canada, the United States, and Germany." *Canadian Social Trends,* (Winter):27–33.

Clark, Warren. 1998. "Religious Observance, Marriage and the Family." *Canadian Social Trends,* (Autumn):2–7.

Cleeland, N. 1991. "Gasping in Smoggy Mexico City Oxygen Kiosk May Prove Helpful." *San Diego Union* (March 9). (Cited in Michael P. Soroka and George J. Bryjak. 1995. *Social Problems: A World at Risk.* Boston: Allyn and Bacon, p. 116.)

Clement, Tony. 1999. "Notes for Remarks." Retrieved March 5, 2003, from **www.ene.gov.on.ca/envision/news/ 03199s.htm**

Clinard, Marshall B., and R. F. Meier. 1989. *Sociology of Deviant Behavior* (7th ed.). Fort Worth, TX: Holt, Rinehart and Winston.

CNN World. 2003. "European Protesters Fill Cities—Largest-Ever Gatherings Reported in London, Madrid." (February 15). Retrieved from **www.cnn.com/2003/WORLD/ meast/02/15/sprj.irq.protests.europe**

Coady, Lynn. 2001. "Mediating Thobani." *Rabble* News (October 10). Retrieved from **www.rabble.ca/everyones_a_critic. shtml?x=2898**

Coale, Ansley. 1973. "The Demographic Transition." Proceedings of the International Population Conference, Liege. Vol. 1, pp. 53–72. (Cited in Weeks, 1992.)

Coalition for Lesbian and Gay Rights in Ontario (CLGRO). 1998. *Young People and Sex.* Pamphlet [online]. (May). Retrieved from **www.web.net/~clgro/consent/htm**

Coca-Cola. 2003a. (February 14). Retrieved from **www.coca-cola.com**

Coca-Cola. 2003b. "Our Company Snapshot: Facts and Figures." Retrieved from **www.cokecce.com/srclib/1.2html**

Cochrane, J., J. Durbin, and P. Goering. 1997. *Best Practices in Mental Health Reform.* Discussion paper prepared for the Federal/Provincial/Territorial Advisory Network on Mental Health. Ottawa: Health Canada.

Cock, Jacklyn. 1994. "Women and the Military: Implications for Demilitarization in the 1990s in South Africa." *Gender and Society,* 8(2):152–169.

Cohen, Lawrence E., and Marcus Felson. 1979. "Social Change and Crime Rate Trends: A Routine Activity Approach." *American Sociological Review,* 44:588–608.

Coleman, Eli. 1981/2. "Developmental Stages of the Coming Out Process." *Journal of Homosexuality,* 7:31–43.

Coleman, James W. 1995. "Respectable Crime." In Joseph F. Sheley (Ed.), *Criminology: A Contemporary Handbook* (2nd ed.). Belmont, CA: Wadsworth, pp. 249–269.

Coles, Gerald. 1987. *The Learning Mystique: A Critical Look at "Learning Disabilities."* New York: Pantheon.

Colhoun, J. 1992. "Census Fails to Quash Report on Iraqi Deaths." *The Guardian* (April 22):5.

Collenette, David. 2002. "Where Ottawa Stands." *Globe and Mail* (June 24):T3.

Collins, Patricia Hill. 1991. *Black Feminist Thought: Knowledge, Consciousness, and the Politics of Empowerment.* New York: Routledge.

Collins, Randall. 1979. *The Credential Society: An Historical Sociology of Education.* New York: Academic Press.

Coltrane, Scott. 1989. "Household Labor and the Routine Production of Gender." *Social Problems,* 36:473–490.

Community Childhood Hunger Identification Project. 1995. *A Survey of Childhood Hunger in the United States.* Washington, DC: Food Research and Action Committee (July).

Comstock, Gary David. 1991. *Violence against Lesbians and Gay Men.* New York: Columbia University Press.

Connell, Christopher. 1995. "Birth Rate for Unmarried Women Surges." *Austin American-Statesman* (June 7):A18.

Corbeil, Jean-Pierre. 1998. "Literacy: Does Language Make a Difference?" *Canadian Social Trends,* (Winter):2–6.

Cormack, Elizabeth. 1999. "New Possibilities for a Feminism 'in' Criminology." *Canadian Journal of Criminology,* 41(2):161–170.

Corporate Watch. 2003. Retrieved from **www.corporate watch.org.uk/**

Corr, Charles A., Clyde M. Nabe, and Donna M. Corr. 1994. *Death and Dying, Life and Living.* Pacific Grove, CA: Brooks/Cole.

Coser, Lewis A. 1969. "The Visibility of Evil." *Journal of Social Issues,* 25:101–109. In Bunis, William K., Angela Yancik, and David Snow. 1996. "The Cultural Patterning of Sympathy toward the Homeless and Other Victims of Misfortune." *Social Problems* (November):387–402.

Cottle, Charles E., Patricia Searles, Ronald J. Berger, and Beth Ann Pierce. 1989. "Conflicting Ideologies and the Politics of Pornography." *Gender and Society,* 3:303–333.

Council of Canadians. 1999. "Trade and Investment Must Serve . . . ." Retrieved March 7, 2003, from **www.canadians.org/display_document.htm?COC_token=1@@465cb4da239ed216035817807630876d&id=332&isdoc=1&catid=133**

Council on Foreign Relations. 2003. "How Did Canada, Australia, and New Zealand Respond to September 11?" (February 22). Retrieved from **www.terrorismanswers.com/coalition/canada.html**

Coverman, Shelley. 1989. "Women's Work Is Never Done: The Division of Domestic Labor." In Jo Freeman (Ed.), *Women: A Feminist Perspective* (4th ed.). Mountain View, CA: Mayfield, pp. 356–368.

Cowan, Gloria, C. Lee, D. Levy, and D. Snyder. 1988. "Domination and Inequality in X-Rated Videocassettes." *Psychology of Women Quarterly,* 12:299–311.

Cowan, Gloria, and Margaret O'Brien. 1990. "Gender and Survival vs. Death in Slasher Films: A Content Analysis." *Sex Roles,* 23:187–196.

Cowgill, Donald O. 1986. *Aging around the World.* Belmont, CA: Wadsworth.

Cowley, Geoffrey. 1997. "Can Marijuana Be Medicine?" *Newsweek* (February 3):22–27.

Cox, Oliver C. 1948. *Caste, Class, and Race.* Garden City, NY: Doubleday.

Crary, David, and Jerry Schwartz. 2001. "A Day of Infamy: World Trade Center Collapses in Terrorist Attack." *Seattle Times* (September 11).

Crombie, David. 2001. "Grow Smart or Grow Worse." *Globe and Mail* (April 4):A15.

Crossette, Barbara. 1996a. "Agency Sees Risk in Drug to Temper Child Behavior: Worldwide Survey Cites Overuse of Ritalin." *New York Times* (February 29):A7.

Crossette, Barbara. 1996b. "U.N. Survey Finds World Rich-Poor Gap Widening." *New York Times* (July 15):A3.

Crossette, Barbara. 1996c. "Hope, and Pragmatism, for U.S. Cities Conference." *New York Times* (June 3):A3.

Crossette, Barbara. 1997. "Democracies Love Peace, Don't They?" *New York Times* (June 1):E3.

Crossette, Barbara. 2000. "Europe Stares at a Future Built by Immigrants." *New York Times* (January 2):WK1, 4.

CTV. 1995. *Hearts of Hate: The Battle For Young Minds.* Toronto: Investigative Productions.

Cullen, Dave. 1999. "The Reluctant Activist." *Salon* (October 15):1–4. Retrieved November 15, 1999, from **www.salon.com/news/feature/1999/10/15/laramie/index. html**

Cumming, Elaine C., and William E. Henry. 1961. *Growing Old: The Process of Disengagement.* New York: Basic Books.

Curatolo, Peter W., and David Robertson. 1983. "The Health Consequences of Caffeine." *Annals of Internal Medicine,* 98:641–653. (Cited in Levinthal, 1996.)

Currah, Paisley. 2001. "Queer Theory, Lesbian and Gay Rights, and Transsexual Marriages." In Mark Blasius (Ed.), *Sexual Identities—Queer Politics*. Princeton, NJ: Princeton University Press, pp. 178–199.

Curran, James, Michael Gurevitch, and Janet Woollacott. 1982. "The Study of the Media: Theoretical Approaches." In Michael Gurevitch, Tony Bennett, James Curran, and Janet Woollacott (Eds.). *Culture, Society and the Media*. London: Methuen, pp. 5–35.

Cushman, John H., Jr. 1997. "E.P.A. Seeks Cut, Not End, to Pollution by Paper Mills." *New York Times* (May 21):A10.

Dagg, Anne Innis, and Patricia J. Thompson. 1988. *MisEducation: Women and Canadian Universities.* Toronto: OISE Press.

Dahl, Robert A. 1961. *Who Governs?* New Haven, CT: Yale University Press.

Daley, Suzanne. 1997. "Zaïre's Fall Jolts Neighboring Angola's Frail Peace." *New York Times* (June 8):3.

Dali Lama. 1990. *Ocean of Wisdom: Guidelines for Living.* New York: Harper & Row.

Daly, Kathleen, and Meda Chesney-Lind. 1988. "Feminism and Criminology." *Justice Quarterly,* 5:497–533.

Daniels, Ronald J. 2002. "Let's Reach for the Gold in Higher Education." *Globe and Mail* (March 1).

Danziger, Sheldon, and Peter Gottschalk. 1995. *America Unequal.* Cambridge, MA: Harvard University Press.

Dauncey, Guy. 2003. "101 Ways to Stop the War on Iraq." Retrieved from **www.earthfuture.com**

Davidson, Julia O'Connell. 1996. "Sex Tourism in Cuba." *Race and Class,* 38(1):39–49.

Davies, Scott, Janice Aurini, and Linda Quirke. 2002. "New Markets for Private Education in Canada." *Education Canada.* Fall: 36–38.

Davis, Kingsley. 1937. "The Sociology of Prostitution." *American Sociological Review,* 2:744–755.

Davis, Kingsley, and Amyra Grossbard-Shechtman (Eds.). 1985. *Contemporary Marriage: Comparative Perspectives on a Changing Institution.* New York: Russell Sage Foundation.

de Broucher, Patrice, and Laval Lavallée. 1998. "Getting Ahead in Life: Does Education Count?" *Canadian Social Trend,* (Summer):11–15.

DeKeseredy, Walter S., and Ronald Hinch. 1991. *Woman Abuse: Sociological Perspectives.* Toronto: Thompson.

Delk, J.L., R.B. Madden, M. Livingston, and T.T. Ryan. 1986. "Adult Perceptions of the Infant as a Function of Gender Labeling and Observer Gender." *Sex Roles,* 15:527–534.

Demczuk, Irene, Michele Caron, Ruth Rose, and Lyne Bouchard. 2002. *Recognition of Lesbian Couples: An Inalienable Right.* Ottawa: Status of Women Canada.

DeMont, John. 2002. "Cleaning Up the Harbour Has a Downside." *Maclean's* (July 29):19.

Denis, Angele. 2001. "Corridors: Language as Trap and Meeting Ground." In Carl E. James and Adrienne Shadd (Eds.), *Talking About Identity: Encounters in Race, Ethnicity and Language.* Toronto: Between the Lines, pp. 133–145.

Denton, M., and Walters, V. 1999. "Gender Differences in Structural and Behavioural Determinants of Health: An Analysis of Social Production of Health." *Social Science and Medicin,* 48:1221–1235.

Department of Finance, Canada. 2003. "Chapter One: The Budget Plan." (February 18). Retrieved from **www.fin.gc.ca/ scripts/register_e.asp**

Department of Justice, Canada. 2001. "The Royal Assent of Bill C-36, The Anti-Terrorism Act." *NewsRoom* (December 18).

DePasquale, Katherine M. 1999. "The Effects of Prostitution." Retrieved December 3, 1999, from **www.feminista.com/ v1n5/depasquale.html**

de Silva, Rex. 1980. "Developing the Third World." *World Press Review* (May):48.

Devereaux, Anna. 1987. "Diary of a Prostitute." *Cosmopolitan* (October 1987):164, 166.

Devor, Aaron. 2003. Interview with Aaron Devor, Dean of Graduate Studies, University of Victoria, by Vicki Nygaard, February 20, 2003. See also Devor's Web site for more information and additional publications at **web.uvic. ca/ ~ahdevor/**

Devor, Holly. 1989. *Gender Blending: Confronting the Limits of Duality.* Bloomington: Indiana University Press.

Devor, Holly. 1997. *FTM: Female to Male Transsexuals in Society.* Bloomington: Indiana University Press.

Dews, Peter B. 1984. "Behavioral Effects of Caffeine." In Peter B. Dews (Ed.), *Caffeine: Perspectives from Recent Research.* Berlin: Springer-Verlag, pp. 86–103. (Cited in Levinthal, 1996.)

Diamond, Jared. 2000. "The Greening of Corporate America." *New York Times* (January 8):A31.

Diamond, Sara. 1986. "Childhood's End: Some Comments on Pornography and the Fraser Committee." In J. Lowman, M.A. Jackson, T.S. Palys, and S. Gavigan (Eds.), *Regulating Sex: An anthology of Commentaries on the Findings of the Badgley and Fraser Reports.* Vancouver: School of Criminology, Simon Fraser University, pp. 143–158.

Diamond, Sara. 1988. "Pornography: Image and Reality." In Arlene Tigar McLaren (Ed.), *Gender and Society: Creating a Canadian Women's Sociology.* Mississauga, ON: Copp Clark Pitman, pp. 390–404.

Dickinson, Harley D. 2000. "Work and Unemployment as Social Issues." In B. Singh Bolaria (Ed.), *Social Issues and Contradictions in Canadian Society* (3rd ed.). Toronto: Harcourt Brace, pp. 26–50.

Dickinson, Harley D. 2002. "Mental Health Policy in Canada: What's the Problem?" In B. Singh Bolaria and Harley D. Dickinson. (Eds.), *Health, Illness, and Health Care in Canada* (3rd ed.). Scarborough, ON: Nelson.

Dietz, P. 1986. "Mass, Serial and Sensational Homicide." *Bulletin of the New England Medical Society,* 62:477–491.

DiFranza, Joseph R., and Robert A. Lew. 1995. "Effect of Maternal Cigarette Smoking on Pregnancy Complications and Sudden Infant Death Syndrome." *The Journal of Family Practice,* 40:385–394.

Dimmock, Gary. 2002. "The Secret Life of a Teenage Cyber Informant." *Vancouver Sun* (June 29):A1, A14.

Dobbin, Murray. 1998. *Myth of the Good Corporate Citizen: Democracy Under the Rule of Big Business.* North York, ON: Stoddart Publishing.

Dobbin, Murray. 2001. "Globalization: A World Ruled by Corporations." *CCPA Monitor* (April). Retrieved from **www.policyalternatives.ca**

Dobrzynski, Judith H. 1996. "Study Finds Few Women in Five Highest Company Jobs." *New York Times* (October 16):C3.

Doezema, Jo. 1998. "Forced to Choose: Beyond the Voluntary v. Forced Prostitution Dichotomy." In Kamala Kempadoo and Jo Doezema (Eds.), *Global Sex Workers: Rights, Resistance and Redefinition.* New York: Routledge, pp. 34–50.

Dollard, John, Neal E. Miller, Leonard W. Doob, O. H. Mowrer, and Robert R. Sears. 1939. *Frustration and Aggression.* New Haven, CT: Yale University Press.

Domhoff, G. William. 1978. *The Powers That Be: Processes of Ruling Class Domination in America.* New York: Random House.

Domhoff, G. William. 1990. *The Power Elite and the State: How Policy Is Made in America.* New York: Aldine de Gruyter.

Donahue, Paul. 2000. "The WTO Protests in Seattle: This Is What Democracy Looks Like." *The Maine Woods: A Publication of the Forest Ecology Network,* (Winter):4–1.

Donavon, Tina. 2001. "Being Transgender and Older: A First Person Account." *Journal of Gay and Lesbian Social Services: Issues in Practice, Policy and Research,* 13(4):19–22.

Donnelly, John. 2003. "CIA Had Idea of Contagion, and of Governments' Reactions." *Boston Globe.* Retrieved April 26, 2003, from **www.boston.com/dailyglobe2/ 117/nation/**

Donziger, Steven R. (Ed.). 1996. *The Real War on Crime: The Report of the National Criminal Justice Commission.* New York: HarperPerennial.

Doyle, James A. 1995. *The Male Experience* (3rd ed.). Madison, WI: Brown and Benchmark.

Draffan, George. 2003. *Directory of Transnational Corporations.* (February 14). **www.endgame.org/dtc/directory. html**

Drohan, Madelaine. 1998. "How the Net Killed the MAI: Grassroots Groups Used Their Own Globalization to Derail Deal." *Globe and Mail* (April 29).

Dua, Enakshi. 1999. "Canadian Anti-Racist Feminist Thought: Scratching the Surface of Racism." In Enakshi Dua and Angela Robertson (Eds.), *Scratching the Surface: Canadian Anti-Racist Feminist Thought.* Toronto: Women's Press, pp. 7–31.

Duffy, Anne, and Rina Cohen. 2001. "Violence Against Women: The Struggle Persists." In Nancy Mandell (Ed.), *Feminist Issues: Race, Class, and Sexuality* (3rd ed.). Toronto: Pearson, pp. 134–165.

Duffy, Ann, and Nancy Mandell. 2001. "The Growth in Poverty and Social Inequality: Losing Faith in Social Justice" in *Canadian Society: Meeting the Challenges of the 21st Century.* Don Mills, ON: Oxford University Press, pp. 77–116.

Dull, Diana, and Candace West. 1991. "Accounting for Cosmetic Surgery: The Accomplishments of Gender." *Social Problems,* 38(1):54–70.

Duncan, David F. 1991. "Violence and Degradation as Themes in 'Adult' Videos." *Psychology Reports,* 69(1):239–240.

Dunlap, David W. 1996. "Role of Openly Gay Episcopalians Causes a Rift in the Church." *New York Times* (March 21):A8.

Dunlap, Riley E. 1992. "Trends in Public Opinion toward Environmental Issues: 1965–1990." In Riley E. Dunlap and Angela G. Mertig (Eds.), *American Environmentalism: The U.S. Environmental Movement, 1970–1990.* New York: Taylor & Francis, pp. 89–113.

Durkheim, Emile. 1933. *Division of Labor in Society.* Trans. George Simpson. New York: Free Press (orig. published in 1893).

Durkheim, Emile. 1964. *The Rules of Sociological Method.* Trans. Sarah A. Solovay and John H. Mueller. New York: Free Press (orig. published in 1895).

Dworkin, Andrea. 1988. *Letters to a War Zone.* New York: Dutton/New America Library.

Dye, Thomas R. 2000. *The Irony of Democracy: An Uncommon Introduction to American Politics* (millennium ed.). Fort Worth, TX: Harcourt College.

Dynes, Wayne R. (Ed.). 1990. *Encyclopedia of Homosexuality.* New York: Garland.

Dyson, Rose A. 2000. *Mind Abuse: Media Violence in an Information Age.* Montreal: Black Rose Books.

Eckersley, Robyn. 2001. "Ecofeminism and Environmental Democracy: Exploring the Connections." *Women & Environments International Magazine,* 52/53(Fall):23–26.

The Ecologist. 1993. *Whose Common Future? Reclaiming the Commons.* Philadelphia: New Society Publishers.

The Economist. 1995. "Size of the Internet" (April 15):102.

The Economist. 2002a. (February 2): 16.

The Economist. 2002b. (June 1):76.

Ecumenical Coalition for Economic Justice. 1996. *Promises to Keep: Miles to Go: An Examination of Canada's Record in the International Year for the Eradication of Poverty.* Toronto: Ecumenical Coalition for Economic Justice.

Eder, Donna. 1985. "The Cycle of Popularity: Interpersonal Relations among Female Adolescents." *Sociology of Education,* 58(July):154–165.

Eder, Donna, and Stephen Parker. 1987. "The Cultural Production and Reproduction of Gender: The Effect of Extracurricular Activities on Peer Group Culture." *Sociology of Education,* 60:200–213.

Editorial Collective. 2001. *Resist: A Grassroots Collection of Stories, Poetry, Photos and Analyses from the Quebec City FTAA Protests and Beyond.* Halifax: Fernwood.

Edmonton Journal. 1992. "Salaries of the Top Brass Fuel Ethical and Political Debates." Ontario: Southam News, (June 27):D1.

Ehrenreich, Barbara. 1997. *Blood Rites: Origins and History of the Passions of War.* New York: Metropolitan Books.

Ehrenreich, Barbara, and Deirdre English. 1995. "Blowing the Whistle on the 'Mommy Track'." In E.D. Nelson and B.W. Robinson (Eds.), *Gender in the 1990s: Images, Realities and Issues.* Toronto: Nelson, pp. 211–215.

Ehrlich, Paul R., and Anne H. Ehrlich. 1991. *The Population Explosion.* New York: Touchstone/Simon & Schuster.

Eichler, Margrit (Ed.). 1995. *Change of Plans: Towards a Non-Sexist City.* Toronto: Garamond Press.

Elliott, Michael. 1999. "The New Radicals." *Newsweek* (December 13):36–39.

Elliott, Patricia, and Nancy Mandell. 2001. "Feminist Theories." In Nancy Mandell (Ed.), *Feminist Issues: Race, Class, and Sexuality* (3rd ed.). Toronto: Prentice Hall, pp. 23–48.

Engelhardt, H. Tristan, Jr. 1996. *Foundations of Bioethics.* New York: Oxford University Press.

Engels, Friedrich. 1972. *The Origin of the Family, Private Property and the State.* [orig. published in 1884]. New York: Pathfinder.

Enloe, Cynthia H. 1987. "Feminists Thinking about War, Militarism, and Peace." In Beth Hess and Myra Marx Feree (Eds.), *Analyzing Gender: A Handbook of Social Science Research.* Newbury Park, CA: Sage, pp. 526–547.

Environment Canada. 2002. Retrieved August 15, 2002, from **www.ec.gc.ca/water/en/e_quickfacts.htm**

Epstein, Cynthia Fuchs. 1988. *Deceptive Distinctions: Sex, Gender, and the Social Order.* New Haven, CT: Yale University Press.

Epstein, Cynthia Fuchs. 1993. *Women in Law* (3rd ed.). Urbana, IL: University of Illinois Press.

Erikson, Kai T. 1962. "Notes on the Sociology of Deviance." *Social Problems,* 9:307–314.

Erikson, Kai T. 1991. "A New Species of Trouble." In Stephen Robert Crouch and J. Stephen Kroll-Smith (Eds.), *Communities at Risk: Collective Responses to Technological Hazards.* New York: Peter Land, pp. 11–29.

Erikson, Kai T. 1994. *A New Species of Trouble: Explorations in Disaster, Trauma, and Community.* New York: Norton.

Essed, Philomena. 1990. *Everyday Racism: Reports from Women of Two Cultures.* Claremont, CA: Hunter House.

Essed, Philomena. 1991. *Understanding Everyday Racism.* Newbury Park, CA: Sage.

Evans, Robert G., Kimberlyn M. McGrail, Steven G. Morgan, Morris L. Barer, and Clyde Hertzeman. 2001. "Apocalpyse Now: Population and the Future of Health Care Systems." *Canadian Journal on Aging,* 20(suppl. 1):160–191.

Eyles, John, S. Martin Taylor, Jamie Baxter, Doug Sider, and Dannis Willms. 1993. "The Social Construction of Risk in a Rural Community: Responses of Local Residents to the 1990 Hagersville (Ontario) Tire Fire." *Risk Analysis,* 13(3):281–290.

Fagot, Beverly I. 1984. "Teacher and Peer Reactions to Boys' and Girls' Play Styles." *Sex Roles,* 11:691–702.

Fair Vote Canada. 2001. "An Overview of the Issues and the Citizens' Campaign for Voting System Reform." Retrieved from **www.fairvotecanada.org**

FAO. 1995. *FAO Yearbook 1995.* Rome, Italy: Food and Agricultural Organization of the United Nations.

Feagin, Joe R. 1975. *Subordinating the Poor: Welfare and American Beliefs.* Englewood Cliffs, NJ: Prentice-Hall.

Feagin, Joe R., and Clairece Booher Feagin. 1997. *Social Problems: A Critical-Conflict Perspective* (5th ed.). Upper Saddle River, NJ: Prentice Hall.

Feagin, Joe R., and Robert Parker. 1990. *Building American Cities: The Urban Real Estate Game* (2nd ed.). Englewood Cliffs, NJ: Prentice-Hall.

Feagin, Joe R., and Melvin P. Sikes. 1994. *Living with Racism: The Black Middle-Class Experience.* Boston: Beacon Press.

Feagin, Joe R., and Hernán Vera. 1995. *White Racism: The Basics.* New York: Routledge.

Federman, Joel. 1998. "Introduction." *National Television Violence Study,* vol. 3. Thousand Oaks, CA: Sage.

Feodorowycz, Orest. 2001. "Homicide in Canada." *Juristat.* 21(9).

Findlay, Deborah A., and Leslie J. Miller. 2002. "Through Medical Eyes: The Medicalization of Women's Bodies." In B. Singh Bolaria and Harley D. Dickinson. (Eds.), *Health, Illness, and Health Care in Canada* (3rd ed.) Scarborough, ON: Nelson.

Fine, Gary Alan. 1987. *With the Boys: Little League Baseball and Preadolescent Culture.* Chicago: University of Chicago Press.

Fine, Michelle. 1991. *Framing Dropouts: Notes on the Politics of an Urban Public High School.* Albany, NY: State University Press of New York.

Fineman, Howard. 1997. "Who Needs Washington?" *Newsweek* (January 27):50–52.

Finkelhor, David. 1984. *Child Abuse: New Theory and Research.* New York: Free Press.

Firestone, Shulamith. 1970. *The Dialectic of Sex.* New York: Morrow.

Fishbein, Diana H., and Susan E. Pease. 1996. *The Dynamics of Drug Abuse.* Boston: Allyn and Bacon.

Fisher, Lawrence M. 1996. "Health on Line: Doctor Is In, and His Disk Is Full." *New York Times* (June 14):C1, C8.

Flanagan, William G. 1995. *Urban Sociology: Images and Structure* (2nd ed.). Boston: Allyn and Bacon.

Fleras, Augie. 2001. *Social Problems in Canada: Conditions, Constructions, and Challenges* (3rd ed.). Toronto: Prentice Hall.

Fleras, Augie, and Jean Leonard Elliott. 1992. *The Challenge of Diversity: Multiculturalism in Canada.* Scarborough, ON: Nelson.

Fleras, Augie, and Jean Leonard Elliott. 1996. *Unequal Relations: An Introduction to Race, Ethnic and Aboriginal Dynamics in Canada.* Scarborough, ON: Prentice Hall.

Fleras, Augie, and Jean Leonard Elliott. 1999. *Unequal Relations: An Introduction to Race, Ethnic, and Aboriginal Dynamics in Canada* (3rd ed.). Scarborough, ON: Prentice Hall/Allyn and Bacon.

Fleras, Augie, and Jean Leonard Elliott. 2003. *Unequal Relations: An Introduction to Race and Ethnic Dynamics in Canada* (4th ed.). Toronto, ON: Prentice Hall.

Fleras, Augie, and Jean Lock Kunz. 2001. *Media and Minorities: Representing Diversity in a Multicultural Canada.* Toronto: Thompson.

Florida, Richard. 2002. "Toronto 2020." *Globe and Mail* (June 24):T8.

Flynn, Karen. 1998. "Feeding Kids on Tuna and Bologna: The Impact of the Cuts on Single Black Women in Toronto." In Luciana Ricciutelli, June Larkin, and Eimear O'Neill (Eds), *Confronting the Cuts: A Sourcebook for Women in Ontario.* Toronto: Inanna, pp. 143–148.

Fong, Eric, and Kumiko Shibyuya. 2000. "The Spatial Separation of the Poor in Canadian Cities." *Demography*, 37(4): 449–459.

Forcese, D. 1997. *The Canadian Class Structure* (4th ed.). Toronto: McGraw-Hill Ryerson.

Foreman, Judy. 1996. "Caring for Parents Long-Distance Is a Baby Boomer's Nightmare." *Austin American-Statesman* (November 3):E1, E14.

Fox, Mary Frank. 1995. "Women and Higher Education: Gender Differences in the Status of Students and Scholars." In Jo Freeman (Ed.), *Women: A Feminist Perspective* (5th ed.). Mountain View, CA: Mayfield, pp. 220–237.

Frank, Jeffrey. 2000. "Fifteen Years of AIDS in Canada." In *Canadian Social Trends 3.* Ottawa: Minister of Supply and Services Canada, and Toronto: Thompson.

Frankenberg, Ruth. 1993. *White Women, Race Matters: The Social Construction of Whiteness.* Minneapolis: University of Minnesota Press.

Frederick, Judith A., and Monica Boyd. 1998. "The Impact of Family Structure on High School Completion." *Canadian Social Trends,* (Spring):12–18.

Freedman, Jonathan L. 2002. *Media Violence and Its Effect on Aggression: Assessing the Scientific Evidence.* Toronto: University of Toronto Press.

Freeze, Colin. 2001. "Support for Death Penalty Plunges." *Globe and Mail* (February 16):A1.

Freidan, Betty. 1963. *The Feminine Mystique.* New York: Norton.

Freiler, Christa, and Judy Cerny. 1998. *Benefiting Canada's Children: Perspectives on Gender and Social Responsibility.* (March). Ottawa: Research Directorate, Status of Women Canada.

French, Dolores, with Linda Lee. 1988. *Working: My Life as a Prostitute.* New York: E.P. Dutton.

Freudenberg, Nicholas, and Carl Steinsapir. 1992. "Not in Our Backyards: The Grassroots Environmental Movement." In Riley E. Dunlap and Angela G. Mertig (Eds.), *American Environmentalism: The U.S. Environmental Movement, 1970–1990.* New York: Taylor & Francis, pp. 27–37.

Freund, Matthew, Nancy Lee, and Terri Leonard. 1991. "Sexual Behavior of Clients with Street Prostitutes in Camden, New Jersey." *Journal of Sex Research,* 28(4) (November): 579–591.

Frideres, James S. 2000. "First Nations: Walking the Path of Social Change." In B. Singh Bolaria (Ed.), *Social Issues and Contradictions in Canadian Society* (3rd ed.). Toronto: Harcourt Brace, pp. 195–227.

Frideres, Jim S. 2002. "Overcoming Hurdles: Health Care and Aboriginal People." In B. Singh Bolaria and Harley D. Dickinson. (Eds.), *Health, Illness, and Health Care in Canada* (3rd ed.). Scarborough, ON: Nelson.

Friedan, Betty. 1993. *The Fountain of Age.* New York: Simon & Schuster.

Friedman, Thomas L. 2000a. "Boston E-Party." *New York Times* (January 1):A31.

Friedman, Thomas L. 2000b. "The Spirit of Y2K." *New York Times* (January 7):A23.

Friedmann, John. 1995. "The World City Hypothesis." In Paul L. Knox and Peter J. Taylor (Eds.), *World Cities in a World-System.* Cambridge, England: Cambridge University Press, pp. 317–331.

Friedman, George, and Meredith Friedman. 1996. *The Future of War: Power, Technology, and American World Dominance in the 21st Century.* New York: Crown.

Friedrichs, David O. 1996. *Trusted Criminals: White Collar Crime in Contemporary Society.* Belmont, CA: Wadsworth.

Friend, Tim. 1996. "Teens and Drugs: Today's Youth Just Don't See the Dangers." *USA Today* (August 21):1A, 2A.

Fudenberg, H.H. 1995. "Gulf War Syndrome: A Scientific Analysis of the Government's Mistreatment of Gulf War Veterans, Part I." Conference report (June 2):17–19. Retrieved from **www.nitrf.org/gulf.html**

Fullilove, Mindy Thompson, E. Anne Lown, and Robert E. Fullilove. 1992. "Crack 'Hos and Skeezers: Traumatic Experiences of Women Crack Users." *Journal of Sex Research,* 29(2):275–288.

Gabor, Thomas. 1995. *Responding to School Violence: An Assessment of Zero Tolerance and Related Policies.* Ottawa: Solicitor General of Canada.

Gabriel, Trip. 1995a. "A New Generation Seems Ready to Give Bisexuality a Place in the Spectrum." *New York Times* (June 12):C10.

Gabriel, Trip. 1995b. "Some On-Line Discoveries Give Gay Youths a Path to Themselves." *New York Times* (July 2):1, 9.

Gabriel, Trip. 1996. "High-Tech Pregnancies Test Hope's Limit." *New York Times* (January 7):1, 10–11.

Gailey, Christine Ward. 1987. "Evolutionary Perspectives on Gender Hierarchy." In Beth B. Hess and Myra Marx Ferree

(Eds.), *Analyzing Gender: A Handbook of Social Science Research.* Newbury Park, CA: Sage, pp. 32–67.

Gamson, Joshua. 1994. *Claims to Fame: Celebrity in Contemporary America.* Berkeley, CA: University of California Press.

Gamson, Joshua. 1996. "Must Identity Movements Self-Destruct? A Queer Dilemma." In Steven Seidman (Ed.), *Queer Theory/Sociology.* Cambridge, MA: Blackwell, pp. 395–420.

Gamson, William. 1990. *The Strategy of Social Protest* (2nd ed.). Belmont, CA: Wadsworth.

Gans, Herbert. 1982. *The Urban Villagers: Group and Class in the Life of Italian Americans* (updated and expanded ed.; orig. published in 1962). New York: Free Press.

Gardner, Carol Brooks. 1995. *Passing By: Gender and Public Harassment.* Berkeley, CA: University of California Press.

Gardner, Tracey A. 1994. "Racism in Pornography and the Women's Movement." In Alison M. Jaggar (Ed.), *Living with Contradictions: Controversies in Feminist Social Ethics.* Boulder, CO: Westview, pp. 171–176.

Garreau, Joel. 1991. *Edge City: Life on the New Frontier.* New York: Doubleday.

Gawin, F. H., and E. H. Ellinwood, Jr. 1988. Cocaine and Other Stimulants: Actions, Abuse, and Treatment. *New England Journal of Medicine,* 318:1173–1182.

Gee, Ellen, and M. Kimball. 1987. *Women and Aging.* Toronto: Butterworths.

Gee, Ellen M. and Susan A. McDaniel. 1991. "Pension Politics and Challenges: Retirement Policy Implications." *Canadian Public Policy-Analyse de politiques,* 17(4):456–472.

Gelfand, Donald E. 1994. *Aging and Ethnicity: Knowledge and Services.* New York: Springer.

Gerbner, George, 1995. "Television Violence: The Power and the Peril." In Gail Dines and Jean M. Humez (Eds.), *Gender, Face, and Class in Media: A Text-Reader.* Thousand Oaks, CA: Sage, pp. 547–557.

Gerson, Kathleen. 1993. *No Man's Land: Men's Changing Commitments to Family and Work.* New York: Basic Books.

Gerstel, Naomi, and Harriet Engel Gross. 1995. "Gender and Families in the United States: The Reality of Economic Dependence." In Jo Freeman (Ed.), *Women: A Feminist Perspective* (5th ed.). Mountain View, CA: Mayfield, pp. 92–127.

Gertler, Meric S. 2001. "Urban Economy and Society in Canada: Flows of People, Capital and Ideas." *Isuma,* 2(3):119–130.

Gessen, Masha. 1993. "Lesbians and Breast Cancer." *The Advocate* (February 9):22–23.

Gfellner, Barbara M., and John D. Hundleby. 1995. "Patterns of Drug Use among Native and White Adolescents: 1990–1993." *Canadian Journal of Public Health,* 86:95–97.

Gibbs, Lois Marie, as told to Murray Levine. 1982. *Love Canal: My Story.* Albany, NY: State University of New York Press.

Gibbs, Nancy. 1996. "Cause Celeb: Two High-Profile Entertainers Are Props in a Worldwide Debate over Sweatshops and the Use of Child Labor." *Time* (June 17): 28–30.

Gibson, James William, and Francesca M. Cancian. 1990. "Is War Inevitable?" In Francesca M. Cancian and James William Gibson (Eds.), *Making War, Making Peace: The Social Foundations of Violent Conflict.* Belmont, CA: Wadsworth, pp. 1–10.

Gil, Vincent E., Marco S. Wang, Allen F. Anderson, Guo Matthew Lin, and Zongjian Oliver Wu. 1996. "Prostitutes, Prostitution and STD/HIV Transmission in Mainland China." *Social Science and Medicine,* 42(1):141–153.

Gilbert, Gustave. 1995. *Nuremberg Diary.* Cambridge, MA: DaCapo Press.

Gilbert, Richard J. 1986. *Caffeine: The Most Popular Stimulant.* New York: Chelsea House.

Gilder, George. 1981. *Wealth and Poverty.* New York: Basic Books.

Gillis, Charlie. 2001. "Racial Profiling Inevitable: Courts Expected to Permit Practice at Points of Entry." *National Post* [online] (October 10). Retrieved from **www.geocities. com/CapitolHill/2381/CanadaCustomsandRevenue Agency/cdnracialprofileinevitable.html**

Giobbe, Evelina. 1993. "Surviving Commercial Sexual Exploitation." In Diana E. H. Russell (Ed.), *Making Violence Sexy: Feminist Views on Pornography.* New York: Teachers College Press, pp. 37–41.

Giobbe, Evelina. 1994. "Confronting the Liberal Lies about Prostitution." In Alison M. Jaggar (Ed.), *Living with Contradictions: Controversies in Feminist Social Ethics.* Boulder, CO: Westview, pp. 120–136.

Gizewksi, Peter. 1994. "Military Activity and Environmental Security: The Case of Radioactivity in the Arctic in CARC." *Northern Perspectives* [online], 21(4/Winter). Retrieved from **www.carc.org/pubs/v21no4/military.htm**

Gladwell, Malcolm. 1997. "Damaged: Why Do Some People Turn into Violent Criminals?" *The New Yorker* (February 24–March 3):132–147.

Glaser, Barney, and Anselm Strauss. 1968. *Time for Dying.* Chicago: Aldine.

Glazier, Richard H., Elizabeth M. Badley, Julie E. Gilbert, and Lorne Rothman. 2000. "The Nature of Increased Hospital Use in Poor Neighbourhoods: Findings from a Canadian Inner City." *Canadian Journal of Public Health,* 91(4): 268–273.

Gleick, Elizabeth. 1996. "The Children's Crusade." *Time* (June 3): 30–35.

Glick, Paul C., and Sung-Ling Lin. 1986. "More Young Adults Are Living with Their Parents: Who Are They?" *Journal of Marriage and the Family,* 48:107–112.

Global Custodian. 1997. "Custody: Canadian Clubbed." (Spring). Retrieved from **www.assetpub.com/archive/gc/ 97-01gcspring/ spring97GC016a.html**

Global Policy Forum. 2003. "The Threat of U.S. War Against Iraq." (Feb. 26). Retrieved from **www.globalpolicy.org/security/issues/iraq/attackindex.htm**

Goffman, Erving. 1961. *Asylums: Essays on the Social Situation of Mental Patients and Other Inmates.* Chicago: Aldine.

Gold, Rachel Benson, and Cory L. Richards. 1994. "Securing American Women's Reproductive Health." In Cynthia Costello and Anne J. Stone (Eds.), *The American Woman, 1994–1995.* New York: Norton, pp. 197–222.

Goldberg, Carey, 1996. "A Victory for Same-Sex Parenting, at Least." *New York Times* (December 5):A20.

Goldberg, Carey. 1997. "Quiet Roads Bringing Thundering Protests." *New York Times* (May 23):A8.

Goldberg, Joshua. 1998. Personal correspondence to a friend. Author's Files. Victoria, BC.

Goldberg, Robert A. 1991. *Grassroots Resistance: Social Movements in Twentieth Century America.* Belmont, CA: Wadsworth.

Golden, Anne, William H. Currie, Elizabeth Greaves, and E. John Latimer. 1999. *Taking Responsibility for Homelessness: An Action Plan for Toronto Overview and Recommendations.* Toronto: City of Toronto.

Golden, Stephanie. 1992. *The Women Outside: Meanings and Myths of Homelessness.* Berkeley, CA: University of California Press.

Goldie, Terry (Ed). 2001. *In a Queer Country: Gay and Lesbian Studies in the Canadian Context.* Vancouver: Arsenal Pulp Press.

Goldstein, Joshua. 2001. *War and Gender: How Gender Shapes the War System andVice Versa.* Cambridge, MA: Cambridge University Press.

Goode, Erich. 1989. *Drugs in American Society* (3rd ed.). New York: McGraw-Hill.

Goode, William J. 1976. "Family Disorganization." In Robert K. Merton and Robert Nisbet (Eds.), *Contemporary Social Problems* (4th ed). New York: Harcourt Brace Jovanovich, pp. 511–554.

Goode, William J. 1982. "Why Men Resist." In Barrie Thorne with Marilyn Yalom (Eds.), *Rethinking the Family: Some Feminist Questions.* New York: Longman, pp. 131–150.

Goodman, Emily Jane. 1999. "Seducers, Harassers, and Wimps in Black Robes." *New York Times* (December 19):AR47, 51.

Goodman, Peter S. 1996. "The High Cost of Sneakers." *Austin American-Statesman* (July 7):F1, F6.

Gordon, David M. 1996. *Fat and Mean: The Corporate Squeeze of Working Americans and the Myth of Managerial "Downsizing."* New York: Martin Kessler Books/ The Free Press.

Gordon, Frances Linzee. 2000. *Lonely Planet Guide to Ethiopia, Eritrea, and Djibouti* (1st ed.). Victoria, Australia: Lonely Planet.

Gordon, Milton M. 1964. *Assimilation in American Life: The Role of Race, Religion, and National Origins.* New York: Oxford University Press.

Gordon, Robert M. 2000. "Criminal Business Organizations, Street Gangs and 'Wanna-be' Groups: A Vancouver Perspective." *Canadian Journal of Criminology,* 42(1):39–60.

Gottdiener, Mark. 1985. *The Social Production of Urban Space.* Austin, TX: University of Texas Press.

Gover, Tzivia. 1996a. "Fighting for Our Children." *The Advocate* (November 26):22–30.

Gover, Tzivia. 1996b. "Occupational Hazards." *The Advocate* (November 26):36–38.

Gover, Tzivia. 1996c. "The Other Mothers." *The Advocate* (November 26):31.

Graham, Ian D., and Paul M. Baker. 1989. "Status, Age, and Gender: Perceptions of Old and Young People." *Canadian Journal on Aging,* 8(3):255–267.

Graham, John R., Karen J. Swift, and Roger Delaney. 2000. *Canadian Social Policy: An Introduction.* Scarborough, ON: Prentice Hall/Allyn and Bacon.

Graveline, Fyre Jean. 2000. "Lived Experiences of an Aboriginal Feminist Transforming the Curriculum." In Carl E. James (Ed.), *Experiencing Difference.* Halifax: Fernwood, pp. 283–293.

Gray, Paul. 1996. "Gagging the Doctors." *Time* (January 8):50.

Green, K. 1985. "Identification of the Facets of Self-Health Management." *Evaluation and the Health Professions,* 8:323–338.

Greenberg, Edward S., and Benjamin I. Page. 1993. *The Struggle for Democracy.* New York: HarperCollins.

Greene, Mark. 2003. Press Release for The Lysistrata Project. Retrieved March 2, 2003, from **www.pecosdesign. com/lys/press1**

Greene, Vernon L., and J. I. Ondrich. 1990. "Risk Factors for Nursing Home Admissions and Exits." *Journal of Gerontology,* 45:S250–S258.

Greenpeace. 1996. "History of Nuclear Weapons Testing." **http://archive.greenpeace.org/~comms/nukes/ctbt/read9.html**

Grillo, Trina, and Stephanie M. Wildman. 1996. "Obscuring the Importance of Race: the Implication of Making Comparisons Between Racism and Sexism (or Other isms)." In Stephanie M. Wildman (Ed.), *Privilege Revealed: How Invisible Preference Undermines America.* New York: New York University Press, pp. 85–102.

Grobe, Jeanine (Ed.). 1995. *Beyond Bedlam: Contemporary Women Psychiatric Survivors Speak Out.* Chicago: Third Side Press.

Gross, Leonard. 1983. *How Much Is Too Much: The Effects of Social Drinking.* New York: Random House.

Guma, Greg. 2001. "Corporate Media and the Indy Challenge— A Talk for FTAA Convergence Conference." The MediaChannel (April 14). Retrieved from **www.media-channel. org**

Guslits, Mark. 2002. "*Let's Build* Leads Toronto's Affordable Housing Plans." *Canadian Housing,* 19(1):23–24.

Gutstein, Donald. 2000. "Blindspots: Big Business Escapes the Critical Media Spotlight." *Media Magazine*, (Winter). Retrieved from **www.caj.ca/mediamag**

Hacker, Andrew. 1995. *Two Nations: Black and White, Separate, Hostile, Unequal* (rev. ed.). New York: Ballantine Books.

Hackett, Robert A, Richard Gruneau, Donald Gutstein, Timothy A. Gibson, and NewsWatch Canada. 1999. *The Missing News: Filters and Blind Spots in Canada's Press*. Aurora, ON: Canadian Centre for Policy Alternatives/Garamond Press.

Haddock, Vicki. 1999. "Study: Kids Are Hooked on Media." *Austin American-Statesman* (November 21):A32.

Hadekel, Peter. 2002. "Down from the Summit." *Montreal Gazette* (June 29).

Hagan, John, John H. Simpson, and A.R. Gillis. 1987. "Class in the Household: A Power-Control Theory of Gender and Delinquency." *American Journal of Sociology*, 92:788–816.

Hall, Roberta M., with Bernice R. Sandler. 1982. *The Classroom Climate: A Chilly One for Women?* Washington, DC: Association of American Colleges, Project on the Status and Education of Women.

Hall, Roberta M. 1984. *Out of the Classroom: A Chilly Campus Climate for Women*. Washington, DC: Association of American Colleges, Project on the Status and Education of Women.

Hamilton, James T. 1998. *Channeling Violence: The Economic Market for Violent Television Programming*. Princeton, NJ: Princeton University Press.

Hannigan, John A. 1995. *Environmental Sociology: A Social Constructionist Perspective*. New York: Routledge.

Hansell, Saul. 1996. "Identity Crisis: When a Criminal's Got Your Number." *New York Times* (June 16):E1, E5.

Hansell, Saul. 2000. "America Online Agrees to Buy Time Warner for $165 Billion; Media Deal Is Richest Merger." *New York Times* (January 11):A1, C11.

Hantover, Jeffrey P. 1998. "The Boy Scouts and the Validation of Masculinity." In Michael S. Kimmel and Michael A. Messner (Eds.), *Men's Lives* (4th ed.). Boston: Allyn and Bacon, pp. 101–108.

Hardina, Donna. 1997. "Workfare in the U.S.: Empirically Tested Programs or Ideological Quagmire?" In Eric Shragge (Ed.), *Workfare: Ideology for a New Under-Class*. Toronto: Garamond Press, pp. 131–148.

Hardy, Eric S. 1996. "Annual Report on American Industry." *Forbes* (January 1):76–79.

Harlow, C. W. 1991. *Female Victims of Violent Crime*. Washington, DC: U.S. Department of Justice, Bureau of Justice Statistics.

Harper, Charles L. 2001. *Environment and Society Human Perspectives on Environmental Issues* (2nd ed.). Upper Saddle River, NJ: Prentice Hall.

Harper's. 2002. "Harper's Index." (March 13).

Harris, Judith R. 1998. *The Nurture Assumption: Why Children Turn Out the Way They Do*. New York: Free Press.

Harrison, Susan. 1997. "Working with Women." In Susan Harrison and Virginia Carver (Eds.), *Alcohol and Drug Problems: A Practical Guide for Counsellors*. Toronto: Addiction Research Foundation, pp. 219–244.

Hartley, Nina. 1994. "Confessions of a Feminist Porno Star." In Alison M. Jaggar (Ed.), *Living with Contradictions: Controversies in Feminist Social Ethics*. Boulder, CO: Westview, pp. 176–178.

Hartmann, Heidi. 1976. "Capitalism, Patriarchy, and Job Segregation by Sex." *Signs: Journal of Women in Culture and Society*, 1(Spring):137–169.

Hartmann, Heidi. 1981. "The Family as the Locus of Gender, Class, and Political Struggle: The Example of Housework." *Signs*, 6:366–394.

Hauchler, Ingomar, and Paul M. Kennedy (Eds.). 1994. *Global Trends: The World Almanac of Development and Peace*. New York: Continuum.

Havighurst, Robert J., Bernice L. Neugarten, and Sheldon S. Tobin. 1968. "Disengagement and Patterns of Aging." In Bernice L. Neugarten (Ed.), *Middle Age and Aging*. Chicago: University of Chicago Press, pp. 161–172.

Hawaleshka, Danylo. 2002. "Measuring Health Care." *Maclean's* (June 17):23–31.

Hawley, Amos. 1950. *Human Ecology*. New York: Ronald Press.

Hawley, Amos. 1981. *Urban Society* (2nd ed.). New York: Wiley.

Hay-Edie, David. 2002. "The Military's Impact on the Environment: A Neglected Aspect of the Sustainable Development Debate." In *A Briefing Paper for States and Non-Governmental Organisations*. (August). Geneva: International Peace Bureau.

Hays, Constance L. 1995. "If the Hair Is Gray, Con Artists See Green: The Elderly Are Prime Targets." *New York Times* (May 21):F1, F5.

Hays, Mathew. 1997. "Kathleen Shannon Falks about Being Captured on Media." *Montréal Mirror*. Retrieved August 21, 1997, from **www.montrealmirror.com/archives/1997/082197/film4.html**.

Health Canada. 1993. *Family Violence and Substance Abuse*. Ottawa: National Clearinghouse on Family Violence.

Health Canada. 1998. *Canada's Drug Strategy*. Ottawa: Minister of Public Works and Government Services Canada.

Health Canada. 2001. "Marijuana for Medical Purposes." Retrieved March 1, 2002, from **www.hc-sc.gc.ca/english/protection/marijuana.html**

Health Canada. 2002. "45 000 Deaths a Year." Retrieved March 15, 2002, from **www.gosmokefree.ca**

Hendrick, Dianne. 1999. "Youth Court Statistics 1997–98: Highlights." Canadian Centre for Justice Statistics (Eds.), *The Juristat Reader: A Statistical Overview of the Canadian Justice System*. Toronto: Thompson, pp. 85–100.

Hendriks, Aart, Rob Tielman, and Evert van der Veen. 1993. *The Third Pink Book: A Global View of Lesbian and Gay Liberation and Oppression*. Buffalo, NY: Prometheus.

Hennessy, Rosemary, and Chrys Ingraham. 1997. "Introduction: Reclaiming Anticapitalist Feminism." In Rosemary Hennessy and Chrys Ingraham (Eds.), *Materialist Feminism: A Reader in Class, Difference, and Women's Lives*. New York: Routledge, pp.1–16.

Henry, Frances, and Carol Tator. 1999. "State Policy and Practices as Racialized Discourse: Multiculturalism, the *Charter*, and Employment Equity." In Peter S. Li (Ed.), *Race and Ethnic Relations in Canada* (2nd ed.). Don Mills, ON: Oxford University Press, pp. 88–115.

Henry, Frances, and Carol Tator. 2000. "The Theory and Practice of Democratic Racism in Canada." In Madeline A. Kalbach and Warren E. Kalbach (Eds.), *Perspectives on Ethnicity in Canada: A Reader*. Toronto: Harcourt Brace, pp. 285–302.

Henry, Francis, Carol Tator, Winston Mattis, and Tim Rees. 2000. *The Colour of Democracy: Racism in Canadian Society*. (2nd ed.). Toronto: Harcourt Brace.

Herbert, Bob. 1995. "Not a Living Wage." *New York Times* (October 9):A11.

Herek, Gregory M. 1995. "Psychological Heterosexism and Anti-Gay Violence: The Social Psychology of Bigotry and Bashing." In Michael S. Kimmel and Michael A. Messner (Eds.), *Men's Lives* (3rd ed.). Boston: Allyn and Bacon, pp. 341–353.

Herman, Edward S., and Noam Chomsky. 1988. *Manufacturing Consent: The Political Economy of the Mass Media*. New York: Pantheon Books.

Hessing, Melody. 1993. "Mothers' Management of Their Combined Workloads: Clerical Work and Household Needs." *Canadian Review of Sociology and Anthropology*, 301:37–63.

Hessing, Melody. 1995. "The Sociology of Sustainability: Feminist Eco/nomic Approaches to Survival." In Michael D. Mehta and Eric Ouellet (Eds.), *Environmental Sociology Theory and Practice*. North York, ON: Captus Press, pp. 231–254.

Hewa, Soma. 2002. "Physicians, the Medical Profession, and Medical Practice." In B. Singh Bolaria and Harley D. Dickinson. (Eds.), *Health, Illness, and Health Care in Canada* (3rd ed.). Scarborough, ON: Nelson.

Higley, Stephen Richard. 1995. *Privilege, Power and Place: The Geography of the American Upper Class*. Lanham, MD: Rowman & Littlefield.

Hills, Stuart L. 1971. *Crime, Power, and Morality*. Scranton, PA: Chandler.

Hirschi, Travis. 1969. *Causes of Delinquency*. Berkeley, CA: University of California Press.

Hirschi, Travis, and Michael J. Hindelang. 1977. "Intelligence and Delinquency: A Revisionist Review." *American Sociological Review*, 42:571–586.

Hochschild, Arlie Russell, with Ann Machung. 1989. *The Second Shift: Working Parents and the Revolution at Home*. New York: Viking/Penguin.

Hoffman, Andrew J. 1994. "Love Canal Lives." *E Magazine* (November–December):19–22.

Hollinger Press. 2003. Homepage. (January 13). Retrieved from **www.hollinger.com**

Holloway, Kelly. 2002. "Black Students Slam U of T for Law Tuition Hike." *Varsity* (February 25).

Holmes, Ronald M. 1983. *The Sex Offender and the Criminal Justice System*. Springfield, IL: Charles C. Thomas.

Holmes, Robert M. 1988. *Serial Murder*. Beverl y Hills, CA: Sage.

Holt, John C. 1964. *How Children Fail*. New York: Dell.

hooks, bell. 1984. *Feminist Theory: From Margin to Centre*. Boston: South End Press.

Hooyman, Nancy R., and H. Asuman Kiyak. 1996. *Social Gerontology: A Multidisciplinary Perspective*. Boston: Allyn and Bacon.

Houseknecht, Sharon, Suzanne Vaughn, and Anne Macke. 1984. "Marital Disruption among Professional Women: The Timing of Career and Family Events." *Social Problems*, 31(1):273–284.

Hoynes, William. 2002. "Why Media Mergers Matter." (January 16). Retrieved from **www.opendemocracy.net/ debates/article-8-24-47.jsp**

Hulchanski, J. David. 1990. "Planning New Urban Neighbourhoods: Lessons from Toronto's St. Lawrence Neighbourhood." In *UBC Planning Papers*. Vancouver: School of Community and Regional Planning, University of British Columbia.

Human Resources Development Canada (HRDC). 2002. *Advancing the Inclusion of Persons With Disabilities*. Ottawa: Government of Canada report (December). Retrieved from **www.hrdc-drhc.gc.ca/hrib/sdd-dds/odi/documents/AIPD/ fdr000.shtml**

Human Suffering Index. 1992. Washington, DC: Population Crisis Committee (now Population Action International).

Husk, Norma. 1998. "Men's Resistance to Men's Education: The Personal is Political." *Canadian Women's Studies*, 17–4:107–112.

Huston, Aletha C. 1985. "The Development of Sex Typing: Themes from Recent Research." *Developmental Review*, 5:2–17.

Hynes, Samuel. 1997. *The Soldiers' Tale: Bearing Witness to Modern War*. New York: Allen Lane/Penguin.

IDFA, NMPF, and USDEC. 2002. "News Release: U.S. Dairy Industry Applauds WTO Ruling Against Canada on Compliance with Dairy Export Subsidies." (June 25). Retrieved from **www.idfa.org/news/releases/2002/usdairy. cfm**

Illich, Ivan. 1975. *Medical Nemesis*. London: Calder and Brown.

Immem, Wallace. 2002. "Village Scores High Marks for Quality of Urban Life." *Globe and Mail* (August 5):A10.

Inciardi, James, Dorothy Lockwood, and Anne E. Pottieger. 1993. *Women and Crack-Cocaine*. New York: Macmillan.

Indymedia. 2003. "Historic Global Resistance." (February 12). **http://seattle.indymedia.org**

Infertility Awareness Association of Canada. 2003. Retrieved April 20, 2003, from **www.iaac.ca/english/articles/insurance.asp**

Ingram, Gordon Brent. 2001. "Redesigning Wreck: Beach Meets Forest as Location of Male Homoerotic Culture and Placemaking in Pacific Canada." In Terry Goldie (Ed.), *In a Queer Country: Gay and Lesbian Studies in the Canadian Context*. Vancouver: Arsenal Pulp Press, pp. 188–208.

International Labour Organization. 2003. Retrieved from **www.ilo.org/public/english/**

International Peace Bureau. 2001. Retrieved from **www.ipb.org**

Ipsos-Reid. 2002. "Canadians Say Computer Hardware (86%) and Teacher Training (82%) are the Two Main Barriers to Greater Use of Computers and Internet in Schools. Retrieved July 10, 2002, from **www.ipsos-reid.com**

Jackson, Robert, and Doreen Jackson. 1996. *Canadian Government in Transition: Disruption and Continuity*. Scarborough, ON: Prentice Hall.

Jaffee, David. 1990. *Levels of Socio-economic Development Theory*. Westport, CT: Praeger.

JAMA: The Journal of the American Medical Association. 1996. "Health Care Needs of Gay Men and Lesbians in the United States" (May 1):1354–1360.

Janhevich, Derek E. 1999. "The Changing Nature of Fraud in Canada." In Canadian Centre for Justice Statistics (Eds.), *The Juristat Reader: A Statistical Overview of the Canadian Justice System*. Toronto: Thompson, pp. 283–296.

Jankowski, Martín Sánchez. 1991. *Islands in the Street: Gangs and American Urban Society*. Berkeley, CA: University of California Press.

Jiwani, Yasmin. 1997. "Reena Virk: The Erasure of Race." The FREDA Centre for Research on Violence against Women and Children, Simon Fraser University, BC. (December). Retrieved from **www.harbour.sfu.ca/freda/articles/virk.htm**

Johnson, Bruce D., Paul J. Goldstein, Edward Preble, James Schmeidler, Douglas S. Lipton, Barry Spunt, and Thomas Miller. 1985. *Taking Care of Business: The Economics of Crime by Heroin Abusers*. Lexington, MA: Lexington Books.

Johnson, Holly. 1996. *Dangerous Domains: Violence against Women in Canada*. Toronto: Nelson.

Jolin, Annette. 1994. "On the Backs of Working Prostitutes: Feminist Theory and Prostitution Policy." *Crime and Delinquency*, 40(1):69–83.

Jones, Charles, Lorna Marsden, and Lorne Tepperman. 1990. *Lives of Their Own: The Individualization of Women's Lives*. Don Mills, ON: Oxford University Press.

Josephson, Wendy L. 1995. *Television Violence: A Review of the Effects on Children of Different Ages*. Ottawa: Department of Canadian Heritage. Retrieved February 21, 2003, from **www.media-awareness.ca/eng/med/home/resource/tvviorp.htm**

JUMP. 2002. Retrieved from **www.jumptutoring.org**

Jung, John. 1994. *Under the Influence: Alcohol and Human Behavior*. Pacific Grove, CA: Brooks/Cole.

Kadie, Carl. 1993. *Computers and Academic Freedom* [online]. Retrieved from **www.eff.org.CAF/news/nov_28_1993**

Kairos. 2003. "A Hopeful Step in a Long Journey: A Report on Iraq Peace Events Held on 18 January 2003." (January 18). Retrieved from **www.kairoscanada.org/english/programme/iraq/eventsreport(030118).htm**

Kalish, Richard A. 1985. *Death, Grief, and Caring Relationships* (2nd ed.). Monterey, CA: Brooks/Cole.

Kaminer, Wendy. 1990. *A Fearful Freedom: Women's Flight from Equality*. Reading, MA: Addison-Wesley.

Kane, Hal. 1995. "Leaving Home." *Transaction: Social Science and Modern Society* (May–June):16–25.

Kantrowitz, Barbara. 1993. "Live Wires." *Newsweek* (September 6): 42–48.

Kapadia, Reshma. 2003. "AOL-TW May Write Down Billions Again." *Kansas City Star* (January 8). Retrieved from **www.kansascity.com/mld/kansascity/business/4902614.htm**

Kaplan, Robert D. 1996. "Cities of Despair." *New York Times* (June 6):A19.

Katz, Janet, and William J. Chambliss. 1995. In Joseph F. Sheley (Ed.), *Criminology: A Contemporary Handbook* (2nd ed.). Belmont, CA: Wadsworth, pp. 275–303.

Kazemipur, Abdolmohammad, and Shiva S. Halli. 2000. *The New Poverty in Canada: Ethnic Groups and Ghetto Neighbourhoods*. Toronto: Thompson.

Kazempur, Abdolmohammed, and Shiva S. Halli. 2001. The changing colour of poverty in Canada. *Canadian Review of Sociology and Anthropology*. 38(2): 217–238.

Katz, Stephen. 2000. "Busy Bodies: Activity, Aging, and the Management of Everyday Life." *Journal of Aging Studies*, 14(2):135–152.

Kelber, Harry. 2002. "President Bush Offers Flimsy Reasons for Waging a Reckless War against Iraq." *Labor Educator* [online] (August 21). Retrieved from **www.laboreducator.org/bshirq.htm**

Kemp, Alice Abel. 1994. *Women's Work: Degraded and Devalued*. Englewood Cliffs, NJ: Prentice Hall.

Kempadoo, Kamala. 1998. "Introduction: Globalizing Sex Workers' Rights." In Kamala Kempadoo and Jo Doezema (Eds.), *Global Sex Workers: Rights, Resistance and Redefinition*. New York: Routledge, pp. 1–28.

Kempe, C. Henry, F. Silverman, B. Steele, W. Droegemueller, and H. Silver. 1962. "The Battered-Child Syndrome." *Journal of the American Medical Association*, 181:17–24.

Kempe, Ruth S., and C. Henry Kempe. 1978. *Child Abuse*. Cambridge, MA: Harvard University Press.

Kendall, Diana. 2000. *Sociology in Our Times: The Essentials* (2nd ed.). Belmont, CA: Wadsworth.

Kendall, Diana. 2001. *Social Problems in a Diverse Society* (2nd ed.). Needham Heights, MA: Allyn & Bacon. See p. 28.

Kennedy, Paul. 1993. *Preparing for the Twenty-First Century*. New York: Random House.

Kessler, Ronald C. 1994. "Lifetime and 12-Month Prevalence of DSM-III-R Psychiatric Disorders in the United States: Results of the National Comorbidity Survey." *JAMA, The Journal of the American Medical Association*, 271 (March 2): 654D.

Kessler-Harris, Alice. 1990. *A Woman's Wage: Historical Meanings and Social Consequences*. Lexington, KY: University Press of Kentucky.

"Ketupa.net media profiles: Black and Hollinger." (April 2003). **www.ketupa.net/black1.htm**

Khayatt, Didi. 2001. "Addendum to What Makes Lesbianism Thinkable? Theorizing Lesbianism From Adrienne Rich to Queer Theory." In Nancy Mandell (Ed.), *Feminist Issues: Race, Class and Sexuality*. Toronto: Prentice Hall, pp. 49–74.

Kidron, Michael, and Ronald Segal. 1995. *The State of the World Atlas*. New York: Penguin.

Kiel, Douglas P., David T. Felson, Marian T. Hanna, Jennifer J. Anderson, and Peter W. F. Wilson. 1990. "Caffeine and the Risk of Hip Fracture: The Framington Study." *American Journal of Epidemiology*, 132:675–684.

Kilbourne, Jean. 1999. *Deadly Persuasion: Why Women and Girls Must Fight the Addictive Power of Advertising*. New York: Free Press.

Kimber, Stephen. 2002. "Last Word: The Last Spike." *Media Magazine*, (8(4/ Winter). Retrieved from **www.caj.ca/mediamag/winter2002/lastword.html**

Kimmel, Michael S. 1987. "The Contemporary 'Crisis' in Masculinity in Historical Perspective." In Harry Brod (Ed.), *The Making of Masculinities*. Boston: Allen and Unwin, pp. 121–153.

Kimmel, Michael S. (Ed.). 1990. *Men Confront Pornography*. New York: Crown Books.

King, Leslie, and Madonna Harrington Meyer. 1997. "The Politics of Reproductive Benefits: U.S. Insurance Coverage of Contraceptive and Infertility Treatments." *Gender and Society*, 11(1):8–30.

King-Irani, Laurie. 2002. "Fundamentalisms, Media, and the New McCarthyism: How Demagogues are Hijacking Washington, DC." A presentation delivered at the 7th annual "Common Terms: The Dialogue of Civilizations" conference in Beirut, Lebanon. The Electronic Intifada. (December 13). **http://electronicintifada.net/v2/article990.shtml**

Kingsley, Cherry, and Melanie Mark. 2000. *Sacred lives: Canadian Aboriginal Children and Youth Speak Out About Sexual Exploitation*. Vancouver: Save the Children Canada.

Kingstone, Barbara. 2002. "Invisible Women." *Forever Young*, (June):42.

Kinsman, Gary. 1996. *The Regulation of Desire: Homo and Hetero Sexualities* (2nd ed., rev.). Montreal: Black Rose Books.

Kipnis, Laura. 1996. *Bound and Gagged: Pornography and the Politics of Fantasy in America*. New York: Grove Press.

Kirsch, Max H. 2000. *Queer Theory and Social Change*. London: Routledge.

Kitzinger, Celia. 1987. *The Social Construction of Lesbianism*. London: Sage.

Kivel, Paul. 1996. *Uprooting Racism: How White People Can Work for Racial Justice*. Philadelphia: New Society Publishers.

Klein, Naomi. 2000. *No Logo: Taking Aim at the Brand Bullies*. Toronto: Vintage.

Klein, Naomi. 2002. *Fences and Windows: Dispatches from the Front Lines of the Globalization Debate*. Ed. Debra Ann Levy. Toronto: Vintage.

Klockars, Carl B. 1979. "The Contemporary Crises of Marxist Criminology." *Criminology*, 16:477–515.

Knapp, Caroline. 1996. *Drinking: A Love Story*. New York: Dial.

Knight, Graham. 1998. "The Mass Media." In Robert Brym (Ed.), *New Society: Sociology for the 21st Century*. Toronto: Harcourt Brace, pp.103–127.

Knox, Paul L., and Peter J. Taylor (Eds.). 1995. *World Cities in a World-System*. Cambridge, England: Cambridge University Press.

Kolata, Gina. 1996a. "Experts Are at Odds on How Best to Tackle Rise in Teen-Agers' Drug Use." *New York Times* (September 18):A17.

Kolata, Gina. 1996b. "On Fringes of Health Care, Untested Therapies Thrive." *New York Times* (June 17):A1, C11.

Kosmin, Barry A., and Seymour P. Lachman. 1993. *One Nation under God: Religion in Contemporary American Society*. New York: Crown Trade Paperbacks.

Kremarik, Frances. 2000. "One Hundred Years of Urban Development." *Canadian Social Trends*, (Winter):18–22.

Krohn, Marvin. 1995. "Control and Deterrence Theories of Criminality." In Joseph F. Sheley (Ed.), *Criminology: A Contemporary Handbook* (2nd ed.). Belmont, CA: Wadsworth, pp. 329–347.

Kübler-Ross, Elisabeth. 1969. *On Death and Dying*. New York: Macmillan.

Kunisawa, Byron. 1996. "Designs of Omission." Workshop handout. Cultural Solutions. Author's Files, Victoria, BC. Retrieved from **www.byronkunisawa.com**

Kurz, Demie. 1989. "Social Science Perspectives on Wife Abuse: Current Debates and Future Directions." *Gender and Society*, 3(4):489–505.

Kurz, Demie. 1995. *For Richer, for Poorer: Mothers Confront Divorce*. New York: Routledge.

Lalonde, Marc. 1974. *A New Perspective on the Health of Canadians*. Ottawa: Minister of Supply and Services.

Lamanna, Marianne, and Agnes Riedmann. 1994. *Marriages and Families: Making Choices and Facing Change* (5th ed.). Belmont, CA: Wadsworth.

Langelan, Martha J. 1993. *Back Off! How to Confront and Stop Sexual Harassment and Harassers*. New York: Fireside/Simon & Schuster.

Langlois, Stéphanie, and Peter Morrison. 2002. "Suicide Deaths and Attempts." *Social Trends*, (Autumn):20–25.

Lappé, Frances Moore, and Paul Martin Du Bois. 1994. *The Quickening of America: Rebuilding Our Nation, Remaking Our Lives.* San Francisco: Jossey-Bass.

Laqueur, Thomas. 1992. *Making Sex: Body and Gender from the Greeks to Freud.* Cambridge, England: Harvard University Press.

Larkin, June. 1994. *Sexual Harassment: High School Girls Speak Out.* Toronto: Second Story Press.

Larkin, June, and Pat Staton. 1998. "If We Can't Get Equal, We'll Get Even: A Transformative Model of Gender Equity." *Canadian Women's Studies,* 17–4:16–22.

Lasswell, Harold D. 1969. "The Structure and Function of Communication in Society." In Wilbur Schramm (Ed.), *Mass Communications.* Urbana, IL: University of Illinois Press, pp. 103–130.

Lauderback, David, and Dan Waldorf. 1993. "Whatever Happened to ICE: The Latest Drug Scare." *Journal of Drug Issues,* 23:597–613.

Lauer, Robert H. 1995. *Social Problems and the Quality of Life* (6th ed.). Madison, WI: Brown.

Lauer, Robert H., and Jeannette C. Lauer. 1991. "The Long-Term Relational Consequences of Problematic Family Backgrounds." *Family Relations,* 40:286–290.

Laurence, Leslie, and Beth Weinhouse. 1994. *Outrageous Practices: The Alarming Truth About How Medicine Mistreats Women.* New York: Fawcett Columbine.

Law Commission of Canada. 2002. "Renewing Democracy: Debating Electoral Reform in Canada." Retrieved from **www.lcc.gc.ca**

Laxer, James. 2002. "Casus Belli." Retrieved from **www.james laxer.com/casus.htm**

Layton, Jack. 2000. *Homelessness: The Making and Unmaking of a Crisis.* Toronto: Penguin/McGill Institute.

Leaper, Campbell. 1994. *Childhood Gender Segregation: Causes and Consequences.* San Francisco: Jossey-Bass.

Leaper, C., K. Anderson, and P. Sanders. 1998. "Moderators of Gender Effects of Parents' Talk to Their Children: A Meta-Analysis." *Developmental Psychology,* 34:3–27.

Lee, Felicia R. 1996. "Infertile Couples Forge Ties within Society of Their Own." *New York Times* (January 9):A1, A7.

Lee, Kevin K. 2000. *Urban Poverty in Canada: A Statistical Profile.* Ottawa: Canadian Council on Social Development.

Lefrançois, Guy R. 1999. *The Lifespan* (6th ed.). Belmont, CA: Wadsworth.

Lehmann, Jennifer M. 1994. *Durkheim and Women.* Lincoln, NE: University of Nebraska Press.

Lehne, Gregory K. 1995. "Homophobia among Men: Supporting and Defining the Male Role." In Michael S. Kimmel and Michael A. Messner (Eds.), *Men's Lives* (3rd ed.). Boston: Allyn and Bacon, pp. 325–336.

Leinen, Stephen. 1993. *Gay Cops.* New Brunswick, NJ: Rutgers University Press.

Leland, John. 1995. "Bisexuality." *Newsweek* (July 17):44–50.

Lemert, Edwin. 1951. *Social Pathology.* New York: McGraw-Hill.

Lengermann, Patricia Madoo, and Jill Niebrugge-Brantley. 1992. "Contemporary Feminist Theory." In George Ritzer (Ed.), *Contemporary Sociological Theory* (3rd ed.). New York: McGraw-Hill, pp. 308–357.

Leong, Wai-Teng. 1991. "The Pornography 'Problem': Disciplining Women and Young Girls." *Media, Culture, and Society,* 13:91–117.

Levin, Jack, and Jack McDevitt. 1993. *Hate Crimes: The Rising Tide of Bigotry and Bloodshed.* New York: Plenum.

Levin, William C. 1988. "Age Stereotyping: College Student Evaluations." *Research on Aging,* 10(1):134–148.

Levine, Peter. 1992. *Ellis Island to Ebbets Field: Sport and the American Jewish Experience.* New York: Oxford University Press.

Levinthal, Charles F. 1996. *Drugs, Behavior, and Modern Society.* Boston: Allyn and Bacon.

Lewin, Tamar. 1995. "The Decay of Families Is Global, Study Says." *New York Times* (May 30):A5.

Lewis, Oscar. 1966. *La Vida: A Puerto Rican Family in the Culture of Poverty—San Juan and New York.* New York: Random House.

Lexchin, Joel. 2002. "Profits First: The Pharmaceutical Industry in Canada. In B. Singh Bolaria and Harley D. Dickinson. (Eds.), *Health, Illness, and Health Care in Canada* (3rd ed.). Scarborough, ON: Nelson.

Ley, D.F., and L.S. Bourne. 1993. "Introduction: The Social Context and Diversity of Urban Canada." In L.S. Bourne and D.F. Ley (Eds.), *The Changing Social Geography of Canadian Cities.* Montreal: McGill-Queen's University Press, pp. 3–30.

Lian, Jason Z., and David Ralph Matthews. 1998. "Does the Vertical Mosaic Still Exist? Ethnicity and Income in Canada, 1991." *Canadian Review of Sociology and Anthropology,* 35(4):461–481.

Liberty. 2001. "You Could See the Shame on Their Faces." Eds. *The Editorial Collective in Resist: A Grassroots Collection of Stories, Poetry, Photos and Analyses from the Quebec City FTAA Protests and Beyond.* Halifax: Fernwood.

Liebow, Elliot. 1993. *Tell Them Who I Am: The Lives of Homeless Women.* New York: Free Press.

Lill, Wendy. 2001. "Media Chaos Reigns in Canada." Retrieved December 20, 2001 from **www.mediachannel.org/ownership**

Lin Lap-Chew 1999. "Global Trafficking in Women: Some Issues and Strategies." *Women's Studies Quarterly,* 1(2):11–18.

Lindsey, Linda L. 1994. *Gender Roles: A Sociological Perspective* (2nd ed.). Englewood Cliffs, NJ: Prentice-Hall.

Lips, Hilary M. 1993. *Sex and Gender: An Introduction* (2nd ed.). Mountain View, CA: Mayfield.

Ljunggren, David. 2003. "Canada Sending Up to 2,000 Troops to Afghanistan." Reuters (February 13). Retrieved from **www.reuters.com**

Logan, Ron. 2001."Crime Statistics in Canada, 2000." *Juristat,* 21(8).

Lombardi, Emilia L., Riki Anne Wilchins, Dana Priesling, and Diana Malouf. 2001. "Gender Violence: Transgender Experiences with Violence and Discrimination." *Journal of Homosexuality,* 42(1):89–101.

Lomborg, Bjorn. 2001. *The Skeptical Environmentalist: Measuring the Real State of the World.* Cambridge, UK: Cambridge University Press.

Lommo, Charlene. 2001. "Adult Correctional Services in Canada." *Juristat,* 21(5).

London, Kathryn A. 1991. "Advance Data Number 194: Cohabitation, Marriage, Marital Dissolution, and Remarriage: United States 1988." U.S. Department of Health and Human Services. Vital and Health Statistics of the National Center, January 4.

London, Kathryn A., and Barbara Foley Wilson. 1988. "Divorce." *American Demographics,* 10(10):23–26.

Lorber, Judith. 1986. "Dismantling Noah's Ark." *Sex Roles,* 14(11–12):567–579.

Lorber, Judith. 1994. *Paradoxes of Gender.* New Haven, CT: Yale University Press.

Los Angeles Times. 1988. "If Only the Spirit of Giving Could Continue" (December 25).

Lottes, Ilsa. 1993. "Reactions to Pornography on a College Campus: For or Against?" *Sex Roles: A Journal of Research,* 29(1–2):69–90.

Loury, Glenn C. 1997. "Integration Has Had Its Day." *New York Times* (April 23):A21.

Lowman, John. 2000. "Violence and the Outlaw Status of (Street) Prostitution in Canada." *Violence Against Women,* 6(9/ September):987–1011.

Lowman, John, Chris Atchison, and Laura Fraser. 1997. *Sexuality in the 1990s: Survey Results—Men Who Buy Sex, Phase Two* [online]. **http://users.uniserve.com/~lowman/ICSS/icss.htm**

Lowman, John, and Laura Fraser. 1995. *Violence Against Persons Who Prostitute: The Experience in British Columbia.* Ottawa: Department of Justice Canada.

Luckenbill, David F. 1977. "Criminal Homicide as a Situated Transaction." *Social Problems,* 25:176–186.

Luffman, Jacqueline. 1998. "When Parents Replace Teachers: The Home Schooling Option." *Canadian Social Trends,* (Autumn).

Luker, Kristin. 1996. *Dubious Conceptions: The Politics of Teenage Pregnancy.* Cambridge, MA: Harvard University Press.

Lundy, Katherine Coleman. 1995. *Sidewalk Talk: A Naturalistic Study of Street Kids.* New York: Garland.

Lunman, Kim. 2002. "Privacy Watchdog Sues RCMP Over Cameras." *Globe and Mail* (June 22):A1.

Lytton, H., and D.M. Romney. 1991. "Parents' Differential Socialization of Boys and Girls: A Meta-Analysis." *Psychological Bulletin,* 109:267–296.

Maccoby, Eleanor E., and Carol Nagy Jacklin. 1987. "Gender Segregation in Childhood." *Advances in Child Development and Behavior,* 20:239–287.

MacCorquodale, Patricia, and Gary Jensen. 1993. "Women in the Law: Partners or Tokens?" *Gender and Society,* 7(4):582–593.

MacDonald, Eleanor. 2000. "Critical Identities: Rethinking Feminism Through Transgender Politics" (1998). In Barbara Crow and Lise Gotell (Eds.), *Open Boundaries: A Canadian Women's Studies Reader.* Toronto: Prentice Hall, pp. 282–290.

MacDonald, Kevin, and Ross D. Parke. 1986. "Parental-Child Physical Play: The Effects of Sex and Age of Children and Parents." *Sex Roles,* 15:367–378.

Macdonald, Scott. 1995. "The Role of Drugs in Workplace Injuries: Is Drug Testing Appropriate?" *Journal of Drug Issues,* 25(4):703–723.

Macfarlane, Ronald, Monica Campbell, and Sheela V. Basrur. 2000. *Toronto's Air: Let's Make It Healthy.* Toronto: Toronto Public Health.

Macionis, John J. and Linda M. Gerber. 2002. *Sociology* (4th Can. ed.). Toronto: Pearson.

MacIssac, Rob. 2002. "Regional Thinking." *Globe and Mail* (June 24):T3.

MacKinnon, Catharine. 1987. *Feminism Unmodified: Discourses on Life and Law.* Cambridge, MA: Harvard University Press.

Mackenzie, Hugh. 2002. "Cutting Classes: Elementary and Secondary Funding in Ontario." The Canadian Centre for Policy Alternatives. Retrieved July 20, 2002, from **www.policyalternatives.ca**

Mackie, Marlene. 1987. *Constructing Women and Men: Gender Socialization.* Toronto: Holt, Rinehart.

Mackie, Marlene. 1991. *Gender Relations in Canada: Further Explorations.* Toronto: Harcourt Brace.

Mackie, Richard. 2002. "Official Attacks Mandatory Retirement." *Globe and Mail* (June 14):A10.

Maclean's. 1999, 2002. "Annual Poll." (December 20 and 30 respectively).

MacLeod, Jay. 1995. *Ain't No Makin' It: Aspirations and Attainment in a Low-Income Neighborhood.* Boulder, CO: Westview Press.

MacMillan, Craig S., and Myron G. Claridge. 1998. "Criminal Proceedings as a Response to Hate." Paper presented at the "Hatred in Canada" conference, University of Victoria, Victoria, BC. (September).

Macy, Marianne. 1996. *Working Sex: An Odyssey into Our Cultural Underworld.* New York: Carroll & Graf.

Madden, Patricia A., and Joel W. Grube. 1994. "The Frequency and Nature of Alcohol and Tobacco Advertising in Televised Sports, 1990 through 1992." *The American Journal of Public Health,* 84(2):297–300.

Makin, Kirk. 2002. "Ontario Court Upholds Parents' Right to Spank." *Globe and Mail. (*January 16):A1, A8.

Malarek, Victor. 2002. "Ontario Teens Suing School Board Over Bullying." *Globe and Mail* (June 3):A4.

Males, Mike. 1994. "Bashing Youth: Media Myths about Teenagers." *Extra!* (March/April). Retrieved November 11, 1999, from **www.fair.org/extra/9403/bashing-youth.html**

Malette, Louise, and Marie Chalouh (Eds.). 1991. *The Montreal Massacre.* Marlene Wildman (Trans.). Charlottetown, PEI: gynergy books.

Malinowski, Bronislaw. 1964. "The Principle of Legitimacy: Parenthood, the Basis of Social Structure." In Rose Laub Coser (Ed.), *The Family: Its Structure and Functions.* New York: St Martin's Press.

Malthus, Thomas R. 1965. *An Essay on Population.* New York: Augustus Kelley, Bookseller (orig. published in 1798).

Mandel, Ruth B. 1981. *In the Running: The New Woman Candidate.* New Haven, CT: Ticknor & Fields.

Manitoba Addictions Awareness Week. 2002. *2001 Youth Survey.* Winnipeg: Addictions Foundation of Manitoba.

Manley, John. 2002. "The Economic and the Fiscal Update to the House of Commons Standing Committee on Finance." Presented by the Honourable John Manley, P.C., M.P. Halifax, Nova Scotia. (October 30).

Mann, P. 1993. *Hostile Hallways: The AAUW Survey on Sexual Harassment in America's Schools.* Washington, DC: AAUW Educational Foundation Council.

Mann, Patricia S. 1994. *Micro-Politics: Agency in a Post-Feminist Era.* Minneapolis: University of Minnesota Press.

Marable, Manning. 1995. *Beyond Black and White: Transforming African-American Politics.* New York: Verso.

Marger, Martin. 1999. *Social Inequality: Patterns and Processes.* Toronto: Mayfield.

Marger, Martin N. 1994. *Race and Ethnic Relations: American and Global Perspectives.* Belmont, CA: Wadsworth.

Marshall, Barbara L. 2000. *Configuring Gender: Explorations in Theory and Politics.* Peterborough, ON: Broadview Press.

Marshall, Robert. 2001. "Where Can We Get the Best Care? *Maclean's* (June 11):31–43.

Marshall, Victor W. 1980. *Last Chapters: A Sociology of Aging and Dying.* Monterey, CA: Brooks/Cole.

Marshall, Victor W., and Judith Levy. 1990. "Aging and Dying." In Robert H. Binstock and Linda George (Eds.), *Handbook of Aging and the Social Sciences* (3rd ed). New York: Academic Press.

Martin, Carol L. 1989. "Children's Use of Gender-Related Information in Making Social Judgments." *Developmental Psychology,* 25:80–88.

Martin, Patricia Yancy. 1992. "Gender, Interaction and Inequality in Organizations." In Cecilia Ridgeway (Ed.), *Gender, Interaction and Inequality.* New York: Springer-Verlag, pp. 208–231.

Martin, Teresa Castro, and Larry L. Bumpass. 1989. "Recent Trends in Marital Disruption." *Demography*, 26:37–51.

Marx, Karl, and Friedrich Engels. 1971. "The Communist Manifesto." [orig. published in 1847]. In Dirk Struik (Ed.), *The Birth of the Communist Manifesto.* New York: International.

Marx, Karl, and Friedrich Engels. 1976. *The Communist Manifesto.* New York: Pantheon (orig. published in 1848).

Massey, Douglas S. 2002. "A Brief History of Human Society: The Origin and Role of Emotion in Social Life." *American Sociological Review*, 67(1):1–29.

Massey, Douglas S., and Nancy A. Denton. 1992. *American Apartheid: Segregation and the Making of the Underclass.* Cambridge, MA: harvard University Press.

Massey, James L., and Marvin D. Krohn. 1986. "A Longitudinal Examination of an Integrated Social Process Model of Deviant Behavior." *Social Forces*, 65:106–134.

Mastrofski, Stephen D. 1995. "The Police." In Joseph F. Sheley (Ed.), *Criminology: A Contemporary Handbook* (2nd ed.). Belmont, CA: Wadsworth, pp. 373–405.

Mathis, Nancy. 1996. "Clinton Urges Student Uniforms." *Houston Chronicle* (February 25):6A.

matthewsplace.com. 1999. "Dennis Shepard's Statement to the Court" (November 4). Retrieved November 15, 1999, from **www.matthewsplace.com/dennis2.htm**

Maugh, T. 1990. "Sex: American Style Trend to the Traditional." *Los Angeles Times* (February 18):A1, A22.

Maxwell, Milton A. 1981. "Alcoholics Anonymous." In Martin S. Weinberg, Earl Rubington, and Sue Kiefer Hammersmith (Eds.), *The Solution of Social Problems: Five Perspectives* (2nd ed.). New York: Oxford University Press, pp. 152–156.

Mayall, Alice, and Diana E. H. Russell. 1993. "Racism in Pornography." In Diana E. H. Russell (Ed.), *Making Violence Sexy: Feminist Views on Pornography.* New York: Teachers College Press, pp. 167–177.

Maynard, Joyce. 1994. "To Tell the Truth." In Jay David (Ed.), *The Family Secret: An Anthology.* New York: William Morrow, pp. 79–85.

McAdie, Patricia. 1998. "The Abandonment of the Pursuit of Equity and the Implications for Education." *Canadian Women's Studies*, 17(4):6–15.

McCall, Nathan. 1994. *Makes Me Wanna Holler: A Young Black Man in America.* New York: Random House.

McChesney, Robert W. 1999. *Rich Media, Poor Democracy: Communication Politics in Dubious Times.* Urbana, IL: University of Illinois Press.

McChesney, Robert W. 2001. "Global Media, Neoliberalism and Imperialism." Media Channel, 52(10/March). Retrieved from **www.mediachannel.org/ownership**

McCluskey, Peter. 2002. "Keeping the Peace." CBC News [online]. Retrieved from **www.cbc.ca/news/indepth/peacekeepers/index.html**

McDonald, L. 2000. "Alarmist Economics and Women's Pensions." In Ellen M. Gee and Gloria M.Gutman (Eds.), *The Overselling of Population Aging: Apocalyptic Demography, Intergenerational Challenges, and Social Policy.* Don Mills, ON: Oxford University Press: 114–128.

McDonald, Lynn, Brooke Moore, and Natalya Timoshkina. 2000. *Migrant Sex Workers from Eastern Europe and the Former Soviet Union: The Canadian Case.* Ottawa: Research Directorate, Status of Women Canada.

McElroy, Wendy. 2001. "Free Speech Protects All Speech." FOX News Channel (October 16). Retrieved from **www.foxnews. com/story/0,2933,36565,00.html**

McElvogue, Louise. 1997. "Making a Killing Out of Nature." *Television Business International* (November):52.

McIntosh, Peggy. 1995. "White Privilege and Male Privilege: A Personal Account of Coming to See Correspondences through Work in Women's Studies." In Margaret A. Andersen and Patricia Hill Collins (Eds.), *Race, Class, and Gender: An Anthology.* Belmont, CA: Wadsworth, pp. 76–87.

McKenna, Barry. 1999. "U.S. Election Strategy Helps Shape WTO Agenda." *Globe and Mail* (November 29):A9.

McKinlay, John B. 1994. "A Case for Refocusing Upstream: The Political Economy of Illness." In Peter Conrad and Rochelle Kern (Eds.), *The Sociology of Health and Illness.* New York: St. Martin's Press, pp. 509–530.

McLanahan, Sara, and Gary D. Sandefur. 1994. *Growing Up with a Single Parent: What Hurts, What Helps.* Cambridge, MA: Harvard University Press.

McLaughlin, Hannah. 1995. "Homophobia in the Schools." In Katherine Arnup (Ed.), *Lesbian Parenting Living with Pride and Prejudice.* Charlettetown, PEI: gynergy books, pp. 238–250.

McMullin, J.A., and Victor W. Marshall. 1996. "Family, Friends, Stress, and Well-Being: Does Childlessness Make a Difference?" *Canadian Journal on Aging,* 15(3):355-373.

McMullin, J.A., and Victor W. Marshall. 1999. "Structure and Agency in the Retirement Process: A Case Study of Montreal Garment Workers." In C.D. Ryff and Victor W. Marshall (Eds.), *The Self and Society in Aging Processes.* New York: Springer-Verlag, pp. 305–338.

McNamara, Robert P. 1994. *The Times Square Hustler: Male Prostitution in New York City.* Westport, CT: Praeger.

McNeill, J.R. 2000. *Something New Under The Sun: An Environmental History of the Twentieth-Century World.* New York: Norton.

McPherson, Barry D. 1990. *Aging as a Social Process: An Introduction to Individual and Population Aging* (2nd ed.). Toronto: Butterworths.

McWilliams, Peter. 1996. *Ain't Nobody's Business If You Do: The Absurdity of Consensual Crimes in Our Free Country.* Los Angeles: Prelude Press.

Mead, Margaret. 1966. "Marriage in Two Steps." *Redbook,* 127:48–49, 85–86.

Mead, Rebecca. 1994. "Playing It Straight: In and Out of the Closet." *New York* (June 20):40–46.

Mehta, Bina, and Kevin Spooner. 2000. "Glimpses of a Canadian Interracial Relationship." In Carl E. James (Ed.), *Experiencing Difference.* Halifax: Fernwood, pp. 150–162.

Mellor, Mary. 1997. *Feminism and Ecology.* New York: New York University Press.

Merton, Robert. 1938. "Social Structure and Anomie." *American Sociological Review,* 3(6):672–682.

Merton, Robert King. 1968. *Social Theory and Social Structure* (enlarged ed.). New York: Free Press.

Michael, Robert T., John H. Gagnon, Edward O. Laumann, and Gina Kolata. 1994. *Sex in America: A Definitive Survey.* New York: Warner Books.

Michelson, William H. 1976. *Man and His Urban Environment: A Sociological Approach.* Don Mills, ON: Addison-Wesley.

Mick, Hayley. 2001. "Thobani." *UBC Journalism Review* [Thunderbird Online], 4(2). (December). Retrieved from **www.journalism.ubc.ca/thunderbird.html**

Middlestaedt, Martin. 2001. "Poll Finds Global Climate Change Hot Issue." *Globe and Mail.* (July 10): A4.

Mies, Maria. 1986. *Patriarchy and Accumulation on a World Scale: Women in the International Division of Labour.* UK: Zed Books.

Mies, Maria, and Vandana Shiva. 1993. *Ecofeminism.* Atlantic Highlands, NJ: Zed Books.

Mighton, John. 2002. "Breaking the Cycle of Ignorance." *JUMP Teaching Manual.* Toronto: Junior Undiscovered Math Prodigies.

Migration News. 2002. "Canada: Immigration, Border." *Migration News,* 9(12, December). Retrieved from **www.migration. ucdavis.edu:80/mn/archive_mn/dec_2002-06mn.html**

Milan, Anne. 2000. "One Hundred Years of Families." *Canadian Social Trends,* (Spring):2–12.

Milkman, Harvey, and Stanley Sunderwirth. 1987. *Craving for Ecstasy: The Consciousness and Chemistry of Escape.* Lexington, MA: Heath.

Millar, Alison E. 2002. *Leaving the Trade: Exiting Experiences of Former Sex Trade Workers in the CRD.* Unpublished master's thesis, University of Victoria, Department of Sociology, Victoria, BC.

Millar, Wayne J. 2001. "Patterns of use—alternate health care practitioners." *Health Reports,* 13(1):19–20.

Miller, Casey, and Kate Swift. 1991. *Words and Women: New Language in New Times* (updated). New York: Harper-Collins.

Miller, Eleanor M. 1986. *Street Woman.* Philadelphia: Temple University Press.

Miller, J.R. 2002. "Residential Schools." *The Canadian Encyclopedia.* Retrieved October 20, 2002, from **www. thecanadianencyclopedia.com/index.cfm?PgNm= TCE&TCE_Version=A&ArticleId=A0011547&MenuC losed=0**

Miller, James. 1996. "Out Family Values." In Marion Lynn (Ed.), *Voices: Essays on Canadian Families.* Toronto: Nelson.

Miller, Michael W. 1994. "Quality Stuff: Firm Is Peddling Cocaine, and Deals Are Legit." *Wall Street Journal* (October 17):A1, A14.

Mills, C. Wright. 1959a. *The Power Elite*. Fair Lawn, NJ: Oxford University Press.

Mills, C. Wright. 1959b. *The Sociological Imagination*. London: Oxford University Press.

Milner, Henry (Ed). 1999. *Making Every Vote Count: Reassessing Canada's Electoral System*. Peterborough, ON: Broadview Press.

Minnich, Elizabeth Kamarck. 1995. "Transforming Knowledge." In Sheila Ruth (Ed.), *Issues in Feminism* (3rd ed.). Mountain View, CA: Mayfield, pp. 413–429.

Minow, Newton N., and Craig L. LaMay. 1999. "Changing the Way We Think." In Robert M. Baird, William E. Loges, and Stuart E. Rosenbaum (Eds.), *The Media and Morality*. Amherst, NY: Promethus Books, pp. 309–330.

Mintz, Beth, and Michael Schwartz. 1985. *The Power Structure of American Business*. Chicago: University of Chicago Press.

Mitchell, Alanna. 2000. "Waste Not: How Tricks from Tiny Holland Can Tame Canada's Garbage Beast." *Globe and Mail* (November 18):F4–5.

Moloney, Paul. 2002. "Canadian Cities to Urge Ottawa for Tax Powers." *Toronto Star* (May 23):A9.

Monahan, John. 1992. "Mental Disorder and Violent Behavior: Perceptions and Evidence." *American Psychologist*, 47:511–521.

Mooney, Linda A., David Knox, Caroline Schacht, and Adie Nelson. 2001. *Understanding Social Problems* (1st Can. ed.). Scarborough, ON: Nelson Thomson Learning.

Mooney, Linda A., David Knox, Caroline Schacht, and Adie Nelson. 2003. *Understanding Social Problems* (2nd Can. ed.). Scarborough, ON: Nelson Thomson Learning.

Moore, Aaron James. 2003. "Who Owns What: CJR's Web Guide to What the Major Media Companies Own." *Columbia Journalism Review* [online] (January 14). Retrieved from **www.cjr.org**

Morel, Sylvie. 2002. *The Insertion Model or the Workfare Model? The Transformation of Social Assistance within Quebec and Canada*. Ottawa: Research Directorate, Status of Women Canada.

Morgan, Robin. 1993. *The Word of a Woman: Selected Prose 1968–1992*. London: Virago Press.

Morgan, S. Philip, Diane N. Lye, and Gretchen A. Condran. 1988. "Sons, Daughters, and the Risk of Marital Disruption." *American Journal of Sociology*, 94(1):110–129.

Moriarty, T.J. 2003. "Born Soldiers: Birth Defects From Service in the Gulf? *LIFE* Magazine's Full-Court Press." OLNews@aol.com (February 2).

Mosher, Steven W. 1994. *A Mother's Ordeal: One Woman's Fight against China's One-Child Policy*. New York: Harper-Perennial.

Muggeridge, Peter. 2001. "Report on Ageism." *CARPNews* (December 5).

Murphy, Barbara. 2000. *On the Street: How We Created Homelessness*. Ontario: J. Gordon Shillingford Publishing Inc.

Muszynski, Alicja. 2000. "The Social Construction/Deconstruction of Sex, Gender, Race and Class." In B. Singh Bolaria (Ed.), *Social Issues and Contradictions in Canadian Society* (3rd ed.). Toronto: Harcourt Brace, pp. 95–131.

Muto, Sheila. 1995. "Student Uniforms Pay Off, One School District Says." *New York Times* (September 20):B6.

Mydans, Seth. 1997. "Brutal End for an Architect of Cambodian Brutality." *New York Times* (June 14):5.

Myers, Steven Lee. 1997. "Converting the Dollar into a Bludgeon." *New York Times* (April 20):E5.

Myles, John. 2000. "The Maturation of Canada's Retirement Income System: Income Levels, Income Inequality and Low Income among Older Persons." *Canadian Journal on Aging*. 19(3):287–316.

Nader, Ralph. 2000. *Cutting Corporate Welfare*. New York: Seven Stories Press.

Nangeroni, Nancy R. 2001. *Transgenderism: Transgressing Gender Norms. GenderTalk*. Retrieved from **www.gendertalk. com/ tgism/tgism.shtml**

Nath, Pamela S., John G. Borkowski, Thomas L. Whitman, and Cynthia J. Schellenbach. 1991. "Understanding Adolescent Parenting: The Dimensions and Functions of Social Support." *Family Relations*, 40:411–420.

National Council of Welfare. 2001a. *Child Poverty Profile— 1998*. Ottawa: Minister of Public Works and Government Services Canada.

National Council of Welfare. 2001b. *The Cost of Poverty*, 115 (Winter 2001–2). Ottawa, ON: Minister of Public Works and Government Services Canada.

National Council on Crime and Delinquency. 1969. *The Infiltration into Legitimate Business by Organized Crime*. Washington, DC: National Council on Crime and Delinquency.

National Film Board of Canada (NFB). 1973. *The October Crisis*. Director Pierre Perrault.

National Firearms Association. 2002. "NFA Press Release." (November 7). Retrieved from **www.nfa.ca**

National Library of Canada. 2001. "Prelude to Confederation: The Making of Canada." Retrieved from **www. nlc-bnc.ca/nlc-search-bin/search/l=e**

National Library of Canada. 2003. "First Among Equals: The Prime Minister in Canadian Life and Politics." (February 21). Retrieved from **www.nlc-bnc.ca/history/4/h4-2231-e.html**

National Public Radio (USA). 1992. Untitled report on parental responses to children. (July 23).

National Television Violence Study. 1998. "Executive Summary," *National Television Violence Study*, vol. 3. Retrieved October 31, 1999, from **www.ccsp. ucsb.edu/execsum.pdf**

National Victims Resource Center. 1991. *Juvenile Prostitution: Fact Sheet*. Rockville, MD: Victims Resource Center.

Nava, Michael, and Robert Dawidoff. 1994. *Created Equal: Why Gay Rights Matter to America*. New York: St. Martin's Press.

Navarro, Mireya. 1996. "Marijuana Farms Are Flourishing Indoors, Producing a More Potent Drug." *New York Times* (November 24):13.

Naylor, C. David. 1999. "Health Care in Canada: Incrementalism under Fiscal Duress." *Health Affairs*, 18(3):9–26.

Naylor, Tom. 2002. *Wages of Crime: Black Markets, Illegal Finance and the Underworld Economy.* Montreal: McGill-Queen's University Press.

Nechas, Eileen, and Denise Foley. 1994. *Unequal Treatment: What You Don't Know about How Women Are Mistreated by the Medical Community.* New York: Simon & Schuster.

Nelson, Adie and Barrie W. Robinson. 2002. *Gender in Canada* (2nd ed.). Toronto: Pearson.

Nelson, Fiona. 1996. *Lesbian Motherhood: An Exploration of Canadian Lesbian Families.* Toronto: University of Toronto Press.

Neve, Alex. 2003. "The Refugee Appeal Division (RAD) Must Be Implemented—Take Action Now." Amnesty International. Retrieved from **www.amnesty.ca/Refugee/actRAD.htm**

New York Times. 1993. "Despite 6-Year U.S. Campaign, Pornography Industry Thrives" (July 4):10.

New York Times. 1994a. "Car Bomb Kills 3 in Beirut; Arabs Accuse Israel" (December 22):A5.

New York Times. 1994b. "Jordan Dooms 11 Militants" (December 22):A5.

New York Times. 1996. "The Megacity Summit" (April 8):A14.

Newman, Zoe. 2001. "The Bisexuality Wars: The Perils of Identity as Marginality." In Terry Goldie (Ed.), *In a Queer Country: Gay and Lesbian Studies in the Canadian Context.* Vancouver: Arsenal Pulp Press, pp. 122–137.

Niebuhr, Gustav. 1996. "Bishop Who Ordained Gay Deacon Is Accused of Heresy." *New York Times* (Februrary 28):A8.

North American Commission for Environmental Cooperation (CEC). 2001. Retrieved August 12, 2002, from **www.cec.org/pubs_docs/documents/index.cfm?varlan=english&ID=141**

North American Commission for Environmental Cooperation (CEC). 2002. Highlights from *The North American Mosaic: A State of the Environment Report.* Retrieved July 16, 2002, from **www.cec.org/files.PDFPUBLICATIONS/soehigh_en.PDF**

Novak, Mark. 1997. *Aging and Society a Canadian Perspective* (3rd ed.). Toronto: Nelson.

Oakes, Jeannie. 1985. *Keeping Track: How Schools Structure Inequality.* New Haven, CT: Yale University Press.

O'Connell, Helen. 1994. *Women and the Family.* Prepared for the UN-NGO Group on Women and Development. Atlantic Highlands, NJ: Zed Books.

Oliver, Melvin L., and Thomas M. Shapiro. 1995. *Black Wealth/White Wealth: A New Perspective on Racial Inequality.* New York: Routledge.

Olsen, Gregg M. 2002. *The Politics of the Welfare State: Canada, Sweden, and the United States.* Don Mills, ON: Oxford University Press.

Olzak, Susan, Suzanne Shanahan, and Elizabeth H. McEneaney. 1996. "Poverty, Segregation, and Race Riots: 1960 to 1993." *American Sociological Review,* 61(August):590–613.

Omi, Michael, and Howard Winant. 1994. *Racial Formation in the United States: From the 1960s to the 1990s* (2nd ed.). New York: Routledge.

O'Neil, Peter. 2001. "Feminist's Anti-U.S. Speech Causes Uproar—Hedy Fry Jeered by Opposition for Sitting Silent." *Vancouver Sun* (October 2).

O'Neill, Terry. 2001. "As Chrétien Moves Closer, Multiculturalism Is Shown to Have Given Birth to Ingrates Who Hate." *Report: Canada's Independent News Magazine* (October 22).

Ontario Association of Interval and Transition Houses. 1998. "Locked In, Left Out: Impacts of the Budget Cuts on Abused Women and Their Children." In Luciana Ricciutelli, June Larkin, and Eimear O'Neill (Eds.), *Confronting the Cuts: A Sourcebook for Women in Ontario.* Toronto: Inanna, pp. 29–38.

Orenstein, Peggy. 1996. "For Too Many Schoolgirls, Sexual Harassment Is Real." *Austin American-Statesman* (October 4):A15.

Organisation of Economic Co-operation and Development (OECD). 1997. *Draft of the Multilateral Agreement on Investment, Consolidated Text and Commentary,* Paris, (May 13):II.

Otis, Leah. 1985. *Prostitution in Medieval Society.* Chicago: University of Chicago Press.

Ouimet, Marc. 1999. "Crime in Canada and in the United States: A Comparative Analysis." *Canadian Review of Sociology and Anthropology,* 36(3):389–408.

Overall, Christine. 2000. "Heterosexuality and Feminist Theory." In Barbara A. Crow and Lise Gotell (Eds.), *Open Boundaries: A Canadian Women's Studies Reader.* Toronto: Prentice Hall/Allyn and Bacon, pp. 262–269.

Owens, Anne Marie. 2002. "Feminist Shifts Focus to Boys." *National Post.* Retrieved June 27, 2002, from **www.nationalpost.com**

Oxfam Canada. 2002. "Coffee Facts." Retrieved September 19, 2002, from **www.oxfam.ca/news/MakeTradeFair/Launch02.htm**

Palen, J. John, and Bruce London. 1984. *Gentrification, Displacement, and Neighborhood Revitalization.* Albany, NY: State University of New York Press.

Parenti, Michael. 1998. *America Besieged.* San Francisco: City Lights Books.

Parker, Robert Nash. 1995. "Violent Crime." In Joseph F. Sheley (Ed.), *Criminology: A Contemporary Handbook* (2nd ed.). Belmont, CA: Wadsworth, pp. 169–185.

Parry, A. 1976. *Terrorism: From Robespierre to Arafat.* New York: Vanguard Press.

Parsons, Talcott. 1951. *The Social System.* New York: Free Press.

Parsons, Talcott. 1955. "The American Family: Its Relations to Personality and to the Social Structure." In Talcott Parsons and Robert F. Bales (Eds.), *Family, Socialization, and Interaction Process.* Glencoe, IL: Free Press, pp. 3–33.

Parsons, Talcott. 1966. *Societies: Evolutionary and Comparative Perspectives.* Englewood Cliffs, NJ: Prentice Hall.

Pateman, Carole. 1994. "What's Wrong with Prostitution?" In Alison M. Jaggar (Ed.), *Living with Contradictions: Controversies in Feminist Social Ethics.* Boulder, CO: Westview, pp. 127–132.

Paul, Pamela. 2002. *The Starter Marriage and the Future of Matrimony.* New York: Random House.

Pear, Robert. 1996. "Health Costs Pose Problems for Millions, a Study Finds." *New York Times* (October 23):A14.

Pear, Robert. 1997. "Academy's Report Says Immigration Benefits the U.S." *New York Times* (May 18):1, 15.

Pearce, Diana M. 1978. *The Feminization of Poverty: Women, Work, and Welfare.* Chicago: University of Illinois Press.

Pepler, Debra, Wendy Craig, and J. Connolly. 1997. *Bullying and Victimization: The Problems and Solutions for School Aged Children.* Ottawa: National Crime Prevention Council of Canada.

Perdue, William Dan. 1993. *Systemic Crisis: Problems in Society, Politics, and World Order.* Fort Worth, TX: Harcourt Brace Jovanovich.

Perelle, Robin. 2002. "Staying Alive: Police Ourselves—Meeting." *XTRA! West News* (November 14):7.

Perry, David C., and Alfred J. Watkins (Eds.). 1977. *The Rise of the Sunbelt Cities.* Beverly Hills, CA: Sage.

Perry-Jenkins, Maureen, and Ann C. Crouter. 1990. "Men's Provider Role Attitudes: Implications for Household Work and Marital Satisfaction." *Journal of Family Issues,* 11:136–156.

Peterborough Social Planning Council. 1998. "A Report on Hunger in Peterborough." In Luciana Ricciutelli, June Larkin, and Eimear O'Neill (Eds.), *Confronting the Cuts: A Sourcebook for Women in Ontario.* Toronto: Inanna, pp. 124–132.

Petersen, John L. 1994. *The Road to 2015: Profiles of the Future.* Corte Madera, CA: Waite Group Press.

Peterson, V. Spike, and Anne Sisson Runyan. 1993. *Global Gender Issues.* Boulder, CO: Westview Press.

Petras, James F. 1983. *Capitalist and Socialist Crises in the Late Twentieth Century.* Totowa, NJ: Rowman and Allenheld.

Pheasant, Valerie Bedassigae. 2001. "My Mother Used to Dance." In Carl E. James and Adrienne Shadd (Eds.), *Talking About Identity: Encounters in Race, Ethnicity and Language.* Toronto: Between the Lines, pp. 38–43.

Phillips, Peter. 1999. *Censored 1999: The News That Didn't Make the News.* New York: Seven Stories Press.

Picard, Andre. 2001. "Fattest and Fittest." *Globe and Mail* (July 21):F8.

Pierce, Jennifer L. 1995. *Gender Trials: Emotional Lives in Contemporary Law Firms.* Berkeley, CA: University of California Press.

Pocklington, Tom, and Allan Tupper. 2002. *No Place to Learn: Why Universities Aren't Working.* Vancouver: UBC Press.

Pollack, Andrew. 1996. "Square Pegs Stay Home from Japan's Schools." *New York Times* (September 15):A4.

Ponse, Barbara. 1978. *Identities in the Lesbian World: The Social Construction of Self.* Westport, CT: Greenwood Press.

Pope, C. Arden III, Richard T. Burnett, Michael J. Thun, Eugenia E. Calle, Daniel Krewski, Kazuhiko Ito, and George D. Thurston. 2002. "Lung Cancer, Cardio-pulmonary Mortality, and Long-Term Exposure to Fine Particulate Air Pollution." *Journal of the American Medical Association,* 287(9):1132–1141.

Popenoe, David. 1988. *Disturbing the Nest: Family Change and Decline in Modern Societies.* New York: Aldine de Gruyter.

Popenoe, David. 1995. "The American Family Crisis." *National Forum: The Phi Kappa Phi Journal,* 73(Summer 1995):15–19.

Popenoe, David. 1996. *Life without Father: Compelling New Evidence That Fatherhood and Marriage Are Indispensable for the Good of Children and Society.* New York: Martin Kessler/Free Press.

Porteous, S. 1998. *Organized Crime: Impact Study (Highlights).* Ottawa: Solicitor General of Canada.

Potterat, John J., Donald E. Woodhouse, John B. Muth, and Stephen Q. Muth. 1990. "Estimating the Prevalence and Career Longevity of Prostitute Women." *Journal of Sex Research,* 27(May):233–243.

Pran, Dith. 1997. *Children of Cambodia's Killing Fields.* New Haven, CT: Yale University Press.

Press Campaigns. 2003. Home Page. (January 14). Retrieved from **www.presscampaigns.org**

Priest, Lisa. 2001. "Street Deaths Spark Calls for Shelters." *Globe and Mail* (December 28):A18.

Public Citizen. 2003. "Global Trade Watch." Retrieved from **www.citizen.org/trade/issues/mai/articles.cfm?ID=1500**

Purvis, Andrew. 1996. "The Global Epidemic: AIDS Is Tightening Its Grip on the Developing World." *Time* (December 30):76–78.

Quadagno, Jill, and Catherine Fobes. 1995. "The Welfare State and the Cultural Reproduction of Gender." *Social Problems,* 42(2):171–190.

Queen, Carol. 1997. *Real Live Nude Girl: Chronicles of Sex-Positive Culture.* Pittsburgh, PA: Cleis Press.

Rank, Mark Robert. 1994. *Living on the Edge: The Realities of Welfare in America.* New York: Columbia University Press.

Rankin, Robert P., and Jerry S. Maneker. 1985. "The Duration of Marriage in a Divorcing Population: The Impact of Children." *Journal of Marriage and the Family,* 47(February):43–52.

Raphael, Ray. 1988. *The Men from the Boys: Rites of Passage in Male America.* Lincoln, NE: University of Nebraska Press.

Ratner, Robert S. 1997. "Many Davids, One Goliath." In William K. Carroll (Ed.), *Organizing Dissent: Contemporary Social Movements in Theory and Practice*. Toronto: Garamond Press, pp. 271–286.

Rawls, John. 1971. *A Theory of Justice*. Cambridge, MA: Harvard University Press.

Rebick, Judy. 2001a. "PR Can Help Solve Canada's Democracy Deficit." *Policy Options*, 22(6/July–August):15.

Rebick, Judy. 2001b. "Soaked in Sensorship." (October 5). Retrieved from **www.cbc.ca**

Reckless, Walter C. 1967. *The Crime Problem*. New York: Meredith.

Reinharz, S. 1992. *Feminist Methods in Social Research*. New York: Oxford University Press.

Reiss, I. L. 1986. *Journey into Sexuality: An Exploratory Voyage*. Englewood Cliffs, NJ: Prentice-Hall.

Relman, Arnold S. 1992. "Self-Referral—What's at Stake?" *New England Journal of Medicine*, 327 (November 19): 1522–1524.

Renner, Michael. 1993. *Critical Juncture: The Future of Peacekeeping*. Washington, DC: Worldwatch Institute.

Renzetti, Claire M., and Daniel J. Curran. 1995. *Women, Men, and Society* (3rd ed.). Boston: Allyn and Bacon.

Reskin, Barbara F., and Heidi Hartmann. 1986. *Women's Work, Men's Work: Sex Segregation on the Job*. Washington, DC: National Academy Press.

Reskin, Barbara F., and Irene Padavic. 1994. *Women and Men at Work*. Thousand Oaks, CA: Pine Forge.

Reynolds, Cecilia. 2001. "The Educational System." In Nancy Mandell (Ed.), *Feminist Issues: Race, Class, and Sexuality* (3rd ed.). Toronto: Pearson, pp. 242–259.

Reynolds, Helen. 1986. *The Economics of Prostitution*. Springfield, IL: Charles C. Thomas.

Ricciutelli, Luciana, June Larkin, and Eimear O'Neill. 1998. "Preface." In Luciana Ricciutelli, June Larkin, and Eimear O'Neill (Eds.), *Confronting the Cuts: A Sourcebook for Women in Ontario*. Toronto: Inanna, pp. Iiii.

Rich, Adrienne. 1984. "Compulsory Heterosexuality and Lesbian Existence." In Ann Snitnow, Christine Stansell, and Sharon Thompson (Eds), *Desire: The Politics of Sexuality*. London: Virago Press, pp. 212–241.

Richardson, Laurel. 1993. "Inequalities of Power, Property, and Prestige." In Virginia Cyrus (Ed.), *Experiencing Race, Class, and Gender in the United States*. Mountain View, CA: Mayfield, pp. 229–236.

Risman, Barbara J. 1987. "Intimate Relationships from a Microstructural Perspective: Men Who Mother." *Gender and Society*, 1:6–32.

Ritzer, George. 1995. *Expressing America: A Critique of the Global Credit Card Society*. Thousand Oaks, CA: Pine Forge.

Roberts, Nickie. 1992. *Whores in History: Prostitution in Western Society*. London: HarperCollins.

Robertson, Angela. 1999. "Continuing on the Ground: Feminists of Colour Discuss Organizing." In Enakshi Dua and Angela Robertson (Eds.), *Scratching the Surface: Canadian Anti-Racist Feminist Thought*. Toronto: Women's Press, pp. 309–329

Robinson, David, Frank J. Porporino, William A. Millson, Shelley Trevethan, and Barry McKillop. 1999. "The One-Day Snapshot of Inmates in Canada's Adult Correctional Facilities." In Canadian Centre for Justice Statistics (Eds.), *The Juristat Reader: A Statistical Overview of the Canadian Justice System*. Toronto: Thompson, pp. 54–66.

Rochlin, M. 1982. "The Heterosexual Questionnaire." *Changing Men*, (Spring).

Rogers Communication. 2003. "Investor Relations." Retrieved from **www.rogers.com/english/investorrelations/index.html**

Romero, Mary. 1992. *Maid in the U.S.A.* New York: Routledge.

Roos, Noralou P., and L.L. Roos. 1994. "Small Area Variations, Practice Style, and Quality of Care." In R.G. Evans, M.L. Barer, and T.R. Marmor (Eds.), *Why Are Some People Healthy and Others Not? The Determinants of Health of Populations*. Hawthorne, NY: Aldine de Gruyter.

Roos, Patricia A., and Barbara F. Reskin. 1992. "Occupational Desegregation in the 1970s: Integration and Economic Equity?" *Sociological Perspectives*, 35:69.

Ropers, Richard H. 1991. *Persistent Poverty: The American Dream Turned Nightmare*. New York: Plenum.

Rose, Arnold. 1951. *The Roots of Prejudice*. Paris: UNESCO.

Rosenberg, Janet, Harry Perlstadt, and William Phillips. 1993. "Now That We Are Here: Discrimination, Disparagement and Harassment at Work and the Experience of Women Lawyers." *Gender and Society*, 7(3):415–433.

Rosenthal, Carolyn J. 1987. "Aging and Intergenerational Relations in Canada." In Victor W. Marshall (Ed.), *Aging in Canada Social Perspectives* (2nd ed.). Markham, ON: Fitzhenry and Whiteside, pp. 311–342.

Rosenthal, Elisabeth. 1997. "The H.M.O. Catch: When Healthier Isn't Cheaper." *New York Times* (March 16):E1, E4.

Rosenwein, Rifka. 2000. "Why Media Mergers Matter." *Brill's Content* (January):93–95.

Ross, David P., Katherine J. Scott, and Peter J. Smith. 2000. *The Canadian Fact Book on Poverty*. Ottawa: Canadian Council on Social Development.

Rossi, Peter H. 1989. *Down and Out in America: The Origins of Homelessness*. Chicago: University of Chicago Press.

Rothchild, John. 1995. "Wealth: Static Wages, Except for the Rich." *Time* (January 30):60–61.

Rothman, Robert A. 1993. *Inequality and Stratification: Class, Color, and Gender* (2nd ed.). Englewood Cliffs, NJ: Prentice-Hall.

Rowan, Ruby. 2001. "Sleeping with the Enemy and Liking It: Confessions of a Bi-Sexual Feminist." In Allyson Mitchell, Lisa Bryn Rundle, and Lara Karaian (Eds.), *Turbo Chicks: Talking Young Feminisms*. Toronto: Sumach Press, pp. 238–244.

Rowland, Robyn, and Renate Klein. 1996. "Radical Feminism: History, Politics, Action." In Diane Bell and Renate Klein (Eds.), *Radically Speaking: Feminism Reclaimed*. London: Zed Books, pp. 9–36.

Roy, Arundati. 2003. "Confronting Empire." People's Summit Port Alegre, Brazil. January 27, 2003. Retrieved from **www.dawn.com/2003/02/10/op.htm**

Rubin, J.Z., F.J. Provenzano, and Z. Luria. 1974. "The Eye of the Beholder: Parents' Views on Sex of Newborns." *American Journal of Orthopsychiatry*, 44:512–519.

Rubin, Lillian B. 1976. *Worlds of Pain: Life in the Working-Class Family*. New York: Basic Books.

Rubin, Lillian B. 1994. *Families on the Fault Line*. New York: HarperCollins.

Russell, Diana E. H. 1993. "Introduction." In Diana E. H. Russell (Ed.), *Making Violence Sexy: Feminist Views on Pornography*. New York: Teachers College Press, pp. 1–20.

Ryan, William. 1976. *Blaming the Victim* (rev. ed.). New York: Vintage.

Sacco, Vincent F., and Leslie W. Kennedy. 1998. *The Criminal Event* (2nd ed.). Scarborough, ON: Nelson.

Sachs, Aaron. 1994. "The Last Commodity: Child Prostitution in the Developing World." *World Watch*, 7(4) (July–August):24–31.

Sadker, Myra, and David Sadker. 1994. *Failing at Fairness: How America's Schools Cheat Girls*. New York: Scribner.

Safilios-Rothschild, Constantina. 1969. "Family Sociology or Wives' Family Sociology? A Cross-Cultural Examination of Decision-Making." *Journal of Marriage and the Family*, 31(2):290–301.

Sallot, Jeff. 1999. "Latimer Sentence Too Harsh, Poll Told." *Globe and Mail* (January 11):A5.

Sambugaro, Elaine. 2000. "Money Laundering Is on the Rise." *Metro* (October 25):10–11.

Sampson, Robert J. 1986. "Effects of Socioeconomic Context on Official Reactions to Juvenile Delinquency." *American Sociological Review*, 51(December):876–885.

Sanday, Peggy Reeves. 1996. *A Woman Scorned: Acquaintance Rape on Trial*. New York: Doubleday.

Sanger, David E. 2000. "In Leading Nations, a Population Bust?" *New York Times* (January 1):YNE8.

Sapon-Shevin, Mara. 1993. "Gifted Education and the Protection of Privilege: Breaking the Silence, Opening the Discourse." In Lois Weis and Michelle Fine (Eds.), *Beyond Silenced Voices: Class, Race, and Gender in United States Schools*. Albany, NY: State University of New York Press, pp. 25–44.

Sassen, Saskia. 1995. "On Concentration and Centrality in the Global City." In Paul L. Knox and Peter J. Taylor (Eds.), *World Cities in a World-System*. Cambridge, England: Cambridge University Press, pp. 63–75.

Satzewich, Victor. 1989. "Racism and Canadian Immigration Policy: The Government's View of Caribbean Migration, 1962–66." *Canadian Ethnic Studies*, 30(1):77–97.

Saunders, John. 2001. "Furor Erupts as Police Seize Spanked Children." *Globe and Mail* (July 6):A1, A7.

Sawyer, Janet. 1989. "Internalized Dominance." *Quarterly Change*, 1(4):16–23.

Scheff, Thomas J. 1977. "The Distancing of Emotion in Ritual." *Current Anthropology*, 18:483–505. In Bunis, William K., Angela Yancik, and David Snow. 1996. "The Cultural Patterning of Sympathy toward the Homeless and Other Victims of Misfortune." *Social Problems* (November): 387–402.

Schetagne, Sylvain, Andrew Jackson, and Shelley Harman. 2001. *Gaining Ground: The Personal Security Index, 2001*. Ottawa: Canadian Council on Social Development.

Schiller, Herbert I. 1996. *Information Inequality: The Deepening Social Crisis in America*. New York: Routledge.

Schlaadt, R.G. 1992. *Alcohol Use and Abuse*. Guilford, CT: Duskin.

Schneider, Keith. 1993. "The Regulatory Thickets of Environmental Racism." *New York Times* (December 19): E5.

Schur, Edwin M. 1965. *Crimes without Victims: Deviant Behavior and Public Policy*. Englewood Cliffs, NJ: Prentice-Hall.

Scott, Alan. 1990. *Ideology and the New Social Movements*. Boston: Unwin & Hyman.

Scott, Denise Benoit. 1996. "Shattering the Instrumental-Expressive Myth: The Power of Women's Networks in Corporate-Government Affairs." *Gender and Society*, 10(3):232–247.

Seabrook, Jeremy. 2002. *The No-Nonsense Guide to Class, Caste, and Hierarchies*. Carlisle, England: Carel Press.

Seager, Joni. 1997. *The State of Women in the World Atlas* (2nd ed.). London: Penguin.

Searight, H. Russel, and Priscilla R. Searight. 1988. "The Homeless Mentally Ill: Overview, Policy Implications, and Adult Foster Care as a Neglected Resource." *Adult Foster Care Journal*, 2:235–259.

Seavor, Jim. 1996. "Closing the Books on Homophobia." *Austin American-Statesman* (November 24):E11.

Segal, Lynn. 1990. "Pornography and Violence: What the 'Experts' Really Say." *Feminist Review*, 36:29–41.

Segall, Alexander, and Neena L. Chappell. 2000. *Health and Health Care in Canada*. Toronto: Prentice Hall.

Seidman, Steven. 1992. "An Investigation of Sex-Role Stereotyping in Music Videos." *Journal of Broadcasting & Electronic Media* (Spring):212.

Sen, Amartya. 1999. *Development as Freedom*. New York: Knopf.

Serbeh-Dunn, Gifty, and Wayne Dunn. 2001. "We Are All the Same—Just Because You Are Black Doesn't Matter." In Carl E. James and Adrienne Shadd (Eds.), *Talking About Identity: Encounters in Race, Ethnicity and Language*. Toronto: Between the Lines, pp. 267–276.

Sexually Exploited Youth Committee of the Capital Regional District. 1997. *Report of the Sexually Exploited Youth*

Committee of the Capital Regional District, Victoria, British Columbia. Victoria, BC: City of Victoria.

Sforza, Michelle, and Mark Vallianatos. 1997. "NAFTA & Environmental Laws: Ethyl Corp. v. Government of Canada: Chemical Firm Uses Trade Pact to Contest Environmental Law." Retrieved from **www.globalpolicy. org/socecon/envronment/ethyl.htm**

Shaw, Randy. 1999. *Reclaiming America: Nike, Clean Air, and the New National Activism.* Berkeley, CA: University of California Press.

Shea, Christopher. 1996. "A Scholar Links Sexual Orientation to Gender Roles in Childhood." *Chronicle of Higher Education* (November 22):A11, A12.

Shedler, J., and J. Block. 1990. "Adolescent Drug Users and Psychological Health." *American Psychologist,* 45:612–630.

Sheehan, Molly O. 2002. "CFC Use Declining." *Vital Signs 2002: The Trends That are Shaping Our Future.* New York: Norton.

Sheff, David. 1995. "If It's Tuesday, It Must Be Dad's House." *New York Times Magazine* (March 26):64–65.

Sheldon, William H. 1949. *Varieties of Delinquent Youth: An Introduction to Constitutional Psychiatry.* New York: Harper.

Sheley, Joseph F. (Ed.). 1995. *Criminology* (2nd ed.) Belmont, CA: Wadsworth.

Shelton, Beth Ann. 1992. *Women, Men and Time: Gender Differences in Paid Work, Housework and Leisure.* Westport, CT: Greenwood.

Shenon, Philip. 1996. "AIDS Epidemic, Late to Arrive, Now Explodes in Populous Asia." *New York Times* (January 21): A1.

Sher, Kenneth J. 1991. *Children of Alcoholics: A Critical Appraisal of Theory and Research.* Chicago: University of Chicago Press.

Sherman, Lawrence, Patrick R. Gratin, and M.E. Buerger. 1989. "Routine Activities and the Criminology of Place." *Criminology,* 27(1):27–55.

Shibutani, Tamotsu. 1970. "On the Personification of Adversaries." In Tamotsu Shibutani (Ed.), *Human Nature and Collective Behavior.* Englewood Cliffs, NJ: Prentice-Hall, pp. 223–233.

Shilts, Randy. 1988. *And the Band Played On: Politics, People, and the AIDS Epidemic.* New York: Penguin.

Short, G. 1991. "Combating Anti-Semitism: A Dilemma for Antiracist Education." *British Journal of Educational Studies,* 39(1).

Shragge, Eric. 1997. "Workfare: An Overview." In Eric Shragge (Ed.), *Workfare: Ideology for a New Under-Class.* Toronto: Garamond Press, pp. 17–34.

Shrybman, Steven. 1999. *A Citizens Guide to the World Trade Organization.* Ottawa: Canadian Centre for Policy Alternatives/Lorimer.

Sidel, Ruth. 1996. *Keeping Women and Children Last: America's War on the Poor.* New York: Penguin.

Siegel, Arthur. 1996. *Politics and the Media in Canada* (2nd ed.). Toronto: McGraw-Hill Ryerson.

Silverman, R.A., J.J. Teevan, and V.F. Sacco (Eds.). 1996. *Crime in Canadian Society* (5th ed.). Toronto: Harcourt Brace.

Simmel, Georg. 1950. *The Sociology of Georg Simmel.* Trans. Kurt Wolff. Glencoe, IL: Free Press (orig. written in 1902–1917).

Simon, Brenda M. 1999. "*United States v. Hilton.*" *Berkeley Technology Law Journal* 14:385–403.

Simon, David R. 1996. *Elite Deviance* (5th ed.) Boston: Allyn and Bacon.

Singer, Bennett L., and David Deschamps. 1994. *Gay and Lesbian Stats.* New York: New Press.

Single, Eric, Linda Robson, and Jurgen Rehm and Xiadi Xie. 1999. "Morbidity and Mortality Attributable to Alcohol, Tobacco and Illicit Drug Use in Canada." *American Journal of Public Health,* 89:385–390.

Single, Eric, Linda Robson, Xiadi Xie, and Jurgen Rehm. 1996. *The Cost of Substance Abuse in Canada.* Ottawa: Canadian Centre on Substance Abuse.

Single, Eric, Minh Van Truong, Edward Adlaf, and Anca Ialomiteanu (Eds.). 1999. *Canadian Profile Alcohol, Tobacco and Other Drugs/Profil Canadien L'alcool, le tabac et les autres drogues.* Toronto: Centre for Addiction and Mental Health, and Ottawa: Canadian Centre on Substance Abuse.

Sivard, Ruth L. 1991. *World Military and Social Expenditures— 1991.* Washington, DC: World Priorities.

Sivard, Ruth L. 1993. *World Military and Social Expenditures— 1993.* Washington, DC: World Priorities.

Skolnick, Arlene. 1991. *Embattled Paradise: The American Family in an Age of Uncertainty.* New York: HarperCollins.

Skolnick, Jerome H. 1975. *Justice without Trial* (2nd ed.). New York: Wiley.

Sleeter, Christine E. 1996. "White Silence, White Solidarity." In Noel Ignatiev and John Garvey (Eds.), *Race Traitor.* New York: Routledge, pp. 257–265.

Small, Shirley. 1978. "Canadian Narcotics Legislation, 1908–1923: A Conflict Model Interpretation." In William K. Greenaway and Stephen L. Brickey (Eds.), *Law and Social Control in Canada.* Scarborough, ON: Prentice Hall.

Smith, Michael D. 1993. "Women's Fear of Male Violence." *Canada Watch,* 1:68–70.

Snell, Cudore L. 1995. *Young Men in the Street: Help-Seeking Behavior of Young Male Prostitutes.* Westport, CT: Praeger.

Snitow, Ann Barr. 1994. "Mass Market Romance: Pornography for Women Is Different." In Alison M. Jaggar (Ed.), *Living with Contradictions: Controversies in Feminist Social Ethics.* Boulder, CO: Westview, pp. 181–188.

Snow, David A., and Leon Anderson. 1991. "Researching the Homeless: The Characteristic Features and Virtues of the Case Study." In Joe R. Feagin, Anthony M. Orum, and Gideon Sjoberg (Eds.), *A Case for the Case Study.* Chapel Hill: University of North Carolina Press, pp. 148–173.

Snyder, Benson R. 1971. *The Hidden Curriculum.* New York: Knopf.

Soble, Alan. 1986. "Pornography in Capitalism: Powerlessness." In Alan Soble, *Pornography: Marxism, Feminism and the Future of Sexuality*. New Haven, CT: Yale University Press, pp. 78–84.

Solicitor General of Canada (Porteus, S.D.). 1998. *Organized Crime Impact Study: Highlights*. Public Works and Government Services Canada [online]. Retrieved from **www.sgc.gc.ca**

Solyom, Catherine. 2001. "Pigment Matters in Montreal: Survey." *Gazette* (October 26).

Spafford, Marlee M., Neepun Sharma, Vicki L. Nygaard, and Christina Kahlou. 2002. "Diversity within the Profession, Part 1: Trends and Challenges." *Optometric Education*, 27(4/Summer):114–121.

Spanier, Graham, and Paul Glick. 1981. "Marital Instability in the U.S.: Some Correlates and Recent Changes." *Family Relations*, 30(July):329–338.

Spears, John, and Richard Brennan. 2002. "Smog Blamed on Coal-Fired Power Plants." *Toronto Star* (August 13):A18.

Special Committee on Pornography and Prostitution. 1985. *Pornography and Prostitution in Canada: Report of the Special Committee on Pornography and Prostitution*. Ottawa: Department of Justice Canada.

Spoto, Antonio. 2003. "The World Enters the Nuclear Era." (February 22). Retrieved from **www.geocities.com/ iturks/html/nuclear.html#inizio**

Squires, Gregory D. 1994. *Capital and Communities in Black and White: The Intersections of Race, Class, and Uneven Development*. Albany, NY: State University of New York Press.

Sridhara, B.A. 2003. "Media, Democracy and Citizenship." (January). Retrieved from **www.indiatogether.org/ 2003/jan/med-hoot0301.htm**

Standing Committee on Canadian Heritage. 2002. "Friends of Canadian Broadcasting." **http://friendscb.ca/issues heritagectte.htm**

Stanko, Elizabeth. 1990. *Everyday Violence: How Women and Men Experience Sexual and Physical Danger*. London: HarperCollins.

Stanley, Alessandra. 1995. "Russian Mothers, from All Walks, Walk Alone." *New York Times* (October 21):A1.

Stanley, Julia P. 1972. "Paradigmatic Woman: The Prostitute." Paper presented at South Atlantic Modern Language Association, Jacksonville, FL, cited in Jessie Bernard, *The Female World*. New York: Free Press, 1981.

Stasiulis, Daiva K. 1999. "Feminist Intersectional Theorizing." In Peter S. Li (Ed.), *Race and Ethnic Relations in Canada* (2nd ed.). Don Mills, ON: Oxford University Press, pp. 347–397.

Statistics Canada. 1994. *Selected Characteristics of Persons with Disabilities Residing in Households*. Ottawa: Ministry of Industry Science, and Technology.

Statistics Canada. 1998a. "Deaths 1996." *The Daily* (April 16).

Statistics Canada. 1998b. "National Longitudinal Survey of Children and Youth, 1996–97." *The Daily* (October 28).

Statistics Canada. 1999a. "Assets and Debts Held by Family Units, Canada and Provinces, 1999." Retrieved April 23, 2003 from **www.statcan.ca/english/pgdb/ famil99d.htm**

Statistics Canada. 1999b. *A Portrait of Seniors in Canada* (3rd ed.). Ottawa: Ministry of Industry.

Statistics Canada. 1999c. *Work Absence Rates, 1987–1998*. Ottawa: Labour and Household Surveys Analysis Division.

Statistics Canada. 2000. "Family Income, 1998." *The Daily* (June 12).

Statistics Canada. 2001a. "Crime Comparisons Between Canada and the United States." *The Daily* (December 18).

Statistics Canada. 2001b. "How Healthy Are Canadians?" *Health Reports*, 12(3).

Statistics Canada. 2001c. "Measuring Student Knowledge and Skills: The Performance of Canada's Youth in Reading, Mathematics and Science. *The Daily* (December 4).

Statistics Canada. 2001d. "School Performance of Children from Immigrant Families." *The Daily* (November 14).

Statistics Canada. 2001e. "Social Indicators." *Canadian Social Trends*, (Winter):25.

Statistics Canada. 2001f. "Trends in the Use of Private Education." *The Daily* (July 4).

Statistics Canada. 2001g. "University Tuition Fees." *The Daily* (August 27).

Statistics Canada. 2001h. *Women in Canada: Work Chapter Updates*. Ottawa: Ministry of Industry.

Statistics Canada. 2002a. "Average Earnings by Sex and Work Pattern." CANSIM II, Table 202-0102. Retrieved from **www.statcan.ca/english/Pgdb/labor01a.htm**

Statistics Canada. 2002b. "Changes in Unmet Health Care Needs." *The Daily* (March 13).

Statistics Canada. 2002bb. "Health Indicators." Retrieved April 5, 2002 from **www.statcan.ca/english/freepub/82-221-XIE/syst.htm**

Statistics Canada. 2002c. "Control and Sale of Alcoholic Beverages." *The Daily* (July 12).

Statistics Canada. 2002d. "Defending Science." *The Economist* (Feb. 2):15–16.

Statistics Canada. 2002e. "Distance to School and University Participation." *The Daily* (June 24).

Statistics Canada. 2002f. "Divorces." *The Daily* (December 2).

Statistics Canada. 2002g. "Family Income, 2000." *The Daily* (July 18).

Statistics Canada. 2002h. "Family Income, 2000." *The Daily* (October 30).

Statistics Canada. 2002i. "Family Violence: Impacts and Consequences of Spousal Violence." *The Daily* (June 26).

Statistics Canada. 2002j. "Housing: An Income Issue." *The Daily* (June 21).

Statistics Canada. 2002k. "Human Activity and the Environment: Annual Statistics." *The Daily* (November 6).

Statistics Canada. 2002l. *Low Income Cutoffs from 1992 to 2001 and Low Income Measures from 1991 to 2000.* Ottawa: Minister of Industry.

Statistics Canada. 2002m. "National Longitudinal Survey of Children and Youth: Childhood Obesity 1994 to 1999." *The Daily* (October 18).

Statistics Canada. 2002n. "Police Expenditures and Personnel in Canada 2001." *The Daily* (February 12).

Statistics Canada. 2002o. *Population Tabulation.* Retrieved from www.statcan.ca

Statistics Canada. 2002p. "Profile of Canadian Families and Households: Diversification Continues. Retrieved October 22, 2002, from **www12.statcan.ca/english/census01/ release/index.cfm**

Statistics Canada. 2002q. "Profile of the Canadian Population by Age and Sex: Canada Ages." Retrieved February 6, 2003, from **www12.statcan.ca/english/census01/products/ analytic/companion/age/contents.cfm**

Statistics, Canada. 2002r. "A Profile of the Canadian Population: Where We Live." 2001 Census Analysis Series. Retrieved March 30, 2002, from **www.statcan.ca/english/dai-quo/ note.htm**

Statistics Canada. 2002s. "Social Indicators." *Canadian Social Trends,* (Spring):27.

Statistics Canada. 2002t. "Therapeutic Abortions." *The Daily* (January 18).

Statistics Canada. 2002u. "2001 Census: Collective Dwellings." Retrieved November 6, 2002, from **www12.statcan. ca/ english/census01/products/analytic/companion/coll/ contents.cfm**

Statistics Canada. 2002v. "2001 Census: Marital Status, Common-Law Status, Families, Dwellings, and House-holds." *The Daily* (October 22).

Statistics Canada. 2002w. "Wealth Inequality, 1984–1999." *The Daily* (February 22).

Statistics Canada. 2002x. "Youth in Transition Survey." *The Daily* (January 23).

Statistics Canada. 2003. "Census of Population: Immigration, Birthplace and Birthplace of Parents, Citizenship, Ethnic Origin, Visible Minorities and Aboriginal Peoples." *The Daily* (January 21).

Steering Committee of the Physicians' Health Study Group. 1989. "Final Report on the Aspirin Component of the Ongoing Physician's Health Study." *New England Journal of Medicine,* 321:129–135.

Stefanac, Suzanne. 1993. "Sex and the New Media." *New Media* (April):38–45.

Steffensmeier, Darrell, and Emilie Allan. 1995. "Criminal Behavior: Gender and Age." In Joseph F. Sheley (Ed.), *Criminology: A Contemporary Handbook* (2nd ed.). Belmont, CA: Wadsworth, pp. 83–143.

Stein, Peter J. 1976. *Single.* Englewood Cliffs, NJ: Prentice-Hall.

Stein, Peter J. (Ed.). 1981. *Single Life: Unmarried Adults in Social Context.* New York: St. Martin's Press.

Steinberg, Michelle. 2001. "If You Thought NAFTA Spelled Trouble." *Media Reader Quarterly.* Retrieved February 17, 2003, from **www.mediareader.org**

Steingart, R. M., M. Packer, P. Hamm, and others. 1991. "Sex Differences in the Management of Coronary Artery Disease." *New England Journal of Medicine,* 325:226–230.

Stern, M., and K.H. Karraker. 1989. "Sex Stereotyping of Infants: A Review of Gender Labelling Studies." *Sex Roles,* 20:501–522.

Stevens, Patricia E. 1992. "Lesbian Health Care Research: A Review of the Literature from 1970 to 1990." *Health Care for Women International,* 13.

Stevens, William K. 1997. "How Much Is Nature Worth? For You, $33 Trillion." *New York Times* (May 20):B7, B9.

Stewart, Charles T., Jr. 1995. *Healthy, Wealthy, or Wise? Issues in American Health Care Policy.* Armonk, NY: M.E. Sharpe.

Stoll, Clifford. 1996. "Invest in Humanware." *New York Times* (May 19):E15.

Stoller, Robert J. 1991. *Porn: Myths for the Twentieth Century.* New Haven, CT: Yale University Press.

Strom, Stephanie. 2000. "Tradition of Equality Fading in New Japan." *New York Times* (January 4):A1, A6.

Sturgeon, Noel. 1997. *Ecofeminist Natures: Race, Gender, Feminist Theory and Political Action.* New York: Routledge.

Sullivan, A. 1997. "The Conservative Case." In A. Sullivan (Ed.), *Same Sex Marriage: Pro and Con.* New York: Vintage, pp. 146–154.

Sullivan, Maureen. 1996. "Rozzie and Harriet? Gender and Family Patterns of Lesbian Coparents." *Gender and Society,* 10(6):747–767.

Sullivan, Teresa A., Elizabeth Warren, and Jay Lawrence Westbrook. 1989. *As We Forgive Our Debtors: Bankruptcy and Consumer Credit in America.* New York: Oxford University Press.

Sullivan, Thomas J. 1997. *Introduction to Social Problems* (4th ed.). Boston: Allyn and Bacon.

Sutherland, Edwin H. 1939. *Principles of Criminology.* Philadelphia: Lippincott.

Sutherland, Edwin H. 1949. *White Collar Crime.* New York: Dryden.

Swanson, Jean. 1997. "Resisting Workfare." In Eric Shragge (Ed.), *Workfare: Ideology for a New Under-Class.* Toronto: Garamond Press, pp. 149–170.

Swanson, Jean. 2001. *Poor-Bashing: The Politics of Exclusion.* Toronto: Between the Lines.

Swingewood, Alan. 2000. *A Short History of Sociological Thought* (3rd ed.). London: Macmillan Press.

Swol, Karen. 1999. "Private Security and Public Policing in Canada." In Canadian Centre for Justice Statistics (Eds.), *The Juristat Reader: A Statistical Overview of the Canadian Justice System.* Toronto: Thompson, pp. 15–25.

Sydie, Rosalind A. 1983. "Sociology and Gender." In M. Michael Rosenberg et al. (Eds.), *An Introduction to Sociology.* Toronto: Methuen, pp. 185–223.

Tadic, Vela, and Karen Hughes. 1998. "Sexual Harassment in the Service Economy: Exploring Women's Retail Work in Canada." *Canadian Women's Studies*, 18(1):86–91.

Tait, Heather. 1999. "Educational Achievement of Young Aboriginal Adults." *Canadian Social Trends*, (Spring).

Tannen, Deborah. 1990. *You Just Don't Understand: Women and Men in Conversation*. New York: William Morrow.

Tannen, Deborah. 1994. *Gender and Discourse*. New York: Oxford University Press.

Tavris, Carol. 2002. "Are Girls Really as Mean as Books Say They Are?" *Chronicle of Higher Education*, 48(43):B7–B9.

Taylor, Leanne E. 2000. "Black, White, Beige, Other? Memories of Growing Up Different." In Carl E. James (Ed.), *Experiencing Difference*. Halifax: Fernwood, pp. 59–70.

Taylor, Verta, and Nicole C. Raeburn. 1995. "Identity Politics as High-Risk Activism: Career Consequences for Lesbian, Gay, and Bisexual Sociologists." *Social Problems*, 42(2):252–273.

Teeple, Gary. 2000. "The Decline of the Canadian Welfare State: Policies and Implications of Retrenchment." In B. Singh Bolaria (Ed.), *Social Issues and Contradictions in Canadian Society* (3rd ed.). Toronto: Harcourt Brace, pp. 434–468.

Telegdi, Andrew. 2002. Statement made at the 37th Parliament, 2nd Session. *Hansard* (November 7):No. 024.

Tepperman, Lorne, and Jenny Blain. 1999. *Think Twice! Sociology Looks at Current Social Issues*. Upper Saddle River, NJ: Prentice Hall.

Terkel, Studs. 1996. *Coming of Age: The Story of Our Century by Those Who've Lived It*. New York: St. Martin's Griffin.

Thobani, Sunera. 2001a. Speech at the "Women's Resistance: From Victimization to Criminalization" conference (October 1). Transcript provided by the Cable Public Affairs Channel. Retrieved from **www.casac.ca/conference01/ conf01_thobani.htm**

Thobani, Sunera. 2001b. "War Frenzy." (October 15). Retrieved from **www.casac.ca/conference01/ thobani_ response.htm**

Thomas, Cal. 1996. "Overrule Same-Sex Marriage." *Austin American-Statesman* (December 6):A15.

Thomas, Gale E. 1995. "Conclusion: Healthy Communities as a Basis for Healthy Race and Ethnic Relations." In Gail E. Thomas (Ed.), *Race and Ethnicity in America: Meeting the Challenge in the 21st Century*. Bristol, PA: Taylor & Francis, pp. 335–342.

Thomas, Mikhail. 2002. "Adult Criminal Court Cases." *Juristat*, 22(2).

Thompson, Jon, Patricia Baird, and Jocelyn Downie. 2001. *The Olivieri Report: The Complete Text of the Report of the Independent Inquiry Commissioned by the Canadian Association of University Teachers*. Toronto: Lorimer.

Thomson, Elizabeth, and Ugo Colella. 1992. "Cohabitation and Marital Stability: Quality or Commitment?" *Journal of Marriage and the Family*, 54:259–267.

Thorne, Barrie. 1998. "Girls and Boys Together . . . But Mostly Apart: Gender Arrangements in Elementary School." In Michael S. Kimmel and Michael A. Messner (Eds.), *Men's Lives* (4th ed.). Boston: Allyn and Bacon, pp. 81–100.

Thornton, Michael C., Linda M. Chatters, Robert Joseph Taylor, and Walter R. Allen. 1990. "Sociodemographic and Environmental Correlates of Racial Socialization by Black Parents." *Child Development*, 61:401–409.

Tierney, John. 1994. "Porn, the Low-Slung Engine of Progress." *New York Times* (January 9):H1, H18.

Time. 1996. "A Journey of 10,000 Miles Begins with the Shoes." *Time* (June 17):78.

Time. 1999b. "A Week in the Life of a High School" (October 25). Retrieved November 11, 1999, from **www.time.com**

Toner, Robin. 1995. "No Free Rides: Generational Push Has Not Come to Shove." *New York Times* (December 31): E1, E4.

Toner, Robin, and Robert Pear. 1995. "Medicare, Turning 30, Won't Be What It Was." *New York Times* (July 23):1, 12.

Toronto Dominion Bank. 2002. "A Choice Between Investing in Canada's Cities or Disinvesting in Canada's Future: Executive Summary." Retrieved November 1, 2002, from **www.td.com/economics/index.html**

Torrey, E. Fuller. 1998. *Nowhere to Go: The Tragic Odyssey of the Homeless Mentally Ill*. New York: Harper and Row.

Tovee, M.J., S.M. Mason, J.L. Emery, S.E. McCloskey, and E.M. Cohen-Tovee. 1997. "Supermodels: Stick Insects or Hourglasses." *Lancet*, 350 (9089):1474–1475.

Tower, Cynthia Crosson. 1996. *Child Abuse and Neglect* (3rd ed.). Boston: Allyn and Bacon.

Towle, Evan B., and Lynn M. Morgan. 2002. "Romancing the Transgender Native: Rethinking the Use of the 'Third Gender' Concept." *GLQ: A Journal of Lesbian and Gay Studies*, 8(4):469–497.

Townson, Monica. 2003. "Women's Poverty Rates Reach 20-Year High." *Straight Goods* (February 19). Retrieved from **www.straightgoods.com**

Trice, Harrison M., and Paul Michael Roman. 1970. "Delabeling, Relabeling, and Alcoholics Anonymous." *Social Problems*, 17(4):538–546.

Trocmé, Nico, Bruce MacLaurin, Barbara Fallon, Joanne Daciuk, Diane Billingsley, Marc Tourigny, Micheline Mayer, John Wright, Ken Barter, Gale Burford, Joe Hornick, Richard Sullivan, and Brad McKenzie. 2001. *Canadian Incidence Study of Reported Child Abuse and Neglect: Final Report*. Ottawa: Minister of Public Works and Government Services.

Tumulty, Karen. 1996. "Why Subsidies Survive." *Time* (March 25):46–47.

Turk, Austin T. 1966. "Conflict and Criminality." *American Sociological Review*, 31:338–352.

Turk, Austin T. 1971. *Criminality and Legal Order*. Chicago: Rand McNally.

Turner, Francis J. 1995. "Social Welfare in Canada." In Joanne C. Turner and Francis J. Turner (Eds.), *Canadian Social Welfare* (3rd ed.). Scarborough, ON: Allyn and Bacon, pp. 2–11.

Turner, Richard. 1999. "All Carnage, All the Time." *Newsweek* (August 23):45.

Turpin, Jennifer, and Lester R. Kurtz. 1997. "Introduction: Violence The Micro/Macro Link." In Jennifer Turpin and Lester R. Kurtz (Eds.), *The Web of Violence: From Interpersonal to Global.* Urbana and Chicago: University of Illinois, pp. 1–27.

Tyson, Eric K. 1993. "Credit Crackdown: Control Your Spending Before It Controls You." *San Francisco Examiner* (November 28):E1. (Cited in Ritzer, 1995.)

Tyyska, Vappu. 2001. *Long and Winding Road Adolescents and Youth in Canada Today.* Toronto: Canadian Scholars' Press.

UNAIDS. 2002a. Retrieved February 13, 2003, from **www. unaids.org/worldaidsday/2002/press/EpiCoreSlides2002/ EPIcore_en/Slide1.GIF**

UNAIDS. 2002b. Retrieved from **www.unaids.org/ worldaidsday/2002/press/EpiCoreSlides2002/EPIcore_ en/Slide4.gif**

United Nations. 1995. *The World's Women 1995: Trends and Statistics.* New York: United Nations.

United Nations. 2003a. Homepage. (February 20). Retrieved from **www.un.org**

United Nations. 2003b. "NPT Brief Background." (February 12). Retrieved from **www.un.org/Depts/dda/WMD/ treaty**

United Nations Development Programme (UNDP). 1999. *Human Development Report: 1999.* New York: Oxford University Press.

United Nations Development Programme (UNDP). 2001. *Human Development Report 2001.* New York: Oxford University Press.

United Nations Environment Programme (UNEP). 2003. *The UN World Water Development Report.* Retrieved March 5, 2003, from **www.unesco.org/water/wwap/wwdr/index. shtml**

United Nations Environment Programme (UNEP). 1992. *Status of Desertification and Implementation of the United Nations Plan of Action to Combat Desertification.* Nairobi, Egypt: United Nations.

United Nations (UN) Human Development Index. 1995. **http://unstats.un.org/unsd**

United Nations (UN) Security Council. 2003. "Iraq Memorandum." Presented by France, Russia, and Germany (February 24). Retrieved from **www.globalpolicy.org/ security**

U.S. Bureau of the Census. 1998. *Statistical Abstract of the United States, 1998* (118th ed.). Washington, DC: U.S. Government Printing Office.

U.S. Bureau of the Census. 1999. "Poverty in the United States: 1998." Retrieved November 17, 1999, from **www.census. gov/hhes/www/povty98.html**

Urschel, Joe. 1996. "How Girls Get Scared Away from Computers." *USA Today* (June 26):1D–2D.

Valdivia, Angharad N.1995. *Feminist Media Studies in a Global Setting: Beyond Binary Contradictions and Into Multicultural Spectrums in Feminism, Multiculturalisms, and the Media.* Thousand Oaks, CA: Sage.

Valpy, Michael. 2002. "Carey Speaks Out on Homosexuality." *Globe and Mail* (October 22):A8.

Valverde, Mariana. 1985. *Sex, Power and Pleasure.* Toronto: Women's Press.

Valverde, Mariana. 1998. "Sexuality." In Robert J. Brym (Ed.), *New Society: Sociology for the 21st Century* (2nd ed.). Toronto: Harcourt Brace, pp. 74–102.

Valverde, Mariana. 2000. "Lesbianism: A Country That Has No Language" (1987). In Barbara A. Crow and Lise Gotell (Eds.), *Open Boundaries: A Canadian Women's Studies Reader.* Toronto: Prentice Hall/Allyn and Bacon, pp. 255–261.

van Dijk, Jan J.M., Pat Matthews, and M. Killans. 1990. *Experiences of Crime around the World: Key Findings from the 1989 International Crime Survey.* Deventer, Netherlands: Klower.

Vanneman, Reeve, and Lynn Weber Cannon. 1987. *The American Perception of Class.* Philadelphia: Temple University Press.

Vartiainen, Erkki, Meri Paavola, Alfred McAlister, and Pekka Puska. 1998. "Fifteen-Year Follow-up of Smoking Prevention Effects in the North Karelia Youth Project." *American Journal of Public Health,* 88:81–85.

Veteran Affairs Canada. 1999. "Quick Facts." Retrieved from **www.vacacc.gc.ca/general/sub.cfm? source=teach_ resources/quickfact**

Veteran Affairs Canada. 2002. "Veteran's Week 2002: Remembering Our Past, Preserving our Future." Retrieved from **www.vac-acc.gc.ca**

Vetter, Harold J., and Gary R. Perlstein. 1991. *Perspectives on Terrorism.* Pacific Grove, CA: Brooks/Cole.

Vissing, Yvonne M. 1996. *Out of Sight, Out of Mind; Homeless Children and Families in Small-Town America.* Lexington, KY: University of Kentucky Press,

Vito, Gennaro F., and Ronald M. Holmes. 1994. *Criminology: Theory, Research and Policy.* Belmont, CA: Wadsworth.

Viviano, Frank. 1995. "The New Mafia Order." *Mother Jones* (May–June):45–55.

Vozoris, Nicholas, Barbara Davis, and Valerie Tarasuk. 2002. "The Affordability of a Nutritional Diet for Households on Welfare in Toronto." *Canadian Journal of Public Health,* 93:36–40.

Wagner, David. 1993. *Checkerboard Square: Culture and Resistance in a Homeless Community.* Boulder, CO: Westview.

Waldron, I. 1997. "Changing Gender Roles in Health Behavior." In D. Gochman (Ed.), *Handbook of Health Behavior Research I: Personal and Social Determinants.* New York: Plenum, pp. 303–328.

Walker, S.G. 1994. *Weapons Use in Canadian Schools.* Ottawa: Solicitor General of Canada.

Walker, S.L. 1994. "Critics Fume at Mayor of World Smog Capital. *San Diego Union-Tribune* (April 22). (Cited in

Michael P. Soroka and George J. Bryjak, *Social Problems: A World at Risk*. 1995. Boston: Allyn and Bacon, p. 115.)

Wallerstein, Immanuel. 1984. *The Politics of the World Economy*. Cambridge, England: Cambridge University Press.

Wallerstein, Immanuel. 1999. *The End of the World as We Know It: Social Science for the Twenty-First Century*. Minneapolis: University of Minnesota Press.

Wallerstein, Judith, and Sandra Blakeslee. 1989. *Second Chances: Men, Women and Children a Decade after Divorce*. New York: Ticknor & Field.

Wallis, Claudia. 1994. "A Class of Their Own." *Time* (October 31):53–61.

Wanner, Richard A. 1999. "Trends in Educational Opportunity in Canada, 1920–1994." *Canadian Review of Sociology and Anthropology*, 36(3):409–42.

Ward, Martha C. 1999. *A World Full of Women* (2nd ed.). Boston: Allyn and Bacon.

Warr, Mark. 1995. "Public Perceptions of Crime and Punishment." In Joseph F. Sheley (Ed.), *Criminology: A Contemporary Handbook* (2nd ed.). Belmont, CA: Wadsworth, pp. 15–31.

Warshaw, Robin. 1994. *I Never Called It Rape*. New York: HarperPerennial.

Waters, Malcolm. 1995. *Globalization*. New York: Routledge.

Watson, Roy E. L., and Peter W. DeMeo. 1987. "Premarital Cohabitation Versus Traditional Courtship and Subsequent Marital Adjustment: A Replication and a Follow-Up." *Family Relations*, 36:193–197.

Wednesday Report. 2002. "Canada in Afghanistan." (January). Retrieved from **www.mobrien.com/twr/Canada_in_Afghanistan.htm**

Weedon, Chris. 1999. *Feminism, Theory and the Politics of Difference*. Oxford, England: Blackwell.

Weeks, John R. 1998. *Population: An Introduction to Concepts and Issues* (7th ed.). Belmont, CA: Wadsworth.

Weinberg, Martin S., and Colin Williams. 1975. *Male Homosexuals*. New York: Penguin.

Weinberg, Martin S., Earl Rubington, and Sue Kiefer Hammersmith. 1981. *The Solution of Social Problems: Five Perspectives* (2nd ed.). New York: Oxford University Press.

Weinberg, Martin S., Colin J. Williams, and Douglas W. Pryor. 1994. *Dual Attraction: Understanding Bisexuality*. New York: Oxford University Press.

Weiner, Jonathan. 1990. *The Next One Hundred Years: Shaping the Fate of Our Living Earth*. New York: Bantam.

Weisner, Thomas S., Helen Garnier, and James Loucky. 1994. "Domestic Tasks, Gender Egalitarian Values, and Children's Gender Typing in Conventional and Nonconventional Families." *Sex Roles*, 30:23–54.

Weiten, Wayne, and Margaret A. Lloyd. 1994. *Psychology Applied to Modern Life: Adjustment in the 90s*. Pacific Grove, CA: Brooks/Cole.

Weitz, Rose. 1996. *The Sociology of Health, Illness, and Health Care: A Critical Approach*. Belmont, CA: Wadsworth.

Weitzman, Lenore J. 1985. *The Divorce Revolution*. New York: Free Press.

Wellman, David T. 1993. *Portraits of White Racism* (2nd ed.). New York: Cambridge University Press.

Westoff, Charles F. 1995. "International Population Policy." *Society* (May–June):11–15.

Wildman, Stephanie M., and Adrienne D. Davis. 2002. "Making Systems of Privilege Visible." In Paula S. Rothenberg (Ed.), *White Privilege: Essential Readings on the Other Side of Racism*. New York: Worth, pp. 89–96.

Wilkie, Jane Riblett. 1993. "Changes in U.S. Men's Attitudes toward the Family Provider Role, 1972–1989." *Gender and Society*, 7(2):261–279.

Wilkinson, Sue, and Celia Kitzinger. 1996. "The Queer Backlash." In Diane Bell and Renate Klein (Eds.), *Radically Speaking: Feminism Reclaimed*. London: Zed Books, pp. 375–382.

Williams, Cara. 2001. "Family Disruptions and Childhood Happiness." *Canadian Social Trends*, (Autumn):2–4.

Williams, Christine L. 1995. *Still a Man's World: Men Who Do Women's Work*. Berkeley, CA: University of California Press.

Williams, Robin M., Jr. 1970. *American Society: A Sociological Interpretation* (3rd ed.). New York: Knopf.

Williamson, Robert C., Alice Duffy Rinehart, and Thomas O. Blank. 1992. *Early Retirement: Promises and Pitfalls*. New York: Plenum.

Willis, Ellen. 1981. *Beginning to See the Light*. New York: Knopf.

Willis, Ellen. 1983. "Feminism, Moralism, and Pornography." In Ann Snitow, Christine Stansell, and Sharon Thompson (Eds.), *Powers of Desire: The Politics of Sexuality*. New York: Monthly Review Press, pp. 460–466.

Wilson, David (Ed.). 1997. "Globalization and the Changing U.S. City." *The Annals of the American Academy of Political and Social Science*, 551(May). Special Issue. Thousand Oaks, CA: Sage.

Wilson, Susannah J. 2001. "Paid Work, Jobs and the Illusion of Economic Security." In Nancy Mandell (Ed.), *Feminist Issues: Race, Class, and Sexuality* (3rd ed.). Toronto: Pearson, pp. 219–241.

Wilson, William Julius. 1996. *When Work Disappears: The World of the New Urban Poor*. New York: Knopf.

Wilton, Tamsin. 2000. *Sexualities in Health and Social Care: A Textbook*. Buckingham, England: Open University Press.

Winsor, Hugh. 2002. "CBC Shouldn't Shun Its Strongest Fans." *Globe and Mail* (April 25):A16.

Wirth, Louis. 1938. "Urbanism as a Way of Life." *American Journal of Sociology*, 40:1–24.

Wirth, Louis. 1945. "The Problem of Minority Groups." In Ralph Linton (Ed.), *The Science of Man in the World Crisis*. New York: Columbia University Press, p. 38.

Wolf, Robin. 1996. *Marriages and Families in a Diverse Society*. New York: HarperCollins.

Wolff, Lee, and Dorota Geissel. 2000. "Street Prostitution in Canada." In *Canadian Social Trends 3*. Ottawa: Minister of

Supply and Services Canada, and Toronto: Thompson, pp. 253–257.

Wolfgang, Marvin E., and Franco Ferracuti. 1967. *The Subculture of Violence: Towards an Integrated Theory in Criminology.* Beverly Hills, CA: Sage.

Women's International Network. 1995. "Sex Trade Flourishing in Japan." *WIN News* 21(1) (Winter):42.

Wood, Julia T. 2001. *Gendered Lives: Communication, Gender and Culture* (4th ed.). Belmont, CA: Wadsworth/Thomson Learning.

Woods, Catherine. 1998. "TV and Media Imperialism." *MTheory,* 2(Fall). Retrieved from **www.mala.bc.ca/soules/mtheory/vol2/index.htm**

Woods, James D., with Jay H. Lucas. 1993. *The Corporate Closet: The Professional Lives of Gay Men in America.* New York: Free Press.

Woog, Dan. 1995. *School's Out: The Impact of Gay and Lesbian Issues on America's Schools.* Boston: Alyson Publications.

World Bank. 1995. *World Development Report: 1995.* New York: Oxford University Press.

World Health Organization (WHO). 1946. *Constitution of the World Health Organization.* New York: World Health Organization Interim Commission.

World Health Organization (WHO). 2002. *World Report on Violence and Health.* Retrieved February 15, 2003, from **www5.who.int/violence_injury_prevention/main.cfm?p=0000000117**

World Health Organization (WHO). 2003. Retrieved February 16, 2003, from **www.who.int/nut/obs.htm**

World Resources Institute. 1992. *World Resources 1992–93.* New York: Oxford University Press.

Wortley, Scot. 1999. "A Northern Taboo: Research on Race, Crime, and Criminal Justice in Canada." *Canadian Journal of Criminology,* 41(2):261–274.

Wren, Christopher. 1996. "Teen-Agers Find Drugs Easy to Obtain and Warnings Easy to Ignore." *New York Times* (October 10):A12.

Wright, Erik Olin. 1979. *Class Structure and Income Determination.* New York: Academic Press.

Wright, Erik Olin. 1985. *Class.* London: Verso.

Wright, Erik Olin. 1997. *Class Counts: Comparative Studies in Class Analysis.* Cambridge, England: Cambridge University Press.

Wright, Erik Olin, Karen Shire, Shu-Ling Hwang, Maureen Dolan, and Janeen Baxter. 1992. "The Non-Effects of Class on the Gender Division of Labor in the Home: A Comparative Study of Sweden and the U.S." *Gender and Society,* 6(2):252–282.

Wright, Quincy. 1964. *A Study of War.* Chicago: University of Chicago Press.

Wright, Richard T., and Scott Decker. 1994. *Burglars on the Job: Streetlife and Residential Break-ins.* Boston: Northeastern University Press.

WuDunn, Sheryl. 1995. "Japanese Cult: A Strong Lure and a Danger to Challenge." *New York Times* (March 24):A1.

WuDunn, Sheryl. 1996. "In Japan, Even Toddlers Feel the Pressure to Excel." *New York Times* (January 23):A3.

Yinger, J. Milton. 1994. *Ethnicity: Source of Strength, Source of Conflict?* Albany, NY: SUNY Press.

Yogis, J.A., R.R. Duplak, and J.R. Trainor. 1996. *Sexual Orientation and Canadian Law: An Assessment of Law Affecting Lesbian and Gay Persons.* Toronto: Emond Montgomery.

York, Geoffrey. 2002. "Japan's Students Can't Spell Relax." *Globe and Mail* (June 10):A1, A12.

Young, J. H. 1961. *The Toadstool Millionnaires: A Social History of Patent Medicine in America before Federal Regulation.* Princeton, NJ: Princeton University Press.

Young, Michael Dunlap. 1994. *The Rise of the Meritocracy.* New Brunswick, NJ: Transaction.

Zelizer, Viviana. 1985. *Pricing the Priceless Child: The Changing Social Value of Children.* New Haven, CT: Yale University Press.

Zolf, Larry. 2003. "1970—The October Crisis." *CBC News Online.* Retrieved February 2003 from **www.cbc.ca/millenium/timelines/feature_octobercrisis.html**

NAME INDEX

SUBJECT INDEX

functionalist perspective,   7–8
against homosexuals,   138
interactionist perspective,   11–12
media and,   330–331
against older people,   118
spouse abuse,   267
against women,   73, 91–94, 254
See also violent crime
Violence Against Women Survey,
   206, 207
violent crime
gang violence,   207–208
hate crimes,   208
homicide,   205–206
nature of,   212
sexual assault,   206–207
social response to murder,   206
visible minorities, spatial separation of,
   382
visionary-type serial killer,   205
votes, voting
Canadian voting system,
   290–308
gender gap in voting,   289–308
right to vote,   308
voter apathy,   289–308
Vriend decision,   132

W

wages
downsizing and,   38
and free trade,   298
gender gap in,   87, 90–93
globalization and,   24, 297–298
in split-labour market theory,   64
wage squeeze,   38
Walkerton contaminated water,   359
"wannabe" groups,   207
war
biological and chemical weapons,
   400–401

casualties,   397
characteristics of,   395–396
civilian casualties,   398
conflict perspectives,   411–412
economic costs,   399–400
and environmental degradation,
   400–401
feminist perspectives,   412–413
forms of,   395
functionalist perspective,   411
interactionist perspective,   412
nuclear arms,   397–398
opposing,   414
psychological trauma,   399
in twenty-first century,   413–414
war system,   395
"War on Terrorism,"   403
water shortages,   359–361
wealth
and family types,   26
global economic disparity,   23–24
and income gap,   26–27
and life chances,   25, 26
Weberian concept of,   25
Weberian concept of class,   25
welfare policies and programs
Canadian and European policies
   compared,   40
fiscal retrenchment and,   29,
   36–37
government expenditure on,   38
underlying premises of,   38–39
welfare state
creation of,   35–36
white collar crime. *See* occupational
   crime
White privilege,   51–52
White supremacism. *See* hate groups,
   organized
White victimization, discourse of,   60
wine,   179

withdrawal management (detox)
   services,   196
withdrawal symptoms,   179
women
in business,   95
and career advancement,   94–95,
   99
health issues of,   121
and housework,   95–97
life expectancy of,   231
and medical profession,   245
and middle age,   112
in nursing homes,   119
and pornography,   169
stereotyping of,   332–333
trafficking of,   154–155
unpaid work,   254
workfare,   36–39
working poor,   28
World Social Forum,   306
World Wildlife Fund,   430

X

Xanith,   77

Y

young adulthood,   109
"young-old,"   113
youth crime,   212–213
youth groups (gangs),   207
youth movements (gangs),   207

Z

zero population growth,   353

NUMBERS/SYMBOLS

!Kung,   128